# THE CHURCH OF GOD IN CHRIST
# PRESIDI

## Bishop J. Drew Sheard

## Seeking the Heart of God
### Colossians 3:1 -3; Matthew 6:33; 2 Chronicles 7:14

Order materials today from the Power for Living Series:

Church Of God In Christ Publishing House
806 East Brooks Road, Memphis, Tennessee 38116
P.O. Box 161330, Memphis, Tennessee 38116
Toll Free: 1-877-746-8578 | Fax: (901) 743-1555
Website: www.cogicpublishinghouse.net
Email: sales@cogicpublishinghouse.net

# CHURCH OF GOD IN CHRIST, INC.
## ANNUAL SUNDAY SCHOOL LESSON COMMENTARY 2021–2022
## INTERNATIONAL SUNDAY SCHOOL LESSONS
### Volume I of II

# TABLE OF CONTENTS

Greetings From the Presiding Bishop........................vi

Greetings From the Chairman of the
Publishing Board..............................................vii

Greeting From the Chairman of Marketing .......... viii

Greetings From the Voice of Marketing....................ix

Greetings From the COGIC-UMI
Sunday School Liaison .........................................x

Visionary Leadership Collage
In the Time of Crisis .........................................xi

Greeting From the Publishing Board .....................xvi

2021-2022 COGIC Teaching Tips by Quarter........ xvii

How to Use This Commentary ............................ xviii

## Fall Quarter 2021

### TRADITIONS AND WISDOM

Quarter-At-A-Glance ................................................ 19
Teacher's Tips............................................................20
Quarterly Quiz ........................................................27

### LESSONS
### Unit 1 • Teaching and Learning

#### SEPTEMBER

5   Righteousness and Wisdom
    Proverbs 3:1–12 .................................................30
12  From Generation to Generation
    Proverbs 4:10–15, 20-27......................................38
19  Teaching Values
    Proverbs 15:21–33 ..............................................46
26  Wisdom and Discernment
    Proverbs 25:1–10 ................................................54

#### OCTOBER

3   An Ordered Life
    Proverbs 29:16–27 ..............................................62
10  The Superiority of Wisdom
    Ecclesiastes 9:13–18 ...........................................70
17  Wisdom For Aging
    Ecclesiastes 11:9-12:7, 13....................................77
24  Tradition and Love
    Song of Solomon 4:8–5:1a...................................85

### Unit 2 • Jesus Teaches Wisdom

31  Living as God's People
    Matthew 5:1–12 ..................................................94

#### NOVEMBER

7   Forgiving as God's People
    Matthew 5:17–26 ...............................................102
14  Loving as God's People
    Matthew 5:43–48 ............................................... 111
21  Praying as God's People
    Matthew 6:5–15...................................................118
28  Facing Life without Worry
    Matthew 6:25–34 ................................................126

## Winter Quarter 2021–2022

### GOD ESTABLISHES A FAITHFUL PEOPLE

Quarter-At-A-Glance ............................................. 133
Teacher's Tips.........................................................134
Quarterly Quiz .......................................................139

### LESSONS
### Unit 1 • God's Covenant

#### DECEMBER

5   A Blessing for All Nations
    Genesis 12:1–9....................................................142
12  A Promise to Abraham
    Genesis 15:1–6, 12–18.........................................150
19  The Lord Provides
    Genesis 22:1-2, 6-14............................................158
26  According to the Promise
    Luke 1:46–55 ......................................................165

### Unit 2 • God's Protection

#### JANUARY

2   God Watches Over Joseph
    Genesis 39:7–21a................................................. 171
9   Joseph Finds Favor
    Genesis 41:37-45, 50-52 ..................................... 179
16  God Preserves a Remnant
    Genesis 45:3-15 .................................................. 187
23  Joseph Transmits Abraham's Promise
    Genesis 50:15-26................................................. 194
30  Out Of Egypt
    Exodus 15:1-3,19, 22-26......................................201

# TABLE OF CONTENTS

**Unit 3 • God's Redemption**

**FEBRUARY**
6   Justified by Faith in Christ
    Galatians -2:15–21.............................208
13  Freed From Law through Christ
    Galatians 3:1–14 ..............................215
20  Heirs to the Promise
    Galatians 3:15–18; 4:1–7 ....................223
27  Fruits of Redemption
    Galatians 5:22–6:10...........................230

**Spring Quarter 2022**

**GOD'S CREATIVE WORD**
Quarter-At-A-Glance ..............................238
Teacher's Tips......................................239
Quarterly Quiz .....................................246

**LESSONS**
**Unit 1 • The Word Was in the Beginning**

**MARCH**
6   Wisdom's Part in Creation
    Proverbs 8:22–35................................249
13  The Word Became Flesh
    John 1:1–14.......................................256
20  The Wedding at Cana
    John 2:1–12 ......................................264
27  God's Word Saves
    John 3:11–21......................................272

**APRIL**
3   Jesus Testifies to the Truth
    John 18:28-37.....................................280
10  The Living Word
    John 20:1-10, 19-20.............................288

**Unit 2 • The Word Is Here and Now**

**APRIL**
17  Cleansing the Temple
    John 2:13–22 .....................................295
24  Woman of Samaria
    John 4:7–15, 23–26, 28–30....................303

**MAY**
1   Healing the Blind Man
    John 9:1–17 .......................................313

**Unit 3 • The Word Will Be**
8   The Bread of Life
    John 6:22–35......................................323
15  The Good Shepherd
    John 10:7–18.......................................333
22  The Resurrection and the Life
    John 11:17–27......................................342
29  The Way, the Truth, and the Life
    John 14:1–14.......................................350

**Summer Quarter 2022**

**GOD'S CALL FOR JUSTICE**
Quarter-At-A-Glance ..............................361
Teacher's Tips......................................362
Quarterly Quiz .....................................367
**LESSONS**
**Unit 1 • Justice Defined**

**JUNE**
5   Rules for Just Living
    Exodus 23:1–9.....................................370
12  Living as God's Just People
    Leviticus 19:9–18, 33–37 ......................378
19  Celebrate Jubilee-
    Leviticus 25:8–12, 25, 35–36, 39–40,
    47–48, 55...........................................387
26  The Heart of the Law
    Deuteronomy 10:12–22; 16:18–20............397

**Unit 2 • Justice Enacted**

**JULY**
3   Samuel Administers Justice
    1 Samuel 7:3–11, 15–17.........................407
10  David Embodies God's Justice
    2 Samuel 23:1-7; 1 Chronicles 18:14.........415
17  Solomon Judges with Wisdom and Justice
    1 Kings 3:16–28; 2 Chronicles 9:8............424
24  A King Acts on a Widow's Behalf
    2 Kings 8:1–6 .....................................434
31  Jehoshaphat Makes Judicial Reforms
    2 Chronicles 19:4–11 ...........................441

# TABLE OF CONTENTS

**Unit 3 • Justice Promised**

**AUGUST**

7   Praise for God's Justice
Psalm 146:1–10 .................................................448

14   God Promised a Righteous Lord
Isaiah 9:2–7 ......................................................455

21   God Promised a Righteous Branch
Jeremiah 23:1–6; 33:14–18 ...............................463

28   God Promised To Be with Us
Ezekiel 34:23–31 ..............................................471


Answers to the Quarterly Quizzes .........................478
2021 - 2022 Uniform Lesson Series Outline ..........481
Glossary...............................................................497
Affirmation of Faith .............................................500
COGIC Doctrine ..................................................502

# FROM THE PRESIDING BISHOP'S DESK

Greetings in the matchless name of our Lord and Savior, Jesus Christ.

2021-2022 is upon us, and we optimistically, yet cautiously, look forward to this next year. The past year has been the most challenging we have ever experienced. A relentless, microscopic virus catapulted the entire world into a tailspin. Schools, malls, airports, and even our churches were forced to close as we sought alternate ways of functioning. Our day-to-day lives were upended, and many of us were faced with the unbearable losses of friends, family, and co-laborers.

How much longer will we be forced to endure, and when will this end? When will normalcy return? These are questions that have been asked but cannot be answered with any amount of certainty. As believers, it is this time that we faithfully place our uncertain futures in the hands of a loving and faithful God. A God who promised never to leave or forsake us. Now is when we must trust in the Lord with all of our hearts and not lean to our limited and finite understanding.

We must continue to dedicate ourselves to trusting God in all circumstances knowing that even when the road is rough and the journey tumultuous, we maintain unyielding confidence in the God of our salvation.

Regardless of the many hardships, we have endured, let us now focus on this next season with hope and anticipation, trusting that God will sustain us. Jeremiah 17:7-8 declares, "Blessed is the man who trusts in the Lord. He is like a tree planted by water that sends out its roots by the stream and does not fear when heat comes, for its leaves remain green, and is not anxious in the year of drought, for it does not cease to bear fruit."

Be encouraged, knowing that no matter what the season may bring, God is with us.


In His service
Presiding Bishop J. Drew Sheard
Eighth in Succession
Church Of God In Christ, Inc.

# THE VOICE OF THE CHAIRMAN
# OF THE PUBLISHING BOARD

Blessings in the name of our Lord and Savior, Jesus Christ,

2021 has been a transformative year for the world, the various world governments, the church, and, more importantly, the everyday people of this world. This Pandemic transformed the mindset of people all around the world. We have been reshaped against our will and forced to live life on a survivalist level. Yet, while the unpredictable cares of this world have consumed us, God has been faithful to us. The Apostle Paul, in Philippians 2:5, says, "Let this mind be in you as it also was in Christ Jesus." Because we have lost so many leaders and loved ones, taking on the mind of Christ has been the only way we have been able to pick up the broken pieces and continue this journey called life. We are hurt. Our hearts are broken. But with the mind of Christ, we take on the very attributes of Jesus Christ himself. "For we have not an high priest which cannot be touched with the feeling of our infirmities; but was in all points tempted like as we are, yet without sin" (Hebrews 4:15). So, we can stand amid our mountain and say, "Be thou there removed" (from Mark 11:23). With the mindset of Christ, we can display the very wisdom of Christ; as the Bible says that "he that winneth souls is wise" (from Proverbs 11:30).

Do you not know my brothers and sisters that there is nothing in this world that can defeat the mindset of Christ? With Christ's mindset and the indwelling of the Holy Spirit, we become unbeatable in our thoughts, in our actions, and our abilities. I know it seems like we are always going through a lot, but these challenges test our mindsets to see how we perform under pressure: Will we act Christlike or act sinfully? Will we hit the mark or miss the mark and be forced to retake the test? Yes, sometimes we fall short, but when we do, we gain a better understanding of ourselves and an appreciation for Christ as we retake the test. When we learn how to appreciate ourselves, we can share that appreciation with others and connect, not just spiritually but physically and mentally as well. We have to connect with people because if this Pandemic has taught us anything, it has taught us that we waste away without human interaction.

One of Christ's ultimate goals for us is the power of unity. When we are unified, we can accomplish amazing feats as humans and even more mind-blowing feats as Christians. So, the thought that I leave with you in this letter is to let us become better and not bitter. Let us not dwell on the losses but seek out the victory that is still to be obtained because even though we have lost those dear to us, they have already received their reward, and they would want us to keep pushing and striving to obtain ours.

God bless you, and may the Lord continue to abound in your lives.

Bishop Uleses C. Henderson, Jr., Esq.
Chairman of the Publishing Board

# THE FOREWORD
# FROM THE CHAIRMAN OF MARKETING

Dear Saints of God,

Peace and grace be multiplied unto you.

I would like to give God praise for His goodness, grace, and mercy towards you and me. With great joy, zeal, and excitement, I also would like to congratulate our newly elected Presiding Bishop and Chief Apostle, the honorable Bishop J. Drew Sheard, the eighth in succession. Let us all join together to uphold our leader and the entire Church Of God In Christ in prayer. I am confident I speak for all of us when I say Bishop Sheard; you have our unending love and support!

Without equivocation, this past year was one of the most trying times we have ever witnessed as a country and certainly a denomination. We have lost some great leaders and Saints of God who will never be forgotten. Yet and still, the Church Of God In Christ is alive and well. In these days and times, with everyone and everything pulling for your time and attention, it is essential not to lose your passion for God. Like any healthy relationship, you must work hard at remaining dedicated to passionately carrying out God's mandate for your personal life and that of the Church. Jesus reminds us that we are the "salt of the earth, and the light of the world" (Matthew 5:13-16). I pray you continue to make a difference in your spheres of influence. I believe this excellent Church Of God In Christ material will serve you exquisitely in helping to keep that fire burning within you for passionate ministry.

I implore each of you as you study these lessons to remember that we are called into community. Indeed, we are a community of believers. We need each other. We are much more effective in reaching this sin-cursed world with the Gospel of Jesus Christ when we see ourselves as a body of believers in community with one another. The German theologian Dietrich Bonhoeffer said, "The church is her true self only when she exists for humanity."

In this 21 century the Church Of God In Christ has not lost our identity. We are still doing the work of ministry and making a difference in our communities. That is why it is so important to keep your church exposed to our Christian Education literature, especially for our young people. It is fresh, vibrant, innovative, and relevant. I sincerely pray that as you study this material, the Holy Ghost minister's life into you and everything that is important to you.

Bishop Reggie C. Witherspoon, Sr.
Chairman of Marketing
Church Of God In Christ Publishing Board

*"Now to Him who is able to keep you from stumbling, and to present you faultless before the presence of His glory with exceeding joy, to God our Savior, who alone is wise, be glory and majesty, dominion and power, both now and forever. Amen" (Jude 24,25 NKJV).*

# THE VOICE OF MARKETING

Blessings in the name of the Lord Jesus Christ,

I greet you with a renewed mind and with a refreshed Spirit. After the 2020 COVID-19 PANDEMIC, I found myself turning to the Word of God more and more, just like a tree that was planted by the rivers of living water. I had to tap into the spring inside of me to keep pressing forward no matter what obstacles came my way. When the George Floyd Murder gripped the entire country and then the world, I found myself finding my strength and my peace in the Lord; I had to put on the mind of Christ. For it is the mind of Christ that gives us peace when everything around us is chaotic. It is the mind of Christ that gives us the wisdom to solve the unsolvable solutions of man. With the mind of Christ, I can push, strive, and move forward with the vision of God.

With the mind of Christ, I obtain wisdom, and I obtain strength, I obtain a more determined faith; it is with the Mind of Christ that the Holy Ghost can speak to my spirit and calm me. It is with the mind of Christ that my love for man continues to grow. To take on the mind of Christ, we become more and more like Christ, and we strive for perfection; we strive for due diligence and justice. Don't you understand, my brothers and sisters, that with the Mind of God, we can stand still and see the salvation of the Lord? Can you not feel Him touch you? Can you not feel Him move within you? Can you not feel Him speaking to your mind and your soul? If the answer is no, then I ask you to put on the Mind of Christ. If the answer is yes that I ask that you grow deeper within Christ so that his presence grows stronger and stronger.

Sunday School is where we learn about the Mind of Christ and how to apply the mind of Christ. So, I ask you that in this 2021-2022 year, promise yourself that you will take on the Mind of Christ. Promise yourself that you will take out the time, spread the teachings of Christ Jesus to other people, and help them take on the mind of Christ because we are stronger together united under the Blood of Jesus Christ.

God Bless you,

Mother Sandra S. Jones
Senior Marketing Consultant
Church Of God In Christ Publishing Board

# THE VOICE OF THE COGIC LIAISON

Once more, I want to thank you for your commitment to the literature produced by your own Publishing House. Your support over the years has been appreciated. God has been faithful to us during one of the most unprecedented occurrences in the world. The Coronavirus seized the world and took many lives; however, we do not sorrow as those who have no hope; we trust God's sovereignty.

Your purchase of the Annual Commentary lets me know that you value the wealth of information contained herein. Pastors find they can prepare Sunday morning messages that coincide with the Sunday school lesson, thus reinforcing the subject matter, which helps the believer live out the Word of God. This year's focus of wisdom, the covenant relationship God establishes with His people, the call to justice, and the creative Word of God are needed topics for the body of Christ.

The Fall quarter is directing all our readers to the importance of letting your desire to learn and to know be an essential part of your spiritual experience. The first two months place a priority on wisdom in your Christian walk. You will be studying out of what is called the wisdom books. Wisdom has equal importance to knowledge. Knowledge is of little help if you do not know when, where, and how to apply it. In November, you will focus on the four most important teachings of Jesus, forgiveness, prayer, love, and faith, that exhibit true Christian character.

In the Winter quarter, we examine how God establishes a faithful people through His covenant, protection, and redemptive power. We see God's promise to Abraham and the promises to Abraham fulfilled in Joseph, his great-grandson. Finally, we learn through the Apostle Paul that we are heirs to this promise as children grafted because of Jesus' death, burial, and resurrection.

In the Spring quarter, the study of God's creative Word became flesh through his son Jesus, who is the bread of life and the good Shepherd. The Word made flesh is the bread of life, the way, the truth, and the life. The Summer quarter addresses God's concern for justice. As we study, we see justice defined, enacted, and promised in Scripture.

As you study through this year's Annual Lesson Commentary, I know you will be blessed.

Until the next time,

Bishop J. L. Whitehead, Jr., M.Div., COGIC Liaison

Review Team,
Evangelist Irether Sanford, Doctoral Candidate, Dr. Adrienne Israel, Elder Scott Bradley, B.A., Dr. Harold Bennett, Dr. Avery Brown,

# VISIONARY LEADERSHIP
## *In the Time of Crisis*

Presiding Bishop J. Drew Sheard's visionary leadership has provoked phenomenal growth and the implementation of innovative programs in both his local church and the International church. The leaders and citizens of Detroit and throughout the state of Michigan recognize his leadership acumen. Bishop Sheard's ideas have propelled him to the forefront of both the civic and religious community, and have gained him recognition as a "bridge builder" to other denominations. Below are some of the accomplishments through God's guidance he has achieved. This is an excerpt from an interview.

1.  What are the civic programs and partnerships that Bishop has with Governor Whitmer, as well as any programs he partnered with the Mayor of Detroit?

    A. Ecumenical Round Table - Executive Board Member - provides advise to Governor Whitmer on religious and community affairs for the State of Michigan.

    B. Urban Alliance of Michigan – founder and sponsor is Wayne County Executive Warren

    C. Evans and the organizational purpose is to unite urban elected officials, clergy and civic leaders in the State of Michigan to address common issues and share information that impact the communities represented by the membership.

2.  What were the support efforts to ministries during the COVID-19 pandemic?

    A. Food Distribution Partnerships (1.4 tons of food distributed over last 9 months):

       a. LaGrasso Bros Produce, (liaison State of Michigan)
       b. Prairie Farms Dairy (liaison World Vision)
       c. Compassion International (direct contact)

    B. Personal Protection Equipment (PPE)

       a. TCF Bank - Financial remuneration to individuals for purchases
       b. City of Detroit, Wayne County and DTE - PPE provided for distribution

    C. COVID-19 Testing – Sponsorship of a Detroit Regional Drive-thru program in partnership with Wayne State University and Detroit Medical Center (DMC)

    D. Wayne County COVID-19 Relief Grant Program - $50,000 for:

       a. Food purchases through the use of gift cards and turkey giveaways
       b. Utility, medical and rental payment assistance

3. How was the $100,000 raised for churches suffering during the pandemic? Did local Detroit families benefit?

The funds were raised through STRETCH which is an arm of J.D. Sheard Ministries dedicated to helping pastors pivot and remain relevant in their concepts and ideas in terms of all aspects of ministry in light of the pandemic. The funds were raised through PayPal's Go Fund Me Campaign. Pastors nationwide were eligible to apply for relief and awards were determined by a multi-denominational committee.

4. What other social, or charitable programs in Detroit does Bishop Sheard support/partner with?

   a. DTE Community Liaison Outreach Partner – assisting those who have difficulty paying utility bills.

   b. Detroit Medical Center (DMC) Ministerial Advisory Council (MAC) – objective is to effectively improve health outcomes in Metropolitan Detroit through collaborations with faith-based leaders.

5. Does GEI have any upcoming events, or support programs happening in 2021 such as continued food donations or fundraising for other churches?

   a. Gleaners and Forgotten Harvest partnership for ongoing monthly food distributions

6. How has Bishop Sheard had an impact on the City?

Bishop Sheard continues to impact the City of Detroit by continuously seeking to enrich the physical and spiritual lives of residents. Through the employment of creative and innovative methods of ministry individuals are impowered to prosper and have fulfilling lives.

# Bishop J. Drew Sheard and Lady Karen C. Sheard & family.

# COVID TESTING

# PRAYER WALK

# FOOD BANK

# Greater Emmanuel Institutional COGIC
## WOMEN'S DAY WORSHIP

# Church Of God In Christ **Publishing House**

*806 E. Brooks Rd • Memphis, Tennessee 38116 • 901.744.0477 Office • 901.743.1555 Fax*

**www.cogicpublishinghouse.net • Toll Free: 1-877-746-8578**

**Bishop J. Drew Sheard**
*Presiding Bishop*

**Bishop Uleses Henderson, Jr.**
*Chairman*

**Bishop Reggie Witherspoon**
*Secretary*

**Terri L. Hannett**
*Executive Director*

Dear Saints,

We greet you in the name of our Lord and Savior, Jesus Christ.

The year 2020 brought many challenges that caused the world to grind to a halt. The lingering effect of the Coronavirus yet has its grip upon the world. As believers, we are confident and secure in the knowledge that our God is Sovereign. We trust Him.

We saw the effects of the Coronavirus on the ministry of the Publishing House **_and felt the constraints of the government-mandated shutdown_**. We thank those who were able to continue the support of the Publishing House through your quarterly purchases. Many were not engaged in Sunday school due to the shutdown and because members experienced layoffs and other challenges. As most of us return to our houses of worship, we ask you to continue to support The Church Of God In Christ Publishing House!

The Publishing Board is excited to share with you the new *"Legacy Edition"* of the Annual Lesson Commentary, The Annual Interpretative Expository, and the quarterly curriculum for Fall 2021. The *Legacy Edition* follows the ISSL Uniform series of lessons. Additional insights have been added to this series that broaden the scope of the lesson content. As many of you know, we utilize the Uniform Lesson Series outline that most other denominations use. Our COGIC review team reads the lessons and makes changes and adjustments to ensure that the content aligns with our doctrinal belief. **_The Publishing Board wants to ensure that our lessons do not veer from the foundation of the Church Of God In Christ and that the emerging doctrine of inclusion is not a part of our curriculum._**

**_Because the review team has seen the rise of doctrines that do not line up with Scripture, the Publishing Board is transitioning to writers within our great church to write all lessons based on the ISSL Uniform series outline._** To accomplish this, we have to prepare in advance, and therefore, beginning Fall 2021, our books will not be succinct with the current Uniform Lessons series; however, we rest assured in the knowledge that God's Word is evergreen! It never returns void, and it is always relevant and life-changing!

The board, therefore, determined the *Legacy Edition* would help us during this transformation. We are thrilled to inform you that following this transition, your Sunday School materials will be authored exclusively by members of the Church Of God In Christ. Likewise, we have added the outline of the 2021-2022 Uniform Lesson Series in the Annual Commentary.

*"So will My word be which goes out of My mouth; It will not return to Me void (useless, without result), Without accomplishing what I desire, And without succeeding in the matter for which I sent it" (Isaiah 55:11, AMP).*

Again, thank you for your continued support, and I pray that you will journey with us as we transition for transformation.

For the Kingdom,
Publishing Board
Church Of God In Christ, Inc.

" The Lord gave the word; great was the company of those who published it" Psalm 68:11

# 2021-2022 COGIC TEACHING TIPS BY QUARTER

Teaching Tips are general principles designed to assist pastors, Sunday school superintendents, teachers, volunteers, small group leaders, Bible study teacher and parents. Thank you to Evangelist Waynell Henson for coordinating this year's writers.

## FALL 2021

- **Ministry Beyond the Church Walls,** *Evangelist Sharon Green*
- **Six Ways to "Make it Stick",** *Sister Angela Sims*
- **Yes Lord- Our Anthem and the Key to our Mental Wellness,** *Chantelle Bittings, LCPC*

## WINTER 2021 – 2022

- **Teaching Those with Different Learning Styles,** *Sis. Angela Moore*
- **Keeping Your Students Engaged,** *Kacey R. Pringle*

## SPRING 2022

- **Ten Tips for Sunday School Excellence,** *Evangelist Patricia Johnson*
- **Pay Attention to What You're Paying Attention To!,** *Dr. Missionary Kishki Kamaranell Hall*
- **Kahoot! A Youth Perspective on The Use of Technology in Sunday School,** *Alyssa Grace Henson*

## SUMMER 2022

- **Checking for Understanding,** *Patrick Guy*
- **The Relevant Sunday School – 2021 & Beyond: How to "Keep The Burning",** *Ja'Qyrie Wheeler*

# HOW TO USE THIS COMMENTARY

Welcome to the *The Church Of God In Christ Annual Sunday School Lesson Commentary 2021-2022*! This Bible study guide accomplishes the Christian education goals of the International Sunday School Department (ISSD) to equip and edify God's people through a systematic study of God's Holy Word.

In-Depth lessons are divided into four quarters—Fall (September-November), Winter (December-February), Spring (March-May), and Summer (June-August). Each quarter is comprised of three units, which contain four to five lessons that are perfect for Sunday School, weekly Bible studies, small groups or individual study.

Scriptures that are studied in this commentary are based on The International Bible Lessons for Christian Teaching, which is the standard of Scriptures to study the entire Bible over a period of seven years. *The Church Of God In Christ Annual Sunday School Lesson Commentary 20XX-20XX* brings biblical teaching to life with:

- Parallel King James Version with the Amplified Bible

- Contextual exegesis of passages by theologians and Bible scholars

- Background on the people, setting and circumstance of events

- Greek and Hebrew word studies with explanations

- Questions for small group discussions and individual reflection

- Teaching tips by ISSD leadership to enhance your Sunday School

- Challenges for a Spirit-filled relationship with God that results in holy living

## EACH LESSON IS ORGANIZED WITH:

**Lesson Aims**—Teaching and learning objectives based on Bloom's Taxonomy

**Light On The Word**—Overview of the lesson

**Life Need for Today's Lesson**—Answers a universal need for believers

**Introduction**—Summary of the lesson

**Bible Learning**—Two- or three-point outline of the lesson

**Search the Scriptures**—Questions and Answers about the previous text

**Light On The Word**—Commentary on the Scriptures

**Bible Application**—Practical suggestions to apply the lesson

**Students' Responses**—Practical steps for personal application

**Prayer**—Heartfelt entreaty based on the lesson

**Dig a Little Deeper**—In-depth analysis of an aspect of the lesson

The International Sunday School department guarantees that after diligent study, instruction, and application, no student, teacher, or Sunday School will ever remain the same!

# QUARTERLY COMMENTARY

## TEACHER'S TIPS

### " MINISTRY BEYOND THE CHURCH WALLS"
Evangelist Sharon Green

### "SIX WAYS TO 'MAKE IT STICK' "
Sister Angela Sims

### "YES LORD- OUR ANTHEM AND THE KEY TO OUR MENTAL WELLNESS"
Chantelle Bittings, LCPC

## QUARTERLY QUIZ

# MINISTRY BEYOND THE CHURCH WALLS

## By Evangelist Sharon Green

"Then shall the King say unto them on his right hand, Come, ye blessed of my Father, inherit the kingdom prepared for you from the foundation of the world: For I was an hungered, and ye gave me meat: I was thirsty, and ye gave me drink: I was a stranger, and ye took me in: Naked, and ye clothed me: I was sick, and ye visited me: I was in prison, and ye came unto me." - Matthew 25:34-36

As we look at the role of the church, there are times that we get stuck "having church" instead of "being the church." As I sought the Lord on what work He would have our congregation accomplish in our community, He took me to a familiar scripture. In Matthew 35:31-33, the Word of God tells us when the Son of man shall come in his glory, and all the holy angels with him, then shall he sit upon the throne of his glory: And before him shall be gathered all nations: and he shall separate them one from another, as a shepherd divideth his sheep from the goats: And he shall set the sheep on his right hand, but the goats on the left." He mentions six (6) areas of ministry that those on the right had performed:

1. Food ministry

2. Water ministry

3. Housing the Homeless ministry

4. Clothing closet

5. Sick and Shut-in ministry

6. Prison ministry

This tells us that the work of the church is outside of the church walls. Therefore, it is critical that we are observant of our environment. I believe that 2020 has ushered in greater opportunities for ministry within our neighborhoods. Our homeless numbers have continued to increase annually nationwide. The increase in rent prices is makes housing less affordable, thereby placing many more at risk of becoming unhoused. The pandemic not only added to the numbers of at-risk residents but has also increased food disparities for many others living in the "country of abundance" having to consume unsafe drinking water. In attempting to address these issues, Jesus said it best in Matthew 9:37 when He said to his disciples, "The harvest truly is plenteous, but the labourers are few; Pray ye therefore the Lord of the harvest, that he will send forth labourers into his harvest." He has done so; it is you and me.

Higher Praise Tabernacle is located in the High Desert Region of San Bernardino County. The community that we reside and worship in has the second-highest homeless population in our county. Therefore, our church felt it was critical to join the fight against homelessness, and in 2009, Victor Valley Family Resource Center, a 501(c)3 nonprofit to provide temporary housing, case management, Life Skills, Work Readiness, and other supportive services to assist in eradicating homelessness in our community. We began by opening a four-bedroom house to provide temporary housing for up to twenty-four months to those experiencing mental health challenges. Since that time, we have opened three additional homes to expand our housing to those exiting incarceration and college students experiencing homelessness. As a result, Victor Valley Family Resource Center has a 93% success rate in assisting our clients' transition back into society.

Our newest project is the James A. Lewis Sr. Senior Housing Project (in honor of the late Bishop James A. Lewis) and Cross/Green Senior Center. Both projects are single-family residences that will house up to 16 people. These homes provide housing to active seniors from the age of 55 and over. In addition, it provides affordable, permanent housing and meals to those living on a limited income or that choose not to live alone. With seniors becoming our most vulnerable population, resources provided by our nonprofit are critical to the senior's success.

Since the current pandemic is creating a health and economic crisis in America and around the world, it creates a wealth of ministering opportunities for the body of Christ. With seniors becoming our most vulnerable population, resources provided by our nonprofit are critical to our client's success.

The Lord has blessed us to win souls by fulfilling our assignment outside of the walls of the church building. He has allowed VVFRC to be the vessel He used to change Fair Housing Laws nationwide (Victor Valley Family Resource Center vs. The City of Hesperia.) We are now one of the leading transitional housing agencies in San Bernardino County. We are now a multi-million dollar organization through providing the six service ministries in Matthew chapter 25.

Evangelist Sharon Green is the Administrator/Teacher of Higher Praise Tabernacle North. She is the Founder and Executive Director of Victor Valley Family Resource Center (VVFRC), the nonprofit service center of Higher Praise Tabernacle. VVFRC provides transitional housing for those experiencing homelessness with a focus on those exiting prison. Sharon Green is the proud wife of Pastor Christopher Green. She is a member of Southern California First Jurisdiction - Bishop Joe L. Ealy, Prelate, Mother Barbara Bryant, Supervisor.

# SIX WAYS TO "MAKE IT STICK"

*CREATIVE IDEAS TO MAKE THE SUNDAY SCHOOL LESSON
COME ALIVE IN THE HEART OF THE LISTENER*

## By Sister Angela Sims

Sunday School teachers have the rewarding task of presenting life-changing biblical lessons. We pray, study, and thoroughly prepare so that each lesson can impact the lives of our students. We teach as a mission to share the Word of God and aid others in their walk in Christ. It's a calling! However, I believe every teacher has had a time where they walked away from their class wondering, "Did they get it?" Therefore, I've compiled six creative ways to "Make it Stick" or make a lasting impact in the hearts of your students.

1. Make it Personal – Individuals could read the amazing Sunday School lessons themselves. Still, the benefit of having you as a teacher is the ability to hear YOUR experiences and YOUR perspective. Share a personal story. Express what that scripture means to you. Forget the PowerPoint and just speak from the heart. Someone may not remember what's on page 17, but they will remember the story of how a particular scripture got you through a dark time in your life.

2. When in doubt, Act it out – A great way to make the Word come alive is to act out the story in the lesson, and the possibilities are endless. Here are a few examples:

- If you are studying the last supper, set the table and actually re-enact the whole scenario.

- Kids are taught that Christmas is Jesus' birthday. Have an actual birthday party with cake and balloons. It will help them connect the significance of birth with Christmas.

- Create jail bars and portray Paul and Silas' experience in the jail.

3. Games create excitement – Games are for more than just kids. They can be great learning activities for all ages.

- When studying the crucifixion of Jesus – set class up like an episode of CSI and "investigate" the facts and timeline of the crime.

- Create a puzzle. Make large puzzle pieces and place a part of the lesson on each piece. When the class has read each part of the lesson, they get that puzzle piece, ultimately gaining all the "pieces of the puzzle" or the whole lesson.

- Recreate any TV game show. For example, you could play Let's Make a Deal, and behind curtain, #1, #2, and #3 are choices you can make in life, but only one choice is the actual biblical way, and that's the prize.

4. Make it musical – Music has a way of transcending cultures, generations, languages and is a

great learning aid. Write a catchy phrase or song that you sing every Sunday. Play a gospel song each week that is complimentary to the lesson. Melodies and rhymes are easier to remember. For example, growing up, we learned bible scripture songs in Sunshine Band. Several decades later, I can still quote those scriptures Word for Word.

5. Repetition is Key – Some of the best praise and worship songs are simple yet powerful due to repetition. One idea is to go around the room and have each student say the same scripture allowing the entire class to hear it many times. The repetition helps retention. Say this with me, With HIS stripes, we are healed. With his STRIPES, we are healed. With his stripes, WE are healed. With his stripes, we are HEALED. Now imagine a room full of believers declaring this promise from God over and over again. It's POWERFUL!

6. Follow-up during the week – Sunday School doesn't have to end when the bell rings. Connect with your class during the week. Text, email, or use social media to reiterate the week's lesson. Share how you've applied the lesson in your life that week. Sharing experiences also helps to create community and a sense of support among the group.

No matter what delivery method you choose, if you seek God and follow His direction, your delivery will be just right! Let's Pray…I pray that each teacher experiences the supernatural power of the Holy Spirit in their class. Lord, let each lesson captivate the ears of the listener and initiate a desire for more of God. I declare miracles, signs, and wonders to flow. Lord, teach our minds and nurture our hearts. In Jesus' name. AMEN.

Sister Angela Sims is a member at Mt. Carmel Church of God in Christ under the leadership of her brother, Pastor Jason Sims. She is the full-time Church Administrator. The daughter of the late Bishop Ervin J. Sims and Supervisor Mary K. Sims, she is an Author, Marketing and Administration Consultant. She is the owner of PurpleCraftDiva.com - "Where Encouragement and Creativity Meet." Angela is a member of Missouri Western Second Ecclesiastical Jurisdiction – Bishop John Mark Johnson, Prelate, Mother Mary K. Sims, Supervisor.

# YES LORD- OUR ANTHEM AND THE KEY TO OUR MENTAL WELLNESS

## By Chantelle Bittings, LCPC

It is our call to action, our acknowledgment of the sovereignty of God, and our ultimate surrender to His will for our lives. Yes Lord, allows us to reset our priorities. We are saying yes to the people and things that are important to God for our lives. We are saying yes to strength. We are saying yes to joy. We are saying yes to peace. We are saying yes to being whole in our bodies, our spirits, and our minds.

Isaiah 26:3- Thou wilt keep him in perfect peace, whose mind is stayed on thee: because he trusteth in thee.

How do we maintain peace of mind when so much is going on in the world around us? Mental wellness is something that we do not talk about often in the church. However, it is vital for the wholeness of every believer. As a mental health clinician, I feel that we must be careful how we separate issues of the mind from the rest of the body. As Christians, we are quick to judge people with mental health issues as if the mind is disconnected from the rest of the body. When people have high blood pressure or diabetes, we do not question the need to see a doctor. The pulpit and the professional counselors are not in competition. We must learn to partner in order to promote wellness in our congregations. Of course, we all know that God is the Master Physician, but please know that He has equipped therapists, social workers, psychologists, and psychiatrists to help the people of God.

As we teach our Sunday School classes, we must remember that some people struggle with mental wellness. For far too long, the church has propped up the misconception that Christians are immune to issues of mental illness. Whether the excuse given was a lack of faith or spiritual warfare, too often, we have written off mental health issues and, as a result, turned our back on our fellow brothers and sisters in Christ in their time of need. The ramifications of 2020 will be studied for years to come. We are one year into a pandemic that has completely changed how we work, go to school, and even have church. There has been social injustice and unrest. We have lost some of our nearest and dearest. People are hurting, confused, depressed, and full of anxiety. The counselors' virtual offices are full. People are searching for answers. Depression and anxiety rates are increasing. We must be equipped to help those who we fellowship with, worship with, and with whom we attend Sunday School.

The first step is that we must realize that this conversation is necessary. We must have conversations in our classes. Every Sunday School teacher should be able to refer to a mental health professional in the area of their church. We must continue to promote mental wellness with love. We must continue to say Yes Lord.

Y: Yield to His plan

E: Execute by His power

S: Submit to His process


L: Listen to your Sisters and Brothers

O: Offer support and mental health services

R: Receive one another with love

D: Discuss mental wellness in our classes

For more information on mental wellness, please visit my website: www.cbittingstherapy.com.

Chantelle Bittings is a lifetime member of the Rehoboth Ministries Church of God in Christ, in Park Forest, IL. She serves in various positions in the church, including district Youth Chairlady and chair of First Jurisdiction of Illinois Mental Health Council. She is a devoted wife to Elder Thomas Bittings and the mother of two sons, Thomas and Gaston Bittings. She is a Licensed Clinical Professional Counselor and finds great joy in helping others. Chantelle is the author of "I am Enough: 14 days of Self-Worth, Strength, and Encouragement." She is a member of Illinois First Jurisdiction – Bishop Ocie Booker, Prelate, Mother Shirley Hughes, Supervisor.

## Adrienne Israel
*Biographical Sketch*

Missionary Dr. Adrienne Israel is a member of Wells Memorial Church of God in Christ in Greensboro, NC., where the Pastor is Superintendent Dr. Herman G. Platt. Wells Memorial is part of the Greater North Carolina Jurisdiction, Prelate is Bishop Leroy Jackson Woolard and Supervisor, Mother Harrizene Keyes. Dr. Israel has been a member of Wells Memorial since she was saved through the ministry of the late Bishop Ithiel Clemmons in 1983. She is the author of Amanda Berry Smith: From Washerwoman to Evangelist (1998) which chronicles the life of the Methodist Holiness Movement leader who inspired Bishop C.H. Mason. She is coauthor with Dr. Goldie Wells of Women in Ministry, the textbook for the Jurisdictional Institutes. She currently teaches Sunday School, is a member of the Business and Professional Women's Federation, and Chair of the Wells Memorial Board of Trustees.

A native of Massillon, Ohio, Missionary Israel earned a Bachelor's Degree in English and Master's degree in African Studies from Howard University, and a Doctorate in History from the Johns Hopkins University. She taught African and African American History at Guilford College for 38 years where she was the Vice President of Academic Affairs and Academic Dean for 13 years before retiring in May 2019.

## Arthur A. Porter Sr.

**Degrees:** BA Management and Psychology, Master of Divinity Old Testament and Psychology of Religion, Doctor of Ministry Leadership

- **Title:** Admin. Asst.
- **Local church:** Senior Pastor New Nation Church Of God In Christ
- **Jurisdiction:** Montana
- **Jurisdictional Prelate:** Bishop Phillip Henry Porter
- **Jurisdictional Supervisor:** Missionary Katherine Porter

Arthur A. Porter Sr., is married to First Lady Donna Porter, father and Senior Pastor of New Nation COGIC in Aurora, Colorado. Administrative Assistant, author, and former adjunct faculty at Iliff School of Theology, and Denver Seminary.

# QUARTERLY QUIZ

These questions may be used in two ways: as a pretest at the beginning of the quarter; as a review at the end of the quarter; or as a review after each lesson. Questions are based on the Scripture text of each lesson (King James Version).

## LESSON 1

1. Whose path is directed (Proverbs 3:6)?

_____

_____

2. Who does the Lord correct (Proverbs 3:12)?

_____

_____

## LESSON 2

1. According to Solomon's teaching, what would give life (Proverbs 4:13)?

_____

_____

2. What flows out of the heart (Proverbs 4:23)?

_____

_____

## LESSON 3

1. What does God do to the "house" of the proud (Proverbs 15:25)?

_____

_____

2. Whose prayers are of particular interest to God (Proverbs 15:29)?

_____

_____

## LESSON 4

1. Whose glory is it to conceal a thing (Proverbs 25:2)?

_____

_____

2. What happens when the wicked is taken from before the king (Proverbs 25:5)?

_____

_____

## LESSON 5

1. What are the benefits of disciplining a child (Proverbs 29:17)?

_____

_____

2. What is the biggest problem with hasty and rash words and actions (Proverbs 29:20)?

_____

_____

## LESSON 6

1. What method of war did the powerful king attempt to use against a small city (Ecclesiastes 9:14)?

_____

_____

# QUARTERLY QUIZ

2. Who or what can destroy the peace brought about by wisdom (Ecclesiastes 9:18)?

_____

_____

## LESSON 7

1. "Childhood and youth are_____" (Ecclesiastes 11:10).

_____

_____

2. "Remember now thy _____ in the days of thy _____, while the evil_____ come not, nor the years _____ _____, when thou shalt say, I have no pleasure in them" (Ecclesiastes 12:1).

_____

## LESSON 8

1. Which lands and features of these territories are used to describe the pre-marriage distance of this couple (Song of Solomon 4:8)?

_____

_____

2. What major metaphor is used to describe a woman's body (Song of Solomon 4:12, 16, 5:1a)?

_____

_____

## LESSON 9

1. "Blessed are the _____: for they shall obtain _____" (Matthews 5:7);

_____

_____

2. "Blessed are the _____: for they shall be called the children od God" (Matthew 5:9).

_____

_____

## LESSON 10

1. Based on Matthew 22-24, what can Christians do to help serve as peacemakers in the workplace and church?

_____

_____

2. If we expect or want people to forgive us when we hurt someone or inadvertently make a mistake, why is it so difficult for some Christians to repay the same kindness to persons who offend us? Please include yourself if applicable.

_____

_____

## LESSON 11

1. God sends rain on the just and the unjust (Matthew 5:45). Why do you think He gives certain blessings to all and not just a few? Do you think there are some examples in our society where people exercise the "right" to limit certain blessings or opportunities to only a few? Explain.

_____

_____

2. What does Matthew 5:48 say about how we should act because of who God is?

_____

_____

## LESSON 12

1. What did Jesus say about why hypocrites pray (Matthew 6:5)?

_____

_____

2. What does Matthew 6 tell us happens if we do not forgive others (Matthew 6:15)?

_____

_____

## LESSON 13

1. "But seek ye _____ the _____ of _____, and his _____; and all these things shall be added unto you" (Matthew 6:33).

_____

_____

2. Take therefore no _____ for the _____: for the _____ shall take _____ for the things of itself. _____ unto the day is the _____ thereof" (Matthew 6:34).

_____

_____

*Answers to Quarterly Quiz Can be found on page 478

# RIGHTEOUSNESS AND WISDOM

**BIBLE BASIS:** Proverbs 3:1–12

**BIBLE TRUTH:** Trusting in God's wisdom helps develop strong faith.

**MEMORY VERSE:** "Trust in the LORD with all thine heart; and lean not unto thine own understanding" (Proverbs 3:5, KJV).

**LESSON AIM:** By the end of the lesson, we will: IDENTIFY God's principles for living purposeful lives; TRUST that God's wisdom reveals purpose and meaning of life; and SEEK God's wisdom when making choices in daily life.

**BACKGROUND SCRIPTURES:** Proverbs 3:1 – 35—Read and incorporate the insights gained from the Background Scriptures into your study of the lesson.

## TEACHER PREPARATION

**MATERIALS NEEDED:** Bibles (several different versions), Quarterly Commentary/Teacher Manual, Adult Quarterly, teaching resources such as charts, worksheets/handouts, paper, pens, and pencils.

**OTHER MATERIALS NEEDED / TEACHER'S NOTES:**

_____

_____

## LESSON OVERVIEW

**LIFE NEED FOR TODAY'S LESSON**
To recognize the relationship between righteousness and wisdom.

**BIBLE APPLICATION**
To use biblical principles of wisdom in our lives.

**BIBLE LEARNING**
To understand how wisdom protects and preserves God's people.

**STUDENTS' RESPONSES**
Students will identify God's principles for living purposeful lives.

## LESSON SCRIPTURE

### PROVERBS 3:1-12, KJV

**1** My son, forget not my law; but let thine heart keep my commandments:

### PROVERBS 3:1-12, AMP

**1** My son, do not forget my teaching, But let your heart keep my commandments;

**2** For length of days, and long life, and peace, shall they add to thee

**3** Let not mercy and truth forsake thee: bind them about thy neck; write them upon the table of thine heart:

**4** So shalt thou find favour and good understanding in the sight of God and man.

**5** Trust in the LORD with all thine heart; and lean not unto thine own understanding.

**6** In all thy ways acknowledge him, and he shall direct thy paths.

**7** Be not wise in thine own eyes: fear the LORD, and depart from evil.

**8** It shall be health to thy navel, and marrow to thy bones.

**9** Honour the LORD with thy substance, and with the firstfruits of all thine increase:

**10** So shall thy barns be filled with plenty, and thy presses shall burst out with new wine.

**11** My son, despise not the chastening of the LORD; neither be weary of his correction:

**12** For whom the LORD loveth he correcteth; even as a father the son in whom he delighteth.

**2** For length of days and years of life [worth living] And tranquility and prosperity [the wholeness of life's blessings] they will add to you.

**3** Do not let mercy and kindness and truth leave you [instead let these qualities define you]; Bind them [securely] around your neck, Write them on the tablet of your heart.

**4** So find favor and high esteem In the sight of God and man.

**5** Trust in and rely confidently on the LORD with all your heart. And do not rely on your own insight or understanding.

**6** In all your ways know and acknowledge and recognize Him, And He will make your paths straight and smooth [removing obstacles that block your way].

**7** Do not be wise in your own eyes; Fear the LORD [with reverent awe and obedience] and turn [entirely] away from evil.

**8** It will be health to your body [your marrow, your nerves, your sinews, your muscles—all your inner parts]. And refreshment (physical well-being) to your bones.

**9** Honor the LORD with your wealth and with the first fruits of all your crops (income);

**10** Then your barns will be abundantly filled And your vats will overflow with new wine.

**11** My son, do not reject or take lightly the discipline of the LORD [learn from your mistakes and the testing that comes from His correction through discipline]; Nor despise His rebuke,

**12** For those whom the LORD loves He corrects, Even as a father corrects the son in whom he delights.

## BIBLICAL DEFINITIONS

**A. Depart (Proverbs 3:7)** *cuwr* (Heb.)—Avoid, shun.

**B. Firstfruits (v. 9)** *re'shiyth* (Heb.)—Beginning, best, chief.

## LIGHT ON THE WORD

The first chapters of Proverbs provide an introduction that explains the book's scope, intention, and background. In most Bibles, **Proverbs 1** is labeled as "The Purpose of Proverbs," chapter two is an invitation to the benefits of wisdom, and chapter three outlines the benefits of applying this wisdom by trusting God.

## TEACHING THE BIBLE LESSON

## LIFE NEED FOR TODAY'S LESSON

**AIM: That your students will recognize the need to honor God in all things.**

## INTRODUCTION

### Spiritual Wisdom for Today

Though many regard the book of Proverbs as primarily a collection of wise sayings by King Solomon, we would do well to regard the Holy Spirit as the ultimate source. The proverbs are just as timely to be practiced today as when they were first given.

## BIBLE LEARNING

**AIM: That your students will be able to identify the benefits of God's Word.**

## I. SOLOMON ADVISES HIS SON (Proverbs 3:1-6)

The first ten chapters of Proverbs give advice from King Solomon to his son. Solomon knew that if his son kept a persistent and continual

regard for God's precepts, promises, and provision, he would lead a life of unspeakable advantages.

### Listen, My Son (verses 1-6)!

**1 My son, forget not my law; but let thine heart keep my commandments; 2 For length of days, and long life, and peace, shall they add to thee. 3 Let not mercy and truth forsake thee: bind them about thy neck; write them upon the table of thine heart: 4 So shalt thou find favour and good understanding in the sight of God and man. 5 Trust in the LORD with all thine heart; and lean not unto thine own understanding. 6 In all thy ways acknowledge him, and he shall direct thy paths.**

**Chapter 3** begins with the affectionate and familial language of endearment, "my son." Like the son, we are admonished not to forget the "law" or the teachings and commandments that begin in **verse 3**. "Forget" refers to willful, deliberate neglect and diversion of attention (**cf. Proverbs 2:17**). With the same deliberate intention of not forgetting, the son is admonished in the same verse to "keep" or "retain" the commandments. Although this passage applies to the Scripture as we now have it, the law and commandments to which the writer alludes are those listed from **verse 3** onward.

According to **verse 2** the reward of obedience is a long and peaceful life. The expression, "length of days" signifies the prolonging life to the duration of its appointed limit. It is important to note that "length of days" is represented as a blessing in the Old Testament that depended on the fulfillment of certain conditions. This is life in a qualitative sense—a life worth living, the good life, indicated by "peace." Peace is more than just a matter of inner tranquility or absence of trouble.

"Mercy" and "truth" are the two basic covenant

terms in Israel. However, the exhortation in **verse 3** to hold on to mercy and truth is more than emphasizing trust in God's fidelity to the covenant. It includes internal character. It is firmness and constancy in keeping and executing one's promise. The command is to "bind (mercy and truth) about thy neck." We are to "write (mercy and truth) on the table" of our hearts. This further indicates that the character is in view rather than the behavior of the reader. By "binding" and "writing" the teachings become a part of the disciple's nature and an indelible part of his/her character.

The fourth verse states the outcome and provides the final motivation for obedience explained in **verses 1** and **3**: "Favour and good understanding" by God and by people. The Hebrew word for "understanding," refers to "regard and reputation". Both God and humans will approve such a person. To find favor "in the sight of God" is to be acceptable to God and enjoy a sense of His approval. Favor "in the sight of . . . man" is that which others feel toward those whose character can be found blameless.

There are two commands in **verse 5**. The first is to trust God with all one's heart. "Trust" carries the force of relying on someone for security; one's confidence is to be in the Lord and not in human understanding. To trust in God is to believe that He can and will do what He has promised. The call here is for a trust characterized by total commitment—"with all your heart" (**verse 5, NIV**) and "in all your ways" (**verse 6, NIV**). We are to commit all our concerns to Him so that we can be directed, ordered and overruled as His infinite wisdom sees best. "Trust in God" means giving up confidence or trust in your own understanding exclusively. The command to trust God "with all your heart" (**Proverbs 3:5**) means that the total personality is to be committed to God's care, although it emphasizes the mind and volition. **Verses 5b and 7a** prohibit depending on one's own understanding and intellectual pride. We are to use our understanding, but we must not transfer to our intellect any measure of dependence that should be placed on God alone. These expressions call for absolute obedience and surrender in every realm of life. Relying on one's own human (natural) understanding, or setting a high value on one's own wisdom are the opposite of a trusting dependence on God. The commitment of the heart to God means that all the beliefs and decisions of life are to be submitted to God. Human wisdom is inadequate, but divine wisdom is sufficient for guidance in life.

**Verse 6** literally translates as "in all your ways, know Him." To know God in all our ways means giving constant attention to the divine will and presence in all things, even in those areas that we sometimes consider minor. When obedient faith is present, the Lord will direct or "make straight" the believer's paths in spite of difficulties and hindrances. We are to acknowledge God:

(1) by referring everything to Him; (2) by praying for and expecting His divine guidance; and (3) by consulting and applying His will as revealed in His Word. We must think well, consult wisely, act diligently, and trust wholly. God will direct our lives and enable us to reach our destination.

## SEARCH THE SCRIPTURES
### QUESTION 1
What are the advantages of keeping God's Word in the heart?

**God will give long life, peace, favor, and recognition for good character in the sight of God and man.**

## LIGHT ON THE WORD
### Taking Solomon's Lesson to Heart
Solomon admonished his son to do more than memorize the Scriptures. He encouraged his son to keep God's commandments in his heart.

While the mind records words, the heart paints pictures with detail and emotions, and gives purpose and inspiration to mere words. The heart retains what the mind forgets. In order to depend on God's promises and faithfulness during difficult times, we must wear them as a treasured necklace that must never be removed.

## II. THREE EXHORTATIONS
## (Proverbs 3:7-12)

Solomon was an exhorter, one who inspired others to action through encouragement. In **verses 7 through 12,** he gave his son three exhortations, each enforced with a good reason.

### The Benefits Of Wisdom (verses 7-12)

**7 Be not wise in thine own eyes: fear the LORD, and depart from evil. 8 It shall be health to thy navel, and marrow to thy bones. 9 Honour the LORD with thy substance, and with the firstfruits of all thine increase: 10 So shall thy barns be filled with plenty, and thy presses shall burst out with new wine. 11 My son, despise not the chastening of the LORD; neither be weary of his correction: 12 For whom the LORD loveth he correcteth; even as a father the son in whom he delighteth.**

**Verses 7 and 8** are essentially a repetition of **verses 5 and 6,** where the writer urges the reader to trust in the Lord. Here the author urges us not to take ourselves too seriously, but to reverence the Lord and avoid evil. The admonition is a warning against self-sufficiency, self-conceit and self-reliance. To be "wise in thine own eyes" is to be in an utterly hopeless situation. Trust in God means giving up confidence in yourself and allowing God to become both teacher and father. Even when a person acquires wisdom, he or she must hold to humility and not allow confidence in intellect and learning to displace the demand for faith and confidence in God.

**Verse 9** emphasizes an important element in a person's relationship with God. We must honor Him with our wealth and first fruits as a sacrifice in recognition that God is our source. This admonition reminds the faithful of their religious duties to God. "Honour," as in this Scripture, sometimes implies giving gifts or benefits (**Numbers 22:37; 24:11; Judges 9:9).** This refers to our "substance" or literally the product of one's righteous labors. "First fruits" refers to topmost, first in its kind, or simply, the best. "Increase" or abundance refers to the produce of the earth— one's own crops and husbandry. The implication of these words is that we must give to the Lord from the entire range of our possessions. Our profession of faith in Christ is a mockery unless it affects how we spend our money as well as all other concerns of life. Our possessions ought to be consecrated to God, spent in conscious obedience to His will and used for His glory. This includes the sustenance of worship, the support and extension of missions, the relief of the poor, the sick, the needy, the widow and orphan (**cf. James 1:27).**

The command to give is followed by the promise of blessings in the "barns" or storehouses and the wine "presses." When one honors God with a portion of one's increase, he or she will receive material blessings. We can and should trust God with our gifts and for our material needs. **Verses 9 and 10** explain a principle of stewardship rather than a guarantee of material wealth and prosperity. The promise echoes the language of Moses in **Deuteronomy 28:1–8,** where God promises that in return for full obedience, He will command a blessing upon the "storehouses" (**verse 8)** and industry.

The final instruction of **verse 11** warns not to rebel against the Lord's discipline, because it is evidence of His love. The verb "despise" is "to reject" and "to condemn." "Chastening" means "correction" not by reproof only (as in **Proverbs 6:23; 8:30)** but by punishment also (**Proverbs 13:24; 22:15).** To "be weary" means to loathe, abhor, feel disgust or vexation toward someone. So the expression "neither be weary" reinforces the previous phrase "despise not" and represents a more deeply seated aversion to God's plans. The word "correction" is here used to mean "chastening" or "punishment." To loathe the correction of God is to allow the aversion to estrange us completely from Him. If we are spiritually "weary of his correction"—if we "resent his rebuke" (**Proverbs 3:11, NIV**)—we are rejecting a belief in the truth that "all things work together for good to them that love God" (**Romans 8:28**).

The final verse of our lesson provides the motive for submissiveness to God's corrections—they are the corrections of covenantal love. The writer employs the familial relationship of father and son in order to reconcile us to God's corrections. God corrects those He loves after the same manner as a father corrects the son he loves—an idea that is taken from **Deuteronomy 8:5.** When we learn the truth of this passage, we shall be drawn to, rather than repelled from God by His corrections. We must not engage in indignant questioning, scornful rebellion and proud efforts of indifference to pain or pleasure. We must accept suffering as an act of divine love, not repudiate it and rebel against one's condition.

## QUESTION 2

What is the importance today of this section of Scripture, beginning with "Be not wise in thine own eyes"?

**The admonitions to give to God of our first fruits and to embrace God's chastisement might be seen today as unusual and even foolish. Verse 7 reminds us that we should not look for wisdom on our own. Instead we must look to God for understanding and His principles will become clear.**

## LIGHT ON THE WORD

### Spiritual Therapy: Navel and Bone

Compliance with the wisdom of these verses is therapeutic: obedience will bring health to the body and nourishment for the frame. The healing that the fear of the Lord and avoidance of evil brings, is first spiritual. The benefit of true wisdom is physical health and vigor. The navel and the bones are symbols for the whole body. Knowledge of God that leads to spiritual well-being has its effects on psychological and physical aspects of human personality. As health to the navel and marrow to the bones represent physical strength, so the fear of the Lord is the spiritual strength of God's children.

## BIBLE APPLICATION

**AIM: That your students will accept King Solomon's wisdom for modern society.**

### Accept Responsibility

The cares of life are choking the strength out of families. Financial challenges, underemployment, depression, and addictions are just a few of the things that pull families apart. Today, many parents are too worried, too busy, and too overwhelmed to take time with their children. As a result, we find many children sexting, murdering, failing school, doing drugs, and having babies. In **Proverbs 3,** Solomon models the importance of making time to teach his son how to live. How can the Church and members of its spiritual community empower parents to become active participants in their children's lives, in spite of life's challenges? How can the total community accept responsibility for life-instruction of our youth? This is critical and we must all work to make it happen.

## STUDENTS' RESPONSES

**AIM: That your students will identify areas in their lives where Solomon's words are needed.**

If it is not us personally, then we all know people who are struggling to raise their children. Try your best not to judge yourself or them as bad parents, commit to do better yourself, or to help them do better. Pray for direction, and ask God for help. This week, engage in one of these activities or encourage someone else to do so:

- Find a counselor

- Attend a parenting support group

- Talk with your pastor or other godly parents

- Get active in your child's school

- Talk to and spend time with your child

With God, it is possible to restore and resurrect parent-child relationships. In fact, that is the best way to model God's parental care for us as we learn His righteousness and wisdom.

## PRAYER

Dear Lord, help us to be obedient as sons and daughters who desire to please You and to help our children honor You as well. In Jesus' name. Amen.

## DIG A LITTLE DEEPER

Christian consultant, Larry Julian, has helped many business leaders put Proverbs 3:5 into practice by discovering how to make decisions based on God's principles rather than the "bottom line." As a result, they fostered workplace environments of excellence and respect in which employees are content and genuinely striving to serve others. As customers and clients realized their corporations had their best interests at heart, these businesses flourished.

Following God's principles yielded good results because the leaders lined up the purpose of their companies with God's purpose for their lives. Trusting God equipped them to make wise decisions when faced with hard choices. As a result, they succeeded without becoming "slaves" to "the bottom line."

If someone observed your life, who and what would they say you trust? What would you say is your purpose in life? Is it the same as the work you do or the business you run? How can you determine to be successful by following God's principles even when they conflict with the demands of the "bottom line"?

[1]Larry Julian, God is my CEO: Following God's Principles in a Bottom-Line World (Avon, MA: Adams Media Corporation, 2002), Introduction and pp. 8-12.

## HOW TO SAY IT

Chronicles. KRON-ih-kuhlz.

Septuagint. SEP-too-uh-jint'.

### DAILY HOME BIBLE READINGS

**MONDAY**
The Sun of Righteousness
(Malachi 4:1–6)

**TUESDAY**
Remember All the Commandments
(Numbers 15:37–41)

**WEDNESDAY**
God Is Our Help and Shield
(Psalm 115:3–11)

**THURSDAY**
God's Abundant Blessings
(2 Corinthians 9:6–12)

**FRIDAY**
Wisdom in Relationships
(Proverbs 3:27–35)

**SATURDAY**
The Profit from Wisdom
(Proverbs 3:13–26

**SUNDAY**
Trust in the Lord
(Proverbs 3:1-12)

## PREPARE FOR NEXT SUNDAY

Read **Proverbs 4:10-15, 20-27** and study "From Generation to Generation."

**Sources:**

Baltes, A. J., ed. Biblespeech.com. http://biblespeech.com (accessed July 6, 2010). Clarke, Adam. Clarke's Commentary, Vol. 2: Job–Malachi. Nashville, TN: Abingdon,

n.d.

Clifford, Richard J. Proverbs. Louisville, KY: Westminster John Knox Press, 1999. Garrett, Duane A. Proverbs, Ecclesiastes, Song of Songs. New American Commentary,

Vol. 14. Nashville, TN: Broadman, 1993.

Hebrew and Greek Lexicons. Bible Study Tools.com. http://www.biblestudytools.com/lexicons (accessed September 16, 2010).

Horton, Robert Forman. The Book of Proverbs. New York: A.C. Armstrong, 1891. Kidner, Derek. Proverbs: An Introduction and Commentary. Downers Grove, IL:

InterVarsity Press, 1964. 64.

Merrim-Webster Online Dictionary. Merriam-Webster, Inc. http:// www.merriam-webster.com (accessed July 6, 2010).

Moffatt, James. A New Translation of the Bible: Containing the Old and New Testaments.

London: Hodder and Stoughton, 1935. 695.

Strong, James. New Exhaustive Strong's Numbers and Concordance with Expanded Greek-Hebrew Dictionary. Seattle, WA: Biblesoft, and International Bible Translators, 1994.

## COMMENTS / NOTES:

# FROM GENERATION TO GENERATION

**BIBLE BASIS:** Proverbs 4:10–15, 20–27

**BIBLE TRUTH:** To live life to the fullest, we must make good choices and keep a righteous path.

**MEMORY VERSE:** Take fast hold of instruction; let her not go: keep her; for she is thy life (Proverbs 4:13, KJV).

**LESSON AIM:** By the end of the lesson, we will: EXPLAIN how the teachings from the proverb promote wise living; CONSIDER living wisely and following a straight path; and DEVELOP a strategy for making good choices and living a godly life.

**BACKGROUND SCRIPTURES:**

Proverbs 4:1-27—Read and incorporate the insights gained from the Background Scriptures into your study of the lesson.

## TEACHER PREPARATION

**MATERIALS NEEDED:** Bibles (several different versions), Quarterly Commentary/Teacher Manual, Adult Quarterly, teaching resources such as charts, worksheets/handouts, paper, pens, and pencils.

**OTHER MATERIALS NEEDED / TEACHER'S NOTES:**

_____

_____

## LESSON OVERVIEW

**LIFE NEED FOR TODAY'S LESSON**
To develop a strategy for making good choices and living a godly life.

**BIBLE LEARNING**
To learn the instructions of Proverbs 4.

**BIBLE APPLICATION**
To use Proverbs four as a blueprint for positive living.

**STUDENTS' RESPONSES**
Students will discern how this biblical advice benefits each generation—past, present and future.

## LESSON SCRIPTURE

### PROVERBS 4:10–15, 20–27, KJV

**10** Hear, O my son, and receive my sayings; and the years of thy life shall be many.

### PROVERBS 4:10-15, 20–27, AMP

**10** Hear, my son, and accept my sayings, And the years of your life will be many.

11 I have taught thee in the way of wisdom; I have led thee in right paths.

12 When thou goest, thy steps shall not be straitened; and when thou runnest, thou shalt not stumble.

13 Take fast hold of instruction; let her not go: keep her; for she is thy life.

14 Enter not into the path of the wicked, and go not in the way of evil men.

15 Avoid it, pass not by it, turn from it, and pass away.

## PROVERBS 4:20-27, KJV

20 My son, attend to my words; incline thine ear unto my sayings.

21 Let them not depart from thine eyes; keep them in the midst of thine heart.

22 For they are life unto those that find them, and health to all their flesh.

23 Keep thy heart with all diligence; for out of it are the issues of life.

24 Put away from thee a froward mouth, and perverse lips put far from thee.

25 Let thine eyes look right on, and let thine eyelids look straight before thee.

26 Ponder the path of thy feet, And let all thy ways be established, years of your life will be many.

27 Turn not to the right hand nor to the left: remove thy foot from evil.

11 I have instructed you in the way of [skillful and godly] wisdom; I have led you in upright paths.

12 When you walk, your steps will not be impeded [for your path will be clear and open]; And when you run, you will not stumble.

13 Take hold of instruction; [actively seek it, grip it firmly and] do not let go. Guard her, for she is your life.

14 Do not enter the path of the wicked, And do not go the way of evil men.

15 Avoid it, do not travel on it; Turn away from it and pass on.

## PROVERBS 4:20-27, AMP

20 My son, pay attention to my words and be willing to learn; Open your ears to my sayings.

21 Do not let them escape from your sight; Keep them in the center of your heart.

22 For they are life to those who find them, And healing and health to all their flesh.

23 Watch over your heart with all diligence, For from it flow the springs of life.

24 Put away from you a deceitful (lying, misleading) mouth, And put devious lips far from you.

25 Let your eyes look directly ahead [toward the path of moral courage] And let your gaze be fixed straight in front of you [toward the path of integrity].

26 Consider well and watch carefully the path of your feet, And all your ways will be steadfast and sure.

27 Do not turn away to the right nor to the left [where evil may lurk]; Turn your foot from [the path of] evil.

## BIBLICAL DEFINITIONS

A. **Incline (Proverbs 4:20)** *natah* (Heb.)—To stretch out, extend, offer.
B. **Perverse (v. 24)** *lezuwth* **(Heb.)**—Deviant, crooked.

## LIGHT ON THE WORD

In our lesson text, we find Solomon teaching his children how to shun peer pressure. It may be hard for us to imagine the kind of trouble children in Solomon's day got into, and we probably don't believe it was anything like the trouble children get into today. But as Solomon wrote in **Ecclesiastes 1:9 (NIV)**, "There is nothing new under the sun."

## TEACHING THE BIBLE LESSON

## LIFE NEED FOR TODAY'S LESSON

AIM: That your students will compare the two paths of life.

## INTRODUCTION

### You Must Choose

The way of wisdom might be synonymous with "the paths of righteousness" identified in **Psalm 23:3**, but it is not an actual path or walkway. It is metaphorical for choosing a godly lifestyle. Everyone must choose.

## BIBLE LEARNING

AIM: That your students will identify the benefits and consequences of lifestyle choices.

## I. TWO PATHS, TWO DIFFERENT OUTCOMES (Proverbs 4:10–15)

Simply put, Solomon taught that life is a two-way street and that his children could go the right way (the way of wisdom) or in the wrong direction (the path of the wicked).

Solomon allowed his children to choose by

telling them in effect, "I have led you in the right paths; the rest is up to you." Solomon taught his children by example and showed them how to hide God's Word in their hearts, how to recognize ungodliness, and how to shun evil. Though he was not a perfect man, his children were witnesses to the blessings of God upon Solomon's life.

### Listen Carefully! (verses 10-15)

**10 Hear, O my son, and receive my sayings; and the years of thy life shall be many. 11 I have taught thee in the way of wisdom; I have led thee in right paths. 12 When thou goest, thy steps shall not be straitened; and when thou runnest, thou shalt not stumble. 13 Take fast hold of instruction; let her not go: keep her; for she is thy life. 14 Enter not into the path of the wicked, and go not in the way of evil men. 15 Avoid it, pass not by it, turn from it, and pass away.**

**Proverbs 4:10** begins with the admonition to "hear" or obey. There must be attentiveness and a willingness to appropriate what is taught. The consequence is that the life of the pupil "shall be many," which means he or she will be given a long life. Beginning from **verse 11,** the father/teacher gives additional reasons why his authority should be respected and the teaching followed. Solomon uses the image of a road to make a comparison as he explains the wisdom of his instruction.

In **verse 12,** Solomon explains that living according to wisdom is like walking or running on a safe road, a road that is well defined. On this right path, the feet can tread on good surface and take a course that will be free of unnecessary obstacles. Progress will be certain. "Thy steps shall not be straitened," means the journey will not encounter restraint, confinement, or rebuke. The implied opposite is that those who walk in a troubled and uneven path, are apt to stumble and fall. Likewise, those under the influence of sound biblical teachings ponder their paths and carefully examine circumstances as they occur. The fear of God leads them to act in an upright, honest manner. Thus their way in business and life is clear. They are without fear of being tripped by unpredictable and seemingly insurmountable obstacles.

The admonitions of **verse 13** challenge us to urgent faithfulness. Not only is wisdom the means of making progress in life, it is life itself. Anything so essential must be enthusiastically maintained. The believer must not let go of the truths of God's words and must not allow God's words to go unheeded. "Instruction" refers to discipline, such as parental counsel. It is our duty to hold to the truth that God has revealed to us and to attend to the commandments that He has sent us. But it is also for our own soul's profit. Divine truth is not a luxury; it is a necessity for life.

**Verse 14** begins a command to avoid evil association, which is a source of mischief to everyone, but especially to the young, who are more imitative and whose habits are undergoing development. "Evil men" are bloodthirsty men of violence. The warning is to avoid evil ways and evil people by not starting on the wicked path of life. The rapid sequence of imperatives in **verse 15** stresses the urgency of the matter. In addition, the expressions used continue the comparison of lifestyle with traveling along a path—only now the lifestyle to consider is evil.

Phrases such as "avoid it" and "pass not by it" state in the strongest terms to get as far away from evil as possible. Whether for the sake of worldly gain, or through a desire to please others, never approach the pathway where you would not wish to be found when God calls you into the eternal world. The serious purpose of our soul should be to shun every appearance of evil.

## SEARCH THE SCRIPTURES
### QUESTION 1
Why might Solomon have used a "path" metaphor?

**Life is a journey and we must choose which path to take. Our decisions are consistent with our character. Our roads in life reflect what we value. Solomon urges that we take only the path of wisdom and right.**

## LIGHT ON THE WORD
### Walk This Way!
Solomon warned that the way of wisdom would not always be easy, and that it was not a popular road. He stressed the importance of choosing the way of wisdom so that his children's lives would be consistent and wholesome. Solomon's father, David, had children by each of his many wives. Despite the blended family, these were considered fully David's children and they were fully brothers and sisters to each other. In Solomon's family, his brother, Absalom, had his brother, Amnon, killed for raping his sister, Tamar. Later Absalom tried to steal his father's kingdom. When David was advanced in years, Solomon's brother, Adonijah, tried to have himself declared king instead of Solomon. Solomon apparently recognized, as we must, that adherence to God's Word can break the cycle of violence and sexual sin that can ruin a family. Solomon taught that the way of wisdom is a path to long life, prosperity, and happiness.

## II. PRACTICE MAKES PERFECT (Proverbs 4:20–27)

To Solomon, it was not enough to tell his children to choose the way of wisdom and not give them practical tips on doing so. In these verses, he advised them to: (1) guard their hearts, (2) set a guard over their mouths, (3) attend to what they see or look upon, and (4) be considerate in all they do.

### Pay Attention! (verses 20-27)

**20 My son, attend to my words; incline thine ear unto my sayings. 21 Let them not depart from thine eyes; keep them in the midst of thine heart. 22 For they are life unto those that find them, and health to all their flesh. 23 Keep thy heart with all diligence; for out of it are the issues of life. 24 Put away from thee a froward mouth, and perverse lips put far from thee. 25 Let thine eyes look right on, and let thine eyelids look straight before thee. 26 Ponder the path of thy feet, and let all thy ways be established. 27 Turn not to the right hand nor to the left: remove thy foot from evil.**

In **verse 20,** Solomon's son is first advised to heed the wise words of the father. The word "attend" means to incline the ear attentively. The restating of this phrase in the same verse underscores its importance. **Verse 21** instructs the believer to guard wisdom in the heart for it is the wellspring of life. The heart is the starting point of life's activities **(Proverbs 23:19);** it determines the course of life. "Heart" refers not to the physical organ, but to the mind and the entire personality of the individual. The capacity to live with joy and vigor ultimately comes from within and not from circumstances. The corrupt heart draws one down to the grave, but wisdom protects the heart from that corruption. John Flavel, in his book Keeping the Heart, very wisely observed, "The greatest difficulty in conversion is to win the heart to God; and the greatest difficulty after conversion is to keep the heart with God" (Flavel, 2). The reason for heeding the instruction is that the father's words of wisdom given in **verse 22** are the means of life and health. The human condition apart from God is regarded as a condition of death or enfeebled by sickness, but obeying wise advice can restore the listener to life, health, and soundness. Wisdom does not automatically come to a person. In Hebrew, the verb "to find"

used in **verse 22,** suggests a deliberate effort to get possession of and procure wisdom. The "health" that is promised in verse 22 is physical, emotional, and spiritual—the whole person.

God's words bring deliverance from the evils that harm and hinder life. Nothing preserves soul and body in a healthier state than when we keep before our eyes and carry in our hearts good doctrine. In **verse 22,** "All their flesh" implies the completeness of the restoration; it is not confined to one part, but pervades the whole body.

The living stream "issues" from the physical heart in its normal, healthy condition, to vitalize and nourish every part of the body **(verse 23).** This truth also applies to spiritual things. The streams of spiritual life proceed from Him to all the powers and faculties of the soul. We must, therefore, be vigilant about our treatment of wisdom. The Hebrew term for "diligence" is very emphatic; it means "to set double guards" such as those which provide high-level security. This forcefulness of expression plainly implies how difficult it is to "keep" our hearts, and how dangerous to neglect them! Care must be taken that the fountain not be stopped up nor injured. We must be circumspect and careful with the thoughts we express.

In **verse 24,** after the father challenges his son to store wisdom in his heart and watch over his heart with all diligence, he gives the son a series of instructions involving his mouth, eyes, and feet. Centuries later, Paul referred to our bodies as "members of Christ" that we can use either as instruments of righteousness or unrighteousness **(1 Corinthians 6:15–20).** The commands in **Proverbs 4:24–27** concerning our mouths, eyes, and feet can be obeyed only when we are watching over our hearts with full vigilance. The heart works in tandem with the tongue and as such, starts with it. As the source of life, the heart sends up the thoughts that the tongue expresses in words. Words flow out of the heart. A believer must avoid the words that swerve from truth and purity to lies, deceit, and wrong discourse of every kind. Instead, righteousness must control the tongue, and twisted and crooked speech must be shunned. The final exhortation returns to the imagery of the path (verses 25–27). The idea is that one should not be distracted from the way of wisdom (verse 25). "Look straight before thee" is an expression of unswerving directedness toward a goal. The person who does this pursues wisdom single-mindedly. They do not look to the right or the left to check out other options. They are not distracted by temptation to leave the correct path. The foolish person is always looking around for different objects of desire. As the story of John Bunyan in Pilgrim's Progress well illustrates, temptations lie on both sides of the way, requiring one to focus directly ahead and walk without deviating to either side, without even glancing at them. As the author of Proverbs often states, winking or squinted eyes are symptoms of unreliability and guile (Proverbs 6:13; 10:10; 16:30). The wise person will have an unswerving directness, but the fool is easily distracted (Proverbs 17:24).

Verse 24 warns us not to allow our feet to take us down the wrong path. Proverbs speaks of the foolish as having "feet that are quick to rush into evil" (Proverb 6:18, NIV; see also Proverbs 1:16). By contrast, the wise stay on the path of life, the path of righteousness. Proverbs 15:21 says that "a man of understanding keeps a straight course" (NIV). By contrast, the foolish man follows paths that are "crooked" (Proverbs 2:15). Having feet that stay on the path of righteousness demonstrates a single-minded pursuit of wisdom. The word "ponder" means "to make level," "to weigh," and, metaphorically, "to consider or to deliberate." The sense is that one must consider undertakings well by examining them thoroughly beforehand and pondering whether they are right and proper.

Proverbs 4:27 is closely connected with and more fully explains verses 25 and 26. As in verse 25, the gaze is to be concentrated; the feet are not to deflect nor turn aside to byways. Nothing is to be permitted to divert the believer from the right way, neither adversity, nor prosperity, nor anything that can possess the power of temptation. The disciple must not allow anything to turn him or her aside from the path of virtue, honesty, and fair dealings in all matters of faith.

## QUESTION 2

How does the "body" metaphor provide warnings for those who follow God?

**The rest of the chapter consists of warnings, which are permeated by a metaphorical use of body parts. The ear is to remain keen for listening to wise advice (verse 20); the eyes are to stay fixed on right teaching (verses 21, 25), and the feet are to stay on the right path (verses 26–27). The mouth and lips must shun using twisted words (verse 24). Above all, the heart must be guarded by sound doctrine (verses 21, 23). If the son listens to his father, his whole body will be healthy (verse 22). By using ears, eyes, and heart, the teacher is exhorting the whole person to receive the teaching.**

**Answers will vary.**

## LIGHT ON THE WORD

### The Path of the Wicked

The path of the wicked is another metaphor used to characterize the route of the ungodly. The path of the wicked is wide and dark, but may be fun and seemingly prosperous. It does not have a "Do Not Enter" sign before it, but a discerning person might see other warning signs. A person on the path of the wicked does not care about godly things. They entertain evil thoughts and do evil things. They do what they want to do because they believe that life is too short not to have fun—regardless of the consequences to themselves and others.

## BIBLE APPLICATION

**AIM: That your students will consider how society distracts us today.**

### The Pressure to Keep Up

The word "pressure" when related to teenagers, is called "peer pressure", but concerning adults, is called "keeping up with the Joneses". Using peers as a benchmark for where one should be is dangerous and leads to other evils. Keeping up with the Joneses has plagued African American communities and many others with debt, depression, and fear. How can the church promote wisdom in all aspects of life? Is this more or less difficult in an uncertain economy?

## STUDENTS' RESPONSES

**AIM: That your students will consider how the "paths" are represented today.**

Today, what seems right may not be right. Consider this scenario:Kim had gone to three stores looking for the colorful bracelets her eight-year-old daughter, Destiny, wanted for her birthday.

When Kim and Destiny went into the fourth store, Destiny ran right to the bracelets. "Mom, they're here!"

Kim snatched a couple of bags of bracelets and led her daughter to the counter. "Praise the Lord," she told the cashier.

"Praise Him, sister," the cashier responded. "So, you're a believer?" "Yes, ma'am."

"Well, you should know what these bracelets mean. Your daughter is too young to know. Girls her age like them because they're colorful and are cute animal shapes, but older girls give them to boys because the colors stand for certain sexual acts. I know it sounds crazy, but what is

innocent today might mean meet-me-behind-the-bleachers tomorrow."

What deceptive "road signs" can you find in our society?

## PRAYER

Lord God, help us to keep our eyes, ears, hearts, and feet focused on following Your path. In Jesus' name. Amen.

## DIG A LITTLE DEEPER

It may be a good idea to begin each day with a plan and a prayer to guard our hearts against sin **(Luke 11:4b),** but are planning and praying enough? According to business analyst, Roger Martin, even a strategic plan does not assure success because "discomfort is part of the process." When athletes who have failed to practice before a game pray for victory before a game but fail to practice beforehand because the coach was "too hard," should they be surprised when they lose the game? Plans and prayer may fail to yield success if we stay in our "comfort zone."

Apostle Paul reminds us to examine ourselves **(2 Corinthians 13:5)** and avoid complacency **(1 Corinthians 10:12).** After honestly looking at ourselves in the mirror of God's word, how do we handle the discomfort that results from what we see?

Instead of simply revising our plan for the day and spending more time in prayer, Richard Foster proposes the balanced use of "the disciplines of life in the spirit: meditation, prayer, fasting, and studying" the word of God. These disciplines are not laws that yield the "external righteousness of the scribes and Pharisees" but sustained actions that "facilitate the transformation of the heart." Practicing the disciplines opens us up experiencing a change of heart graciously awarded by God, and to purifying our hearts (**1 John 3:3**).

## HOW TO SAY IT

Deuteronomy.    doo'tuh-RON-uh-mee .

Pharisee.        FAIR-uh-see.

Flavel, John. Keeping the Heart. http://www.the-highway.com/heart1_Flavel.html (accessed June 7, 2010).

Garrett, Duane A. Proverbs, Ecclesiastes, Song of Songs. New American Commentary, Vol. 14. Nashville, TN: Broadman. 1993.

Hebrew and Greek Lexicons. Bible Study Tools.com. http://www.biblestudytools.com/lexicons (accessed September 16, 2010).

Merriam-Webster Online Dictionary. Merriam-Webster, Inc. http:// www.merriam-webster.com (accessed July 6, 2010).

Plaut, W. Gunther. Book of Proverbs. New York, NY: Union of American Hebrew Congregations, 1961.

Strong, James. New Exhaustive Strong's Numbers and Concordance with Expanded Greek-Hebrew Dictionary. Seattle, WA: Biblesoft, and International Bible Translators, 1994.

## DAILY HOME BIBLE READINGS

### MONDAY
Guard Your Heart and Mind
(Proverbs 23:15–19)

### TUESDAY
Walk Uprightly
(Psalm 84:8-12)

### WEDNESDAY
Keep God's Commandments
(Joshua 23:1–8)

### THURSDAY
Lifelong Protection
(Psalm 91:9–16)

### FRIDAY
Walk in Your Parents' Paths
(Proverbs 1:8–15)

### SATURDAY
Prize Wisdom
(Proverbs 4:1–9)

### SUNDAY
Walk the Straight Path
(Proverbs 4: 10-15,20-27)

## COMMENTS / NOTES:

## PREPARE FOR NEXT SUNDAY

Read **Proverbs 15:21-33** and study "Teaching Values."

**Sources:**

Baltes, A. J., ed. Biblespeech.com. http://biblespeech.com (accessed July 6, 2010).

Clarke, Adam. Clarke's Commentary, Vol. 2: Job–Malachi. Nashville, TN: Abingdon, n.d. 712. Clifford, Richard J. Proverbs. Louisville, KY: Westminster John Knox Press, 1999.

# TEACHING VALUES

**BIBLE BASIS:** Proverbs 15:21–33

**BIBLE TRUTH:** Godly wisdom is necessary to live well and to succeed.

**MEMORY VERSE:** He that refuseth instruction despiseth his own soul: but he that heareth reproof getteth understanding (Proverbs 15:32, KJV).

**LESSON AIM:** By the end of this lesson, we will: DISCUSS the advice given in the lesson that promotes godly wisdom; REFLECT on experiences of following both good and bad advice; and DECIDE to follow the advice offered in the proverb.

**BACKGROUND SCRIPTURES:** Proverbs 10:1–15:33— Read and incorporate the insights gained from the Background Scriptures into your study of the lesson.

## TEACHER PREPARATION

**MATERIALS NEEDED:** Bibles (several different versions), Quarterly Commentary/Teacher Manual, Adult Quarterly, teaching resources such as charts, worksheets/handouts, paper, pens, and pencils.

**OTHER MATERIALS NEEDED / TEACHER'S NOTES:**

_____

_____

## LESSON OVERVIEW

**LIFE NEED FOR TODAY'S LESSON**
To embrace the values extolled in Proverbs 15.

**BIBLE LEARNING**
To recognize that without advice and support, the path of life is downward.

**BIBLE APPLICATION**
To desire an orderly life based on the wisdom of Proverbs.

**STUDENTS' RESPONSES**
Students will translate these proverbs into life lessons for today.

## LESSON SCRIPTURE

### PROVERBS 15:21–33, KJV

**21** Folly is joy to him that is destitute of wisdom: but a man of understanding walketh uprightly.

### PROVERBS 15:21–33, AMP

**21** Foolishness is joy to him who is without heart and lacks [intelligent, common] sense,

22 Without counsel purposes are disappointed: but in the multitude of counsellors they are established.

23 A man hath joy by the answer of his mouth: and a word spoken in due season, how good is it!

24 The way of life is above to the wise, that he may depart from hell beneath.

25 The LORD will destroy the house of the proud: but he will establish the border of the widow.

26 The thoughts of the wicked are an abomination to the LORD: but the words of the pure are pleasant words.

27 He that is greedy of gain troubleth his own house; but he that hateth gifts shall live.

28 The heart of the righteous studieth to answer: but the mouth of the wicked poureth out evil things.

29 The LORD is far from the wicked: but he heareth the prayer of the righteous.

30 The light of the eyes rejoiceth the heart: and a good report maketh the bones fat.

31 The ear that heareth the reproof of life abideth among the wise. 32 He that refuseth instruction despiseth his own soul: but he that heareth reproof getteth understanding.

33 The fear of the LORD is the instruction of wisdom; and before honour is humility.

But a man of understanding walks uprightly [making his course straight].

22 Without consultation and wise advice, plans are frustrated, But with many counselors they are established and succeed.

23 A man has joy in giving an appropriate answer, And how good and delightful is a word spoken at the right moment—how good it is!

24 The [chosen] path of life leads upward for the wise, That he may keep away from Sheol (the nether world, the place of the dead) below.

25 The Lord will tear down the house of the proud and arrogant (self-righteous), But He will establish and protect the boundaries [of the land] of the [godly] widow.

26 Evil plans and thoughts of the wicked are exceedingly vile and offensive to the LORD, But pure words are pleasant words to Him.

27 He who profits unlawfully brings suffering to his own house, But he who hates bribes [and does not receive nor pay them] will live.

28 The heart of the righteous thinks carefully about how to answer [in a wise and appropriate and timely way], But the [babbling] mouth of the wicked pours out malevolent things.

29 The Lord is far from the wicked [and distances Himself from them], But He hears the prayer of the [consistently] righteous [that is, those with spiritual integrity and moral courage].

30 The light of the eyes rejoices the hearts of others, And good news puts fat on the bones.

31 The ear that listens to and learns from the life-giving rebuke (reprimand, censure) Will remain among the wise.

**32** He who neglects and ignores instruction and discipline despises himself, But he who learns from rebuke acquires understanding [and grows in wisdom].

**33** The [reverent] fear of the LORD [that is, worshiping Him and regarding Him as truly awesome] is the instruction for wisdom [its starting point and its essence]; And before honor comes humility.

## BIBLICAL DEFINITIONS

A. **Abomination (Proverbs 15:26)** *towè-bah* (Heb.)—A disgusting thing.
B. **Reproof (vv. 31, 32)** *towkechah* (Heb.)—Rebuke, correction, punish, chastisement.

## LIGHT ON THE WORD

Most of the verses in **Proverbs 15** are composed of two-sentence couplets that extend or balance a single illustration. Each proverb sets before us advantages and disadvantages, blessings and curses, or choices made by the wise and the foolish. **Proverbs 15** has three sections that teach us how to speak wisely, live life happily, and embrace the blessings of good advice.

## TEACHING THE BIBLE LESSON

## LIFE NEED FOR TODAY'S LESSON

AIM: **That your students will recall the wisdom of the Proverbs in times of trouble and joy.**

## INTRODUCTION

### The Importance of Advice

Solomon explained that it is easier to know what to do when one seeks the advice of others. In this fatherly advice, Solomon encouraged his children to shy away from making decisions alone and to avoid hasty decision-making. Obtaining counsel from others promotes sound judgment, support, and success.

## BIBLE LEARNING

AIM: **That your students will align their daily actions with God's Word.**

## I. RIGHT ACTIONS
## (Proverbs 15:21–24)

Merriam-Webster defines "folly" as "lack of good sense," which leads to terrible results and, in some cases, tragic outcomes. The focus of this week's lesson is folly and the serious urgency it demands.

### Don't Face It Alone (verses 21-24)
**21 Folly is joy to him that is destitute of wisdom: but a man of understanding walketh uprightly. 22 Without counsel purposes are disappointed: but in the multitude of counsellors they are established. 23 A man hath joy by the answer of his mouth: and a word spoken in due season, how good is it! 24 The way of life is above to the wise, that he may depart from hell beneath.**

Foolish people isolate themselves when they make decisions. This generally comes from overconfidence that leads them to failure. The stumbling occurs when the person comes upon defeating circumstances that they could have been prepared for or even foreseen if only the person had used wisdom. Nevertheless, the fool delights in folly and does not seem to comprehend the outcome of an immoral deed. A foolish person follows any whim and finds delight in impulsive behavior because he or she "is destitute of wisdom." To find joy and satisfaction in folly are definitely signs of stupidity, because folly can bring disaster.

In contrast, the wise person has insight, appreciates the potential for danger, and, therefore, walks "uprightly" or in a "straight course." **Verse 21b** underscores the importance of good judgment and suggests that a valuable lifestyle must be maintained by wise decisions. In fact, **verse 22 e**xplains that a successful plan requires using good advice; this general observation has value on the personal and national level. Imprudent action brings disaster; prudent action gives security. Failure to seek advice is a sign of pride, but seeking advice from many counselors can avert disaster.

**Verses 21** and **22** concentrate on the disappointment of foolish and unwise decisions. **Verse 23** provides a contrast and speaks of the joy that comes with the answer spoken in wisdom. "A word spoken in due season" is advice given at the right moment and in the most suitable manner, when the occasion and the interests at stake demand it. The latter part of **verse 23** points out that content and timing are synonymous in importance. The well thought out and appropriate instruction requires knowledge and wisdom. Obviously good advice and good timing do notalways coincide. One of the ideals of the sage was to have the right word at the right time, as this verse indicates.

**Verse 24** contrasts living with death and going to the grave. Seeking wisdom brings a promise of long life. Foolish decisions and choices can be detrimental to life itself.

## SEARCH THE SCRIPTURES
### QUESTION 1
What primary benefit of wisdom is listed in Proverbs 15:24?

**Those who seek wisdom avoid hell.**

## LIGHT ON THE WORD
### Plotting Disaster
In contrast to **Proverbs 11:14,** where the national interest is at the forefront, consultation here is advised for more personal matters. If a person determines the nature of a matter, and goes about its resolution hastily and precipitously, without mature deliberation, without consulting and taking the advice of others in forming a strategy to bring about desired results, it generally comes to nothing. Plans created by one person tend to be less effective than they could be. Wise planning encourages participation and counsel from a variety of people.

## II. RIGHT RESPONSE
## (Proverbs 15:25-27)

**Proverbs 15:21-24** gave a view of earthly behaviors. Verses 25-27 introduce God's concern for rightly responding to life's decisions.

### What God Requires (verses 25-27)
**25 The LORD will destroy the house of the proud: but he will establish the border of the widow. 26 The thoughts of the wicked are an abomination to the LORD: but the words of the pure are pleasant words. 27 He that is greedy of gain troubleth his own house; but he that hateth gifts shall live.**

The Lord administers His justice through righteousness. He brings down the proud but protects the needy. The proud, self-confident man shall be uprooted along with his family, his household, and his wealth. The second part of **verse 25** refers to the particular vulnerability of widows in Israelite society. Widows had no one but themselves to mount a defense against encroachments and oppression (**Isaiah 1:23; Jeremiah 7:6**). The widow often typifies weakness and desolation in the Scriptures (see **Deuteronomy 10:18; Psalm 146:9**). Because of family, society, and circumstances, the widow was humble or weak, depending only on God for help. These verses explain that God will take the widow under His protection and see to it that her property is secured. Scripture amply confirms that the Lord champions the cause of the widow, the orphan, the poor, and the needy.

**Verse 26** refers to wicked plans or designs. These are an abomination to the Lord as are the devices of the wicked. On the one hand, the intentions or "thoughts of the wicked" are thoughts that will harm other people. On the other hand, the Lord is pleased with plans that have righteous intentions. The phrase "but the words of the pure are pleasant words" means literally that words of a soothing, comforting tone are pure in a ceremonial sense, as a pure and acceptable offering. "Pleasant words" are not sweet nothings. They are the opposite of the wicked plans of **verse 26** and thus express the virtuous designs of the just.

Those who are secure in their circumstances will not succumb to the evil devices of avarice. The "greedy" is the one who wants a big cut, who is in a hurry to get rich, and who is not particular about how it happens. In **Proverbs 15:27**, "gifts" could be innocent enough, but they could also be bribes that alter one's values. Hating bribes is the safest path to follow.

### QUESTION 2

What will God do for the widow? (Proverbs 15:25)

**He will enlarge the widows' border, meaning give protection and support when they have nowhere to turn.**

**Answers will vary.**

## LIGHT ON THE WORD
### Right Speaking

Right speaking includes knowing when to speak, speaking with pure motives and good intentions, and speaking profitably, truly, and pertinently. A fool speaks wrongly. Foolish words are ill timed. The person who says whatever comes to his mind speaks with evil intent and dishonors the hearers. Thus, it is the right word spoken at the right time. It may not be the word that is sought and asked for. It may even be an unwelcome word, a startling word, a word of rebuke. Whether by way of advice and counsel, or of exhortation and instruction, or of comfort, the Lord provides such words to His people.

## III. SPEAK WELL, THINK RIGHT (Proverbs 15:28-30)

While speaking well is a strength, speaking right is vital. An articulate person speaks well—he knows how to express himself, pronounces his words precisely, and is verbally captivating—but a wise person speaks right. It is of great importance not only to consider the matter, but also the manner of our utterances.

### Right Speaking (verses 28-30)
**28 The heart of the righteous studieth to answer: but the mouth of the wicked poureth out evil things. 29 The LORD is far from the wicked: but he heareth the prayer of the righteous. 30 The light of the eyes rejoiceth the heart: and a good report maketh the bones fat.**

Speech is the one thing that many think they

have a right to squander. There is probably no more common recklessness than that of the tongue. In **verse 28,** we find a contrast between deliberate speech and a deluge of thoughtless words. The righteous person "weighs" or "meditates" on how to answer. The thoughtful discourse of the just is the opposite of the rash, actually "evil" speech of the "wicked." Those who are wise are cautious in how they answer, as opposed to the wicked, who blurt out vicious things.

Wicked words are typical of wicked people. Wickedness puts distance between God and thesinner **(Exodus 33:3; Isaiah 59:2).** Those who turn their ears away from hearing God's words are inattentive to God's commands, thus making their prayers abominable to God **(Psalm 10:1; Proverbs 15:8; 28:9).** The distance of God from humans is expressed as His not hearing their prayers (e.g., **Psalm 10:1**). The wicked keep a distance from Him; so He is "far" from them–– an idea that signifies He is inaccessible or deaf to their appeals. Of course, a prayer of repentance by the wicked is the exception, for by it they would become the righteous. But God is near the righteous and hears their prayer. The prayers of the just gives delight to God **(Proverbs 8).**

Good news is uplifting to hear. A "cheerful look," (NIV) may indicate the gleam in the eyes of someone who tells good news, as the parallel second clause suggests. The idea of "health to the bones" (NIV) comes from a Hebrew expression found in the KJV "maketh the bones fat," and it is a symbol of health and prosperity. These are the results of right speaking.

### Right Thinking (verses 31–33)
**31 The ear that heareth the reproof of life abideth among the wise. 32 He that refuseth instruction despiseth his own soul: but he that heareth reproof getteth understanding. 33 The fear of the LORD is the instruction of wisdom; and before honour is humility.**

The hinge on which right speaking and right actions swing is right thinking. **Verse 31** shows how someone who listens to "constructive criticism" will feel comfortable among wise people. The development of wisdom requires a willingness to hear and integrate perspectives that may run counter to previously held convictions. This is the implication of the word "reproof," which means "censure." This is also in opposition to the "scorner" of **Proverbs 15:12** and to anyone who will not listen to reproof. A listener who hears a rebuke receives it gratefully and obeys it.

To abide "among the wise" implies that either a person who listens to reproof will thereby be made wise and be esteemed as one of that number.

**Verse 32** emphasizes the reward of teachability (compare with **Proverbs 5:12**). Note the connection between discipline and understanding, and the neglect of discipline and death. If embracing instruction leads to the preservation of life, he that "refuseth" willfully rejects and despises instruction—throws it all in the way of danger. This willful rejection of wise counsel istantamount to considering one's "own soul" as vile and worthless, as the word "despise" signifies. Discipline is often at odds with youthful inclinations, but accepting discipline is both necessary and important to spiritual development. Being a good disciple demands being a good listener, which in turn implies a willingness to receive rebuke.

The verse takes up the theme of "fear of the LORD" from **Proverbs 1:7** and **9:10** is the subject of **verse 33.** Humble submission, in faith to the Lord, is not only the beginning of wisdom but also its continuance. The last part of **Proverbs 15:33,** "before honour is humility" has its contrast in **Proverbs 18:12,** where pride leads to destruction. Here humility brings honor. It is the over- estimation of self that makes us contemptuous toward others. A person who fears God must be humble. Just as the fear of God leads to wisdom, it may be said that humility leads to the honor and glory of being wise and reckoned thusly among the wise (**verse 31**). God shall honor those who have the humility to accept Him and His guidance.

## SEARCH THE SCRIPTURES

### QUESTION 3

What does it mean to "abide among the wise"?

**This means becoming a wise person and living a wise lifestyle. It can also mean being respected by those who are considered wise. In the final sense, it is being recognized by God for wise actions and thought.**

**Answers will vary.**

## LIGHT ON THE WORD

### Avoid Moral Suicide

According to the Septuagint (the Greek version of the Old Testament commonly designated by LXX), a willful person commits moral suicide because he does not follow the path of life. He is like a sick man who "thrusts away" the wholesome medicine that offers his only hope of cure. In contrast, the person who hears reproof acquires understanding.

## BIBLE APPLICATION

**AIM: That your students will be able to consider how poor choices result from a lack of advice.**

### Flawed Patterns of Thinking

Some families have been raised to keep quiet about their plans, pregnancies, dreams, and goals for fear of being jinxed, ridiculed, or talked about. Such behavior shuns seeking wisdom and good advice. These unwise decisions have led to disparities in education, entrepreneurship, and homeownership. How can we change these patterns and encourage our youth, our churches, and our communities to seek support and guidance from others?

## STUDENTS' RESPONSES

**AIM: That your students will identify personal sources for advice and wisdom**

### Seeking Advice

Are you one to seek advice from others? If so, with whom do you consult? Sometimes family and friends may not be the best people to consider when you need advice. This is especially true if they are not supportive or experienced in the area about which you have questions. Do you have an important decision to make? If you are on the cusp of a new venture or a major decision, prayerfully identify at least two to three supportive and experienced people you can talk to about your plans. Don't forget to take a list of questions you have and to ask God for boldness in seeking advice.

## PRAYER

Dear God, help us to be wise in our decision-making and to seek wise counsel. In Jesus' Name, Amen.

## DIG A LITTLE DEEPER

Television shows featuring experts that give advice enjoy considerable popularity. They tell us how to solve family problems, handle health issues, finances, dating, and even how to remodel your house. Are all these programs reliable or are they simply geared to building an audience? How can we decide who to ask for advice and whether we should take it?

Sometimes those who have experience in our area of concern appear to be the best people to consult. Some look for credentials when deciding who to ask, others think an older person is the best choice. Noted pastor and teacher Warren Wiersbe warned, "Not everybody who grows old, grows up. There is a vast difference between age and maturity." Drawing from the book of James, Wiersbe adds that there is a difference between knowledge and wisdom: "knowledge enables us to take things apart, but wisdom enables us to put things together and relate God's truth to daily life."

The most reliable source of human advice is likely to be someone whose experience has yielded both knowledge and maturity: a Christian who has "grown up" as evidenced by the spiritual fruit on display in his or her life. Are you one of those who have the maturity to advice others, and do you associate with others who are?

Warren W. Wiersbe, Be Mature: How to break the mold of spiritual immaturity and grow up in Christ (Wheaton, IL: Victor Books, 1978), 5 and 103-105.

## HOW TO SAY IT

| | |
|---|---|
| Sheol. | Shē-ōl. |
| Achan. | Ay-kan. |
| Achor. | Ay-kor. |
| Jericho. | Je-ri-kō. |
| Gehazi. | Ge-Ha-dzi. |
| Abomination. | ab-o-mi-na-sion. |
| Septuagint. | SEP-too-uh-jint'. |
| Naaman. | Nay-a-man. |

## DAILY HOME BIBLE READINGS

### MONDAY
A Wise Child
(Proverbs 10:1–5)

### TUESDAY
Wise Words
(Proverbs 10:18–22)

### WEDNESDAY
Wisdom and Wealth
(Proverbs 10:23–28)

### THURSDAY
The Wicked and the Foolish
(Proverbs 12:12–16)

### FRIDAY
A Righteous Life
(Proverbs 14:27–34)

### SATURDAY
The Better Way
(Proverbs 15:15–19)

### SUNDAY
Instruction in Wisdom
(Proverbs 15:21–33)

## PREPARE FOR NEXT SUNDAY

Read **Proverbs 25:1-10** and study "Wisdom and Discernment."

Sources:
Baltes, A. J., ed. Biblespeech.com. http://biblespeech.com (accessed July 6, 2010).
Clarke, Adam. Clarke's Commentary, Vol. 2: Job–Malachi. Nashville, TN: Abingdon, n.d. Garrett, Duane A. Proverbs, Ecclesiastes, Song of Songs. New American Commentary,
Vol. 14. Nashville, TN: Broadman, 1993.
Hebrew and Greek Lexicons. Bible Study Tools.com. http://www.biblestudytools.com/lexicons (accessed September 16, 2010).
Kidner, Derek. Proverbs: An Introduction and Commentary. Downers Grove, IL: InterVarsity Press, 1964.
Merriam-Webster Online Dictionary. Merriam-Webster, Inc. http:// www.merriam-webster.com (accessed July 6, 2010).
Murphy, Roland E. Proverbs. Nashville, TN: Thomas Nelson, 1998.
Strong, James. New Exhaustive Strong's Numbers and Concordance with Expanded Greek-Hebrew Dictionary. Seattle, WA: Biblesoft, and International Bible Translators, 1994.
Warren W. Wiersbe, Be Mature: How to break the mold of spiritual immaturity and grow up in Christ (Wheaton, IL: Victor Books, 1978), 5 and 103-105.

# WISDOM AND DISCERNMENT

**BIBLE BASIS:** Proverbs 25:1-10

**BIBLE TRUTH:** Godly wisdom helps us purify our lives, relationships, and workplaces.

**MEMORY VERSE:** Debate thy cause with thy neighbour himself; and discover not a secret to another (Proverbs 25:9, KJV).

**LESSON AIM:** By the end of this lesson, we will: KNOW the wisdom of following godly advice in dealing with others; FEEL what it means to treat others as we desire to be treated; and DO an intentional act that promotes harmony with others.

**BACKGROUND SCRIPTURES:** Proverbs 25:1–28— Read and incorporate the insights gained from the Background Scriptures into your study of the lesson.

## TEACHER PREPARATION

**MATERIALS NEEDED:** Bibles (several different versions), Quarterly Commentary/Teacher Manual, Adult Quarterly, teaching resources such as charts, worksheets/handouts, paper, pens, and pencils.

**OTHER MATERIALS NEEDED / TEACHER'S NOTES:**

_____

_____

## LESSON OVERVIEW

**LIFE NEED FOR TODAY'S LESSON**
To remember that we they can promote harmony with others.

**BIBLE LEARNING**
To realize that wisdom should build our relationships with others.

**BIBLE APPLICATION**
To begin to understand that wisdom should purify our relationships with others.

**STUDENTS' RESPONSES**
Students will discern how important godly wisdom is.

## LESSON SCRIPTURE

### PROVERBS 25:1-10, 20, KJV

**1** These are also proverbs of Solomon, which the men of Hezekiah king of Judah copied out.

### Proverbs 25:1-10, AMP

**1** These are also the proverbs of Solomon, which the men of Hezekiah king of Judah copied:

**2** It is the glory of God to conceal a thing: but the honour of kings is to search out a matter.

**3** The heaven for height, and the earth for depth, and the heart of kings is unsearchable.

**4** Take away the dross from the silver, and there shall come forth a vessel for the finer.

**5** Take away the wicked from before the king, and his throne shall be established in righteousness.

**6** Put not forth thyself in the presence of the king, and stand not in the place of great men:

**7** For better it is that it be said unto thee, Come up hither; than that thou shouldest be put lower in the presence of the prince whom thine eyes have seen.

**8** Go not forth hastily to strive, lest thou know not what to do in the end thereof, when thy neighbour hath put thee to shame.

**9** Debate thy cause with thy neighbour himself; and discover not a secret to another:

**10** Lest he that heareth it put thee to shame, and thine infamy turn not away.

**2** It is the glory of God to conceal a matter, But the glory of kings is to search out a matter.

**3** As the heavens for height and the earth for depth, So the hearts and minds of kings are unsearchable.

**4** Take away the dross from the silver, And there comes out [the pure metal for] a vessel for the silversmith [to shape].

**5** Take away the wicked from before the king, And his throne will be established in righteousness.

**6** Do not be boastfully ambitious and claim honor in the presence of the king, And do not stand in the place of great men;

**7** For it is better that it be said to you, "Come up here," Than for you to be placed lower in the presence of the prince, Whom your eyes have seen.

**8** Do not rush out to argue your case [before magistrates or judges]; Otherwise what will you do in the end [when your case is lost and] When your neighbor (opponent) humiliates you?

**9** Argue your case with your neighbor himself [before you go to court]; And do not reveal another's secret,

**10** Or he who hears it will shame you, And the rumor about you [and your action in court] will have no end.

## BIBLICAL DEFINITIONS

A. **Unsearchable (Proverbs 25:3)** *cheqer* (Heb.)—Incomprehensible; beyond human investigation.

B. **Debate (v. 9)** *riyb* (Heb.)—To strive or plead; to contend against, argue or make a complaint against.

## LIGHT ON THE WORD

Solomon was the third king of Israel and David's son. He reigned for 40 years from around 971 to 931 B.C. Solomon is attributed with 3000 proverbs and 1005 songs. He was David's chosen heir; he built God's Temple in Jerusalem as well as great works that secured the water supply and defended the city of Jerusalem. After Solomon's death, the Kingdom was divided into two. The Northern Kingdom was Israel; the Southern Kingdom was Judah.

Hezekiah was a descendant of David's bloodline. He was the son and successor of Ahaz. Hezekiah was the 15th king of Judah, the Southern Kingdom He ruled from around 715 to 686 B.C. He began his 29-year reign at the age of 25. Hezekiah was a patron of respect, who removed idolatrous practices and centers, and resumed observance of Passover and temple worship. He prompted civil and religious reform.The "Men of Hezekiah" or "Friends of Hezekiah" were scribes or counselors of that compiled and edited 137 proverbs during the reign of King Hezekiah in order to reveal the traditional wisdom and sayings while elevating the forgotten wisdom of David and Solomon.

### TEACHING THE BIBLE LESSON

### LIFE NEED FOR TODAY'S LESSON

**AIM: That your students will appreciate that wisdom should guide their relationships with other.**

## INTRODUCTION

### The Book of Proverbs and Solomon's Reign

The Book of Proverbs was primarily written by Solomon with contributions from Agur son of Jakeh and Lemuel, a king that received words of wisdom from his mother about wine, women, and legal rights of the weak and poor. Proverbs gives instruction in wisdom, ways of life in God's world, and the preparation for life. The men of Hezekiah transcribed or copied the proverbs and did not author them.

During the early part of Solomon's reign, he wrote and gathered the book of Proverbs. Solomon passed on his practical advice through the short, concise sentences that communicate moral truth. Forty-seven times the book conveys information about wisdom, or essentially, "the skill of living." The wisdom revealed in the book of Proverbs is practical to promote prosperity, productivity, and responsibility in humanity.

### BIBLE LEARNING

**AIM: That your students will desire godly wisdom**

## I. GODLY WISDOM SHOULD BUILD RELATIONSHIPS (Proverbs 25:1-3)

In **Proverbs 25,** we read that Hezekiah's men transcribed Solomon's wisdom. Solomon and Hezekiah were both patrons of wisdom in Israel. They were scholarly kings who lived during a time when governmental power and academic power were closely associated. **Proverbs 25** through **29** constitute a book within the book of Proverbs. This section gives insight to relationships with kings, but the information can be used to develop good and equitable relationships. The Scripture gives instruction for leaders and individuals who seek to become leaders.

### The Proverbs of Solomon
### (verses 1-3)

**1 These are also proverbs of Solomon, which the men of Hezekiah king of Judah copied out. 2 It is the glory of God to conceal a thing: but the honour of kings is to search out a matter. 3 The heaven for height, and the earth for depth, and the heart of kings is unsearchable.**

**Proverbs 25:2** refers to the "glory of God," which is God's overwhelming presence, the display of who God is. God's glory is the ultimate power, perfection, and transcendence. Although God's glory is incomprehensible, Solomon instructs humanity to study and search God's Word (**verses 2–3**). The more believers know God, the more we will reflect God's glory. Although difficult at times, the instruction is to search and study God's Word so that His Word can help us in building relationships. God does not reveal all of who He is to us because we cannot comprehend it. God's being is concealed and we search to know Him better throughout our lives. That is wisdom. That's why a wise king will search out a matter for understanding. As Solomon searched the heart of the true mother when he issued an order to divide a child, a king must seek the truth to rule righteously (refer to **1 Kings 3:24–28**).

This section of the book contains additional proverbs attributed to Solomon that were collected by the men of King Hezekiah (715–687 B.C.). The word "also" connects this portion of the collection with **Proverbs 10:1** and **24:23**. These scribes or scholars "copied out" the sayings (i.e., transcribed them from one book to another). The fact that "men" transcribed these proverbs, instead of referring to a single scribe, most likely refers to the entire process of "writing," "arranging," and the "collation of texts."

## SEARCH THE SCRIPTURES
### QUESTION 1
The men of what king copied these proverbs?

"These are also proverbs of Solomon, which the men of Hezekiah king of Judah copied out."

## LIGHT ON THE WORD
### The Wicked and the Righteous
In Proverbs, one finds numerous examples that contrast the wicked with the righteous. In particular, the wicked represent persons who live outside the confines of a faithful relationship with God and His people. Such persons transgress God's Law with seeming impunity, show injustice toward others, and, overall, exhibit self-centered living. In our day, persons usually are exalted to lofty positions of influence and power based upon academic credentials, social contacts, or outstanding personality traits. However, notice that the writer focuses on the character of those who surround the king. The need for a king to surround himself with honest servants is frequently emphasized (see **Psalm 101**). This is in agreement with the idea that justice is the foundation of his throne (**Proverbs 16:12; 20:28; 29:14**).

## II. PURIFICATION IS A MUST
## (Proverbs 25:4-5)

As the refiner separates the dross from the silver, which mars its beauty and purity, so should the king exclude from his presence and counsels the reckless and the base. Just as it is impossible to have a sterling silver vessel until the silver has been purified, no nation can have a king who is a public blessing until the wicked—all the bad counselors, wicked and interested ministers, and flatterers—are banished from the cabinet and positions of power. When the wise and good are the king's only ministers and advisers, then the throne will be established in righteousness, and his administration be a universal blessing. Any court, pure or vicious, has immense influence on the manners and morals of the community. This is also true of individuals. We should be careful to realize this when seeking advice, choose our company wisely, and be careful whom we allow to speak into our lives.

### A Separation (verses 4-5)
**4 Take away the dross from the silver, and there shall come forth a vessel for the finer. 5 Take away the wicked from before the king, and his throne shall be established in righteousness.**

In **verse 4,** the writer employs the imagery of purification of metals as the basis of his analogy in **verse 5.** The "dross" in **verse 4** is analogous to the wicked or scoundrels in **verse 5** to show the polluting influence of the wicked when allowed into the corridors of power. Thus, the writer compares the scoundrels in the king's presence to the dross in refining silver. The king must take steps to root out wicked and corrupt officials if he is to lay a solid foundation for a good and just rule. A mark of the wise king or ruler is that he ensures he has surrounded himself with officials and counselors marked by integrity.

The "dross" that exists within society and a kingdom are evil individuals, conspirators, and liars who seek to create problems, division, and difficulty. An evil advisor can create chaos in the workplace, home, or social environment. When the "dross" is taken out of a kingdom, a relationship, or a community, the result is a relationship based on righteousness and honor. Wisdom purifies relationships.

### QUESTION 2
What happens when the "dross" is taken out of a kingdom, a relationship, or a community?

**One can have a relationship based on righteousness and honor.**

**Answers will vary.**

## LIGHT ON THE WORD
### What Wisdom Teaches
**Verses 4** and **5** discuss getting to the best by stripping away anything that is hiding true value. These are examples of the value of wisdom. Humility and self-denial are important lessons thatare taught by wisdom. The message of **verses 6** and **7** is reiterated in **Luke 14:7–11.** Do not seek a place of honor where you will receive attention. Instead, seek to accomplish the purpose that God has given to you. Solomon instructed individuals not to pursue the best or most prominent places in life. Instead, individuals should purposely take the lowest place. On the other hand, society encourages individuals to strive for the most recognizable or viewed position––the place of recognition and believed honor. In **Luke 14,** Jesus taught that individuals should not seek social recognition through relationships, appearance, titles, or material possession. Jesus instructed individuals to seek positions where they can serve and allow God to lift them to places of prominence as God purposes.

## III. LET WISDOM GUIDE YOUR RELATIONSHIPS(Proverbs 25:6-7)

Solomon instructed believers to live humbly and modestly in order to be advanced instead of being put "lower in the presence of the prince." God will lift up and honor believers according to His perfect plan.

### Oh, to Have Wisdom (verses 6-7)!
**6 Put not forth thyself in the presence of the king, and stand not in the place of great men: 7 For better it is that it be said unto thee, Come up hither; than that thou shouldest be put lower in the presence of the prince whom thine eyes have seen.**

These verses deal with the actions of those in the court of the king or in the presence of someone who is great. Nothing in conduct is unimportant. Fitting and graceful manners should become our routine. It is wiser to wait to be promoted than to risk demotion by self-promotion. Self- respect is complemented by deference. Promoting yourself while in court may risk public humiliation, but it would be an honor to have everyone in court hear the promotion from the king himself. This is the paradox of Christianity: Humility leads to exaltation, but grasping at more than our due is to lose all and earn condemnation. We must avoid presumption in any of its forms—it is an offense hateful to humankind and God.

## SEARCH THE SCRIPTURES

### QUESTION 3
Why is self-promotion deemed unwise?

**It earns condemnation and is an offense to humankind.**

## LIGHT ON THE WORD

### Disputes Damage Relationships
There are important lessons to learn from **Proverbs 25:8.** First, disputes are unavoidable. In view of conflict and complicated interests—individual, domestic, social, economic, civic, international—differences and difficulties often arise amongst us. There are always and will be conflicts of opinion—wishes and purposes clash; their divergence may result in dissension, including in Christian congregations. Second, the temptation is to be hasty either in jumping to conclusions or in acting rashly. Using the judicial system to mediate conflicts, including those between neighbors, can be one hastily applied result of struggles. But often these actions do no good other than to permanently damage relationships.

## IV. DISPUTES ERECT BARRIERS
(Proverbs 25:8-10)

Disputes erect a barrier between us and our neighbors and make it difficult, if not entirely impossible, to ever again live alongside one another in harmony. Instead, disputes handled unwisely sow seeds of bitterness and discord, which will bear fruit throughout our days. Rather than spreading disharmony and friction, Christians must seek to be peacemakers who love God, each other, and our neighbors.

### Think Before You Act (verses 8-10)
**8 Go not forth hastily to strive, lest thou know not what to do in the end thereof, when thy neighbour hath put thee to shame. 9 Debate thy cause with thy neighbour himself; and discover not a secret to another: 10 Lest he that heareth it put thee to shame, and thine infamy turn not away.**

According to societal standards today, almost all disputes can be handled in the court system. Both parties meet in a courtroom where a judge listens to both sides and makes a decision based on the evidence that is presented. A third party settles the differences that created the disagreement. While some disputes demand court action or outside mediation, Solomon's advice is to discuss differences instead of rushing to court. He instructs that: (1) we should try to handle complaints and disagreements on a private level instead of going to court; (2) we should not complain to others about our neighbor, friend, or coworker; (3) we should not discuss with others what we have discussed with another person in secret because the result will only create trouble and negatively affect our reputations; and (4) after the disagreement has been discussed, end it privately and we will not endure shame.

### QUESTION 4
Why shouldn't we rush into disputes?

**We should strive to be "peacemakers".**

59

Answers will vary.

## BIBLE APPLICATION

**AIM: That your students will begin to understand that just as God has forgiven us of our trespasses, we should forgive others**

### The Way of Peace

In **Proverbs 25:10,** the writer exposes what is at stake when one goes about with rash, impetuous behavior. Settling matters peaceably and privately can prevent escalation in a public arena, where many times things can be misconstrued, a person's reputation can be slandered, or even violence can result. The example given in this verse is about a person who reveals someone else's secret. When the person learns of the indiscretion, the shame suffered by the guilty party leads to a bad reputation that is difficult to overcome. In a case such as this reputation and friendship are ruined. Wisdom dictates that we always seek to maintain peace

## STUDENT RESPONSES

**AIM: That your students will desire to use wisdom in their relationships.**

### Reaching Out in Relationship

Exercising wisdom in handling and building relationships is not easy. Consider this scenario.

Frantically, Brenda knocked at her neighbor's door. When Veronica opened the door, Brenda asked, "Can you please take me to work? My car won't start! If I'm late another day, I will lose my job."

Immediately, Veronica grabbed her jacket and rushed to take Brenda to work. Later that day, Veronica saw Brenda at the local store, but Brenda didn't speak. Veronica had always spoken to Brenda, but she didn't receive the same response in return.

After Brenda and Veronica had been neighbors for 12 years, Veronica was accustomed to being ignored by Brenda. However, Veronica always treated Brenda with love and compassion.

Several weeks later, Brenda called Veronica to drive her to the hospital. Her brother was ill. The entire trip, Veronica spoke but Brenda barely responded. After they arrived at the hospital, Brenda got out of the car without saying anything.

As Veronica drove home, she prayed for Brenda and her family, and decided that she did not want to be treated disrespectfully by Brenda anymore. Veronica asked God to give her instructions on how to deal with Brenda.

How can Veronica continue to reveal God's love to Brenda when her actions are not reciprocated?

## PRAYER

Father in heaven; help us to represent You well as we reach out to others in relationship. Help us to be examples of peacemakers. In Jesus' Name we pray, Amen.

## DIG A LITTLE DEEPER

When conflict erupts in our churches or neighborhoods, do we call the church elders, other respected community members, or the police to make peace? In 2020 when violence against unarmed African Americans seemed to crescendo, some suggested that social workers or others trained in conflict resolution should accompany or replace police officers called to the scene. They hoped this would prevent more violence and help restore communities.

Ideally, the church is a community. Nevertheless, even in church unresolved conflict can create major problems (**1 Corinthians 1:11 and James 4:1-4**). Feeling disrespected and disregarded or wanting more influence and power create major conflict inside and outside the church. Theologian Dr. Marva Dawn proposes that to build relationships that promote genuine respect and appreciation for our differences, Christians should apply the twelfth chapter of Romans in our churches. She says "Christian community sets us free from comparing ourselves with others and having to prove our own importance." What do you think? Where would you begin to make this biblical ideal reality?

Marva J. Dawn, The Hilarity of Community: Romans 12 and How to be the Church (Grand Rapids, Michigan: William B. Eerdmans Publishing Company, 1992), 72.

## DAILY HOME BIBLE READINGS

### MONDAY
The Creator's Hiddenness
(Isaiah 45:9–17)

### TUESDAY
Asking for Wisdom
(2 Kings 3:5–14)

### WEDNESDAY
Humbly Seeking God
(2 Chronicles 7:12–18)

### THURSDAY
Words Fitly Spoken
(Proverbs 25:11–15)

### FRIDAY
Wisdom with Neighbors
(Proverbs 25:16–20)

### SATURDAY
The Wisdom of Self-Control
(Proverbs 25:21–28)

### SUNDAY
Wisdom and Government
(Proverbs 25:1–10)

## PREPARE FOR NEXT SUNDAY

Read **Proverbs 29:16-27,** and study "An Ordered Life."

**Sources:**

Baltes, A. J., ed. Biblespeech.com. http://biblespeech.com (accessed July 6, 2010).

Clarke, Adam. Clarke's Commentary. Vol. 2: Job–Malachi. Nashville, TN: Abingdon, n.d. Clifford, Richard J. Proverbs. Louisville, KY: Westminster John Knox Press, 1999.

Emerson, Ralph Waldo. "Manners," Essays: Second Series. Boston: Phillips, Sampson & Company, 1850. 104.

Garrett, Duane A. Proverbs, Ecclesiastes, Song of Songs. New American Commentary, Vol. 14.

Nashville, TN: Broadman, 1993.

Hebrew and Greek Lexicons. Bible Study Tools.com. http://www. biblestudytools.com/lexicons (accessed September 16, 2010).

Kidner, Derek. Proverbs: An Introduction and Commentary. Downers Grove, IL: InterVarsity Press, 1964.

Merriam-Webster Online Dictionary. Merriam-Webster, Inc. http://www. merriam-webster.com (accessed July 6, 2010).

Murphy, Roland E. Proverbs. Nashville, TN: Thomas Nelson Publishers, 1998.

Roger Martin, "The Big Lie of Strategic Planning," Harvard Business Review <hbr.org/2014/01>.

Richard J. Foster, Celebration of Discipline: the Path to Spiritual Growth (New York: Harper Collins, 1998), 7-9.

Warren W. Wiersbe, Be Mature: How to break the mold of spiritual immaturity and grow up in Christ (Wheaton, IL: Victor Books, 1978), 5 and 103-105.

Marva J. Dawn, The Hilarity of Community: Romans 12 and How to be the Church (Grand Rapids, Michigan: William B. Eerdmans Publishing Company, 1992), 72.

## COMMENTS / NOTES:

_____

_____

_____

_____

_____

_____

_____

_____

_____

_____

_____

_____

_____

_____

_____

_____

_____

_____

_____

# AN ORDERED LIFE

**BIBLE BASIS:** Proverbs 29:16–27

**BIBLE TRUTH:** God calls us to trust in Him as our source for an ordered life.

**MEMORY VERSE:** The fear of man bringeth a snare: but whoso putteth his trust in the LORD shall be safe (Proverbs 29:25, KJV).

**LESSON AIM:** By the end of the lesson, we will: KNOW the relationship between an orderly life and trust in God; FEEL what it means to live an ordered life; and CREATE a strategy, based on godly principles, to live an ordered life.

**BACKGROUND SCRIPTURES:** Proverbs 28:1–29:27— Read and incorporate the insights gained from the Background Scriptures into your study of the lesson.

## TEACHER PREPARATION

**MATERIALS NEEDED:** Bibles (several different versions), Quarterly Commentary/Teacher Manual, Adult Quarterly, teaching resources such as charts, worksheets/handouts, paper, pens, and pencils.

**OTHER MATERIALS NEEDED / TEACHER'S NOTES:**

_____

_____

## LESSON OVERVIEW

### LIFE NEED FOR TODAY'S LESSON
To determine the relationship between an orderly life and trust in God.

### BIBLE LEARNING
To know what the Bible says about those things that cause disarray in our lives.

### BIBLE APPLICATION
To desire to change actions that push us outside of godly principles.

### STUDENTS' RESPONSES
Students will discern godly principles to live an ordered life.

## LESSON SCRIPTURE

### PROVERBS 29:16-27, KJV

**16** When the wicked are multiplied, transgression increaseth: but the righteous shall see their fall.

### PROVERBS 29:16-27, AMP

**16** When the wicked are in authority, transgression increases, But the righteous will see the downfall of the wicked.

**17** Correct thy son, and he shall give thee rest; yea, he shall give delight unto thy soul.

**18** Where there is no vision, the people perish: but he that keepeth the law, happy is he.

**19** A servant will not be corrected by words: for though he understand he will not answer.

**20** Seest thou a man that is hasty in his words? there is more hope of a fool than of him.

**21** He that delicately bringeth up his servant from a child shall have him become his son at the length.

**22** An angry man stirreth up strife, and a furious man aboundeth in transgression.

**23** A man's pride shall bring him low: but honour shall uphold the humble in spirit.

**24** Whoso is partner with a thief hateth his own soul: he heareth cursing, and bewrayeth it not.

**25** The fear of man bringeth a snare: but whoso putteth his trust in the LORD shall be safe.

**26** Many seek the ruler's favour; but every man's judgment cometh from the LORD. **27** An unjust man is an abomination to the just: and he that is upright in the way is abomination to the wicked.

**17** Correct your son, and he will give you comfort;Yes, he will delight your soul.

**18** Where there is no vision [no revelation of God and His word], the people are unrestrained;But happy and blessed is he who keeps the law [of God].

**19** A servant will not be corrected by words alone;For though he understands, he will not respond [nor pay attention].

**20** Do you see a [conceited] man who speaks quickly [offering his opinions or answering without thinking]? There is more hope for a [thickheaded] [a]fool than for him.

**21** He who pampers his slave from childhood Will find him to be a son in the end.

**22** An angry man stirs up strife, And a hot-tempered and undisciplined man commits many transgressions.

**23** A man's pride and sense of self-importance will bring him down, But he who has a humble spirit will obtain honor.

**24** Whoever is partner with a thief hates his own life; He hears the curse [when swearing an oath to testify], but discloses nothing [and commits perjury by omission].

**25** The fear of man brings a snare, But whoever trusts in and puts his confidence in the Lord will be exalted and safe.

**26** Many seek the ruler's favor, But justice for man comes from the Lord.

**27** An unjust man is repulsive to the righteous, And he who is upright in the way [of the Lord] is repulsive to the wicked.

## BIBLICAL DEFINITIONS

A. **Transgression (Proverbs 29:16)** *peshà* (Heb.)—Rebellion or sin against God or others; violation of a law.

B. **Correct (v. 17)** *yacar* (Heb.)—To instruct, chasten, discipline, punish or admonish.

## LIGHT ON THE WORD

The book of Proverbs reveals two major themes: wisdom and folly. Wisdom is "knowledge, understanding, discretion, obedience, and instruction based on God's Word and our reverence of God." Folly is "everything that contradicts wisdom." King Solomon is the sage that provided these insights on the perplexities of life **(Proverbs 1:6).**

## TEACHING THE BIBLE LESSON

## LIFE NEED FOR TODAY'S LESSON

**AIM: That your students will recognize how God's plan is superior to and in contrast with the world's sense of order.**

## INTRODUCTION

### Solomon's Wisdom

Because proverbs were not generally written, memorization was an effective way of teaching and learning them. The short, concise phrases that comprise Proverbs lend themselves to revealing and remembering divine truths.

## BIBLE LEARNING

**AIM: That your students will understand how a lack of discipline will destroy lives and society.**

## I. GOD COMMANDS SELF-CONTROL (Proverbs 29:16–22)

Proverbs teaches that a moral individual recognizes the immorality that exists within society. Immorality is more pronounced when sin flourishes and moral decay increases. Such times demand a prophet who is God's servant and who gives God's vision. A prophet imparts knowledge, understanding, and faith. Because a deficiency in hearing the Word of God leads to rebellion, prophetic exhortation is necessary for a viable, godly society. When society heeds the revelation and submits to God's Word, a blessing is pronounced on God's people.

**Weighing Your Words (verses 16-22)**
**16 When the wicked are multiplied, transgression increaseth: but the righteous shall see their fall. 17 Correct thy son, and he shall give thee rest; yea, he shall give delight unto thy soul. 18 Where there is no vision, the people perish: but he that keepeth the law, happy is he.**

In **Proverbs 29,** the just and the wicked are contrasted. The reign of the just person is beneficial to all, for it ensures the "great glory" of the populace. The rule of the wicked has the effect of driving people into hiding to get out of the way of injustice (cf. **Proverbs 28:12).** The first part of **Proverbs 29:16** affirms that when "the wicked are multiplied," transgression thrives. The second part of **verse 16** does not say how or when the victory of the just is signaled, we know, however, that the righteous will "see their downfall." Regardless of how much wickedness spreads in the land, right will win out.

Proverbs provides numerous references to discipline within the home. This advice is good in our times as well. Discipline or correction is not a popular word; it is sometimes equated or confused with child abuse. However, the writer of Proverbs focuses on discipline in a positive way, expressing the satisfaction and joy that parents will experience in correcting their children and witnessing the wisdom that emerges as a result. The first part of **Proverbs 29:17** is parallel to the second, but adds the thought of "delight." The word "delight" is a metaphor for the joy a responsible son brings. Used together, "delight" and "rest" suggest the image of a parent taking a deep breath and letting out a sigh of relief and pleasure at a child who has turned out well.

Discipline, as described above, provides the wisdom to understand God's vision. **Verse 18** is very popular and refers to divine revelation, vision, and law. Whether understood as prophetic vision or revelation, **Proverbs 29:18** underscores the significance of leadership and personal commitment that are truly spiritual and godly. If there is no revelation from God, people can expect spiritual and political anarchy. A nation's well being depends on obedience to divinerevelation. In addition, the one who keeps the law is a happy person. "The law" is not merely the Mosaic Law or the Ten Commandments; the law is the true proclamation of God's Word.

**19 A servant will not be corrected by words: for though he understand he will not answer. 20 Seest thou a man that is hasty in his words? there is more hope of a fool than of him. 21 He that delicately bringeth up his servant from a child shall have him become his son at the length. 22 An angry man stirreth up strife, and a furious man aboundeth in transgression.**

Everyone, regardless of position or status, requires discipline to recognize how to behave and speak in civil ways. **Verse 19** highlights the problem in any situation where people are unresponsive or silently disobedient. We have all experienced situations where people practice sullen behavior in order to cause strife. **Verse 19** teaches that those who know better, because they have been instructed properly but still disobey, will be punished. Neither life nor the Lord ignores such behavior.

**Proverbs 29** is also a strong condemnation of frivolity and rashness of speech. **Verse 20** applies to those who speak hastily without considering the implications of what they say. The person who is in a hurry to open his or her mouth may do so with the best of intentions. However, the words may turn out to be unhelpful and ruffle rather than soothe a difficult situation or strained relationship. Repeatedly engaging in such behavior is evidence of the person's foolishness. By the same token, the words "delicately bringeth up" in **verse 21,** refers to spoiling a person by pampering at the expense of discipline.

Anger brings strife. Using synonymous parallelism, **Proverbs 29:22** focuses on "an angry man" and "a furious man." The angry man stirs up dissension and causes sin in himself and in others. The word translated as "furious," literally means "heat." A furious person is hotheaded. This is the opposite of the person who knows how to restrain temper and tongue. An angry or hotheaded person is to be avoided because he or she "aboundeth in transgressions" **(Proverbs 29:22)** and, ultimately, will pay the penalty for the multitude of sins **(Proverbs 19:19).**

## SEARCH THE SCRIPTURES
### QUESTION 1
Where in the family does God place the responsibility for discipline?

**God places the responsibility with parents. In Solomon's time, this reference was primarily to fathers. Today, all parents or guardians are equally responsible for providing a sense of discipline and right conduct in a child's life.**

## LIGHT ON THE WORD
### The Need for Restraint
Because continual, thoughtless conversation may lead to sin, Solomon reminds us that

wisdom restrains the tongue. Rashly spoken words put the speaker on the level of a hopeless fool. In fact, because the individual believes there is no need for advice from others, hasty speech often reveals self-conceit and pride. Solomon's advice serves us well today. Trouble and strife within a family, neighborhood, or a workplace can provoke discord among individuals and ultimately throughout society. Unnecessary and undisciplined anger leads to sin and creates chaos.

Troublemakers do not promote peace; uncontrolled anger leads to sin. Make no mistake: There is a difference between righteous indignation—that takes a stand—and uncontrolled, unbridled anger that leads to sin. God, therefore, demands self-control.

## II. GOD COMMANDS HUMILITY (Proverbs 29:23–25)

Because people depend on themselves rather than God, Solomon taught that pride can lead people to live independently from God. Ultimately this shows that they do not trust God. Society encourages people to seek high positions where they will be praised, but God commands humility.

### The Place of Honor and Trust
### (verses 23-25)

**23 A man's pride shall bring him low: but honour shall uphold the humble in spirit. 24 Whoso is partner with a thief hateth his own soul: he heareth cursing, and bewrayeth it not. 25 The fear of man bringeth a snare: but whoso putteth his trust in the LORD shall be safe.**

In our competitive world "humility" is not rated very highly. Instead, it is seen as a sign of weakness rather than strength of character. The writer of Proverbs explains that a humble spirit brings honor and respect. **Proverbs 29:23** contrasts consequences: pride leads to abasement, but humility brings exaltation. The humble person does not seek honor, but by his or her life and action unconsciously attains it.

In the same manner that a person, who aids and abets a crime, is considered guilty, **verse 24** describes a person who is "partner with a thief" as engaging in spiritual self-hatred. The Old Testament (**Leviticus 5:1; Judges 17:2**), holds that if a theft was committed, the person wronged or the judge pronounced a curse on the thief and on anyone who was privy to the crime and refrained from giving information or refused to speak up. As such, a witness, who saw and knew of a crime and was silent during the formal proceedings, must bear his iniquity; he is not only an accomplice, but he is also a perjurer. One sin leads to another.

The final contrast in **verse 25** is between "the fear of man" and "his trust in" the Lord. Fear here is an inordinate fear of harm or suffering from others, particularly those in position of authority. It is opposed to trust in God, because it arises from a distrust of God's promises and providence. Such fear becomes a snare, which is an occasion for committing sins. Fearfulness allows others to control your life, letting their opinions and attitudes put subtle pressure on you. Fear can even hinder you from speaking the truth or doing what is right. Consequently, fear brings punishment from God. In contrast, the person who trusts in the Lord, who walks in God's ways, and completely relies on Him for protection from the schemes and malice of the wicked, shall be safe. That person shall be preserved from all evil, through God's watchful providence.

## SEARCH THE SCRIPTURES

### QUESTION 2
What qualities are valued and what benefits are found in Proverbs 29:24-25?

**Humility exalts and trusting God brings**

safety. When we are arrogant and believe in what we can achieve, we distort God's plan for our lives and our interactions with others.

Answers will vary.

## LIGHT ON THE WORD
### Right Is Right!

**Proverbs 29:24** confirms a truth that our court system carries out today. It states that if people partner with a thief and do not disclose the truth, they become the thief's accomplices and failure to tell the truth about that becomes perjury. The result will be punishment. A silent witness is guilty before God even though friends, family, and co-workers may not know. Seen and unseen wrongdoing do not please God. In our society today, there is a code among our youth that says "Don't Snitch." This flies in the face of Scripture and until we accept that everyone has a responsibility to what is right, we will live in turmoil and chaos. We must each accept our responsibility for doing what's right—all the time!

## III. GOD IS IN CONTROL (Proverbs 29:26–27)

Our legal system offers temporary relief from injustice. Ultimately, individuals will not be satisfied with a ruler's temporary favor. If believers trust in God with a committed faith, they will recognize that God demands justice. Thus, we must look to God and seek His favor because God is sovereign—in control of His universe and never out of control of it. As believers, then, we must make a choice between the path of righteousness and the way of immorality. We walk uprightly when we obey God's commands and depend upon Him. When we choose to obey God, we have security in the eternal promise of God and not the temporal objects and people in the world.

### The Ultimate Judge (verses 26-27)
**26 Many seek the ruler's favour; but every man's judgment cometh from the LORD. 27 An unjust man is an abomination to the just: and he that is upright in the way is abomination to the wicked.**

The contrast in the final verses is between seeking the grace of a ruler and finding justice from the Lord. Many try in times of need, by fair or surreptitious means, to curry favor with an important person. **Verse 26** reminds us that our destiny does not lie in their hands but in the hands of God, who has supreme judgment. It is proper that we seek recourse in our justice system, but it is a great miscalculation to assume that true justice depends on a human ruler and that supplication must be directed first to her or him. True justice ultimately comes from God, whose approval or disapproval is final and indisputable regardless of what we are promised or given by earthly officials or rulers, most of whom are prejudiced and certainly fallible.

As the verse shows, virtue and vice are antagonists. An "unjust" person considers the "upright" or "just" person an abomination. The just are those who are in covenant relationship with God through their faith. How we feel about the unjust is a reflection of our relationship with God. We should not harbor personal ill will or want others to suffer. Rather, we should pray for their salvation. We fall into a mistake, if not into a sin, when we allow ourselves to find pleasure in witnessing or dwelling on the humiliation or sorrow of the wicked.

This passage also declares that the wicked hate the just because their convictions, lifestyle, inclinations, and habits, represent the good that God wants all people to display. Living in harmony with God's plan and discipline for an ordered life is a public condemnation of the negative lifestyles of those who reject God.

## SEARCH THE SCRIPTURES

### QUESTION 3

Where do we find examples of people seeking "the ruler's favor" today?

**Answers will vary.**

## LIGHT ON THE WORD

### Recognize the Times

Moral decay has risen because societal moral standards have declined. Today as in biblical times, the transgressions increase as sinners become bolder. Sometimes things seem so bad that it is hard to believe that God will intervene, but He will. The psalmist David reminds us to, "Wait for the LORD and keep his way," because God will change things according to His time **(Psalm 37:34,** NIV). The wicked will be cut off and fall; the righteous will witness the downfall of the sinners. In the meanwhile, we cannot give up or give in. We must continue to exhibit God's truth to the world through our deeds and our actions.

## BIBLE APPLICATION

**AIM: That students will be able to stay strong in their commitment to God's Way.**

### Hang On!

Security is the comfort, protection, and safety that an unchanging God offers through the promise of eternal life. Because the standards of the world constantly change through various styles, designs, and fads, there is no security other than in God. Therefore, the temporary satisfaction that the world offers cannot compare to the eternal power, love, and security we find in God.

## STUDENTS' RESPONSES

**AIM: That your students will plan a strategy to remain strong in spite of the actions of the unjust around them.**

### What You Can Do

This week, pray that you will increase your trust in God and find more security in your life. Study Scripture on God's unchanging nature. Make a choice to live an ordered life based on godly principles. Today's lesson reminds us to trust in God to have that sense of security. By believing in His promises, we can wholeheartedly trust God to order our lives.

## PRAYER

Dear God, help us to seek Your wisdom and to display it in our actions and our words so that this world will benefit from Your love. In Jesus' name. Amen.

## DIG A LITTLE DEEPER

Raising children to become law abiding, self-controlled adults can be more than challenging in our culture of intensifying resistance to authority. Since the Bible infers that ordered lives are central to God's expectations for His people, how do we reconcile our society's emphasis on personal freedom and "doing your own thing" with teaching children to have ordered lives and doing so ourselves?

The word, ordered, is variously defined as regulated, systematized, ordained, and structured by commands. Paul urged the church at Corinth to conduct their services "decently and in order" **(1 Corinthians 14:40** NKJV). King David asked God to order or "direct his steps by (or in) His word" **(Psalm 119:133 NKJV)**.

A Christian publication lists 12 Scriptural Principles of Child Rearing. Two of them are "have your emotions under control when instructing a child" and being consistent: two steps toward our becoming what we want them to be which may be the only way to effectively teach them.

Vine's Expository Dictionary of New Testament Words, complete and unabridged (Westwood, NJ: Barbour and company, Inc., 1952); James Strong, Strong's Exhaustive Concordance of the Bible (Nashville, TN, n.d.); and Merriam-Webster's collegiate Dictionary, 11th edition (Springfield, MA, 2005).

<vision.org/family-relationships-12 scriptural –principles-of-child-rearing-1086>*

## HOW TO SAY IT

Mephibosheth.    Me·phib'o·sheth.

Ziba.    Zi-ba.

## PREPARE FOR NEXT SUNDAY

Read **Ecclesiastes 9:13-18** and study "The Superiority of Wisdom."

**Sources:**

Baltes, A. J., ed. Biblespeech.com. http://biblespeech.com (accessed July 6, 2010). Clifford, Richard J. Proverbs. Louisville, KY: Westminster John Knox Press, 1999. Garrett, Duane A. Proverbs, Ecclesiastes, Song of Songs. New American Commentary,

Vol. 14. Nashville, TN: Broadman, 1993.

Hebrew and Greek Lexicons. Bible Study Tools.com. http://www.biblestudytools.com/lexicons (accessed September 16, 2010).

Kidner, Derek. Proverbs: An Introduction and Commentary. Downers Grove, IL: InterVarsity Press, 1964.

Merriam-Webster Online Dictionary. Merriam-Webster, Inc. http:// www.merriam-webster.com (accessed May 4, 2009).

Murphy, Roland E. Proverbs. Nashville, TN: Thomas Nelson Publishers, 1998.

The Teacher's Bible Commentary. Nashville, TN: Broadman and Holman Publishers, 1972.

*Due to the nature of the internet, links referenced may or may not be active at the time of this publication.

## DAILY HOME BIBLE READINGS

### MONDAY
Impartiality in Judgment
(Deuteronomy 1:9–17)

### TUESDAY
The Danger of Pride
(2 Chronicles 32:20–26)

### WEDNESDAY
The Wisdom of Justice
(Proverbs 28:1–5)

### THURSDAY
Wisdom in Wealth and Poverty
(Proverbs 28:8–16)

### FRIDAY
Walking in Wisdom
(Proverbs 28:20-28)

### SATURDAY
The Wisdom of the Righteous
(Proverbs 29:2–11)

### SUNDAY
Wisdom in Practice
(Proverbs 29:16–27)

## COMMENTS / NOTES:

# THE SUPERIORITY OF WISDOM

**BIBLE BASIS:** Ecclesiastes 9:13–18

**BIBLE TRUTH:** We should not ignore the quiet, thoughtful words of the wise.

**MEMORY VERSE:** Then said I, Wisdom is better than strength: nevertheless the poor man's wisdom is despised, and his words are not heard (Ecclesiastes 9:16, KJV).

**LESSON AIM:** By the end of the lesson, we will: DISCUSS the underlying message in the parable of the poor, wise man; TRUST the superiority of wisdom over force; and EXAMINE our attitudes about listening to the thoughtful words of the wise.

**BACKGROUND SCRIPTURES:** Ecclesiastes 9:13–10:20— Read and incorporate the insights gained from the Background Scriptures into your study of the lesson.

## TEACHER PREPARATION

**MATERIALS NEEDED:** Bibles (several different versions), Quarterly Commentary/Teacher Manual, Adult Quarterly, teaching resources such as charts, worksheets/handouts, paper, pens, and pencils.

**OTHER MATERIALS NEEDED / TEACHER'S NOTES:**

_____

_____

## LESSON OVERVIEW

### LIFE NEED FOR TODAY'S LESSON
To apply God's wisdom, which confounds those who trust in their own strength.

### BIBLE LEARNING
To discuss the underlying message in the parable of the poor, wise man.

### BIBLE APPLICATION
To begin to understand our attitudes about listening to the thoughtful words of the wise.

### STUDENTS' RESPONSES
Students will begin observing life as evidence of God's truth and faithfulness to His Word.

## LESSON SCRIPTURE

### ECCLESIASTES 9:13-18, KJV

**13** This wisdom have I seen also under the sun, and it seemed great unto me:

## LESSON SCRIPTURE

### ECCLESIASTES 9:13-18, AMP

**13** This [illustration of] wisdom I have also seen under the sun, and great it was to me:
**14** There was a little city with few men in it and

**14** There was a little city, and few men within it; and there came a great king against it, and besieged it, and built great bulwarks against it:

**15** Now there was found in it a poor wise man, and he by his wisdom delivered the city; yet no man remembered that same poor man.

**16** Then said I, Wisdom is better than strength: nevertheless the poor man's wisdom is despised, and his words are not heard.

**17** The words of wise men are heard in quiet more than the cry of him that ruleth among fools.

**18** Wisdom is better than weapons of war: but one sinner destroyeth much good.

a great king came against it and besieged it and built great battlements against it.

**15** But there was found in it a poor wise man, and by his wisdom he rescued the city. Yet no man [seriously] remembered that poor man.

**16** But I say that wisdom is better than strength, though the poor man's wisdom is despised and his words are not heeded.

**17** The words of wise men heard in quietness are better than the shouting of one who rules among fools.

**18** Wisdom is better than weapons of war, but one sinner destroys much good.

## BIBLICAL DEFINITIONS

A. **Preacher (Ecclesiastes 1:1, 2, 12)** *qoheleth* (Heb.)—A teacher, preacher, or lecturer; the author of Ecclesiastes.

B. **Wisdom (9:13, 15, 16, 18)** *chokmah* (Heb.)—Biblical wisdom is knowing what is the right thing to do and doing it. Its beginning is the fear of the Lord **(Proverbs 1:7).**

## LIGHT ON THE WORD

The author of Ecclesiastes calls himself "teacher." The King James Version calls him "preacher." The author describes himself as the son of David **(Ecclesiastes 1:1)** and the "king over Israel in Jerusalem" **(Ecclesiastes 1:12)** All the kings in the line of David were called sons of David, but only Solomon reigned over all of Israel. The author also describes himself as having much wisdom **(Ecclesiastes 1:16)**, great

opportunities for pleasure **(Ecclesiastes 2:3)**, extensive building programs **(Ecclesiastes 2:4–6)**, unequaled wealth **(Ecclesiastes 2:7–8)**, and the author of many proverbs **(Ecclesiastes 12:9)**. All of these things lead many to conclude that King Solomon is the author of Ecclesiastes.

the author of many proverbs **(Ecclesiastes 12:9)**. All of these things lead many to conclude that King Solomon is the author of Ecclesiastes.

## TEACHING THE BIBLE LESSON

## LIFE NEED FOR TODAY'S LESSON

**AIM: That your students will realize that God knows their value, even when others forget.**

## INTRODUCTION

### Under the Sun

We can get into real trouble if we take material out of context from the book of Ecclesiastes. The preacher or teacher looked at things first from an earthly perspective. The key phrase is "under the sun," which we see in the first verse of today's Scripture passage. When we look at things only from an earthly perspective, we can become very cynical. The greedy and the corrupt often seem to come out ahead. But we need to turn to the end of Ecclesiastes to find out the conclusion of the preacher's search for the meaning of life. God knows all and sees all, so no one will be able to fool Him.

## BIBLE LEARNING

AIM: That your students will be able to recount the parable of the poor wise man.

## I. THE POOR BUT WISE MAN (Ecclesiastes 9:13–16)

Three Old Testament books are commonly defined as the wisdom literature: Job, Proverbs, and Ecclesiastes. (Some scholars also include Psalms and Song of Solomon, though these are also regarded as poetic literature). These books contain wise sayings, common sense, observations on life, principles of good governance, and wisdom from the spiritual perspective. The Bible concludes that the fear of the Lord is the beginning of true wisdom (Proverbs 1:7). In most Scripture, the term "wisdom" refers to spiritual understanding and obedience. However, in thisinstance, it is human reason that is the measure. The first assessment of this observation is that the following parable is a great example of wisdom.

### The Parable Revealed (verses 13-16)
**13 This wisdom have I seen also under the sun, and it seemed great unto me: 14 There was a little city, and few men within it; and there came a great king against it, and besieged it, and built great bulwarks against it: 15 Now there was found in it a poor wise man, and he by his wisdom delivered the city; yet no man remembered that same poor man.**

**16 Then said I, Wisdom is better than strength: nevertheless the poor man's wisdom is despised, and his words are not heard.**

Verse 13 reveals that Ecclesiastes is written from Solomon's perspective as an older man, who has lived long enough to see that life is not always as simple as we would wish. The key to Ecclesiastes is the phrase "under the sun." This phrase is used 29 times in the book of Ecclesiastes. This is a reference to the meaning of life on earth. Ecclesiastes does not raise the question of an afterlife.

Verses 14 and 15 provide the story of a city taken captive by a great king. Essentially we are left to our imaginations as to what sort of military equipment was used against this small town with very few men able to defend it. Since cities in those days were surrounded with heavy stone walls, the city could have been besieged in a number of ways. Perhaps a device was created to knock down the walls to gain entrance. Maybe a ramp of soil and stones was constructed, which extended partway up the wall so that warriors went up the ramp with a battering ram to knock down the walls. A portable tower might have been used to climb the wall. The only thing we know for sure is that the conquering king built "bulwarks," a term that can refer to "a besieging tower, a hold, a net, or a snare." But we are left with no real details.

Again we can only imagine that this walled city had a variety of defenses. They could have poured boiling water or boiling oil upon the invaders. They could have hidden behind a shield- like portable wall and shot arrows at their enemies. The exact details are not necessary for us tounderstand this text because this is a parable and we will soon see the preacher's point of the story. What we do know, however, is that the city and its citizens were not totally destroyed because of the advice of this poor but wise man.

We do not know what the wise words of the commoner in the preacher's story were, but here is the moral of the story. This poor man's wise words saved the city, but rather than the wise man receiving great honor, he was soon forgotten. Is this fair? Is it possible? Everyone likes a story with a happy ending, but this one does not end that way. We all like to see people give honor to those who are wise and bring about good results. We like to hear that talented people receive rewards, even if they happen to come from circumstances of poverty. But we all know that life is not that way.

If this story were a fairy tale, it would have a happy ending. The poor, but wise man would be honored by everyone. A statue would be erected in his honor. He might even be elected to high office! But that didn't happen. Soon his wisdom, that saved the city, was forgotten, and he was forgotten as well. He went back to being a "nobody," living in poverty. In fact, in the future, when his wisdom could have continued to profit the little city, no one paid any attention to what he said.

Society despises the poor and ignores the gifts, such as wisdom, that God bestows on them. But whether society notices or not, this parable explains that wisdom is better than strength. The writer of Ecclesiastes still says that wisdom is better than strength, even if no one pays any attention to words of wisdom. The wisdom of the poor man is still better than the brute force of the powerful king. In order for this to be true, we need to look at things from an eternal perspective. In heaven, the poor, but wise man will finally be rewarded.

## SEARCH THE SCRIPTURES

### QUESTION 1
What happened to the poor man after he saved the city?

**He was forgotten and disregarded because he was poor.**

## LIGHT ON THE WORD
### Our Greater Vision
Job had similar concerns to that of the writer of Ecclesiastes. Since he had been living a godly life, he wondered why he was suffering. Many people expect God to bless those who obey God and punish those who do not. But Job wonderfully concludes that this life on earth is not all there is. In **Job 19:25–27,** NIV, we read these wonderful words, "I know that my Redeemer lives, and that in the end he will stand upon the earth. And after my skin has been destroyed, yet in my flesh I will see God; I myself will see him with my own eyes—I, and not another. How my heart yearns within me!"

Only with eternity in view can we make sense of the suffering and injustice in this world. When we remember that God will make all things right in the end, it makes sense to pursue wisdom and justice. There may be no happy ending here on earth, but we know that our just and loving God will make all things right. The preacher and Job were living on the other side of the Cross. But because of Jesus, we can be assured that we shall live forever and there will be a happy ending.

## II. THE BENEFIT OF WISDOM OVER FOLLY (Ecclesiastes 9:17–18)

A wise mentor-teacher once said that when a classroom of noisy children makes you feel like yelling at them, lower your voice instead. The children will get very quiet as they try to hear what you are saying. This quiet style of administration is advocated in these two verses. This wisdom can also be applied to warring factions of any kind—the gangs in a neighborhood, the faculty of a school, the employees in an office, and even the members of church committees! Are we among those who listen to the agitators, or, are we willing to listen to quiet words of wisdom and peace?

## Speak Softly (verses 17-18)

**17 The words of wise men are heard in quiet more than the cry of him that ruleth among fools. 18 Wisdom is better than weapons of war: but one sinner destroyeth much good.** The phrase "heard in quiet" in verse 17 refers not to the manner in which the crowd received the words of wisdom, but to the way that they were delivered. The wise person is speaking in a gentle, but sure voice. Meanwhile, the ruler among the fools shouts and pushes his way to get the attention of the people. The word "fools" can mean "silly, stupid, or foolish." This verse suggests that not only did the ruler rule over fools, but that he himself was a fool. In contrast to the ruler of fools, the truly wise person gives advice in a quiet manner. Because he or she is counting on wisdom in words rather than dash and splash, the wise person speaks from a calm spirit within.

**Verse 18** encapsulates wisdom that could end wars in our time, if people really followed these words. Peace negotiators may come with words of wisdom that, if heeded, could prevent wars. While the negotiator sits down, listens to both sides, and comes up with a solution that is agreeable to all sides, all that is needed to stop negotiations is one rebellious person with a loud mouth or worse yet, with weapons of war. It takes only one hotheaded leader to sabotage the peace process, and thus many people are slaughtered, women are raped, people are starved, and families are torn apart and displaced. This sinner may stir up a crowd of fools, and soon many people are hurt or even killed.

## SEARCH THE SCRIPTURES

### QUESTION 2

Who can be identified as a destructive force?

One sinner! Far-reaching and insidious, sin destroys the sinner and those around the sinner. Sin has lasting impact and can cause generations of harm. Sin can destroy families, communities, and nations. There is no way to know the breadth of destruction sin can cause.

Answers willl vary.

## LIGHT ON THE WORD

### A Happy Ending

The book of Ecclesiastes does not address the issue of life after death. It looks at life only through the observation of what can be known. We, however, have a better view of a better ending. Our revelation of Jesus Christ assures us that God will make all things right. We can keep on believing in God's justice and love, in spite of some of the injustices we see in this world. As Christians, we are sure of the resurrection of our Savior and we know that we shall oneday rise from the dead to live forever with Him. We know that Jesus will make all things right in the end, and so we put our trust in Him when things on earth are unfair. It is this trust that enables us to go on following the wise way. Even if the forces of corruption seem to be winning, we know that wisdom is better than power that is not restrained by goodness.

## BIBLE APPLICATION

**AIM: That your students will consider God's opinion of their actions and attitudes.**

### A Better View

The writer of Ecclesiastes is viewing a story from the viewpoint of life "under the sun." This is the opposite of viewing things from the perspective of eternity. How do you think God views the poor, but wise man? How should our view of eternity affect how we judge the activities we see around us?

## STUDENTS' RESPONSES

**AIM: That your students will apply the wisdom of the lesson to their lives.**

How many scenarios can you imagine that apply the wisdom on today's lesson? Here's one to consider.

The parents' school council meeting was getting louder and louder. The council president was upset about her daughter getting bad grades in Mr. Washington's class. "I think we ought to get rid of him!" she shouted.

"Did he say why your daughter was getting bad grades?" Ms. Jones asked quietly.

"Oh, he's giving too much homework, and she's not getting it done," the president answered indignantly.

"Well, I make my son do his homework right after school, and he is doing very well in Mr. Washington's class," Ms. Jones quietly interjected.

The other parents weren't saying anything. They knew that the principal and the president were good friends. The principal would probably do whatever the president told her to do.Do you think the schoolchildren will profit from the principal listening to the powerful parents' school council president? Why is it that people are more likely to listen to an outspoken leader than to the wise words of a person with no power? In what other area do you see this happen?

## PRAYER

Lord, help us to speak soft words of wisdom that save our families, our communities, our cities, and our nation. Give us wisdom in all things. In Jesus' name. Amen.

## DIG A LITTLE DEEPER

In the senior class yearbook, who gets selected as the most likely to succeed? In crowded lines after Christmas, who gets a refund first: the quiet and soft-spoken who defer to others or those with strong opinions and loud voices who wear the latest styles and drive expensive cars?

Lazarus, the beggar, illustrates how the poor manifest wisdom when they hear and obey God's word and the rich who do not lack of wisdom and suffer the consequences (**Luke 16: 19-31**).

If we believe that Martin Luther King was right when he said that equality means being judged by the "content of our character," rather than how we look, why do we determine whether someone's ideas are valid based on how they look? King gave away the money he received with the Nobel Peace Prize, and when he died, he left his family very little monetarily, yet he was one of his century's wisest men. As King and other leaders planned the Poor People's Campaign, they wore casual clothes in public: denim pants and jackets. Were they less effective than when they were in suits and ties? Would you have still followed their leadership?

Martin Luther King, Jr., August 28, 1963.

## HOW TO SAY IT

Ecclesiastes.      E-KLE-se-as-tes.

## DAILY HOME BIBLE READINGS

### MONDAY
Hope in God's Steadfast Love
(Psalm 33:13–22)

### TUESDAY
Two Are Better than One
(Ecclesiastes 4:4–12)

### WEDNESDAY
Fear God!
(Ecclesiastes 5:1-7)

### THURSDAY
Consider the Word of God
(Ecclesiastes 7:1–14)

### FRIDAY
Wisdom and Success
(Ecclesiastes 10:5–11)

### SATURDAY
Wisdom with Words
(Ecclesiastes 10:12–20)

### SUNDAY
Wisdom Is Better than Might
(Ecclesiastes 9:13–18)

## PREPARE FOR NEXT SUNDAY

Read **Ecclesiastes 11:9—12:7, 13** and study "Wisdom for Aging."

**Sources:**

Adeyemo, Tokunboh, ed., et al. Africa Bible Commentary: A One-Volume Commentary Written by 70 African Scholars. Nairobi, Kenya: Word Alive Publishers, 2006.

Baltes, A. J., ed. Biblespeech.com. http://biblespeech.com (accessed June 25, 2010). Bartholomew, Craig G. Ecclesiastes. Grand Rapids, MI: Baker Academic, 2009.

Hebrew and Greek Lexicons. Bible Study Tools.com. http://www.biblestudytools.com/lexicons (accessed September 16, 2010).

Merriam-Webster Online Dictionary. Merriam-Webster, Inc. http:// www.merriam-webster.com (accessed June 25, 2010).

Miller, Stephen R. "The Book of Ecclesiastes." Holman Illustrated Bible Dictionary. Chad Brand, Charles Draper and Archie England, gen. eds. Nashville, TN: Holman Bible

Publishers, 2003. 452–455.

Seow, C. L. Ecclesiastes: A New Translation with Introduction and Commentary. From

The Anchor Bible. New York, NY: Doubleday, 1997.

Strong's Concordance with Hebrew and Greek Lexicon. Eliyah.com. http:// www.eliyah.com/lexicon.html (accessed June 29, 2010)

## COMMENTS / NOTES:

# WISDOM FOR AGING

**BIBLE BASIS:** Ecclesiastes 11:9–10, 12:1-7,13

**BIBLE TRUTH:** It is important to seek God's wisdom early in life.

**MEMORY VERSE:** Let us hear the conclusion of the whole matter: Fear God, and keep his commandments: for this is the whole duty of man (Ecclesiastes 12:13, KJV).

**LESSON AIM:** By the end of the lesson, we will: UNDERSTAND the importance of seeking God early in our lives; REFLECT on the meaning of life as we move toward death; and IDENTIFY ways to honor God with our lives.

**BACKGROUND SCRIPTURES:** Ecclesiastes 11:7–12:14—Read and incorporate the insights gained from the Background Scriptures into your study of the lesson.

## TEACHER PREPARATION

**MATERIALS NEEDED:** Bibles (several different versions), Quarterly Commentary/Teacher Manual, Adult Quarterly, teaching resources such as charts, worksheets/handouts, paper, pens, and pencils.

**OTHER MATERIALS NEEDED / TEACHER'S NOTES:**

_____

_____

## LESSON OVERVIEW

**LIFE NEED FOR TODAY'S LESSON**
To understand the importance of seeking God early in our lives.

**BIBLE LEARNING**
To reflect on the meaning of life as we move through life's stages.

**BIBLE APPLICATION**
To recall the words of Ecclesiastes 12:13 as a mantra for daily living.

**STUDENTS' RESPONSES**
Students will praise God daily for His many benefits.

## LESSON SCRIPTURE

### ECCLESIASTES 11:9–10; 12:1-7, 13, KJV

9 Rejoice, O young man, in thy youth; and let thy heart cheer thee in the days of thy youth, and walk in the ways of thine heart, and in the sight of thine eyes: but know thou, that

### ECCLESIASTES 11:9–10; 12:1-7, 13, AMP

9 Rejoice, young man, in your childhood, and let your heart be pleasant in the days of your young manhood. And walk in the ways of your heart and in the desires of your eyes, but know

for all these things God will bring thee into judgment.

**10** Therefore remove sorrow from thy heart, and put away evil from thy flesh: for childhood and youth are vanity.

**12:1.** Remember now thy Creator in the days of thy youth, while the evil days come not, nor the years draw nigh, when thou shalt say, I have no pleasure in them;

**2** While the sun, or the light, or the moon, or the stars, be not darkened, nor the clouds return after the rain:

**3** In the day when the keepers of the house shall tremble, and the strong men shall bow themselves, and the grinders cease because they are few, and those that look out of the windows be darkened,

**4** And the doors shall be shut in the streets, when the sound of the grinding is low, and he shall rise up at the voice of the bird, and all the daughters of musick shall be brought low;

**5** Also when they shall be afraid of that which is high, and fears shall be in the way, and the almond tree shall flourish, and the grasshopper shall be a burden, and desire shall fail: because man goeth to his long home, and the mourners go about the streets:

**6** Or ever the silver cord be loosed, or the golden bowl be broken, or the pitcher be broken at the fountain, or the wheel broken at the cistern.

**7** Then shall the dust return to the earth as it was: and the spirit shall return unto God who gave it.

**12:13** Let us hear the conclusion of the whole matter: Fear God, and keep his commandments: for this is the whole duty of man.

that God will bring you into judgment for all these things.

**10** Therefore, remove sorrow and anger from your heart and put away pain from your body, for childhood and the prime of life are fleeting.

**12:1** Remember [thoughtfully] also your Creator in the days of your youth [for you are not your own, but His], before the evil days come or the years draw near when you will say [of physical pleasures], "I have no enjoyment and delight in them";

**2** before the sun and the light, and the moon and the stars are darkened [by impaired vision], and the clouds [of depression] return after the rain [of tears];

**3** in the day when the keepers of the house (hands, arms) tremble, and the strong men (feet, knees) bow themselves, and the grinders (molar teeth) cease because they are few, and those (eyes) who look through the windows grow dim;

**4** when the doors (lips) are shut in the streets and the sound of the grinding [of the teeth] is low, and one rises at the sound of a bird and the crowing of a rooster, and all the daughters of music (voice, ears) sing softly.

**5** Furthermore, they are afraid of a high place and of dangers on the road; the almond tree (hair) blossoms [white], and the grasshopper (a little thing) is a burden, and the [a]caperberry (desire, appetite) fails. For man goes to his eternal home and the mourners go about the streets and market places.

**6** Earnestly remember your Creator before the silver cord [of life] is broken, or the golden bowl is crushed, or the pitcher at the fountain is shattered and the wheel at the cistern is crushed;

**7** then the dust [out of which God made man's body] will return to the earth as it was, and the spirit will return to God who gave it. from your heart and put away pain from your body, for childhood and the prime of life are fleeting.

**12:13** When all has been heard, the end of the matter is: fear God [worship Him with awe-filled reverence, knowing that He is almighty God] and keep His commandments, for this applies to every person.

## BIBLICAL DEFINITIONS

A. **Vanity (Ecclesiastes 11:8, 10; 12:8)** *hebel* (Heb.)—Transient, fleeting, and without substance.

B. **Judgment (11:9)** *mishpat*—The time of giving final account to God.

## LIGHT ON THE WORD

Wise, God-fearing people in every generation have known that life is fragile, brief, and not without urgency. Consequently, the counsel necessary to pursue a meaningful life is relevant for all people, in every place, at all times. Solomon's advice to make the most of one's youth, before the difficult days of old age and death arrive, was good counsel during Old Testament times— and still is now.

## TEACHING THE BIBLE LESSON

## LIFE NEED FOR TODAY'S LESSON

**AIM: That your students will use these principles as grounding for daily living.**

## INTRODUCTION

### What Is Life About?

The writer of Ecclesiastes had a deep and abiding desire to make sense out of life. He recognized that, except for death, judgment, and the fleeting days of youth, nothing seemed to be permanent. The effects of aging were overwhelmingly obvious and God's ways did not always meet his expectations. Consequently, his search for meaning in life was haunted by an anxiety that caused him to view human striving as "vanity" and "chasing after the wind." In an attempt to find a way out of this dilemma, he resorts to reason and concludes that life and human striving are futile for those who disregard God.

## BIBLE LEARNING

**AIM: That your students will put life's trials and joys in perspective.**

## I. REJOICE IN LIFE (Ecclesiastes 11:9–10)

One of the greatest challenges of life is to truly live while we are alive. God wants us to enjoy life and be sure that our desires are in line with the word of God.. The enjoyment of life and the pursuit of one's desires however, are to be governed and managed by a keen awareness of one's accountability to God.

### Live Life (verses 9-10)

**9 Rejoice, O young man, in thy youth; and let thy heart cheer thee in the days of**

thy youth, and walk in the ways of thine heart, and in the sight of thine eyes: but know thou, that for all these things God will bring thee into judgment. 10 Therefore remove sorrow from thy heart, and put away evil from thy flesh: for childhood and youth are vanity.

**Verse 9** expresses the advice an older person might give to a younger person: "Make the most of your younger years." At first it may appear that Solomon is encouraging young men to live a life of folly. The phrase to "walk in the ways of [your] heart" is not an invitation for young people to go out and do whatever they'd like to do. However, Solomon reminds the young man that God will judge unless our wants are attuned to what God wants from us and for us. Solomon also reminds us that someday, all our words and works will be weighed by God's eternal evaluation.

In light of God's future judgment, Solomon advised youth to put away or avoid the grief that sin and evil produce.. Solomon reminds us that youth is fleeting. Although we should enjoy life during our youth, we should live in a way that glorifies God. This is timely advice for those teens and young adults who are impatient, lack self-control, or focus on pleasing themselves.

## SEARCH THE SCRIPTURES

### QUESTION 1
What suggestions do you have for putting away sin?

**To put away sin, we must engage in practices that strengthen our ability to withstand the pull of sin. Young people, indeed all people, must set their affections on God, pray for direction, praise God for His mercy, study the Bible, and adhere to sound teaching in order to learn of God and His joy.**

## LIGHT ON THE WORD
### Perspective on Judgment
The use of the word "judgment" in **verse 9** should be understood in the light of the Olympian athlete who trains diligently, and after giving all in competition, awaits expectantly to receive the appropriate recognition and reward. In biblical thought, judgment is not a moment to be feared. It is a crowning moment to be welcomed by all those who have spent their days celebrating life and pursuing the desires of their heart in ways that honor God. Verse 10 begins our consideration of the brevity of life and the urgency of employing one's youthful years wisely.

## II. HONOR GOD AND LIVE VIGILANTLY (Ecclesiastes 12:1-7)

The motivation to enjoy life and to pursue the heart's desires is sparked, in part, by the brevity of life and fleetingness of youth. Therefore, one's youthful days should be taken seriously, and the opportunities presented during youth should be promptly acted upon out of reverence for God.

The book of Ecclesiastes offers no illusions about the potential effects of the aging process and the certainty of death. If one continues to live, aging and death are imminent and inescapable.

### Observing Life's Signs (verses 1-7)
1 Remember now thy Creator in the days of thy youth, while the evil days come not, nor the years draw nigh, when thou shalt say, I have no pleasure in them; 2 While the sun, or the light, or the moon, or the stars, be not darkened, nor the clouds return after the rain: 3 In the day when the keepers of the house shall tremble, and the strong men shall bow themselves, and the grinders cease because they are few, and those that look out of the windows be darkened, 4 And the doors shall be shut in the streets,

**when the sound of the grinding is low, and he shall rise up at the voice of the bird, and all the daughters of musick shall be brought low; 5 Also when they shall be afraid of that which is high, and fears shall be in the way, and the almond tree shall flourish, and the grasshopper shall be a burden, and desire shall fail: because man goeth to his long home, and the mourners go about the streets: 6 Or ever the silver cord be loosed, or the golden bowl be broken, or the pitcher be broken at the fountain, or the wheel broken at the cistern. 7 Then shall the dust return to the earth as it was: and the spirit shall return unto God who gave it.**

Where human life is concerned, the aging process affects, in a variety of ways, one's capacity to function. Modern people have humorously referred to the five B's of old age: baldness, bifocals, bridges, bulges, and bunions. The metaphors in **verses 2** through **7** are more sobering and so difficult to understand that even Bible scholars are not in agreement about what each word picture means. Nevertheless, the message of **verses 2** through **5** is intended to give urgency to the invitation of **verse 1** to "remember . . . thy Creator in the days of thy youth." Since God is our Creator, we'd better follow His Word if we want our lives to run as smoothly as possible.

Remembering your Creator in your youth does not suggest that opportunities vanish with one's aging years. What is at stake is the potential impact of the aging process upon one's capacity to maximize life's pleasures and take advantage of the capacity we have to honor God. In other words, we are to begin early in life to enjoy life by living vigilantly, "soberly, righteously, and godly, in this present world" (from **Titus 2:12**).

In **Ecclesiastes 12:2,** the deteriorating days of old age are depicted as a cloudy period. The phrase "keepers [or guardians] of the house" in

**verse 3** is a reference to muscular arms that are now weakening and beginning to tremble. The "strong men" may refer to the once-strong legs that are beginning to become feeble. "Grinders" are probably an older person's loss of teeth. "Those that look out of the windows," may refer to the dimming eyesight often associated with old age.

The closed doors to the house in **verse 4** could present a picture of becoming so hard of hearing that we feel like the world is being shut out. "The sound of the grinding is low" indicates that the older person no longer hears sounds, like the familiar sound of grinding wheat, as distinctly as in younger years. The "daughters of musick" is perhaps a reference to songs and also indicates a time of diminished hearing.

**Verse 5** is difficult for the scholars to translate. The first part undoubtedly refers to the aging individual's increasing fears and difficulty with heights. The almond tree has pretty pink petals at first, but then it bursts into an all-white color, similar to the change experienced by a

white-haired elderly individual. "The grasshopper shall be a burden" is translated in the NIV as "the grasshopper drags himself along," bringing to mind the slow and stiff walk of an elderly person.

The next phrase, "desire shall fail," may refer to a caper berry that was considered in the ancient Middle East to be an aphrodisiac or love-potion. This is why the King James translators rendered it "desire." The aging person's appetites (whether for sex or food) diminish. The final portion ofthe text touches on the inevitability of death— despite the fact that those who will mourn you are going about their lives seemingly oblivious to the plight you face.

**Verse 6** may be painting two pictures: (1) a lamp with oil and (2) a well with water. Lamps during biblical times usually looked like clay dishes with a wick sitting in oil in the dish. The wick would stay lit as long as oil was present. The author may have pictured a "golden [lamp] bowl" hung on a "silver cord" that was broken or smashed. As a result, the lamp became useless. A well (or cistern) during biblical times might have had a "wheel" that attached a bucket or "pitcher" to a rope that went down into the well to obtain water below. If the bucket were to strike the well's side, it might also become broken. These images refer to the end of life. Just as useful devices and their parts eventually wear out, our lives eventually come to an end.

"Dust to dust and ashes to ashes" is the familiar refrain at funerals. In **verse 7**, the "dust" of our bodies returns to the dust of the earth, and "the spirit" returns to God who gave us breath and life (cf. **Genesis 2:7).** The primary emphasis on "spirit" refers to how God is the source of life and keeps us alive. For Christians, this means that our physical bodies go down to the grave at death, but our spirits go to be with God until the final resurrection. Those that do not know God will also be resurrected at the final judgment, but they will not face God's reward for accepting Jesus Christ as Lord and Savior. The day will indeed come, when we all must stand before God. Are you prepared to meet God? The only way to prepare for that day is to believe that Christ died for you and to receive God's gift of eternal life as part of His family.

Death is a normal part of life and must not be feared as a signal to inevitable uselessness and worthlessness. While death's coming may occasion grief and sorrow, God has ordained its place in the unfolding mystery of His ways. Since God has ordained death, we can honor Him by accepting what He has ordained.

## QUESTION 2
In the 21st Century, we see ads for medications and remedies that are expected to stave off the aging process. How do these modern conveniences line up with the Ecclesiastical writer's view?

**There is nothing man or science can do to stop the inevitable. If we dye our hair, get a facelift, take vitamins, we may feel better longer; but, God has ordered our lives from birth to death. The inevitable end of life must be faced with the recognition that we must live with joy so that our lives honor God.**

**Answers will vary.**

## LIGHT ON THE WORD
### Wells
Usually, it is understood and accepted that each of the objects in **verse 6** are used to draw water from a well, but that the objects themselves do not last forever. Moreover, wells sometimes dry up and become useless. This, too, is understandable and accepted as par for the course of life. So also should it be where human death is concerned. By that same token, our lives are like wells that hold God's desires and strength for each of us. We must reach deeply into God's love and His will for us to drink fully of life. God is the One who holds our eternal future in His hands. No matter what else this world holds out to us, we need to remember that God is the Almighty God.

## III. THE DUTY OF HUMANKIND (Ecclesiastes 12:13)

Now we come to the end of the book of Ecclesiastes and the author gives us his conclusion. The "fear of the Lord" is reverential awe of Him. In our efforts to make the Christian faith more palatable to the modern mind, we have soft-pedaled fear of the Lord. We need to remember who God is—the Creator of the universe and all that is in it.

### Our Duty (verse 13)
**13 Let us hear the conclusion of the whole matter: Fear God, and keep his**

**commandments: for this is the whole duty of man.**

Ecclesiastes contains the meditations of a man who has lived to see old age. He has seen that we must fear the Lord and obey Him. The Hebrew word for "fear" means "to revere" or "to dread." The fear of God must open us to see His awesomeness and His holiness, and cause us to tremble when we think about disobeying Him. We are sinful beings unable to enter into God's presence,even though we desperately want to. How can we come before Him? Through Jesus who sacrificed Himself on the Cross-, we are able to enter the presence of God **(Hebrews 10:19–22)**. Because of Jesus' sacrifice for us, we desire to please God and obey Him. Whether male or female, our primary task in life is to bow down in reverence before God and obey Him.

## SEARCH THE SCRIPTURES
### QUESTION 3
How does verse Ecclesiastes 12:13 address the "busy-ness" of life today?

**We can never be so busy that we fail to meet the obligation of our "whole duty." Fearing and obeying God will help us focus every aspect of our lives—home, work, personal, and social.**

Answers will vary.

## LIGHT ON THE WORD
### The Blessing of God
While we may reflect with gratitude on the blessings of our earlier years, the reality is that the days of our youth pass all too quickly. Youth and vitality do not continue unabated forever. We are challenged to adapt ourselves to the diminishing abilities of increased age. The question is: Can we do so gracefully? Can we stand face to face with the aging process and embrace the inevitable approach of death as a

time of reunion, renewal, and fulfillment? Those who keep God first and who are confident of His goodness can truly enjoy and celebrate life.

## BIBLE APPLICATION
**AIM: That your students will be able to apply this advice to modern situations.**
### Living Life's Lessons
Those who have reached longevity learn to distinguish between what is urgent and what is important, what needs attention and what can be overlooked. Such wisdom is garnered from experiencing life at close range. Their years of experience and seasoned perspectives are quite informative. With the passing of each year comes some change in our bodies and in our environment. The aging process and change are inevitable. Like birth, childhood, and youth, the effects of advanced aging, change, and death are inescapable.

## STUDENTS' RESPONSES
**AIM: That your students will reflect on their responses to the stages of life.**
### Approaching Life Today...
How should we approach the life-lessons of today's text? Spend some time reflecting upon the days of your youth, and thank God for the distance He has brought you. Recommit yourself to Him. Ask God to give you sufficient grace to manage the diminishing abilities of your own aging and to give you wisdom in taking care of the one body He has given you. Ask God to supply you with the resources necessary to enjoy and celebrate life in ways that honor Him through all the days and stages of your life.

## PRAYER
Lord, help us to face life with an appreciation for what You have given us so that we may honor You in all our ways and throughout our days. In

Jesus' name we pray. Amen.

## DIG A LITTLE DEEPER

Physicians acknowledge that good eating habits improve health as we age. Following a Mediterranean diet delays the onset of Parkinson's disease in women for up to 17 years and men, up to eight. Whatever our state of health, God empowers us to live fully at every stage of life. Moses died at 120, with his eyesight and physical strength intact (**Deuteronomy 34:7**).

Yet most of us face the situation Paul described as "Paul the aged" (**Philemon 9**). He told the Corinthians his "outward man is perishing" and his body a "tent" was being destroyed (**2 Corinthians 4:16**). Yet his inner life was being renewed daily, and he knew that God would provide a mansion for him, a new indestructible body after his old one died. Since in old age men and women can serve God if they are "reverent and sober" (**Titus 2:2-3**), and beginning good eating habits while young produces good results as we age, how much more will good spiritual habits adopted in our youth pay off when we are old?

"Diet and Parkinson's Disease," Focus on Healthy Aging, Icahn School of Medicine at Mount Sinai, Vol. 24, No.4, April 2021, p. 2.

## HOW TO SAY IT

Ecclesiastes.        E-KLE-se-as-tes.

## DAILY HOME BIBLE READINGS

**MONDAY**
Do Not Forsake Me
(Psalm 71:1–12)

**TUESDAY**
Nothing New Under the Sun?
(Ecclesiastes 1:1–11)

**WEDNESDAY**
Nothing to Be Gained?
(Ecclesiastes 2:1–11)

**THURSDAY**
Toiling for the Wind
(Ecclesiastes 5:10–20)

**FRIDAY**
Everything Has Its Time
(Ecclesiastes 3:1–8))

**SATURDAY**
Ignorance of God's Work
(Ecclesiastes 11:1–8)

**SUNDAY**
Remember Your Creator
(Ecclesiastes 11:9–12:7, 13)

## PREPARE FOR NEXT SUNDAY

Read Song of **Solomon 4:8–5:1a** and study "Tradition and Love."

**Sources:**
Baltes, A. J., ed. Biblespeech.com. http://biblespeech.com (accessed November 4, 2009).
Bible Study Tools.com. Old Testament Hebrew Lexicons. http://www.biblestudytools.com/lexicons/hebrew/kjv (accessed June 10, 2010).
Hebrew and Greek Lexicons. Bible Study Tools.com. http://www.biblestudytools.com/lexicons (accessed September 16, 2010).
Leupold, H. C. Exposition of Ecclesiastes. Columbus, OH: The Wartburg Press, 1952.
Seow, C. L. Ecclesiastes: A New Translation with Introduction and Commentary. The Anchor Bible. New York, NY: Doubleday, 1997.

# TRADITION AND LOVE

**BIBLE BASIS:** Song of Solomon 4:8–5:1a

**BIBLE TRUTH:** God ordained committed relationships.

**MEMORY VERSE:** Awake, O north wind; and come, thou south; blow upon my garden, that the spices thereof may flow out. Let my beloved come into his garden, and eat his pleasant fruits (Song of Solomon 4:16,KJV).

**LESSON AIM:** By the end of the lesson, we will: DISCUSS the beauty and wonder of love in a committed relationship; REFLECT on our attitude about love and commitment; and EXPLAIN how to build a relationship that honors a marriage commitment.

**BACKGROUND SCRIPTURES:** Song Of Solomon 4:8–5:1a— Read and incorporate the insights gained from the Background Scriptures into your study of the lesson.

## TEACHER PREPARATION

**MATERIALS NEEDED:** Bibles (several different versions), Quarterly Commentary/Teacher Manual, Adult Quarterly, teaching resources such as charts, worksheets/handouts, paper, pens, and pencils.

**OTHER MATERIALS NEEDED / TEACHER'S NOTES:**

_____

_____

## LESSON OVERVIEW

### LIFE NEED FOR TODAY'S LESSON
To know that Song of Solomon presents a timely message about marital relationships.

### BIBLE LEARNING
To recognize the language of love contained in Song of Solomon.

### BIBLE APPLICATION
To reflect on modern attitudes about love and commitment.

### STUDENTS' RESPONSES
Students will understand how to build a relationship that honors a marriage commitment.

## LESSON SCRIPTURE

### SONG OF SOLOMON 4:8-5:1a, KJV

8 Come with me from Lebanon, my spouse, with me from Lebanon: look from the top of

### SONG OF SOLOMON 4:8-5:1a, AMP

8 "Come away with me from Lebanon, my [promised] bride, May you come with me

Amana, from the top of Shenir and Hermon, from the lions' dens, from the mountains of the leopards.

9 Thou hast ravished my heart, my sister, my spouse; thou hast ravished my heart with one of thine eyes, with one chain of thy neck.

10 How fair is thy love, my sister, my spouse! how much better is thy love than wine! and the smell of thine ointments than all spices!

11 Thy lips, O my spouse, drop as the honeycomb: honey and milk are under thy tongue; and the smell of thy garments is like the smell of Lebanon.

12 A garden inclosed is my sister, my spouse; a spring shut up, a fountain sealed.

13 Thy plants are an orchard of pomegranates, with pleasant fruits; camphire, with spikenard,

14 Spikenard and saffron; calamus and cinnamon, with all trees of frankincense; myrrh and aloes, with all the chief spices:

15. A fountain of gardens, a well of living waters, and streams from Lebanon.

16 Awake, O north wind; and come, thou south; blow upon my garden, that the spices thereof may flow out. Let my beloved come into his garden, and eat his pleasant fruits.

5:1a I am come into my garden, my sister, my spouse:

from Lebanon. Journey down from the top of Amana, From the summit of Senir and Hermon, From the dens of lions, From the mountains of leopards.

9 "You have ravished my heart and given me courage, my sister, my [promised] bride; You have ravished my heart and given me courage with a single glance of your eyes, With one jewel of your necklace.

10 "How beautiful is your love, my sister, my [promised] bride! How much better is your love than wine, And the fragrance of your oils Than all kinds of balsam and spices.

11 "Your lips, my [promised] bride, drip honey [as the honeycomb]; Honey and milk are under your tongue, And the fragrance of your garments is like the fragrance of Lebanon.

12 "A garden enclosed is my sister, my [promised] bride—A rock garden locked, a spring sealed up.

13 "Your shoots are an orchard of pomegranates, [A paradise] with precious fruits, henna with fragrant plants,

14 Fragrant plants and saffron, calamus and cinnamon, With all trees of frankincense, Myrrh and aloes, along with all the finest spices.

15 "You are a fountain in a garden, A well of fresh and living water, And streams flowing from Lebanon."

16 ""Awake, O north wind, And come, south wind [blow softly upon my garden]; Make my garden breathe out fragrance, [for the one in whom my soul delights], Let its spices flow forth. Let my beloved come into his garden And eat its choicest fruits."

5:1a "I have come into my garden, my sister, my [promised] bride.

## BIBLICAL DEFINITIONS

A. **Sister (Song of Solomon 4:9)** *àchowth* (Heb.)—A term of endearment meaning "beloved;" it denotes an intimate relationship.

B. **Enclosed (v. 12)** *naàl* (Heb.)—Something that is locked, bolted, or shut up.

## LIGHT ON THE WORD

In biblical times, couples did not meet, date, fall in love, and then marry. Rather, marriage was a vastly different four-step process that had little to do with emotional involvement. Marriage was an arranged contract between two families who sought alliances with each other for various social, territorial, or financial reasons. The bridegroom's father paid a "bride price" to the bride's family. The couple began a year-long betrothal period after their parents ratified the contract.

During that betrothal period, the groom-to-be prepared the home and the future bride prepared for new responsibility as a wife. Sex between the couple or with others, was forbidden (cf. **Deuteronomy 22:13-21; 23-24; 28:2).**

Complete abstinence was required. After the successful completion of the betrothal, the couple fulfilled their legal (and social) responsibility to marry. Wedding feasts often lasted a week and provided opportunity for family and friends to applaud the new alliance and celebrate the marriage consummation.

## TEACHING THE BIBLE LESSON

## LIFE NEED FOR TODAY'S LESSON

**AIM: That your students will consider how marriages today can benefit from this lesson text.**

## INTRODUCTION
### Solomon's Words

Son of King David and Bathsheba, Solomon was part of the lineage of Jesus. The third king of Israel, Solomon reigned for 40 years and was known for his unequalled wisdom, vast wealth, and impressive Temple construction project. Solomon's wisdom was a gift of God. Some of Solomon's wisdom is contained in the three thousand proverbs and more than one thousand songs he wrote. The Song of Solomon—also dubbed the "Song of Songs"—is attributed to KingSolomon. It is a text to which Christians can turn for encouragement as they contemplate love and commitment.

## BIBLE LEARNING

**AIM: That your students will discuss the invitation of love presented in Song of Solomon.**

## I. INVITATION TO LOVE (Song of Solomon 4:8–9)

Every marriage begins with an invitation to love, the point at which a relationship becomes more serious and leads to the exchange of vows. In today's text, the groom-to-be issues the invitation to love and awaits his beloved's response.

### A Call to Love (verses 8-9)

**8 Come with me from Lebanon, my spouse, with me from Lebanon: look from the top of Amana, from the top of Shenir and Hermon, from the lions' dens, from the mountains of the leopards. 9 Thou hast ravished my heart, my sister, my spouse; thou hast ravished my heart with one of thine eyes, with one chain of thy neck.**

The man calls for his lover to come to him from Lebanon, the country to the immediate North of Israel. Shenir or Hermon is a mountain range that extends into Lebanon and includes Mount Amana. This text creates the perception of separation by distance. The mention of lions and leopards paints a picture of danger, mystique, grandeur, and power. He is saying that his beloved is inaccessible to him. In his mind she might as well be at the top of a distant mountain. He wants her to be closer.

The New International Version translates this "ravished my heart". The man's reference to the woman as "sister" was a common expression of romantic affection in the Ancient Near East.

## SEARCH THE SCRIPTURES

## QUESTION 1

What informal sentences can you use to express the feelings in **verses 8** and **9**?

Two theologians suggest the following as less formal ways to capture the sentiment being expressed. These were "I am hopelessly in love with you" (Garrett, 406) and "You drive me crazy!" (Longman, 151).

## LIGHT ON THE WORD

### The Biblical Tradition of Marriage

By Solomon's day, many men had strayed from God's one-wife design for marriage. Most had multiple wives. Few, however, could attest to having as many as Solomon. He had 700 wives and 300 concubines (**1 Kings 11:1–13**). Concubines, considered to be secondary wives, held lower social rank than women who bore the title "wife." The foreign women in his life influenced Solomon's worship of foreign gods. However, he may have had a change of heart later in life (**Ecclesiastes 12:13**).

## II. LOVE EXPRESSED (Song of Solomon 4:10–15)

How can married or dating couples express love verbally? First, mediate on a beloved's good or sweet qualities! Second, extol a spouse's physical attributes. Third, consider the beauty, joy, and value that your beloved adds to your life.

### How Do I Love Thee (verses 10-15)?

**10 How fair is thy love, my sister, my spouse! how much better is thy love than wine! and the smell of thine ointments than all spices! 11 Thy lips, O my spouse, drop as the honeycomb: honey and milk are under thy tongue; and the smell of thy garments is like the smell of Lebanon. 12 A garden inclosed is my sister, my spouse; a spring shut up, a fountain sealed. 13 Thy plants are an orchard of pomegranates, with pleasant fruits;**

**camphire, with spikenard, 14 Spikenard and saffron; calamus and cinnamon, with all trees of frankincense; myrrh and aloes, with all the chief spices: 15 A fountain of gardens, a well of living waters, and streams from Lebanon.**

Having described the impact the woman has on him in **verses 8** and **9,** the man now focuses on the sensory experience of her love. A man of fewer words would simply say, "I love everythingabout you." But that would not do justice to her beauty. The only fitting way to communicate his captivation with her is to use finely crafted metaphors that compare her attributes to the finest and best things known in the ancient world. Wine is used as an analogy for love **(Song of Solomon 1:2; 1:4).** In **verse 10,** the comparison of her love with wine says that her love is elegant and has an intoxicating effect. Her "ointments" are her perfumes. By comparing her scent to the most prized fragrances of the day, the man is saying that not only does he prefer her to anyone or anything else, but she is also the gold standard.

Honey and honeycomb were highly prized luxury items in the Ancient Near East. "Milk and honey" are common expressions in the Old Testament used to indicate fertility, prosperity, and an abundance of the best things in the ancient world. Such delicacies cannot be properly enjoyed quickly, but must be savored. At the time of Solomon, Lebanon was renowned for its cedar forests. There is something ideal about the aroma of Lebanon and her aroma is likewise a very fine thing. Note that in the first seven verses of Song of **Solomon 4,** her hair is compared to a flock of goats and her breasts are compared to gazelles. This kind of metaphor references a shared standard of excellence.

The appeal of the woman is based not only on her excellent physical features, but on her skill in self-presentation, her air of nobility, and her overpowering charm. The fact that she has saved herself for him and has waited for the right time to consummate their love intensifies his desire for her. Gardens in the Ancient Near East had more in common with our parks than what we typically think of as a "garden." Gardens were not simply thought of as a place to grow things. Gardens were regarded as sources of great beauty and pleasure, a feast to the senses of sight, smell, and taste. By using this garden metaphor, the man is building anticipation for the day his lover gives herself fully to him. Fountains were another source of pleasure to the ancients and a metaphor for sexual pleasure. A fountain satisfies the eye as well as refreshing the skin and quenching the thirst.

In **Song of Solomon 4:12,** "inclosed" implies that the woman is "shut up" or "sealed" so that no one has enjoyed the sexual pleasure she has to offer. Of course, her virginity is evidence of hermoral integrity. The overriding thought here is that she recognizes that her sexuality is a valuable commodity—too valuable to be wasted on the wrong man or used at the wrong time.

In **verse 13,** the man extends the garden metaphor to praise the excellence of the woman's love by listing a variety of plants found in her garden. The list of plants is impressive. Pomegranates are an edible fruit slightly smaller than a grapefruit with a reddish color. Inside its thick skin are roughly 600 arils—seeds covered with juicy pulp. "Camphire" is henna, a shrub that is still used today to make orange dye for hair and nails. "Spikenard" is nard, an aromatic plant native to the Himalays, China, and Japan used to make perfume that was quite costly in ancient times. **Mark 14:3** and **John 12:3** report that the perfume used to anoint Jesus at Bethany was pure nard of extravagant cost. "Saffron" is a type of crocus with purple flowers native to Asia, Asia Minor, and the eastern Mediterranean. It produces oil with a sweet, spicy floral scent. "Calamus" is an aromatic reed or sweet cane, probably imported from northern India **(cf. Jeremiah 6:20).** "Cinnamon" can refer to the aromatic bark of a number of trees. "Frankincense" and "myrrh" are fragrant tree gum. Along with gold, they were the tribute gifts given to Jesus by the Magi (**Matthew 2:11**). **John 19:39** reveals that a large amount of myrrh and aloe was used by Nicodemus in the wrapping and burial of Jesus' body. Calamus, cinnamon, and myrrh were ingredients in the anointing oil used by the temple priests (**Exodus 30:23**).

The chances are low that any one garden would contain all of these items. The man is speaking of an ideal "dream" garden where all of the plants are beautiful and many appeal to more than one sense. This list contains items that were highly prized and extremely valuable. To him, she is beyond comparison. She has no equal.

Although fountains and springs have already been mentioned in **verse 12,** the focus there was on her desirability and inaccessibility. Verse 15 focuses on the water imagery as a refreshing and sustaining quality of her love. A well of "living water" is a supply of water that never runs dry. Her appeal is lasting, and the satisfaction she offers her lover will never diminish. Known for its beautiful mountain ranges, Lebanon was a source of mountain streams fed by melting snow. All of these water sources provide fresh, high-quality water.

## QUESTION 2

Why do the references to different spices help us to understand the depth of love expressed in verses 10-15?

**Answers will vary.**

## LIGHT ON THE WORD

### Talking About Love

What might be the root of an inability to express love? Consider two options. (1) Past experiences. These include verbal abuse, childhood sexual or physical abuse, a failed marriage, or even wrong advice. Whatever the cause, couples can look to God for healing and wholeness, knowing He designed marriage to be the place for couples to experience satisfying love. (2) Harsh words. Sometimes familiarity breeds contempt in marriage as evidenced by how spouses speak to each other. After all, "Even so the tongue is a little member, and boasteth great things. Behold, how great a matter a little fire kindleth!" (**James 3:5**). Couples are reminded: "Let no corrupt communication proceed out of your mouth, but that which is good to the use of edifying, that it may minister grace unto the hearers" (**Ephesians 4:29**).

## III. LOVE ENJOYED(Song of Solomon 4:16–5:1a)

Solomon's poetic words were the appetite for building a marriage that honors a marriage commitment. The key is to assure that external situations strengthen, not weaken, marriage commitments. For the first time in this poem, the woman responds to her lover. These final verses show the importance of not stirring up or awakening love before the right time.

**Complete Love (verses 4:16–5:1a)**
**4:16 Awake, O north wind; and come, thou south; blow upon my garden, that the spices thereof may flow out. Let my beloved come into his garden, and eat his pleasant fruits. 5:1a I am come into my garden, my sister, my spouse:**

In **verse 16,** the time has come for their love to be consummated. The references to north and south wind are a bit mysterious, but may simply indicate that all the gates that had been lockedare now open. In any case, "blow upon my garden" clearly suggests physical contact. The clause "that the spices thereof may flow out" indicates that it is time for her beauty to be fully enjoyed—for the spices to be tasted—but only by one man. Whereas she was simply "a garden" in **verse 12,** she now refers to herself as "his garden"—she belongs to him and is eager for him to exercise his ownership on their wedding day.

The husband's reply to his bride confirms that sexual union has occurred. He echoes her acknowledgment of ownership: "my garden." The language of "come into" speaks to more than just the act of sexual intercourse; it describes a new stage in their relationship. His position is one of great privilege and pleasure, but also of great responsibility. "My garden" reminds us that marital relationships take time, attention, and effort in order to grow and flourish. This final verse speaks of the sexual pleasure and commitment to love his wife faithfully by attending to her needs for the rest of his life.

## SEARCH THE SCRIPTURES

### QUESTION 3

What primary principle can be understood from verses 4:16 and 5:1a?

**These lines express the beauty of sexual intimacy within the confines of marriage and lifelong commitment. They reveal the fallacy of engaging in casual sexual activity.**

**Answers will vary.**

## LIGHT ON THE WORD

### For Singles, Too

It is important to note that Song of Solomon is applicable for singles, as well. The analogy of the "enclosed garden" reminds singles to reserve intimacy for marriage and to seek other ways to express love when they are in a committed relationship. This means (1) looking beyond physical attributes to the other person's heart, the spiritual and natural character of the person; (2) not buying into society's "ticking clock" mantra, and (3) expressing love in non-physical ways.

## BIBLE APPLICATION

**AIM: That your students will be able to explain modern views of the text.**

### Understanding the Song of Solomon

Until the 19th century, Jewish and Christian communities both interpreted Song of Solomon as an allegory of God's love for His people. Although we no longer see this book as an analogy of Christ's love for the church, the attitude of the husband is a reminder that Jesus loved the church, sacrificing Himself for her, faithfully nourishing and cherishing her **(Ephesians 5:25–29).** In the realm of human relationships, Song of Solomon is recognized as love poetry that celebrates erotic love as something that is beautiful—a good gift of God for which we should be thankful.

However, the book is also clear that sexual expression carries responsibilities with it, and it must conform to God's law in order to be a blessing. We are repeatedly warned against stirring up or awakening love until the right time **(Song of Solomon 2:7; 3:5; 8:4).** Although there is no explicit mention of a marriage ceremony in the book, there can be no doubt that the author only condones sexual intercourse within the bounds of marriage.

## STUDENTS' RESPONSES

**AIM: That your students will discuss how to sustain committed relationships and marriage.**

Building a Relationship That Honors a Marriage Commitment

Many priorities vie for a couple's attention, but nothing is as important as their devotion to God and each other. Building a relationship that honors a marriage commitment means managing the health and vibrancy of relationships so that they thrive. Like **1 Corinthians 13,** these affirmations about love can help you focus. (1) True love surpasses all else. After the honeymoon, couples need to continually prioritize their lives to give preference to caring for their relationship. (2) True love is satisfying. It quenches emotional and physical appetites. (3) True love is physical. Solomon celebrated the beauty of sex in the confines of marriage. Marital sex is passionate and fulfilling; it catapults a couple back to the Garden of Eden where they are vulnerable to each other in order to freely give and receive love. (4) True love is faithful. The couple needs to know they can trust each other. Infidelity is a sin and a serious breach of one's wedding vows and committed promise. (5) True love is a mix of sweet and bitter herbs. Only in fairy tales do couples live happily ever after without disagreements, trials, or struggles. Health concerns, financial problems, and other issues impact relationships. Couples must consider all of this and commit to nurturing their relationship through all the situations they will face together.

## PRAYER

Lord God, help us to honor You as we honor our commitments in marriage and in singleness. In Jesus' Name we pray. Amen.

## DIG A LITTLE DEEPER

Because of its erotic images, Christians often wonder why the Song of Solomon is included in the Holy Bible. Some have interpreted this love song as a metaphor or image representing an ardent relationship between God and Israel or between Jesus Christ and the Church, the bride of Christ (**Revelation 21:2b**).

Nevertheless, the Song of Solomon was written to celebrate attraction and the physical expression of love between married couples. One commentator asserts that its vivid imagery is valuable for believers because it "suggests that love and sex both need to be understood and

managed wisely." (Cultural Backgrounds Study Bible, NKJV)

The Song of Solomon also illustrates the differences between lust that quickly fades and erotic love that can sustain genuine passion between husbands and wives in every stage of life. Since the modern music industry has commercialized sexuality by promoting sin, how can Christians find music or poetry that enhance their love and encourage them to be faithful to their spouses? Could this be why the Song was canonized for both the Christian and Hebrew Bibles and has been read or sung to benefit believers for thousands of years?

## HOW TO SAY IT

Amana. a-ma'-na.

Calamus. kal'-a-mus.

Camphire. kam'-fir.

Hermon. hur'-mon.

Saffron. saf'-run.

Shenir. she'-ner.

Spikenard. spik'-nard.

Grand Rapids, MI: William B. Eerdmans, 2001. 148–59.
NET Bible Study Dictionary. http://www.net.bible.org/dictionary (accessed May 29, 2010).

## DAILY HOME BIBLE READINGS

### MONDAY
God Blessed Them
(Genesis 1:26–31)

### TUESDAY
One Flesh
(Genesis 2:18–24) )

### WEDNESDAY
The Consequences of Unfaithfulness
(Jeremiah 3:1–5)

### THURSDAY
A Covenant of Love
(Hosea 2:16–23) )

### FRIDAY
The Source of Love
(1 John 4:7–12) )

### SATURDAY
The Expectations of Love
(1 Corinthians 13)

### SUNDAY
How Sweet Is Love!
(Song of Solomon 4:8–5:1a)

## COMMENTS / NOTES:

## PREPARE FOR NEXT SUNDAY

Read **Matthew 5:1-12** and study "Living as God's People."

**Sources:**

Baker's Evangelical Dictionary. Bible Study Tools.com. http://www.biblestudytools.com/dictionaries/bakers-evangelical-dictionary (accessed May 23, 2010).

Baltes, A. J., ed. Biblespeech.com. http://biblespeech.com (accessed November 5, 2009).

Beers, V. Gilbert. The Victor Handbook of Bible Knowledge. Wheaton, IL: Victor Books, 1981. 224–25, 228–31.

Elwell, Walter A., ed. Baker's Evangelical Dictionary of Biblical Theology. Grand Rapids, MI: Baker Books, 1996.

ESV Study Bible, The. Wheaton, IL: Crossway Bibles, 2008. 1221–22.

Garrett, Duane A. Proverbs, Ecclesiastes, Song of Songs. New American Commentary, Vol. 14. Nashville, TN: Thomas Nelson Publishers, 1993. 406.

Longman, Tremper III. Song of Songs, New International Commentary on the Old Testament.

# LIVING AS GOD'S PEOPLE

**BIBLE BASIS:** Matthew 5:1-12

**BIBLE TRUTH:** God's reign on earth is already a blessing.

**MEMORY VERSE:** Blessed are they which do hunger and thirst after righteousness: for they shall be filled (Matthew 5:6, KJV).

**LESSON AIM:** By the end of the lesson, we will: DISCUSS the blessings outlined in the Beatitudes; REFLECT on examples of blessings of God's reign already present on the earth; and IDENTIFY ways to apply the Beatitudes to our daily lives.

**BACKGROUND SCRIPTURES:** Matthew 5:1–12— Read and incorporate the insights gained from the Background Scriptures into your study of the lesson.

## TEACHER PREPARATION

**MATERIALS NEEDED:** Bibles (several different versions), Quarterly Commentary/Teacher Manual, Adult Quarterly, teaching resources such as charts, worksheets/handouts, paper, pens, and pencils.

**OTHER MATERIALS NEEDED / TEACHER'S NOTES:**

_____

_____

## LESSON OVERVIEW

**LIFE NEED FOR TODAY'S LESSON**
To apply the Beatitudes to our daily lives.

**BIBLE LEARNING**
To begin to understand that when we trust Christ for our salvation and enter into the kingdom of God, He provides His children with an abundance of gifts.

**BIBLE APPLICATION**
To be overwhelmed with delight at the many gifts that God gives His children.

**STUDENTS' RESPONSES**
Students will praise God for His many blessings.

## LESSON SCRIPTURE

### MATTHEW 5:1-12, KJV

**1** And seeing the multitudes, he went up into a mountain: and when he was set, his disciples came unto him:

### MATTHEW 5:1-12 AMP

**1** When Jesus saw the crowds, He went up on the mountain; and when He was seated, His ] disciples came to Him.

**2** Then He began to teach them, saying,

2 And he opened his mouth, and taught them, saying,

3 Blessed are the poor in spirit: for theirs is the kingdom of heaven.

4 Blessed are they that mourn: for they shall be comforted.

5 Blessed are the meek: for they shall inherit the earth.

6 Blessed are they which do hunger and thirst after righteousness: for they shall be filled.

7 Blessed are the merciful: for they shall obtain mercy.

8 Blessed are the pure in heart: for they shall see God.

9 Blessed are the peacemakers: for they shall be called the children of God.

10 Blessed are they which are persecuted for righteousness' sake: for theirs is the kingdom of heaven.

11 Blessed are ye, when men shall revile you, and persecute you, and shall say all manner of evil against you falsely, for my sake.

12 Rejoice, and be exceeding glad: for great is your reward in heaven: for so persecuted they the prophets which were before you.

3 "Blessed [spiritually prosperous, happy, to be admired] are the poor in spirit [those devoid of spiritual arrogance, those who regard themselves as insignificant], for theirs is the kingdom of heaven [both now and forever].

4 "Blessed [forgiven, refreshed by God's grace] are those who mourn [over their sins and repent], for they will be comforted [when the burden of sin is lifted].

5 "Blessed [inwardly peaceful, spiritually secure, worthy of respect] are thegentle [the kind-hearted, the sweet-spirited, the self-controlled], for they will inherit the earth.

6 "Blessed [joyful, nourished by God's goodness] are those who hunger and thirst for righteousness [those who actively seek right standing with God], for they will be [completely] satisfied.

7 "Blessed [content, sheltered by God's promises] are the merciful, for they will receive mercy.

8 "Blessed [anticipating God's presence, spiritually mature] are the pure in heart [those with integrity, moral courage, and godly character], for they will see God.

9 "Blessed [spiritually calm with life-joy in God's favor] are the makers and maintainers of peace, for they will [express His character and] be called the sons of God.

10 "Blessed [comforted by inner peace and God's love] are those who are persecuted for [c]doing that which is morally right, for theirs is the kingdom of heaven [both now and forever].

11 "Blessed [morally courageous and spiritually alive with life-joy in God's goodness] are you when people insult you and persecute you, and falsely say all kinds of evil things against you because of [your association with] Me.

**12** Be glad and exceedingly joyful, for your reward in heaven is great [absolutely inexhaustible]; for in this same way they persecuted the prophets who were before you.

## BIBLICAL DEFINITIONS

A. **Blessed (Matthew 5:3-11)** *makarios* (Gk.)—Fortunate, happy.

B. **Kingdom (vv. 3, 10)** *basileia* (Gk.)— Royal dominion; God's rule.

## LIGHT ON THE WORD

**Matthew 5–7 is** known as the Sermon on the Mount and is a collection of Jesus' teachings on spiritual maturity. The Sermon on the Mount can be summarized in one verse: "Be ye therefore perfect, even as your Father which is in heaven is perfect" (**Matthew 5:48**). Jesus' sermon explained how His followers could be perfect, meaning mature and complete in Christ and all that God intended for His children to be.

## TEACHING THE BIBLE LESSON

## LIFE NEED FOR TODAY'S LESSON

**AIM: That your students will know what it means to become a part of the kingdom of God.**

## INTRODUCTION

### The Sermon on the Mount

The Sermon on the Mount contrasts a new way of following God with the old way taught by the scribes and Pharisees. The religious leaders emphasized strict observance of the letter of the law. Jesus elaborated on the spirit of the law and displayed the heart of God revealed in the law.

Jesus taught His committed followers the proper character, duties and attitudes, as well as the dangers and rewards of being a Christian disciple. He wanted His followers to know what it meant to become a part of the kingdom of God (i.e., yield to God as the king and ruler of one's entire life, to live as a citizen of the kingdom).

## BIBLE LEARNING

**AIM: That your students will also yield to God as the King and Ruler of their entire lives.**

## I. GOD'S CHILDREN ARE KINGDOM CHILDREN (Matthew 5:1-2)

The night before, Jesus had gone up into the mountain and prayed. In the morning, He chose His 12 disciples and then Jesus began this sermon. Other devoted disciples were also part of the crowd on the mountain, along with a multitude of people.

In this sermon, Jesus made God's expectations clear to His apostles and close followers. He also told them what to expect as a result of their allegiance and devotion to God. He preached this sermon to the unbelievers in the crowd as well, encouraging them to join those who were already a part of the kingdom.

### Jesus Teaches His Followers (verses 1-2)

**1 And seeing the multitudes, he went up into a mountain: and when he was set, his disciples came unto him: 2 And he opened his mouth, and taught them, saying,**

**Verse 1** seems to suggest that there were two different types of people in the crowd. The first represented the larger group (mentioned in **Matthew 4:25),** who came from different regions around Jerusalem. The people that made up the second group were Jesus' disciples, among whom were those Jesus had called earlier to follow Him **(Matthew 4:18–22).** This smaller group probably sat in a semicircle close to Him, and the rest of the crowd formed a larger semicircle down the slope of the mountain. The Greek word means "to sit down," "settle down," or "sojourn." This means that Jesus sat down as He taught the people, which was customary for teachers in Jewish circles (see **Matthew 13:2; 23:2; Luke 4:20–21).**

"And he opened his mouth, and taught them" **(Matthew 5:2)** is a familiar phrase that is usually used to introduce an important teaching. The phrase may also demonstrate a conscious and deliberate decision on the part of the Teacher to teach, seizing the opportunity afforded Him by the surging crowd to set forth the fundamental ordinances of the kingdom.

To whom does the pronoun in "taught them" refer? At first glance, one might assume that the immediate antecedent is "his disciples" in **verse 1.** However, at the conclusion of the sermon, one observes that "the people were astonished at his doctrine: For he taught them as one having authority, and not as the scribes" **(Matthew 7:28–29).**

## SEARCH THE SCRIPTURES

### QUESTION 1
Who was doing the teaching of the Sermon on the Mount?

**Jesus was doing the teaching.**

## LIGHT ON THE WORD
### Ten Statements of Blessings

The beginning of the Sermon on the Mount consists of 10 statements of blessing. These declarations are referred to as "the Beatitudes." The word "blessed" introduces someone who is to be congratulated. Many Bible translators use the word "happy" instead of "blessed," but a temporary mental state like happiness is not what is being described here. "Blessed" is a condition of life and describes one who is fortunate or well-off.

## II. GOD BLESSES KINGDOM CHILDREN (Matthew 5:3-6)

During times of popularity, it's easy to witness and take a stand for Christ. But, what about, when people ridicule you for your faith? In times of opposition and times of peace, remember all that God has and is. All of that is available to His children.

### Oh, to be Blessed by Jesus (verses 3-6)!

**3 Blessed are the poor in spirit: for theirs is the kingdom of heaven. 4 Blessed are they that mourn: for they shall be comforted. 5 Blessed are the meek: for they shall inherit the earth. 6 Blessed are they which do hunger and thirst after righteousness: for they shall be filled.**

Jesus' sermon began by addressing those who are "poor in spirit" **(verse 3).** He is speaking to the meek who are humbly trusting God, even though their loyalty may result in oppression and material disadvantage. The poor in spirit are individuals who are "empty before God"— humble in heart. Daily, they reach up unfilled hands to the Heavenly Father and receive grace.

This "poor in spirit" group has been promised the "kingdom of heaven." This is not an identifiable place. If you can, imagine each believer surrounded by the presence of God, and His, precious gifts. This kind of "place" exists wherever Jesus reigns as King; His power and might are evident.

"They that mourn" are the next group Jesus addresses **(verse 4)**. The verb "mourn" denotes loud wailing, such as a lament for the dead or grieving over a severe, painful loss. This sorrow is the recognition of the power of sin and of our helplessness toward it and escape a constant repentant distress cry. This kind of mourning requires a special kind of comfort; therefore, God Himself addresses this cry. God's comfort flows to a believer in distress. This verse is often used to comfort those grieving over a death or a loss, but the verse is really speaking to those who have suffered because of their loyalty to God.

The next group addressed is the "meek" **(verse 5)**. Meekness is an inward virtue that displays itself when a person is wronged or abused. It is not weakness. A meek person will react not with bitterness, anger, or violence, but instead with mildness, gentleness, and patience.

Jesus is the greatest example of meekness. He totally relied on God to take vengeance on His enemies. He constantly entrusted Himself to the Heavenly Father who promised that He wouldget what He was due. For people who have this inner attitude, the divine blessing constantly follows them in this life.

The righteous are the next group addressed in the Beatitudes **(verse 6)**. Those in God's kingdom hunger and thirst for forgiveness, and God satisfies that need daily. People cannot achieve righteousness unless they believe on Jesus Christ as Lord and Savior.. Once again, the believer has to turn to God and receive the gift of righteousness. The moment faith in Christ is wrought, the believer is declared righteous and through the power of the Holy Ghost is enabled to live a righteous life.

## SEARCH THE SCRIPTURES

## QUESTION 2
How does one obtain righteousness?

**He/she must turn to God and receive the gift of righteousness by faith.**

**Answers will vary.**

## LIGHT ON THE WORD
### God's Children Bless One Another
The next three beatitudes are more active, particularly in regard to our behavior toward others. Christians receive God's mercy in abundance. He forgives His undeserving children for a multitude of sins. Mercy is not merely an emotion ("Oh-h-h, I'm so sorry.") but a practical action ("Here, let me help.").

## III. BELIEVERS' BEHAVIOR TOWARD OTHERS (Matthew 5:7-9)

The simplest way to talk about the beatitude in **Matthew 5:7** is in terms of reaping and sowing (i.e., you reap what you sow), but in a positive sense. The word "mercy" contains the idea of both forgiveness and compassion (i.e., showing kindness). Both understandings of mercy are common themes in Matthew's Gospel (in the Lord's Prayer, **6:12–15;** in Jesus' teachings and parables, **9:13; 12:7; 18:33–34).** The reward for showing mercy is obtaining (i.e., also receiving) mercy, not necessarily from other people or from the immediate recipients, but from the Lord.

Although showing mercy to others is not always grounds for God's mercy, it can be its"occasional ground," as someone put it **(Matthew 6:14–15).** Mercy is part of God's character and is not dependent on our merciful acts; it is in God's nature and a gift to sinful man.

### Let Others See Jesus in You
### (verses 7-9)
**7 Blessed are the merciful: for they shall**

obtain mercy. **8 Blessed are the pure in heart: for they shall see God. 9 Blessed are the peacemakers: for they shall be called the children of God.**

The phrase "pure in heart" (**verse 8**) means singleness of heart and refers to a child of God who is honest and has no hidden motives or selfish interests. It denotes one who loves God wholeheartedly and shows it outwardly in sincere service to others.

Those with a pure heart are promised that they shall see God. Viewing God fully will only be realized in heaven, when we shall see Him just as He is. The greatest joy for the Christian in heaven will be to see God. However, the person who is free from sin, cleansed and forgiven, will begin to see God in His true character and will experience His presence here on earth.

"Peacemakers" (**verse 9**) are rare in our society. We live in a world of people who pour forth violence, conflict, and anger. The absence of selfish ambition and a concern for the good of others are pleasing to God.

The peacemaker is—first of all—at peace with God. When believers are filled with God's sweet peace, peace with others is a natural result. A peacemaker is a reconciler. This includes reconciling others to God, a chief responsibility of all Christians (**2 Corinthians 5:19–20**).

## SEARCH THE SCRIPTURES

### QUESTION 3
The "peacemaker" is first of all at peace with?
**God**

## LIGHT ON THE WORD

### God's Children Are under Persecution
The Beatitudes emphasize rewards in the kingdom of God. Yet, as God's children display the character of God on earth, not everyone is going to encourage the Christian in his or her positive, godly attitudes. Jesus walked this earth as a perfect man, and yet He endured suffering and persecution—and God's children will encounter the same.

## IV. SUFFERING IS A PART OF BELIEVERS' LIVES (Matthew 5:10-12)
The tone of the phrase "they which are persecuted" (verse 10) seems to indicate those who have allowed themselves to be persecuted. They did not flee from persecution but willingly submitted to it when it came to them. And they endured "for righteousness sake." Their whole lives, their character, and their actions stood as a rebuke to the world, and, therefore, the world persecuted them. By taking this kind of stand for God in opposition to the world, they displayed the grace and gifts provided in the kingdom of God.

### Lord, Help Me to Hold Out (verses 10-12)!
**10 Blessed are they which are persecuted for righteousness' sake: for theirs is the kingdom of heaven. 11 Blessed are ye, when men shall revile you, and persecute you, and shall say all manner of evil against you falsely, for my sake. 12 Rejoice, and be exceeding glad: for great is your reward in heaven: for so persecuted they the prophets which were before you.**

Jesus says that in the face of this kind of persecution, we are to rejoice. Jesus endured the Cross "for the joy that was set before him" (**Hebrews 12:2**). "Blessed" are those believers who are persecuted, insulted, and lied about because they dare to take a stand for Christ (**Matthew 5:11**). Jesus encourages this group to be happy and to be glad. Why? He does so because those who suffer with Christ will experience the comfort that He experienced.

They will also receive a future reward. In heaven, a "crown of reward" is waiting for all who have shared in His sufferings.

Jesus also mentions the prophets, the martyrs of the past who gave up their lives for God. When we suffer persecution for Christ's sake, we can have joy because we are part of this great company of believers.

## SEARCH THE SCRIPTURES

### QUESTION 4

The evil that humanity says against believers should be_____ Matthew 5:11).

**False**

## BIBLE APPLICATION

**AIM: That your students will begin to understand and praise God for His blessings and for not leaving or forsaking them in times of trouble.**

### A Steadfast Faith in God!

Jesus urges His disciples to rejoice with exceeding gladness even in the face of their tribulations. The first reason is that they will be greatly rewarded for their faith––that their reward will be great in heaven. The second reason is that they are in the same company with the Old Testament prophets before them, who were likewise persecuted.

The beatitude of **Matthew 5:11–12** does not imply that Christians, or believers, should seek persecution (though it should not surprise us when it occurs), nor does it permit retreat from it or seek revenge. Rather, it speaks of steadfast faith in the Lord under any and all circumstances with humility and singleness of heart and continuing reliance on and faithfulness to God, irrespective of what may come our way, good and bad.

## STUDENTS' RESPONSES

**AIM: That your students will always delight in God's many blessings. Which of God's Gifts Should You Open First?**

When Lydia, our firstborn, was a baby, my husband and I agreed to raise her differently. At Christmas time, we wanted to place the main emphasis on the birth of Christ and not merely on an abundance of gifts received. However, we forgot about the gifts Lydia would receive from her grandmothers, her aunts, and others. On Christmas morning, Lydia, who was now two, was surrounded by brightly colored packages. She was so excited; she hardly knew which one to open first.

## PRAYER

Father in heaven, thank You, for Your many blessings. Thank You for being our God! In Jesus' name we pray. Amen.

## DIG A LITTLE DEEPER

How can Americans living in the richest country in history believe that the poor, mourning, persecuted and reviled, the peacemakers and those hungering and thirsting after righteousness be happy? Does being "heavenly minded" make one "no earthly good? How could this be when Jesus called his disciples the "salt of the earth" and "light of the world" **(Matthew 5:13-14)?**

Theologian Howard Thurman reminds us that "Jesus was a poor Jew" (emphasis added) who "in his poverty (was) more truly Son of man" than if he had been born rich. Jesus also said it was extremely unlikely that the rich would enter the Kingdom of Heaven but added that "with God, all things are possible" **(Matthew 19: 23-26).**

Is Jesus saying we can live blessed lives only if we keep heaven in view while suffering on earth for doing his will? Since His church has always included both rich and poor, how do we undertake the inner transformation which produces characteristics that are essential to living as His people regardless of socio-economic status?

Howard Thurman, Jesus and the Disinherited (Richmond, IN: Friends United Press edition, 1981), p. 17.

## HOW TO SAY IT:

Beatitudes. Be AT-i-toods.

## DAILY HOME BIBLE READINGS

### MONDAY
A Lowly Spirit
(Proverbs 16:16–20)

### TUESDAY
Comfort for All Who Mourn
(Isaiah 61:1–7)

### WEDNESDAY
The Inheritance of the Meek
(Psalm 37:10–17)

### THURSDAY
The Way of Righteousness
(Isaiah 26:7–11)

### FRIDAY
BeMerciful
(Luke 6:32–36)

### SATURDAY
The Strength of My Heart
(Psalm 73:10–26)

### SUNDAY
Blessed by God
(Matthew 5:1–12)

## PREPARE FOR NEXT SUNDAY

Read **Matthew 5:17-26,** and study "Forgiving as God's People."

Sources:
Baltes, A. J., ed. Biblespeech.com. http://biblespeech.com (accessed July 1, 2010). Gardner, Richard. "Matthew." Believers Church Bible Commentary. Scottsdale, PA:
Herald Press, 1991. 95.
Hebrew and Greek Lexicons. Bible Study Tools.com. http://www.biblestudytools.com/lexicons (accessed September 16, 2010).
Vine's Expository Dictionary of New Testament Words, complete and unabridged (Westwood, NJ: Barbour and company, Inc., 1952); James Strong, Strong's Exhaustive Concordance of the Bible (Nashville, TN, n.d.); and Merriam-Webster's collegiate Dictionary, 11th edition (Springfield, MA, 2005).
<vision.org/family-relationships-12 scriptural –princiles-of-child-rearing-1086>
Martin Luther King, Jr., August 28, 1963.
"Diet and Parkinson's Disease," Focus on Healthy Aging, Icahn School of Medicine at Mount Sinai, Vol. 24, No.4, April 2021, p. 2. Howard Thurman, Jesus and the Disinherited (Richmond, IN: Friends United Press edition, 1981), p. 17.

## COMMENTS / NOTES:

_____
_____
_____
_____
_____
_____
_____
_____
_____
_____
_____
_____
_____
_____
_____
_____
_____
_____
_____
_____
_____
_____

# FORGIVING AS GOD'S PEOPLE

**BIBLE BASIS:** Matthew 5:17–26

**BIBLE TRUTH:** As people of God, living in harmony with others is important..

**MEMORY VERSE:** Therefore if thou bring thy gift to the altar, and there rememberest that thy brother hath ought against thee; Leave there thy gift before the altar, and go thy way; first be reconciled to thy brother, and then come and offer thy gift (Matthew 5:23–24 KJV).

**LESSON AIM:** By the end of the lesson, we will: DISCUSS the beauty and wonder of love in a committed relationship; REFLECT on our attitude about love and commitment; and EXPLAIN how to build a relationship that honors a marriage commitment.

**BACKGROUND SCRIPTURES:** Matthew 5:17–26—Read and incorporate the insights gained from the Background Scriptures into your study of the lesson.

## TEACHER PREPARATION

**MATERIALS NEEDED:** Bibles (several different versions), Quarterly Commentary/Teacher Manual, Adult Quarterly, teaching resources such as charts, worksheets/handouts, paper, pens, and pencils.

**OTHER MATERIALS NEEDED / TEACHER'S NOTES:**

_____

_____

## LESSON OVERVIEW

**LIFE NEED FOR TODAY'S LESSON**
To know what Jesus taught about the relationship between reconciliation and forgiveness.

**BIBLE LEARNING**
To reflect more on reconciliation as God's people.

**BIBLE APPLICATION**
To begin to understand the consequences of anger and how to improve relationships.

**STUDENTS' RESPONSES**
Students will seek to repair a damaged relationship.

## LESSON SCRIPTURE

### MATTHEW 5:17-26, KJV

**17** Think not that I am come to destroy the law, or the prophets: I am not come to destroy, but to fulfil.

### MATTHEW 5:17-26, AMP

**17** "Do not think that I came to do away with or undo the [a]Law [of Moses] or the [writings

18 For verily I say unto you, Till heaven and earth pass, one jot or one tittle shall in no wise pass from the law, till all be fulfilled.

19 Whosoever therefore shall break one of these least commandments, and shall teach men so, he shall be called the least in the kingdom of heaven: but whosoever shall do and teach them, the same shall be called great in the kingdom of heaven.

20 For I say unto you, That except your righteousness shall exceed the righteousness of the scribes and Pharisees, ye shall in no case enter into the kingdom of heaven.

21 Ye have heard that it was said by them of old time, Thou shalt not kill; and whosoever shall kill shall be in danger of the judgment:

22 But I say unto you, That whosoever is angry with his brother without a cause shall be in danger of the judgment: and whosoever shall say to his brother, Raca, shall be in danger of the council: but whosoever shall say, Thou fool, shall be in danger of hell fire.

23 Therefore if thou bring thy gift to the altar, and there rememberest that thy brother hath ought against thee;

24 Leave there thy gift before the altar, and go thy way; first be reconciled to thy brother, and then come and offer thy gift.

25 Agree with thine adversary quickly, whiles thou art in the way with him; lest at any time the adversary deliver thee to the judge, and the judge deliver thee to the officer, and thou be cast into prison.

26. Verily I say unto thee, Thou shalt by no means come out thence, till thou hast paid the uttermost farthing.

of the] Prophets; I did not come to destroy but to fulfill.

18 For I assure you and most solemnly say to you, until heaven and earth pass away, not the smallest letter or stroke [of the pen] will pass from the Law until all things [which it foreshadows] are accomplished. 19 So whoever breaks one of the least [important] of these commandments, and teaches others to do the same, will be called least [important] in the kingdom of heaven; but whoever practices and teaches them, he will be called great in the kingdom of heaven.

20 "For I say to you that unless your righteousness (uprightness, moral essence) is more than that of the scribes and Pharisees, you will never enter the kingdom of heaven.

21 "You have heard that it was said to the men of old, 'You shall not murder,' and 'Whoever murders shall be guilty before the court.'

22 But I say to you that everyone who continues to be angry with his brother or harbors malice against him shall be guilty before the court; and whoever speaks [contemptuously and insultingly] to his brother, 'Raca (You empty-headed idiot)!' shall be guilty before the supreme court (Sanhedrin); and whoever says, 'You fool!' shall be in danger of the fiery hell.

23 So if you are presenting your offering at the altar, and while there you remember that your brother has something [such as a grievance or legitimate complaint] against you,

24 leave your offering there at the altar and go. First make peace with your brother, and then come and present your offering.

25 Come to terms quickly [at the earliest opportunity] with your opponent at law while you are with him on the way [to court], so that your opponent does not hand you over to the

judge, and the judge to the guard, and you are thrown into prison.

**26** I assure you and most solemnly say to you, you will not come out of there until you have paid the last cent.

## BIBLICAL DEFINITIONS

A. **To fulfill (Matthew 5:17)** *pleroo* (Gk.)—To accomplish or complete something.

B. **Be reconciled (v. 24)** *diallasso* (Gk.)—Conciliated; caused the nature of a broken relationship to change.

## LIGHT ON THE WORD

On the heels of a triumphant victory in the wilderness, Jesus begins His public ministry. His fame spread rapidly, due in part to Jesus' astounding power to heal various diseases. While the "multitudes" followed Jesus to receive healing, many of the religious leaders shunned commitment to Him or His teaching. This did not stop Jesus from healing, teaching and preaching God's Word to others.

### TEACHING THE BIBLE LESSON

### LIFE NEED FOR TODAY'S LESSON

AIM: That your students will learn more about how Jesus came to fulfill the law.

## INTRODUCTION

### The Danger of Not Forgiving

It is quite dangerous for us not to forgive. We are responsible to make sure we don't tempt our brother to sin by leaving conflicts unresolved. We must do everything in our power to eradicate the poison of resentment from our lives as well as the lives of others. Our faithfulness to do so is far more important than even the most solemn act of worship.

## BIBLE LEARNING

AIM: **That your students will understand how Jesus came to fulfill the Law.**

## I. JESUS' OBEDIENCE TO GOD (Matthew 5:17-18)

Jesus prepares His listeners for what He is about to say by explaining that His teaching does not destroy, but rather fulfills the Old Testament. The Greek word translated "destroy" in other contexts, means "dissolve, disunite, subvert, demolish." Here it means "do away with, annul, make invalid." To "fulfill" the law and prophets, then, would be to uphold the Laws of the Old Testament, and to bring to fulfillment their Messianic and kingdom prophecies.

### His Purpose Was Finished (verses 17-18)

**17 Think not that I am come to destroy the law, or the prophets: I am not come to destroy, but to fulfil. 18 For verily I say unto you, Till heaven and earth pass, one jot or one tittle shall in no wise pass from the law, till all be fulfilled.**

Jesus lived a life on earth that honored God and was marked by obedience, self-denial, and love. Before dying, Jesus declared, "When Jesus therefore had received the vinegar, he said, It is finished: and he bowed his head, and gave up the ghost" (**John 19:30, KJV**). Jesus finished the work of fulfilling the Law, but not in ways people expected. For example, the scribes were outraged what Jesus told a sick man, "And, behold, they brought to him a man sick of the palsy, lying on a bed: and Jesus seeing their faith said unto the sick of the palsy; Son, be of good cheer; thy sins be forgiven thee" (**Matthew 9:2**).

Knowing the bystanders' emerging criticism, Jesus queried, "For whether is easier, to say, Thy sins be forgiven thee; or to say, Arise, and walk?" (**Mathew 9:5**). Jesus continued by saying, "But that ye may know that the Son of man hath power on earth to forgive sins, (then saith he to the sick of the palsy,) Arise, take up thy bed, and go unto thine house (**Matthew 9:6**).

## SEARCH THE SCRIPTURES

### QUESTION 1
Did Jesus come to fulfill or destroy the Law?

**Jesus came to fulfill the Law.**

## LIGHT ON THE WORD

### The Perfect Sacrifice
The law exacted punishment for sin, but also provided a system of sacrifices for unintentional and intentional sin (**Leviticus 4**). The sacrifices of animals, however, could not completely atone for sin and only foreshadowed the atonement of Jesus Christ. For Jesus, fulfilling the Law meant becoming the sacrificial Lamb slain for humankind's sins. **Galatians 1:4** says, "Who gave himself for our sins, that he might deliver us from this present evil world, according to the will of God and our Father." Beholding Jesus, "The next day John seeth Jesus coming unto him, and saith, Behold the Lamb of God, which taketh away the sin of the world." (**John 1:29**). His was a one-time-only sacrifice that completely fulfilled the Law (**Hebrews 10:12**).

## II. HYPOCRISY CONDEMNED (Matthew 5:19-20)

In Jesus' day, the Pharisees and scribes were the epitome of hypocrisy. On one occasion Jesus said, "But woe unto you, scribes and Pharisees, hypocrites! for ye shut up the kingdom of heaven against men: for ye neither go in yourselves, neither suffer ye them that are entering to go in" (**Matthew 23:13**). Ironically, they accused Him of hypocrisy because Jesus ate with known sinners, offered compassion to tax collectors and harlots, and associated with non-Jews.

### "Least and Righteous" (verses 19-20)
**19 Whosoever therefore shall break one of these least commandments, and shall teach men so, he shall be called the least in the kingdom of heaven: but whosoever shall do and teach them, the same shall be called great in the kingdom of heaven. 20 For I say unto you, That except your righteousness shall exceed the righteousness of the scribes and Pharisees, ye shall in no case enter into the kingdom of heaven.**

The consequence for living in deliberate violation of God's Law is being called "least" in the kingdom of heaven. What God wants is not a display of religious behavior that impresses others, but our wholehearted submission to His will. It is impossible to rise to greatness in God's eyes without a firm commitment to total obedience.

The scribes and Pharisees were some of the spiritual elite in Jesus' day. The scribes were the expert teachers and interpreters of the Law. The Pharisees were a Jewish religious party whose name comes from the Aramaic, meaning "separated." Among other things, they attempted to distinguish themselves through fastidious obedience to the Law (**Philippians 3:4-6**). However, they also added human traditions to the Laws of God and modified God's Laws through their interpretations and traditions. Because their lives were so dominated by conformity to their religious rules, they were highly regarded by the Jewish people for their outward appearance of righteousness.

Jesus' statement that our righteousness must exceed that of the Pharisees would have shocked His audience. Most of His hearers would have assumed that if anyone could make it to heaven on

the basis of their good works, it would be the Pharisees. Doubtless they would have thought, "If even the Pharisees aren't good enough, is there any hope for the rest of us?" But Jesus' point is not that we must do more than the Pharisees, but that their righteousness is not true righteousness.

## SEARCH THE SCRIPTURES

### QUESTION 2
Describe what "least" means in verse Matthew 5:19.

**"Least" means the consequence for living in deliberate violation of God's Law.**

**Answers will vary.**

## LIGHT ON THE WORD

### Don't Be a Hypocrite
Jesus' life and ministry proved that the Law requires more than outward obedience. It requires a change of heart, evidenced by authentic living free from hypocrisy. This kind of lifestyle promotes reconciliation, allowing us to exist harmoniously with others. Jesus warned, "…Take heed and beware of the leaven of the Pharisees and of the Sadducees. Beware of the yeast of the Pharisees and Sadducees" (**Matthew 16:6**). He later helped the disciples understand that "yeast" referred to the false teaching among

the Pharisees and Sadducees—a small amount could rise and spread (**Matthew 16:7–12**).

## III. HARMONIOUS LIVING (Matthew 5:21-26)

The Sixth Commandment prohibited murder (**Exodus 20:13**). Strict adherence to the Law taught that the commandment referred to killing a person. Jesus, however, helped listeners understand that the spirit of the Law meant much more. For example, anger is akin to murder and has its own consequences. On another occasion, Jesus explained: "But those things which proceed out of the mouth come forth from the heart; and they defile the man. For out of the heart proceed evil thoughts, murders, adulteries, fornications, thefts, false witness, blasphemies" (**Matthew 15:18– 19**).

### Living in Peace, Joy, and Forgiveness (verses 21-26)
**21 Ye have heard that it was said by them of old time, Thou shalt not kill; and whosoever shall kill shall be in danger of the judgment: 22 But I say unto you, That whosoever is angry with his brother without a cause shall be in danger of the judgment: and whosoever shall say to his brother, Raca, shall be in danger of the council: but whosoever shall say, Thou fool, shall be in danger of hell fire.**

Jesus now begins to address specific commandments from God's Law to show just how the scribes and Pharisees have misunderstood and misrepresented them. He starts with the Sixth Commandment, found in **Exodus 20:13**: "Thou shalt not kill." The Old Testament Law required that anyone guilty of murder (intentional, unjustified homicide) be put to death. Those guilty of unintentional homicide (manslaughter) could avoid the death penalty, but did have to stand before the congregation for judgment to determine whether or not it really was manslaughter

(**Numbers 35:12**). Any conviction required a trial and the testimony of at least two witnesses (**35:30**). But Jesus reveals that simply abstaining from murder does not count as true righteousness. He lists two common offenses that reveal a murderous heart: anger and ridicule.

The anger at issue here is clearly unjustified anger, even though the best Greek manuscripts do not include the phrase "without a cause." Jesus Himself was sometimes angry (**Matthew 21:12– 13; Mark 3:5**), but His anger was always justified and was directed at those whose evil was exposed by their hypocrisy and their exploitation of the vulnerable. In brief, the anger that qualifies as a violation of God's Law is: (1) anger that is unjustly aroused, such as Cain's jealous anger of Abel (**Genesis 4:5–6**); and (2) anger that is not swiftly resolved, making it likely that we will sin (**Ephesians 4:26–27**).

Most scholars take the Aramaic term "Raca" to mean "empty-headed, numbskull, fool." The Greek word for "you fool" is an adjective used elsewhere in the New Testament to mean "foolish." Any words that communicate to someone that he or she is worthless are a violation of true righteousness, whether or not that violation is punished by a human authority.

**23 Therefore if thou bring thy gift to the altar, and there rememberest that thy brother hath ought against thee; 24 Leave there thy gift before the altar, and go thy way; first be reconciled to thy brother, and then come and offer thy gift.**

The altar in question here is the temple altar and the gift is the offering being brought for sacrifice. This teaching underscores the priority of forgiveness in two ways. First, it warns us against the hypocrisy of pretending to be at peace with God when we are at odds with others. If our faith is genuine, God's forgiveness of us in Christ transforms us and makes us willing to pursue reconciliation with others. Secondly, Jesus is saying forgiveness is so important that we need to pursue reconciliation, even in situations when others—not ourselves—are the angry ones.

**25 Agree with thine adversary quickly, whiles thou art in the way with him; lest at any time the adversary deliver thee to the judge, and the judge deliver thee to the officer, and thou be cast into prison. 26 Verily I say unto thee, Thou shalt by no means come out thence, till thou hast paid the uttermost farthing.**

Jesus ends His interpretation of the Sixth Commandment by discussing the urgency and wisdom of forgiveness. The Greek word translated "agree with" literally means "give of yourself wholly to an idea or a person." The Greek word translated "adversary" refers to an opponent in a lawsuit. Because of the preceding verses, we know that Jesus is not speaking only of legal affairs, but is using a legal situation as an example to make His point. He is speaking about our need to reconcile as quickly as possible in any kind of conflict. Just as in the preceding situation with the brother, who is right and who is wrong is irrelevant. The word translated "farthing" referred to the smallest Roman coin. Unresolved conflict creates situations in which others may seek to get "every last penny" from us. Failure to reconcile quickly can have dramatic, painful, and even permanent consequences. It is a foolish and unnecessary risk to let a matter wait. The best time to attempt reconciliation will always be right now!

## SEARCH THE SCRIPTURES

### QUESTION 3
A "farthing" referred to what?

**The smallest Roman coin.**

## LIGHT ON THE WORD

### Fostering Reconciliation

When we live harmoniously with other people, we can foster reconciliation. As we do, we experience:

The power of forgiveness. Forgiveness promotes reconciliation on two levels: between God and humankind, and between people. The power of forgiveness allows us to heal past, present, and future emotional wounds. A commitment to forgive future offenses acknowledges the inevitable: someone will probably offend you daily and vice versa.

The peace of forgiveness. Forgiveness promotes inner peace. **Psalm 32:3–4** offers a glimpse of the turmoil of unforgiveness, while **verses 1 and 2** describe the peace received from being forgiven.

The joy of forgiveness. Forgiveness not only promotes peace, it also sparks joy. That's true whether we are forgiving someone or being forgiven. To experience the fullness of joy, dare to be the first to say, "I'm sorry."

## BIBLE APPLICATION

**AIM: That your students will better understand how forgiving others as God's people is necessary to help us draw closer to God and have healthier lives**

### An Estranged Relationship

Becari sat in the examination room, anxiously awaiting the cardiologist and the results from a recent battery of tests. He hoped to learn the source of persistent chest and back pains. A non-smoker and non-drinker, Becari was 40, physically fit, and had no family history of cardiac problems. Despite this, he was advised to see a cardiologist when nothing eased his discomfort. After meeting with the doctor, Becari left relieved that he did not have heart disease. At the same time, he was a bit dismayed at some of the doctor's suggestions to reduce stress, including improving personal relationships. Becari knew that included his estranged father.

Damaged relationships are particularly troublesome, impacting one's mental, physical, and emotional health. Working to resolve issues with family, friends, and co-workers can go a long way in promoting physical and social well-being.

## STUDENTS' RESPONSES

**AIM: That your students will learn how to give and receive forgiveness.**

### The Power of Forgiveness

Many people feel forgiveness should be earned. But that is not a scriptural approach. Scripture encourages us to forgive unconditionally—and repeatedly (**Matthew 18:21–23**). Tap into the power of forgiveness. This week, ask God to help you identify harmful habits that block forgiveness. Allow Him to open your eyes to the way in which you extend—and receive forgiveness. Then take every opportunity to grasp or extend forgiveness in a Christ-honoring manner.

## PRAYER

Help us Lord to be who You want us to be. Guide our tongues and our minds to be on one accord with You. Thank You for caring for us and forgiving us. As we reconcile ourselves to one another, let us stay focused on You and in Your Word. In the name of Jesus we pray. Amen.

## DIG A LITTLE DEEPER

Forgiveness is the primary and foundational principle of the Bible and our Christian faith. After Adam and Eve sinned, atonement became necessary. Atonement is at-one-ment, by which reconciliation with God is accomplished through the death of Christ. Like atonement, or at-one-ment, God's commandments are about relationship. The law was created for our relationship with God and others, so that in our families, churches, and communities, and government, relationships will be conciliatory—meaning, loving, caring, and equitable relationships. The commandments guide us in our relationship with God and with one another. Jesus came to fulfill the law through His atoning death on the cross. Forgiveness became the seal of approval for atonement involving repentance, redemption, and reconciliation, with the ultimate goal being reconciliation. We don't always want to forgive but in order to heal we must forgive. We forgive not for the sake of the person who did us wrong—but in order to heal and restore broken and lost relationships.

The three Biblical principles when it comes to forgiveness are repentance, redemption, and reconciliation. According to **John 3:16-17** forgiveness always involves repentance, redemption, and reconciliation. Atonement means that I am engaged in the hard work to restore the relationship to its original or even better state. *Kaparah1* is the Hebrew word for atonement, which also means to wipe clean.

Spilling grape juice on the carpet requires not only an apology, because the stain is still there. Atonement requires me to get the carpet clean so that no more stain remains. The power of forgiveness lies in the fact that God, in **Genesis 3:21,** performs the act of atonement. "God made garments of skin for Adam and his wife and clothed them." Adam and Eve tried to cover themselves, but their attempt to cover themselves, was inadequate. So, covers by taking the skins from animals, the shedding of innocent blood. These animals had to die so that appropriate coverings and atonement could be made for Adam and his wife Eve.

("H3722 - kāpar - Strong's Hebrew Lexicon (KJV)." Blue Letter Bible. Web. 29 Mar, 2021. <https://www.blueletterbible.org//lang/lexicon/lexicon.cfm?Strongs=H3722&t=KJV>.).

## HOW TO SAY IT

| | |
|---|---|
| Jot. | Jät. |
| Tittle. | TIT-uhl. |
| Pharisee. | FA-ruh-see. |
| Raca. | rhak-ah'. |

## DAILY HOME BIBLE READINGS

### MONDAY
A Covenant of Forgiveness
(Hebrews 10:11–18)

### TUESDAY
Rejoicing in God's Forgiveness
(Psalm 32:1–5)

### WEDNESDAY
The Prayer of Faith
(James 5:13–18)

### THURSDAY
Forgive and Be Forgiven
(Luke 6:37–42)

### FRIDAY
How Often Should I Forgive?
(Matthew 18:21–35)

### SATURDAY
Forgiveness Begets Love
(Luke 7:40–47)

### SUNDAY
First Be Reconciled
(Matthew 5:17–26)

## PREPARE FOR NEXT SUNDAY

Read **Matthew 5:43-48,** and study "Loving as God's People."

**Sources:**
Baltes, A. J., ed. Biblespeech.com. http://biblespeech.com (accessed May 29, 2010). Beers, V. Gilbert. The Victor Handbook of Bible Knowledge. Wheaton, IL: Victor Books,
1981. 374–76, 389, 390–91.
Brand, Chad, Charles Draper and Archie England, gen. eds. Holman Illustrated Bible Dictionary. Nashville, TN: Holman Bible Publishers, 1998. 596.
Doriani, Daniel M. Matthew. Reformed Expository Commentary, Vol. 1. Phillipsburg, NJ: P&R Publishing, 2008. 138–49.
ESV Study Bible, The. Wheaton, IL: Crossway Bibles, 2008. 1828–29.
Hebrew and Greek Lexicons. Bible Study Tools.com. http://www.biblestudytools.com/lexicons (accessed September 16, 2010).
Henry, Matthew. Concise Commentary on the Whole Bible. Nashville, TN: Thomas Nelson, n.d. 864–66.
Merriam-Webster Online Dictionary. Merriam-Webster, Inc. http://www.merriam-webster.com (accessed May 8, 2010).
Morris, Leon. The Gospel According to Matthew. Grand Rapids, MI: William B. Eerdmans, 1992. 106–17.

**COMMENTS / NOTES:**

# LOVING AS GOD'S PEOPLE

**BIBLE BASIS:** Matthew 5:43–48

**BIBLE TRUTH:** Adopting an attitude of love is Jesus' expectation for all people.

**MEMORY VERSE:** But I say unto you, Love your enemies, bless them that curse you, do good to them that hate you, and pray for them which despitefully use you, and persecute you; That ye may be the children of your Father which is in heaven: for he maketh his sun to rise on the evil and on the good, and sendeth rain on the just and on the unjust (Matthew 5:44–45, KJV).

**LESSON AIM:** By the end of the lesson, we will: DISCUSS Jesus' teachings concerning loving and praying for our enemies; CONSIDER the relationship between loving our enemies and being a child of God; and DECIDE to pray daily for our enemies.

**BACKGROUND SCRIPTURES:** Matthew 5:43–48—Read and incorporate the insights gained from the Background Scriptures into your study of the lesson

## TEACHER PREPARATION

**MATERIALS NEEDED:** Bibles (several different versions), Quarterly Commentary/Teacher Manual, Adult Quarterly, teaching resources such as charts, worksheets/handouts, paper, pens, and pencils.

**OTHER MATERIALS NEEDED / TEACHER'S NOTES:**

_____

_____

## LESSON OVERVIEW

**LIFE NEED FOR TODAY'S LESSON**
To reflect on the power of love and its transforming power.

**BIBLE LEARNING**
To understand that Jesus taught that we should love our enemies.

**BIBLE APPLICATION**
To practice loving our enemies.

**STUDENTS' RESPONSES**
Students will see the importance of love for others.

## LESSON SCRIPTURE

### MATTHEW 5:43-48, KJV

**43** Ye have heard that it hath been said, Thou shalt love thy neighbour, and hate thine enemy.

### MATTHEW 5:43-48, AMP

**43** "You have heard that it was said, 'You shall love your neighbor (fellow man) and hate your enemy.'

**44** But I say unto you, Love your enemies, bless them that curse you, do good to them that hate you, and pray for them which despitefully use you, and persecute you;

**44** But I say to you, [a]love [that is, unselfishly seek the best or higher good for] your enemies and pray for those who persecute you,

**45** That ye may be the children of your Father which is in heaven: for he maketh his sun to rise on the evil and on the good, and sendeth rain on the just and on the unjust. sun to rise on the evil and on the good, and sendeth rain on the just and on the unjust.

**45** So that you may [show yourselves to] be the children of your Father who is in heaven; for He makes His sun rise on those who are evil and on those who are good, and makes the rain fall on the righteous [those who are morally upright] and the unrighteous [the unrepentant, those who oppose Him].

**46** For if ye love them which love you, what reward have ye? do not even the publicans the same?

**46** For if you love [only] those who love you, what reward do you have? Do not even the tax collectors do that?

**47** And if ye salute your brethren only, what do ye more than others? do not even the publicans so?

**47** And if you greet only your brothers [wishing them God's blessing and peace], what more [than others] are you doing? Do not even the Gentiles [who do not know the Lord] do that?

**48** Be ye therefore perfect, even as your Father which is in heaven is perfect.

**48** You, therefore, will be perfect [growing into spiritual maturity both in mind and character, actively integrating godly values into your daily life], as your heavenly Father is perfect.

## BIBLICAL DEFINITIONS

A. **Neighbor (Matthew 5:43)** *plesion* (Gk.)—Any other person; fellow hu-mankind.

B. **Perfect (v. 48)** *teleios* (Gk.)—A state of being completely mature, complete.

## LIGHT ON THE WORD

Enemies. Holman's Illustrated Dictionary defines "enemy" as "adversary or foe; one who dislikes or hates and seeks to harm the person." The Israelites were instructed to treat their neighbors well. They were warned, "Do not hate a fellow Israelite in your heart. Rebuke your neighbor frankly so you will not share in their guilt" (**Leviticus 19:17, NIV**). Over time, the Jewish people began using a strict interpretation of "neighbor," limited to only Jews. People of other nations or religions were treated as non-neighbors or enemies.

## TEACHING THE BIBLE LESSON

## LIFE NEED FOR TODAY'S LESSON

**AIM: That your students will learn the importance of love as God loves.**

## INTRODUCTION

### Jesus' Challenge

The Jews' keen hatred of Samaritans, for

example, was legendary—so much so that Jesus deliberately cast a Samaritan as a hero in a parable depicting what makes a real neighbor. He told the story on an occasion when He was tested by a teacher of the Law who wanted to know what to do to inherit eternal life. Jesus in turn asked him what the law required. "And he answering said, Thou shalt love the Lord thy God with all thy heart, and with all thy soul, and with all thy strength, and with all thy mind; and thy neighbour as thyself" (**Luke 10:27**).

Jesus challenged them to be like their Father in heaven. God pours out blessings on His enemies, giving them plenty of sunshine and rain. Christ's comment here may have been to prevent the elitism the Jews exhibited because they were God's chosen people.

## BIBLE LEARNING

AIM: **That your students will better understand that Jesus is committed to the foundation of love**.

## I. UNLIKE THE WORLD
## (Matthew 5:43, 46–47)

Jesus' audience has heard the commandment "Love thy neighbor," which is found in **Leviticus 19:18.** However, Jesus' quote of the commandment is different from the Old Testament in two ways: it is missing "as yourself," and in its place is added "and hate thine enemy." It seems most likely that Jesus is using the words of the Jewish teachers of the day, who have twisted God's standard in their interpretation of the Law.

### Jesus Reminds Them (verse 43)
**43 Ye have heard that it hath been said, Thou shalt love thy neighbor, and hate thine enemy.**

The Bible is realistic about the fact that some will ultimately oppose God, and their destruction

will be a vindication of God and His people. The Psalms even talk of hating evildoers and idolaters (**Psalm 26:5; 31:6**) and of God's hatred for evildoers (**Psalms 5:5**). But the Scriptures also require God's people to welcome outsiders (**Leviticus 19:33–34**). And Jesus' own example was to lovingly reach out to hardened "sinners" such as the Samaritan woman and Zacchaeus, the tax collector. So the clear mandate for us is to hope, pray, and work for the salvation—not the destruction—of unbelievers. One day we will rejoice in God's victory over His enemies, but right now, we do not know who will be saved in the end. We should never presume that any individual or group is beyond hope. The apostle Paul is proof that even a hardened enemy of Jesus can be dramatically converted through God's grace. The Christian has no justification for hatred of any "neighbor."

## SEARCH THE SCRIPTURES
### QUESTION 1
Jesus repeated that the Israelites had heard that they were to _____their_____, and _____ their _____ (Matthew 5:43).

**love, their neighbors, and hate their enemies**

## LIGHT ON THE WORD
### Jesus Continued to Teach
Continuing His "Sermon on the Mount" in **Matthew 5,** Jesus touches on another thorny subject: treatment of one's enemies. As was His practice, Jesus dealt directly with the topic. He openly refuted practices that made people shun, rather than embrace, others. His message was especially needed given the Jews' manner of treatment of their enemies, especially those of different ethnic and social status.

## II. LIKE THE FATHER
## (Matthew 5:44-48)

The enemies in question here are not simply

people who dislike us. The Greek word for "enemies" is an adjective meaning "hated, hostile" that is used in the New Testament as a noun. The Greek word translated "persecute" means "to make to run or flee, to pursue, to harass, trouble, molest." So the enemies of whom Jesus speaks are those who are actively trying to do us harm, or those who would do us harm if they could.

### Loving Your Enemy (verses 44-45)

**44 But I say unto you, Love your enemies, bless them that curse you, do good to them that hate you, and pray for them which despitefully use you, and persecute you; 45 That ye may be the children of your Father which is in heaven: for he maketh his sun to rise on the evil and on the good, and sendeth rain on the just and on the unjust.**

The Greek word for "love" used in this passage is agape which is not based on feelings or affinity but seeks opportunities to promote the welfare of others. Consider, then, what Jesus is teaching. He instructs us to intentionally move toward those who want to harm us and take action, when possible, to secure their well-being.

Although Jesus does not here explain the purpose for such a difficult teaching, we see it clearly and powerfully in His example. When one of the disciples attempted to defend Jesus by force on the night of His arrest and cut off the ear of the high priest's servant, Jesus healed the ear (**Luke 22:49–51**). And while Jesus was still on the Cross, He asked the Father to forgive those responsible for His death (**Luke 23:34**). Love for enemies is not a suicide mission, but a rescue mission founded on self-sacrificial love. Christ calls His followers to advance His kingdom by joining Him in this mission of self-sacrifice (**I Peter 2:21–24**). In the days of the early church, Stephen and Paul both stand out as examples of this kind of love (**Acts 7:60; I Corinthians 4:12–13**).

The phrase "may be the children" is literally "may become sons" in the Greek text. "Become" is the common Greek word with a wide range of meanings, most commonly "to be born or produced." Here Jesus' message is not that we become children of God by loving like God, but

that we grow into our identity as God's children as we learn to love. The increasing resemblance with our Heavenly Father proves that we really are His.

God's love for even His enemies is seen in ways so ordinary that they are easy to overlook: the fact that the sun rises and rain falls the world over, regardless of who lives where. The Greek word for "just" means "righteous, upright, and virtuous." Jesus is articulating the concept theologians have termed "common grace": even though God's saving grace is only experienced through faith in Christ, all humanity experiences some undeserved favor. God sustains the functions of the universe that make it possible for us to live.

**46 For if ye love them which love you, what reward have ye? do not even the publicans the same? 47 And if ye salute your brethren only, what do ye more than others? do not even the publicans so?**

Jesus' point with His questions in **Matthew 5:46–47** is not that we can earn something from God by loving others well enough, or that God judges human righteousness by comparing us to each other, but that people who pride themselves on their religious perfection aren't actually meeting any higher standard than people widely regarded as scoundrels. The Greek word translated "reward" means "wages," and it is used in **Romans 4:4** to refer to what we expect God to give us in return for living righteously. The religious elite assumed that they were earning points from God through their elaborate rituals and stringent rule keeping, but Jesus is showing us that true righteousness will distinguish itself in an entirely different kind of love than what their religion produced. The shocking truth is that human-powered religion apart from faith in Jesus Christ and the love this faith produces, make us any more righteous in God's eyes than a hardened sinner.

**48 Be ye therefore perfect, even as your Father which is in heaven is perfect.**

"Therefore" reminds us to think of what we have already heard so far in the Sermon on the Mount, but especially **verses 44** through **47,** in order to understand what comes next. What we have heard is that external righteousness, even when it conforms to the Old Testament Law, is totally inadequate in God's eyes. The best behavior that religion can produce in us makes us no better than a tax collector—and everybody knew that tax collectors are not viewed as being anywhere near holy enough to be approved by God.

## SEARCH THE SCRIPTURES
### QUESTION 2
Who did Jesus say that the Israelites were also to love and pray for? (Matthew 5:44)

**The Israelites were to love their enemies and pray for those who despitefully used them.**

## LIGHT ON THE WORD
### Living Up to God's Standards
The only right way to live is to pursue perfection and live up to God's standards. The Greek word translated "perfect" is used in the New Testament to mean "mature, complete" **(Colossians 4:12; James 1:4)** and that is a very, very high standard, and it is unreachable apart from God's work in our life.

## BIBLE APPLICATION
**AIM: That your students will begin to understand that past hurts may cause us to be skeptical about truly forgiving others.**

### A Bitter Taste
Sharon reread the e-mail that had popped into her inbox earlier today from her favorite social media site. She could not fathom why Kelly wanted to be one of her "friends." The last time she saw Kelly was the day they both were kicked out of college a decade earlier for hacking into their college's supposedly secure exam portal. Kelly was the culprit, but no one believed that the computer whiz, Sharon, had not enticed her Christian roommate to access the site. It had taken Sharon three years and thousands of dollars to clear her name. More so, the situation had left a bitter taste in Sharon's mouth for so-called Christians who used other people for their personal gain.

Ironically, it was the success of her legal battle that led Sharon to make Jesus her Savior. Back then, she had even gone through the motions of forgiving Kelly, but then she never expected to see her old "roomie" again. Now this! What to do?

## STUDENTS' RESPONSES
**AIM: That your students will know how to express prayers for others through writing.**

### Prayer Journaling
A prayer journal is a useful tool for recording petitions. It also helps us to see the faithfulness of God. The answers may not be what we thought they would be, but they are always what we need. Even if you have never used a prayer journal, try it for at least this week. Record your petitions, and include those for your enemies. Then remember to go back and jot down any answers you received, including any internal or external changes you see as a result of your prayer.

## PRAYER

Dear Lord, help me to learn how to love my enemies in ways that are pleasing to You. Help me to pray for those who are my enemies, and help those who think of me as an enemy to pray for me. Allow each of us to reach out and show love to each other. In Jesus' name we pray. Amen.

## DIG A LITTLE DEEPER

If we love God, we will love others. If we do not love God, we will not love others. And the way we treat God is how we will treat others. In essence, others get the overflow of our relationship with God. "Let us make man in our image, after our likeness **(Genesis 1:26),**" is about relationship and informs us about God's purely relational intentions towards humankind. God creates humankind in relationship through relationship and for relationship. So, relationships become critical because God is relational, thus freedom from hatred of self and others cannot happen in the absence of authentic relationship. And thus, helping free us from impersonal and adversarial approaches in relationships. Authentic relationships come through embracing God's relational image and intentions towards all human beings. God acts in and through relationship. We are created good, yet we struggle to understand ourselves as created in the image of God and that we are valid, viable and valuable.

God is the source of authentic love from which all love flows. But because of the fall, humankind has distorted self-images, which cause humankind to revert back to negative and stereotypical sinful relationships.

The true image of God is to be found in relations, that is human persons are fundamentally relational beings, related to God, and to other humans. God created in humanity an essential relationality that mirrors the relationality inherent in the Trinity itself.

## HOW TO SAY IT

Despitefully.     di-spīt- fUH-lē.

### DAILY HOME BIBLE READINGS

**MONDAY**
Commandment
(Matthew 22:34–40)

**TUESDAY**
Loving Your God
(Deuteronomy 6:1–9)

**WEDNESDAY**
Loving Your Neighbor
(Leviticus 19:13–18)

**THURSDAY**
Loving the Alien
(Leviticus 19:33–37)

**FRIDAY**
Loving Your Wife
(Ephesians 5:25–33)

**SATURDAY**
Loving Your Husband and Children (Titus 2:1–5)

**SUNDAY**
Loving Your Enemies
(Matthew 5:43-48)

## PREPARE FOR NEXT SUNDAY

Read **Matthew 6:5-15** and learn about "Praying as God's People."

**Sources:**

Beers, V. Gilbert. The Victor Handbook of Bible Knowledge. Wheaton, IL: Victor Books, 1981. 442.

Butler, Bradley S. "Enemy." Holman Illustrated Bible Dictionary. Chad Brand, Charles Draper and Archie England, gen. eds. Nashville, TN: Holman Bible Publishers, 1998. 487.

Clendenen, E. Ray. "Blessing and Cursing." Holman Illustrated Bible Dictionary. Chad Brand, Charles Draper and Archie England, gen. eds. Nashville, TN: Holman Bible Publishers, 1998. 223–24.

Doriani, Daniel M. Matthew. Reformed Expository Commentary, Vol. 1. Phillipsburg, NJ: P&R Publishing, 2008. 186–95.

ESV Study Bible, The. Wheaton, IL: Crossway Bibles, 2008. 1830–31.

Hebrew and Greek Lexicons. Bible Study Tools.com. http://www.biblestudytools.com/lexicons (accessed September 16, 2010).

Henry, Matthew. Concise Commentary on the Whole Bible. Nashville, Tennessee: Thomas Nelson, n.d. 866.

Lanier, Daniel. "Love." Holman Illustrated Bible Dictionary. Chad Brand, Charles Draper and Archie England, gen. eds. Nashville, TN: Holman Bible Publishers, 1998. 1054–55.

Merriam-Webster Online Dictionary. Merriam-Webster, Inc. http://www.merriam-webster.com (accessed May 8, 2010).

Morris, Leon. The Gospel According to Matthew. Grand Rapids, MI: William B. Eerdmans, 1992. 129–34.

## COMMENTS / NOTES:

# PRAYING AS GOD'S PEOPLE

**BIBLE BASIS:** Matthew 6:5–15

**BIBLE TRUTH:** Jesus taught that it is more important to develop our inner relationship with God through prayer.

**MEMORY VERSE:** But thou, when thou prayest, enter into thy closet, and when thou hast shut thy door, pray to thy Father which is in secret; and thy Father which seeth in secret shall reward thee openly (Matthew 6:6, KJV).

**LESSON AIM:** By the end of the lesson, we will: SUMMARIZE Jesus' teaching about prayer; BECOME CONVINCED that Jesus' model of praying should be our guide; and DECIDE to model our prayers after the Lord's Prayer.

**BACKGROUND SCRIPTURES:** Matthew 6:5–15— Read and incorporate the insights gained from the Background Scriptures into your study of the lesson.

## TEACHER PREPARATION

**MATERIALS NEEDED:** Bibles (several different versions), Quarterly Commentary/Teacher Manual, Adult Quarterly, teaching resources such as charts, worksheets/handouts, paper, pens, and pencils.

**OTHER MATERIALS NEEDED / TEACHER'S NOTES:**

_____

_____

## LESSON OVERVIEW

**LIFE NEED FOR TODAY'S LESSON**
Students will be able to summarize Jesus' teaching about prayer.

**BIBLE APPLICATION**
To understand that prayer is a way to seek God for all of our needs.

**BIBLE LEARNING**
To show how God's teachings on prayer were different from how some understood prayer.

**STUDENTS' RESPONSES**
Students should decide to model their prayers after the Lord's Prayer.

## LESSON SCRIPTURE

### MATTHEW 6:5-15, KJV

**5** And when thou prayest, thou shalt not be as the hypocrites are: for they love to ray standing in the synagogues and in the corners

### MATTHEW 6:5-15, AMP

**5** "Also, when you pray, do not be like the hypocrites; for they love to pray [publicly] standing in the synagogues and on the of the streets, that they may be seen of men. Verily I say unto you, They have their reward.

**6** But thou, when thou prayest, enter into thy closet, and when thou hast shut thy door, pray to thy Father which is in secret; and thy Father which seeth in secret shall reward thee openly.

**7** But when ye pray, use not vain repetitions, as the heathen do: for they think that they shall be heard for their much speaking.

**8** Be not ye therefore like unto them: for your Father knoweth what things ye have need of, before ye ask him.

**9** After this manner therefore pray ye: Our Father which art in heaven, Hallowed be thy name.

**10** Thy kingdom come, Thy will be done in earth, as it is in heaven.

**11** Give us this day our daily bread.

**12.** And forgive us our debts, as we forgive our debtors.

**13** And lead us not into temptation, but deliver us from evil: For thine is the kingdom, and the power, and the glory, for ever. Amen.

**14** For if ye forgive men their trespasses, your heavenly Father will also forgive you:

**15** But if ye forgive not men their trespasses, neither will your Father forgive your trespasses.

corners of the streets so that they may be seen by men. I assure you and most solemnly say to you, they [already] have their reward in full. 6 But when you pray, go into your most private room, close the door and pray to your Father who is in secret, and your Father who sees [what is done] in secret will reward you.

**7** "And when you pray, do not use meaningless repetition as the Gentiles do, for they think they will be heard because of their many words.

**8** So do not be like them [praying as they do]; for your Father knows what you need before you ask Him.

**9** "Pray, then, in this way: 'Our Father, who is in heaven, Hallowed be Your name.

**10** Your kingdom come, Your will be done On earth as it is in heaven.

**11** 'Give us this day our daily bread.

**12** 'And forgive us our debts, as we have forgiven our debtors [letting go of both the wrong and the resentment].

**13** 'And do not lead us into temptation, but deliver us from evil. For Yours is the kingdom and the power and the glory forever. Amen.]'

**14** For if you forgive others their trespasses [their reckless and willful sins], your heavenly Father will also forgive you.

**15** But if you do not forgive others [nurturing your hurt and anger with the result that it interferes with your relationship with God], then your Father will not forgive your trespasses.

## BIBLICAL DEFINITIONS

A. **Pray (Matthew 6:5–7)** *proseucho-mai* (Gk.)—Make earnest supplication; worship of God.

B. **Forgive (vv. 12, 14, 15)** *aphiemi* (Gk.)—To release from an obligation, debt or guilt.

## LIGHT ON THE WORD

Jesus taught that the true righteousness of the kingdom must be applied in life's everyday activities. He cautioned against practicing piety to impress other people. Almsgiving was designed to be a display of mercy, but the Pharisees had distorted the showing of mercy by using it to demonstrate their devotion to religious duties in almsgiving and prayer. Jesus also taught that those who give without fanfare and quietly pray will receive their rewards.

### TEACHING THE BIBLE LESSON

### LIFE NEED FOR TODAY'S LESSON

AIM: That your students will better understand why Jesus teaches the importance of prayer.

### INTRODUCTION

#### Prayer Time

Prayer is the communication from the heart of a person to the ear of God. Throughout the Old and New Testaments, we find God answering the prayers of those persons who needed Him. The Hebrews, while in Egypt, cried out because of their hard taskmasters, and God sent Moses to deliver them (**Exodus 3:1–4:17**). David prayed for forgiveness and restoration after being caught in sin, and God heard his prayer (**Psalm 51**). Elisha prayed for his servant's eyes to be opened to see the army of the Lord, and God made it so (**2 Kings 6:17**). Peter prayed and Tabitha woke up from the dead (**Acts 9:40–41**). Both faith (**Mark 11:24**) and forgiveness (**Mark 11:25**) are needed in order for prayers to be answered.

### BIBLE LEARNING

AIM: That your students will know God's view on prayer.

## I. OUR PRAYING (Matthew 6:5–13)

Jesus gave instructions to guide us in our praying. He taught that prayer should be done confidentially. It is not wrong to pray in public, but it is not right to pray in public if you are not in the habit of praying in private. It is not wrong to seek God's help or bless our food. Our Lord prayed privately (**Mark 1:35**); so did Elisha (**2 Kings 4:32–33**) and Daniel (**Daniel 6:10**). We should pray sincerely and not use empty phrases, because God knows what we need before we ask (**Matthew 6:7–8**). Repetitious requests are done in vain when we babble without a sincere heart's desire to seek and do God's will (**6:9–13**).

#### How to Pray (verses 5-6)

**5 And when thou prayest, thou shalt not be as the hypocrites are: for they love to pray standing in the synagogues and in the corners of the streets, that they may be seen of men. Verily I say unto you, They have their reward. 6 But thou, when thou prayest, enter into thy closet, and when thou hast shut thy door, pray to thy Father which is in secret; and thy Father which seeth in secret shall reward thee openly.**

The previous verses in this chapter tell us to do our giving to the needy without seeking a public pat on the back. **Verses 5** and **6** apply this same "secrecy" principle to prayer. Jesus declared that praying to impress others makes people hypocrites. He described the hypocrites as those who found conspicuous places to stand and pray in the synagogue and even on the street corners.

Their objective was to have everyone see them

and admire their devotion and dedication.

Instead, we should go into a secret closet and, even though no one else may know what we are doing, God will see, know, and reward us. This is not to say we should avoid praying in public, but we should not pray to show the public how pious and spiritual we are. Even in public, our motivation should be to glorify and seek God and God alone.

**7 But when ye pray, use not vain repetitions, as the heathen do: for they think that they shall be heard for their much speaking. 8 Be not ye therefore like unto them: for your Father knoweth what things ye have need of, before ye ask him.**

In **verse 7,** Jesus continued His instructions about prayer. Not only are we to avoid praying in order to be seen by others, but we are to avoid the practice that was common to the Gentiles of using lots of words to try to impress or manipulate God. The Gentiles had so many gods and so many names for them that they would try to list them all to make sure they included the right one. Also, they would try to flatter the gods in order to convince them to answer the prayer. Jesus said, specifically, do not be like them. He assures us that God, our Father, the omniscient One (all-knowing), knows already what we need even before we ask. And God cannot be manipulated. God stands ready to answer our prayers and bless us because of the love He has for us.

**9 After this manner therefore pray ye: Our Father which art in heaven, Hallowed be thy name.**

Jesus started by affirming that God is the Father, the One in the heavens. This was typical of many formal Jewish prayers. In this prayer, God is addressed as "Father," not as "Daddy." This is His title. He is the parent, and then we are reminded that our Father is the God of heaven. He is absolute holiness. He is our Father, the Father of all who have received Jesus Christ as Savior.

This is both a personal request and a missionary request. We are asking that we personally would do nothing that would bring shame to the name of God. We should want to act and speak in such a way that others will give honor to our God instead of saying that if that's what Christians are like, they want no part of such a faith and such a God. In addition, this is a request that people all over would come to worship and honor the Lord our God. We are asking God to help us share

the Good News in any way we can—whether by praying, giving, or telling the person next door about salvation in Jesus Christ.

**10 Thy kingdom come. Thy will be done in earth, as it is in heaven.**

In one respect, this refers to the end times, when there will be fulfillment of all prophecies and expectations. At that time, God's kingdom will prevail, and God will rule and reign on earth as He does in heaven. This is what we look forward to as Christians, and we seek to make it a reality in our daily lives as we wait for the kingdom to come in totality. We are also praying that God will reign as King in our hearts. When Jesus said that His kingdom was near (**Matthew 3:2; 4:17; Mark 1:15**), He was inviting people to make Him the King of their hearts right then and there. He desires to have complete rule in our lives today as well.

The second half of **Matthew 6:10** continues with the desire for the coming of the kingdom, that is, God's ultimate will for the earth and humanity. As we pray these words, we have to consider what we are doing day-to-day to witness to God's kingdom on earth. It is also a prayer for God's will to be done in our individual lives. We can ask this prayer in complete confidence because we know that God loves us and would not do anything in our lives that ultimately would be bad for us. We can pray this in confidence because God has all wisdom. While something we desire may look good to us today, God can see in the future whether it truly will be good.

## 11 Give us this day our daily bread.

At this point the "we" petitions begin, as we request things from God. Some scholars have debated over whether this means literal bread in terms of our daily physical needs, or whether "daily bread" should be taken in the spiritual sense or even in the understanding of what will be consumed at the heavenly banquet. It was once thought to be a made-up word, and then one day some archaeologists found it on a fragment of paper—a grocery-shopping list with the daily needs written on it. This is a simple request. We are not asking God to set up a large bank account for us. We are simply asking Him to give us what we need for today. Elsewhere in Scripture, we are advised to be wise in financial matters; but here we are trusting children just asking Him for what is needful for today.

## 12 And forgive us our debts, as we forgive our debtors.

This verse literally means that we are asking God to forgive us in the same proportion in which we forgive others. That is pretty scary. This means that if we say, "I will never forgive so-and-so for what he has done" or "I will never forget what you did to me," we are actually asking God not to forgive us! Human forgiveness and God's forgiveness are all wrapped up together.

## 13 And lead us not into temptation, but deliver us from evil: For thine is the kingdom, and the power, and the glory, for ever. Amen.

This is a difficult passage to understand, because it implies God actively "leads" us into temptation. The expression is intended as a petition for God's help when we face the inevitable temptations and trials that come in this life. The epistle of James cautions us never to say that God is tempting us (**James 1:13–14**). Most scholars agree that this means God doesn't allow us to be tempted or tested beyond our ability to persevere. There is a very popular saying inspired by **I Corinthians 10:13,** that especially in times of trial, "God won't put more on you than you can bear," and without giving you a way to escape.

Then the Lord's Prayer continues with a request to be delivered from evil (**Matthew 6:13**). The more accurate translation of the Greek word is used here as "evil one." When times of testing come, as they will, then we pray to be delivered from the evil one—Satan. The devil "comes only to steal, kill, and destroy" (**John 10:10, NIV**). These two petitions in **Matthew 6:13**—to resist temptation and to be rescued from evil—go together.

## SEARCH THE SCRIPTURES

### QUESTION 1

Share a time when you wanted God to forgive you, but you did not want to forgive someone else. After reading verse 12 and its explanation, how would you do things differently?

**Answers will vary.**

## LIGHT ON THE WORD

### The Model Prayer

Jesus gave His followers a model prayer known as the Lord's Prayer. We should use this prayer as a pattern; Jesus said to pray "after this manner" (**verse 9**). The purpose of prayer is to glorify God, and these are the guidelines for prayer: (1) it should involve worship, reverence, and exaltation of our Father; (2) it should concern itself with the work God is engaged in, namely, the establishment of God's kingdom and His will being done on earth; (3) it should be concerned with daily needs; (4) it should contain confession and seek forgiveness; and finally, (5) it should seek protection and deliverance from the evil one.

## II. OUR FORGIVING (Matthew 6:14-15)

We sing and pray the Lord's Prayer so often that it can become rote and lose its meaning for us. But when we look at it with fresh eyes, the prayer can come alive again and give us, as Jesus intended, clear instructions on how to pray effectively.

### If We Forgive…If We Do Not Forgive… (verses 14-15)

**14 For if ye forgive men their trespasses, your heavenly Father will also forgive you: 15 But if ye forgive not men their trespasses, neither will your Father forgive your trespasses.**

Finally, Jesus goes back to the subject of forgiveness in verses 14 and **15**. These verses are not part of the Lord's Prayer, but are included to emphasize the importance of forgiveness and the fact that it must go two ways in the life of the Christian.

## SEARCH THE SCRIPTURES

### QUESTION 2
Complete the following sentence.

For if ye forgive men their _____, your _____ Father also forgive _____ : But if ye _____ men their trespasses, _____ will your Father trespasses (Matthew 6:14-15).

**Trespasses, heavenly, will, you: forgive, not, neither, forgive, your**

## LIGHT ON WORD

### Forgiveness
How serious are we in wanting God's kingdom to come and His will to be done? Do we live as kingdom people, aware of whom and whose we are? How easy or difficult is it for us to forgive others when they do something wrong to us? How satisfied are we with having just our daily needs met, as opposed to all our wants and desires met? And, in the course of going about our daily lives, how much awareness do we show—in our thoughts, actions, and treatment of others—of the truth of **Matthew 6:14–15?** These are all questions that arise when we take time to really reflect and meditate on the Lord's Prayer.

## BIBLE APPLICATION

**AIM: That your students will begin to understand that God forgives us and expects us to forgive others.**

### Lord, I Need to Hear from You!
Virginia sat at her desk with her hands folded together, head bowed, and eyes closed. It was the lunch hour, and she had decided to forget her lunch in favor of prayer. She needed to hear from God. After nine years of employment at the university, it looked as though she was going to be fired.

She had transferred into the position only seven months ago, when her former job had been phased out. Up until now, her work record had been impeccable. Now her new supervisor was telling her that her work was unsatisfactory. "Dear Lord," she prayed. "Please give me the strength to endure whatever comes my way and help me to have the right attitude, especially toward my supervisor. I trust in You and not the situation. Show me what to do, Lord."

Have you ever had something happen to you that was not in your control? Where did you turn? Examine God's teachings on prayer and see another way for you to respond through your action, words, and thought.

## STUDENTS' RESPONSES

**AIM: That your students will realize that**

prayer is vital in our lives today.

### Let Us Pray—Today!

Prayer is needed more today than ever. This week, set aside a specific time each day for prayer. **Psalm 63:1 (KJV)** says, "Early will I seek thee." Ask the Father to bring to your mind those people who have hurt you or persecuted you. Then ask Him to help you to forgive those people. If you can contact any of them, do so, and resolve whatever differences you may have. Remember, prayer changes things.

## PRAYER

O Father, help us to open our eyes and hearts to love and forgive others as You so graciously do for us. In Jesus' name we pray. Amen.

## DIG A LITTLE DEEPER

Jesus, disciples asked Him to "teach us to pray." They understood where His power and strength came from. They saw Jesus "still away" in the early morning hours just before sunrise to talk to His Father hours before He began each day. They knew prayer was the source of His strength, and where His power came from because they witnessed his devotion to prayer each and every day of His life. Jesus, disciples would follow the same example for the rest of their life on earth.

Prayer is authentic communication with God who loves us, understands us, and provides all of our needs according to "His riches in glory in Christ Jesus concerning us." Prayer is talking to our loving Father, who gives us good success, strength, and courage so that we prosper wherever we go. When we pray, we are talking to a loving Father, who delivers us from the curse of the enemy, who wraps us in His love and protection. A loving Father YHVH Roi, who shepherds us so, that we do not want. A loving Father YHVH Jireh, who provides for every one of our needs. A loving Father YHVH M' Kaddesh who sanctifies us. A loving Father

YHVH Tisikenu, who makes us righteous.

Our prayer life is the key to fulfillment and purpose. And our commitment to daily prayer is the avenue through which God is invited to get God involved in earth's affairs. Satan works overtime to over load the saints with activity and busyness to keep us from devotion to pray, which is the main source of power for success in the kingdom of God.

## HOW TO SAY IT

Babbling. BAB-ling.

Hypocrites. HIP-o-krits.

Pagans. PA-gans.

### DAILY HOME BIBLE READINGS

**MONDAY**
A Prayer for Deliverance
(Genesis 32:6–12)

**TUESDAY**
A Prayer for Forgiveness
(Numbers 14:13–19)

**WEDNESDAY**
A Prayer for God's Blessing
(2 Samuel 7:18–29)

**THURSDAY**
A Prayer for Healing
(1 Kings 17:17–23)

**FRIDAY**
A Prayer of Thanksgiving
(Isaiah 12)

**SATURDAY**
God's Assurance for Prayer
(Jeremiah 29:10–14)

**SUNDAY**
The Practice of Prayer
(Matthew 6:5–15)

## PREPARE FOR NEXT SUNDAY

Read **Matthew 6:25-34,** and study "Facing Life without Worry."

**Sources:**

Barclay, William. The Gospel of Matthew, Vol. 1 (Chapters 1 to 10). Rev. ed. Philadelphia, PA: The Westminster Press, 1975. 219–24.

Greek and Hebrew Lexicons. Eliyah.com. http://www.eliyah.com/lexicon.html/greek/kjv (accessed June 1, 2010).

## COMMENTS / NOTES:

# FACING LIFE WITHOUT WORRY

**BIBLE BASIS:** Matthew 6:25-34

**BIBLE TRUTH:** God is the Great Provider.

**MEMORY VERSE:** "But seek ye first the kingdom of God, and his righteousness; and all these things shall be added unto you. Take therefore no thought for the morrow: for the morrow shall take thought for the things of itself. Sufficient unto the day is the evil thereof" (Matthew 6:33–34, KJV).

**LESSON AIM:** By the end of the lesson, we will: REVIEW Jesus' teaching about God as the great provider; REFLECT on what can and cannot relieve worry and stress; and DECIDE to express reliance on God to meet needs.

**BACKGROUND SCRIPTURES:** Matthew 6:19–34— Read and incorporate the insights gained from the Background Scriptures into your study of the lesson.

## TEACHER PREPARATION

**MATERIALS NEEDED:** Bibles (several different versions), Quarterly Commentary/Teacher Manual, Adult Quarterly, teaching resources such as charts, worksheets/handouts, paper, pens, and pencils.

**OTHER MATERIALS NEEDED / TEACHER'S NOTES:**

_____

_____

## LESSON OVERVIEW

### LIFE NEED FOR TODAY'S LESSON
To know that problems in our lives may be out of control to some degree, but how we respond to these difficult issues is under our control.

### BIBLE LEARNING
To begin to understand that God expects His children to trust and rely on Him.

### BIBLE APPLICATION
To know that we need to seek God first in our lives.

### STUDENTS' RESPONSES
Students will not worry about tomorrow because the Almighty God is in control.

## LESSON SCRIPTURE

### MATTHEW 6:25-34, KJV

**25** Therefore I say unto you, Take no thought for your life, what ye shall eat, or what ye shall drink; nor yet for your body, what ye shall put

### MATTHEW 6:25-34, AMP

**25** "Therefore I tell you, stop being worried or anxious (perpetually uneasy, distracted) about your life, as to what you will eat or what on. Is not the life more than meat, and the body than raiment?

26 Behold the fowls of the air: for they sow not, neither do they reap, nor gather into barns; yet your heavenly Father feedeth them. Are ye not much better than they?

27 Which of you by taking thought can add one cubit unto his stature?

28 And why take ye thought for raiment? Consider the lilies of the field, how they grow; they toil not, neither do they spin:

29 And yet I say unto you, That even Solomon in all his glory was not arrayed like one of these.

30 Wherefore, if God so clothe the grass of the field, which to day is, and to morrow is cast into the oven, shall he not much more clothe you, O ye of little faith?

31 Therefore take no thought, saying, What shall we eat? or, What shall we drink? or, Wherewithal shall we be clothed?

32 (For after all these things do the Gentiles seek:) for your heavenly Father knoweth that ye have need of all these things.

33 But seek ye first the kingdom of God, and his righteousness; and all these things shall be added unto you.

34 Take therefore no thought for the morrow: for the morrow shall take thought for the things of itself. Sufficient unto the day is the evil thereof.

you will drink; nor about your body, as to what you will wear. Is life not more than food, and the body more than clothing?

26 Look at the birds of the air; they neither sow [seed] nor reap [the harvest] nor gather [the crops] into barns, and yet your heavenly Father keeps feeding them. Are you not worth much more than they?

27 And who of you by worrying can add one [a]hour to [the length of] his life?

28 And why are you worried about clothes? See how the lilies and wildflowers of the field grow; they do not labor nor do they spin [wool to make clothing],

29 yet I say to you that not even Solomon in all his glory and splendor dressed himself like one of these.

30 But if God so clothes the grass of the field, which is alive and green today and tomorrow is [cut and] thrown [as fuel] into the furnace, will He not much more clothe you? You of little faith!

31 Therefore do not worry or be anxious (perpetually uneasy, distracted), saying, 'What are we going to eat?' or 'What are we going to drink?' or 'What are we going to wear?'

32 For the [pagan] Gentiles eagerly seek all these things; [but do not worry,] for your heavenly Father knows that you need them.

33 But first and most importantly seek (aim at, strive after) His kingdom and His righteousness [His way of doing and being right—the attitude and character of God], and all these things will be given to you also.

34 "So do not worry about tomorrow; for tomorrow will worry about itself. Each day has enough trouble of its own.

## BIBLICAL DEFINITIONS

### A. Lay (not) up (Matthew 6:19-21)

*thesaurizo* (Gk.)—This word is discussed as background for the text of today's lesson; it is important to know that in the Greek, the verb "lay up" and the noun "treasures"
are both rooted in the same word.

### B. Take (no) thought (Matthew 6:25, 27, 28, 31, 34) *merimnao* g—"Be anxious" in contemporary translations.

## 'LIGHT ON THE WORD

### Grass.

During biblical times, fuel was scarce in Israel and Judah. Withered plants of all kinds were used for fuel. The term in **verse 30** (KJV) that is translated "grass" actually includes all sorts of vegetation not classified as trees, including the beautiful lilies mentioned in **verses 28** and **29**. Even the magnificent plants that displayed God's care in creation ended up as fuel to be used by the people that He valued and loved.

### Solomon.

He reigned from approximately 960–922 B.C. and was known as Israel's richest king. When he asked God for wisdom, God also granted him long life, fame, and great riches (**1 Kings 3:6–14**).

## TEACHING THE BIBLE LESSON

## LIFE NEED FOR TODAY'S LESSON

AIM: That your students will see that God is Sovereign (in control of His universe).

## INTRODUCTION

### Jesus' Methods of Teaching

Jesus always used illustrations in His sermon so that His listeners could understand. For instance, those who heard this message knew of the wealth of Solomon and could probably visualize how beautifully he was clothed in the richest cloth with elaborate ornamentation. Jesus also used objects that were right in front of Him. As He sat upon the mountain, He may even have picked one of the wildflowers right beside Him as He spoke of the lilies of the field as "one of these" (**Matthew 6:29**) and gestured toward the birds that flew overhead (**verse 26**) as He told the people that they were much more important to God than these creatures. Therefore, to fully understand God's Word, we have to dig a little to discover the setting and ideas of the people of the time in which the Scripture was written. We can also look for contemporary illustrations to help listeners understand what God is saying today.

## BIBLE LEARNING

AIM: That your students will know that God cares about their needs, and He will provide.

## I. GOD CARES FOR HIS CHILDREN (Matthew 6:25-31)

The promise of God's kingdom resides in our hearts if we are Christians (**see 1 Peter 1:3–5**). This hope is not like the wistful wishing that accomplishes nothing ("Oh, how I wish I could have a vacation"). It is a "favourable and confident expectation . . . a purifying power" (Vine's Expository Dictionary). The kingdom of God resides in us! Heaven is not just a future element; it also has a present-tense impact on our lives as believers.

In this section of today's text, Jesus gives us a simple instruction, followed by three examples that every hearer could easily understand. In Eugene Peterson's paraphrase of Scripture entitled The Message, he interprets Jesus' teaching in **Matthew 6:25** thusly: "If you decide for God, living a life of God-worship, it follows that you don't fuss about what's on the table at mealtimes or whether the clothes in your closet are in fashion. There is far more to your life than the food you put in your stomach, more to your outer appearance than the clothes you hang on your body."

### God Does Indeed Care
### (verses 25-31)

**25 Therefore I say unto you, Take no thought for your life, what ye shall eat, or what ye shall drink; nor yet for your body, what ye shall put on. Is not the life more than meat, and the body than raiment? 26 Behold the fowls of the air: for they sow not, neither do they reap, nor gather into barns; yet your heavenly Father feedeth them. Are ye not much better than they? 27 Which of you by taking thought can add one cubit unto his stature? 28 And why take ye thought for raiment? Consider the lilies of the field, how they grow; they toil not, neither do they spin: 29 And yet I say unto you, That even Solomon in all his glory was not arrayed like one of these. 30 Wherefore, if God so clothe the grass of the field, which to day is, and to morrow is cast into the oven, shall he not much more clothe you, O ye of little faith? 31 Therefore take no thought, saying, What shall we eat? or, What shall we drink? or, Wherewithal shall we be clothed?**

First, Jesus uses birds to support His argument that He is indeed the Great Provider. They don't plant seeds, harvest, or store crops, yet they are well cared for. It is important to note that the birds are not self-sufficient creatures. Their care comes from the Father. Jesus then simply, pointedly asks, "Are you not of more value than they?" **(verse 26, NKJV)**.

Next, He asks a rhetorical question: "Which of you by taking thought can add one cubit unto his stature?" **(Matthew 6:27)** We can't make ourselves grow any taller, no matter how hard we wish to! Some commentators have interpreted

this verse to mean a continuance of life (adding days to our lives) rather than an increase in height. Either way, our most intensive worrying will not add a centimeter to our height or a second to our lives. Those things are out of our control.

Jesus' third examples **(verses 28–30)** were the common field lilies and the grass. The common field lilies were simple, prolific wildflowers. It is as though He pointed to the dandelions that pepper our landscapes and asked us to consider their growth. (Well, lilies are prettier!) These flowers did not work or weave their own garments, yet they were  more  beautifully  adorned than the wealthiest king that Israel had ever known.

In **verse 31,** Jesus delivers the punch line: If God takes such good care of some of the simplest of His creation, then, He can be trusted to take care of our needs. Food and clothing are some of our most basic necessities. He doesn't promise designer clothing or gourmet cuisine. He promises that He will care for us. We are of much greater value to Him than a flower or bird.

## SEARCH THE SCRIPTURES

### QUESTION 1
What three examples did Jesus give to illustrate the Father's care?

**He spoke of "the fowls of the air", "the lilies of the field" and "the grass of the field".**

## LIGHT ON THE WORD
### Anxiety Is Not Your Friend

Anxiety robs us of our ability to trust God's care for us. Worry causes us to try to figure out a way to obtain for ourselves which God has already promised to supply. Worry leaves us hopeless and fearful. Jesus diagnoses the problem for us in this section. The next section of today's study provides His cure for our worries.

## II. KEEP FIRST THINGS FIRST
## (Matthew 6:32-34)

Jesus reemphasizes the command "do not worry." In light of God's providential care, there is no need to fret about food, drink, or clothing. He lists the common questions that go through the minds of those who worry. Such questions are useless and unprofitable because they do not serve any helpful purpose (**Matthew 6:27**). He continues by saying that worrying too much about all the earthly needs is the mark of the Gentile—"all these things do the Gentiles (pagans) seek" (**verse 32**). Gentiles here are those who have no relationship with the Lord—those who do not trust in the providential power of God to provide for His own people. It is also useless and indeed foolhardy to fret about food, drink, and clothes since the Lord is always aware of our circumstances and knows what our needs are, including the above-mentioned necessities.

Christ's disciples should therefore lead lives that contrast those of the pagans who have no trust in God's fatherly care for them and whose fundamental goals are materialistic.

### Don't Let Worry Rule Your Life
### (verses 32-34)!

**32 (For after all these things do the Gentiles seek:) for your heavenly Father knoweth that ye have need of all these things. 33 But seek ye first the kingdom of God, and his righteousness; and all these things shall be added unto you. 34 Take therefore no thought for the morrow: for the morrow shall take thought for the things of itself. Sufficient unto the day is the evil thereof.**

Jesus gently reminded His hearers that the Father knew their needs (**verse 32**). Too many people spend their lives chasing after ways to get their needs (and, too often, their wants) met. By focusing on this, they have put the cart before the horse. Jesus ends this passage by giving a practical application of how a God-seeking life should function. Trusting God with each day and leaving tomorrow in His hands further limits the possibility for anxiety to rule our lives.

Jesus said, "But seek ye first the kingdom of God, and his righteousness; and all these things shall be added unto you" (**verse 33**). Carl Henry wrote, "The sons of the Kingdom should therefore live in complete trust that God will supply the necessary provisions for the physical life; they are not to be pressed by anxiety and worry for these things. Ambition is to be directed toward the Kingdom of God and God's righteousness, rather than the acquisition of wealth" (The Biblical Expositor, 31).

In **verse 34,** Jesus concludes this section with another negative imperative: "do not worry." In view of the assurance that God will meet the needs of those who commit themselves to His kingdom and righteousness, "take . . . no thought for the morrow" ("do not worry about tomorrow," [NIV]). The phrase "for the morrow shall take thought for the things of itself" is a way of saying, "Leave tomorrow's problems for that day" or "allow nature to take its course," as people would say. Focus on today's issues; they are enough for today. Don't add tomorrow's "evil" or "trouble" to today's. God's grace for today is sufficient for today and should not be wasted on tomorrow's worries. God will provide new grace to meet whatever trouble tomorrow may bring.

## SEARCH THE SCRIPTURES

### QUESTION 2
What does it mean, in practical terms, to seek God first?

**Answers will vary.**

## LIGHT ON THE WORD

### Seeking the Kingdom of God

We live in an extremely materialistic culture. It is so easy to get locked in to the lie that who you are equals the pile of stuff you can accumulate. Those who do not have the ability to contribute financially are assigned a lesser value than those who have big earning power. God, on the other hand, values every person, and is not at all impressed by our material possessions.

By learning to seek His kingdom first, you declare to the world around you that you serve a radically different King. Desiring Him above all else will help to set everything else in proper, eternal perspective. It has the added bonus of subduing worry, which can also be a powerful statement to the world around you that your King is completely trustworthy.

## BIBLE APPLICATION

**AIM: That your students will begin to understand that God's kingdom is more important than seeking material possessions.**

### Why Worry?

At the conclusion of a sermon about worry, a pastor passed out blank envelopes and sheets of paper to his congregation. Each person in the church that morning was instructed to list all the things that were troubling him or her, no matter how big or small. They were then instructed to place the list in the envelopes and address the envelopes to themselves.

A month later, the pastor mailed the envelopes out to his congregation. With few exceptions, most of the congregation saw their month-old concerns in a whole new light. Though some troubles were ongoing in the lives of the people, the majority of the worries that seemed so enormous at the time the lists were penned had diminished drastically in urgency and intensity. Bills had gotten paid, arguments had been resolved, problems at work had changed, and

health problems had been healed. This simple experiment taught the congregation a lesson about the nature of worries that none of them would soon forget.

## STUDENTS' RESPONSES

**AIM: That your students will commit to replace worry with trust in Almighty God in all things.**

Make a list of everything that is worrying you today, date it, place it in an envelope, and do not

open it for a month. While you are listing your concerns, pray about each one. When you open your envelope a month from now, you will have a fresh perspective (and answered prayer) about today's problems. You can trust God—you are of great value to Him!

## PRAYER

Father in heaven, help us to give You our worries and trust in Your sovereign power. Help us to seek first the kingdom of heaven and always remember that You love and care for us. In Jesus' name we pray. Amen.

## DIG A LITTLE DEEPER

The key element that Jesus describes to deal with worry is found in **Matthew 6:33-34.**

Worry is not just a serious problem. Worry is a sickness that manifests itself in many ways. Excessive worrying can cause digestive disorders, muscle tension, suppression of the immune system, short-term memory loss, and even premature coronary artery disease, and heart attacks. However, the greatest problem with worrying is it affects us spiritually. "For therin is the righteousness of God revealed from faith to faith; as it is written, "The just shall live by faith (Romans 1:17)." "But without faith it is impossible to please him, for he that cometh to God must believe that he is, and that he is a rewarder of them that diligently seek him (Hebrews 11:6)." Physicians prescribe medication, counseling, and psychological treatment. But God's Word says, "Thou wilt keep him in perfect peace, whose mind is stayed on thee, because he trusteth in thee **(Isaiah 26:3)."** Jesus taught us the wisdom given by God that was born in the bosom of heaven about how not to worry about the comforts and necessities but care for the Soul, for out of the soul prosperity comes.

## HOW TO SAY IT

Pagans. PAY-gans.

## PREPARE FOR NEXT SUNDAY

Read G**enesis12:1-9** and study "A Blessing for All Nations."

**Sources:**
Baltes, A. J., ed. Biblespeech.com. http://biblespeech.com (accessed July 6, 2010).

Hebrew and Greek Lexicons. Bible Study Tools.com. http://www.biblestudytools.com/lexicons (accessed September 16, 2010).

Ladd, George Eldon. The Biblical Expositor: The Living Theme of The Great Book. Carl Henry, ed. Philadelphia, PA: A. J. Holman, 1960. 31.

Merriam-Webster Online Dictionary. Merriam-Webster, Inc. http://www.merriam-webster.com (accessed July 6, 2010).

Peterson, Eugene H. The Message: The Bible in Contemporary Language. Colorado Springs, CO: NavPress Publishing Group, 2002. 1755.

Vine, W. E., Merrill F. Unger and William White Jr. Vine's Expository Dictionary. Nashville, TN: Thomas Nelson Publishers, 1996. 562–63.

## DAILY HOME BIBLE READINGS

### MONDAY
Do Not Fret
(Psalm 37:1–8)

### TUESDAY
The Consequences of Worry
(Matthew 13:18–23)

### WEDNESDAY
Guard Against Worry
(Luke 21:29–36)

### THURSDAY
Do Not Be Afraid
(Matthew 10:24–31)

### FRIDAY
The Spirit as Our Resource
(Matthew 10:16–20)

### SATURDAY
Give Your Worries to God
(1 Peter 5:6–11)

### SUNDAY
Don't Worry about Tomorrow
(Matthew 6:25–34)

## COMMENTS / NOTES:

# QUARTERLY COMMENTARY

## TEACHER'S TIPS

### " TEACHING THOSE WITH DIFFERENT LEARNING STYLES"

Sis. Angela Moore

### "KEEPING YOUR STUDENTS ENGAGED"

Kacey R. Pringle

## QUARTERLY QUIZ

# TEACHING THOSE WITH DIFFERENT LEARNING STYLES

## By Sis. Angela Moore

You are standing in front of your class. You see different people from different backgrounds, with different experiences, from all walks of life. Everyone--from child to adult--is different, including their learning style. It is time to step out of the box and rethink teaching. Our goal is to help everyone understand the Word of God as much as possible, utilizing their learning style.

### What is a Learning Style?

A learning style is a preferred way that someone understands, processes, and remembers information. Have you ever found yourself engaged or distracted while in a learning environment? If so, it is possible your learning style may or may not have been utilized.

### Learning Styles

There are seven learning styles: visual, verbal, aural (auditory-musical), physical, logical, social, and solitary. Most of us learn applying multiple styles, but one usually dominates the others. It is important to teach using different styles so the lesson can reach a wider audience. Let us explore the different learning styles!

### Visual

A visual learner is someone who uses pictures, images, and spatial (see the task in whole, but not in details) understanding. They picture what they are learning. Take Matthew 7:3-5, for example: "The Beams and the Motes." In the scriptures, Jesus uses a visual teaching method to help His audience to understand the topic of judging. If you are a visual learner, you probably "pictured" an object sticking out of someone's eye. When teaching a visual learner, try to provide visual aids such as photos, word images, diagrams, and maps along with the lesson so that students can mentally gather detailed information.

### Verbal

A verbal learner may use both written and spoken words. In Mark 16:15, Jesus tells His disciples to preach the gospel to every creature. You will have some students that prefer teaching! They will most likely also take notes. For these students, provide or encourage them to get a writing utensil, paper, and highlighter.

### Musical/Auditory

A musical/auditory learner learns best from what they hear, vocally or musically. Colossians 3:16 tells us to teach and admonish in psalms, hymns, and spiritual songs! In Exodus 15:21, Miriam sings of how the Lord delivered the Hebrew children from their enemies and tells of their enemies' demise. Songs that describe a story are remembered for generations. Please consider adding a song that is related to your lesson.

### Physical/Kinesthetic

A physical/kinesthetic learner is someone who requires physical engagement in their learning. They use the sense of touch. In Jeremiah 27, Jeremiah wore a yoke around his neck to signify the bondage of the children of Israel. For the kinesthetic learner, engage your students in a lesson demonstration, skit, or craft with easily obtainable materials.

## Logical Mathematical

A logical mathematical learner is someone who will need background information that leads to the current lesson. For example, Matthew chapter one talks about the genealogy of Jesus Christ until His birth. In your lesson, include the background scriptures that give context to the current lesson.

## Social

A social learner enjoys table talk, group and class discussions. In Mark 8:27, Jesus asked His disciples, "Whom do men say that I am?" which engaged His disciples in a discussion of His identity. Allowing the class to discuss the lesson helps them to understand and remember what is taught.

## Solitary

A solitary learner is someone who enjoys or prefers learning alone. Many Biblical figures, such as Daniel, Elijah, John the Baptist, Anna the Prophetess, and Jesus, spent time alone praying, studying, and hearing from God. Encourage your students to study before and after class. For these students, homework and pre-work may benefit them.

Most people have more than one learning style, so incorporating at least two to three is encouraged; that way, all or most of the class will understand the lesson.

### References:
Holy Bible KJV
www.learning-style-online.com
www.engage-education.com
www.wordsthatgivelife.com

www.verywellfamily.com
www.teach.com  www.ignitestudentlife.com
www.study.com  www.biblebible.com

Sis. Angela Moore serves as the Sunday School Superintendent in her local church, Burning Bush International Ministries Church of God in Christ in Westland, Michigan, under the leadership of her Pastor, Bishop Don W. Shelby, Jr., and First Lady, Evangelist Bonita A. Shelby.

Sis. Angela Moore is married to Elder Andrew Moore, Sr.

The couple has three children. She is a member of Michigan Southwest Fifth Jurisdiction, Bishop Don W. Shelby Jr., Prelate.

# KEEPING YOUR STUDENTS ENGAGED

## By Kacey R. Pringle

Effective teachers are always on the prowl for new and exciting teaching strategies to keep their students motivated and engaged.

With all of the information available, it's hard to decide which teaching strategies are suitable for your classroom. Sometimes, the old tried-and-true ones that you have been using in your classroom just happen to work the best, and that's okay.

Here are a few teaching strategies that I use in my classroom and are a staple in most classrooms. Depending upon your style, preference, and your students, choose the ones that suit your needs.

### 1. Differentiated Instruction: Learning Stations

Differentiated instruction strategies allow teachers to engage each student by accommodating their specific learning styles. According to Howard Gardner's Multiple Intelligences Theory, every person has a different mind, and therefore each person learns and understands information differently. Differentiating instruction offers a way to meet all students' needs. One helpful strategy to differentiate instruction is learning stations. Learning stations can easily be designed to enable students with diverse learning needs to learn at their pace and readiness level. Teachers can set up each station where students will complete the same task but at the level and style that is specifically designed for them.

### 2. Cooperative Learning: The Jigsaw Method

Cooperative learning gives students the opportunity to work with others and see different points of view. Students learn more effectively when working together rather than apart, and it is also known to improve self-confidence in students. The jig-saw method is especially effective because each student is responsible for one another's learning. Students find out quickly that each group member has something equally important to contribute to the group to make the task a successful one. Students are exposed to and use many skills throughout this strategy: communication, problem-solving skills, cognition, and critical thinking — all of which are essential to be successful.

### 3. Utilizing Technology in the Classroom

Integrating technology is a great way to empower students to stay connected in this technological era. Technology-rich lessons have been found to keep students motivated and engaged longer. Some examples of utilizing technology in the classroom are to create web-based lessons or multimedia presentations such as a video, animation, or some type of graphic. In addition, you can use a tablet or an iPad, taking your class on a virtual field trip, participating in an online research project, or even creating a class website. Any of these technology integration strategies will have a positive impact on student learning.

## 4. Inquiry-Based Instruction

Inquiry-based learning implies involving students in the learning process so they will have a deeper understanding of what they are learning. We are born with the instinct to inquire — as babies; we use our senses to make connections to our surroundings. Inquiry-based learning strategies are used to engage students to learn by asking questions, investigating, exploring, and reporting what they see. This process leads students to a deeper understanding of the content that they are learning, which helps them to apply these concepts in new situations. The inquiry-based learning strategy is a great tool to do just that.

## 5. Incorporate Mystery into Your Lessons

Learning may be the most fun for your students when they don't know what to expect. Try to incorporate a sense of surprise and mystery into your lessons. When you're about to unveil a new lesson, give students a clue before the start of the lesson. This is a fun way to make your lesson mysterious, and you may find that your students are actually looking forward to finding out what they'll be learning about next.

An experienced teacher knows that not every teaching strategy that you use will be an effective one. There will be some hits and misses, and depending upon your teaching style and the ways your students learn, you will figure out which strategies work and which do not. It may take some trial and error, but it doesn't hurt to try them all.

**References:**

Cox, J. (2019). K-12 Resources by Teachers, For Teachers.

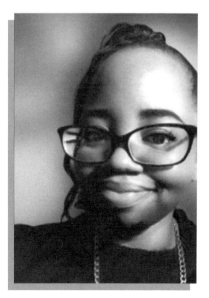

Kacey is the daughter of Pastor Isaac and Lady Patricia Pringle. She is a faithful member of Temple of Joy Church of God in Christ where she serves in the local and Jurisdictional Music Departments, Women's Department, and Sunday school. She is a qualified teacher and has worked in the educational field for 15 years. She currently teaches first grade at Scotland Park Elementary School in Wichita Falls, Texas. She is a member of Texas Northwest Jurisdiction - Bishop William Watson, III, Prelate, Supervisor Mary Barnes, Jurisdictional Supervisor.

## Patricia Johnson

- Bachelor, Political Science and Master, Christian Ministry
- District Missionary and Jurisdictional Field Representative
- Chosen By God Ministries, Evangelist Patricia Johnson, Pastor
- Greater Maryland First Jurisdiction
- Bishop Joel Harley Lyles

Evangelist Patricia Johnson, affectionately known as "Pastor Patti", is a trailblazer as she endeavors fulfill God's call on her life. Pastor Johnson is Assistant Director of Human Resources for State agency with over 9,000 employees. She provides executive level leadership for human resources operations across a statewide agency responsible for custody and community corrections. Pastor Patti is the proud mother of two beautiful daughters, Ebone and Jenelle. She loves God and God's people. Her scripture mediation is Philippians 1:6 "Being confident of this very thing, that he which hath begun a good work in you will perform it until the day of Jesus Christ:"

## Arthur A. Porter Sr.

**Degrees:** BA Management and Psychology, Master of Divinity Old Testament and Psychology of Religion, Doctor of Ministry Leadership

- **Title:** Admin. Asst.
- **Local church:** Senior Pastor New Nation Church Of God In Christ
- **Jurisdiction:** Montana
- **Jurisdictional Prelate:** Bishop Phillip Henry Porter
- **Jurisdictional Supervisor:** Missionary Katherine Porter

Arthur A. Porter Sr., is married to First Lady Donna Porter, father and Senior Pastor of New Nation COGIC in Aurora, Colorado. Administrative Assistant, author, and former adjunct faculty at Iliff School of Theology, and Denver Seminary.

# QUARTERLY QUIZ

These questions may be used in two ways: as a pretest at the beginning of the quarter; as a review at the end of the quarter; or as a review after each lesson. Questions are based on the Scripture text of each lesson (King James Version).

## LESSON 1

1. Why did Jesus emphasize the correct attitude towards money in Matthew 6:25–34?

_____

_____

2. Why is Jesus' caution not to worry or be anxious such good advice?

_____

_____

## LESSON 2

1. Why does Jesus' calming the storm contribute to the disciples understanding that Jesus is God (Matthew 8:23–27)?

_____

_____

2. What does Jesus being asleep teach about His humanity?

_____

_____

## LESSON 3

1. Why does Jairus bother Jesus when his daughter is already dead (Matthew 9:18–26)?

_____

_____

2. What was the role of the woman's knowledge of the Law in her healing (Matthew 9:20–22)?

_____

_____

## LESSON 4

1. After demonstrating such power to feed the multitude, why does Jesus pray (Matthew 14:22–23)?

_____

_____

2. Although Peter began to sink, is there anything remarkable about his experience (vv. 24–27)?

_____

_____

## LESSON 5

1. Why is leprosy such a dreadful disease (Leviticus 13:45–46; Luke 17:11–19)?

_____

_____

2. Why are the lepers an example that we must testify about what Jesus has done in our lives?

_____

_____

# QUARTERLY QUIZ

**LESSON 6**

1. Restate Paul's purpose in writing, which he expressed in his prayer in Romans 1:8–17.

_____

_____

2. When Paul describes his readiness to preach, what do you "hear"?

_____

_____

**LESSON 7**

1. Explain how Abraham's faith produces justice or righteousness (Romans 4:1–3).

_____

_____

2. Explain why Paul's letter is a relief to the Gentile believers (vv. 9–12)?

_____

_____

**LESSON 8**

1. Define justification based on Romans 5:1–5.

_____

_____

2. Define reconciliation; define atonement (Romans 5:9–11).

_____

_____

**LESSON 9**

1. According to Romans 10:5, why did God give Moses the Law if the Law could not save?

_____

_____

2. Define righteousness.

_____

_____

**LESSON 10**

1. Why is the faith of the past (as explained in Hebrews 11) instructive or a teaching tool for us today?

_____

_____

2. Why are (1) respect or reverence for God and (2) obedience to God's commands demonstrations of faith?

_____

_____

**LESSON 11**

1. Why was it necessary for the author of Hebrews to encourage the audience to hold fast to their faith?

_____

_____

2. Why is the writer's warning about willful, deliberate sin so stern (vv. 26–27)?

_____

_____

# QUARTERLY QUIZ

## LESSON 12

1. False teachers deny that Jesus Christ came in the flesh.

_____

_____

2. What role does the Holy Spirit play in the believer's life?

_____

_____

## LESSON 13

1. According to 2 Corinthians 4:16–18, how does understanding suffering and glory help us handle life's challenges?

_____

_____

2. Why is the imagery or metaphor of moving from a tent to a building inspiring (2 Corinthians 5:1–5)?

_____

_____

*Answers to Quarterly Quiz Can be found on  page 478

# A BLESSING FOR ALL NATIONS

**BIBLE BASIS:** Genesis 12:1-9

**BIBLE TRUTH:** Because of their faith in God's promises, Abram and Sarai risked everything in their old age to move their family and all their possessions to a new land.

**MEMORY VERSE:** "And I will make of thee a great nation, and I will bless thee, and make thy name great; and thou shalt be a blessing" (Genesis 12:2, KJV).

**LESSON AIM:** By the end of this lesson, we will: LEARN the story of God's call and promise to Abram; REFLECT on the joy that Abram and Sarai's faith gave to them from obeying the Lord; and DECIDE what we are willing to sacrifice to claim the promises of God.

**BACKGROUND SCRIPTURES:** Genesis 12:1 - 9--Read and incorporate the insights gained from the Background Scriptures into your study of the lesson.

## TEACHER PREPARATION

**MATERIALS NEEDED:** Bibles (several different versions), Quarterly Commentary/Teacher Manual, Adult Quarterly, teaching resources such as charts, worksheets/handouts, paper, pens, and pencils.

**OTHER MATERIALS NEEDED / TEACHER'S NOTES:**

_____

_____

## LESSON OVERVIEW

**LIFE NEED FOR TODAY'S LESSON**
To determine what students are willing to sacrifice to claim the promises of God.

**BIBLE LEARNING**
To understand that God's promises to Abram included a promise to bless all people on the earth through him; a promise which was fulfilled when God sent Jesus, a descendant of Abram, to be our Savior.

**BIBLE APPLICATION**
We must commit to obey God's Word.

**STUDENTS' RESPONSES**
That your students will commit to doing the will of God.

## LESSON SCRIPTURE

### GENESIS 12:1-9, KJV

**1** Now the LORD had said unto Abram, Get thee out of thy country, and from thy kindred,

### GENESIS 12:1–9, AMP

**1** Now [in Haran] the Lord had said to Abram "Go away from your country, And from and from thy father's house, unto a land that I will shew thee:

2 And I will make of thee a great nation, and I will bless thee, and make thy name great; and thou shalt be a blessing:

3 And I will bless them that bless thee, and curse him that curseth thee: and in thee shall all families of the earth be blessed.

4 So Abram departed, as the LORD had spoken unto him: and Lot went with him: and Abram was seventy and five years old when he departed out of Haran.

5 And Abram took Sarai his wife, and Lot his brother's son, and all their substance that they had gathered, and the souls that they had gotten in Haran; and they went forth to go into the land of Canaan; and into the land of Canaan they came.

6 And Abram passed through the land unto the place of Sichem, unto the plain of Moreh. And the Canaanite was then in the land.

7 And the LORD appeared unto Abram, and said, Unto thy seed will I give this land: and there builded he an altar unto the LORD, who appeared unto him.

8 And he removed from thence unto a mountain on the east of Bethel, and pitched his tent, having Bethel on the west, and Hai on the east: and there he builded an altar unto the LORD, and called upon the name of the LORD.

9 And Abram journeyed, going on still toward the south.

your relatives And from your father's house, To the land which I will show you;

2 And I will make you a great nation, And I will bless you [abundantly], And make your name great (exalted, distinguished); And you shall be a blessing [a source of great good to others];

3 And I will bless (do good for, benefit) those who bless you, And I will curse [that is, subject to My wrath and judgment] the one who curses (despises, dishonors, has contempt for) you. And in you all the families (nations) of the earth will be blessed."

4 So Abram departed [in faithful obedience] as the Lord had directed him; and Lot [his nephew] left with him. Abram was seventy-five years old when he left Haran.

5 Abram took Sarai his wife and Lot his nephew, and all their possessions which they had acquired, and the people (servants) which they had acquired in Haran, and they set out to go to the land of Canaan. When they came to the land of Canaan,

6 Abram passed through the land as far as the site of Shechem, to the [great] terebinth (oak) tree of Moreh. Now the Canaanites were in the land at that time.

7 Then the Lord appeared to Abram and said, "I will give this land to your descendants." So Abram built an altar there to [honor] the Lord who had appeared to him.

8 Then he moved on from there to the mountain on the east of Bethel, and pitched his tent, with Bethel on the west and Ai on the east; and there he built an altar to the Lord and called on the name of the Lord [in worship through prayer, praise, and thanksgiving].

**9** Then Abram journeyed on, continuing toward the Negev (the South country of Judah).

## BIBLICAL DEFINITIONS

A. **Blessing (Genesis 12:2)** *berakah* (Heb.)—Prosperity, benediction, benefit, favor, peace, and invocation of good.

B. **Seed (Genesis 12:7)** *zara`* (Heb.)—Offspring, issue, progeny, posterity, family, race.

## LIGHT ON THE WORD

In the preceding chapter (**Genesis 11:10–32**), we learn that Abram was a descendant of Noah's son Shem. Genesis 11 ends with Abram's father, Terah, leading his family from his native land, Ur of the Chaldees, to make their way to the land of Canaan, but instead, the group settles in Haran (**Genesis 11:31**). It is noted in **verse 32**, however, that Terah remained in Haran until his death. Geographically, scholars maintain that Haran was perched between Ur and Canaan, so they were in the middle of their intended destination. Terah's name was believed to mean, "delay," and we learn in **Joshua 24:2** that he was an idol worshiper. We will see why Abram and Sarai's faith and obedience were pivotal to the blessing for all nations as God separates him from his people.

## TEACHING THE BIBLE LESSON

## LIFE NEED FOR TODAY'S LESSON

**AIM: That your students will be willing to sacrifice to claim the promises of God.**

## INTRODUCTION

### Abram's Ancestry

Up to this point there was no distinction between people and races as we think of today. After the Flood, the people were dispersed at the Tower of Babel (**Genesis 11:1–9**). The Bible depicts a detailed review of Shem's descendants—Noah's eldest son. It is out of Shem's lineage, through Abram, that God would call out a people unto Himself to be witnesses in the earth of His greatness. They would receive the blessing for serving the one true and living God in the midst of universal idolatry. Ultimately, Abram's seed through 42 generations would bring forth the Messiah who would reconcile the world back to the Father (**Matthew 1:1–17**). Abram exemplifies the faith necessary to obtain righteousness and access to the promises of God through Jesus Christ.

## BIBLE LEARNING

**AIM: That your students will learn that God's promises to Abram included a promise to bless all people on the earth through him; because Jesus, our Savior, was a descendant of Abram.**

## I. A BLESSING FOR ALL NATIONS (Genesis 12:1-9)

Abram was the youngest son of Terah, a descendant of Noah's son Shem. According to Stephen's account in **Acts 7:2-4**, the God of glory appeared to Abram while he was in

Mesopotamia, which was before he settled in Haran. Therefore, when Abram heard God's call (**Genesis 12:1**), this was his second encounter with the Lord Jehovah, and it's believed to be not long after his father's death. Abram was told to leave his country and his family, and uproot his home to go to a place the Lord would soon reveal.

### God's Call for a Blessed Nation
### (verses 1–3)

**1 Now the LORD had said unto Abram, Get thee out of thy country, and from thy kindred, and from thy father's house, unto a land that I will shew thee: 2 And I will make of thee a great nation, and I will bless thee, and make thy name great; and thou shalt be a blessing: 3 And I will bless them that bless thee, and curse him that curseth thee: and in thee shall all families of the earth be blessed.**

The Scripture does not indicate that there was a discussion after this command was given, but that Abram moved at God's Word. Abram was surrounded by people, including his own family, who were polytheistic (worshiped multiple gods). For him to hear the voice of the true and living God was monumental. Because of his obedience, Abram is forever etched as "the father of faith." With this second encounter, however, God made Abram a promise to bless him and make him a great nation, to make his name great and for him to be a blessing (**verse 2**). This promise from God was astounding from humanity's perspective, due to Abram's age (**verse 4**), and as first noted in **Genesis 11:30**, his wife Sarai was barren. God gave Abram further motivation to adhere to His command with the pronouncement of future blessings. For leaving his father's house, Abram would receive a father's blessing—a namesake. God gave Abram His sovereign promise to fulfill His Word to make a great nation from him and to make his name great. Abram went from not having any children, and with no hope of ever being a

father, to having the promise of an entire nation coming from his loins.

In **Genesis 12:3**, God established His relationship and the power of this connection by stating that He would bless those who blessed Abram and curse those who cursed him. God's presence is marked in the lives of those chosen by Him. Verse 3 ends with the most important component of this promise: God commits to blessing all the families of the earth through Abram. Abram's seed birthed three world religions; Judaism, Christianity, and Islam (Ishmael) all lay claim to him as father. However, the ending of this verse points to the coming Christ who would bring salvation and restoration to the world. Abram's seed is the divinely appointed channel through which blessing would come to all humankind by faith in Jesus Christ (**Galatians 3:6–7, 14**).

## SEARCH THE SCRIPTURES
### QUESTION 1
What was God's promise to Abram?

**He promised to make a nation of Abram's descendants, to bless him, to make his name great, to make him a blessing to others, to bless those who blessed him, to curse those who cursed him, and to bless everyone through his descendant.**

## LIGHT ON THE WORD
### Keep Moving
Oftentimes, when God gives us a directive, it may not come with full disclosure of the details—like what we have to go through to get to the promise. Just like Jesus, Abram teaches us to keep moving forward by focusing on God's promise (**Hebrews 12:2**).

## II. ABRAM DEPARTED
## (Genesis 12:4–6)

Abram followed God's spoken command and departed from his familiar surroundings to a place unknown. Abram, after having departed once with his kindred from his native land of Ur, was once again a nomad, and at the age of 75, he was leaving Haran. He took with him his wife, all their possessions, his nephew Lot, and his servants.

### Abram's Response to God's Call
### (verses 4-6)

**4 So Abram departed, as the LORD had spoken unto him: and Lot went with him: and Abram was seventy and five years old when he departed out of Haran. 5 And Abram took Sarai his wife, and Lot his brother's son, and all their substance that they had gathered, and the souls that they had gotten in Haran; and they went forth to go into the land of Canaan; and into the land of Canaan they came. 6 And Abram passed through the land unto the place of Sichem, unto the plain of Moreh. And the Canaanite was then in the land.**

We can imagine how very unsettling it must have been for Abram to be uprooted again and to move everything he owned to answer God's call. However, in spite of the circumstances, Abram walked in obedience and trusted God based on what God had revealed to him. He went forward and began the journey. His father, Terah, stopped short his migration to Canaan (**see Genesis 11:31, NIV**). When God declares a call on your life, not everyone is privy to see the revelation of God's plan. Therefore, even close relatives may need to be left behind.

In **Genesis 12:6**, Abram arrives in Canaan and the land is already occupied by the Canaanites. He is yet again a stranger in a strange land. He was put in an uncomfortable position by coming into a land that was promised to him, but was already inhabited, which could have been a reason to give up. But Abram continued to follow God and remain confident that he heard God correctly.

## QUESTION 2

How did Abram respond to God's command?

**He gathered together his family and all his possessions and went wherever God was going to lead him.**

**Answer will vary.**

## LIGHT ON THE WORD
### God Appears

In this instance, rather than just speaking to Abram, God appeared in the form of a theophany—God appeared in human form. He showed Abram once again the land He was going to bless Abram with and repeated His promise to give him seed or offspring. Abram yet again heard a word from the Lord declaring that he would not only receive this land that is already occupied, but that his children would live in it. In response to God's appearance, Abram built an altar unto the Lord. The proper response to God's presence and confirmation of His promise is worship. Abram had God's continued assurance that he would receive that which God had spoken, and by making a personal appearance, it further sealed the guarantee.

## III. ABRAM'S RELATIONSHIP WITH GOD (Genesis 12:7-9)

Abram continued to move forward at God's command and thus declared his own allegiance to serve God alone. In spite of the culture around him, which had a god for everything, Abram is the father of a monotheistic religion that is based on a relationship with the true and living God.

## God's Promise of Generational Blessings
### (verses 7-9)

**7 And the LORD appeared unto Abram, and said, Unto thy seed will I give this land: and there builded he an altar unto the LORD, who appeared unto him. 8 And he removed from thence unto a mountain on the east of Bethel, and pitched his tent, having Bethel on the west, and Hai on the east: and there he builded an altar unto the LORD, and called upon the name of the LORD. 9 And Abram journeyed, going on still toward the south.**

Abram pitched his tent, and wherever he pitched his tent, he built an altar unto the Lord. He remained in constant contact with Him through worship and prayer as he called on the name of the Lord. Abram lived a disciplined life of worship and walked in obedience by listening for the voice of the Lord God. Abram's faithful response to God's promise to make him a great nation required a close relationship and strict adherence to God's instructions. Abram would have been shortsighted if he only thought of the personal impact of this promise, but because the call was greater than he could ever imagine, he was willing to make the sacrifice with his wife by his side.

## SEARCH THE SCRIPTURES

### QUESTION 3

When Abram arrived in the land that God promised to give him, how did he express his thankfulness to God?

He built an altar unto the Lord.

Answer will vary.

## LIGHT ON THE WORD

### A Blessing for All Nations

No one enjoys being uprooted, especially when one has been settled in a place for an extended period of time and enjoys a comfortable living. Abram and his family had lived in Ur of Chaldees with his father and brothers. During Abram's time, Ur of Chaldees was a port city that offered wealth and prosperity to its inhabitants, but for some unexplained reason, Terah, Abram's father, moved himself and his extended family to Haran. It was in Haran that God spoke to Abram. God first called to Abram while he was living in Ur of Chaldees (**see Genesis 15:7 and Acts 7:2**).

## BIBLE APPLICATION

**AIM: That your students will begin to understand that we are reaping the benefits of the blood, sweat, and tears of our heroes and heroines of the Civil Rights Movement, as well as the ancestors before them who sacrificed so that we might have freedom to be whatever God called us to be.**

### Following the Vision

Like Abram, Dr. Martin Luther King did not live to see the fullness of this vision of freedom, but he moved at God's Word and did as he was instructed, walking in love. He trusted God and sacrificed his own personal comfort and gain by believing that God would do what He said. We can continue to honor Dr. King's legacy by showing our willingness to submit to God's plan no matter where it takes us as we serve others and strive to move toward successful lives of freedom.

## STUDENTS' RESPONSES

**AIM: That your students will pray and assess their own ambitions, goals, and interests to see if they line up with God's Word.**

Ask your students to reflect on today's lesson, and think of things God has promised in their lives that will bless them and others now as well as in generations to come. What are they willing to risk to follow through with God's plan and bring Him glory, even at the risk of their own comfort? Encourage them to allow the Holy Spirit to speak to them about anything that needs adjustment.

## PRAYER

Dear Father, help us to be sensitive to Your leading in our lives. Help us to listen and then obey. In Jesus' Name we pray. Amen.

## DIG A LITTLE DEEPER

When we consider the concepts of "blessing" and "name," we might consider the meaning of "Nation." "Nation," in this regard, means a new species, essentially different from all other nations and people on the earth. "A great nation" and a "great name," to be allied and aligned to heaven as no other nation and people on earth is. They are to be God's people in image, likeness, and essence. A nation called and blessed by God to be the godly conscience and righteous influnce in the earth. God reestablishes through Abraham and Sarai His original covenant with Adam and Eve. In **Genesis 1:28,** God blessed them to be fruitful, multiply, replenish, and rule the earth. God's blessing and all God has for humankind are exemplified in Adam and Eve and reestablished through Abraham and Sarah. The blessings of God for us are demonstrated in three ways according to **Genesis 1:28** fruitfulness, multiplying, and dominion. Blessings are often thought of as material things and human happiness, but the blessings of God are all that God owns, and God bestows divine assistance, favor, and power to receive all his blessings. God owns it all "the earth is the Lord's, and the fullness thereof; the world,and they that dwell therin"**(Psalm 24:1).** That is the essence of Blessing! God's blessings are primarily relationship-dependnt and established through a special relationship with God and with each other.

God's blessings and all God has for humankind are exemplified in Adam and Eve and reestablished through Abraham and Sarah. The blessings of God for us are demonstrated in three ways according to **Genesis 1:28**: fruitfulness, multiplying, and rulership. Blessings are often thought of as material things and human happiness, but the blessings of God are all that God owns, and God bestows divine assistance, favor, and power to receive all His blessings. God owns it all "the earth is the Lord's, and the fulness thereof; the world, and they that dwell therein" **(Psalm 24:1).** That is the essence of Blessing! God's blessings are primarily relationship dependent and established through a special relationship with God and with each other.

## HOW TO SAY IT

Haran.  Kaw-rawn'

Canaan. Ken-ah'-an.

Moreh.  Mo-reh'.

Sichem. Shek-em'.

## DAILY HOME BIBLE READINGS

### MONDAY
Abraham's Story
(Acts 7:1–8)

### TUESDAY
A God So Near
(Deuteronomy 4:5–9)

### WEDNESDAY
The Lord Heard Our Voice
(Deuteronomy 26:1–11)

### THURSDAY
Look to Abraham
(Isaiah 51:1–6)

### FRIDAY
Abraham, Our Ancestor?
(Matthew 3:1–10)

### SATURDAY
We Have This Hope
(Hebrews 6:13–20)

### SUNDAY
God's Call to Bless
(Genesis 12:1–9)

## PREPARE FOR NEXT SUNDAY

Read **Genesis 15:1–6, 12–18**, and next week's lesson, "A Promise to Abraham."

**Sources:**
"Abraham." Christian Answers.net. http://www.christiananswers.net/dictionary/abraham.html (accessed June 25, 2010).
"Genesis." Scofield Reference Notes. Bible Study Tools.com. http://www.biblestudytools.com/commentaries/scofieldreferencenotes/genesis/genesis-11.html (accessed June 25, 2010 and June 29, 2010).
"Genesis 12." Net Bible.org. http://www.Net.Bible.org (accessed July 12, 2010).
Hebrew Greek Key Word Study Bible, King James Version. 2nd ed. Chattanooga, TN: AMG Publishers, 1991. 1648, 1657.
Henry, Matthew. The Matthew Henry Study Bible, King James Version. Iowa Falls, IA: World Bible Publishers, 1994. 34–35.
Mays, James L., gen. ed. Bible Commentary. San Francisco, CA: HarperCollins, 2000.
Skinner, John. A Critical and Exegetical Commentary of Genesis. Edinburgh, UK: Morrison and Gibb Limited, 1980.
Smith's Bible Dictionary. Peabody, MA: Hendrickson Publishers, 1999. 109.
Von Rad, Gerhard. Genesis: A Commentary. Philadelphia, PA: Westminster Press, 1972.]

# A PROMISE TO ABRAHAM

**BIBLE BASIS:** Genesis 15:1–6, 12–18

**BIBLE TRUTH:** Even though Abram and Sarai were well beyond the age of childbearing, Abram believed God when he was told that he would have descendants more numerous than the stars.

**MEMORY VERSE:** "And he believed in the LORD; and he counted it to him for righteousness" (Genesis 15:6, KJV).

**LESSON AIM:** By the end of the lesson, we will: REVIEW God's promise of a child to Abram and Sarai; APPRECIATE God's ability to accomplish what seems impossible; and EXERCISE faith in God's power to manifest present-day promises..

**BACKGROUND SCRIPTURES:** Genesis 12:1-9-Read and incorporate the insights gained from the Background Scriptures into your study of the lesson.

## TEACHER PREPARATION

**MATERIALS NEEDED:** Bibles (several different versions), Quarterly Commentary/Teacher Manual, Adult Quarterly, teaching resources such as charts, worksheets/handouts, paper, pens, and pencils.

**OTHER MATERIALS NEEDED / TEACHER'S NOTES:**

_____

_____

## LESSON OVERVIEW

### LIFE NEED FOR TODAY'S LESSON
That students will appreciate God's ability to accomplish what seems impossible.

### BIBLE LEARNING
To understand that God's promises to Abram included a future time of slavery before He made a great nation of Abram's descendants.

### BIBLE APPLICATION
To learn that God keeps His promise.

### STUDENTS' RESPONSES
Students will learn that God can be trusted to keep His promises.

## LESSON SCRIPTURE

### GENESIS 15:1-6, 12-18, KJV

1 After these things the word of the LORD came unto Abram in a vision, saying, Fear

### GENESIS 15:1-6, 12-18, AMP

1 After these things the word of the Lord came to Abram in a vision, saying, "Do not be

not, Abram: I am thy shield, and thy exceeding great reward.

2 And Abram said, LORD God, what wilt thou give me, seeing I go childless, and the steward of my house is this Eliezer of Damascus?

3 And Abram said, Behold, to me thou hast given no seed: and, lo, one born in my house is mine heir.

4 And, behold, the word of the LORD came unto him, saying, This shall not be thine heir; but he that shall come forth out of thine own bowels shall be thine heir.

5 And he brought him forth abroad, and said, Look now toward heaven, and tell the stars, if thou be able to number them: and he said unto him, So shall thy seed be.

6 And he believed in the LORD; and he counted it to him for righteousness.

15:12 And when the sun was going down, a deep sleep fell upon Abram; and, lo, an horror of great darkness fell upon him.

13 And he said unto Abram, Know of a surety that thy seed shall be a stranger in a land that is not theirs, and shall serve them; and they shall afflict them four hundred years;

14 And also that nation, whom they shall serve, will I judge: and afterward shall they come out with great substance.

15 And thou shalt go to thy fathers in peace; thou shalt be buried in a good old age.

16 But in the fourth generation they shall come hither again: for the iniquity of the Amorites is not yet full.

17 And it came to pass, that, when the sun went down, and it was dark, behold a smoking furnace, and a burning lamp that passed between those pieces.

afraid, Abram, I am your shield; Your reward [for obedience] shall be very great."

2 Abram said, "Lord God, what reward will You give me, since I am [leaving this world] childless, and he who will be the owner and heir of my house is this [servant] Eliezer from Damascus?"

3 And Abram continued, "Since You have given no child to me, one (a servant) born in my house is my heir."

4 Then behold, the word of the Lord came to him, saying, "This man [Eliezer] will not be your heir but he who shall come from your own body shall be your heir."

5 And the Lord brought Abram outside [his tent into the night] and said, "Look now toward the heavens and count the stars—if you are able to count them." Then He said to him, "So [numerous] shall your descendants be."

6 Then Abram believed in (affirmed, trusted in, relied on, remained steadfast to) the Lord; and He counted (credited) it to him as righteousness (doing right in regard to God and man).

15:12 When the sun was setting, a deep sleep overcame Abram; and a horror (terror, shuddering fear, nightmare) of great darkness overcame him.

13 God said to Abram, "Know for sure that your descendants will be strangers [living temporarily] in a land (Egypt) that is not theirs, where they will be enslaved and oppressed for four hundred years.

14 But on that nation whom your descendants will serve I will bring judgment, and afterward they will come out [of that land] with great possessions.

**18** In the same day the LORD made a covenant with Abram, saying, Unto thy seed have I given this land, from the river of Egypt unto the great river, the river Euphrates:

**15** As for you, you shall [die and] go to your fathers in peace; you shall be buried at a good old age.

**16** Then in the fourth generation your descendants shall return here [to Canaan, the land of promise], for the wickedness and guilt of the Amorites is not yet complete (finished)."

**17** When the sun had gone down and a [deep] darkness had come, there appeared a smoking brazier and a flaming torch which passed between the [divided] pieces [of the animals].

**18** On the same day the Lord made a covenant (promise, pledge) with Abram, saying, "To your descendants I have given this land, From the river of Egypt to the great river Euphrates.

## BIBLICAL DEFINITIONS

A. **Bowels (Genesis 15:4)** *me`ah* (Heb.)—Womb, intestines, the abdomen.
B. **Righteousness (v. 6)** *tsedaqah* (Heb.)—Rightness, rectitude, virtue, pros-perity, piety.

## LIGHT ON THE WORD

In **Genesis 12–14**, Abram migrated from Canaan to Egypt to Negeb to Hebron, always building an altar unto the Lord for worship. Along the way, he also had some missteps and situations that could have derailed him, but he remained faithful to the Lord his God. In the process, God continued to reinforce His promise of land and a multitude of descendants to Abram **(Genesis 13:14–18).** However, Abram was still childless, but he vowed to stay singularly focused on pleasing the Lord first. It is at this point that we begin today's lesson.

## TEACHING THE BIBLE LESSON

## LIFE NEED FOR TODAY'S LESSON

**AIM: That your students will be willing to exercise faith in God's power to fulfill present-day promises.**

## INTRODUCTION

### A Promise Reaffirmed

In **Genesis 12,** Abram was 75 years old and Sarai was already 65. We don't know how old Abram was when **chapter 15** opens, but he clearly needed God to reaffirm the promise that He was going to make a nation from Abram's descendants. It wasn't until Abram was 100 years old and Sarai was 90 that God finally fulfilled the promise and they had baby Isaac. But God renews the promise to Abram in today's Scripture with some powerful object lessons.

## BIBLE LEARNING

**AIM: That your students will learn that God renewed His promises to Abram and gave him some of the details.**

## I. A PROMISE TO ABRAHAM (Genesis 15:1-6, 12-18)

Time was passing by and Abram and Sarai still did not have a son. God lovingly renewed the covenant with Abram by promising them many descendants and giving Abram the greatest gift of all—the promise that He, Himself, would be Abram's greatest heritage.

### God Reinforces His Promise to Abram (Genesis 15:1–3)

**1 After these things the word of the LORD came unto Abram in a vision, saying, Fear not, Abram: I am thy shield, and thy exceeding great reward. 2 And Abram said, LORD God, what wilt thou give me, seeing I go childless, and the steward of my house is this Eliezer of Damascus? 3 And Abram said, Behold, to me thou hast given no seed: and, lo, one born in my house is mine heir.**

After protecting Abram from some foolish mistakes and defeating his enemies, God came to Abram in a vision with words of comfort: "Fear not, Abram: I am thy shield, and thy exceeding great reward" (**Genesis 15:1**). The Lord reinforced that He would give Abram safety and security and that he would not want for anything, because everything he needed was to be found in the self-existent, eternal, and almighty God. Because Abram declared that God was his source of blessing, God Himself was all the reward and protection Abram would ever need.

In **verses 2 and 3,** Abram responded to God's declaration of blessing by acknowledging God's sovereign Lordship. Yet Abram expressed great concern, because due to his and Sarai's advanced age a slave born in his house would be the heir. In this era, it was a disgrace for a husband and wife not to produce children (especially sons) because children marked fruitfulness and continuation of the family lineage and property. This greatly disturbed Abram, and he expressed his concern to God, because this did not seem to be according to God's promises to him.

## SEARCH THE SCRIPTURES

### QUESTION 1

What was the great reward that God promised to Abram?

**He promised that He, Himself, would be Abram's great reward. God would be all that Abram would need.**

## LIGHT ON THE WORD

### Trust the Details to God

Often we worry about all the details. How is God going to do this and how is He going to do that? Instead we need to keep on trusting in God to work out all the details involved in keeping His promises to us (Psalm 37:5).

## II. GOD ANSWERS (Genesis 15:4–6)

Abram could see no other way—his servant Eliezer was going to inherit his estate. Abram really valued Eliezer, and Eliezer trusted in God just as Abram did (**See Genesis 24**). But God had promised Abram that he and Sarai would give birth to children and so God had to encourage him that He would bring this about.

### God Unveils Details of His Promise to Abram (verses 4–6)

**4 And, behold, the word of the LORD came unto him, saying, This shall not be thine heir; but he that shall come forth out of thine own bowels shall be thine heir. 5 And he brought him forth abroad, and said, Look now toward heaven, and**

tell the stars, if thou be able to number them: and he said unto him, So shall thy seed be. 6 And he believed in the LORD; and he counted it to him for righteousness.

God assured Abram that Eliezer would not be his heir, but that Abram's heir would come from his "own bowels" (Genesis 15:4), meaning through his own body. God brought Abram outside and by using the stars in the sky; He gave Abram another visual of how vast Abram's descendants would be. The common eye cannot count the number of stars in the sky or the amount of dust of the earth. Yet, this is how innumerable Abram's offspring would be, and God assured Abram that it would come from his own loins.

After receiving yet another visual of God's promise and confirmation that a son would come through his blood, Abram believed God, which forever placed him in right standing with the Lord (verse 6) and in the Faith Hall of Fame (Hebrews 11:8,11).

## QUESTION 2
What visual did the Lord give Abram to show him how many descendants he would have?

**God showed him the stars in the sky to show him how many descendants he would have (too many to count).**

**Answer will vary.**

## LIGHT ON THE WORD
### Believe the Lord
God made some awesome promises to Abram—promises that would be humanly impossible to keep. God promised Abram that he would father a child in his old age and that his descendants would be too many to count. Abram's simple response to God was to believe.

## III. ABRAM'S RELATIONSHIP WITH GOD (Genesis 15:12-16)

Abram continued to move forward at God's command and thus declared his own allegiance to serve God alone. In spite of the culture around him, which had a god for everything, Abram is the father of a monotheistic religion that is based on a relationship with the true and living God.

### God Foretells Abram and His Seed's Future (15:12–16)
**12 And when the sun was going down, a deep sleep fell upon Abram; and, lo, an horror of great darkness fell upon him. 13 And he said unto Abram, Know of a surety that thy seed shall be a stranger in a land that is not theirs, and shall serve them; and they shall afflict them four hundred years; 14 And also that nation, whom they shall serve, will I judge: and afterward shall they come out with great substance. 15 And thou shalt go to thy fathers in peace; thou shalt be buried in a good old age. 16 But in the fourth generation they shall come hither again: for the iniquity of the Amorites is not yet full.**

Then God caused Abram to go into a deep sleep (verse 12). In this state, the Lord gave Abram a preview of events in his descendants' futures, including the migration to Egypt—first in peace, then as slaves. God even specified the amount of time (400 years) for their captivity (verse 13). Although Abram's seed would be afflicted, God assured him that his descendants would benefit from God's promise to him. Most notably, they would walk away from slavery with great substance. God then gave Abram the personal prophecy that Abram would live in peace, the rest of his days because God would provide divine protection for him, and all connected to him in his lifetime. He would live a rich and fruitful life and would die at "a good old age" (verse 15) because of his faithfulness.

## SEARCH THE SCRIPTURES

### QUESTION 3
What did God say would happen to Abram's descendants for 400 years?

**They would go to a foreign land for 400 years and eventually would be slaves, but in the end God would deliver them and give them great riches.**

## LIGHT ON THE WORD

### Blessings May Be Preceded by Hard Times
Abram did not have to experience slavery, but his descendants did. Sometimes it's not us, but members of our family who suffer. But we can rest assured that if we and our family trust in God, He will bring about blessings in the end.

## IV. A SOLEMN PROMISE FROM GOD (Genesis 15:17-18)

Abraham had a tremendous responsibility. Very few people of his time understood that there is only one true God and believed in Him. But from Abraham would come a nation that was to be entrusted with recording God's Word and preserving it; being a witness to the world of the one true God; and giving birth to the Savior of the world. This was such an awesome promise that it could only come clothed in the majesty of God.

### God Ratifies His Covenant with Abram (verses 17–18)
**17 And it came to pass, that, when the sun went down, and it was dark, behold a smoking furnace, and a burning lamp that passed between those pieces. 18 In the same day the LORD made a covenant with Abram, saying, Unto thy seed have I given this land, from the river of Egypt**

**unto the great river, the river Euphrates:**

God ratified His covenant with Abram through this sacrifice, thus giving Abram the confirmation he desired. God further guaranteed the demarcation of the Promised Land where Abram's seed would dwell and take ownership (verse 18). Although God had given His promise before concerning the land, this time He reinforced the covenant with specific details. The Lord does not forget what He says He will do.

### QUESTION 4
What two things did Abraham see when the sun went down?

**He saw a smoking furnace and a burning lamp.**

## LIGHT ON THE WORD

In today's lesson, once again Abram received God's promise of a namesake and a nation being birthed through him in old age, but because he had no children at the time, he wondered how those things would happen.

## BIBLE APPLICATION

**AIM: That your students will begin to understand that waiting on God may not be easy.**

### Waiting on God
There are single adults who are so discouraged during their season of singleness that they either make wrong choices—thus disobeying God—or they live with discontentment and bitterness, which displeases God. They neglect to be fruitful for the kingdom. No matter what you are waiting on God to do in your life, you must remain faithful to God's Word and trust that His promises are true. **Isaiah 1:19 (NKJV)** says, "If you are willing and obedient, you shall eat the good of the land."

## STUDENTS' RESPONSES

**AIM: That your students will wait on God to fulfill His promises to them.**

Whatever you are waiting on God to do for you, whatever the breakthrough you seek, don't give up for He who has promised is faithful. Decide today that you are going to believe God in spite of the circumstances.

## PRAYER

Dear Father, we thank You that You always keep Your promises to us, even though we may have to go through some hard times first. Help us to wait patiently, in faith believing. In Jesus' Name we pray. Amen.

## DIG A LITTLE DEEPER

### Faith in God is Accounted as Righteousness!

Abraham and Sara were well beyond human childbearing age, but they were not beyond spiritual childbearing age. They would have both physical and spiritual descendants more numerous than the stars because they believed God and acted in faith according to what God promised.

God created humans in the image of God so humans can participate in God's dominion, being fruitful and bringing forth not only physical but spiritual children. Imago Dei is a gift given to us by God so that we might manifest God's personal presence in creation. This gift, plus the covenantal narrative in (**Genesis 1:26-28**), is prologue to a much larger narrative. In (**Genesis 15:1-6, 12-18**), Faith in God, seeing the invisible and believing the impossible no matter the conditions or circumstances. "Abram believed the LORD, and he credited it to him as righteousness." Only faith in God through righteousness brings us back into the image of God.

We live in a world of distractions and devourers of our faith. "And when the fowls came down upon the carcasses," Abram drove the distractions and devourers away. God made a covenant with him. The lie of Satan in Eden's garden is that God cannot be trusted and believed. But Abraham believed God and God made a covenant with him. God created us for a covenantal relationship. God only has covenantal relationships.

God's image in humans is described in (**Genesis 5:1-4**). Adam was made in the image of God but when Adam's son, Seth, was born, he was born sinful, defiled and mortal, like Adam. Not only a man like Adam, consisting of body and soul, but a sinner like Adam. This was the reverse of that Divine likeness in which Adam was made; having lost it, he could not pass the divine image on to his seed without faith in God that is accounted as righteousness.

## HOW TO SAY IT

| | |
|---|---|
| Mahazeh. | Makh-az-eh. |
| Masheq. | Meh'-shek. |
| Zara. | Zah'-rah. |
| Tardemah. | Tar-day-maw. |
| Amorites. | Am-uh-rahyt. |

## DAILY HOME BIBLE READINGS

### MONDAY
The Faith of Abraham
(Hebrews 11:8–16)

### TUESDAY
Abraham's Faith Tested
(Hebrews 11:17–22)

### WEDNESDAY
Righteousness by Faith
(Romans 4:9–15)

### THURSDAY
Strong in Faith
(Romans 4:16–25)

### FRIDAY
An Everlasting Covenant
(Psalm 105:4–11)

### SATURDAY
The Eternal Covenant
Hebrews 13:17–21)

### SUNDAY
A Covenant with God
(Genesis 15:1–6, 12–18)

Read **Genesis 22:1-2, 6-14** and next week's lesson, "The Lord Provides,"

**Sources:**
Aalders, G. Charles. Bible Student's Commentary: Genesis, Volume 1. Grand Rapids, MI: Zondervan, 1981.

Berrigan, Daniel. Genesis: Fair Beginnings, Then Foul. Lanham, MD: Rowman & Littlefield Publishers, 2006. 129.

"Genesis." Scofield Reference Notes. Bible Study Tools.com. http://www.biblestudytools.com/commentaries/scofield-reference-notes/genesis/genesis-15.html#Ge15_18 (accessed June 25 & June 30, 2010).

Hebrew Greek Key Word Study Bible King James Version. 2nd ed. Chattanooga, TN: AMG Publishers, 1991. 1648.

Henry, Matthew. The Matthew Henry Study Bible, King James Version. Iowa Falls, IA: World Bible Publishers, 1994. 40–41.

McKeown, James. Genesis: The Two Horizons Old Testament Commentary. Grand Rapids, MI: William B. Eerdmans, 2008. 90, 94.

Walton, John H. Genesis: The NIV Application Commentary. Grand Rapids, MI: Zondervan, 2001. 420–23.

**COMMENTS / NOTES:**

# THE LORD PROVIDES

**BIBLE BASIS:** Genesis 22:1–2, 6–14

**BIBLE TRUTH:** Abraham was unquestioning in his faith and devotion to God, who eventually rescinded His demand to kill Isaac.

**MEMORY VERSE:** And he said, Lay not thine hand upon the lad, neither do thou any thing unto him: for now I know that thou fearest God, seeing thou hast not withheld thy son, thine only son from me (Genesis 22:12, KJV).

**LESSON AIM:** By the end of the lesson, we will: LEARN of Abraham's willingness to sacrifice his only son to please God; IMAGINE the unquestioning faith Abraham exhibited; and COMMIT to increasing faith in God and obedience to Him.

**BACKGROUND SCRIPTURES:** Genesis 22:1-14--Read and incorporate the insights gained from the Background Scriptures into your study of the lesson.

## TEACHER PREPARATION

**MATERIALS NEEDED:** Bibles (several different versions), Quarterly Commentary/Teacher Manual, Adult Quarterly, teaching resources such as charts, worksheets/handouts, paper, pens, and pencils.

**OTHER MATERIALS NEEDED / TEACHER'S NOTES:**

_____

_____

## LESSON OVERVIEW

### LIFE NEED FOR TODAY'S LESSON
That students will learn that we can trust God when we take a leap of faith and totally obey Him.

### BIBLE LEARNING
To understand that Abraham was put to the ultimate test of loyalty and faith in God as he was commanded to give up the son he waited for so long.

### BIBLE APPLICATION
To learn that God will provide for us when we totally obey Him.

### STUDENTS' RESPONSES
Students will commit to increasing faith in God and obedience to Him.

### LESSON SCRIPTURE

#### GENESIS 22:1-2, 6-14, KJV

**1** And it came to pass after these things, that God did tempt Abraham, and said unto him, Abraham: and he said, Behold, here I am.

#### GENESIS 22:1-2, 6-14, AMP

**1** Now after these things, God tested [the faith and commitment of] Abraham and said

**2** And he said, Take now thy son, thine only son Isaac, whom thou lovest, and get thee into the land of Moriah; and offer him there for a burnt offering upon one of the mountains which I will tell thee of.

**22:6** And Abraham took the wood of the burnt offering, and laid it upon Isaac his son; and he took the fire in his hand, and a knife; and they went both of them together.

**7** And Isaac spake unto Abraham his father, and said, My father: and he said, Here am I, my son. And he said, Behold the fire and the wood: but where is the lamb for a burnt offering?

**8** And Abraham said, My son, God will provide himself a lamb for a burnt offering: so they went both of them together.

**9** And they came to the place which God had told him of; and Abraham built an altar there, and laid the wood in order, and bound Isaac his son, and laid him on the altar upon the wood.

**10** And Abraham stretched forth his hand, and took the knife to slay his son.

**11** And the angel of the LORD called unto him out of heaven, and said, Abraham, Abraham: and he said, Here am I.

**12** And he said, Lay not thine hand upon the lad, neither do thou any thing unto him: for now I know that thou fearest God, seeing thou hast not withheld thy son, thine only son from me.

**13** And Abraham lifted up his eyes, and looked, and behold behind him a ram caught in a thicket by his horns: and Abraham went and took the ram, and offered him up for a burnt offering in the stead of his son.

to him, "Abraham!" And he answered, "Here I am."

**2** God said, "Take now your son, your only son [of [a]promise], whom you love, Isaac, and go to the region of [b]Moriah, and offer him there as a burnt offering on one of the mountains of which I shall tell you."

**22:6** Then Abraham took the wood for the burnt offering and laid it on [the shoulders of] Isaac his son, and he took the fire (firepot) in his own hand and the [sacrificial] knife; and the two of them walked on together.

**7** And Isaac said to Abraham, "My father!" And he said, "Here I am, my son." Isaac said, "Look, the fire and the wood, but where is the lamb for the burnt offering?"

**8** Abraham said, "My son, God will provide for Himself a lamb for the burnt offering." So the two walked on together.

**9** When they came to the place of which God had told him, Abraham built an altar there and arranged the wood, and bound Isaac his son and placed him on the altar, on top of the wood.

**10** Abraham reached out his hand and took the knife to kill his son.

**11** But the Angel of the Lord called to him from heaven and said, "Abraham, Abraham!" He answered, "Here I am."

**12** The Lord said, "Do not reach out [with the knife in] your hand against the boy, and do nothing to [harm] him; for now I know that you fear God [with reverence and profound respect], since you have not withheld from Me your son, your only son [of promise]."

**13** Then Abraham looked up and glanced around, and behold, behind him was a ram caught in a thicket by his horns. And Abraham went and took the ram and offered it up for a

**14** And Abraham called the name of that place Jehovah-jireh: as it is said to this day, In the mount of the LORD it shall be seen.

**14** So Abraham named that place The Lord Will Provide. And it is said to this day, "On the mountain of the Lord it will be seen and provided."

## BIBLICAL DEFINITIONS

A. **Tempt (Genesis 22:1)** *nacah* (Heb.)—To test, prove, put to the proof, to qualify.

B. **Know (v. 12)** *yada`* (Heb.)—To ascertain by seeing, be assuredly aware, with certainty.

## LIGHT ON THE WORD

Isaac was the promised son of Abraham and Sarah. His name means "laughter." In their old age, God brought joy and fulfillment to them. Abraham and Sarah received their namesake who would go on to inherit the land promised to the patriarch and continue the blessing of Abraham through his son Jacob. Isaac was the only biblical patriarch whose name was not changed, and the only one who did not leave Canaan.

## TEACHING THE BIBLE LESSON

## LIFE NEED FOR TODAY'S LESSON

**AIM: That your students will be willing to exercise faith in God's power to fulfill present-day promises.**

## INTRODUCTION

### A Promise Reaffirmed

God appeared to Abram and Sarai on two more occasions prior to the birth of the promised child as outlined in Scripture. The Lord appeared to reinforce His covenant to make a great nation from them by giving them a son, He changed their names to Abraham (meaning "father of multitudes") and Sarah (which means "princess"), and He gave them a sign of His covenant by instilling circumcision of all males **(Genesis 17).** Then an angel of the Lord appeared to tell Abraham and Sarah that in due season, approximately one year later, a child would come. At the age of 100 and 90 respectively, Abraham and Sarah became the proud parents of Isaac. The impossible had happened, and they conceived a child in their old age **(Genesis 17:19–21).**

## BIBLE LEARNING

**AIM: That your students will learn that God provides as He promises.**

### I. THE LORD PROVIDES (Genesis 22:1-2, 6-14)

At the close of the previous chapter, **Genesis 21:22–34,** Abraham made a covenant with King Abimelech of Gerar, who had an interest in striking a political alliance with Abraham because he could see that God was with him. Upon making an agreement of peace and to dig a well, Abraham staked his claim by planting a grove in Beer-sheba and named it in the Lord's honor as an outward sign in a pagan and idolatrous world that he served the everlasting

God (**Genesis 21:22**). **Genesis 22** opens with, "And it came to pass after these things, that God did tempt (tested) Abraham."

### God's Command for a Sacrifice
### (Genesis 22:1–2)

**1 And it came to pass after these things, that God did tempt Abraham, and said unto him, Abraham: and he said, Behold, here I am. 2 And he said, Take now thy son, thine only son Isaac, whom thou lovest, and get thee into the land of Moriah; and offer him there for a burnt offering upon one of the mountains which I will tell thee of.**

It may appear strange, that God would tell Abraham to take the son that he and Sarah waited so long for, and offer him up as a sacrifice, when God clearly did not want His people to act like the other nations around who offered up child sacrifices (**Leviticus 18:21; Deuteronomy 18:10**). God's command for Abraham to offer Isaac as a sacrifice, gave us a picture of God's release of His own Son Jesus for the redemption of the world. Abraham had a love relationship with the Lord and once again he listened to the Lord, presented himself ready to obey, and upon instruction, he got up and moved at God's Word. Out of His love for us, Jesus also presented Himself ready and moved at the Father's command to be the propitiation (sacrifice) for our sins (**1 John 4:10**).

## SEARCH THE SCRIPTURES

### QUESTION 1

What test did God give Abraham?

**God asked Abraham to sacrifice Isaac, his only son.**

## LIGHT ON THE WORD

### When God Asks the Hard Things

God made it clear after asking Abraham to sacrifice his son, that in the future God would only demand that of Himself when He gave His only Son for us. Any other child sacrifice has been ruled out. However, God may ask some hard things of us. Maybe you will be called to a life of singleness—no marriage and no children. Maybe there are other tough things you will have to sacrifice to prove your love for God. Nothing should be too hard when we consider that God went through and sacrificed His only Son.

## II. GOD ANSWERS (Genesis 22:6-8)

Abram could see no other way, his servant Eliezer was going to inherit his estate. Abram really valued Eliezer and Eliezer trusted in God just as Abram did (**see Genesis 24**). But God had promised Abram that he and Sarai would give birth to a child and so God had to encourage him that He would bring this about.

### Abraham's Sojourn of Faith
### (verses 6–8)

**6 And Abraham took the wood of the burnt offering, and laid it upon Isaac his son; and he took the fire in his hand, and a knife; and they went both of them together. 7 And Isaac spake unto Abraham his father, and said, My father: and he said, Here am I, my son. And he said, Behold the fire and the wood: but where is the lamb for a burnt offering? 8 And Abraham said, My son, God will provide himself a lamb for a burnt offering: so they went both of them together.**

What an ominous responsibility it must have been for Abraham to carry the very instruments he would use to kill his son. Isaac unknowingly was carrying the wood that he would lie upon and in doing so, would lay down his life out of love and obedience to his father and his God. This is quite a picture prefiguring Jesus carrying the Cross to Calvary for our sins, out of love and obedience. It has been widely believed and portrayed in children's Bible stories and films that Isaac was a small child. However, traditional Jewish sources maintain that he was an adult or at least over the age of 12, which is considered to be an adult in Jewish custom (The Jewish Study Bible, 44–46). In light of Isaac's perceived age, it makes this story even more powerful because his father was now a very old man, and Isaac could have refused to go with him or turned back when he didn't see the lamb. Abraham replied to Isaac's question by prudently stating that "God will provide himself a lamb for a burnt offering" **(Genesis 22:8, KJV)**. Abraham did not lie to his son by not telling him what God commanded or what his pending fate involved. He trusted God, did not give cause for alarm, and was unwavering in his faith that somehow God was going to take care of His request. We read in **Hebrews 11:19** that Abraham believed that God would raise up Isaac from the dead. The father and son continued on this journey of faith and sacrifice together.

## QUESTION 2

How did Abraham answer Isaac when he asked where the sacrifice was?

**Abraham told Isaac that God would provide a lamb for the sacrifice.**

**Answers will vary.**

## LIGHT ON THE WORD

### Incredible Faith in an Incredible God

Abraham's obedience to the Lord in taking steps to sacrifice his only son is incredible. We cannot understand why God would even suggest this except to provide a picture to us of what it meant to God to sacrifice His only Son for us. Our understanding of our Father's sacrifice of His Son means that we must understand the Trinity. The Father was in the Son every step He took on the road to Calvary. He was sharing

everything with His Son, because of His love not only for us, but also for Jesus. The only time the Father had to look away from His only Son was when Jesus took our sins on Himself as He hung on the Cross. If the Father could do this for us, there is no sacrifice that would be too great for us to make for Him.

## III. ABRAM'S RELATIONSHIP WITH GOD (Genesis 22:9-10)

### Abraham's Willingness to Obey God (verses 9–10)

**9 And they came to the place which God had told him of; and Abraham built an altar there, and laid the wood in order, and bound Isaac his son, and laid him on the altar upon the wood. 10 And Abraham stretched forth his hand, and took the knife to slay his son.**

Abraham already committed in his heart to follow through with what the Lord God commanded, and Isaac was willing to obey his father's command. One can only imagine the pain in their eyes as they continued to believe God, but Abraham moved forward with this sacrifice. After years of waiting for the promise to make him the father of many nations, his seed was lying on the altar prepared to die.

## SEARCH THE SCRIPTURES

### QUESTION 3

What steps of obedience did Abraham take in order to obey God's command?

**He built an altar, laid the wood on it, tied up Isaac and laid him on the altar, and then he took his knife and raised it to kill his only son.**

## LIGHT ON THE WORD

### Instant Obedience

Abraham had his knife ready to kill his only son. We read in **Hebrews 11:17-19** that Abraham believed that God would raise Isaac from the dead. But as soon as the angel of the Lord called out his name, he said, "Here am I." In spite of all that God was calling Abraham to do, he was instantly ready to obey God.

## IV. GOD WILL PROVIDE
## Genesis 22:11-14

### God's Provision of a Sacrifice
### (verses 11–14)

**11 And the angel of the LORD called unto him out of heaven, and said, Abraham, Abraham: and he said, Here am I. 12 And he said, Lay not thine hand upon the lad, neither do thou any thing unto him: for now I know that thou fearest God, seeing thou hast not withheld thy son, thine only son from me. 13 And Abraham lifted up his eyes, and looked, and behold behind him a ram caught in a thicket by his horns: and Abraham went and took the ram, and offered him up for a burnt offering in the stead of his son. 14 And Abraham called the name of that place Jehovah-jireh: as it is said to this day, In the mount of the LORD it shall be seen.**

Abraham's obedience revealed that he revered God with his whole heart. Then Abraham turned around to see a ram that God had provided for the sacrifice. Abraham formally named the place of this sacrifice Jehovah-jireh, in honor of God's provision. This sacrifice reflects the fact that Jesus was our substitute, taking on the sins of the world.

### QUESTION 4
What sacrifice did God provide?

**God provided a ram in the thicket.**

## LIGHT ON THE WORD

In today's lesson, we see that when God demands something so hard that it sounds impossible, the Lord will make a way out.

## BIBLE APPLICATION

**AIM: That your students will begin to understand that God demands our obedience, even when it's hard to do.**

### Giving Our Best

As Christians, we will face decisions that demonstrate where we stand and what is truly in our hearts. The God and Father of our Lord and Savior Jesus Christ gave His very best, and we must resolve as the Body of Christ to do the same for Him.

## STUDENTS' RESPONSES

**AIM: That your students will wait on God to fulfill His promises to them.**

Whatever you are waiting on God to do for you, whatever the breakthrough you seek, don't give up for He who has promised is faithful. Decide today that you are going to believe God in spite of the circumstances.

## PRAYER

Dear Father, we thank You that You always keep Your promises to us, even though we may have to go through some hard times first. Help us to wait patiently, in faith believing. In Jesus' Name we pray. Amen.

## DIG A LITTLE DEEPER

Faith and obedience go together Abraham's faith in God was obedience to God. We need both a relationship and obedience to God. Both faith and obedience, are required in order for God to work in our lives and our circumstances. The child must have faith in the parent and be obedient if they are going to successfully overcome obstacles and grow in life. It is the same with God, obedience is the evidence of our faith. Faith that succeeds also obeys. "Faith without works is dead" **(James 2:26).** Meaning faith requires obedient corresponding action.

Jesus said to His disciples, "O faithless and perverse generation, how long shall I be with you? How long shall I bear with you? **(Matthew 17:17)"** Jesus rebuked the demon out of the child and His disciples asked Jesus, "Why could we not cast it out?" Jesus said to them, "Because of your unbelief, if you have faith as a mustard seed, you will say to this mountain, 'Move from here to there,' and it will move; and nothing will be impossible for you.

Jesus helped his disciples develop spiritually and transform the lives of people who in turn helped transform others. Jesus demonstrated how to overcome obstacles and how to grow.

Jesus taught them that their faith and obedience, gives them power over their conditions and obstacles. When they believed and obeyed transformation took place in their lives as well as others lives.

## HOW TO SAY IT

| | |
|---|---|
| Haran. | Kaw-rawn' |
| Canaan. | Ken-ah'-an. |
| Moriah. | Mor-i-ah'. |

### DAILY HOME BIBLE READINGS

**MONDAY**
All Your Needs
(Philippians 4:15–20)

**TUESDAY**
Born through the Promise
(Galatians 4:21–28)

**WEDNESDAY**
Not Withholding His Only Son
(Genesis 22:15–19)

**THURSDAY**
Faith Completed by Works
(James 2:14–24)

**FRIDAY**
Concern for Our Descendants
(Joshua 22:21–29)

**SATURDAY**
Righteousness and Justice
(Proverbs 21:1–5)

**SUNDAY**
The Challenge to Commitment
(Genesis 22:1–2, 6–14)

## PREPARE FOR NEXT SUNDAY

Read **Luke 1:46–55,** and next week's lesson, "According to the Promise."

Sources:
Berlin, Adele, and Marc Brettler, eds. The Jewish Study Bible. New York, NY: Oxford University Press, 2004. 44–46.
"Genesis 22." Net Bible.org. http://www.Net.Bible.org (accessed July 25, 2010).
Henry, Matthew. The Matthew Henry Study Bible, King James Version. Iowa Falls, IA: World Bible Publishers, 1994. 60.
Mays, James L., gen. ed. Bible Commentary. San Francisco, CA: HarperCollins, 2000.
Skinner, John. A Critical and Exegetical Commentary of Genesis. Edinburgh, UK: Morrison and Gibb Limited, 1980.
Von Rad, Gerhard. Genesis: A Commentary. Philadelphia, PA: Westminster Press, 1972.

# ACCORDING TO THE PROMISE

**BIBLE BASIS:** Luke 1:46–55

**BIBLE TRUTH:** God fulfilled His promise to Adam and Eve, Sarah and Abraham, and all who followed Him through Mary who was promised a son, Jesus.

**MEMORY VERSE:** And Mary said, My soul doth magnify the Lord, And my spirit hath rejoiced in God my Saviour (Luke 1:46–47, KJV).

**LESSON AIM:** By the end of the lesson, we will: REVIEW Mary's song praising God's faithfulness; APPRECIATE the faithfulness of God's people from generation to generation; and EXAMINE areas in our lives where our faithfulness to God can be strengthened.

**BACKGROUND SCRIPTURES:** Galatians 3:6-18--Read and incorporate the insights gained from the Background Scriptures into your study of the lesson.

## TEACHER PREPARATION

**MATERIALS NEEDED:** Bibles (several different versions), Quarterly Commentary/Teacher Manual, Adult Quarterly, teaching resources such as charts, worksheets/handouts, paper, pens, and pencils.

**OTHER MATERIALS NEEDED / TEACHER'S NOTES:**

_____

_____

## LESSON OVERVIEW

### LIFE NEED FOR TODAY'S LESSON
That students will learn that God is able to use us, no matter what our earthly situation is.

### BIBLE LEARNING
To understand that Mary praised God because He has promised to make her the mother of His Son.

### BIBLE APPLICATION
To learn that God desires that we be faithful and thankful for all His good promises.

### STUDENTS' RESPONSES
Students will thank God for His promises in whatever situation they find themselves.

## LESSON SCRIPTURE

### LUKE 1:46-55, KJV

46 And Mary said, My soul doth magnify the Lord,

### LUKE 1:46-55, AMP

46 And Mary said," My soul magnifies and exalts the Lord,

**47** And my spirit hath rejoiced in God my Saviour.

**48** For he hath regarded the low estate of his handmaiden: for, behold, from henceforth all generations shall call me blessed.

**49** For he that is mighty hath done to me great things; and holy is his name.

**50** And his mercy is on them that fear him from generation to generation.

**51** He hath shewed strength with his arm; he hath scattered the proud in the imagination of their hearts.

**52** He hath put down the mighty from their seats, and exalted them of low degree.

**53** He hath filled the hungry with good things; and the rich he hath sent empty away.

**54** He hath helped his servant Israel, in remembrance of his mercy;

**55** As he spake to our fathers, to Abraham, and to his seed for ever.

**47** And my spirit has rejoiced in God my Savior.

**48** "For He has looked [with loving care] on the humble state of His maidservant; For behold, from now on all generations will count me blessed and happy and favored by God!

**49** "For He who is mighty has done great things for me; And holy is His name [to be worshiped in His purity, majesty, and glory].

**50** "And His mercy is upon generation after generation Toward those who [stand in great awe of God and] fear Him.

**51** "He has done mighty deeds with His [powerful] arm; He has scattered those who were proud in the thoughts of their heart.

**52** "He has brought down rulers from their thrones, And exalted those who were humble.

**53** "He has filled the hungry with good things; And sent the rich away empty-handed.

**54** "He has helped His servant Israel, In remembrance of His mercy,

**55** Just as He promised to our fathers, To Abraham and to his descendants forever."

## BIBLICAL DEFINITIONS

A. **Magnify (Luke 1:46)** *megaluno* (Gk.)—Root word for "Magnificat," Mary's song of praise, which is the first word of Mary's song in the Latin Vulgate scriptural text, and it means "glorify."
B. **Soul (v. 46)** *psuche* (Gk.)—The seat of feelings, emotion, desire, and affection.

## LIGHT ON THE WORD

Mary sang the beautiful words of today's Scripture passage while she was visiting Elizabeth, her relative. Elizabeth and her husband, Zechariah, were elderly, childless couple. They had prayed many years for a child until they reached the age where they no longer expected God to answer this request. Both Elizabeth and Zechariah were of the tribe of Aaron, so Zechariah was in rotation for serving at the Temple in Jerusalem.

After Luke's introduction to his Gospel record, he plunges right into the story of the birth of John the Baptist. It was Zechariah's turn to serve at the Temple, a great privilege for a godly Jew. As he went in to burn incense, suddenly the angel Gabriel was standing beside the incense altar (**Luke 1:11**). Zechariah had the same reaction that all who have ever been visited by an angel, he was afraid.

After telling him not to be afraid, Gabriel told Zechariah that God was answering his and Elizabeth's prayer for a child, a very special child that they were to name "John" (**v. 13**). Unfortunately, Zechariah found this hard to believe, and so he became speechless until after the birth of John, their baby. John grew up to be the prophet we know as John the Baptist (or Baptizer).

## TEACHING THE BIBLE LESSON

## LIFE NEED FOR TODAY'S LESSON

**AIM: That your students will look beyond their present circumstances to see God's blessings for them.**

## INTRODUCTION

### An Angel Visits Mary

Word must have traveled, in spite of the lack of modern communication devices, because Mary heard that her elderly relative was now pregnant. Mary was on the other end of the age spectrum, probably only around 15 years old, the age when women of those days usually got married. Gabriel had also visited Mary to tell her that she would be pregnant in the most miraculous way ever (**verses 26–38**). Mary was going to give birth to the Son of God and this would be a virgin birth.

## BIBLE LEARNING

**AIM: That your students will learn that the promises given in the Old Testament were fulfilled in Jesus Christ.**

# I. THE LORD FULFILLS HIS PROMISES (Luke 1:46-49)

Shortly after Gabriel's announcement to Mary, she hurried to see Elizabeth (about an 80-mile hike). As soon as she walked in the door and Elizabeth heard her, baby John in her womb leaped in praise at the presence of the Baby who was growing within Mary. At this time, Elizabeth was already six months pregnant, while Mary's pregnancy had just begun. After Elizabeth had finished praising God for the coming Savior, Mary began singing a song of praise to God that reminds us very much of Hannah's song of praise when she became pregnant with baby Samuel in answer to her prayers. The similarity of Mary's prayer to others in the Bible makes us think that Mary studied Scripture and meditated upon it even in an era when women had little access to formal education.

### God's Personal Blessings on Mary
### (Luke 1:46–49)

**46 And Mary said, My soul doth magnify the Lord, 47 And my spirit hath rejoiced in God my Saviour. 48 For he hath regarded the low estate of his handmaiden: for, behold, from henceforth all generations shall call me blessed. 49 For he that is mighty hath done to me great things; and holy is his name.**

This stanza of Mary's song sings of how blessed she is. From a worldly perspective, this would seem to be the opposite of Mary's situation. Mary came from Nazareth, a town that was so poor that many of its few inhabitants lived in caves. She was engaged to a very godly man with a respectable job, but now she was pregnant—and not by him. Where are the blessings in such a situation?

First, she rejoices because God is her Savior. Every Christian, regardless of his or her situation, should remember that the greatest blessing is to have God as Savior. Then, thinking upon the news from angel Gabriel, Mary praises God for choosing her for this blessing, in spite of her humble status—she is poor and a woman, two things that in that era assigned one to an automatic inferior status. But Mary does not see her lowly status as a disadvantage in the sight of the Lord. God delights in blessing the ones who are of a very humble socio-economic status, but who put all of their trust in the Lord.

## SEARCH THE SCRIPTURES

### QUESTION 1
What is the first thing that Mary thanked God for in her song?

**She rejoiced that God was her Savior.**

## LIGHT ON THE WORD

### God's Blessings on His People
Mary has trust in the Lord showing mercy to His people, because she knows that Scripture details how God had blessed His people in the past. This is more than simple optimism. This is hope based upon knowledge of how God has worked in the past. Based upon how He has blessed His people, Mary knows that He will continue to do so in the future.

## II. GOD FULFILLS HIS PROMISES TO HIS PEOPLE (Luke 1:50–53)

Mary brings to bear the merciful attributes of God, His consistency, and His faithfulness. In **verse 50,** she celebrates God's mercy on all those who "fear" Him, meaning those who venerate or reverence Him. The fear of God is verifiable by the people's obedience and keeping of God's Law. God's mercy is accorded specifically to the people of Israel in keeping with God's promises, which started with Abraham (**Genesis 17:7; 18:18; 22:17**). This mercy is demonstrated in the display of God's strength and power (**Luke 1:51–53**).

### God's Blessings on His People (verses 50–53)
**50 And his mercy is on them that fear him from generation to generation. 51 He hath shewed strength with his arm; he hath scattered the proud in the imagination of their hearts. 52 He hath put down the mighty from their seats, and exalted them of low degree. 53 He hath filled the hungry with good things; and the rich he hath sent empty away.**

As we look closely at the things that Mary sings about concerning how God acts, we see that when Jesus came to the earth, He brought about a moral revolution. He is using His mighty arm to sweep aside the proud. Pride has no place in the Christian, because our standard is Jesus Christ. When we see ourselves compared to Him, we realize how far we are from how God desires us to be.

Then we see a social revolution. Jesus brings an end to the labels and titles that people think elevate them. In the sight of our Lord, the lowest person is just as important as the person with money and power.

Next, there is an economic revolution. Just think about the first Christians in **Acts 2:44–45.** No one went hungry in that first Christian community, because the rich sold their riches so the poor could have the basic necessities of life. Probably that ideal community existed for only a short time, but no Christians should go hungry while others have abundance. We live in a very materialistic and greedy society, but Christians should have a different set of values than that of the world.

### QUESTION 2
Who will experience God's mercy?

**God's mercy is on those who fear (respect, revere, adore) Him.**

**Answers will vary.**

168

## LIGHT ON THE WORD

### The Most Wonderful Promise Fulfilled

"God may not come when you want Him to, but He always comes on time." People were waiting hundreds of years and some were waiting thousands of years, for God to send our Savior. But finally, God sent Him! And you and I can look back at our promised Savior, already come.

## III. GOD'S PROMISES TO US AND TO OUR FAMILIES (Luke 1:54-55)

### God's Faithfulness in Sending the Messiah (verses 54–55)

**54 He hath helped his servant Israel, in remembrance of his mercy; 55 As he spake to our fathers, to Abraham, and to his seed for ever.**

Mary acknowledges that all these great and revolutionary changes in us can only come about through the coming of the Messiah that God had promised to send. Mary is thinking about God's promises to Abraham, Father of her people; but God promised Mother Eve back in **(Genesis 3:15)** that He would send a Savior that we all so much need **(see also Genesis 4:25).** God is always faithful to keep His promises, even if we have to wait!

## SEARCH THE SCRIPTURES

### QUESTION 3

What does God promise to do for His people?

**He promised to show them mercy forever.**

**Answers will vary.**

## LIGHT ON THE WORD

In today's lesson, we see that Mary reveals the excellent nature of God: His divine power and authority over all things both spiritual and human (**Luke 1:49, 51**); His holiness (**verse 49**); His mercy and justice (**verse 50**);

and His faithfulness and trustworthiness in fulfilling His promises (**verses 54–55**). Through the incarnation of Christ, we realize the omnipotence, holiness, mercy and justice, and faithfulness of God.

## BIBLE APPLICATION

**AIM: That your students will see that God always keeps His promises, even if we have to wait a long, long time for them to be fulfilled.**

### God Is Faithful to Us

God is faithful to us. Are we faithful to Him? Do we wait patiently? Or do we worry and try to take things into our own hands? Think back to all the times that God has fulfilled His promises to you. Thank Him now and trust Him for the future.

## STUDENTS' RESPONSES

**AIM: That your students will praise God for keeping all His promises to them.**

Today's entire Scripture passage consists of a song of worship and thanksgiving. The proper response to God's many fulfilled promises to us is praise. We can thank God for the big things like our salvation and the daily things He does for us, even the air we breathe.

## PRAYER

Dear Father, we thank You for fulfilling Your greatest promise and that is sending Jesus Christ, our Savior. In Jesus' Name we pray. Amen.

## DIG A LITTLE DEEPER

God's promises require our participation. His promises are Yes, and Amen. Our yes, and our amen must be action oriented. God did not overpower Mary against her will God needed her participation. Everything God promises requires belieivng God and acting on His promises. "Abraham believed God, and it was accounted to him for righteousness" **(James 2:23).** Believing and acting is righteousness Scripture Being human without believing God is maddening! Believing God liberates us from negative limitations and influence and replaces the human limitations with godly possibilities. Our faith in God allows us dominion and power over every kind of negative experience or influence. "For all the promises of God in Him are yea, and in Him Amen, unto the glory of God unto yea by us" **(2 Corinthians 1:20).** The promises of God provides a new reality and identity, not because of our intelligence, resumé, or political or social status, but because God stands on his promises. Our faith in God, is an endowment through Jesus, adopted into the family of God we are accepted through Christ as God accepts His own Son. As joint- heirs with christ we share the same inheritance, God fulfilled His promise to Adam and Eve, Sarah and Abraham, and all who followed Him. We are heirs of God and joint- heirs with christ, we suffer with Him, so that we may be also glorified together **(Romans 8:17).**

## HOW TO SAY IT

Annakims. AN-uh-kims.

Chaldees. KAL-dees'.

Debir. DEE-buhr.

Eleazar. El'ee-AY-zuhr.

Negev. NEG-ev.

Seir. SEE-uhr.

### DAILY HOME BIBLE READINGS

**MONDAY**
God Is Faithful
(2 Corinthians 1:18–22)

**TUESDAY**
A Faithful Heart
(Nehemiah 9:6–10)

**WEDNESDAY**
Descendants of Abraham
(Galatians 3:6–12)

**THURSDAY**
Inheritance through the Promise
(Galatians 3:13–18)

**FRIDAY**
Jesus' Birth Foretold
(Luke 1:26–38)

**SATURDAY**
Elizabeth's Blessing
(Luke 1:39–45)

**SUNDAY**
Mary's Song of Praise
(Luke 1:46–55))

## PREPARE FOR NEXT SUNDAY

Read **Genesis 39:7–21a** , and next week"s lesson "God Watches over Joseph."

**Sources:**

Baltes, A. J., ed. Biblespeech.com. http://www.biblespeech.com (accessed August 11, 2010).

Cox, Steven L. "Angel." Holman Illustrated Bible Dictionary. Nashville, TN: Holman Reference, 2003. 66–67.

# GOD WATCHES OVER JOSEPH

**BIBLE BASIS: Genesis 39:7–21a**

**BIBLE TRUTH:** Potiphar's complete faith in Joseph's integrity, Joseph's faith in and loyalty to God, and Joseph's loyalty to Potiphar led Joseph to decline [reject] his mistress's sexual demands.

**MEMORY VERSE:** There is none greater in this house than I; neither hath he kept back any thing from me but thee, because thou art his wife: how then can I do this great wickedness, and sin against God? (Genesis 39:9, KJV).

**LESSON AIM:** By the end of the lesson, we will: EXAMINE Joseph's loyalty and faithfulness to Potiphar; REFLECT on how loyalty influences decisions and behavior; and COMMIT to faithfulness and loyalty in our relationship with God.

**BACKGROUND SCRIPTURES: Genesis 39:1 - 23** Read and incorporate the insights gained from the Background Scriptures into your study of the lesson.

## TEACHER PREPARATION

**MATERIALS NEEDED:** Bibles (several different versions), Quarterly Commentary/Teacher Manual, Adult Quarterly, teaching resources such as charts, worksheets/handouts, paper, pens, and pencils.

**OTHER MATERIALS NEEDED / TEACHER'S NOTES:**

_____

_____

## LESSON OVERVIEW

**LIFE NEED FOR TODAY'S LESSON**
That students will learn that God is able to help them live lives of sexual purity.

**BIBLE LEARNING**
To understand that Joseph refused to give in to the sexual inducements of Potiphar's wife.

**BIBLE APPLICATION**
To learn that God desires our faithfulness to Him, especially in the area of sexual purity.

**STUDENTS' RESPONSES**
Students will ask God to help them to be true to Him, especially in the area of sex, whether it is to celibacy outside of marriage or faithfulness inside of marriage.

## LESSON SCRIPTURE

### GENESIS 39:7-21, KJV

**7** And it came to pass after these things, that his master's wife cast hereyes upon Joseph; and she said, Lie with me.

### GENESIS 39:7-21, AMP

**7** Then after a time his master's wife looked at Joseph with desire, and she said, "Lie with me."

8 But he refused, and said unto his master's wife, Behold, my master wotteth not what is with me in the house, and he hath committed all that he hath to my hand;

9 There is none greater in this house than I; neither hath he kept back any thing from me but thee, because thou art his wife: how then can I do this great wickedness, and sin against God?

10 And it came to pass, as she spake to Joseph day by day, that he hearkened not unto her, to lie by her, or to be with her.

11 And it came to pass about this time, that Joseph went into the house to do his business; and there was none of the men of the house there within.

12 And she caught him by his garment, saying, Lie with me: and he left his garment in her hand, and fled, and got him out.

13 And it came to pass, when she saw that he had left his garment in her hand, and was fled forth,

14 That she called unto the men of her house, and spake unto them, saying, See, he hath brought in an Hebrew unto us to mock us; he came in unto me to lie with me, and I cried with a loud voice:

15 And it came to pass, when he heard that I lifted up my voice and cried, that he left his garment with me, and fled, and got him out.

16 And she laid up his garment by her, until his lord came home.

17 And she spake unto him according to these words, saying, The Hebrew servant, which thou hast brought unto us, came in unto me to mock me:

8 But he refused and said to his master's wife, "Look, with me in the house, my master does not concern himself with anything; he has put everything that he owns in my charge.

9 He is not greater in this house than I am, nor has he kept anything from me except you, because you are his wife. How then could I do this great evil and sin against God [and your husband]?"

10 And so it was that she spoke to Joseph [persistently] day after day, but he did not listen to her [plea] to lie beside her or be with her.

11 Then it happened one day that Joseph went into the house to attend to his duties, and none of the men of the household was there in the house.

12 She caught Joseph by his [outer] robe, saying, "Lie with me!" But he left his robe in her hand and ran, and got outside [the house].

13 When she saw that he had left his robe in her hand and had run outside.

14 she called to the men of her household and said to them, "Look at this, your master has brought a Hebrew [into the household] to mock and insult us; he came to me to lie with me, and I screamed.

15 When he heard me screaming, he left his robe with me and ran outside [the house]."

16 So she left Joseph's [outer] robe beside her until his master came home.

17 Then she told her husband the same story, saying, "The Hebrew servant, whom you brought among us, came to me to mock and insult me.

18 then as soon as I raised my voice and screamed, he left his robe with me and ran outside [the house]."

18 And it came to pass, as I lifted up my voice and cried, that he left his garment with me, and fled out.

19 And it came to pass, when his master heard the words of his wife, which she spake unto him, saying, After this manner did thy servant to me; that his wrath was kindled.

20 And Joseph's master took him, and put him into the prison, a place where the king's prisoners were bound: and he was there in the prison.

21a But the LORD was with Joseph.

19 And when Joseph's master heard the words of his wife, saying, "This is the way your servant treated me," his anger burned.

20 So Joseph's master took him and put him in the prison, a place where the king's prisoners were confined; so he was there in the prison.

21 But the LORD was with Joseph.

## BIBLICAL DEFINITIONS

A. **Mock (Genesis 39:14)** *tsachaq* (Heb.)—To laugh and make fun of.

B. **Hebrew Servant (v. 17)** `*ebed* (Heb.)—Proper name for some sort of a servant, slave, or attendant.

## LIGHT ON THE WORD

Joseph is the beloved son of Jacob and the firstborn son of his father's favorite wife, Rachel. The richly ornamented coat worn by Joseph was given to him by his father. This gesture of kindness served as confirmation of paternal favor. The eldest son, Reuben, had forfeited his birthright as heir when he committed incest **(Genesis 35:22; 49:3–4; 1 Chronicles 5:1–2)**. Simeon and Levi, next in line, were ruled out because of their violence at Shechem **(Genesis 49:5–7)**. The fourth son, Judah, was the next heir. However, Joseph, the 11th in order, is believed by some scholars to be the recipient of the birthright.

## TEACHING THE BIBLE LESSON

## LIFE NEED FOR TODAY'S LESSON

**AIM: That your students will be faithful to the Lord in the area of sexual purity, especially when the situation is very difficult.**

## INTRODUCTION

### Joseph Is Sold into Slavery by His Brothers

Joseph was his father's favorite and although he was a very good son, he had a habit of talking himself up. So, out of great jealousy, his brothers sold him into slavery to a band of wandering Ishmaelites. In **Genesis 39**, we learn that Joseph was sold by the Ishmaelites to an Egyptian named Potiphar, a very high official of Pharaoh's **(Genesis 37:28; 39:1)**. Joseph lived in Potiphar's house and was appointed to a position of authority.

## BIBLE LEARNING

**AIM: That your students will learn that Joseph was in a very difficult situation in which his boss's wife was trying to have sex with him.**

## I. REFUSING TO GIVE IN (Genesis 39:7-12)

The position of Potiphar's wife has given this text special attention. She remains unnamed and has a role of grand consequence and tremendous freedom. She utilizes her liberty with authority as she confronts Joseph. Her power is displayed boldly as she commands Joseph, "Lie with me" (Genesis 39:7). In her statement, she relinquishes all preludes to intimacy and gets right down to business. Her attitude is one of control rather than love; she is the master's wife, a woman who demands, not seduces. Joseph refuses her orders and responds to her with equal authority. Joseph turns down an invitation to engage in sexual immorality. In doing so, he gives a testimony of faithful service to both God and Potiphar.

Joseph reiterates to Potiphar's wife that he has been given power over her husband's household. He has authority over and access to all things, except her. In his rhetorical question, "How then can I do this great wickedness, and sin against God?" (Genesis 39:9), Joseph declares that such an act of adultery is not without great consequences. This is more than a sin against another man; this act involves disobedience against the Lord. In order to remain true to God, he must also remain true to his master, Potiphar.

Potiphar's wife does not accept Joseph's replies. She is relentless and continues her onslaught of sexual advances. Nevertheless, Joseph repeatedly denies her sexual overtures. He avoids her at all cost. Finally, on one occasion while working alone in the house, Joseph encounters her again, and she grabs his cloak and demands that he sleep with her. Joseph runs out of the house leaving his cloak behind.

### Refusing to Give In (Genesis 39:7–12)

**7 And it came to pass after these things, that his master's wife cast her eyes upon Joseph; and she said, Lie with me. 8 But he refused, and said unto his master's wife, Behold, my master wotteth not what is with me in the house, and he hath committed all that he hath to my hand; 9 There is none greater in this house than I; neither hath he kept back any thing from me but thee, because thou art his wife: how then can I do this great wickedness, and sin against God? 10 And it came to pass, as she spake to Joseph day by day, that he hearkened not unto her, to lie by her, or to be with her. 11 And it came to pass about this time, that Joseph went into the house to do his business; and there was none of the men of the house there within. 12 And she caught him by his garment, saying, Lie with me: and he left his garment in her hand, and fled, and got him out.**

Joseph had become the property of Potiphar and served him, but Potiphar had enough sense and insight to recognize that there was something different about this foreigner. Every task he assigned Joseph was successfully completed. Because of his integrity, Joseph was promoted quickly to oversee all the work and people in Potiphar's house.

Even though Joseph was far away from his family, God never left him. God showed the young man loyalty, and blessed the work of his hands. As God showed loyalty to Joseph, Joseph was loyal to Potiphar. Thus, God blessed Potiphar for Joseph's sake. No matter what situation young Joseph encountered on his journey to greatness, it was evident that God was with him. The favor of Joseph's life was not only appealing to Potiphar, but also to Potiphar's wife. Perhaps because Moses did not find it necessary to identify her, we are not given "Mrs. Potiphar's" first name. What she meant for evil, God worked it for good in Joseph's life.

## SEARCH THE SCRIPTURES

### QUESTION 1

What did Potiphar's wife do with Joseph's garment?

**"And she laid up his garment by her, until his lord came home."**

## LIGHT ON THE WORD

### Potiphar's Wife Makes a Terrible Accusation

With Joseph's garment in her hand and Joseph in her power, Potiphar's wife conjures up a story of lies and deception. She accuses Joseph of attempted rape. She not only fabricates a story of sexual assault, but she also slanders the integrity of Potiphar's household. Her remark, "This Hebrew has been brought to us to make sport of us!" (**Genesis 39:14, NIV**), suggests that Joseph has a condescending attitude toward her, his master Potiphar, and his entire household.

By blaming her husband, Potiphar's wife raises the stakes. When she recounts the lie to her husband, she strategically uses the words, "That Hebrew slave that you brought us…" (**Genesis 39:17, NIV**), emphasizing that her husband hired Joseph and brought his supposedly wicked influence into their home. Her assertion is clever; the blame is now on Potiphar's shoulders. He is literally forced to make a hasty decision. She shrewdly implies that Potiphar's integrity is in question.

## II. IN SPITE OF UNJUST CIRCUMSTANCES, GOD IS WITH JOSEPH (Genesis 39:13-21a)

Joseph is placed into another pit and launched into another tribulation. Again, he is not given the opportunity to tell his side of the story or argue against any evidence found against him. He is plunged into his master's prison. Joseph is a victim of a false accusation. Although he

is silenced and thrown into jail, God is with him. Potiphar gave up on him, yet Joseph knew God would not forget him. He did not forget God's promises to him. Joseph refused to give up and remained faithful. He sustained harsh mistreatment and injustice. Truly, the favor of the Lord was with him for his punishment could have been death instead of prison.

Sometimes our decision to remain loyal to God places us on the receiving end of someone else's scorn and anger. Nevertheless, God honors our allegiance to Him. Our commitment to live in accordance with God's Word will orchestrate our choices, navigate our paths, and dictate our behavior. The Lord was with Joseph, and He is with us when we stand on the principles of His Word. Do not give up and compromise what we know is the right thing to do. Do not surrender the opportunity to experience a deeper, richer, and enduring relationship with Jesus Christ. Don't give up doing what is right!

### Refusing to Give Up
### (verses 13–21a)

**13 And it came to pass, when she saw that he had left his garment in her hand, and was fled forth, 14 That she called unto the men of her house, and spake unto them, saying, See, he hath brought in an Hebrew unto us to mock us; he came in unto me to lie with me, and I cried with a loud voice: 15 And it came to pass, when he heard that I lifted up my voice and cried, that he left his garment with me, and fled, and got him out. 16 And she laid up his garment by her, until his lord came home. 17 And she spake unto him according to these words, saying, The Hebrew servant, which thou hast brought unto us, came in unto me to mock me: 18 And it came to pass, as I lifted up my voice and cried, that he left his garment with me, and fled out. 19 And it came to pass, when his master heard the words of his wife, which she spake unto him, saying,**

**After this manner did thy servant to me; that his wrath was kindled. 20 And Joseph's master took him, and put him into the prison, a place where the king's prisoners were bound: and he was there in the prison. 21 But the LORD was with Joseph, and shewed him mercy, and gave him favour in the sight of the keeper of the prison.**

Potiphar did not bother to ask Joseph what happened, or why he thought he could get away with having sexual intercourse with his wife, especially in his house. Instead, he consigned Joseph to a prison that is reserved for the royal servants of the king. Moses does not infer whether Potiphar may have been reluctant to turn Joseph over to the prison, nor does he identify the other prisoners, at least at this time. Still, Moses made this point clear: "But the LORD was with Joseph" (**Genesis 39:21a**).

Though Joseph was wrongfully accused, and his integrity tested by a brazen woman, he could rest assured that, no matter the outcome, God was with him. At the time, Joseph may have felt God was a million miles away, and there was no hope for him in prison. But he received special grace and favor to resist sexual temptation and remained truthful to Potiphar and his God. Jehovah Jireh [God] was truly Joseph's provider, and He demonstrated His nearness to the young Hebrew in prison, too.

### QUESTION 2
How did Potiphar react when he heard his wife's words?

**"His wrath was kindled"—he was very angry. Answers will vary.**

### LIGHT ON THE WORD
What are we willing to leave behind and give up for the sake of our Christian integrity? So many Christians fall in the area of sexual temptation.

Too often, we compromise our Christian values for the sake of self-gratification. Instead of running from temptation, we start walking toward it. We fail also to realize that infidelity does not happen in a vacuum; this sin hurts other people, rips apart families, destroys our testimony and reputation, and strips us of our integrity. Sometimes we have to do like Joseph and literally run from sin!

### BIBLE APPLICATION
**AIM: That your students will see that if they are faithful and obedient to God, He will stay with them.**

#### God Has a Plan
Joseph could not see how his circumstances could be good, but God was using this as an important plan for Joseph's future and for the future of the Jewish people.

### STUDENTS' RESPONSES
**AIM: That your students will commit to faithfulness and loyalty in their relationship with God, because they are trusting that God is working everything out according to His plan for them.**

Peer pressure, loneliness, and a desire to be needed are some reasons why Christians get involved in sexual misconduct. Many individuals want to share their struggles and are afraid of being judged. Over the next week, ask the Lord to lay on your heart someone who is struggling with faithfulness and integrity. Pray and ask the Lord what you can do to help. Follow the Lord's instruction as He guides you in approaching this individual.

### PRAYER
Dear Father, we ask You to help us to be faithful in obeying You, especially in the area of sexual temptations. In Jesus' Name we pray. Amen.

## DIG A LITTLE DEEPER

Diabolical evil renders Joseph a slave and a prisoner, but he rejects unrighteousness and embraces loyalty and faithfulness. Joseph overcame the hatred of his brothers and rejected Potiphar's wife's sexual demands. He embraces loyalty and faithfulness to God and Potiphar, and as a result, God blessed Joseph. Loyal, faithful relationships are critical elements in the story and life of Joseph because sin is not only against people; it is against God **(Genesis 39:9)**. God's blessings are connected to relationships. You don't have a money problem but a relationship problem. After the fall, humans continue dominion but in a sinful, twisted way. Hierarchical, dominating, and oppressive rather than functioning as stewards and thus as a manifestation of God's glory. God summons Joseph into a morally accountable relationship with God and others. His difficult and painful trials finally come to a fantastic and glorious crescendo, as God exalts him to second in command in Egypt. Pain and evil don't have to make us bitter but can make us better. False accusations and evil are opportunities for learning and growth. Human nature says to fight back, hate back, deny and defy, but our God nature says have dominion over that which sin has caused and become a fruitful life-giver. Where death and destruction attempt to stake a claim, cause life to come forth by being faithful. The purpose for Joseph's life is succinctly stated in **Genesis 50:20** "But as for you, you meant evil against me; but God meant it for good, to bring it about as it is this day, to save many people alive".

### DAILY HOME BIBLE READINGS

**MONDAY**
A Man Sent Ahead
(Psalm 105:16–22)

**TUESDAY**
Joseph's Story
(Acts 7:9–16)

**WEDNESDAY**
Facing Temptation
(Luke 22:39–46)

**THURSDAY**
Enduring Temptation
(1 Corinthians 10:1–13)

**FRIDAY**
Choosing the Way of Faithfulness
(Psalm 119:25–32)

**SATURDAY**
A Responsible Servant
(Genesis 39:1–6)

**SUNDAY**
Guided by a Loving Lord
(Genesis 39:7–21a)

## HOW TO SAY IT

Potiphar.      Pot'-i-far.

Joseph.        Jo'-sef.

Hearkened.     Har-kined.

Garment.       Gar'-mint.

## PREPARE FOR NEXT SUNDAY

Read **Genesis 41:37–45, 50–52**, and next week's lesson, "Joseph Finds Favor."

**Sources:**

Berlin, Adele, and Marc Brettler, eds. The Jewish Study Bible. New York, NY: Oxford
University Press, 2004. 78–79.

Bruce, F. F. et al., eds. Zondervan Bible Commentary. Grand Rapids, MI: Zondervan
Publishing, 2008. 50.

Elwell, Walter A., and Philip W. Comfort. Tyndale Bible Dictionary. Wheaton, IL: Tyndale House Publishers, 2001. 736.

Hayford, Jack W., Litt.D. et al., eds. The New Spirit-Filled Life Bible, NKJV. Nashville,
TN: Thomas Nelson Publishers, 2002. 57–58.

Life Application Study Bible (NLT). Wheaton, IL: Tyndale House, 1996.

MacArthur, John. The MacArthur Study Bible, NKJV. Nashville, TN: Thomas Nelson
Publishers, 1997. 72–73.

Mattingly, Gerald L. "Midan, Midianites." The Harper Collins Bible Dictionary. Paul J. Achtemeir et al., eds. San Francisco, CA: HarperCollins Publishers, 1996. 682–683.

The New Interpreters Bible, Vol. I. Nashville, TN: Abingdon Press, 2002. 607–12.

The New Strong's Exhaustive Concordance of the Bible. Nashville, TN: Thomas Nelson Publishers, 1990.

"Potiphar." The Harper Collins Bible Dictionary. Paul J. Achtemeir et al., eds. San Francisco, CA: HarperCollins Publishers, 1996. 867–68

## COMMENTS / NOTES:

# JOSEPH FINDS FAVOR

**BIBLE BASIS:** Genesis 41:37–45, 50–52

**BIBLE TRUTH:** Because Joseph interpreted the dreams of the Egyptian king and had a plan for survival of the nation in a time of famine, Pharaoh had faith in Joseph's abilities, elevated him to the second position in all of Egypt, and gave him responsibility for ruling the day-to-day activities of the kingdom..

**MEMORY VERSE:** "And Pharaoh said unto his servants, Can we find such a one as this is, a man in whom the Spirit of God is?" (Genesis 41:38, KJV).

**LESSON AIM:** By the end of the lesson, we will: STUDY how Joseph's faithfulness is rewarded; EXPLORE how superior performance can lead to honor; and COMMIT to responsible actions and superior performance.

**BACKGROUND SCRIPTURES:** Genesis 41:1-52--Read and incorporate the insights gained from the Background Scriptures into your study of the lesson.

## TEACHER PREPARATION

**MATERIALS NEEDED:** Bibles (several different versions), Quarterly Commentary/Teacher Manual, Adult Quarterly, teaching resources such as charts, worksheets/handouts, paper, pens, and pencils.

**OTHER MATERIALS NEEDED / TEACHER'S NOTES:**

_____

_____

## LESSON OVERVIEW

**LIFE NEED FOR TODAY'S LESSON**
That students will learn that God rewards those who are faithful and obedient to Him.

**BIBLE LEARNING**
To understand that Joseph was rewarded for his faithfulness after a long period of undeserved shame.

**BIBLE APPLICATION**
To learn that God will reward those who are obedient to Him, even though they may go through long periods of trials.

**STUDENTS' RESPONSES**
Students will persevere in their obedience to God, even when they must experience difficulties at first.

## LESSON SCRIPTURE

**GENESIS 41:37-45, 50-52, KJV**

**37** And the thing was good in the eyes of Pharaoh, and in the eyes of all his servants.

**GENESIS 41:37-45, 50-52, AMP**

**37** Now the plan seemed good to Pharaoh and to all of his servants.

**38** And Pharaoh said unto his servants, Can we find such a one as this is, a man in whom the Spirit of God is?

**39** And Pharaoh said unto Joseph, Forasmuch as God hath shewed thee all this, there is none so discreet and wise as thou art:

**40** Thou shalt be over my house, and according unto thy word shall all my people be ruled: only in the throne will I be greater than thou.

**41** And Pharaoh said unto Joseph, See, I have set thee over all the land of Egypt.

**42** And Pharaoh took off his ring from his hand, and put it upon Joseph's hand, and arrayed him in vestures of fine linen, and put a gold chain about his neck;

**43** And he made him to ride in the second chariot which he had; and they cried before him, Bow the knee: and he made him ruler over all the land of Egypt.

**44** And Pharaoh said unto Joseph, I am Pharaoh, and without thee shall no man lift up his hand or foot in all the land of Egypt.

**45** And Pharaoh called Joseph's name Zaphnath-paaneah; and he gave him to wife Asenath the daughter of Poti-pherah priest of On. And Joseph went out over all the land of Egypt.

**41:50** And unto Joseph were born two sons before the years of famine came, which Asenath the daughter of Poti-pherah priest of On bare unto him.

**51** And Joseph called the name of the firstborn Manasseh: For God, said he, hath made me forget all my toil, and all my father's house.

**52** And the name of the second called he Ephraim: For God hath caused me to be fruitful in the land of my affliction.

**38** So Pharaoh said to his servants, "Can we find a man like this [a man equal to Joseph], in whom is the divine spirit [of God]?"

**39** Then Pharaoh said to Joseph, "Since [your] God has shown you all this, there is no one as discerning and clear-headed and wise as you are.

**40** You shall have charge over my house, and all my people shall be governed according to your word and pay respect [to you with reverence, submission, and obedience]; only in [matters of] the throne will I be greater than you [in Egypt]."

**41** Then Pharaoh said to Joseph, "See, I have set you [in charge] over all the land of Egypt."

**42** Then Pharaoh took off his signet ring from his hand and put it on Joseph's hand, and dressed him in [official] vestments of fine linen and put a gold chain around his neck.

**43** He had him ride in his second chariot; and runners proclaimed before him, "[Attention,] bow the knee!" And he set him over all the land of Egypt.

**44** Moreover, Pharaoh said to Joseph, "Though I am Pharaoh, yet without your permission shall no man raise his hand [to do anything] or set his foot [to go anywhere] in all the land of Egypt [all classes of people shall submit to your authority]."

**45** Then Pharaoh named Joseph Zaphenath-paaneah; and he gave him Asenath, the daughter of Potipherah, priest of On (Heliopolis in Egypt), as his wife. And Joseph went out over all the land of Egypt [to inspect and govern it].

land of Egypt [to inspect and govern it].

**41:50** Now two sons were born to Joseph before the years of famine came, whom

Asenath, the daughter of Potiphera, priest of On, bore to him.

51 Joseph named the firstborn Manasseh (causing to forget), for he said, "God has made me forget all my trouble and hardship and all [the sorrow of the loss of] my father's household."

52 He named the second [son] Ephraim (fruitfulness), for "God has caused me to be fruitful and very successful in the land of my suffering."

## BIBLICAL DEFINITIONS

A. **Manasseh (Genesis 41:50–51)** *Me-nashsheh* (Heb.)—Grandson of Jacob; the firstborn son of Joseph and his Egyptian wife, Asenath; the name means "causing to forget."

B. **Ephraim.(v. 52)** *'Ephrayim* (Heb.)—Joseph's younger son, born of Joseph and Asenath before the seven years of famine in Egypt; He was the ancestor of an Israelite tribe, and his name came to designate the Northern Kingdom of Israel.

## LIGHT ON THE WORD

While Joseph languishes in prison, Pharaoh of Egypt has two disturbing dreams. In the first dream, the setting is the Nile, Egypt's lifeline. The first dream

depicts seven lean and fat cows that come out to the Nile and begin to graze. After that, seven hideous and scrawny cows appear and eat the fat ones. In the second dream, seven plump and choice ears of grain grow on one stalk; then seven ears of grain, skinny and parched by the hot desert wind, blossom on that stalk and consume the hearty grain. The dreams imitate each other, and Pharaoh is extremely troubled by these imaginings. The strange makeup of the dreams appears to point to a very gloomy future, a disturbance that Pharaoh cannot control or change. Pharaoh beckons experts to give meaning to the dreams, but none of them provide a suitable analysis.

## TEACHING THE BIBLE LESSON

## LIFE NEED FOR TODAY'S LESSON

**AIM: That your students will commit to responsible actions and superior performance.**

## INTRODUCTION

### Joseph Proves His Wisdom and Is Rewarded

Joseph does more than interpret Pharaoh's dreams. He gives Pharaoh instructions on what he should do to avoid catastrophic damage to the country. He urges Pharaoh to implement a plan to address these events. Pharoah has to make a wise decision and select a man who is judicious and intelligent, someone that can strategically develop a plan of action that enables Egypt to tackle the food crisis in a way that brings the maximum possible safety to all. No doubt, shrewd administrators should also be selected for the job. However, Joseph is confident that God has prepared him for any responsibility that will unfold. Joseph proposes a plan that requires enough food (20 percent of the crop), each year to be stored during the years of prosperity in order to provide a reserve for the years of food crisis. The plan would be implemented by Joseph, yet would be under the authority of Pharaoh.

Little did Joseph know that his ability to interpret dreams would alter his life forever. Joseph, a man once sold into slavery and sentenced to prison, is now catapulted to Pharaoh's palace. Joseph, a man once overconfident in his own human frailties, now stands at the feet of an Egyptian Pharaoh. He is a man now humbled by life circumstances and is on the brink of becoming the second most powerful man in Egypt.

## BIBLE LEARNING

**AIM: That your students will learn that Joseph's faithfulness was rewarded.**

## I. THE FAVOR OF GOD (Genesis 41:37–45)

It is important to recognize that Joseph did not run after fame. He did not bribe his way to the top or manipulate his circumstances. He relied on God and remained obedient to the Lord. Even after experiencing hardship, Joseph endured and waited on the Lord. When it came time for him to stand before Pharaoh, Joseph performed honorably. He did not blame the cupbearer or anyone else for his time in prison. He spoke with confidence and wisdom. He won the heart and favor of Pharaoh, an Egyptian ruler, who neither knew nor served his God. We should see from this study that the Lord has the supernatural ability to work in the lives of those inside and outside the faith community. When we are faithful to our Lord, God can elevate us to positions where we have favor even with those who do not know Jesus. In the positions God calls us to serve, we have the ability to make

enormous contributions that will impact our society for the good. In order for God to use us, however, we must commit to acting responsibly.

This story reminds us of how God works through a humbled heart. Joseph was pulled up from the lowest rungs to lead a people from the highest levels of authority. God worked through the lives of an Egyptian Pharaoh and Hebrew servant. Joseph had no idea that he would be crowned prime minister of Egypt. It is amazing what God can do through our lives when we commit to serving Him faithfully.

**The Favor of God (Genesis 41:37–45)**
**37 And the thing was good in the eyes of Pharaoh, and in the eyes of all his servants. 38 And Pharaoh said unto his servants, Can we find such a one as this is, a man in whom the Spirit of God is? 39 And Pharaoh said unto Joseph, Forasmuch as God hath shewed thee all this, there is none so discreet and wise as thou art: 40 Thou shalt be over my house, and according unto thy word shall all my people be ruled: only in the throne will I be greater than thou. 41 And Pharaoh said unto Joseph, See, I have set thee over all the land of Egypt. 42 And Pharaoh took off his ring from his hand, and put it upon Joseph's hand, and arrayed him in vestures of fine linen, and put a gold chain about his neck; 43 And he made him to ride in the second chariot which he had; and they cried before him, Bow the knee: and he made him ruler over all the land of Egypt. 44 And Pharaoh said unto Joseph, I am Pharaoh, and without thee shall no man lift up his hand or foot in all the land of Egypt. 45 And Pharaoh called Joseph's name Zaphnath-paaneah; and he gave him to wife Asenath the daughter of Potipherah priest of On. And Joseph went out over all the land of Egypt.**

Pharaoh concludes that Joseph's ability to

interpret his dreams serves as evidence that the hand of God rested upon him. There is no way mere human understanding could accomplish this feat; only a divinely inspired revelation could provide such an analysis. Pharaoh decides to make Joseph the prime minister in charge of the palace and the country (verse 40). He is second in command only to Pharaoh, with full range of authority (verses 41, 43). No one has authority to rebel or lift a hand against Joseph. With such authority given to him, Joseph is marked as a wise and discerning man. Pharaoh's position is elevated as well, for it takes an astute leader to recognize wisdom in someone else (verse 44).

Verses 41 through 44 illustrate an act of installation. Joseph is promoted and formally given symbols that designate his new status. Pharaoh gives Joseph his signet ring, gold chain, and garments of royalty. These items signify his prominent new role. Joseph rides in a royal chariot throughout the city while the Egyptians cry out to him, bending their knees in honor of him and acknowledging his role as ruler of Egypt. Pharaoh renames Joseph and calls him Zaphenath-paaneah, which means "God speaks and lives." Pharaoh also gives Joseph a wife from a noble family. Joseph is now established as a man of great esteem, status, and success.

## SEARCH THE SCRIPTURES

### QUESTION 1
What items did Pharaoh give Joseph to signify his new status in Egypt?

He gave Joseph his own ring, plus he dressed him in fine linen, and gave him a gold chain.

## LIGHT ON THE WORD

### Joseph Arrives at a Time of Blessing
Thirty years old and 13 years after his enslavement, Joseph is carrying out the economic program in Egypt. The fruitfulness of the land mirrors Joseph and Asenath's life together. They have two sons, Ephraim and Manasseh. Joseph names them in recognition of God's involvement in his life: Manasseh, because God has enabled Joseph's slavery in Canaan and Egypt to be forgotten; and Ephraim, because God has brought Joseph prosperity in the very land in which he has experienced so much misfortune. These names reveal Joseph's life experience of seeing God's preserving and prospering activity in the midst of great personal hardship.

## II. THE FRUITFULNESS OF GOD (Genesis 41:50–52)

Pharaoh completed the transformation of his new prime minister. He altered his Hebrew name, from Joseph to Zaphnath-Paaneah. The Coptic language states that the name may mean "a revealer of secrets," or "a man in whom secrets are revealed." MacArthur states that Joseph's new name probably meant "the Nourisher of the Two Lands, the Living One," or "for God speaks, and He lives."

### The Fruitfulness of God (Genesis 41:50–52)

**50 And unto Joseph were born two sons before the years of famine came, which Asenath the daughter of Poti-pherah priest of On bare unto him. 51 And Joseph called the name of the first-born Manasseh: For God, said he, hath made me forget all my toil, and all my father's house. 52 And the name of the second called he Ephraim: For God hath caused me to be fruitful in the land of my affliction.**

Then Pharaoh gave Joseph an Egyptian wife named Asenath. Her name meant "one who belongs to the goddess Neith." Moses affirms that she was the daughter of "Potiphera, a priest of On" (verse 45). The name Potiphera in Egyptian means "he whom Ra has given."

Potiphera was probably a very important figure in an Egyptian cult. On was one of the four great Egyptian cities called Heliopolis and was the place where they worshiped the sun god, "Ra." The priests of On often engaged in widely varied commercial, political, and cultic responsibilities. Thus, Joseph was enveloped in Egyptian culture, but never lost his faith and commitment to Jehovah God.

Jewish tradition came to interpret Asenath as a prototype of Judaism conversion. Her powerful story is told at length in an important Hellenistic novella Joseph and Asenath. Joseph was now an "Egyptian" ruler and the prime minister of Pharaoh's entire kingdom. He settled in Egypt and began a family before the famine engulfed the land. He had two sons, born to Asenath. The first was named Manasseh, and the English translation of the Hebrew means "cause to forget" or "forgetful." The second son was called Ephraim, and from the Hebrew, the English word would be "double fruit" or "fruitful." Joseph's experience was tragic, from the time he left his father's home, until his ascendancy to prime minister. From a human perspective, the young man did not want to remember all he endured. His son Manasseh would affirm that Joseph had "turned the corner" on his oppression and difficulties ("toil," **verse 51**), because he had put his trust in the Lord.

Consequently, his son Ephraim would always remind Joseph, that only through God's grace and favor, Joseph had been promoted in Egypt and received increase (was "fruitful") and influence as a result of his faithfulness to the Lord. Even in "the land of [his] affliction," Joseph recognized the centrality of God's compassion and grace. Separation from his father and all that he held dear had not diminished Joseph's perspective that he was still in the hands of God.

## SEARCH THE SCRIPTURES

## QUESTION 2

What names did Joseph give his children and why?

**He called the first son Manasseh, because the Lord made him forget all his toil and his father's house. He called the second son Ephraim, which meant that God had caused him to be fruitful in the land of his affliction. Answers will vary.**

## LIGHT ON THE WORD

Some Christians want quick esteem and instant stardom. We have heard stories of risen and fallen stars, individuals who have plummeted from the height of their success because they lacked the ability to handle the pressure and responsibility. We have also heard stories where God's supposed "favor" has been used to manipulate others for deceitful gain. The church must teach that the favor of God involves commitment and faithfulness to Jesus, and compels superior performance and responsible moral and work ethics.

## BIBLE APPLICATION

**AIM: That your students will continue obeying God, trusting that He will reward them in due time.**

### God's Rewards

God does not always reward us with fame and wonderful jobs in this life. But as **Psalm 23:1** tells us, we shall not want. This means that He will bring us to a place of satisfaction, a place where we need nothing more than what we already have.

## STUDENTS' RESPONSES

**AIM: That your students will not be discouraged in trying times, trusting that good will come to those who display discipline and superior work.**

Ask God to reveal to you where His favor

reigns in your life. Pray and ask God if you are honoring Him with your actions in this area. Listen closely to what He says and commit to changing whatever He tells you to modify.

## PRAYER

Dear Father, we trust that You will reward us in Your time and in Your way. Help us to do our very best in every responsibility we are given. In Jesus' Name, Amen.

## DIG A LITTLE DEEPER

Bishop Tony W. Torain of Baltimore, Maryland preached a message in 2015 entitled "Live in the F.O.G." was an acronym for Favor of God. He encouraged the believers to live victoriously because the Favor of God is over our lives. This grace from God is present in our lives even when there are adversarial circumstances. Joseph demonstates living in the Favor of God consistently throughout his life. His faithfulness and obedience to operating his God-given gifts eventually resulted in promotion. As believers, we must know that the Favor of God is a consistent presence with us and with this knowledge; our lives should be a consistent reflection of God throughout our sphere of influence. What challenges have prevented you from operating your God-given gifts?

### DAILY HOME BIBLE READINGS

**MONDAY**
Interpretations Belong to God
(Genesis 40:1–8)

**TUESDAY**
Restored to Office
(Genesis 40:9–15)

**WEDNESDAY**
The Predictions Come True
(Genesis 40:16–23)

**THURSDAY**
The Interpreter Remembered
(Genesis 41:1–13)

**FRIDAY**
Pharaoh's Dreams
(Genesis 41:14–24)

**SATURDAY**
The Dreams Interpreted
(Genesis 41:25–36)

**SUNDAY**
A Discerning and Wise Leader
(Genesis 41:37–45, 50–52)

## HOW TO SAY IT

| | |
|---|---|
| Pharaoh. | Fair'- oh. |
| Vestures. | Ves-chers. |
| Asenath. | As-uh-nath. |
| Manasseh. | Muh-nas-uh. |
| Ephraim. | Ee-fray-im. |

## PREPARE FOR NEXT SUNDAY

Read **Genesis 45:3-15,** and next week's lesson, "God Preserves a Remnant."

**Sorces:**

Achtemeir, Paul J. et al., eds. The Harper Collins Bible Dictionary. San Francisco,
CA: HarperCollins Publishers, 1996. 82, 544–45, 868.

Berlin, Adele, and Marc Brettler, eds. The Jewish Study Bible. New York, NY: Oxford
University Press, 2004. 81–83.

Bruce, F. F. et al., eds. Zondervan Bible Commentary. Grand Rapids, MI: Zondervan
Publishing, 2008. 50–52.

Elwell, Walter A., and Philip W. Comfort. Tyndale Bible Dictionary. Wheaton, IL: Tyndale House Publishers, 2001. 736–37.

"Genesis 41." John Gill's Exposition of the Bible. Bible Study Tools.com. http://www.biblestudytools.com/commentaries/gills-exposition-of-the-bible/genesis-41-43.html (accessed December 12, 2010).

MacArthur, John. The MacArthur Study Bible. Nashville, TN: Thomas Nelson Publishers, 1997. 74–76.

The New Interpreters Bible, Vol. I. Nashville, TN: Abingdon Press, 2002. 617–24.
The New Strong's Exhaustive Concordance of the Bible. Nashville, TN: Thomas Nelson
Publishers, 1990.

## COMMENTS / NOTES:

# GOD PRESERVES A REMNANT

**BIBLE BASIS:** Genesis 45:3 - 15

**BIBLE TRUTH:** Jacob and Joseph were both faithful to God, and God remained faithful to His promise to Abraham by putting Joseph in a position to save his entire family from starvation..

**MEMORY VERSE:** "So now it was not you that sent me hither, but God: and he hath made me a father to Pharaoh, and lord of all his house, and a ruler throughout all the land of Egypt" (Genesis 45:8, KJV).

**LESSON AIM:** By the end of the lesson, we will: KNOW the story of Joseph reuniting with his brothers; FEEL protected and supported by people in the Faith Community; and PROTECT and support other members of our Faith Community.

**BACKGROUND SCRIPTURES:** Genesis 42:1–38; 45:1–28 -- Read and incorporate the insights gained from the Background Scriptures into your study of the lesson.

## TEACHER PREPARATION

**MATERIALS NEEDED:** Bibles (several different versions), Quarterly Commentary/Teacher Manual, Adult Quarterly, teaching resources such as charts, worksheets/handouts, paper, pens, and pencils.

**OTHER MATERIALS NEEDED / TEACHER'S NOTES:**

_____

_____

## LESSON OVERVIEW

**LIFE NEED FOR TODAY'S LESSON**
That students will learn that God desires His people to care for one another.

**BIBLE LEARNING**
To understand that God cared for Joseph and Jacob's family because they were faithful to Him.

**BIBLE APPLICATION**
Students will learn that God will preserve His people.

**STUDENTS' RESPONSES**
Students will demonstrate acts of caring for members of their class or families throughout this week.

## LESSON SCRIPTURE

### GENESIS 45:3–15, KJV

**3** And Joseph said unto his brethren, I am Joseph; doth my father yet live? And his brethren could not answer him; for

### GENESIS 45:3–15, AMP

**3** Then Joseph said to his brothers, "I am Joseph! Is my father still alive?" But his brothers were speechless, for they were

187

they were troubled at his presence.

**4** And Joseph said unto his brethren, Come near to me, I pray you. And they came near. And he said, I am Joseph your brother, whom ye sold into Egypt.

**5** Now therefore be not grieved, nor angry with yourselves, that ye sold me hither: for God did send me before you to preserve life.

**6** For these two years hath the famine been in the land: and yet there are five years, in the which there shall neither be earing nor harvest.

**7** And God sent me before you to preserve you a posterity in the earth, and to save your lives by a great deliverance.

**8** So now it was not you that sent me hither, but God: and he hath made me a father to Pharaoh, and lord of all his house, and a ruler throughout all the land of Egypt.

**9** Haste ye, and go up to my father, and say unto him, Thus saith thy son Joseph, God hath made me lord of all Egypt: come down unto me, tarry not:

**10** And thou shalt dwell in the land of Goshen, and thou shalt be near unto me, thou, and thy children, and thy children's children, and thy flocks, and thy herds, and all that thou hast:

**11** And there will I nourish thee; for yet there are five years of famine; lest thou, and thy household, and all that thou hast, come to poverty.

**12** And, behold, your eyes see, and the eyes of my brother Benjamin, that it is my mouth that speaketh unto you.

**13** And ye shall tell my father of all my glory in Egypt, and of all that ye have seen; and ye shall haste and bring down my father hither.

stunned and dismayed by [the fact that they were in] Joseph's presence.

**4** And Joseph said to his brothers, "Please come closer to me." And they approached him. And he said, "I am Joseph your brother, whom you sold into Egypt.

**5** Now do not be distressed or angry with yourselves because you sold me here, for God sent me ahead of you to save life and preserve our family.

**6** For the famine has been in the land these two years, and there are still five more years in which there will be no plowing and harvesting.

**7** God sent me [to Egypt] ahead of you to preserve for you a remnant on the earth, and to keep you alive by a great escape.

**8** So now it was not you who sent me here, but God; and He has made me a father to Pharaoh and lord of all his household and ruler over all the land of Egypt.

**9** Hurry and go up to my father, and tell him, 'Your son Joseph says this to you: "God has made me lord of all Egypt; come down to me, do not delay.

**10** You shall live in the land of Goshen [the best pasture land of Egypt], and you shall be close to me—you and your children and your grandchildren, your flocks and your herds and all you have.

**11** There I will provide for you and sustain you, so that you and your household and all that are yours may not become impoverished, for there are still five years of famine to come."'

**12** Look! Your eyes see, and the eyes of my brother Benjamin see, that I am speaking to you [personally in your language and not through an interpreter].

**14** And he fell upon his brother Benjamin's neck, and wept; and Benjamin wept upon his neck.

**15** Moreover he kissed all his brethren, and wept upon them: and after that his brethren talked with him.

**13** Now you must tell my father of all my splendor and power in Egypt, and of everything that you have seen; and you must hurry and bring my father down here."

**14** Then he embraced his brother Benjamin's neck and wept, and Benjamin wept on his neck.

**15** He kissed all his brothers and wept on them, and afterward his brothers talked with him.

## BIBLICAL DEFINITIONS

A. **Earing (Genesis 45:6)** *chariysh* (Heb.)—Plowing; plowing time.

B. **Nourish (v. 11)** *kuwl* (Heb.)—Feed, attend to, contain, sustain, endure.

## LIGHT ON THE WORD

Joseph was a man who honored God, in every situation he found himself; whether it was suffering or success, he honored the one true and living God. Potiphar's wife tried to tempt him, but because Joseph wanted to honor his Master, he would not yield (**Genesis 39:9**). Although God had given him the ability to interpret dreams, Joseph always gave God the credit for being able to do so (**Genesis 40:8**). Even when he was before Pharaoh, he honored God, his maker. Joseph boldly told Pharaoh there would be a specific number of years with plenty of famine that would surely follow (**Genesis 41:14–36**). When Joseph named his own son, Manasseh (which means "to forget"), he was stating that God helped him to forget his sorrow.

## TEACHING THE BIBLE LESSON

## LIFE NEED FOR TODAY'S LESSON

AIM: That your students will not take revenge on those who have hurt them, but will forgive them and embrace them.

## INTRODUCTION

### Joseph Revealed Himself to His Brothers

In today's lesson, Joseph told his brothers who he was and acknowledged that God was responsible for him being in Egypt. After Jacob died, Joseph reassured his brothers that God had ordered his steps, and He did it for the good of all. He further assured them they should not be afraid of him because he was not God (**Genesis 50:15–21**).

## BIBLE LEARNING

AIM: That your students will treat others with respect, even those who have harmed them.

## I. JOSEPH MAKES HIMSELF KNOWN (Genesis 45:3–8)

After having held back his emotions as best he could for quite a while, Joseph told his brothers who he really was: "I am Joseph" (**verse 3**). His brothers did not know him as Joseph. They knew him by his Egyptian name, Zaphnath-paaneah. His Hebrew name had been lost and seemingly forgotten in Egypt. Now he boldly states, "I am Joseph." So they wouldn't be confused about who he really was, he gave them more details: "I am Joseph, your brother" (**verse 4**). In knowing exactly who he was, this would likely humble them as they remembered what they had done. In addition, they might also be hopeful that Joseph might be compassionate toward them.

### Joseph Makes Himself Known
### (Genesis 45:3–8)

**3 And Joseph said unto his brethren, I am Joseph; doth my father yet live? And his brethren could not answer him; for they were troubled at his presence. 4 And Joseph said unto his brethren, Come near to me, I pray you. And they came near. And he said, I am Joseph your brother, whom ye sold into Egypt. 5 Now therefore be not grieved, nor angry with yourselves, that ye sold me hither: for God did send me before you to preserve life. 6 For these two years hath the famine been in the land: and yet there are five years, in the which there shall neither be earing nor harvest. 7 And God sent me before you to preserve you a posterity in the earth, and to save your lives by a great deliverance. 8 So now it was not you that sent me hither, but God: and he hath made me a father to Pharaoh, and lord of all his house, and a ruler throughout all the land of Egypt.**

But now that they knew who Joseph really was, they were afraid and stood in disbelief or amazement, unable to move or speak. Joseph saw their concern and tried to ease their minds. He called out to them, beckoning them closer and assuring them that they didn't have reason to fear. This was reflective of Christ when He manifests Himself. He urges His people to come near to Him as He draws near to them.

A shift was under way in Joseph's character development. At first, when he no longer held back his identity, he was quite emotional. Then he spoke quietly to his brothers and became calm in his demeanor as he offered more details about himself and the depth of his true nature.

Joseph began to assure them of God's sovereignty. He understood and wanted them to understand that whatever they tried to do for evil, God meant it for good and a lot of good came out of it. He did not want them to grieve or be angry with themselves for selling him (**verse 5**). Instead of having a vindictive attitude toward them, he was giving recognition to who God is, what God had done, and what He was going to do. God had a perfect plan in mind and was about to use the brother's sinful acts to preserve a remnant of His chosen people.

In **verses 7** and **8,** Joseph's statements weren't meant to make light of sin or sinners, but rather to illuminate how God does things. This was not to give an excuse for sinning, but rather to appreciate and celebrate the almighty power of God in those things we could refer to as "misfortunes." God is in divine control.

Joseph further explained how long the famine would last, reflecting that it had already been occurring for the past two years. He reassured them that he was in a position to help his family in their dire circumstances. He emphasized that they weren't the ones who sent him ahead to Egypt, but an all-knowing God had done this (**verse 8**). God not only sent Joseph, but God made him "a father" to Pharaoh, "lord of all his house, and a ruler throughout all the land of Egypt" (**verse 8**).

## SEARCH THE SCRIPTURES

### QUESTION 1

When Joseph announced himself to his brothers, and asked if his father was alive, why couldn't his brothers answer him?

They were troubled when they realized who he was.

## LIGHT ON THE WORD

Joseph Assures His Brothers Concerning Their Father

Again in an effort to make his brothers feel more confident and secure, Joseph promised to take care of his father and all his family during the next years of the famine. He urged his brothers to hurry back to Canaan (the Promised Land) to get this news to their father Jacob and let him know about Joseph's authority in Egypt. Joseph was well and had enough power to help them all. "I will nourish thee," promised Joseph (**verse 11**). He was delighted to be in the position to help his father and his family. He was excited for his father to know where God had placed him, and he was eager to relieve his father of the stress of the famine.

## II. JOSEPH SENDS FOR HIS FATHER (Genesis 45:9-15)

Benjamin one of Joseph's brothers, was approximately one year old when Joseph was separated from his family and was too young to have had any involvement in the other brothers' maltreatment. He was to young to have known Joseph before he was sent away, but Joseph remembered him and he hugged Benjamin. They began to weep on each other's neck (**verse 14**). Then Joseph hugged and wept with all of them, and everyone "talked freely" (**verse 15**). Joseph's words and actions made his brothers realize that he was not holding a grudge and was genuinely affectionate toward them. Knowing what God had done for all of them and would do in the future, Joseph was compassionate toward the brothers who had hurt him so much. He did not let past experiences with his brothers defeat the purpose of all that the Lord allowed him to go through. Instead Joseph was warm toward them, and they were able to reciprocate

these feelings.

### Joseph Sends For His Father
(verses 9–15)

**9 Haste ye, and go up to my father, and say unto him, Thus saith thy son Joseph, God hath made me lord of all Egypt: come down unto me, tarry not: 10 And thou shalt dwell in the land of Goshen, and thou shalt be near unto me, thou, and thy children, and thy children's children, and thy flocks, and thy herds, and all that thou hast: 11 And there will I nourish thee; for yet there are five years of famine; lest thou, and thy household, and all that thou hast, come to poverty. 12 And, behold, your eyes see, and the eyes of my brother Benjamin, that it is my mouth that speaketh unto you. 13 And ye shall tell my father of all my glory in Egypt, and of all that ye have seen; and ye shall haste and bring down my father hither. 14 And he fell upon his brother Benjamin's neck, and wept; and Benjamin wept upon his neck. 15 Moreover he kissed all his brethren, and wept upon them: and after that his brethren talked with him.**

Joseph then charged his brothers to hasten and return to their father with the good news of his life, appointment, and favor. Joseph sent his brothers away with a message of hope and celebration. He invited his brothers and father to come and dwell in the land of Goshen, a region in northern Egypt east of the lower Nile, where they could be near him and enjoy all the rights, privileges, and protection suitable to his kin. (The Children of Israel lived there from the time of Joseph to the time of Moses.) Joseph's invitation extended to his brothers' children, their flocks of sheep and goats and their herds of cattle and oxen.

## QUESTION 2

Where was Joseph's family going to live?

His family would live in Goshen, in the northern part of Egypt. Answers will vary.

## LIGHT ON THE WORD

Tragedy is happening all around us and the first question is, why? In recent years, Chicago's public schools have suffered the loss of too many students due to gang and gun violence. God is speaking through these circumstances to show people who He is. It may appear as though the enemy is having his way, but we can be assured that God's plan is being fulfilled for His perfect purpose.

## BIBLE APPLICATION

**AIM: That your students will remember their brothers and sisters when God elevates them to high positions.**

### Treatment of Our Brothers and Sisters in Christ

Living in our world can prove to be disappointing at times. When we come to church, we should expect to be treated differently. Joseph's brothers didn't know what to expect after finding out who Joseph was, the position he held, and remembering what they had done to him. Joseph relieved them of their worries by embracing them and being very kind. As we interact with our brothers and sisters in Christ, let us try to adopt Joseph's attitude toward others, especially family members. Let us remember to be kind and warm to others always.

## STUDENTS' RESPONSES

**AIM: That your students will go home and demonstrate love for their families today.**

Consider this: Satan's plan was to use Pontius Pilate, Judas Iscariot, the mob in the streets, and the cruel Roman soldiers to end the plan God had for Jesus Christ. How did these men's actions actually fulfill God's divine plan of salvation for humankind through His only Son, Jesus Christ? Compare and contrast this example from the New Testament with the actions of Joseph's brothers, before and after they encountered him in Egypt.

## PRAYER

Dear Father, we thank You for the good times that come in our lives. Help us to make sure we help our brothers and sisters in those times. In Jesus' Name, Amen.

## DIG A LITTLE DEEPER

"Get Over It" is a common refrain given when a person begins to rehearse the hurt and pain resulting from a person or action in thier past. While this statement is meant to encourage the person to move beyond this stage, it often results in the devaluing of the person's emotions. As long as the person is in this stage, they are incapable of moving forward with their lives or relationships. Rather than "get over it", we should practice "work through it". Joseph was able to receive his brothers after their mistreatment because he worked through his circumstances with God's help. (**Genesis 45:5-8**) Many families have long-term discord and broken relationships due to past hurts. We are encouraged and challenged by the Word on today to preserve our family relationships.

## HOW TO SAY IT

| Canaan. | KAY-nuhn. |
|---|---|
| Genesis. | JEN-uh-sis. |
| Midianites. | MID-ee-uh-nit'. |
| Pharaoh. | FER-oh, FAY-roh. |

# DAILY HOME BIBLE READINGS

## MONDAY
A Famine in Canaan
(Genesis 42:1–5)

## TUESDAY
Joseph Recognized His Brothers
(Genesis 42:6–17)

## WEDNESDAY
Paying the Penalty
(Genesis 42:18–25)

## THURSDAY
Hold Me Accountable
(Genesis 43:1–14)

## FRIDAY
Benjamin Detained in Egypt
(Genesis 44:1–13)

## SATURDAY
A Father's Suffering
(Genesis 44:24–34)

## SUNDAY
A Brother Revealed
(Genesis 45:3–15)

Read **Genesis 50:15–26,** and next week's lesson, "Joseph Transmits Abraham's Promise."

**Sources:**
Henry, Matthew. "Commentary on Genesis 45." Blue Letter Bible.org. http://www.blueletterbible.org/commentaries/Henry/ (accessed December 11, 2010).

Life Application Study Bible (New Living Translation). Wheaton, IL: Tyndale House, 1996. 81–82.

Merriam-Webster Online Dictionary. Merriam-Webster, Inc. http://www.merriam-webster.com (accessed August 13, 2010).

The Origin of the Amber Plan. Mid Ohio AMBER Alert.org. http://www.midohioamberalert.org/origin_Amber.htm (accessed August 28, 2010).

Youngblood, Ronald F., ed. Nelson's New Illustrated Bible Dictionary. Nashville, TN: Thomas Nelson, 1995. 704–05.

Achtemeir, Paul J. et al., eds. The Harper Collins Bible Dictionary. San Francisco, CA: HarperCollins Publishers, 1996. 82, 544–45, 868.

Berlin, Adele, and Marc Brettler, eds. The Jewish Study Bible. New York, NY: Oxford University Press, 2004. 81–83.

Bruce, F. F. et al., eds. Zondervan Bible Commentary. Grand Rapids, MI: Zondervan Publishing, 2008. 50–52.

Elwell, Walter A., and Philip W. Comfort. Tyndale Bible Dictionary. Wheaton, IL: Tyndale House Publishers, 2001. 736–37.

"Genesis 41." John Gill's Exposition of the Bible. Bible Study Tools.com. http://www.biblestudytools.com/commentaries/gills-exposition-of-the-bible/genesis-41-43.html (accessed December 12, 2010).

MacArthur, John. The MacArthur Study Bible. Nashville, TN: Thomas Nelson Publishers, 1997. 74–76.

The New Interpreters Bible, Vol. I. Nashville, TN: Abingdon Press, 2002. 617–24.

The New Strong's Exhaustive Concordance of the Bible. Nashville, TN: Thomas Nelson Publishers, 1990.

## COMMENTS / NOTES:

_____

_____

_____

_____

_____

_____

_____

_____

_____

_____

_____

_____

_____

_____

_____

_____

_____

_____

_____

_____

_____

# JOSEPH TRANSMITS ABRAHAM'S PROMISE

**BIBLE BASIS:** Genesis 50:15–26

**BIBLE TRUTH:** Because Jacob and Joseph were both faithful to God; Joseph was able to forgive his brothers' treachery from so many years before..

**MEMORY VERSE:** "But as for you, ye thought evil against me; but God meant it unto good, to bring to pass, as it is this day, to save much people alive" (Genesis 50:20, KJV).

**LESSON AIM:** By the end of the lesson, we will: KNOW how Joseph forgave his brothers; FEEL thankful for forgiveness; and FORGIVE those who need to be forgiven in our lives.

**BACKGROUND SCRIPTURES:** Genesis 50:1-26--Read and incorporate the insights gained from the Background Scriptures into your study of the lesson

## TEACHER PREPARATION

**MATERIALS NEEDED:** Bibles (several different versions), Quarterly Commentary/Teacher Manual, Adult Quarterly, teaching resources such as charts, worksheets/handouts, paper, pens, and pencils.

**OTHER MATERIALS NEEDED / TEACHER'S NOTES:**

_____

_____

## LESSON OVERVIEW

**LIFE NEED FOR TODAY'S LESSON**
That students will learn that God wants them to forgive those who have hurt them.

**BIBLE LEARNING**
To understand that God teaches forgiveness all through Scripture.

**BIBLE APPLICATION**
To learn that God gave Joseph a happy ending because he obeyed God and forgave his brothers.

**STUDENTS' RESPONSES**
Students will purge from their hearts any attitudes of anger toward those who have harmed them.

## LESSON SCRIPTURE

### GENESIS 50:15–26, KJV

**15** And when Joseph's brethren saw that their father was dead, they said, Joseph will

### GENESIS 50:15–26, AMP

**15** When Joseph's brothers saw that their father was dead, they said, "What if Joseph peradventure hate us, and will certainly requite us all the evil which we did unto him.

**16** And they sent a messenger unto Joseph, saying, Thy father did command before he died, saying,

**17** So shall ye say unto Joseph, Forgive, I pray thee now, the trespass of thy brethren, and their sin; for they did unto thee evil: and now, we pray thee, forgive the trespass of the servants of the God of thy father. And Joseph wept when they spake unto him.

**18** And his brethren also went and fell down before his face; and they said, Behold, we be thy servants.

**19** And Joseph said unto them, Fear not: for am I in the place of God?

**20** But as for you, ye thought evil against me; but God meant it unto good, to bring to pass, as it is this day, to save much people alive.

**21** Now therefore fear ye not: I will nourish you, and your little ones. And he comforted them, and spake kindly unto them.

**22** And Joseph dwelt in Egypt, he, and his father's house: and Joseph lived an hundred and ten years.

**23** And Joseph saw Ephraim's children of the third generation: the children also of Machir the son of Manasseh were brought up upon Joseph's knees.

**24** And Joseph said unto his brethren, I die: and God will surely visit you, and bring you out of this land unto the land which he sware to Abraham, to Isaac, and to Jacob.

**25** And Joseph took an oath of the children of Israel, saying, God will surely visit you, and ye shall carry up my bones from hence.

carries a grudge against us and pays us back in full for all the wrong which we did to him?"

**16** So they sent word to Joseph, saying, "Your father commanded us before he died, saying,

**17** 'You are to say to Joseph, "I beg you, please forgive the transgression of your brothers and their sin, for they did you wrong."' Now, please forgive the transgression of the servants of the God of your father." And Joseph wept when they spoke to him.

**18** Then his brothers went and fell down before him [in confession]; then they said, "Behold, we are your servants (slaves)."

**19** But Joseph said to them, "Do not be afraid, for am I in the place of God? [Vengeance is His, not mine.]

**20** As for you, you meant evil against me, but God meant it for good in order to bring about this present outcome, that many people would be kept alive [as they are this day].

**21** So now, do not be afraid; I will provide for you and support you and your little ones." So he comforted them [giving them encouragement and hope] and spoke [with kindness] to their hearts.

**22** Now Joseph lived in Egypt, he and his father's household, and Joseph lived a hundred and ten years.

**23** Joseph saw the third generation of Ephraim's children; also the children of Machir, the son of Manasseh, were born and raised on Joseph's knees.

**24** Joseph said to his brothers, "I am about to die, but God will surely take care of you and bring you up out of this land to the land which He promised to Abraham, to Isaac, and to Jacob [to give you]."

26 So Joseph died, being an hundred and ten years old: and they embalmed him, and he was put in a coffin in Egypt

25 Then Joseph made the sons of Israel (Jacob) swear [an oath], saying, "God will surely visit you and take care of you [returning you to Canaan], and [when that happens] you shall carry my bones up from here."

26 So Joseph died, being a hundred and ten years old; and they embalmed him and he was put in a coffin in Egypt.

## BIBLICAL DEFINITIONS

A. **Requite (Genesis 50:15)** *shuwb* (Heb.)—Return again, turn back, turn away, restore.

B. **Sent (v. 16)** *tsavah* (tsaw-VAW) (Heb.)—Charged or commanded by another with a verbal communication.

## LIGHT ON THE WORD

The Lord calls Abraham out of Ur **(Genesis 12:1–3)** and makes promises to him. Included in those promises was that Abraham's seed would be a stranger in a land that wasn't theirs **(Genesis 15:13)**. This prophecy was being fulfilled when Jacob took his entire family to Egypt, where Joseph was the chief official after only Pharaoh, himself. After being afflicted for many years, Joseph earned a reputation as being one who could interpret dreams. One day, the Pharaoh of Egypt had a dream that no one can interpret; and Joseph was called to interpret Pharaoh's dream. Afterward, Pharaoh implemented Joseph's recommendation that he find a discreet, wise overseer of Egypt and selected Joseph for the role **(Genesis 41:25–57)**. As foretold, a severe famine came throughout the region. However, because God had prepared Egypt through Joseph, all countries came there to buy corn as supervised by Joseph **(verse 57)**. Jacob's sons—Joseph's brothers—were impacted by the famine and came to Egypt to have their needs met. Joseph recognized his brothers, although they did not recognize him, and he used this as an opportunity to demonstrate forgiveness.

## TEACHING THE BIBLE LESSON

## LIFE NEED FOR TODAY'S LESSON

**AIM: That your students will not take revenge on those who have hurt them, but will forgive and embrace them.**

## INTRODUCTION

### Joseph's Brothers Were Afraid of Him

Now Jacob, father of Joseph and his brothers was dead. Joseph's brothers were feeling guilty for what they had done to him. They worried that Joseph might have felt a surge of bad memories about his youth, and they became suspicious that he would seek revenge on them. Joseph's actions did not exemplify this at all, he was sincere in his motives and showed them nothing less than complete forgiveness. Still, his brothers were sure Joseph would hate them for what they had done.

## BIBLE LEARNING

**AIM: That your students will treat others with respect, even those who have harmed them.**

## I. JOSEPH'S REASSURANCE OF HIS BROTHERS (Genesis 50:15-21)

In response to their fears these brothers humbled themselves, confessed their wrongdoing, and begged Joseph to forgive them. At first, they sent a message to Joseph and then they went in person, stressing that Jacob told them to ask Joseph to forgive his brothers. Joseph reassured them he indeed forgave them because of what God had done in him. He knew that despite the trauma of his youth, God remained faithful to him and that whatever situation he found himself in, God always brought him out.

### Joseph Reassures
### (Genesis 50:15–21)

**15 And when Joseph's brethren saw that their father was dead, they said, Joseph will peradventure hate us, and will certainly requite us all the evil which we did unto him. 16 And they sent a messenger unto Joseph, saying, Thy father did command before he died, saying, 17 So shall ye say unto Joseph, Forgive, I pray thee now, the trespass of thy brethren, and their sin; for they did unto thee evil: and now, we pray thee, forgive the trespass of the servants of the God of thy father. And Joseph wept when they spake unto him. 18 And his brethren also went and fell down before his face; and they said, Behold, we be thy servants. 19 And Joseph said unto them, Fear not: for am I in the place of God? 20 But as for you, ye thought evil against me; but God meant it unto good, to bring to pass, as it is this day, to save much people alive. 21 Now therefore fear ye not: I will nourish you, and your little ones. And he comforted them, and spake kindly unto them.**

Joseph's brothers even went so far as to say they would be his servants (his "slaves," **verse 18,** NIV). They were really trying to mend the relationship. Joseph felt sad and began to weep, this moment was bittersweet. He was sad because they still felt the need to suspect his motives, even after a lengthy period of his support of them in Egypt. He was moved because he saw their efforts at genuine repentance.

Joseph assured them there was no need to be afraid, he also asked, "Am I in the place of God?" (**verse 19,** NIV), which focused their attention on the true, ultimate source of forgiveness of sin. Joseph reminded his brothers that they were intending to do evil against him, but God used their cruelty to bring about good to people who were not even related to them (the Egyptians). By comforting them he demonstrated there was no need to be afraid. Joseph's attitude helped them to release their fears.

## SEARCH THE SCRIPTURES

### QUESTION 1
Why did Joseph's brothers seek his forgiveness?

**They knew they had done a very evil thing to Joseph.**

## LIGHT ON THE WORD
### Joseph Lived a Long Life
Joseph lived to be 110 years old. He had honored his father and was given many days on this earth. Joseph was given the privilege of seeing his great-grandchildren from both his sons, this was indeed a blessing in itself. God blessed Joseph for his faithfulness.

## II. JOSEPH'S LAST DAYS (Genesis 50:22-26)

Joseph knew his death was approaching and there were some things he wanted those who were still living to know. He had his children, nieces, nephews, and grandchildren make a promise to him. First, he assured them that even though he was about to die, they would still return to Canaan in due time. These words were intended to give them hope and assurance. Joseph had already done a great deal for them and now he was dying. Undoubtedly, their thoughts turned to questions of what would become of them after Joseph, who had nourished them and taken good care of them was gone. Joseph probably sensed their apprehension and tried to offer them comfort.

He went on to say, "God will surely visit you" (**verse 24**). Joseph was passing on, but God's care of them would make up for his absence. Although Joseph had been taking care of them, now they could see that it had been God's doing all along. Through Joseph, God provided comfort for them and they would continue to live comfortably. Joseph further encouraged them, letting them know that God would bring them back to the land of Abraham, Isaac, and Jacob.

Joseph made them promise to bury him in Canaan instead of Egypt where he would die, they honored his request. He was put in a coffin in Egypt, but he wasn't buried until his children had received their inheritance in Canaan.

### Joseph's Last Wish (verses 22–26)

**22 And Joseph dwelt in Egypt, he, and his father's house: and Joseph lived an hundred and ten years. 23 And Joseph saw Ephraim's children of the third generation: the children also of Machir the son of Manasseh were brought up upon Joseph's knees. 24 And Joseph said unto his brethren, I die: and God will surely visit you, and bring you out of this land unto the land which he sware to Abraham, to Isaac, and to Jacob. 25 And Joseph took an oath of the children of Israel, saying, God will surely visit you, and ye shall carry up my bones from hence. 26 So Joseph died, being an hundred and ten years old: and they embalmed him, and he was put in a coffin in Egypt.**

Israel's patriarch Jacob lived 147 years, 17 of them in the land of Goshen (**Genesis 47:27–28**), a fertile region in the eastern delta of the Nile River in Egypt. It is here that Jacob and his family settled once they came into the land. He was finally able to spend the remainder of his life with Joseph, his favorite son (**Genesis 37:3**). Before Jacob died, he blessed all of his sons, emphasizing the promise and provision that would follow God's people throughout their history (**Genesis 49:28**).

Joseph, his 11 brothers, and a large entourage of Egyptians traveled to Canaan to bury Jacob in the cave of Machpelah, the same burial site of Abraham, Sarah, Isaac, Rebekah, and Leah. When the family returned to Egypt, the realization of Jacob's death finally set in with the brothers (**Genesis 49:30**). What would their relationship with Joseph be now that Jacob's powerful influence was gone? Would Joseph finally exact revenge on them for the way they had treated him?

Joseph was an important figure in Egypt, and he had already demonstrated his authority over his brothers see (**Genesis 42–45:3**). Now that Jacob was gone the brothers surmised that Joseph would not only hate them, but he would also "requite [them] all the evil" they had done to him (**Genesis 50:15**). To a large extent the brothers were saying, "Joseph is going to treat us as we have treated him."

Bruce (a Bible scholar) suggests that one of the reasons why the brothers may have been fearful and intimidated by Joseph was the long memory for vengeance that was often prevalent in the Ancient Near East (**Genesis 27:41**). Certainly, an Old Testament concept of "an eye for an eye, and a tooth for a tooth" (**Exodus 21:24; Leviticus 24:19–20; Deuteronomy 19:21**) teaches that revenge is appropriate and just, especially in civil matters. Jesus came to teach us a higher law called love. We may feel that our cause is just and right in retaliating against another, but does that satisfy the purposes and plans of Christ?

## QUESTION 2

What demand did Joseph make to the Children of Israel concerning his death?

**He told them to take his bones back to the Promised Land—"and ye shall carry up my bones from hence."**

## LIGHT ON THE WORD

Faith and forgiveness work together, the same faith to live our lives also gives us the strength to forgive. Joseph had faith in God about the promise, he also had faith in the promise God had given to Abraham and was able to forgive his brothers because he knew they would see the Promised Land. Abraham believed God, and Joseph believed God as demonstrated by the request to have his body buried in the land God had promised his great-grandfather, Abraham.

## BIBLE APPLICATION

**AIM: That your students will remember their brothers and sisters when God elevates them to high positions.**

### Treatment of Our Brothers and Sisters in Christ

Living in our world can prove to be disappointing at times. When we come to church we should expect to be treated differently. Joseph's brothers didn't know what to expect after finding out who Joseph was, the position he held, and remembering what they had done to him. Joseph relieved them of their worries by embracing them and being very kind. As we interact with our brothers and sisters in Christ, let us try to adopt Joseph's attitude toward others, especially family members. Let us remember to be kind and warm to others

always.

## STUDENTS' RESPONSES

**AIM: That your students will go home and demonstrate love for their families today.**

Joseph is an example to us all in how he approached hurtful family issues. He did not let past issues affect how he treated his brothers and neither should we. We should follow his example in both our flesh-and-blood families and our brothers and sisters at church.

## PRAYER

Dear Father, we pray that we will live lives of faith and that we will always be quick to forgive others. In Jesus' Name. Amen.

## DIG A LITTLE DEEPER

We associate promise with positive outcomes or times of celebration. The fulfillment of the promise requires a process. The promise to Abraham required a period where his seed was enslaved in a foreign land. In order o fulfill the promise, Joseph had to be forsaken by his brothers, lied on by his employer, unjustly incarcerated and forgotten by those he helped. Joseph probably at some time was angry toward his brothers and his unfortunate situations. However, over time and through intervention of God, Joseph was able to see his situations as working of God in his life. He did not use those situations to remain bitter toward his family. Through the hand of God, he was able to extend forgiveness to his family and in turn maintain the promise of Abraham. Joseph's behavior is imagery of Jesus who suffered on our behalf and extended forgiveness toward us so that we may have the ultimate promise of eternal life.

## HOW TO SAY IT

Requite. Re-quite.

Egypt. E'-jipt.

Ephraim. Ef"-ra-im.

Machir. Ma'-kir.

## DAILY HOME BIBLE READINGS

### MONDAY
A Divine Confirmation
(Genesis 46:1–7)

### TUESDAY
A Divine Confirmation
(Genesis 46:1–7)

### WEDNESDAY
A Father's Heritage
(Genesis 48:8–16)

### THURSDAY
A Father's Blessing
(Genesis 49:22–26)

### FRIDAY
A Father's Final Wish
(Genesis 49:29—50:6)

### SATURDAY
A Child's Final Duty
(Genesis 50:7–14)

### SUNDAY
Reconciliation in the Family
(Genesis 50:15–26)

## PREPARE FOR NEXT SUNDAY

Read **Exodus 15:1–3, 19, 22–26,** and next week's lesson, "Out of Egypt."

**Sources:**
Achtemeir, Paul J. et al., eds. The Harper Collins Bible Dictionary. San Francisco, CA: HarperCollins Publishers, 1996. 477–79, 544–45.

Baltes, A. J., ed. Biblespeech.com. http://www.biblespeech.com (accessed August 11, 2010).

Berlin, Adele, and Marc Brettler. The Jewish Study Bible. New York, NY: Oxford University Press, 2004. 99–101.

Brown, Raymond E., Joseph A. Fitzmyer, and Roland E. Murphy, eds. Genesis: New Jerome Biblical Commentary. Englewood Cliffs, NJ: Prentice Hall, 1990. 42–43.

Bruce, F. F. et al., eds. Zondervan Bible Commentary. Grand Rapids, MI: Zondervan Publishing, 2008. 57–60.

Henry, Matthew. "Commentary on Genesis 50." Blue Letter Bible.org. http://www.blueletterbible.org/commentaries/Henry/ (accessed September 1, 2010).

Hitchcock, Roswell D. "Abraham." Hitchcock's Bible Names Dictionary. Bible Study Tools.com. http://www.biblestudytools.com/dictionaries/hitchcocks-bible-names/ (accessed September 2, 2010).

MacArthur, John. The MacArthur Study Bible. Nashville, TN: Thomas Nelson, 1997.

## COMMENTS / NOTES:

_____
_____
_____
_____
_____
_____
_____
_____
_____
_____
_____
_____
_____
_____
_____
_____
_____
_____
_____
_____
_____
_____
_____
_____
_____
_____

# OUT OF EGYPT

**BIBLE BASIS:** Exodus 15:1–3, 19, 22–26

**BIBLE TRUTH:** God miraculously led His people out of Egypt, for which they praised Him, but He taught them through many trials.

**MEMORY VERSE:** "For the horse of Pharaoh went in with his chariots and with his horsemen into the sea, and the LORD brought again the waters of the sea upon them; but the children of Israel went on dry land in the midst of the sea" (Exodus 15:19, KJV).

**LESSON AIM:** By the end of the lesson, we will: REVIEW the story of the Israelites' journey of faith through the Red Sea and wilderness; FEEL confidence to trust God during trying times; and REMAIN faithful when times and situations are difficult.

**BACKGROUND SCRIPTURES:** Exodus 1:8-14; 15:1-27--Read and incorporate the insightsgained from the Background Scriptures into your study of the lesson.

## TEACHER PREPARATION

**MATERIALS NEEDED:** Bibles (several different versions), Quarterly Commentary/Teacher Manual, Adult Quarterly, teaching resources such as charts, worksheets/handouts, paper, pens, and pencils.

**OTHER MATERIALS NEEDED / TEACHER'S NOTES:**

_____

_____

## LESSON OVERVIEW

**LIFE NEED FOR TODAY'S LESSON**
That students will keep on trusting in God through their trials and then will thank Him for bringing them through.

**BIBLE LEARNING**
To understand that God desires our thanks for His provisions through our trials.

**BIBLE APPLICATION**
To learn that God led His people out of Egypt and gave them many reasons to thank Him.

**STUDENTS' RESPONSES**
Students will praise God for His many deeds of kindness toward them.

## LESSON SCRIPTURE

### EXODUS 15:1–3, 19, 22–26, KJV

1 Then sang Moses and the children of Israel this song unto the LORD, and spake, saying, I

### EXODUS 15:1–3, 19, 22–26, AMP

1 Then Moses and the children of Israel sang this [a]song to the LORD, singing, "I will sing

will sing unto the LORD, for he hath triumphed gloriously: the horse and his rider hath he thrown into the sea.

2 The LORD is my strength and song, and he is become my salvation: he is my God, and I will prepare him a habitation; my father's God, and I will exalt him.

3 The LORD is a man of war: the LORD is his name.

15:19 For the horse of Pharaoh went in with his chariots and with his horsemen into the sea, and the LORD brought again the waters of the sea upon them; but the children of Israel went on dry land in the midst of the sea.

15:22 So Moses brought Israel from the Red sea, and they went out into the wilderness of Shur; and they went three days in the wilderness, and found no water.

23 And when they came to Marah, they could not drink of the waters of Marah, for they were bitter: therefore the name of it was called Marah.

24 And the people murmured against Moses, saying, What shall we drink?

25 And he cried unto the LORD; and the LORD shewed him a tree, which when he had cast into the waters, the waters were made sweet: there he made for them a statute and an ordinance, and there he proved them,

26 And said, If thou wilt diligently hearken to the voice of the LORD thy God, and wilt do that which is right in his sight, and wilt give ear to his commandments, and keep all his statutes, I will put none of these diseases upon thee, which I have brought upon the Egyptians: for I am the LORD that healeth thee.

to the LORD, for He has triumphed gloriously; The horse and its rider He has thrown into the sea.

2 "The LORD is my strength and my song, And He has become my salvation; This is my God, and I will praise Him; My father's God, and I will exalt Him.

3 "The LORD is a warrior; The LORD is His name.

15:19 For the horses of Pharaoh went with his war-chariots and his charioteers into the sea, and the LORD brought back the waters of the sea on them, but the sons of Israel walked on dry land in the middle of the sea.

15:22 Then Moses led Israel from the Red Sea, and they went into the Wilderness of Shur; they went [a distance of] three days (about thirty-three miles) in the wilderness and found no water.

23 Then they came to Marah, but they could not drink its waters because they were bitter; therefore it was named Marah (bitter).

24 The people [grew discontented and] grumbled at Moses, saying, "What are we going to drink?"

25 Then he cried to the LORD [for help], and the LORD showed him a tree, [a branch of] which he threw into the waters, and the waters became sweet.There the LORD made a statute and an ordinance for them, and there He tested them,

26 saying, "If you will diligently listen and pay attention to the voice of the LORD your God, and do what is right in His sight, and listen to His commandments, and keep [foremost in your thoughts and actively obey] all His precepts and statutes, then I will not put on you any of the diseases which I have put on

the Egyptians; for I am the LORD who heals you."

## BIBLICAL DEFINITIONS

A. **Triumphed (Exodus 15:1)** *ga'ah* (Heb.)—Rose up or was exalted in victory.

B. **Salvation (v. 2)** *yeshuw'ah* (Heb.)—Deliverance, victory, or help.

## LIGHT ON THE WORD

Moses was born to an Israelite mother who put him into the Nile River in a basket **(Exodus 2:2–3)**. He was rescued from the Nile River by the king's daughter. She raised him in the king's palace and Moses received the same quality education as the king's other children. As he grew into adulthood, Moses had compassion for his people. One day he witnessed an Egyptian beating a slave so he intervened and murdered the Egyptian **(Exodus 2:11-15)**. Moses fled Egypt to avoid being executed by the king, and he settled in Midian and married a shepherd's daughter. Moses' wife had a son and he worked as a shepherd until the age of 80.

Moses heard the call of God in the midst of a burning bush and answered the call **(Exodus 3:1-22)**. He expressed doubts the people would accept his call by God to lead them out of Egypt. However, God promised to be with him and sent Aaron his brother to speak for Moses to the Israelites and Pharaoh. The Israelites' situation grew worse and Pharaoh treated them more harshly **(Exodus 5:1-14)**. They complained to Moses. Moses complained to God. God promised that after Pharaoh experienced His powerful hand upon him, he would let the Children of Israel go. God sent 10 plagues on the Egyptians **(Exodus 7:14–11:10)**. At the same time, God instituted the first Passover and not one Israelite was harmed during the plagues. Eventually Pharaoh let the people go, and over two million Israelites and others fled Egypt and God guided them by cloud by day and fire by night. As Moses led them through the wilderness the Egyptian army was in pursuit to stop the Israelites.

## TEACHING THE BIBLE LESSON

## LIFE NEED FOR TODAY'S LESSON

AIM: **That your students will feel confident during trying times.**

## INTRODUCTION

### God Made a Dry Path through the Red Sea

God had promised Moses that He would be with him as he led the Israelites out of Egypt to a land flowing with milk and honey, and Moses trusted God and obeyed. He led the people through the wilderness as the Egyptian army tried one last time to recapture them through the orders of Pharaoh. The Israelites were extremely frightened that they were going to die in the wilderness at the hands of Pharaoh's army. However in spite of the danger, Moses was fearless knowing God was going to somehow deliver them from the threat of the approaching army. God proved in the past He was much more powerful than horses and chariots. "Moses answered the people, 'Do not be afraid. Stand firm and you will see the deliverance the LORD will bring you today. The Egyptians you see today you will never see again. The LORD will fight for you; you need only to be still'" **(Exodus 14:13–14, NIV).**

## BIBLE LEARNING

AIM: That your students will learn that Moses and the Israelites praised God for leading them.

## I. THE VICTORY SONG
## (Exodus 15:1-3, 19)

God promised to deliver the Israelites out of slavery. "For he is faithful that promised" (**Hebrews 10:23**). **Exodus 14** records that God did deliver the Israelites and lead them safely across the Red Sea as Moses stretched his hand out over the water. They walked on dry land to safety, but their enemies drowned when Moses once again stretched his hand out over the water. Moses and the people were in awe of the power of God.

After they landed on dry ground, Moses composed the song presented in **Exodus 15** and he sang it with the men of Israel. Miriam, who was skilled in music, used a timbrel and led the women in singing and dancing (**Exodus 15:20–21**). Singing was a significant part of religious worship, this song is the first one recorded in Scripture. Moses had reasons to sing because God had used him to save the people from slavery. Israel had reason to sing as the chosen people of God who were being redeemed from bondage. Moreover, they were brought safely through the Red Sea and were now on dry land. Their enemies had been destroyed. God had triumphed over Pharaoh and all Egyptians, just as Christ has over Satan and sin through His sacrifice on the Cross. We, too, should sing praises to God for the great things He has done.

### Song of Victory (Exodus 15:1–3, 19)

**1 Then sang Moses and the children of Israel this song unto the LORD, and spake, saying, I will sing unto the LORD, for he hath triumphed gloriously: the horse and his rider hath he thrown into the sea. 2 The LORD is my strength and song, and he is become my salvation: he is my God, and I will prepare him an habitation; my father's God, and I will exalt him. 3 The LORD is a man of war: the LORD is his name. 19 For the horse of Pharaoh went in with his chariots and with his horsemen into the sea, and the LORD brought again the waters of the sea upon them; but the children of Israel went on dry land in the midst of the sea.**

The Israelites declared, "The LORD is my strength and song, and he is become my salvation" (**Exodus 15:2**). They were weak but God gave them strength, even when they experienced sorrow God became their comfort. Sin and death were threatening them, but God was and would be their salvation. However, it was a temporary salvation because Jesus had to come and offer Himself so they and we could have eternal salvation. It was all being done for their ancestors and for their descendants, whom He loved and whom He chose (**Deuteronomy 4:37**). He is a warrior who always overcomes and defeats the enemy (**Exodus 15:3**). God never fails to fulfill His promises! God gave the Israelites courage, strengthened their faith, and removed their fear of the enemy. In the midst of our trials, He will do the same for us.

The words in **verse 19** indicate the conclusion of the song. It simply reiterates the purpose of the song, which was to give praise and express gratitude to God. The more we repeat something the more likely we are to remember it. We should constantly recall and offer praises to God for His great power in saving and delivering us.

### SEARCH THE SCRIPTURES

#### QUESTION 1

Why did Moses create a song?

He sang to praise the Lord for His glorious triumph over Pharaoh's horses and riders.

## LIGHT ON THE WORD

### Marching Orders

After crossing over to dry ground the Israelites refreshed themselves, enjoyed taking the spoils of the enemy, and sat singing praises to God. Moses gave them marching orders because they had remained too long on the shores of the Red Sea. He did not want them to get too comfortable. They had a long journey ahead of them and Moses wanted to reach the Promised Land.

## II. THE FAITH TEST (Exodus 15:22-26)

After marching for three days in the wilderness of Shur, the people and animals were thirsty (**Exodus 15:22**). There was no water in the hot, sandy desert. This was set up by God to see how the people would respond to adversity, and sometimes the trials and suffering we face are tests of our faith. We cannot always understand why these things are happening to us, but we can choose how we respond.

The Israelites reached Marah, and the water was bitter so they could not drink it. Immediately the people began to murmur against Moses, saying, "What shall we drink?" (**Exodus 15:24**). Instead of trusting God to provide for them they complained. How quickly we sometimes forget about the power of God and His promises. Hardships and trials should not cause us to doubt God's faithfulness. If we recall God's works on our behalf in the past, we would have faith to trust Him with our present struggles. He is trustworthy.

### Test of Faith (verses 22–26)

**22 So Moses brought Israel from the Red sea, and they went out into the wilderness of Shur; and they went three days in the wilderness, and found no water. 23 And when they came to Marah, they could not drink of the waters of Marah, for they were bitter: therefore the name of it was called Marah. 24 And the people murmured against Moses, saying, What shall we drink? 25 And he cried unto the LORD; and the LORD shewed him a tree, which when he had cast into the waters, the waters were made sweet: there he made for them a statute and an ordinance, and there he proved them, 26 And said, If thou wilt diligently hearken to the voice of the LORD thy God, and wilt do that which is right in his sight, and wilt give ear to his commandments, and keep all his statutes, I will put none of these diseases upon thee, which I have brought upon the Egyptians: for I am the LORD that healeth thee.**

The people complained to Moses and Moses cried out to the Lord (**Exodus 15:25**). Moses knew the power of God and trusted in His faithfulness to make good on the promises to him and the people. God promised He would bring the Israelites into a land flowing with milk and honey (**Exodus 3:17**). God showed Moses a tree and directed him to cast it into the water (**Exodus 15:25**). The water immediately became pure and sweet, enabling the people to drink it. God had performed another miracle, this was just a test of Israel's faithfulness and obedience.

## QUESTION 2

How did God test Israel's faithfulness?

**They were out in the wilderness for three days without water and then they came to Marah where the water was undrinkable. Answer will vary.**

## LIGHT ON THE WORD

Moses had faith in God, so the Israelites followed him into the Red Sea where God saved them from the Egyptians and from drowning. God is trustworthy, no matter the circumstances we face. This week as you face struggles, pray to the Lord, praise Him for His past faithfulness and ability to help now, and sing songs that encourage and uplift your spirit.

## BIBLE APPLICATION

**AIM: That your students will trust that God is working on their behalf even when trials come their way.**

### God Always Keep His Promises

As we endure daily struggles and trials, we can trust in God. God has proven He is trustworthy because every promise He has made has been fulfilled throughout the generations. How has God proven to you that He is trustworthy?

## STUDENTS' RESPONSES

**AIM: That your students will praise God no matter what the circumstances may be.**

Many people lose their jobs in a bad economy. The high unemployment rates in some communities can lead to home foreclosures, cars repossessed, and family break ups. Some people can lose their health insurance as well and must rely on emergency rooms during illnesses. How can the church be an encouragement to the unemployed who are struggling to survive? What steps can the unemployed take to remain faithful to God in the midst of their trials?

## PRAYER

Dear Father, we praise You for the many wonderful things You have already done for us. Help us to keep on trusting You when we go through trials. In Jesus' Name. Amen.

## DIG A LITTLE DEEPER

How could the children of Israel be bitter with God when He just delivered them from slavery and brought them through the Red Sea? The reality is they had a limited knowledge of God. They were a people of promise who never experienced freedom, who were dependent on oppressors and indoctrinated with false religion. The journey to the fulfillment of the promise would require them to re-engage with God who had been working on their behalf all the time. In 2018-2019 Pew Research concluded we are living in a post-Christian society where there is a continuing decline in people identifying as Protestant and 29% of the public are labled "religiously unaffiliated". Our evangelistic efforts should adapt to a society where there is a limited knowledge of God. We should not be quick to judge or condemn people who do not readily recognize God at work in their lives.

## HOW TO SAY IT

| | |
|---|---|
| Jehovah. | YEH-ho-vah´. |
| Miriam. | Meer-yawm´ |
| Aaron. | A-har-one´. |
| Shur. | Shûwr. |
| Marah. | Ma-rawh. |

## DAILY HOME BIBLE READINGS

### MONDAY
A Mighty Redemption
(Psalm 77:11–20)

### TUESDAY
A Strong People
(Exodus 1:1–7)

### WEDNESDAY
A New King
(Exodus 1:8–14)

### THURSDAY
A Treacherous Plan
(Exodus 1:15–22)

### FRIDAY
A Divine Intervention
(Exodus 15:4–10)

### SATURDAY
An Unsurpassable God
(Exodus 15:11–18)

### SUNDAY
A New Ordinance
(Exodus 15:1–3, 19, 22–26)

## PREPARE FOR NEXT SUNDAY

Read **Galatians 2:15–21,** and next week's lesson, "Justified by Faith in Christ."

**Sources:**

American Tract Society Bible Dictionary. Studylight.com. http://www.studylight.org/dic/ats/view.cgi?number=T674 (accessed May 12, 2010).

Baker's Evangelical Dictionary of Biblical Theology. Studylight.com. http://www.studylight.org/dic/bed/view.cgi?number=T219 (accessed May 12, 2010).

The Commentary Critical and Explanatory on the Whole Bible. Studylight.com.
http://www.studylight.org/com/jfb/view.cgi?book=ex&chapter=015 (accessed May 20, 2010).

The Geneva Study Bible. Crosswalk.com.

http://www.biblestudytools.com/commentaries/geneva-study-bible/exodus/exodus-15.html (accessed May 15, 2010).

Holman Illustrated Bible Dictionary. Studylight.com. http://www.studylight.org/dic/hbd/view.cgi?number=T1742 (accessed May 12, 2010).

John Wesley Explanatory Notes on the Bible. Studylight.com. http://www.studylight.org/com/wen/view.cgi?book=ex&chapter=015 (accessed May 16, 2010).

Life Application Bible––New Revised Standard Version. Wheaton, IL: Tyndale House Publishers, 1989. 118–120.

Miller, Stephen M. The Complete Guide to the Bible. Uhrichsville, OH: Barbour Publishing, 2007. 27–30.

The New John Gill Exposition of the Entire Bible. Studylight.com. http://www.studylight.org/com/geb/view.cgi?book=ex&chapter=015http://studylight.org/com/geb/view.cgi?book=ps&chapter=063&001 - 003 (accessed May 16, 2010).

Scofield, C. I., ed. The New Scofield Study Bible––King James Version. New York, NY: Oxford University Press, 1967. 71–90.

Spence-Jones, H. D. Maurice, ed. The Pulpit Commentary––Vol. 1: Genesis. New York, NY: Funk & Wagnalls, 1890, 2004.

## COMMENTS / NOTES:

_____
_____
_____
_____
_____
_____
_____
_____
_____
_____
_____
_____
_____
_____
_____
_____

# JUSTIFIED BY FAITH IN CHRIST

**BIBLE BASIS:** Galatians 2:15-21

**BIBLE TRUTH:** If, for eternal salvation, we place our faith in any thing or any other person than Christ, our faith is misplaced. In such a case, Paul stated that Jesus died in vain..

**MEMORY VERSE:** "For I through the law am dead to the law, that I might live unto God. I am crucified with Christ: nevertheless I live; yet not I, but Christ liveth in me: and the life which I now live in the flesh I live by the faith of the Son of God, who loved me, and gave himself for me" (Galatians 2:19–20, KJV).

**LESSON AIM:** By the end of the lesson, we will: KNOW Paul's argument against salvation by works; APPRECIATE Christ's saving work on the earth; and DEEPEN our faith in Jesus.

**BACKGROUND SCRIPTURES:** Galatians 1:1–2:21-- Read and incorporate the insights gained from the Background Scriptures into your study of the lesson.

## TEACHER PREPARATION

**MATERIALS NEEDED:** Bibles (several different versions), Quarterly Commentary/Teacher Manual, Adult Quarterly, teaching resources such as charts, worksheets/handouts, paper, pens, and pencils.

**OTHER MATERIALS NEEDED / TEACHER'S NOTES:**

_____

_____

## LESSON OVERVIEW

**LIFE NEED FOR TODAY'S LESSON**
That students will trust in Christ alone for their salvation.

**BIBLE LEARNING**
To understand that Jesus died to take the punishment for our sins and that is all that is needed.

**BIBLE APPLICATION**
To learn that to say that anything else is needed for our salvation is to cheapen the value of Christ's death for us.

**STUDENTS' RESPONSES**
Students will trust in Jesus Christ alone for their salvation.

## LESSON SCRIPTURE

### GALATIANS 2:15-21, KJV

**15** We who are Jews by nature, and not sinners of the Gentiles,

### GALATIANS 2:15-21, AMP

**15** [I went on to say] "We are Jews by birth and not sinners from among the Gentiles;

16 Knowing that a man is not justified by the works of the law, but by the faith of Jesus Christ, even we have believed in Jesus Christ, that we might be justified by the faith of Christ, and not by the works of the law: for by the works of the law shall no flesh be justified.

17 But if, while we seek to be justified by Christ, we ourselves also are found sinners, is therefore Christ the minister of sin? God forbid.

18 For if I build again the things which I destroyed, I make myself a transgressor.

19 For I through the law am dead to the law, that I might live unto God.

20 I am crucified with Christ: nevertheless I live; yet not I, but Christ liveth in me: and the life which I now live in the flesh I live by the faith of the Son of God, who loved me, and gave himself for me.

21 I do not frustrate the grace of God: for if righteousness come by the law, then Christ is dead in vain.

16 yet we know that a man is not justified [and placed in right standing with God] by works of the Law, but [only] through faith in [God's beloved Son,] Christ Jesus. And even we [as Jews] have believed in Christ Jesus, so that we may be justified by faith in Christ and not by works of the Law. By observing the Law no one will ever be justified [declared free of the guilt of sin and its penalty].

17 But if, while we seek to be justified in Christ [by faith], we ourselves are found to be sinners, does that make Christ an advocate or promoter of our sin? Certainly not!

18 For if I [or anyone else should] rebuild [through word or by practice] what I once tore down [the belief that observing the Law is essential for salvation], I prove myself to be a transgressor.

19 For through the Law I died to the Law and its demands on me [because salvation is provided through the death and resurrection of Christ], so that I might [from now on] live to God.

20 I have been crucified with Christ [that is, in Him I have shared His crucifixion]; it is no longer I who live, but Christ lives in me. The life I now live in the body I live by faith [by adhering to, relying on, and completely trusting] in the Son of God, who loved me and gave Himself up for me.

21 I do not ignore or nullify the [gracious gift of the] grace of God [His amazing, unmerited favor], for if righteousness comes through [observing] the Law, then Christ died needlessly. [His suffering and death would have had no purpose whatsoever.]"

## BIBLICAL DEFINITIONS

A. **Nature (Galatians 2:15)** *phusis* (Gk.)—The way of feeling and acting which has become "normal."

B. **Transgressor (2:18)** *parabates* (Gk.)—A person who violates a command or law; someone who goes beyond a boundary or limit.

## LIGHT ON THE WORD

Galatia was a region in the Roman Empire, also located in what is now part of Turkey. The book of Acts records ministry visits from Paul to Antioch in Pisidia, Iconium, Lystra, and Derbe. So when the people in these cities that Paul had led to Christ were being led astray, Paul, as their spiritual father, was rightly concerned.

## TEACHING THE BIBLE LESSON

## LIFE NEED FOR TODAY'S LESSON

**AIM: That your students will feel confident in Christ's death for them.**

## INTRODUCTION

### Paul's Ministry to Gentiles

Paul was originally named Saul after Israel's first king, and he was born in a very religious Jewish family in Tarsus. It was a city which was located in what is modern-day Turkey, but soon the family moved to Jerusalem where he was educated as a Pharisee. The Pharisees were very devoted to the Law, and Paul could see that Christianity was opposed to what Pharisees believed. So Paul became a "missionary" Pharisee, beginning in Jerusalem by rounding up Christians and having them put in prison or even killed. (He was a part of those who saw to it that Stephen was stoned for his faith in Jesus Christ.)

Paul was dramatically converted while he was on the road to Damascus, where he planned to ferret out more Christians and have them put in jail, neverthelesss it was on this road that Jesus Christ spoke to him from heaven and Paul was temporarily blinded, but completely convinced that the only way to salvation was through faith in Jesus Christ.

Shortly after his conversion, Paul concentrated on missionary work to the Gentiles. It was at this time that he was called Paul instead of Saul. Paul was a Gentile name, whereas Saul was a Jewish name. Paul was determined to tear down any barriers for the conversion of Gentiles (non-Jews) to Christ.

So when Jews who may have been converted to Christianity or may really just have been sham Christians who came along and tried to convince Gentile Christians that they had to be circumcised and obey the whole Law in order to be saved. Paul was filled with holy anger and jealousy for the Gospel. Salvation is by grace through faith alone, no works are required for salvation. It is enough that Jesus died on the Cross for us and rose again! To say that anything else is needed is to belittle the Cross.

## BIBLE LEARNING

**AIM: That your students will learn that the Law was not given in order to save people.**

## I. THE PURPOSE OF THE LAW (Galatians 2:15-16)

The Law was given to the Jewish people as a means of identifying themselves as the people of God and was not meant to provide a means of salvation, but it was often interpreted that way. Almost all of the Old Testament prophets condemned this view, God has always accepted people based upon their trust in Him.

Most scholars divide the Law into three areas. The first is the moral law, which is the Ten

Commandments and which is also spelled out in more detail. Jesus helped people to see that it was not meant just to be an outward set of rules, but was meant to be an attitude of the heart described as love for God and love for others. The civil law went into detail on how to live out the moral law in the context in which the Jewish people lived. The ceremonial law had to do with regulations for sacrifices and for the priestly system.

No one would deny that Christians should be following the Ten Commandments, but Paul makes it clear that obeying them does not qualify us for salvation. The civil law was limited to Israel's monarchy, and the ceremonial law was completed with the death and resurrection of Jesus Christ. We no longer need to sacrifice animals to atone for our sins, because our sins have been paid for once and for all in Jesus' death on the Cross. Circumcision was meant to be the unique physical symbol that the Jewish people were God's chosen people. This has been replaced with Christian baptism, and the celebration of the Jewish Passover meal has been replaced with the Lord's Supper.

### Justified by Faith Alone
#### (Galatians 2:15–16)
**15 We who are Jews by nature, and not sinners of the Gentiles, 16 Knowing that a man is not justified by the works of the law, but by the faith of Jesus Christ, even we have believed in Jesus Christ, that we might be justified by the faith of Christ, and not by the works of the law: for by the works of the law shall no flesh be justified.**

In **verses 11** through **14** of **Galatians 2,** Paul recalls a confrontation he had with Peter. As a fellow Jew, Peter's behavior in Antioch toward Gentile Christians was equivalent to treating them as second class citizens in the church. In essence, the actions of Peter and the other Jewish Christians said to the Gentiles that they had to become Jewish in order to be accepted into the community. Paul argues before his fellow Jewish Christians that they should know better than to require the Gentiles to observe the Law as mandatory for salvation. He further argues that if Jewish Christians know that they, who were born Jews, are saved not by works of the Law but by faith in Christ, how can they demand that the Gentiles obey the Law in order to be saved?

## SEARCH THE SCRIPTURES
### QUESTION 1
How does Paul say that people can be justified?

**People can only be justified by faith in Jesus Christ.**

## LIGHT ON THE WORD
### Justification
Paul's message to the Galatians explained that they did not have to become Jewish in order to be Christian. Just as observing the Law did not put the Jewish Christians in right relationship with God, neither would observing the Law put the Galatians in right relationship with God. Rather, both Jewish and Gentile Christians were put right or "justified" by putting their trust in Jesus Christ.

## II. CHRIST LIVES IN ME
## (Galatians 2:17-21)

The Jewish Christians were justified by believing in Christ, which made them equal to their Gentile counterparts in God's sight. They both had to come to God in the same way. Paul did not mean that Christ made the Jews sinners, rather, both Jews and Gentiles were sinners saved by God's grace through faith in Christ.

### Living by Faith (verses 17–21)
**17 But if, while we seek to be justified by Christ, we ourselves also are found sinners, is therefore Christ the minister of**

sin? God forbid. 18 For if I build again the things which I destroyed, I make myself a transgressor. 19 For I through the law am dead to the law, that I might live unto God. 20 I am crucified with Christ: nevertheless I live; yet not I, but Christ liveth in me: and the life which I now live in the flesh I live by the faith of the Son of God, who loved me, and gave himself for me. 21 I do not frustrate the grace of God: for if righteousness come by the law, then Christ is dead in vain.

Paul continued his defense that no human being can be justified before God by works of the Law. He argued that he had already died to the Law when he was saved. Since he now shares in Christ's death and resurrection, the Law free Gospel he shared with the Galatians is sufficient for their salvation. For him to preach otherwise would be the same as returning to the works of the Law. He continued that because Jesus loved him, He died to save him, and to return to the works of the Law would make Jesus' death pointless. Paul wanted the Gentiles to understand that he, a devout Jew, understood that faith in Christ was the only way he could be justified before God.

## QUESTION 2

If righteousness comes by the Law, what then does Paul say is in vain?

Christ's death on the Cross would be unnecessary if there were any other way for us to be saved. Answer will vary.

## LIGHT ON THE WORD

If anything is added to what we need to do to be saved, it is wrong, because our salvation comes by faith alone.

## BIBLE APPLICATION

AIM: That your students will deepen their

faith in the death of Jesus on the Cross for them.

## We Can Have Victory over Sin through the Cross

Galatians 2:19–20 are the key verses for this week's Scripture passage, and verse 20 is especially important in our understanding and appropriation in order to live a victorious Christian life. We read that the two thieves were crucified with Christ (Matthew 27:44; Mark 15:27; John 19:32), and here Paul uses the same words to say that he is crucified with Christ. When we put our trust in Jesus Christ, we are united with Him so closely that we, along with our sins, are nailed to the Cross. Our old way of life is crucified, and we rise again with Him unto new life. In Romans 6:6, the words can be paraphrased to read "the person we formerly were was crucified with him" (Bruce, 144). Just as death is the final barrier to life, so our salvation separates us from our former way of life.

We might expect Paul to say that he now lives in Christ, but instead he says that Christ lives in him. So completely do we reckon ourselves dead to sin, that the "I" no longer exists; it is only Christ who lives through us. We are now living the resurrection life of Christ.

## STUDENTS' RESPONSES

AIM: That your students will understand that their old sinful selves died with Christ on the Cross, so they can now live victorious lives with Christ living in them.

Some may think that salvation by grace through faith means that Christians will feel free to live sinfully, but this is not so. A true understanding of all that happened on the Cross will make Christians see that their old sinful selves are dead, and now they are free to live lives for Christ.

## PRAYER

Dear Father, we thank You so much for sending Your Son, Jesus, to die on the Cross for us. Help us to put our whole trust in Him for our salvation and for our daily living. In Jesus' Name, Amen

## DIG A LITTLE DEEPER

I remember seeing a picture where three different people were trying to watch a game over a fence. Equality gave each person the same box; however, not everyone was able to see the game. Equity gave each person what he or she needed to watch the game. Paul teaches us that justification by faith in Jesus Christ provided access to God. While each person has to believe in Jesus Christ, everyone's path to Jesus might be different. Paul was instructing the Galatian Christians that their path to Jesus was just as valuable as the Jewish Christians. We should be careful we do not create false standards or hold to traditions that judge whether or not someone is really saved.

## HOW TO SAY IT

| | |
|---|---|
| Antioch. | AN-te-ock. |
| Circumcise. | SIR-cum-siz. |
| Crucified. | CRU-ce-fid. |
| Galatians. | Ga-LA-shuns. |
| Transgressor. | Trans-GRES-or. |

### DAILY HOME BIBLE READINGS

**MONDAY**
Our Only Source of Righteousness
(Isaiah 45:20–25)

**TUESDAY**
Righteousness through Faith
(Romans 3:21–26)

**WEDNESDAY**
A Prayer for Mercy
(Luke 18:9–14)

**THURSDAY**
Challenged by a Different Gospel
(Galatians 1:1–10)

**FRIDAY**
Called through God's Grace
(Galatians 1:11–24)

**SATURDAY**
Sent to the Gentiles
(Galatians 2:6–10)

**SUNDAY**
Justified by Faith
(Galatians 2:15–21)

## PREPARE FOR NEXT SUNDAY

Read **Galatians 3:1–14,** and next week's lesson, "Freed from Law through Christ."

Sources:

Baltes, A. J., ed. Biblespeech.com. http://www.biblespeech.com (accessed August 11, 2010).

Barclay, William. The Letters to the Galatians and Ephesians. Translated, with Introductions and Interpretations. Philadephia, PA: Westminster Press, 1956.

Browning, Daniel C. "Law, Ten Commandments, Torah." Holman Illustrated Bible Dictionary. Chad Brand, Charles Draper, Archie England, eds. Nashville, TN: Holman Bible Publishers, 2003. 1609–10.

Bruce, F. F. The Epistle to the Galatians: A Commentary on the Greek Text. The New International Greek Testament Commentary. Grand Rapids, MI: William B. Eerdmans Publishing Company, 1982. 144.

Quarles, Charles L. "Paul." Holman Illustrated Bible Dictionary. Chad Brand, Charles Draper, Archie England, eds. Nashville, TN: Holman Bible Publishers, 2003. 1254–61.

Strong, James. New Exhaustive Strong's Numbers and Concordance with Expanded
Greek-Hebrew Dictionary. Seattle, WA: Biblesoft, and International Bible Translators, 1994.

## COMMENTS / NOTES:

# FREED FROM LAW THROUGH CHRIST

**BIBLE BASIS:** Galatians 3:1–14

**BIBLE TRUTH:** We have to put our trust in Jesus Christ who sacrificed His life on our behalf. The Law cannot save us, only faith in Christ.

**MEMORY VERSE:** "That the blessing of Abraham might come on the Gentiles through Jesus Christ; that we might receive the promise of the Spirit through faith" (Galatians 3:14, KJV).

**LESSON AIM:** By the end of the lesson, we will: UNDERSTAND Paul's contrast of faith in law versus faith in Jesus; FEEL loyalty to Christ; and DEMONSTRATE faith in Christ daily.

**BACKGROUND SCRIPTURES:** Galatians 3:1–14--Read and incorporate the insights gained from the Background Scriptures into your study of the lesson.

## TEACHER PREPARATION

**MATERIALS NEEDED:** Bibles (several different versions), Quarterly Commentary/Teacher Manual, Adult Quarterly, teaching resources such as charts, worksheets/handouts, paper, pens, and pencils.

**OTHER MATERIALS NEEDED / TEACHER'S NOTES:**

_____

_____

## LESSON OVERVIEW

**LIFE NEED FOR TODAY'S LESSON**
That students will trust in Christ alone for their spiritual growth.

**BIBLE LEARNING**
To understand that works of the flesh will not help anyone grow in the Lord.

**BIBLE APPLICATION**
To learn to seek a closer walk with the Lord for spiritual growth.

**STUDENTS' RESPONSES**
Students will trust in the Holy Spirit, not in deadly legalism for spiritual growth.

## LESSON SCRIPTURE

### GALATIANS 3:1-14, KJV

1 O foolish Galatians, who hath bewitched you, that ye should not obey the truth, before

### GALATIANS 3:1-14, AMP

1 you foolish and thoughtless and superficial Galatians, who has bewitched you [that you would act like this], to whom—right before

whose eyes Jesus Christ hath been evidently set forth, crucified among you?

**2** This only would I learn of you, Received ye the Spirit by the works of the law, or by the hearing of faith?

**3** Are ye so foolish? having begun in the Spirit, are ye now made perfect by the flesh?

**4** Have ye suffered so many things in vain? if it be yet in vain.

**5** He therefore that ministereth to you the Spirit, and worketh miracles among you, doeth he it by the works of the law, or by the hearing of faith?

**6** Even as Abraham believed God, and it was accounted to him for righteousness.

**7** Know ye therefore that they which are of faith, the same are the children of Abraham.

**8** And the scripture, foreseeing that God would justify the heathen through faith, preached before the gospel unto Abraham, saying, In thee shall all nations be blessed.

**9** So then they which be of faith are blessed with faithful Abraham.

**10** For as many as are of the works of the law are under the curse: for it is written, Cursed is every one that continueth not in all things which are written in the book of the law to do them.

**11** But that no man is justified by the law in the sight of God, it is evident: for, The just shall live by faith.

**12** And the law is not of faith: but, The man that doeth them shall live in them.

**13** Christ hath redeemed us from the curse of the law, being made a curse for us: for it is written, Cursed is every one that hangeth on a tree:

your very eyes—Jesus Christ was publicly portrayed as crucified [in the gospel message]?

**2** This is all I want to ask of you: did you receive the [Holy] Spirit as the result of obeying [the requirements of] the Law, or was it the result of hearing [the message of salvation and] with faith [believing it]?

**3** Are you so foolish and senseless? Having begun [your new life by faith] with the Spirit, are you now being perfected and reaching spiritual maturity by the flesh [that is, by your own works and efforts to keep the Law]?

**4** Have you suffered so many things and experienced so much all for nothing—if indeed it was all for nothing?

**5** So then, does He who supplies you with His [marvelous Holy] Spirit and works miracles among you, do it as a result of the works of the Law [which you perform], or because you [believe confidently in the message which you] heard with faith?

**6** Just as Abraham BELIEVED GOD, AND IT WAS CREDITED TO HIM AS RIGHTEOUSNESS, [as conformity to God's will and purpose—so it is with you also].

**7** So understand that it is the people who live by faith [with confidence in the power and goodness of God] who are [the true] sons of [a]Abraham.

**8** The Scripture, foreseeing that God would justify the Gentiles by faith, proclaimed the good news [of the Savior] to Abraham in advance [with this promise], saying, "IN YOU SHALL ALL THE NATIONS BE BLESSED."

**9** So then those who are people of faith [whether Jew or Gentile] are blessed and favored by God [and declared free of the guilt of sin and its penalty, and placed in right

**14** That the blessing of Abraham might come on the Gentiles through Jesus Christ; that we might receive the promise of the Spirit through faith.

standing with Him] along with Abraham, the believer.

**10** For all who depend on the Law [seeking justification and salvation by obedience to the Law and the observance of rituals] are under a curse; for it is written, "CURSED (condemned to destruction) IS EVERYONE WHO DOES NOT ABIDE BY ALL THINGS WRITTEN IN THE BOOK OF THE LAW, SO AS TO PRACTICE THEM."

**11** Now it is clear that no one is justified [that is, declared free of the guilt of sin and its penalty, and placed in right standing] before God by the Law, for "THE RIGHTEOUS (the just, the upright) SHALL LIVE BY FAITH."

**12** But the Law does not rest on or require faith [it has nothing to do with faith], but [instead, the Law] says, "HE WHO PRACTICES THEM [the things prescribed by the Law] SHALL LIVE BY THEM [instead of faith]."

**13** Christ purchased our freedom and redeemed us from the curse of the Law and its condemnation by becoming a curse for us—for it is written, "CURSED IS EVERYONE WHO HANGS [crucified] ON A TREE (cross)"—

**14** in order that in Christ Jesus the blessing of Abraham might also come to the Gentiles, so that we would all receive [the realization of] the promise of the [Holy] Spirit through faith.

## BIBLICAL DEFINITIONS

A. **Curse (Galatians 3:10, 13)** *katara* (Gk.)—The act of denouncing.

B. **Faith (v. 14)** *pistis* (Heb.)—A strong conviction that Jesus is the Messiah and the One through whom we can by faith obtain eternal salvation.

## LIGHT ON THE WORD

Judaizers were Jewish Christians who believed that ceremonial practices of the Old Testament were still in effect for the New Testament church. They insisted that Gentile converts to Christianity abide by the ceremonial rite of circumcision. Also, they argued that Paul was not an authentic apostle and that out of a desire to make the Gospel more appealing to Gentiles, he had removed from the Gospel certain legal requirements.

The Gentile Christians had been persuaded by certain teachers to follow a false Gospel **(Galatians 1:6).** The teachers told the Gentile Christians if they wanted to share in Abraham's blessing, they must be circumcised, offer sacrifices, eat kosher foods, and submit themselves to Old Testament Law. This contradicted Paul's message so the false teachers also claimed that Paul did not have the proper authority to preach the Gospel.

## TEACHING THE BIBLE LESSON

## LIFE NEED FOR TODAY'S LESSON

**AIM: That your students will feel confident in the Holy Spirit to help them in their daily walk.**

## INTRODUCTION

### Paul's Ministry to Gentiles

In this letter, Paul rebukes the Gentile Christians for alienating themselves from him and the truth. He vindicates his authority and his teachings as an apostle by showing he received them from Christ Himself. He also presents the doctrine of Christianity, justification by faith, with its relationship to the Law on the one hand and to holy living on the other. Paul spoke to the Galatians in reference to their faith in the Law versus faith in Jesus.

## BIBLE LEARNING

**AIM: That your students will learn that the Law was not given in order to save people.**

## I. GOD'S POWER IS THROUGH THE SPIRIT (Galatians 3:1–5)

In **Galatians 3:1,** Paul asked, "O foolish Galatians, who hath bewitched you, that ye should not obey the truth, before whose eyes

Jesus Christ hath been evidently set forth, crucified among you?" The Galatians had become so intrigued by the false teachings that it was as though they were under a magical spell. Magic was common during that time, and because of that some people did not realize that the mysterious powers came from Satan. This was in direct contradiction to the power of God manifested through the Holy Spirit. Paul wanted to know how they could be so foolish to renounce the Gospel of Christ and turn back to the Law, after having heard, received, and suffered so much for the Gospel.

### The Gift of the Spirit Is by Faith (Galatians 3:1–5)

**1 O foolish Galatians, who hath bewitched you, that ye should not obey the truth, before whose eyes Jesus Christ hath been evidently set forth, crucified among you? 2 This only would I learn of you, Received ye the Spirit by the works of the law, or by the hearing of faith? 3 Are ye so foolish? having begun in the Spirit, are ye now made perfect by the flesh? 4 Have ye suffered so many things in vain? if it be yet in vain. 5 He therefore that ministereth to you the Spirit, and worketh miracles among you, doeth he it by the works of the law, or by the hearing of faith?**

The Galatians knew they had not received the Holy Spirit by obeying the Jewish laws, but by faith. They were now trying to complete their salvation by means of the flesh, flesh refers to human efforts. The Judaizers were emphasizing the need for circumcision and following other Old Testament laws for true salvation, but Paul called it foolishness. We grow spiritually through the Spirit's work in us, not by obeying rules. The power of the Spirit is needed for sanctification (consecration, the act of being set apart).

## SEARCH THE SCRIPTURES

### QUESTION 1
Why did Paul call the Galatians "foolish"?

They foolishly believed that having received salvation through the Spirit, they would now depend upon obedience to the Law.

## LIGHT ON THE WORD

### Abraham's Faith
At least 600 years before God gave Moses the Jewish laws, Abraham was the founding father of the Jewish nation. Paul reminded the people, "Even as Abraham believed God, and it was accounted to him for righteousness. Know ye therefore that they which are of faith, the same are the children of Abraham" (**Galatians 3:6–7**). The real children of God are those who put their faith in God, not the Law. Abraham was saved by his faith (**Genesis 15:6**). Therefore, all nations will be blessed through Abraham if they believe by faith (**Galatians 3:8**).

# II. GOD PLANNED FOR SALVATION TO BE AVAILABLE TO ALL (Galatians 3:6-9)

The true design of God from the beginning was for salvation to be offered to all nations, including Gentiles. Jesus commissioned the apostles to go and evangelize to  the entire world. "But ye shall receive power, after that the Holy Ghost is come upon you: and ye shall be witnesses unto me both in Jerusalem, and in all Judaea, and in Samaria, and unto the uttermost part of the earth" (**Acts 1:8**). Faith is the sole requirement for salvation for all people. We are not bound by the Law; we are justified "by faith" (**Galatians 3:11**).

### Abraham's Covenant of Faith
#### (verses 6–9)
**6 Even as Abraham believed God, and it was accounted to him for righteousness.**

**7 Know ye therefore that they which are of faith, the same are the children of Abraham. 8 And the scripture, foreseeing that God would justify the heathen through faith, preached before the gospel unto Abraham, saying, In thee shall all nations be blessed. 9 So then they which be of faith are blessed with faithful Abraham.**

Paul wants his Gentile readers to know that they have no need to jump through the Judaizers' legalistic hoops. God provided for their salvation when He entered into covenant with Abraham. Thus, Paul's closing statement (which in the Greek emphasizes the results that follow a previous action): "So then," as a result of what God has planned and is currently bringing to pass, "they which be of faith," as opposed to the circumcised who rely on the works of the law, "are blessed with faithful Abraham."

### QUESTION 2
How do we become the children of Abraham?

We become his children through faith in God. Answers will vary.

## LIGHT ON THE WORD

### No One's Perfect!
Whoever subjects themselves to the Law is cursed. "Cursed is every one that continueth not in all things which are written in the book of the law to do them" (**Galatians 3:10**). Paul quoted **Deuteronomy 27:26** to prove that the Law only condemns, we are condemned if we even break one of the Mosaic Laws. Therefore, everyone is condemned to death because no one can keep all of the laws. The Law was a temporary "guardian" to condemn sins, preparing the way for Christ. Once Christ comes, the new age of faith breaks in and we do not need a guardian.

## III. WE CANNOT FIX OURSELVES (Galatians 3:10-14)

We cannot fix our lives on our own,we need God to help us because we are often motivated to submit to the flesh instead of the spirit. "Every time we desire to do good, evil is always present" (**Romans 7:21,** paraphrased). Only God can save and empower us to live holy lives. Paul quoted **Habakkuk 2:4** in saying, "The just shall live by faith" (**Galatians 3:11**). The Galatians were tricked under the penalty of God's curse to keep the whole Law. The only person able to keep the whole Law was Jesus. It's only by trusting in Christ's redemption of humanity that we are freed from the condemnation of sin and given the power to change.

### Freed from the Curse of the Law by Faith (verses 10–14)

**10 For as many as are of the works of the law are under the curse: for it is written, Cursed is every one that continueth not in all things which are written in the book of the law to do them. 11 But that no man is justified by the law in the sight of God, it is evident: for, The just shall live by faith. 12 And the law is not of faith: but, The man that doeth them shall live in them. 13 Christ hath redeemed us from the curse of the law, being made a curse for us: for it is written, Cursed is every one that hangeth on a tree: 14 That the blessing of Abraham might come on the Gentiles through Jesus Christ; that we might receive the promise of the Spirit through faith.**

Christ became the curse for us through condemnation, sufferings, and death that He endured for us. He became a curse for us. "For it is written, Cursed is every one that hangeth on a tree" (**Galatians 3:13;** see also **Deuteronomy 21:23**). If a person was found guilty of a capital offense, his body was hung from a tree. The person was considered under God's curse. Moreover, it demonstrated that God had condemned them and hanging on the tree symbolized divine judgment and rejection. Christ accepted the full punishment of our sins, thus becoming a curse for us. Christians have been made free from the curse of the Law.

## SEARCH THE SCRIPTURES

### QUESTION 3

How did Christ redeem us from the curse of the Law?

**He hung on the tree (Cross) and died for our sins. Answers will vary.**

## LIGHT ON THE WORD

The promise of blessings made to Abraham comes to the Gentiles who believe, these promises made to Abraham were conditional based on faith. Therefore, these conditions could not be altered by the giving of the Law four centuries later. The Galatians needed to reconsider their relationship with Christ. If we base our salvation on works, it is not salvation. We all are made righteous through faith in Jesus Christ (**Romans 3:22–24**). We all have sinned and are in need of redemption, but we are justified freely by the grace of our Lord and Savior, Jesus Christ.

## BIBLE APPLICATION

**AIM: That your students will understand that salvation is through faith in Jesus Christ and His death on the Cross.**

### Salvation through Jesus Christ Alone

In conclusion, even Gentiles have access to this wonderful salvation through Jesus Christ. God chose to use Abraham and His lineage to bestow the blessing on all those who will accept Jesus Christ as Savior. Fully divine and fully human, He is sent because God so loved the world (**John 3:16**). What have you done with Jesus?

## STUDENTS' RESPONSES

**AIM: That your students will receive Christ as Savior, if they have not yet done so, and they will begin walking by faith.**

Jesus wants us to be loyal to Him alone. If we have faith and believe Christ sacrificed Himself on the Cross on our behalf then we are saved. We are to demonstrate our faith in Christ by living holy lives. The only way to conquer the impulses of the flesh is to walk in the Spirit, be led by the Spirit, bear the fruit of the Spirit, and keep connected to the Spirit (**Galatians 5:16, 18, 22, 25**, paraphrased). How? First, pray and ask God to forgive you of all sins. Secondly, seek God for direction in your life. Thirdly, memorize Scriptures that empower you to overcome temptations. Fourth, you have to yield to the power of the Holy Spirit and act accordingly. God will always guide you in the right direction. This is faith in action!

## PRAYER

Dear Father, we thank You that our salvation is by grace alone. Help us to live by faith as well. In Jesus' Name, Amen.

## DIG A LITLLE DEEPER

"Actions speak louder than words". This quote attributed to Abraham Lincoln, means that a person's actions are more powerful than the words they speak. While faith does not come by works, faith without works is dead (**James 2:26**). Now freed from the tentacles of the Law, should propel us to walk closer with Christ. As we grow in our relationship with Christ, one sign of spiritual maturity is the compassion we show for others. Our preaching shoud extend beyond the pulpit and into the community. We should be active in ensuring fairness, justice, compassion, and mercy is evident throughout all aspects of our society.

## HOW TO SAY IT

| | |
|---|---|
| Bithynia. | Bi·thyn·i·an. |
| Cappadocia. | Ka'puh-DOH-shee-uh. |
| Cilicia. | Suh-LISH-ee-uh. |
| Derbe. | DUHR-bee('). |
| Pamphylia. | Pam-FIL-ee-uh. |

### DAILY HOME BIBLE READINGS

**MONDAY**
Blessing All Nations
(Genesis 18:16–21)

**TUESDAY**
Keep the Law and Live
(Leviticus 18:1–5)

**WEDNESDAY**
The Curse of Sin
(Deuteronomy 27:15–26)

**THURSDAY**
The Righteous Live by Their Faith
(Habakkuk 2:1–5)

**FRIDAY**
Faith and Salvation
(Hebrews 10:32–39)

**SATURDAY**
What Do I Still Lack?
(Matthew 19:16–26)

**SUNDAY**
The Blessing for All
(Galatians 3:1–14)

## PREPARE FOR NEXT SUNDAY

Read **Galatians 3:15–18; 4:1–7**, next week's lesson, "Heirs to the Promise."

**Sources:**

Abbott, John C. S., and Jacob Abbott. Illustrated New Testament. Studylight.org. http://www.studylight.org/com/ain/view.cgi?book=ga&chapter=003 (accessed May 25, 2010).

American Tract Society Bible Dictionary. Studylight.org. http://studylight.org/dic/ats/view.cgi?number=T829 (accessed May 25, 2010).

Baker's Evangelical Dictionary of Bible Theology. Studylight.org. http://www.studylight.org/dic/bed/view.cgi?number=T285 (accessed May 25, 2010).

Clarke, Adam. Adam Clarke's Commentary. Studylight.org. http://www.studylight.org/com/acc/view.cgi?book=ga&chapter=003 (accessed May 25, 2010).

Enns, Paul. The Moody Handbook of Theology. Chicago, IL: Moody Press. 1989. 110.

Life Application Study Bible. Wheaton, IL: Tyndale House Publishers, 1996.

Scofield, C. I., ed. The New Scofield Study Bible––King James Version. New York, NY: Oxford

University Press, 1967. 1264–71.

Strong, James. New Exhaustive Strong's Numbers and Concordance with Expanded

Greek-Hebrew Dictionary. Seattle, WA: Biblesoft, and International Bible Translators, 1994. 2003.

www.betterdaysarecoming.com/bible/pronunciation.html. (Accessed 1-12-11).

## COMMENTS / NOTES:

# HEIRS TO THE PROMISE

**BIBLE BASIS:** Galatians 3:15–18; 4:1–7

**BIBLE TRUTH:** Paul states that Gentiles received God's blessing as heirs of Abraham, but had to accept the promise for themselves by maturing in their faith in Jesus Christ..

**MEMORY VERSE:** "Wherefore thou art no more a servant, but a son; and if a son, then an heir of God through Christ" (Galatians 4:7, KJV).

**LESSON AIM:** By the end of the lesson, we will: KNOW Paul's statements about being heirs of Abraham through faith; FEEL secure through faith in Jesus; and PURSUE a relationship with God that will lead to growth in faith.

**BACKGROUND SCRIPTURES:** Galatians 3:15–29; 4:1–5:1 -- Read and incorporate the insights gained from the Background Scriptures into your study of the lesson.

## TEACHER PREPARATION

**MATERIALS NEEDED:** Bibles (several different versions), Quarterly Commentary/Teacher Manual, Adult Quarterly, teaching resources such as charts, worksheets/handouts, paper, pens, and pencils.

**OTHER MATERIALS NEEDED / TEACHER'S NOTES:**

_____

_____

## LESSON OVERVIEW

**LIFE NEED FOR TODAY'S LESSON**
That students will feel secure in Christ through faith.

**BIBLE LEARNING**
To understand that they can be heirs with Abraham through faith.

**BIBLE APPLICATION**
To understand that they can be heirs with Abraham through faith.

**STUDENTS' RESPONSES**
Students will respond to Christ in faith and will grow in Him through faith.

## LESSON SCRIPTURE

### GALATIANS 3:15–18; 4:1–7, KJV

**15** Brethren, I speak after the manner of men; Though it be but a man's covenant, yet if it be confirmed, no man

### GALATIANS 3:15–18; 4:1–7, AMP

**15** Brothers and sisters, I speak in terms of human relations: even though a last will and testament is just a human covenant, yet when disannulleth, or addeth thereto.

**16** Now to Abraham and his seed were the promises made. He saith not, And to seeds, as of many; but as of one, And to thy seed, which is Christ.

**17** And this I say, that the covenant, that was confirmed before of God in Christ, the law, which was four hundred and thirty years after, cannot disannul, that it should make the promise of none effect.

**18** For if the inheritance be of the law, it is no more of promise: but God gave it to Abraham by promise.

**4:1** Now I say, That the heir, as long as he is a child, differeth nothing from a servant, though he be lord of all;

**2** But is under tutors and governors until the time appointed of the father.

**3** Even so we, when we were children, were in bondage under the elements of the world:

**4** But when the fulness of the time was come, God sent forth his Son, made of a woman, made under the law,

**5** To redeem them that were under the law, that we might receive the adoption of sons.

**6** And because ye are sons, God hath sent forth the Spirit of his Son into your hearts, crying, Abba, Father.

**7** Wherefore thou art no more a servant, but a son; and if a son, then an heir of God through Christ.

it has been signed and made legally binding, no one sets it aside or adds to it [modifying it in some way].

**16** Now the promises [in the covenants] were decreed to Abraham and to his seed. God does not say, "And to seeds (descendants, heirs)," as if [referring] to many [persons], but as to one, "And to your Seed," who is [none other than] Christ.

**17** This is what I mean: the Law, which came into existence four hundred and thirty years later [after the covenant concerning the coming Messiah], does not and cannot invalidate the covenant previously established by God, so as to abolish the promise.

**18** For if the inheritance [of what was promised] is based on [observing] the Law [as these false teachers claim], it is no longer based on a promise; however, God granted it to Abraham [as a gift] by virtue of His promise.

**4:1** Now what I mean [when I talk about children and their guardians] is this: as long as the heir is a child, he does not differ at all from a slave even though he is the [future owner and] master of all [the estate];

**2** but he is under [the authority of] guardians and household administrators or managers until the date set by his father [when he is of legal age].

**3** So also we [whether Jews or Gentiles], when we were children (spiritually immature), were kept like slaves under the elementary [man-made religious or philosophical] teachings of the world.

**4** But when [in God's plan] the proper time had fully come, God sent His Son, born of a woman, born under the [regulations of the] Law,

**5** so that He might redeem and liberate those who were under the Law, that we [who believe] might be adopted as sons [as God's children with all rights as fully grown members of a family].

**6** And because you [really] are [His] sons, God has sent the Spirit of His Son into our hearts, crying out, "Abba! Father!"

**7** Therefore you are no longer a slave (bond-servant), but a son; and if a son, then also an heir through [the gracious act of] God [through Christ].

## BIBLICAL DEFINITIONS

A. **Covenant (Galatians 3:15, 17)** *diatheke* (Gk.)—A promise, contract, or a will.

B. **Redeem (4:5)** *exagorazo* (Gk.)—To buy something from someone in order to establish ownership.

## LIGHT ON THE WORD

The Bible contains many promises by God to His people. Significant among God's promises is His promise to bless Abraham with a son, who would become a great nation, and that all the nations of the earth would be blessed by Abraham. God also promised Abraham that his descendants would be too many to count. God's promise to Abraham is in the background as God delivered the Children of Israel from Egyptian slavery and made a covenant with them. Israel descended from Abraham through Isaac. God's presence was continually with the Israelites, who trusted in God's future salvation because of His promise to Abraham.

## TEACHING THE BIBLE LESSON

## LIFE NEED FOR TODAY'S LESSON

**AIM: That your students will feel confident in the Holy Spirit to help them in their daily walk.**

## INTRODUCTION

### Paul's Education

Paul was a very highly educated man. He taught under the supervision of Gamaliel, the most highly respected rabbi (Jewish teacher) of his day. Paul also was familiar with Greek and Roman thought, so he could argue points from both the Jewish point of view and the Gentile point of view. In today's Scripture passages, he makes use of both styles of defense.

## BIBLE LEARNING

**AIM: That your students will learn that the Law was not given in order to save people.**

## I. THE SPIRIT GIVES POWER (Galatians 3:15-18)

We first read of God's promise to Abraham in **Genesis 12:1–7**. God called Abraham to leave his homeland, his relatives, and even his elderly father. God made some wonderful promises to him, but Abraham saw almost none of them fulfilled in his lifetime. God promised that He would make Abraham's descendants into a great nation, that He would make his name famous, and that He would bless Abraham, bless everyone that blessed the Jewish people, and curse those who hurt the Jewish people. In fact, everyone on earth would be blessed through Abraham and his seed.

### The Law and the Promise
### (Galatians 3:15–18)

**15 Brethren, I speak after the manner of men; Though it be but a man's covenant, yet if it be confirmed, no man disannulleth, or addeth thereto. 16 Now to Abraham and his seed were the promises made. He saith not, And to seeds, as of many; but as of one, And to thy seed, which is Christ. 17 And this I say, that the covenant, that was confirmed before of God in Christ, the law, which was four hundred and thirty years after, cannot disannul, that it should make the promise of none effect. 18 For if the inheritance be of the law, it is no more of promise: but God gave it to Abraham by promise.**

Paul points out that in **Genesis 12:7** and elsewhere in Scripture (God repeated His promise over and over to Abraham and to his descendants) the word for "seed" is singular. We might substitute the word "descendant" for "seed" to grasp the meaning. God promised to bless everyone in the world through one of Abraham's descendants in particular, Jesus!

So God's promise to Abraham was fulfilled in Jesus. God made the promise to Abraham and Abraham believed God. God's promise to Abraham was given to him based on his faith alone.

Four hundred and thirty years later, God gave the Law to Moses. Moses and all the Israelites were the descendants of Abraham. God gave the promise to Abraham based upon his faith alone, not by obedience to the Law. We are quite sure of this, because the Law had not yet been given. Do you think that if the Israelites did not obey the Law, that God would not keep His promise to send Jesus? We are so blessed that God kept His promise, in spite of the fact that His people were unable to keep the Law.

## SEARCH THE SCRIPTURES

### QUESTION 1

What was promised to Abraham concerning his seed?

**God gave the promise to the seed (descendant) of David, which is Jesus Christ.**

## LIGHT ON THE WORD

### Slavery in the Roman Empire

Slavery was an integral part of Greco Roman civilization. Slaves accounted for one fifth of the population. People became slaves through various circumstances, including breeding, wars, piracy, debt, and birth to a slave mother. Slaves were the property of their owners and had no legal rights. Slaves functioned broadly within the society from civil service to hard labor. Household slaves were entrusted with the care of the home and child rearing. School age children were under the moral guidance of "pedagogues," or custodians, who also looked after the children's general well-being but were not the children's teachers.

A benevolent master might grant a slave freedom in his will. The slave was freed upon the death of the master. A friend, relative, or other benefactor might also purchase a slave's freedom. "Redemption" means "the act of buying back," as in a purchase from slavery. For the most part, slave masters were not as brutal as American slave masters were; they did not break up families by selling members.

## II. SLAVERY TO THE LAW (Galatians 4:1-3)

From the time the Law was instituted (the first five books of the Old Testament), people sought to have a right relationship with God based upon their obedience to the Law. Day after day, person after person, people failed to live up to the standards of perfection. All that the Law can do for our relationship with God is to point out how sinful we really are.

### Relationship to God Based upon the Law (Galatians 4:1–3)

**1 Now I say, That the heir, as long as he is a child, differeth nothing from a servant, though he be lord of all; 2 But is under tutors and governors until the time appointed of the father. 3 Even so we, when we were children, were in bondage under the elements of the world:**

Although the King James Version uses the word servant, slave is the best translation of this word. Paul explains that living under the law was like the time period in which a rich man's son was growing up. Although he would someday inherit the company his father owns, as long as he is a child, he cannot spend any of the company's money. He may get an allowance, but he cannot dip into the company accounts that he will someday inherit. In fact, his allowance may be no bigger than the slaves that work in his home.

If we as Christians are struggling to live up to legalistic standards, we are not living like true children of God. Paul is inviting us to take hold of our inheritance as grown children of our heavenly Father.

### QUESTION 2

When is an heir the same as a slave or a servant?

**The heir is just the same as a slave when he is still a child. Answers will vary.**

## LIGHT ON THE WORD

### Adoption in the Roman World

The status of children in early Christianity was only a little better than that of slaves. Although freeborn male children would someday inherit their father's property, including the slaves, the children held a subordinate position in the household. Earlier, Paul had described the Jewish people as children under the guardianship of the Law. However, when God's appointed hour had come, He sent Jesus into the world to redeem them from the Law and adopt them as children. Adoption was a common practice in the Greco Roman world. A person could be adopted as an adult, as well as a child. The adoptive parent gave the adopted person a new life with a new family name and status. The adopted person received all the rights and privileges of a natural born child, including the family inheritance.

## III. GOD WANTS TO ADOPT US (Galatians 4:4-7)

The Galatians, in their faith, were in a new relationship with God. Through Christ Jesus, Gentiles were adopted into God's household with the full rights of natural born children with the Holy Spirit as God's witness. As children of God, they were no longer under the slave custodian, but instead as God's children, heirs of God through Christ Jesus.

If we are living in a legalistic kind of limbo, we are missing out on all of our rights as full-grown children of God. Instead of a bunch of laws, we have the Holy Spirit in our hearts. Therefore, our motivation for our behavior is a mature desire to please our heavenly Father. We are not slaves; we are royal heirs! We have much we inherit on earth and even more in heaven to come when we will receive our full inheritance as children of God.

#### Slavery and Adoption (verses 4–7)

**4 But when the fulness of the time was come, God sent forth his Son, made of a woman, made under the law, 5 To redeem them that were under the law, that we might receive the adoption of sons. 6 And because ye are sons, God hath sent forth the Spirit of his Son into your hearts, crying, Abba, Father. 7 Wherefore thou art no more a servant, but a son; and if a son, then an heir of God through Christ.**

At the right time, God sent His Son to redeem all humanity. The same God who made the promise to Abraham now sends His Son in fulfillment of the promise. Christ was sent with the commission to fulfill the Father's promise of salvation through faith. That Christ was God's "Son, made of a woman" indicates His full divinity as well as His full humanity without sin. Therefore, the Savior could be born under the Law and yet not subjected to its bondage. Thus, He identifies with the experience of those under the Law; yet He is without sin.

## SEARCH THE SCRIPTURES

### QUESTION 3

What did God do in the fullness of time (just the right time)?

**He sent His Son. Answers will vary.**

## LIGHT ON THE WORD

With our new status as children of God comes the end of slavery to sin under the Law. We can be children and still be excluded from any inheritance by a will. Such is not the situation of God's children. We are not just children of God in the abstract, nominal sense without any privileges attached. To us belong the full privileges of being His heirs. An heir is one who receives an inheritance without having to work for it. That is what believers have as "Abraham's seed, and heirs according to the promise"

(Galatians 3:29).

## BIBLE APPLICATION

**AIM: That your students will understand that salvation is through faith in Jesus Christ and His death on the Cross.**

### Salvation through Jesus Christ Alone

As God's children, we receive the Spirit of Christ into our hearts, bearing witness of our filial relationship to God. This is a continuous witness, reassuring us of our new relationship to God. Out of respect, the Jews would not call God by the name of Father. It was therefore a very surprising idea, which derives from Christ **(see Mark 14:36)** that we should address God as Father, using the very intimate and affectionate Aramaic term "Abba" (more like "dear Father" than "Daddy"). The term acknowledges the protective power, care, and concern that God the Father shows for us—His children.

## STUDENTS' RESPONSES

**AIM: That your students will appreciate that God made a way for us to be saved.**

The goal of some religions is to make a way to having a relationship with God, but the chief difference between biblical Christianity and all other ways is that other religions say that you must live in such a way as to qualify for that relationship. In other words, your actions, words, and thoughts must be good enough. For this to work, either God must not be holy enough to have high standards, or a person must live a perfect life. Neither position is tenable. To aim to have our good deeds outweigh our bad deeds is just not good enough for our holy God. Despite our sinfulness, God loves us and that is why God had to make a way for us.

## PRAYER

Dear Father, thank You for adopting us as Your

children. Help us to live lives that are worthy of You. In Jesus' Name, Amen.

## DIG A LITTLE DEEPER

The Fourteenth Amendment to the United States Constitution was ratified in 1868 and provided citizenship to all those who were born or nationalized in U.S. This amendment provided citizenship to slaves and equal protection of the law. Similar to the Gentiles who became heirs of the promise through Jesus Christ, slaves received all the rights and privileges of citizenship including the right t vote. Since the enactment of the amendment, African American voting rights have been violated resulting in civil protest and legal action. We are in the midst of a resurgence of attempts by States to prevent free access to voting by black, brown and women voters. Believers are encouraged to be active in ensuring our communities continue to have access to voting rights privilages.

## HOW TO SAY IT

Disannulleth.    Dis-a-NULL-eth.

Differeth.    DIF-er-eth.

Greco-Roman.    GRE-co-RO-man.

Pedagogues.    PED-a-gogs.

### DAILY HOME BIBLE READINGS

**MONDAY**
Ancestor to a Multitude of Nations
(Genesis 17:1–8)

**TUESDAY**
The Promise Is for You
(Acts 2:32–39)

**WEDNESDAY**
The Gift of Righteousness
(Romans 4:1–8)

**THURSDAY**
Now That Faith Has Come
(Galatians 3:19–29)

**FRIDAY**
Until Christ Is Formed in You
(Galatians 4:12–20)

**SATURDAY**
Stand Firm in Christ's Freedom
(Galatians 4:28—5:1)

**SUNDAY**
Heirs to the Promise
(Galatians 3:15–18; 4:1–7)

## PREPARE FOR NEXT SUNDAY

Read **Galatians 5:22–6:10**, and next week's lesson, "Fruits of Redemption."

Sources:
Baltes, A. J., ed. Biblespeech.com. http://www.biblespeech.com (accessed August 11, 2010).
Barclay, William. The Letters to the Galatians and Ephesians. Translated, with Introductions and Interpretations. Philadephia, PA: Westminster Press, 1956.
Bruce, F. F. The Epistle to the Galatians: A Commentary on the Greek Text. The New International Greek Testament Commentary. Grand Rapids, MI: William B. Eerdmans Publishing Company, 1982.
Buttrick, George A., ed. "Promise." The Interpreters' Dictionary of the Bible. Vol. 3. Nashville, TN: Abingdon Press, 1962. 893–94.
Strong, James. Strong's Exhaustive Concordance of the Bible. McLean, VA: MacDonald Publishing Company, n.d.

# FRUITS OF REDEMPTION

**BIBLE BASIS:** Galatians 5:22—6:10

**BIBLE TRUTH:** Paul said that whenever possible, we should work for the good of all, especially for those in the family of faith..

**MEMORY VERSE:** "But the fruit of the Spirit is love, joy, peace, longsuffering, gentleness, goodness, faith" (Galatians 5:22, KJV).

**LESSON AIM:** By the end of the lesson, we will: HEAR Paul's teaching on faithfulness and sharing others' burdens; FEEL compassion and a sense of duty to others; and SUPPORT one another in the faith through service.

**BACKGROUND SCRIPTURES:** Galatians 5:2–6:1--Read and incorporate the insights gained from the Background Scriptures into your study of the lesson.

## TEACHER PREPARATION

**MATERIALS NEEDED:** Bibles (several different versions), Quarterly Commentary/Teacher Manual, Adult Quarterly, teaching resources such as charts, worksheets/handouts, paper, pens, and pencils.

**OTHER MATERIALS NEEDED / TEACHER'S NOTES:**

---

---

## LESSON OVERVIEW

**LIFE NEED FOR TODAY'S LESSON**
That students will demonstrate the fruit of the Spirit in their lives.

**BIBLE LEARNING**
To understand that we are responsible for our own walk with the Lord.

**BIBLE APPLICATION**
To learn how to access the fruit of the Spirit.

**STUDENTS' RESPONSES**
Students will do good to everyone, especially to fellow believers.

## LESSON SCRIPTURE

### GALATIANS 5:22—6:10, KJV

22 But the fruit of the Spirit is love, joy, peace, longsuffering, gentleness, goodness, faith,

### GALATIANS 5:22—6:10, AMP

22 But the fruit of the Spirit [the result of His presence within us] is love [unselfish concern for others], joy, [inner] peace, patience [not the

23 Meekness, temperance: against such there is no law.

24 And they that are Christ's have crucified the flesh with the affections and lusts.

25 If we live in the Spirit, let us also walk in the Spirit.

26 Let us not be desirous of vain glory, provoking one another, envying one another.

6:1 Brethren, if a man be overtaken in a fault, ye which are spiritual, restore such a one in the spirit of meekness; considering thyself, lest thou also be tempted.

2 Bear ye one another's burdens, and so fulfil the law of Christ.

3 For if a man think himself to be something, when he is nothing, he deceiveth himself.

4 But let every man prove his own work, and then shall he have rejoicing in himself alone, and not in another.

5 For every man shall bear his own burden.

6 Let him that is taught in the word communicate unto him that teacheth in all good things.

7 Be not deceived; God is not mocked: for whatsoever a man soweth, that shall he also reap.

8 For he that soweth to his flesh shall of the flesh reap corruption; but he that soweth to the Spirit shall of the Spirit reap life everlasting.

9 And let us not be weary in well doing: for in due season we shall reap, if we faint not.

10 As we have therefore opportunity, let us do good unto all men, especially unto them who are of the household of faith.

ability to wait, but how we act while waiting], kindness, goodness, faithfulness,

23 gentleness, self-control. Against such things there is no law.

24 And those who belong to Christ Jesus have crucified the [I]sinful nature together with its passions and appetites.

25 If we [claim to] live by the [Holy] Spirit, we must also walk by the Spirit [with personal integrity, godly character, and moral courage—our conduct empowered by the Holy Spirit].

26 We must not become conceited, challenging or provoking one another, envying one another.

6:1 Brothers, if anyone is caught in any sin, you who are spiritual [that is, you who are responsive to the guidance of the Spirit] are to restore such a person in a spirit of gentleness [not with a sense of superiority or self-righteousness], keeping a watchful eye on yourself, so that you are not tempted as well.

2 Carry one another's burdens and in this way you will fulfill the requirements of the law of Christ [that is, the law of Christian love].

3 For if anyone thinks he is something [special] when [in fact] he is nothing [special except in his own eyes], he deceives himself.

4 But each one must carefully scrutinize his own work [examining his actions, attitudes, and behavior], and then he can have the personal satisfaction and inner joy of doing something commendable [a]without comparing himself to another.

5 For every person will have to bear [with patience] his own burden [of faults and shortcomings for which he alone is responsible].

**6** The one who is taught the word [of God] is to share all good things with his teacher [contributing to his spiritual and material support].

**7** Do not be deceived, God is not mocked [He will not allow Himself to be ridiculed, nor treated with contempt nor allow His precepts to be scornfully set aside]; for whatever a man sows, this and this only is what he will reap.

**8** For the one who sows to his flesh [his sinful capacity, his worldliness, his disgraceful impulses] will reap from the flesh ruin and destruction, but the one who sows to the Spirit will from the Spirit reap eternal life.

**9** Let us not grow weary or become discouraged in doing good, for at the proper time we will reap, if we do not give in.

**10** So then, while we [as individual believers] have the opportunity, let us do good to all people [not only being helpful, but also doing that which promotes their spiritual well-being], and especially [be a blessing] to those of the household of faith (born-again believers).

## BIBLICAL DEFINITIONS

A. **Longsuffering (Galatians 5:22)** *makrothumia* (Gk.)—The patience and self-restraint of people who could quickly/eas-ily avenge themselves against wrongdoers.

B. **Mocked (6:7)** *mukterizo* (Gk.)—Turned up one's nose at someone as a gesture of ridicule, scorn, or contempt.

## LIGHT ON THE WORD

The apostle Paul challenged the believers of his day to learn what every believer today would do and remember: The key to making progress in the realm of Christian freedom is to keep walking in the Spirit.

Paul is very much aware of the Galatians' need for a power that the Law could not give. The history of the Jewish people consistently revealed that there are some things the Law cannot do (**Romans 7:7–12; 8:3**). Rules and regulations can command, but they cannot empower one to do what is commanded. Rules and regulations serve as a guide or a road map, but they cannot motivate and enable one to follow the direction and guidance given.

If the Galatians were to live free from sin's power to control their lives—if they were to fulfill the

Law—it would be because they surrendered themselves to the enabling power of the Holy Spirit. Only those who have surrendered and who continually surrender themselves to the complete control of the Spirit are empowered to walk according to the Spirit's orders. It is the power of the Holy Spirit that guides and strengthens believers to live righteously and gain victory in their warfare against the desires of the flesh (sinful nature).

## TEACHING THE BIBLE LESSON

## LIFE NEED FOR TODAY'S LESSON

AIM: That your students will feel confident in the Holy Spirit to help them in their daily walk.

## INTRODUCTION

### Living in the Spirit

Paul had just finished telling the Galatians about their freedom in Christ. They were instructed to use their freedom to make doing God's will and lovingly serving others their highest aim. Paul was not, however, unaware of the inner struggle that such freedom would bring. The desires of the sinful nature are always present to dissuade believers from fulfilling the call of God and living ethical and righteous lives.

Christian freedom requires believers to make choices, because there is always the choice to serve the will of God or the desires of the sinful nature. The power to do God's will flows into the hearts of those who are now walking and who make a choice to keep walking in the Spirit.

## BIBLE LEARNING

AIM: That your students will learn that the primary sign of the Spirit-filled life is love.

## I. THE SPIRIT PRODUCES FRUIT (Galatians 5:22-26)

After listing certain manifestations of the sinful nature (the flesh), Paul now mentions some of the manifestations of the Spirit. His listing of the fruit of the Spirit is not meant to be exhaustive, but rather illustrative of the kinds of qualities and behaviors produced by the Spirit.

### Believers Are to Rely on the Spirit to Produce the Fruit of the Spirit (verses 22–26)

**22 But the fruit of the Spirit is love, joy, peace, longsuffering, gentleness, goodness, faith, 23 Meekness, temperance: against such there is no law. 24 And they that are Christ's have crucified the flesh with the affections and lusts. 25 If we live in the Spirit, let us also walk in the Spirit. 26 Let us not be desirous of vain glory, provoking one another, envying one another.**

First, it is worthy to note that Paul's list begins with love, the one quality necessary to create the atmosphere needed for the proper functioning of all the other qualities (**see 1 Corinthians 13**). Moreover, ending the list with temperance (i.e., self control) is a clear indication of our Spirit-led ability to control the desires of the sinful nature.

Leon Morris offers a helpful comment about the phrase "fruit (singular) of the Spirit" in **Galatians 5:22**. Morris suggests that this is not a reference to a "series of fruits" to be distributed among believers "so that one believer has one (and) another (believer has) another. Rather, he is referring to a cluster, such that all these qualities are to be manifested in each believer" (Morris, 173). If Morris is right, then every believer, through the Spirit's grace, has access to all the fruit of the Spirit. Therefore, while the works of the sinful nature lead to destruction, the fruit of the Spirit offers the believer the power to grow in the things of the Spirit.

Given the warfare between the sinful nature and the Spirit, what is the believer's responsibility?

What should the believer do to gain victory over the desires of the sinful nature and to grow in the things of the Spirit? To this question, Paul gives three specific responses. First, believers are not to undo what they have already done. What the believer has nailed to the Cross through repentance and faith is not to be removed. They that are Christ's have crucified the flesh; let the flesh remain dead! Do not bring the flesh to life again by choosing to fulfill its desires.

Second, since the Holy Spirit is the source of the believer's life in Christ, the believer is to allow the Spirit to dominate and control his or her behavior. In other words, "If we live in the Spirit, let us also walk in the Spirit" (**Galatians 5:25**).

Third, the believer must "not be desirous of vain glory" (**verse 26**). This, Paul adds, will disrupt Christian fellowship and create envy within our hearts. The implication is that the desire for vainglory (being conceited) works against the Spirit's desires for God's glory.

## SEARCH THE SCRIPTURES

### QUESTION 1
Name the fruit of the Spirit.

**The fruit of the Spirit is love, joy, peace, longsuffering, gentleness, goodness, faith, meekness, and temperance.**

## LIGHT ON THE WORD

### When a Believer Slips
In these verses, Paul continues to outline the responsibility and expected behavior of those who follow the Spirit's leading. Believers are to be led by the Spirit, and avoid arrogance and self deception. We should also rally 'round one another in the spirit of meekness, especially when another believer has been "overtaken in a fault" (**Galatians 6:1a**).

## II. HELP IN LOVING HUMILITY (Galatians 6:1-5)

Paul is not naive, he recognizes that there will be occasional instances when a believer will be guilty of missing the mark and yielding to the desires of the sinful nature. In these instances, God's plan is to involve the body of believers in the Spirit's redemptive and restorative process. This plan has no place for judging, self deception, or arrogance. Rather, "the spirit of meekness" (**Galatians 6:1a**) is to characterize the congregation. Each believer is to keep in mind that they, too, are vulnerable to the desires of the sinful nature (**verse 1b**).

In addition, believers are to "bear. . . one another's burdens" (**verse 2**). No believer should view himself or herself as being superior to another believer (**verses 3–5**). Paul makes the point that the fruit of the Spirit is to find expression not only through the lives of individual believers, but also through the collective life of the congregation.

### Believers Are to Rally Around One Another in the Spirit of Meekness (Galatians 6:1–5)
**1 Brethren, if a man be overtaken in a fault, ye which are spiritual, restore such an one in the spirit of meekness; considering thyself, lest thou also be tempted. 2 Bear ye one another's burdens, and so fulfil the law of Christ. 3 For if a man think himself to be something, when he is nothing, he deceiveth himself. 4 But let every man prove his own work, and then shall he have rejoicing in himself alone, and not in another. 5 For every man shall bear his own burden.**

Those who are led by the Spirit are called here to be willing and available to help carry one another's loads. We are to support one another by helping bear the weight of hardship. Bearing one another's burdens is not an occasional act, rather it is a way of living and behaving in the Christian community. By so behaving, we like Christ, will have fulfilled the Law.

One of the expressions of the Spirit-led life is a proper and legitimate estimate of oneself. Those who think too highly of themselves are unlikely candidates for bearing another's burdens. Each person should evaluate his or her own behavior. Those who are led by the Spirit have no need to compare themselves with other believers. Proving one's own work, or testing and evaluating one's own actions in the light of God's Word gives a basis for self-evaluation. In fact, rejoicing because one thinks that he or she is better than someone else is in opposition to our life in Christ. It is not the way of the Spirit.

**Verse 5** might appear to contradict **verse 2** where Paul says we should share each other's burdens. Here, Paul says bear your own burden. The meaning is better conveyed by the use of the word "load," which refers to everyone pulling their own weight in relationship to their responsibilities. In other words, you should do your job and not expect someone else to do it for you. This is so that the work of ministry is shouldered by everyone and not by a few; we each have a responsibility to carry part of the load (burden). This personal responsibility is quite different from helping someone who is burdened down with problems. Nowhere in Scripture is laziness a virtue. Our Christian responsibility is to carry our own weight and help bear the misfortunes of others.

## QUESTION 2
"If a man be overtaken in a fault," what should believers do?

Help a believer who is having a difficult time. "Restore such a one in the spirit of meekness; considering thyself, lest thou also be tempted."

## LIGHT ON THE WORD
### Keep on Doing Good
In **verses 6** through **10**, Paul reminds believers to persevere in "doing good." They are to remember those who teach them spiritual truths and persevere in the things of the Spirit. In contrast, he clearly states that to give place to the desires of the sinful nature has both current and eternal consequences. The consequence of pursuing the things of the Spirit is "life everlasting" (**verse 8b**). The consequence of yielding to the desires of the sinful nature is "corruption" (**verse 8a**).

## III. REAPING THE CONSEQUENCES (Galatians 6:6-10)

Therefore, since God cannot be mocked (scornfully disregarded), believers would do well to remember that they will reap the good they have sown if they do not grow weary or give up (**verse 9**). In light of God's approval and external rewards, we are admonished to take advantage of opportunities to do good, especially for fellow believers in Christ.

### Believers Are to Persevere in Doing Good (verses 6–10)
**6 Let him that is taught in the word communicate unto him that teacheth in all good things. 7 Be not deceived; God is not mocked: for whatsoever a man soweth, that shall he also reap. 8 For he that soweth to his flesh shall of the flesh reap corruption; but he that soweth to the Spirit shall of the Spirit reap life everlasting. 9 And let us not be weary in well doing: for in due season we shall reap, if we faint not. 10 As we have therefore opportunity, let us do good unto all men, especially unto them who are of the household of faith.**

In **verse 6**, Paul transitions from bearing burdens to sharing blessings. He admonishes those who hear God's Word to share all good things with their pastors and teachers. The phrase "all good things" does not mean that people are to give all they have to their ministers, but that they should support them and share with them the good things of this life according to their need. In **verse** 7, Paul uses the metaphor of a farmer who sows and reaps the harvest to say that what a believer sows determines what he or she will harvest. Put another way, our choices will determine our consequences. Whether we choose to live in the Spirit or to live in the flesh (sinful nature), the respective consequences will follow.

Believers are encouraged to sow to the Spirit, and refuse to become discouraged. This explains the need for Paul's note of encouragement in **verse 9**. Paul encourages the Galatians not to get tired and give up for there is a reward after all is said and done. In the terms of sowing and reaping, we now have a seasonal opportunity to do what is good and beneficial for others, especially to our brothers and sisters in the family of God.

## SEARCH THE SCRIPTURES

### QUESTION 3
Why do you think that Paul makes it clear that "God is not mocked"?

**Our choices will determine our consequences. Answers will vary.**

## LIGHT ON THE WORD

Every believer who desires to do the will of God has access to the Spirit's guiding and empowering resources. However, to do so, we must continue to walk in the Spirit. Believers have no reason to grow weary and give up. The rewards that follow those who, by the Spirit's enabling, keep choosing to do good are everlastingly beneficial.

## BIBLE APPLICATION

**AIM: That your students will understand that walking in love is the key to the Spirit-led life.**

### Fulfilling the Desires of the Spirit
Those believers who dare to remember and who in remembering take to heart the truth that in love Christ died for us. They will find themselves increasingly compelled and constrained (**2 Corinthians 5:14**) to keep choosing to fulfill the desires of the Spirit by living righteously and walking in love. If we want to have a distinctive witness to the world around us, we have to live in the Spirit's power.

## STUDENTS' RESPONSES

**AIM: That your students will make living in the Spirit the priority in their lives.**

During this week, set aside a day or two to give yourself to prayer and fasting asking God to make you more aware of the presence and leading of His Spirit. In addition to your praying and fasting, set some priorities for the week so that the pressures of your schedule will not deafen you to the Spirit's voice.

## PRAYER

Dear Father, thank You for the Holy Spirit, who empowers us to live lives of love toward one another. In Jesus' Name, Amen.

## DIG A LITTLE DEEPER

TLC had a show entitled "What not To Wear!" The television series featured makeovers by professional stylists. The selected person had to decide to allow the stylist to throw away their clothes in exchange for $5000 to purchase a new wardrobe. The stylist would provide recommendations on what style of clothes would best represent the person. Our Sunday School lesson on today ask the believer to agree to throw away their unspiritual attitudes and behaviors in exchange for spiritual fruit which would best represent Christ in the earth. For this exchange, the believer would receive a crown of eternal life.

## HOW TO SAY IT

Corinthians.    Kuh-RIN(T)-thee-uhnz.

Galatians.    Guh-LAY-shuhnz.

Bruce, F. F. The Epistle to the Galatians: A Commentary on the Greek Text. The New
    International Greek Testament Commentary. Grand Rapids, MI: William B.
    Eerdmans Publishing Company, 1982. 257.

Morris, Leon. Galatians: Paul's Charter of Christian Freedom. Downers Grove, IL:
    InterVarsity Press, 1996. 173.

## COMMENTS / NOTES:

### DAILY HOME BIBLE READINGS

**MONDAY**
Renewed by the Holy Spirit
(Titus 3:1–7)

**TUESDAY**
Chosen to Be Obedient
(1 Peter 1:1–5)

**WEDNESDAY**
Supporting Your Faith
(2 Peter 1:3–8)

**THURSDAY**
Faith Working through Love
(Galatians 5:2–6)

**FRIDAY**
Called to Freedom
(Galatians 5:7–15)

**SATURDAY**
The Works of the Flesh
(Galatians 5:16–21)

**SUNDAY**
Living by the Spirit
(Galatians 5:22—6:10)

Read **Proverbs 8:22-35**, and next week's lesson, "Wisdom's Part in Creation."

**Sources:**
Baltes, A. J., ed. Biblespeech.com. http://www.biblespeech.com (accessed August 11, 2010).

# Spring 2022
# QUARTER AT-A-GLANCE

# QUARTERLY COMMENTARY

## TEACHER'S TIPS

### " TEN TIPS FOR SUNDAY SCHOOL EXCELLENCE"
Evangelist Patricia Johnson

### "PAY ATTENTION TO WHAT YOU'RE PAYING ATTENTION TO!"
Dr. Missionary Kishki Kamaranell Hall

### "KAHOOT! A YOUTH PERSPECTIVE ON THE USE OF TECHNOLOGY IN SUNDAY SCHOOL"
Alyssa Grace Henson

## QUARTERLY QUIZ

# TEN TIPS FOR SUNDAY SCHOOL EXCELLENCE

## By Evangelist Patricia Johnson

*"And whatsoever ye do in word or deed, do all in the name of the Lord Jesus, giving thanks to God and the Father by him"* Colossians 3:17

As Jurisdictional representatives, one of our responsibilities is to educate, equip and empower our District Leaders to impact the local churches. We want them to be able to effectively guide local churches to develop sustaining ministries. This article highlights ten principles for Sunday School excellence. As we review each principle, we will identify actionable items you can implement immediately. Using these principles consistently and intentionally, you will see numerical growth, spiritual transformation, and ministry expansion.

### Administration
Inspiration: "In order for Sunday School to accomplish its mission, people, resources, and programs must be organized and coordinated." Mark W. Cannister

Implementation:  Sunday School lessons should align and incorporate with church events.

### Attracting Leaders
Inspiration: "A believer's basic motivation for service is to serve God. It is a way in which we can be fulfilled as disciples." Dennis Williams

Implementation: Conduct an annual recruitment for teachers and staff. Highlight the benefits of joining your team. Make sure you have a current position outlining the time commitment and performance metrics.

### Care for Members
Inspiration: "People will forget what you said; people will forget what you did, but people will never forget how you made them feel." Maya Angelou
Implementation: Connect with your students at outside events. Show up at school plays, games, and community events.

### Discipleship
Inspiration: "The goal of Christian teaching is Christlikeness in our learners" Rick Yount
Implementation: Assign accountability partners.

### Enrollment
Inspiration: "Establish the role of the roll" Steve Parr
Implementation: Create a prospective class member list from church and community. Endeavor to have one person join your class each month.

### Evangelism
Inspiration: "Go ye therefore and teach all nations....Teaching them to observe all things

whatsoever I commanded you." Jesus (Matthew 28:19-20 KJV)
Implementation: Introduce salvation at least three times during every lesson. Show the class the relevance and need for Jesus.

## Student Engagement
Inspiration: "Students learn what they care about and remember what they understand" Samuel Ericksen
Implementation: Students know their spiritual gifts.

## Teaching
Inspiration: "The people were amazed at his teaching because he taught them as one who had authority, not as the teachers of the law." Mark 1:22 (NIV)
Implementation: Develop a weekly schedule to study, plan and implement your weekly lesson.

## Technology
Inspiration: "Technology will never replace great teachers, but technology in the hands of great teachers is transformational" George Couros
Implementation: Utilize a written, verbal, and video form of social media to connect with your students each week.

## Training
Inspiration: "Biblical educator must not only have knowledge of the material but also an understanding of the student" Douglas Wilson (paraphrase)
Implementation: Read one book with your staff together. Use the book topics/themes as monthly empowerment sessions. Create opportunities to implement learnings from the book.

Evangelist Patricia Johnson serves as the Jurisdictional Field Representative for Greater Maryland First Jurisdiction, Baltimore, Maryland, under the leadership of Bishop Joel H. Lyles. She works with our International Sunday School Department as a writer for Sunday School Expository and as host/producer for #PowerUp. You can check out her weekly videos on "Tips and Tools for Sunday School" Facebook and YouTube pages. She holds a Bachelor's Degree in Political Science and a Master's Degree in Christian Ministry. She is a member of Greater Maryland First Jurisdiction - Bishop Joel H. Lyles, Prelate, Mother Freddie M. Joy, Supervisor.

# PAY ATTENTION TO WHAT YOU'RE PAYING ATTENTION TO!!!

## By Dr. Missionary Kishki Kamaranell Hall

Theodore Roosevelt once stated, *"People don't care how much you know until they know how much you care."*

In 2020, we found ourselves in a global pandemic. Personally, without my approval, I became a remote professor and had to adjust to the circumstances quickly. Business as "usual" couldn't be the focus during "unusual" times. I couldn't focus solely on academics but had to pay attention to the mental and emotional needs of my students. Just as secular educators were forced to adjust, Sunday school teachers must also adapt and reimagine Sunday school in this season. While you're facing your own issues, you have to stand firm on the Word of God that you so adequately teach to pull others through their issues.

People are hurting, grieving, and suffering. Therefore, teachers need to be well equipped to spiritually and naturally handle the various issues of today. The following statement may not be popular or even approved, but it must be said. Sometimes people don't need a lesson shoved in their faces! They simply need to know that you care and you're interested in what they're facing. Yes, they definitely need you to give them the Word of God. They also need hope, love, and compassion.

It is essential that you pay attention to what you are paying attention to in this season. Are you only concerned about covering every part of the lesson, sharing your revelations about the lesson, or leaving some catchy cliché' for the students to remember throughout the week? I pray that above all those things, you are concerned about the people on the other side of your screen (if virtual) or your desk or pew (if in-person). Teachers, never forget to let your students know that you care about where they are. Teachers strive to meet them where they are. Below are suggestions of how you can meet the needs of your students:

1.      **Remain hopeful, which automatically offers hope to students.**

It is imperative that you always inspire and offer hope to your students! Hope is "A feeling of expectation and desire for a certain thing to happen; a feeling of trust!" I would like to personally define hope as "high expectation and trust in God that He will do what He promised to do; deeply rooted faith! Philippians 1:6 offers us hope: Being confident of this very thing that he which hath begun a good work in you will perform it until the day of Jesus Christ. Saints, we can't stop trusting God and expecting great things from our great God. Even in these times, we serve an awesome God. There is HOPE for us today! People are hurting, and many of them feel absolutely hopeless. The last thing we need in the middle of a pandemic is hopeless and discouraged teachers! One way to remain hopeful is not just to teach the Word but pay attention to the Word that you're teaching. Philippians 4:8 specifically lists what to pay attention to in this life. Positive thinking transforms you and your environment! Furthermore, remind the saints that through it all, we don't sorrow as those with no hope (I Thessalonian 4:13).  In order for you to give hope, you (the teacher) must first think and remain hopeful!!

**2.** **Remain a listener-one who offers students a space to express what they feel.**

People need a space outside of their homes to express their hurt, insecurities, doubts, heartaches, and frustrations. As a Sunday school teacher, you should allow them the space to do so. Feel free to allow them a space to share how the lesson relates to them or even what they need to continue their spiritual journey. It's so crucial that you pay attention to the needs of the students and remain intentional about giving them space to vent. In some cases, you may be the solution. Make your Sunday school environment therapeutic. Many of the saints are not in contact with other saints as they once were. Sunday school may be the only place many of them (especially the elderly) get to express themselves and talk to others. Teachers, sometimes it's okay to serve as the facilitator rather than the lecturer. You don't have to do all of the talking. The saints need someone to listen to them. Listening is a powerful ministry that is often overlooked. All educators, when intentional with their attention, possess power to change the world. Pay attention to what you pay attention to in this season.

Dr. Missionary Kishki Kamaranell Hall is an evangelist and motivational speaker of Cleveland, Mississippi. She is an employed educator at Coahoma Community College, where she teaches public speaking and English. She earned a Bachelor of Arts in Mass Communication from Mississippi Valley State University and a Master of Science in Mass Communication from Arkansas State University, both with an emphasis in Radio/TV Broadcasting. In addition, she earned and received the Doctorate of Philosophy (Ph.D.) in Community College Leadership from Mississippi State University.

Dr. Hall is a member of New Morning Star COGIC (Cleveland, MS), Superintendent Walter S. Dixon, Sr., pastor, Northern Mississippi Ecclesiastical Jurisdiction - Interim Bishop is Bishop Sedgwick Daniels, Bishop Designate William Dean, Mother Mary Scott, Supervisor.

# KAHOOT!!
# A YOUTH PERSPECTIVE ON THE USE
# OF TECHNOLOGY IN SUNDAY SCHOOL

## By Alyssa Grace Henson

Perhaps when you read the title of this article, the voice in your head heard a sneeze. And likely, your immediate thought was "bless you." Thank you! However, the title was no sneeze at all. Instead, I hoped to gain your attention to share from my humble middle school perspective about technology use in Sunday School.

Please allow me first to say young people love God. And we love Sunday School! It's just a bit difficult when we are learning using different systems in school and our other extra-curricular activities and come to our classes and have only books. It is always fun and exciting when my teacher brings in a game, a video, or even a song to tell us more about the lesson. Sometimes it is a short clip from a movie or tv show we might recognize. These are always great conversations starters for our class.

I personally really like getting the opportunity to use my cell phone for games and sometimes even social media! I can tell you firsthand those lessons that involve technology are the ones I remember the most. Even in my school work, my teachers use technology; I typically score higher in class. (I love to go for the A grade!). Some of my favorite learning platforms are Kahoot, Blooket quizzes and for learning facts and Quizlet. These are all FREE to use. According to classcraft, "Technology also motivates students to learn. They look forward to having time on their devices to explore and learn things through websites, videos, apps, and games. Students can learn and have fun at the same time, which helps them stay engaged with the material".

Technology is forever evolving into something amazing. I say why not use it all the time! Technology is not just for kids. Adults can use it too. When teachers prepare all those questions for us kids to answer, teachers are learning just as much as we are. Now I know that technology can sometimes be challenging. When our devices freeze or the internet is not working, don't worry and don't consider it frustration or even a failure. think of it as a blessing. When we constantly must look at that same screen with all of those amazing facts on it. You're learning without even knowing it!

If you're not completely sold on how beneficial technology can be, then let me enlighten you some more. Children's brains are still developing. That means our minds are still impressionable when we learn about how not to worry or stress. We really grip on to that. Teens spend seven hours a day on their phones, and tweens spend about the same amount. Why not use some of that time and learn about the bible. Even if you're not tech-savvy, ask one of the kids you teach to help you out?

You can even ask them if they prefer any specific platform! I'll tell you a little secret…we actually like it when you ask for our help! We like to feel valued and share what we know.

Make Sunday School learning and reviews even more exciting by adding some extra creativity. Maybe the game's winner gets to create the next Kahoot, or the class will watch a movie about what you learn that Sunday if everyone comes prepared. The possibilities with technology are endless. Maybe your church doesn't use technology as much as other churches do. That's okay to be a trendsetter!

Maybe you don't know how to present the idea of technology to your class. Many people have been in the exact same spot, and that's okay. Rely on technology and watch a video and read an article. In fact, there is almost nothing we can't learn on "YouTube University." There are so many helpful videos to help with technology and learning to present to classes of all ages and sizes.

Wow! That was a lot to take in but this Sunday, when you are reading the lesson, think about how you can incorporate technology into it!

Alyssa Grace Henson is the 13-year-old daughter of Pastor Aaron & Lady Christine Henson. She is in the 8th grade. She attends Henson Memorial COGIC, where her father is her pastor. She is a member of the praise team, youth department, and graphic media team. She enjoys writing, graphic design, and creating a business advertisements. She is a member of Kansas East Jurisdiction, Bishop L.F.Thuston, Prelate, Mother Novella Singleton, Supervisor Designee.

# DIG DEEPER WRITERS
## SPRING QUARTER

## The Reverend
## Eric James Gréaux, Sr., Ph.D.

Eric Gréaux, is a native of Amityville, New York, where he received his formal education at Our Redeemer Lutheran School, St. Kilian Jr. High School, and St. John the Baptist High School.

During his formative years, he received a sound fundamental foundation in Christian ethics and virtues through the godly example of his parents and godparents at Amityville Gospel Tabernacle. These experiences were strengthened by the training he received from the pastor and Christian Education workers at Faith Temple Church of God in Christ. Eric gave his heart to the Lord on August 15, 1979.

Eric Gréaux earned the Bachelor of Arts in Biblical & Theological Studies from Gordon College, the Master of Arts in Theological Studies from Gordon-Conwell Theological Seminary, and the Ph.D. in New Testament & Early Christian Origins from Duke University.

Dr. Gréaux has held teaching positions at Duke University, Carolina Evangelical Divinity School, Gordon-Conwell Theological Seminary-Charlotte, and Shaw University Divinity School. He is presently serving as Associate Professor of Religion at Winston-Salem State University, where he recently received the Wilma Lassiter Master Teaching Award. Eric holds memberships in the American Academy of Religion, the Society of Biblical Literature, the Evangelical Theological Society, the Institute for Biblical Research, and the Black Religious Scholars Society.

Dr. Gréaux is the author of To the Elect Exiles of the Dispersion ... from Babylon, a study of the function of Old Testament citations and allusions in First Peter. He has written articles that have been published in peer-reviewed journals, and Sunday School material for Urban Ministries, Inc. Dr. Gréaux has lectured and presented papers before numerous colleges, universities, and seminaries across the United States and at the Pontifical Gregorian University in Rome, Italy. In addition, he has traveled to India and Turkey in order to continue his studies and enhance his teaching skills. Dr. Gréaux is the recipient of the Wilma Lassiter Master Teacher Award (2019) and the Wells Fargo Excellence in Teaching Award (2021).

Elder Gréaux is married to the former Loring Bonita Crockett, a native of Boston. They have two sons, Tyler (a student at Gordon College) and Eric Jr. (a student at Appalachian State Universit). They live in Kernersville, NC, where he also serves as Pastor of Triad Ministries Church Of God In Christ. Bishop Leroy Jackson Woolard of Greater North Carolina is his Jurisdictional Prelate.

# QUARTERLY QUIZ

These questions may be used in two ways: as a pretest at the beginning of the quarter; as a review at the end of the quarter; or as a review after each lesson. Questions are based on the Scripture text of each lesson (King James Version).

## LESSON 1

1. Before the mountains and hills, what was "brought forth" (Proverbs 8:25)?

_____

_____

2. You are what if you hear (listen/follow) wisdom (Proverbs 8:33-34)?

_____

_____

## LESSON 2

1. John the Baptist was not the _____ (John 1:8).

_____

_____

2. "He [Jesus] was in the ____, and the world_____ _____ _____ _____, and the world knew him not" (John 1:10).

_____

_____

## LESSON 3

1. Name the town where the wedding took place (John 2:1).

_____

_____

2. Was the master of the banquet surprised at the miracle that happened (John 2:9)?

_____

_____

## LESSON 4

1. John stated that whoever believed in the _____ of _____ would have eternal life (John 3:14-15).

_____

_____

2. God sent Jesus for the whole world so that Jesus would _____ the world (John 3:17)

_____

_____

## LESSON 5

1. The Jewish leaders did not want to go into the hall of judgment because it was _____ (John 18:28).

_____

_____

2. True or False – Pilate wanted the Jews to judge Jesus instead (John 18:31).

_____

_____

## LESSON 6

1. Spell correctly the "full name" of the woman that John notes who went to Jesus' tomb (John 20:1).

_____

# QUARTERLY QUIZ

_____

2. What did Simon Peter (who went in first) and "the other disciple" (John) see in the tomb (John 20:5-7)?

_____

_____

## LESSON 7

1. "And said unto them that sold doves, take these things hence; make not my Father's house an house of _____". (John 2:16).

_____

_____

2. "Jesus answered and said unto them, destroy this _____, and in _____ _____ I will raise it up" (John 2:19).

_____

_____

## LESSON 8

1. What did Jesus mean by "living water" (John 4:10, 13–14)?

_____

_____

2. Based on the Samaritan woman's reaction to her conversation with Jesus, what sort of impact did He have on her (John 4:28–30)?

_____

_____

## LESSON 9

1. "I must work the works of him that sent me, while it is day: the _____ cometh, when no man can work" (John 9:4).

2. "And said unto him, Go, wash in the pool of _____, (which is by interpretation, Sent.) He went his way therefore, and washed, and came seeing" (John 9:7).

_____

_____

## LESSON 10

1. "_____ not for the meat which perisheth, but for that meat which endureth unto everlasting life, which the Son of man shall give unto you: for him hath God the Father sealed" (John 6:27).

_____

_____

2. Who is the Bread of Life, and what does He offer (John 6:33, 35)?

_____

_____

## LESSON 11

1. "_____ _____ _____ _____: by me if any man enter in, he shall be saved, and shall go in and out, and find pasture" (John 10:9).

_____

_____

2. "The _____ cometh not, but for to _____ and to _____, and to _____: I am come that they might have life, and that they might have it more abundantly" (John 10:10).

# QUARTERLY QUIZ

_____

_____

## LESSON 12

1. What is the first thing Martha says to Jesus when she meets Him (John 11:21)?

_____

_____

2. How does Martha understand Jesus' words about her brother rising again (John 11:24)?

_____

_____

## LESSON 13

1. How did Jesus tell the disciples to deal with anxiety in their hearts (John 14:1)?

_____

_____

2. According to Jesus, how can we know the Father (John 14:6–7)?

_____

_____

*Answers to Quarterly Quiz Can be found on page 479*

# WISDOM'S PART IN CREATION

**BIBLE BASIS: Proverbs 8:22–35**

**BIBLE TRUTH: Proverbs speaks of wisdom having a divine origin.**

**MEMORY VERSE: Hear instruction, and be wise, and refuse it not (Proverbs 8:33, KJV).**

**LESSON AIM: By the end of this lesson, we will: EXPLAIN what God's wisdom is;** REFLECT on God's wisdom in our lives; and PRAY for wisdom in our everyday life experiences.

**BACKGROUND SCRIPTURES: Proverbs 8—** Read and incorporate the insights gained from the Background Scriptures into your study of the lesson.

## TEACHER PREPARATION

**MATERIALS NEEDED:** Bibles (several different versions), Quarterly Commentary/Teacher Manual, Adult Quarterly, teaching resources such as charts, worksheets/handouts, paper, pens, and pencils.

**OTHER MATERIALS NEEDED / TEACHER'S NOTES:**

_____

_____

## LESSON OVERVIEW

**LIFE NEED FOR TODAY'S LESSON**
To know that wisdom is an important aspect with God in God's creation.

**BIBLE LEARNING**
To remember that wisdom is to be gained and not wasted.

**BIBLE APPLICATION**
To better understand how we can apply wisdom in our daily lives.

**STUDENTS' RESPONSES**
Students will share thoughts on how wisdom is obtained.

## LESSON SCRIPTURE

### PROVERBS 8:22-35, KJV

**22** The LORD possessed me in the beginning of his way, before his works of old.

**23** I was set up from everlasting, from the beginning, or ever the earth was.

### PROVERBS 8:22-35, AMP

**22** "The Lord created and possessed me at the beginning of His way, Before His works of old [were accomplished].

24 When there were no depths, I was brought forth; when there were no fountains abounding with water.

25 Before the mountains were settled, before the hills was I brought forth:

26 While as yet he had not made the earth, nor the fields, nor the highest part of the dust of the world.

27 When he prepared the heavens, I was there: when he set a compass upon the face of the depth:

28 When he established the clouds above: when he strengthened the fountains of the deep:

29 When he gave to the sea his decree, that the waters should not pass his commandment: when he appointed the foundations of the earth:

30 Then I was by him, as one brought up with him: and I was daily his delight, rejoicing always before him;

31 Rejoicing in the habitable part of his earth; and my delights were with the sons of men.

32 Now therefore hearken unto me, O ye children: for blessed are they that keep my ways.

33 Hear instruction, and be wise, and refuse it not.

34 Blessed is the man that heareth me, watching daily at my gates, waiting at the posts of my doors.

35 For whoso findeth me findeth life, and shall obtain favour of the LORD.

23" From everlasting I was established and ordained, From the beginning, before the earth existed, [I, godly wisdom, existed].

24 "When there were no ocean depths I was born, When there were no fountains and springs overflowing with water.

25 "Before the mountains were settled, Before the hills, I was born;

26 While He had not yet made the earth and the fields, Or the first of the dust of the earth.

27 "When He established the heavens, I [Wisdom] was there; When He drew a circle upon the face of the deep,

28 When He made firm the skies above, When the fountains and springs of the deep became fixed and strong,

29 When He set for the sea its boundary So that the waters would not transgress [the boundaries set by] His command, When He marked out the foundations of the earth—

30 Then I was beside Him, as a master craftsman; And I was daily His delight; Rejoicing before Him always,

31 Rejoicing in the world, His inhabited earth, And having my delight in the sons of men.

32 "Now therefore, O sons, listen to me, For blessed [happy, prosperous, to be admired] are they who keep my ways.

33 "Heed (pay attention to) instruction and be wise, And do not ignore or neglect it.

34 "Blessed [happy, prosperous, to be admired] is the man who listens to me, Watching daily at my gates, Waiting at my doorposts.

35 "For whoever finds me (Wisdom) finds life And obtains favor and grace from the Lord.

## BIBLICAL DEFINTIONS

A. **Hypostatize** (Hy-POST–a-tize)—To think of a concept, abstraction, etc., as having a real, objective existence.

B. **Metaphor**—A figure of speech in which a word or phrase is likened to something, but is not to be taken literally.

## LIGHT ON THE WORD

The book of Proverbs was written as instructional material, to be used as a type of "how to" manual for life. As such the book of Proverbs consists of succinct statements about life and human nature. Similes, metaphors, and other figures of speech are used generously to help give the reader a memorable word picture of a particular truth. In today's passage, wisdom is portrayed as "Lady Wisdom," giving us a unique, down-to-earth perspective on an intangible commodity. We will see wisdom is fulfilled in the person of Jesus Christ, He is wisdom.

## TEACHING THE BIBLE LESSON

## LIFE NEED FOR TODAY'S LESSON

AIM: That your students will appreciate the role that wisdom played in creation.

## INTRODUCTION

In this passage wisdom is personified. Some have called this a "hypostatization"-- thinking of a concept, abstraction, as having real objective existence. It seems more appropriate to think of this passage merely as a metaphor, that is a personification of an attribute of God but not an actual being in any way.

## BIBLE LEARNING

AIM: That your students will desire to acquire wisdom in their lives.

## I. WISDOM'S STORY (Proverbs 8:22–31)

In **Proverbs 8**, we see wisdom existing eternally. A sweeping panorama of creation is covered in **verses 24** through **29**, following the order of God's work listed in Genesis. Wisdom was with God before there was anything created. Wisdom was with God before there were oceans and rivers, before there were mountains and hills. Wisdom was there when God created the heavens and when He "set a compass" (**verse 27**) or "marked out the horizon" (NIV). What an indescribably beautiful picture!

### The Beauty of Wisdom
### (verses 22-31)

**22 The LORD possessed me in the beginning of his way, before his works of old. 23 I was set up from everlasting, from the beginning, Or ever the earth was. 24 When there were no depths, I was brought forth; when there were no fountains abounding with water. 25 Before the mountains were settled, before the hills was I brought forth: 26 While as yet he had not made the earth, nor the fields, nor the highest part of the dust of the world. 27 When he prepared the heavens, I was there: when he set a compass upon the face of the depth: 28 When he established the clouds above: when he strengthened the fountains of the deep: 29 When he gave to the sea his decree, that the waters should not pass his commandment: when he appointed the foundations of the earth: 30 Then I was by him, as one brought up with him: and I was daily his delight, rejoicing always before him; 31 Rejoicing in the habitable part of his earth; and my delights were**

**with the sons of men.**

clouds

The everlasting wisdom of God, an intrinsic fiber of His nature and character that was with Him as He created the world is available to us! When God set the world into motion, wisdom was there. Wisdom was there when God set the boundaries for the oceans, when He set the stars in motion, wisdom was there when He placed the clouds in the sky (**verse 28**). Wisdom is like a skilled artisan, rejoicing in the Master's presence and His creation (**verses 30–31**). Wisdom flowed from God's character, and His wonderful, creation was the result. God desires to give wisdom to those who seek Him. What an incredible thought!

The Hebrew word in Proverbs 8:30 translated as "brought up" means "architect," "master workman," or "skilled workman." The picture is that of wisdom, the faithful master artisan, standing at God's side as He created the universe. "How many are your works, LORD! In wisdom you made them all; the earth is full of your creatures" (**Psalm 104:24, NIV**).

Wisdom was ecstatic, as she was able to enjoy the "handiwork" of God (**Psalm 19:1, NKJV**). This implies a wonderful gathering of wisdom and humankind—do we dare envision a party? We celebrate God's creation in many ways. Each time we enjoy a ride through the countryside and see the bursting forth of the springtime flowers, view snowcapped mountains, or enjoy a picnic on a bright sunny day, we share wisdom's pleasure and joy in Creation. As we look at God's creation, we should praise our Creator: "Oh that men would praise the LORD for his goodness, and for his wonderful works to the children of men!" (**Psalm 107:8**).

## SEARCH THE SCRIPTURES

### QUESTION 1

Wisdom was present when God placed the _____ in the sky.

## LIGHT ON THE WORD
### The Delights of Wisdom

God's creative wisdom is available for the asking. In fact, wisdom "delights" in those who choose her (**verse 31**). Through wisdom, God set the creation in motion; likewise, through wisdom He orders our lives. He is aware of every detail of our lives and delights in giving us the wisdom to know Him more. As we know Him, more we begin to walk in wisdom. It's a circular principle, but one that God longs for us to take hold of. The more we know Him, the more wisdom we receive, and the more wisdom we receive, the more we seek Him.

## II. WISDOM'S INVITATION (Proverbs 8:32–35)

So the plea goes out to all people: "Listen to me; blessed are those who keep my ways" (**verse 32, NIV**). Receive instruction—don't refuse it. Proverbs 19:20 (NIV) says, "Listen to advice and accept discipline, and at the end you will be counted among the wise." Only fools reject instruction that will improve their lives. Respond to God's wisdom! He has made it available to us for our good, and we will be blessed when we choose to live by God's wisdom.

### The Blessings of Wisdom (verses 32-35)

**32 Now therefore hearken unto me, O ye children: for blessed are they that keep my ways. 33 Hear instruction, and be wise, and refuse it not. 34 Blessed is the man that heareth me, watching daily at my gates, waiting at the posts of my doors. 35 For whoso findeth me findeth life, and shall obtain favour of the LORD.**

What kind of blessings can we expect from living a wise life? Peace with God is certainly high on the list. A good reputation is also a benefit. Wisdom affects every area of our lives. If we conduct our interpersonal relationships with wisdom, we will have meaningful friendships and strong family ties. If we practice our business policies with wisdom we will enjoy the blessing of a reputable business. If we live our Christian lives with wisdom we will draw others to Christ. The blessings of wisdom may not always be tangible, but they far outweigh the material blessings that we often desire. Wisdom is worth it.

Wisdom does have another aspect however, it is not only something that God possesses it is something that God gives. We also see that Jesus demonstates wisdom in the New Testament. Jesus is viewed as the ultimate fulfillment of the Old Testament. Proverbs 8:22 tells us that wisdom was with God in the beginning before any of His "works of old." Does this have a familiar ring to it? John 1:1 says, "In the beginning was the Word, and the Word was with God, and the Word was God." Proverbs speaks of wisdom's eternal existence in a way that parallels John's words about Christ. In the Incarnation, Jesus is the complete demonstration of all that is divine including wisdom.

**Proverbs 8:23** says that wisdom was "appointed" (NIV) or "set up" (KJV) from eternity before the beginning! Jesus is the Anointed One, the Everlasting God, He was with God in the beginning, before time began. He has always been and always will be. In fact, without Him, "nothing was made that has been made" (**John 1:3, NIV**). He is and was first. He is and was supreme. He was "rejoicing always before him; Rejoicing in the habitable part" (**Proverbs 8:30–31**). Jesus, Wisdom Himself, rejoices over those who choose Him.

When we choose Jesus, we avail ourselves of a tremendous infinite amount of wisdom. Christ is "the power of God, and the wisdom of God" (**1 Corinthians 1:24**). "Blessed are they that keep my [wisdom's or Jesus'] ways (**Proverbs 8:32**). Hallelujah! What a treasure! When we seek Jesus, we gain wisdom. He is our all in all.

## QUESTION 2

According to Proverbs 8:35, "whoso findeth me [wisdom] findeth _____."

**life**. **Answers will vary**.

## LIGHT ON THE WORD

The Hebrew word for "life" means to be alive in a physical sense. Although we see hints in the Old Testament of eternal life, this idea was not yet fully developed. When Jesus came, our understanding of life after death became clear. We read in John 3:36 that those who believe in Jesus Christ, the Son of God, have everlasting life. Those who do not believe in Him do not have everlasting life in heaven, but God's wrath is on them. The book of Proverbs focuses on wisdom, wisdom that comes from God. This wisdom is incomplete until we receive Jesus Christ, who rightly claims that He is life.

## BIBLE APPLICATION

**AIM: That your students will learn to seek God's wisdom.**

How would your life be different if you sought God's wisdom on a regular basis? This week, try an experiment. Make a conscious effort to gain Godly wisdom before you make a decision or tackle a problem.

## STUDENTS' RESPONSES

**AIM: That your students will know that God's wisdom is available to everyone who desires a deeper relationship with Christ.**

Christ, family, and friendship were the most important things in life for Diane a successful high school principal. She and her best friend, Asia, had gone to high school and college together. Asia had dropped out of college and ran off with her "dream man" without marrying him. It had been a shock because Asia had been president of the College Christian Fellowship. Shortly after that, they had lost touch. One Thursday night, Diane received a call from Asia.

"Asia, is it really you?" Diana cried. "It's been 20 years."

"Girl, it's me!" said Asia. "I'm in town. I'd like to swing by your house later."

When Diane opened the door, Asia's face stole her breath away. Asia was scarecrow thin, and her eyes reflected a life of drug abuse and pain.

Suddenly, Diane realized that at some point in her life, Asia had chosen a life quite different from the one they had shared as young girls in Bible study. The folly of a life consumed by narcotics had blinded Asia and robbed her of the ability to make wise decisions.

Again, God's wisdom is available to everyone who desires a deeper relationship with Christ.

## PRAYER

God wisdom is precious and wonderful to have and to keep. Show us how to use wisdom in our personal and collective lives. Help us to see Jesus as true wisdom for us to have each and every day. In the name of Jesus we pray. Amen.

## DIG A LITTLE DEEPER

### The Authorship of Proverbs

The Bible records that when given the rare opportunity to request to receive anything from God that Solomon asked for "an understanding mind to govern [God's] people" (**1 Kings 3:3-9**). Evidence of the fulfillment is given in the account of how he handles a dispute between two prostitutes (**1 Kings 3:16-28**). As a result, Solomon is considered the wisest man to have ever lived (**1 Kings 4:29-31**). The Bible states that Solomon spoke 3,000 proverbs, and his songs were 1,005. The best of Solomon's songs is the Song of Solomon, identified as "the Song of Songs which is Solomon's" (**1:1**), in other words, his greatest one.

There is no doubt that the book of Proverbs reflects many of Solomon's 3,000 proverbs. From the first verse of Proverbs, we would assume that Solomon was the sole author of Proverbs. However, other authors are also identified throughout the book. For example, the words of Agur, the son of Jakeh (or the man of Massa), are recorded in chapter 30. And the words of King Lemuel are recorded in chapter 31.

Also included in Proverbs are the collected sayings simply identified as the "words of the wise" (**22:17-24:22**), and the "sayings of the wise" (**24:23-34**).

Besides being wise, the Preacher [i.e., Solomon] also taught the people knowledge, weighing and studying and arranging many proverbs with great care (**Eccl 12:9**).

Therefore, we can conclude that Proverbs is an edited work that includes the sayings of Agur, King Lemuel, and other wise people, among whom Solomon was the wisest.

## HOW TO SAY IT

Hypostatize.    Hy-POST–a-tize.

Metaphor.    MET-a-for.

## DAILY HOME BIBLE READINGS

### MONDAY
The Call of Wisdom
(Proverbs 8:1–11)

### TUESDAY
The Gifts of Wisdom
(Proverbs 8:12–21)

### WEDNESDAY
Before the Foundation of the World
(Ephesians 1:3–10)

### THURSDAY
The Handiwork of God
(Psalm 8)

### FRIDAY
The Firstborn of all Creation
(Colossians 1:15–19)

### SATURDAY
Creation Awaits Glory
(Romans 8:18–25)

### SUNDAY
Find Wisdom, Find Life
(Proverbs 8:22–35)

## PREPARE FOR NEXT SUNDAY

Read **John 1:1-14** and study "The Word Became Flesh."

**Sources:**
Adeyemo, Tokunboh, et al., eds. Africa Bible Commentary: A One-Volume Commentary
Written by 70 African Scholars. Nairobi, Kenya: Word Alive Publishers, 2006. 758–59.
Kidner, Derek. The Proverbs: An Introduction & Commentary. The Tyndale Old Testament Commentaries. Downers Grove, IL: InterVarsity Press, 1964.
Old Testament Hebrew Lexicon. Bible Study Tools.com. http://www.biblestudytools.com/lexicons/hebrew (accessed January 7, 2011).
Passage Lookup. Bible Gateway.com. http://www.biblegateway.com/passage (accessed January 7, 2011).
Strong's Exhaustive Concordance of the Bible. McLean, VA: MacDonald Publishing
Company. n.d.

## COMMENTS / NOTES:

# THE WORD BECAME FLESH

**BIBLE BASIS:** John 1:1–14

**BIBLE TRUTH:** Jesus has always been in existence.

**MEMORY VERSE:** And the Word was made flesh, and dwelt among us, (and we beheld his glory, the glory as of the only begotten of the Father,) full of grace and truth (John 1:14, KJV).

**LESSON AIM:** By the end of this lesson, we will: KNOW the importance of the divinity and humanity of Jesus; TRUST in a Savior who is eternal and shares the divine nature with God; and IMAGINE and SHARE how Jesus is the Light in our lives and in the world.

**BACKGROUND SCRIPTURES:** John 1:1–14—Read and incorporate the insights gained from the Background Scriptures into your study of the lesson.

## TEACHER PREPARATION

**MATERIALS NEEDED:** Bibles (several different versions), Quarterly Commentary/Teacher Manual, Adult Quarterly, teaching resources such as charts, worksheets/handouts, paper, pens, and pencils.

**OTHER MATERIALS NEEDED / TEACHER'S NOTES:**

_____

_____

## LESSON OVERVIEW

**LIFE NEED FOR TODAY'S LESSON**
To understand that Jesus is fully divine and fully human.

**BIBLE LEARNING**
To remember that Jesus was personally involved in creation from the beginning.

**BIBLE APPLICATION**
To better understand the role of Jesus as God's agent in creation.

**STUDENTS' RESPONSES**
Students will discuss ways that Jesus is real in their lives.

## LESSON SCRIPTURE

### JOHN 1:1-14, KJV

**1** In the beginning was the Word, and the Word was with God, and the Word was God.

### JOHN 1:1-14, AMP

**1** In the beginning [before all time] was the Word (Christ), and the Word was with God, and [b]the Word was God Himself.

2 The same was in the beginning with God.

3 All things were made by him; and without him was not any thing made that was made.

4 In him was life; and the life was the light of men.

5 And the light shineth in darkness; and the darkness comprehended it not.

6 There was a man sent from God, whose name was John.

7 The same came for a witness, to bear witness of the Light, that all men through him might believe.

8 He was not that Light, but was sent to bear witness of that Light.

9 That was the true Light, which lighteth every man that cometh into the world.

10 He was in the world, and the world was made by him, and the world knew him not.

11 He came unto his own, and his own received him not.

12 But as many as received him, to them gave he power to become the sons of God, even to

 them that believe on his name:

13 Which were born, not of blood, nor of the will of the flesh, nor of the will of man, but of God.

2 He was [continually existing] in the beginning [co-eternally] with God.

3 All things were made and came into existence through Him; and without Him not even one thing was made that has come into being.

4 In Him was life [and the power to bestow life], and the life was the Light of men.

5 The Light shines on in the darkness, and the darkness did not understand it or overpower it or appropriate it or absorb it [and is unreceptive to it].

6 There came a man commissioned and sent from God, whose name was John.

7 This man came as a witness, to testify about the Light, so that all might believe [in Christ, the Light] through him.

8 John was not the Light, but came to testify about the Light.

9 There it was—the true Light [the genuine, perfect, steadfast Light] which, coming into the world, enlightens everyone.

10 He (Christ) was in the world, and though the world was made through Him, the world did not recognize Him.

11 He came to that which was His own [that which belonged to Him—His world, His creation, His possession], and those who were His own [people—the Jewish nation] did not receive and welcome Him.

12 But to as many as did receive and welcome Him, He gave the right [the authority, the privilege] to become children of God, that is, to those who believe in (adhere to, trust in, and rely on) His name—

13 who were born, not of blood [natural conception], nor of the will of the flesh

**14** And the Word was made flesh, and dwelt among us, (and we beheld his glory, the glory as of the only begotten of the Father,) full of grace and truth.

[physical impulse], nor of the will of man [that of a natural father], but of God [that is, a divine and supernatural birth—they are born of God—spiritually transformed, renewed, sanctified].

**14** And the Word (Christ) became flesh, and lived among us; and we [actually] saw His glory, glory as belongs to the [One and] only begotten Son of the Father, [the Son who is truly unique, the only One of His kind, who is] full of grace and truth (absolutely free of deception).

## BIBLICAL DEFINITIONS

A. **Word (John 1:1, 14)** *logos* (Gk.)—The Word; denotes the expression of thought, not the mere name of an object. In John 1:1 and 1:14, Jesus is called "the Word."

B. **Witness (v. 7)** *martus or marturia* (Gk.)—Someone who has seen or heard or knows.

## LIGHT ON THE WORD

The author of the book of John identifies himself as "the disciple whom Jesus loved" (**John 13:23; 19:26; 21:7, 20, NIV**). Most scholars agree that the apostle John is the author of this

book. John was well-known in the early church and was intimately familiar with Jewish life. He

would have been an eyewitness to many of the events recorded in the Gospel of John.

## TEACHING THE BIBLE LESSON

## LIFE NEED FOR TODAY'S LESSON

AIM: That your students will trust that our

Savior is divine and is God.

## INTRODUCTION
### Gnosticism
Many of the early Gentile believers had been exposed to varying strains of Gnosticism (an early heresy) and did not believe in the humanity of Jesus. As people from diverse backgrounds became part of the church, it became necessary for the apostles to correct errors in doctrine as well as encourage the existing believers. In the Gospel of John, the writer seems to be addressing a mixed audience of believers, unbelievers, Jews, and Greeks.

## BIBLE LEARNING

AIM: That your students will learn that Jesus is eternal and human.

## I. JESUS IS THE WORD (John 1:1–3)

The first 14 verses of the book of John summarize the whole Gospel. In these verses, we are introduced to Jesus who He is, what He does, and the role He plays in the eternal plan of God for the world.

### Jesus Is the Word (verses 1-3)

**1 In the beginning was the Word, and the Word was with God, and the Word was God. 2 The same was in the beginning with God. 3 All things were made by him; and without him was not any thing made that was made.**

John began his book with the words "In the beginning," he then introduced Jesus as the Word." The word used here is logos. The Greeks understood logos to mean not only the written or spoken word, but also the thought or reasoning in the mind. John's Greek readers would have understood the nuances of logos, realizing that John was presenting Jesus as the power that controlled all things.

The Jewish believers used the word logos to refer to God and would have connected this concept to the wisdom personified in the Old Testament (**see Proverbs 8**). In tandem with wisdom was ability; in this case, God's wisdom was used to create the universe. Jesus is that wisdom personified, all of these concepts are bound up in the word logos.

John begins the second verse by reiterating the divine preexistent nature of the Word. He proceeds to explain the role of the Word in the beginning. The word "made" means "came into being, happened, or became." John is communicating the idea that this creative work happened out of nothing, that the Word did not rely on preexisting material to create the universe (**Colossians 1:16; Hebrews 1:2**).

John also begins to give us a hint as to the name of the Word by referring to the Word as "him." The Word is more than just an expression of the personality of God; it is the person of Jesus Christ. So John is saying that the Word, which was preexistent with God, was in complete fellowship with God, possessed all the divine nature and characteristics of deity and created everything.

As believers today, when we read John 1:1–3, we may not realize all the nuances that the author intended. But what we must learn from verse 1 is clear: Jesus was, is, and always will be. He is God, and He is the Creator and the Source of all life. The entirety of our Christian faith rests upon accepting these truths.

## SEARCH THE SCRIPTURES

### QUESTION 1

In John 1:1, John calls Jesus

"_____ _____."

**the Word**

## LIGHT ON THE WORD

### Jesus Is Everything to Us

Through Jesus, all things were created. The Bible says, "Without him nothing was made that has been made" (**John 1:3, NIV**). To understand the creation, we must know the Creator.

## II. JESUS IS THE LIGHT (John 1:4-9)

**4 In him was life; and the life was the light of men.**

"Life" in Greek is used throughout the Bible to refer to both physical and spiritual life. It is frequently qualified with the word "eternal." Jesus was the embodiment of the fullness and quality of life that God offers to those who believe (**John 14:6; cp. 10:10**). The life that Jesus was to offer would be the light of all humanity.

**5 And the light shineth in darkness; and the darkness comprehended it not.**

John uses the metaphors of "light" and "darkness" to illustrate the differences between a life of grace, mercy, and forgiveness and a life of sin and death. The word "comprehended" has two possible meanings. One meaning is "understood, perceived, or learned" it communicates the fact that those who live in the darkness do not receive the light because of a lack of

understanding they don't get it. Another meaning is the idea "lay hold of or seized" and communicates the fact that the darkness (perhaps Satan or more generally sinful humanity) will never have the ultimate victory over the light of Jesus.

John is saying that some who see the light will be unable to understand and receive it because Satan has blinded them (**2 Corinthians 4:4**). However John says that no matter how dark the darkness of evil seems in the world, no matter how the global circumstances seem to indicate that the darkness of evil is winning, the darkness cannot overcome the light that comes from the life of Christ.

**6 There was a man sent from God, whose name was John. 7 The same came for a witness, to bear witness of the Light, that all men through him might believe.**

The apostle John goes on to talk about John the Baptist, the ministry of John the Baptist is prominent in the Gospel of John. Here, the apostle John is affirming the prophetic ministry of John the Baptist. Jesus echoed this assertion when He said that John the Baptist was the last of the great Old Testament prophets, who came in the spirit of Elijah (**Matthew 11:9–10; Mark 9:13**). John the Baptist had a unique call and ministry to be a witness of Jesus, the Light (**cp. Matthew 4:4; John 1:4**).

In verse 7, the word "witness" means to affirm by testimony what one has seen, heard, experienced, or known. Therefore, John the Baptist had the prophetic duty of preparing the way for Jesus by preaching the testimonies of God.

The goal of John the Baptist was the same as the goal of John the apostle, to bring humanity to a place of faith in Jesus as Lord and Savior. The author is careful to specify that John the Baptist was not the genuine light, but that he came to "bear witness," to testify of, or report of the One to come. John the Baptist testified to the world of the nature and character of Jesus so that "all men through him might believe."

**8 He was not that Light, but was sent to bear witness of that Light. 9 That was the true Light, which lighteth every man that cometh into the world.**

The apostle John makes it clear that John the Baptist was not the Light, he was only to bear witness of the Light. Like the moon that does not shine its own light but only reflects the light of the sun, so John the Baptist reflects the Light of Jesus Christ, the Son of God. Jesus would be the true Light that would light every person. The word "true" refers to that which is sincere or genuine. The apostle John is saying that John the Baptist pointed others to the light to come, and that Jesus Christ was the authentic Light.

**QUESTION 2**
What role did John the Baptist fulfill before Jesus came?

**He was sent to bear witness of the Light. Answers will vary.**

### LIGHT ON THE WORD

#### Jesus Denied by the World
Although Jesus created the world (**Colossians 1:16**), the world did not recognize Him as Savior (**John 1:10**). Verse 11 says, "He came unto his own, and his own received him not." Jesus came to the Jews first but most of them rejected Him as their Messiah.

### III. JESUS REVEALS GOD'S CHARACTER (John 1:10–14)

Although He had always been omnipresent,

Jesus had now come to be one of us. He came to live with us, to feel our pain, to experience our joy, and to know our sorrow. He experienced human life fully. John and the other disciples knew Him intimately as Teacher and Friend. They ate with Him, talked with Him, laughed with Him, and cried with Him.

### Rejection and Glory (verses 10-14)

**10 He was in the world, and the world was made by him, and the world knew him not. 11 He came unto his own, and his own received him not. 12 But as many as received him, to them gave he power to become the sons of God, even to them that believe on his name: 13 Which were born, not of blood, nor of the will of the flesh, nor of the will of man, but of God. 14 And the Word was made flesh, and dwelt among us, (and we beheld his glory, the glory as of the only begotten of the Father,) full of grace and truth.**

His gift of salvation is offered freely to all, but unless one accepts that salvation, the darkness will continue to obscure the light. When we do receive Jesus, God gives us the right to become His children (**verse 12**). What an amazing statement! We have the right to become God's children. It's not because of anything we have done to deserve it, but because God's grace makes it possible for us to choose to believe and receive Jesus. We are not children in the physical sense; we are spiritual children of our Father. When we receive Christ, we are adopted into the family of God (**see I John 3:1**). We are considered heirs of God (**Galatians 3:29**), eligible to receive all of His promised blessings.

We cannot become God's children by any other means than through salvation in Jesus Christ.

John 1:13 makes it clear that God's children are not born in the natural way of conception and birth. We are born of God spiritually, and He chose us. God chose to send His Son, Jesus, to the earth to take on the form of human flesh. John first introduced us to Jesus as the eternally existing Word of God. Now he reveals another facet of logos Jesus. The One who has always existed, the One who is God, has become a human being (verse 14).

Verse 14 says, "The Word dwelt among us." John's Jewish readers would have understood the word "dwelling" to be connected to the word for "tabernacle." In Old Testament times, the tabernacle was where God's glory dwelled. The disciples watched Him perform miracles, and they knew Him as the Messiah.

### QUESTION 3

In John 1:14, John records that Jesus is full of _____ and _____.

**grace, truth.**

## LIGHT ON THE WORD

### The Power of Salvation

As modern-day believers, we can't physically touch Jesus. He is no longer here in the flesh, yet we can see His glory. We can testify to the miracles He has worked in our lives and the lives of others. We can bear witness to the power of salvation, and we can become like Him. In fact, we should strive to become like Him, because we are frail humans. When we receive the logos, we will begin to reflect the likeness of Him who is the Living Word.

## BIBLE APPLICATION

**AIM: That your students will understand that Jesus came to give a meaningful, real life to all who will receive Him.**

Jesus came into this world in the form of human flesh, yet those around Him did not acknowledge Him for who He is. They chose to continue living in darkness rather than receiving the Light. Things aren't so different in our world today. In modern society, especially in America and other modern societies, many people have become accustomed to a fast-paced hectic lifestyle. They are easily distracted, often bored, or generally dissatisfied with life.

## STUDENTS' RESPONSES

**AIM: That your students will learn that the right theology keeps us in right relationship with God.**

For the past 16 years, Greg had been a member of a group that did not believe that Jesus was the Son of God; they did not believe that Jesus was truly God and truly man. Greg tried and tried to be good enough to be in the number that would go to heaven, however he often slipped. It may have been in small ways, but he knew he was slipping and was not good enough to be in that number.

Then Greg began looking into the Bible for himself, because he desperately wanted to have a right relationship with God. He looked at John 1:1 where he saw that the Word was God and then at verse 14 where it said that the Word was made flesh. He wondered to himself: Who else could that be but Jesus? Then it hit him that the Bible was saying Jesus is God! This is not what those in the group had told him about Jesus.

The clincher was when he read in verse 12 that all he had to do to have that elusive relationship with God was to believe and receive Jesus! Right then and there, that's what Greg did.

## PRAYER

Lord, keep us in Your care, and remind us of the birth, life, death, and resurrection of our Lord and Savior, Jesus the Christ. We bless You, and we praise You. In the name of Jesus we pray. Amen.

## DIG A LITTLE DEEPER

## Heresies regarding the nature of Jesus

Gnosticism (from the Greek gnosis, meaning knowledge) reflects the teachings of a diverse group of people who claimed that they had inside knowledge into various truth regarding the nature of Jesus. Specifically, they taught that the material world was evil and that by knowledge, one could ascend to the pure spirituality of the heavenly realm. We see Paul's initial attempts to address this heresy in Colossians.

Docetism reflects the teachings of a subset of Gnosticism. Docetism comes from the Greek word dokeo, which means to seem or to appear. Docetists taught that Jesus was not a human being with flesh and blood. Rather he was actually a ghost or an apparition who appeared to be human. John addresses this heresy in his epistles, where he endeavors to reaffirm the full humanity and deity of Jesus. Those who deny this teaching are deemed antichrists.

Finally, Arianism was a heresy that developed in the 4th century. As opposed to Docetism that denied the full humanity of Jesus, Arianism denied the full deity of Jesus. In essence, they taught that Jesus was a demigod, i.e., less than God but more than human. This teaching is memorialized in the words of Arius, speaking of Jesus: There was a time when he (i.e., Jesus) was not." In other words, Arius taught that Jesus was some kind of created being. This heresy is reflected in the teachings of Jehovah's Witnesses, who believe that Jesus was the first of God's created beings.

## HOW TO SAY IT

| | |
|---|---|
| Dualistic. | Du-al-IST-ic. |
| Emanation. | Em-a-NA-shun. |
| Preexistence. | Pre-ex-IST-ens. |
| Incarnation. | In-car-NA-shun. |

## DAILY HOME BIBLE READINGS

**MONDAY**
The Beginning of the Year
(Exodus 12:1–8)

**TUESDAY**
The Beginning of Wisdom
(Psalm 111)

**WEDNESDAY**
In the Beginning, God
(Genesis 1:1–5)

**THURSDAY**
From the Foundations of the Earth
(Isaiah 40:21–26)

**FRIDAY**
The Beginning of the Gospel
(Mark 1:1-8)

**SATURDAY**
Beginning from Jerusalem
(Luke 24:44-49)

**SUNDAY**
In the Beginning, the Word
(John 1:1-14)

## PREPARE FOR NEXT SUNDAY

Read **John 2:1-12** and study "The Wedding at Cana."

**Sources:**
New Testament Greek Lexicon. Bible Study Tools.com.
http://www.biblestudytools.com/lexicons/greek (accessed January 7, 2011).
    Passage Lookup. Bible Gateway.com. http://www.biblegateway.com/
    passage (accessed January
7, 2011).
    Tenney, Merrill C. Expositor's Bible Commentary (John and Acts).
    Electronic edition. Edited by
Frank E. Gaebelein. Grand Rapids, MI: Zondervan Publishing, 1992.
    Vincent, Marvin R. Vincent's Word Studies, Vol. 2: The Writings of John.
    Electronic edition.
Hiawatha, IA: Parsons Technology, 1998.

**COMMENTS / NOTES:**

# THE WEDDING AT CANA

**BIBLE BASIS:** John 2:1–12

**BIBLE TRUTH:** Jesus always gives the best to us.

**MEMORY VERSE:** This beginning of miracles did Jesus in Cana of Galilee, and manifested forth his glory; and his disciples believed on him (John 2:11, KJV).

**LESSON AIM:** By the end of this lesson, we will: DISCUSS Jesus' response to Mary; REFLECT on Jesus' transforming power in our lives; and SHARE with others why the power of Jesus is necessary in our lives.

**BACKGROUND SCRIPTURES:** John 2:1–12— Read and incorporate insights gained from the Background Scriptures into your lesson.

## TEACHER PREPARATION

**MATERIALS NEEDED:** Bibles (several different versions), Quarterly Commentary/Teacher Manual, Adult Quarterly, teaching resources such as charts, worksheets/handouts, paper, pens, and pencils.

**OTHER MATERIALS NEEDED / TEACHER'S NOTES:**

_____

_____

## LESSON OVERVIEW

**LIFE NEED FOR TODAY'S LESSON**
To remember Jesus performs miracles that are always blessings.

**BIBLE LEARNING**
Jesus brings joy and hope in unexpected ways.

To better understand how the power of Jesus is real.

**STUDENTS' RESPONSES**
Students will recall situations where they have received or witnessed a miracle.

**BIBLE APPLICATION**

## LESSON SCRIPTURE

### JOHN 2:1-12, KJV

1 And the third day there was a marriage in Cana of Galilee; and the mother of Jesus was there:

### JOHN 2:1-12, AMP

1 On the third day there was a wedding at Cana of Galilee, and the mother of Jesus was there;

**2** And both Jesus was called, and his disciples, to the marriage.

**3** And when they wanted wine, the mother of Jesus saith unto him, They have no wine.

**4** Jesus saith unto her, Woman, what have I to do with thee? mine hour is not yet come.

**5** His mother saith unto the servants, Whatsoever he saith unto you, do it.

**6** And there were set there six waterpots of stone, after the manner of the purifying of the Jews, containing two or three firkins apiece.

**7** Jesus saith unto them, Fill the waterpots with water. And they filled them up to the brim.

**8** And he saith unto them, Draw out now, and bear unto the governor of the feast. And they bare it.

**9** When the ruler of the feast had tasted the water that was made wine, and knew not whence it was: (but the servants which drew the water knew;) the governor of the feast called the bridegroom,

**10** And saith unto him, Every man at the beginning doth set forth good wine; and when men have well drunk, then that which is worse: but thou hast kept the good wine until now.

**11** This beginning of miracles did Jesus in Cana of Galilee, and manifested forth his glory; and his disciples believed on him.

**12** After this he went down to Capernaum, he, and his mother, and his brethren, and his disciples: and they continued there not many days.

**2** and both Jesus and His disciples were invited to the wedding.

**3** When the wine was all gone, the mother of Jesus said to Him, "[a]They have no more wine."

**4** Jesus said to her, "[Dear] woman, [b]what is that to you and to Me? My time [to act and to be revealed] has not yet come."

**5** His mother said to the servants, "Whatever He says to you, do it."

**6** Now there were six stone waterpots set there for the Jewish custom of purification (ceremonial washing), containing twenty or thirty gallons each.

**7** Jesus said to the servants, "Fill the waterpots with water." So they filled them up to the brim.

**8** Then He said to them, "Draw some out now and take it to the headwaiter[of the banquet]." So they took it to him.

**9** And when the headwaiter tasted the water which had turned into wine, not knowing where it came from (though the servants who had drawn the water knew) he called the bridegroom,

**10** and said to him, "Everyone else serves his best wine first, and when people have [c] drunk freely, then he serves that which is not so good; but you have kept back the good wine until now."

**11** This, the first of His signs (attesting miracles), Jesus did in Cana of Galilee, and revealed His glory [displaying His deity and His great power openly], and His disciples believed [confidently] in Him [as the Messiah—they adhered to, trusted in, and relied on Him].

**12** After this He went down to Capernaum, He and His mother and brothers and His disciples; and they stayed there a few days.

## BIBLICAL DEFINTIONS

A. **Firkins (John 2:6)** *metretes* (Gk.)—A measure of capacity for liquids (each firkin equals about 10 gallons).

B. **Purifying (v. 6)** *katharismos* (Gk.)—The process of ritual cleansing, either legal or ceremonial, to purge from the pollution of sin and guilt.

## LIGHT ON THE WORD

God has drawn a veil over most of Jesus' life before He began His public ministry. Both Matthew and Luke record Jesus' birth, some of the incidents surrounding His birth, and early childhood (**Matthew 1:18–2:23; Luke 2:1–40**). The next and last glimpse we get of our Lord before His ministry is the pre-teen Jesus visiting the temple in Jerusalem (**Luke 2:41–52**). There has been a great deal of speculation about the next 18 years of Jesus' life, but Scripture does not reveal anything about those years.

## TEACHING THE BIBLE LESSON

## LIFE NEED FOR TODAY'S LESSON

AIM: That your students will know that God's blessing is upon Jesus.

## INTRODUCTION
### John Is Honored by Jesus

Around A.D. 27, John the Baptist explodes out of the Judean wilderness proclaiming the advent of the Messiah and the arrival of the kingdom of God. One day, as John is baptizing along the Jordan River, Jesus shows up. He presents Himself to John for baptism (**Matthew 3:13**). John realizes who Jesus is and tries to decline the honor, but Jesus convinces him that this is all part of God's plan, and John baptizes Him. As Jesus makes His way out of the water, the heavens open and the Holy Spirit descends upon Jesus in the form of a dove. Then the voice of God calls out from heaven, "This is my beloved Son, whom I love; with him I am well pleased" (**Matthew 3:17, NIV**).

## BIBLE LEARNING

AIM: That your students will learn that Jesus' power makes a difference.

## I. THE MERRY OCCASION (John 2:1–5)

Jewish wedding celebrations often lasted an entire week. The bridegroom's family had the sacred responsibility of providing food and beverages for all their guests for as long as the celebration lasted. In the midst of this celebration the unthinkable happened, the wine ran out. This was a matter of grave concern, it would be considered an insult to all those present and cause the family to become socially marginalized. Mary realized the situation was desperate and immediately turned to Jesus for help.

### Who Was at the Wedding (verses 1-2)?

**1 And the third day there was a marriage in Cana of Galilee; and the mother of Jesus was there: 2 And both Jesus was called, and his disciples, to the marriage.**

Cana of Galilee was located just south of Nazareth where Jesus grew up. The bridegroom may have been related to or maybe a close friend of Mary, Jesus' mother. The language of the passage suggests that Mary had some official function at the wedding, while Jesus and His disciples were invited guests. "Jesus' mother was there, and Jesus and his disciples had also been invited to the wedding" (**from John 2:1–2, NIV**).

Weddings were major events in those days. In small villages, such as Cana, where the people worked hard without much time for recreation, weddings were even more special. The entire village may have participated in the celebration of the couple's union. The actual wedding usually took place on a Wednesday if the bride was a virgin and on Thursday if she was a widow. The phrase "the third day" in verse 1 refers to the succession of incidents recorded in John 1:29 and 1:35.

The series of events began with a celebration at the home of the bride. The bridal party escorted the maiden from her parents' home and then to the home prepared for her by her husband. As the wedding party made its way through the streets, neighbors and townspeople saluted the bride. Many people joined the entourage until it grew into a parade. When the procession arrived at the bride's new home the couple exchanged vows. Then the bride and groom were crowned with garlands and the legal marriage document was signed. After the prescribed washing of hands and prayers, the marriage supper began with the cups being filled.

Marriage is the very first institution established by God (**Genesis 2:24**). The Old Testament repeatedly portrays the intimate relationship between God and Israel as a marriage (see **Isaiah 62:5; Jeremiah 3:14; Hosea 1:2 and 3:1**). In the New Testament, Christ is often referred to as the bridegroom (**Matthew 9:15; John 3:29**). The apostle Paul portrays the relationship between Christ and His church as that of a husband and wife (**II Corinthians 11:2; Ephesians 5:25–27**). The gathering of Christ and His church in heaven at the end of the age is described as a "wedding supper" (**Revelation 19:9, NIV**). When we consider the high esteem God has for marriage, it is highly appropriate that Christ would inaugurate the messianic age with a sign at a wedding.

## SEARCH THE SCRIPTURES
### QUESTION 1
Who was with Jesus at the wedding?

"**And the mother of Jesus was there: And both Jesus was called, and his disciples, to the marriage.**"

## LIGHT ON THE WORD

Mary's urgent request that Jesus do something does not necessarily indicate she expected a miracle. Her husband, Joseph, who is not mentioned again after the temple incident (**Luke 2:41–51**), had probably been dead for a long time.

## II. MARY TURNS TO JESUS FOR HELP (John 2:3-5)

Over the years, Mary had become accustomed to depending on her eldest son in emergencies, and this situation certainly qualified as an emergency. Mary's absolute confidence in Jesus implies that He had seldom disappointed her.

### Mary Brought the Dilemma to Her Son, Jesus (verses 3-5)

**3 And when they wanted wine, the mother of Jesus saith unto him, They have no wine. 4 Jesus saith unto her, Woman, what have I to do with thee? mine hour is not yet come. 5 His mother saith unto the servants, Whatsoever he saith unto you, do it.**

Our Lord's response to His mother seems flippant on the face of it, but Jesus is not being callous or disrespectful. The term "woman" (**John 2:4**) was one of endearment. Jesus used the same word when He lovingly entrusted His mother to John's care from the Cross: "Woman, behold thy son" (**from John 19:26**). It is probably better translated as "Dear woman" (**from John 2:4, NIV**). When the Lord inquires of His mother, "Why do you involve me?" (**from John 2:4, NIV**), it marks the turning point in His relationship with her and His family. From that moment on, the business of His Father would take precedence over the concerns of His mother (**see Luke 2:49–51**).

The phrase "my time has not yet come" (**John 2:4, NIV**) is an idea that will be repeated throughout John's narrative (**compare John 4:21, 23; 5:25; 7:30**). Jesus lived His earthly life according to a heavenly clock. His time on earth was always in His Father's hands. The "hour" Jesus refers to (**John 2:4**) is the final hour of His earthly ministry when He would be manifested as the Christ and share in the glory of God (**John 17:1**).

## QUESTION 2

What is Jesus' response to his mother's request for His assistance?

"Jesus saith unto her, Woman, what have I to do with thee? mine hour is not yet come." Answers will vary.

## LIGHT ON THE WORD

### Mary Believed in Jesus

Mary may or may not have understood what Jesus meant by His response, but she trusted Him to do what was right. She understood that Jesus was much more than just her Son, He was the Son of God. So the mother humbly submitted herself to the Son and instructed the servants, "Do whatever he tells you" (**John 2:5, NIV**).

## III. THE MIRACULOUS OCCURRENCE (John 2:6-11)

Outside the reception room were six large stone pots that contained water used for the ceremonial cleansing of hands. According to Jewish tradition, the primary sources of impurity were contact with dead creatures of any kind, genital flows, and certain skin diseases (**Leviticus 11**). Any impure object or person gave off a secondary degree of impurity to whatever or whomever it came into contact with. Since ultimately everything touches everything else, maintaining ritual purity was a continual battle.

Therefore, whenever new guests arrive at a wedding feast, water from the pots is poured over their hands in a cleansing ritual. Eating with unclean hands was also considered defilement, so water was poured over the hands of the diners before each meal.

### The Good Stuff (verses 6-11)

**6 And there were set there six water-pots of stone, after the manner of the purifying of the Jews, containing two or three firkins apiece. 7 Jesus saith unto them, Fill the waterpots with water. And they filled them up to the brim. 8 And he saith unto them, Draw out now, and bear unto the governor of the feast. And they bare it. 9 When the ruler of the feast had tasted the water that was made wine, and knew not whence it was: (but the servants which drew the water knew;) the governor of the feast called the bridegroom, 10 And saith unto him, Every man at the beginning doth set forth good wine; and when men have well drunk, then that which is worse: but thou hast kept the good wine until now. 11 This beginning of miracles did Jesus in Cana of Galilee, and manifested forth his glory; and his disciples believed on him.**

Each of the water pots had a capacity of two or three firkins of water (**John 2:6**). A firkin is about 10 gallons, so each pot held about 20 to 30 gallons. Jesus commands the servants to fill all the pots with water, and they obediently filled each pot to the brim (**verse 7**). Filling the pots to the brim eliminates the possibility of anything else being added to the pots other than water. Next, Jesus tells the servants to take out some of the wine that is in the pot and give it to the master of the banquet. Again, the servants do as they are instructed.

John does not explain how or when the water in the pots becomes wine. Both the bridegroom and the banquet master were at a loss to explain the source of the new wine but the servants knew.

Traditionally, "good wine " (**verse 10**) was wine that had not lost its sugar content in the fermentation process. Cheaper fermented wine had to be diluted with much more water to ensure that the revelers did not violate the law against drunkenness (**see Deuteronomy 21:20–21; Isaiah 28:7**). In either case, Jewish law mandated mixing all wine with water, the mixture ranged from three to 10 parts water to one part wine. The ratio of water to wine depended on the amount of alcohol in the wine.

The phrase "when men have well drunk" (**John 2:10**) means "become drunk" or "become satisfied" (without reference to drunkenness). The phrase must be translated according to its context. In this case, it is illogical to think that Jesus contributed gallons of wine to an already drunken party.

Our Lord is no mere magician performing magical feats to impress the crowds, He is the Son of God. He affects miracles to help His people and glorify His Father. The significance of Jesus' first miracle lies in the result produced. He transforms what would have been a disaster for the host into a joyous and praiseful moment.

## SEARCH THE SCRIPTURES
### QUESTION 3
The phrase "when men have well drunk" means _____.

**"become drunk" or "become satisfied"**

## LIGHT ON THE WORD
### The New Age of Grace
The supernatural event portrayed the opening of the new age of grace through the new wine of the Gospel and manifested Jesus' glory as the Son of God. The miracle caused Jesus' disciples to put their faith in Him (**verse 11**).

## IV. THE MOVE TO CAPERNAUM (John 2:12)
The belief prompted by the sign was not the complete faith Jesus desired, but it was a step above the disciples initial belief, which was only conjectural. The disciples had seen the miracle with their own eyes and were able to draw their own conclusions that a superior being was in their midst. Jesus proved all His claims through His acts of mercy and power.

### Jesus Leaves the Wedding (verse 12)
**12 After this he went down to Capernaum, he, and his mother, and his brethren, and his disciples: and they continued there not many days.**

Jesus did not stay around to receive public acclaim for this miracle, instead He moved on to Capernaum which was His headquarters for most of His ministry.

### QUESTION 4
Who left the wedding with Jesus?

**Jesus' mother, His brethren, and the disciples. Answers will vary.**

## LIGHT ON THE WORD
### Divine Acts of Love and Power
Miracles are not merely superhuman feats, they are divine acts of love and power. John refers to Jesus' miracles as signs. These signs always point past the event to the source of the event, Jesus Christ. The signs are recorded so that we may believe in the power and person of Jesus Christ and attain eternal life by believing (**1 John 5:13**).

## BIBLE APPLICATION

**AIM: That your students will discover ways to make a positive difference.**

The Gospel of Christ changes people from the inside out. Can you think of any ways God has changed you? This week, make a list of sinful ways or imperfections that God has changed in you. Then make a second list of sinful ways or imperfections you want God to change in you. Be prepared to share your first list with the class next week. Make your second list a matter of prayer and determine to use God's power in you to bring about change.

## STUDENTS' RESPONSES

**AIM: That your students will learn about the miracles that only God can do.**

Eddie's love of the party life was getting out of hand. He reached a critical point one day when he left work for lunch and returned to the office drunk, he was fired on the spot.

When Eddie finally went home, his wife told him that their marriage was over. Walking the streets with no job, no home, and no family, Eddie knew his life had hit rock bottom. He looked up to the sky and cried out, "Dear God, please help me!"

After a while, Eddie passed a little storefront church and something inside him compelled him to go in. The pastor made his way to Eddie and sat down with him, Eddie broke down and tearfully poured out the whole sad story. The pastor told Eddie that in spite of all the mistakes he had made, God still loved him. That day Eddie accepted Christ as His Lord and Savior, and from that moment on he never took another drink. Within a month, he found a new job. A short time later, he and his wife were reunited.

Eddie told his wife that he was sure God performed a miracle in his life. He said, "He changed my life from hopelessness to happiness and our marriage from failure to fantastic. If Jesus can change me, surely He can change anything."

## PRAYER

Lord, Your love, Your miracles, and Your awesomeness are truly blessings to us. Thank You for Your miracles and help us not to take them for granted, but to share Your love and mercy with others. In the name of Jesus we pray. Amen.

## DIG A LITTLE DEEPER

### The Seven Signs of John's Gospel

The key verse for unpacking this Gospel is located in John 20:30-31: "Now Jesus did many other signs in the presence of his disciples which are not written in this book; but these are written that you may believe that Jesus is the Christ, the Son of God, and that by believing you may have life in his name."

The key word is signs (Greek: semeia), which is the term that John uses to refer to the miracles of Jesus. He uses this term because these miracles point away from themselves to Jesus, the miracle-worker. These miracles give Jesus the opportunity to speak about his ministry and himself as the "I am" (**cf. Exod 3:14**). For example, after he feeds the multitude, Jesus talks about himself as the bread of life (**John 6:35**). And just before he opens the eyes of the man who was born blind, Jesus identifies himself as the light of the world (**John 9:5**).

Unlike the other Gospels that record innumerable miracles of Jesus, John chose to record only seven (four of which are unique to John*). These signs are:

- Changing water into wine (2:1-11*)

- Healing the official's son (4:46-54)

- Healing the paralytic (5:1-15*)

- Feeding the multitude (6:5-13) – the only miracles recorded in all four Gospels

- Walking on water (6:16-21)

- Healing the man born blind (9:1-7*)

- Raising Lazarus from the dead (11:1-44*)

John admits that it would be impossible to record everything that Jesus did (**John 21:25**). However, he has selected these seven miracles for the express purpose of getting them to believe that Jesus is the promised Messiah (**2:11; 4:48, 54; 11:45, 47-48**). The result of trusting in Jesus is eternal life.

## HOW TO SAY IT

Geneology.      Je-ne-OL-o-gy.

Lineage.        Li-nē-ij also Li-nij

Messianic.      Mes-e-AN-ik.

Manifestation.  Man-i-fes-TA-shun.

---

**DAILY HOME BIBLE READINGS**

**MONDAY**
Glorify Your Son
(John 17:1–5)

**TUESDAY**
Glory That Comes from God
(John 5:39–47)

**WEDNESDAY**
Glory That Belongs to God
(John 7:10–18)

**THURSDAY**
God Glorifies the Son
(John 8:48–59)

**FRIDAY**
Loving Human Glory
(John 12:36b–43)

**SATURDAY**
Glory for the Sake of Unity
(John 17:20–24)

**SUNDAY**
Glory Revealed
(John 2:1–12)

## PREPARE FOR NEXT SUNDAY

Read **John 3:11-21** and study "God's Word Saves."

**Sources:**

New Testament Greek Lexicon. Bible Study Tools.com. http://www.biblestudytools.com/lexicons/greek (accessed January 7, 2011).

Passage Lookup. Bible Gateway.com. http://www.biblegateway.com/passage (accessed January 7, 2011).

Strong's Exhaustive Concordance of the Bible. McLean, VA: MacDonald Publishing
Company. n.d.

# GOD'S WORD SAVES

**BIBLE BASIS:** John 3:11–21

**BIBLE TRUTH:** Regardless of our choices, God loves us and sent Jesus to restore our relationship with Him..

**MEMORY VERSE:** For God so loved the world, that he gave his only begotten Son, that whosoever believeth in him should not perish, but have everlasting life (John 3:16, KJV).

**LESSON AIM:** By the end of this lesson, we will: KNOW why God gave Jesus to the world; REJOICE for the love of Jesus in the world; and LIST ways we can and do share the love of God.

**BACKGROUND SCRIPTURES:** John 3:11–21; Numbers 21:4–8—Read and incorporate insights gained from the Background Scriptures into your lesson.

## TEACHER PREPARATION

**MATERIALS NEEDED:** Bibles (several different versions), Quarterly Commentary/Teacher Manual, Adult Quarterly, teaching resources such as charts, worksheets/handouts, paper, pens, and pencils.

**OTHER MATERIALS NEEDED / TEACHER'S NOTES:**

_____

_____

## LESSON OVERVIEW

**LIFE NEED FOR TODAY'S LESSON**
To remember why God gave Jesus to the world.

**BIBLE LEARNING**
The Gospel writer John gives us the reassurance of God's everlasting love.

**BIBLE APPLICATION**
To better understand the importance of sharing God's love with others.

**STUDENTS' RESPONSES**
Students will make the time to show the love of Christ.

## LESSON SCRIPTURE

### JOHN 3:11-21, KJV

11 Verily, verily, I say unto thee, We speak that we do know, and testify that we have seen; and ye receive not our witness.

### JOHN 3:11-21, AMP

11 I assure you and most solemnly say to you, we speak only of what we [absolutely] know and testify about what we have [actually] seen [as eyewitnesses]; and [still] you [reject our evidence and] do not accept our testimony.

**12** If I have told you earthly things, and ye believe not, how shall ye believe, if I tell you of heavenly things?

**13** And no man hath ascended up to heaven, but he that came down from heaven, even the Son of man which is in heaven.

**14** And as Moses lifted up the serpent in the wilderness, even so must the Son of man be lifted up:

**15** That whosoever believeth in him should not perish, but have eternal life.

**16** For God so loved the world, that he gave his only begotten Son, that whosoever believeth in him should not perish, but have everlasting life.

**17** For God sent not his Son into the world to condemn the world; but that the world through him might be saved.

**18** He that believeth on him is not condemned: but he that believeth not is condemned already, because he hath not believed in the name of the only begotten Son of God.

**19** And this is the condemnation, that light is come into the world, and men loved darkness rather than light, because their deeds were evil.

**20** For every one that doeth evil hateth the light, neither cometh to the light, lest his deeds should be reproved.

**21** But he that doeth truth cometh to the light, that his deeds may be made manifest, that they are wrought in God.

**12** If I told you earthly things [that is, things that happen right here on earth] and you do not believe, how will you believe and trust Me if I tell you heavenly things?

**13** No one has gone up into heaven, but there is One who came down from heaven, the Son of Man [Himself—whose home is in heaven].

**14** Just as Moses lifted up the [bronze] serpent in the desert [on a pole], so must the Son of Man be lifted up [on the cross],

**15** so that whoever believes will in Him have eternal life [after physical death, and will actually live forever].

**16** "For God so [greatly] loved and dearly prized the world, that He [even] gave His [One and] [a]only begotten Son, so that whoever believes and trusts in Him [as Savior] shall not perish, but have eternal life.

**17** For God did not send the Son into the world to judge and condemn the world[that is, to initiate the final judgment of the world], but that the world might be saved through Him.

**18** Whoever believes and has decided to trust in Him [as personal Savior and Lord] is not judged[for this one, there is no judgment, no rejection, no condemnation]; but the one who does not believe [and has decided to reject Him as personal Savior and Lord] is judged already [that one has been convicted and sentenced], because [b]he has not believed and trusted in the name of the [One and] only begotten Son of God [the One who is truly unique, the only One of His kind, the One who alone can save him].

**19** This is the judgment [that is, the cause for indictment, the test by which people are judged, the basis for the sentence]: the Light has come into the world, and people loved the [c]darkness rather than the Light, for their deeds were evil.

**20** For every wrongdoer hates the Light, and does not come to the Light [but shrinks from it] for fear that his[sinful, worthless] activities will be exposed and condemned.

21 But whoever practices truth [and does what is right—morally, ethically, spiritually] comes to the Light, so that his works may be plainly shown to be what they are—accomplished in God [divinely prompted, done with God's help, in dependence on Him]."

## BIBLICAL DEFINITIONS

A.**Begotten (John 3:16, 18)** *monogenes* (Gk.)—The one who is born; brought forth.

## LIGHT ON THE WORD

Jesus was deep into conversation with Nicodemus one evening. Nicodemus was a respected religious scholar, a Pharisee, and a member of the Jewish ruling council. John does not tell us why Nicodemus came to see Jesus at night. It is possible that he came then because the Pharisees opposed Jesus, and Nicodemus wanted to check out Jesus for himself. Nicodemus seems to be approaching Jesus with a proud attitude. Although he called Jesus "Rabbi" and "teacher" (**John 3:2**), that seems to be all that he was able to admit.

## TEACHING THE BIBLE LESSON

## LIFE NEED FOR TODAY'S LESSON

**AIM:** That your students will understand why Jesus is uniquely qualified to speak of spiritual things.

## INTRODUCTION

### The Pharisees

The Pharisees were members of a Jewish religious sect. They were very concerned with obedience to the Law, and they included their own extensive interpretations of the Law, which were not part of the Old Testament. Because of their emphasis on a legalistic interpretation of Scripture, they came into conflict with Jesus. Jesus pointed to God's concern for love for Him and love for neighbors as being more important than things such as tithing the herbs that grow in our gardens.

## BIBLE LEARNING

**AIM:** That your students will learn that Jesus rebukes spiritual misunderstanding.

## I. JESUS SPEAKS OF HEAVENLY THINGS (John 3:11–13)

Nicodemus was a prominent Pharisee, a member of the Sanhedrin Council, a doctor of the Jewish law, and a spiritual leader. Helacked an understanding of what Jesus was teaching him. However, Jesus makes it clear that He and His followers know the truth through firsthand experience (**John 7:16; 8:38; I John 1:3**). Yet, Nicodemus and the Jewish authorities refused to believe them.

## A Conversation with Nicodemus (verses 11-13)

**11 Verily, verily, I say unto thee, We speak that we do know, and testify that we have seen; and ye receive not our witness. 12 If I have told you earthly things, and ye believe not, how shall ye believe, if I tell you of heavenly things? 13 And no man hath ascended up to heaven, but he that came down from heaven, even the Son of man which is in heaven.**

Jesus mildly rebuked Nicodemus for doubt, and He assured the Pharisee that "we speak [what] we do know, and testify [to what] we have seen" (**verse 11**). Then Jesus asked Nicodemus a rhetorical question: "If I have told you earthly things, and ye believe not, how shall ye believe, if I tell you of heavenly things?" (**verse 12**). If Nicodemus could not accept the basic teaching of redemption, he would never be able to understand the deeper mysteries of God. Jesus used the earthly metaphors of birth and wind to explain heavenly things. Nicodemus probably understood the spiritual truths that Jesus was talking about, but he did not want to believe at this time.

To prove His point, Jesus made an astounding statement: "And no man hath ascended up to heaven, but he that came down from heaven, even the Son of man which is in heaven" (**verse 13**). Jesus is saying that no human has been to heaven except the Son of man who came down from heaven.

## SEARCH THE SCRIPTURES

### QUESTION 1

Jesus told Nicodemus that "no man hath _____ _____ to heaven,…"

Ascended, up

## LIGHT ON THE WORD

### Son of Man

The phrase "Son of man" appears in the Old Testament primarily to specify a member of humanity (**cf. Psalm 8:4**). It was also used to refer to the prophet in the book of Ezekiel. Later, in the apocalyptic book of Daniel, one sees a new development in the use of the phrase. The "Son of man" takes on the character of a divine agent who will carry out judgment and deliverance (**see Daniel 7:13**).

## II. JESUS WILL BE LIFTED UP (John 3:14–15)

Here, Jesus is openly declaring that He came down from heaven to reveal heavenly truths (**verse 14**). To clarify His identity and explain the meaning of His coming down from heaven, Jesus referred to an incident that Nicodemus was certainly aware of.

## Looking to the Cross (verses 14-15)

**14 And as Moses lifted up the serpent in the wilderness, even so must the Son of man be lifted up: 15 That whosoever believeth in him should not perish, but have eternal life.**

Shortly before the Israelites entered the Promised Land, they again complained about their situation. The Lord sent venomous snakes among them that bit the people and many died. Then the Israelites repented of their sin, so God commanded Moses to fashion a bronze serpent and put it on a pole. Anyone who looked up to the serpent would be saved by this simple act of faith (**see Numbers 21:4–9**). In that same way, Jesus came down from heaven to be lifted up on a pole (cross). Whoever will look to the Cross and accept Jesus' sacrifice as an act of faith will be saved.

## QUESTION 2
Moses lifted up what in the wilderness?

**A serpent.**

## LIGHT ON THE WORD
### Jesus Is the Savior
Jesus Christ should be exalted as Savior and Lord in the heart and life of every believer (**2 Peter 3:18**), and He will ultimately be exalted in all the earth (**Philippians 2:8–11**). The One who suffered death for us is the source of life for all who believe.

## III. JESUS SHOWED GOD'S LOVE (John 3:16)

**16 For God so loved the world, that he gave his only begotten Son, that whosoever believeth in him should not perish, but have everlasting life.**

John 3:16 is one of the most beloved verses in all of Scripture. However, in this study, we must also remember that it is found in the context of a conversation between Jesus and Nicodemus.

### God Takes Away Our Sin (verse 16)
Out of the darkness of night under the shadow of uncertainty, Nicodemus came to Jesus the Light of the world. It is in John 3:16 that Nicodemus and each of us find the answer: God takes away our sins and grants us new birth or "everlasting life" because of His unconditional love for us, which is manifested by the sacrifice of His Son and our Savior, Jesus Christ.

## SEARCH THE SCRITURES
### QUESTION 3
God gives everlasting life through whom?

**Jesus**

## LIGHT ON THE WORD
### God's Heart and God's Purpose
This verse reveals God's heart and His purpose is found in verse 16. God's love is so wide that it embraces all persons in "the world." It is so long that it reaches out to "whosoever." The depth of His love is shown by what He was willing to sacrifice on our behalf His "only begotten Son." His love grants us "everlasting life" in heaven in exchange for believing in Jesus Christ, the Son of God, and His sacrifice for us.

## IV. JESUS BRINGS BOTH LOVE AND JUDGMENT (John 3:17–21)

God sent Jesus into a world that already was condemned, so condemnation was not His purpose in coming. Elsewhere in Scripture, we read that Jesus came to judge the world. The judge can declare a person innocent or guilty, and this is the power and authority that Jesus, as the second member of the Trinity, has. So Jesus came to our world when we were already condemned because of our sin, and the purpose of His coming was to save us from this condemnation. The Greek for "condemnation" in some passages, is neutral; it simply means to judge, but in this passage and others in John, it means to condemn.

### Jesus Is the Light of the World (verses 17-21)
**17 For God sent not his Son into the world to condemn the world; but that the world through him might be saved. 18 He that believeth on him is not condemned: but he that believeth not is condemned already, because he hath not believed in the name of the only begotten Son of God. 19 And this is the condemnation, that light is come into the world, and men loved darkness rather than light, because their deeds were evil. 20 For every one that doeth evil hateth the light, neither cometh to the light, lest his deeds should**

be reproved. 21 But he that doeth truth cometh to the light, that his deeds may be made manifest, that they are wrought in God.

We read in **John 1:4–9** that Jesus is the true Light, the only light that can bring light to any one of us. Think of all the dark places of this world such as some bars, clubs, etc, the lights are kept very low so people can do shameful things. If people prefer that no one see the things they are doing, they want to stay where it is figuratively, if not actually, dark. Their pride keeps them from coming to Jesus; they do not want to change.

Jesus desires that we come to Him with all our sinful baggage and let Him wash us clean. Then there is a change in our lives, and we want people to see the change. We want people to see the good things we are doing, not because of self-pride, but because we want to give the glory to God, who is doing these things through us.

## QUESTION 4

But he that _____ _____ cometh to the light, that his _____ may be made manifest, that they are _____ in God.

**Doeth, truth, deeds, and wrought.**

## LIGHT ON THE WORD

### Bad Versus Good

The Greek makes it clear that this is not simply the contrast of doing bad things versus doing good things. The Greek for "evil" refers to many worthless deeds. The Greek for "doeth truth" does not mean good deeds in contrast with evil deeds; it means living by the truth that is in Christ Jesus.

## BIBLE APPLICATION

**AIM: That your students will begin to understand that being a Christian is a lifestyle.**

### Reconciling Our Belief and Actions in Christ

According to several surveys, most citizens consider America to be a Christian nation. Many Americans profess a kind of belief in God and His Son Jesus Christ. Yet this nation is one of the most morally corrupt nations on earth. How do we reconcile our belief in God and Christ with our deeds?

## STUDENTS' RESPONSES

**AIM: That your students will know that we can change to follow God's way.**

Brother Williams is a gifted Christian who serves on the Board of Trustees at his church. However this was not always the case, he is a recovering alcoholic who used to beat his wife and children. After years of tolerating her husband's behavior, Mrs. Williams had finally had enough. One weekend Mr. Williams arrived home drunk as usual and found his wife, children, and all their possessions gone.

Mr. Williams was miserable without his family. One of his coworkers noticed his downward spiral and invited him out to lunch. Mr. Williams confessed to being unable to turn his life around and did not know where he could find help.

His coworker told him about the life-changing relationship he had with Jesus. Then he asked Mr. Williams if he would like to become a new person in Christ. Right there in the restaurant, Brother Williams gave his life to Christ. He no longer drinks; he and his family are reunited and happy.

Brother Williams did not just turn over a "new leaf." He actually became a new person in Christ. In today's lesson, Jesus explains to a religious scholar named Nicodemus what it means to be born again.

## PRAYER

Precious Jesus, thank You for Your abounding love in us and for us. We thank You for giving us so much more than we deserve. Thank You for leading and guiding us to learn how to love and share Your love with one another, while we are learning to love ourselves. In Jesus' name we pray. Amen.

## DIG A LITTLE DEEPER

### Religious groups in the first century Israel

The Jewish historian Josephus (b. A.D. 37) writes extensively about the world in which Jesus lived. One of his most pertinent observations regards the variety of groups that existed in 1st century Palestine.

Jewish philosophy, in fact, takes three forms. The followers of the first school are called Pharisees, of the second Sadducees, of the third Essenes.

Of the two first-named schools, the Pharisees, who are considered the most accurate interpreters of the laws, and hold the position of the leading sect, attribute everything to Fate and to God; they hold that to act rightly or otherwise rests indeed, for the most part with men, but that in each action Fate co-operates. Every soul, they maintain, is imperishable, but the soul of the good alone passes into another body while the souls of the wicked suffer eternal punishment.

The Sadducees, the second of the orders, do away with Fate altogether and remove God beyond, not merely the commission, but they very sight, of evil. They maintain that man has the free choice of good or evil and that it rests with each man's will whether he follows the one or the other. As for the persistence of the soul after death, penalties in the underworld, and rewards, they will have none of them.

Josephus, The Jewish War ii. 119f, 122, 137-42, 152f, 162-66

C.K. Barrett, New Testament Background: Selected Documents (San Francisco: Harper & Row, 1989) 158-59.

## HOW TO SAY IT

Apocalytptic. A-poc-a-LIP-tik

### DAILY HOME BIBLE READINGS

**MONDAY**
The Light of the World
(Matthew 5:13–16)

**TUESDAY**
Lovers of Darkness
(Job 24:13–17)

**WEDNESDAY**
Loving Evil More than Good
(Psalm 52)

**THURSDAY**
Look and Live
(Numbers 21:4–9)

**FRIDAY**
Wrongly Worshiping the Symbol
(2 Kings 18:1–7a)

**SATURDAY**
Light for the Way
(Nehemiah 9:9–15)

**SUNDAY**
Whoever Believes in Him
(John 3:11–21)

## PREPARE FOR NEXT SUNDAY

Read **John 18:28–37**, and study "Jesus Testifies to the Truth."

**Sources:**
Carson, D. A. The Gospel According to John. Grand Rapids, MI: William B. Eerdmans
Publishing Company, 1991.

New Testament Greek Lexicon. Bible Study Tools.com. http://www.biblestudytools.com/lexicons/greek (accessed January 8, 2011).

Passage Lookup. Bible Gateway.com. http://www.biblegateway.com/passage (accessed January 8, 2011).

Strong's Exhaustive Concordance of the Bible. McLean, VA: MacDonald Publishing
Company. n.d.

## COMMENTS / NOTES:

# JESUS TESTIFIES TO THE TRUTH

**BIBLE BASIS:** John 18:28–37

**BIBLE TRUTH:** God's Word is always truth that prevails. .

**MEMORY VERSE:** "Pilate therefore said unto him, Art thou a king then? Jesus answered, Thou sayest that I am a king. To this end was I born, and for this cause came I into the world, that I should bear witness unto the truth.

Every one that is of the truth heareth my voice" (John 18:37, KJV).

**LESSON AIM:** By the end of this lesson, we will: KNOW the meaning of God's love for all; FEEL that we share the truth in Christ; and WITNESS with others how faith impacts our day-to-day behavior.

**BACKGROUND SCRIPTURES:** John 18–19— Read and incorporate insights gained from the Background Scriptures into your lessons.

## TEACHER PREPARATION

**MATERIALS NEEDED:** Bibles (several different versions), Quarterly Commentary/Teacher Manual, Adult Quarterly, teaching resources such as charts, worksheets/handouts, paper, pens, and pencils.

**OTHER MATERIALS NEEDED / TEACHER'S NOTES:**

_____

_____

## LESSON OVERVIEW

**LIFE NEED FOR TODAY'S LESSON**
Remember that the meaning of God's love is for all.

**BIBLE LEARNING**
The truth of God's love is made clear through His sacrifice of His life for us.

**BIBLE APPLICATION**

To appreciate how to witness to others how faith impacts our day-to-day behavior.

**STUDENTS' RESPONSES**
Students will share some insights learned from today's lesson with someone that they may not normally approach.

## LESSON SCRIPTURE

### JOHN 18:28-37, KJV

28 Then led they Jesus from Caiaphas unto the hall of judgment: and it was early; and

### JOHN 18:28-37, AMP

28 Then the Jews led Jesus from Caiaphas to the Praetorium (governor's palace). Now it was early and the Jews did not enter

they themselves went not into the judgment hall, lest they should be defiled; but that they might eat the passover.

29 Pilate then went out unto them, and said, What accusation bring ye against this man?

30 They answered and said unto him, If he were not a malefactor, we would not have delivered him up unto thee.

31 Then said Pilate unto them, Take ye him, and judge him according to your law. The Jews therefore said unto him, It is not lawful for us to put any man to death:

32 That the saying of Jesus might be fulfilled, which he spake, signifying what death he should die.

33 Then Pilate entered into the judgment hall again, and called Jesus, and said unto him, Art thou the King of the Jews?

34 Jesus answered him, Sayest thou this thing of thyself, or did others tell it thee of me?

35 Pilate answered, Am I a Jew? Thine own nation and the chief priests have delivered thee unto me: what hast thou done?

36 Jesus answered, My kingdom is not of this world: if my kingdom were of this world, then would my servants fight, that I should not be delivered to the Jews: but now is my kingdom not from hence.

37 Pilate therefore said unto him, Art thou a king then? Jesus answered, Thou sayest that I am a king. To this end was I born, and for this cause came I into the world, that I should bear witness unto the truth. Every one that is of the truth heareth my voice.

the Praetorium so that they would not be [ceremonially] unclean, but might [be able to] eat [and participate in the Feast of Unleavened Bread which began after] the [a]Passover [supper].

29 So Pilate came out to them and asked, "What accusation do you bring against this Man?"

30 They answered, "If He were not a criminal, we would not have handed Him over to you [for judgment]."

31 Then Pilate said to them, "Take Him yourselves and judge Him according to your own law." The Jews said, "We are not permitted to put anyone to death."

32 This was to fulfill the word which Jesus had spoken to indicate by what manner of death He was going to die.

33 So Pilate went into the Praetorium again, and called Jesus and asked Him, "Are You the King of the Jews?"

34 Jesus replied, "Are you saying this on your own initiative, or did others tell you about Me?"

35 Pilate answered, "I am not a Jew, am I? Your own people and their chief priests have handed You over to me. What have You done [that is worthy of death]?"

36 Jesus replied, "My kingdom is not of this world [nor does it have its origin in this world]. If My kingdom were of this world, My servants would be fighting [hard] to keep Me from being handed over to the Jews; but as it is, My kingdom is not of this world."

37 So Pilate said to Him, "Then You are a King?" Jesus answered, "You say [correctly] that I am a King. This is why I was born, and for this I have come into the world, to testify to the truth. Everyone who is of the truth [who is a friend of

the truth and belongs to the truth] hears and listens carefully to My voice."

## BIBLICAL DEFINITIONS

**A. Passover (John 18:28)** *pecach* (Heb.)—A Jewish celebration commemorating their exodus from bondage in Egypt.

**B. Defilement (v. 28)** *chalal* **(Heb.)**— Unclean. No Hebrew, especially a priest could partake of the Passover Feast and be unclean. To be in a Gentile's presence or building rendered that person unclean.

## LIGHT ON THE WORD

Jerusalem was occupied by the Roman Empire during the days of Jesus. Pontius Pilate served as the Roman Governor of Judea, and Caiaphas, the High Priest, sought a death sentence from Pilate. Pilate, however, did not want the responsibility of sentencing Jesus to death, instead, he relied on public opinion and bartered for the life of Jesus with Barabbas. When the mob chose Barabbas to be released according to custom, Pilate claimed to have found no fault in Him. However, Pilate released Jesus to be crucified (Luke 23:22–25).

## TEACHING THE BIBLE LESSON

## LIFE NEED FOR TODAY'S LESSON

**AIM: That your students will pray that the Holy Spirit will minister to persons who do not know Jesus Christ.**

## INTRODUCTION

### The Passover

Following 400 years of bondage in Egypt, the descendants of Abraham were instructed by Moses to place the blood of a lamb upon the door posts and lintel ("the horizontal beam forming the top of a door" [Wycliffe, 1043]) of their homes. This blood permitted the death angel to pass over the homes of the Hebrew nation, causing Pharaoh to relent and release them from slavery.

## BIBLE LEARNING

**AIM: That your students will better understand the events of Jesus with Caiaphas.**

## I. DEFILED AND UNCLEAN (John 18:28)

Jesus had been questioned in the palace of the High Priest, Caiaphas. There He was ridiculed, challenged, and struck. While there, His disciple Peter denied Him three times. From the palace, Jesus was taken to Pilate's judgment hall. The envoy of priests would not enter the hall of judgment or they would have been defiled, instead they stood outside yelling their accusations against Jesus to Pilate.

### Judgment Hall (verse 28)
**28 Then led they Jesus from Caiaphas unto the hall of judgment: and it was early; and they themselves went not into the judgment hall, lest they should be defiled; but that they might eat the Passover.**

It was "early" in the morning. The Jewish leaders did not want to enter the building where the governor was, lest they should become ceremonially defiled before the Passover (**see Exodus 12:18–19**). Pilate's residence was a place from which leavened bread had not been removed. It was the house of an uncircumcised man (**see Matthew 8:8; Acts 11:3**). The Passover festival probably is meant here, it lasted seven days.

## SEARCH THE SCRIPTURES

### QUESTION 1

Who was the High Priest that Jesus encountered?

**Caiaphas**

## LIGHT ON THE WORD

### Deceitfulness!

Consider the irony of the priests' position, they would not walk into the Hall of Judgment because entering the Gentile building would make them unclean. However, they sought to take the life of the Passover Lamb in the person of Jesus Christ. No wonder Jesus referred to them as hypocrites.

## II. MAKE UP YOUR MIND (John 18:29-31)

According to Roman law, the Jews needed a legitimate complaint against Jesus in order to press charges against Him. The same is true in today's courts of law, a person cannot be indicted for a crime unless proper charges have been filed.

### What's the Charge? (verses 29-31)

**29 Pilate then went out unto them, and said, What accusation bring ye against this man? 30 They answered and said unto him, If he were not a malefactor, we would not have delivered him up unto thee. 31 Then said Pilate unto them, Take ye him, and judge him according to your law. The Jews therefore said unto him, It is not lawful for us to put any man to death:**

Pilate asked the priests, "What accusation bring ye against this man?" (**verse 29**). In their arrogance, the priests replied, "If he were not a malefactor, we would not have delivered him up unto thee" (**verse 30**). In other words, "We would not have brought Jesus to you if He wasn't guilty of a punishable crime." Attempting to avoid sentencing Jesus, Pilate suggested that they try Him by their own law. This met with opposition from the priests because they were prevented by the Mosaic Law from giving anyone the death sentence. They wanted Jesus to die, but sought to make Pilate a pawn who would administer the death penalty in their stead. This would let them off the hook.

### QUESTION 2

What group according to John bought charges against Jesus?

**The Jewish priests. Answers will vary.**

## LIGHT ON THE WORD

### The Leaders Wanted Jesus to Die

Only a Roman official could allow death by crucifixion (**this may be deduced from verse 32**). The leaders wanted the death of Jesus by crucifixion (**see 19:15; Deuteronomy 21:23; cp. John 3:14; 8:28; 12:32–34**), instead of by stoning (**see John 8:1–11, 59; 10:31; cp. Acts 7:54–8:2**), probably so that He would be seen as a curse. Crucifixion was a way for the leaders of the Jews to dishonor Jesus, but God used it to take away the sins of the world (**cp. Genesis 50:19–20; Romans 8:28; Galatians 3:13–14**).

## III. THOUGHT YOU KNEW (John 18:32)

Jesus told him that there is a sense in which He is the head of a kingdom, but His kingdom is not of this world. It is not a kingdom as the world understands kingdoms. If His kingdom were of this world, His servants would support Him at this very moment, and they would fight to free Him.

### Jesus Knows Everything (verse 32)

**32 That the saying of Jesus might be fulfilled, which he spake, signifying what death he should die.**

One of God's characteristics is that He is omniscient; He knows all things. Jesus had already shared His coming demise with His disciples (**Matthew 20:17–19; John 3:14**). Isaiah the prophet spoke of our Savior's suffering in Isaiah 53:5, "But he was wounded for our transgressions, he was bruised for our iniquities: the chastisement of our peace was upon him; and with his stripes we are healed." Jesus knew the price that must be paid for humankind's sin. He was willing to die, even the death of the Cross (**Philippians 2:8**).

## SEARCH THE SCRIPTURES

### QUESTION 3

Jesus spoke what _____ that he should _____.

**Death, die**

## LIGHT ON THE WORD

### The Divine Purpose

The Jewish leaders' determination to secure a crucifixion fulfills the divine purpose (**John 3:14; 19:36–37**). The Gospel of John points out again and again the conformity of the life of Jesus with the affirmations of the Scriptures. The Jewish leaders prided themselves in rejecting Jesus, they were in fact witnessing for Him (**see John 5:39–40**).

## IV. THE KINGSHIP OF CHRIST (John 18:33–37)

Pilate was looking for a way out of the predicament the Jews had put him in, he was well aware of Jesus being tried before the High Priest. In fact, when Pilate thought Jesus could be tried in another jurisdiction, he sent Jesus to Herod (**Luke 23:7**).

### Is Jesus the King of the Jews? (verses 33-37)

**33 Then Pilate entered into the judgment hall again, and called Jesus, and said unto him, Art thou the King of the Jews? 34 Jesus answered him, Sayest thou this thing of thyself, or did others tell it thee of me? 35 Pilate answered, Am I a Jew? Thine own nation and the chief priests have delivered thee unto me: what hast thou done? 36 Jesus answered, My kingdom is not of this world: if my kingdom were of this world, then would my servants fight, that I should not be delivered to the Jews: but now is my kingdom not from hence. 37 Pilate therefore said unto him, Art thou a king then? Jesus answered, Thou sayest that I am a king. To this end was I born, and for this cause came I into the world, that I should bear witness unto the truth. Every one that is of the truth heareth my voice.**

Pilate finds Jesus back in his court, frustrated, he asks Jesus, "Are thou the King of the Jews?" (**John 18:33**). This line of questioning was an attempt to establish a rebellion that as the governor he would be able to crush. If he could establish that Jesus posed a military threat to the Roman Empire, his problem would be solved.

Instead, Jesus let Pilate know that His kingdom is not of this world. If it were, His followers would have fought the Jews who arrested Him and they wouldn't be having this conversation. Rather, His kingdom is God's and not Caesar's, and ultimately the reign of God will extend to the ends of the earth but not yet. His kingdom is the true kingdom, and those who understand the truth of Jesus' words are of His kingdom. The apostle Paul explained it in this way: "For the preaching of the cross is to them that perish foolishness; but unto us which are saved it is the power of God" (**1 Corinthians 1:18**).

## QUESTION 4

Jesus declared that He was or was not the king of the Jews?

**Jesus declared that He was not the king of the Jews. Answers will vary.**

## LIGHT ON THE WORD

### Jesus and the Father

People who accept the One sent from God are in the truth (**John 3:21; 6:42; 17:2**), Jesus is the perfect expression of the Father for humankind. He showed it by His deeds and His words (**John 1:18; 17:8, 14**). He introduces the believer to the fellowship with the Father (**John 1:4; 3:16; 17:3**).

## BIBLE APPLICATION

**AIM: That your students will begin to understand that Jesus represents the Truth.**

### Nothing but the Truth

"Do you solemnly swear to tell the whole truth and nothing but the truth, so help you God?"

The court clerk's words echoed in Rodney's mind, his thoughts raced over the events of the past few weeks. How had he ended up in this hearing? He and his friends only meant to have some fun, and no one was supposed to get hurt.

As his thoughts tumbled over each other, he knew he couldn't go against the code of the streets because that could endanger him. After all, he knew what happened to those who ratted on his friends.

Then Rodney remembered Mrs. Miller's Sunday school class, he loved getting up on Sunday morning and walking around the corner to the little sanctified church! How many years had it been since he had gone to church?

Mrs. Miller taught her class that God sees everything we do, and she said even God knows what we are thinking. As Rodney began to recall those lessons from long ago, he thought about one lesson in particular. His childhood teacher taught that it is best to tell the truth, even if it hurts.

That Sunday school lesson from days gone by began to make sense. As he raised his head, he replied, "Yes, I do swear to tell the whole truth."

## STUDENTS' RESPONSES

**AIM: That your students will reflect on ways to help others.**

Many churches have outreach activities with their communities such as food banks, support groups, bill assistance, housing, and the list goes on. What other practical ways can the church be an expression of truth to the world around us?

## PRAYER

Dear God, You continually bless us with Your love, Your mercy, and Your presence in our lives. Thank You for standing up for us through the ridicule and suffering that began even before You were nailed to the Cross. Thank You, and we love You. In the name of Jesus we pray. Amen.

## DIG A LITTLE DEEPER

### The Trials of Jesus during Passion Week

The last week of Jesus' life on earth was filled with many significant events: the so-called Triumphal Entry into Jerusalem, the Last Supper with his disciples, his prayer in the Garden of Gethsemane.  Preceding his crucifixion, Jesus endured a number of trials.

The first trial (**recorded in John 18:13-23**) was held before Annas, the father-in-law of Caiaphas, the high priest that year.  The second trial (**recorded in Matt 26:57-68; Mark**

14:53-65; John 18:24) is before Caiaphas and the Sanhedrin. The accusation is that Jesus claimed to be the Messiah, the Son of God. They considered this blasphemy and, therefore, worthy of death.

The third trial (**Mark 15:1a and Luke 22:66-71**) is before the Sanhedrin (that ruling body of 70 men in Israel). Again, the accusation is blasphemy, and Jesus is declared guilty. Because they do not have the authority to carry out capital punishment, Jesus is sent to Roman officials.

The fourth trial (**Matt 27:11-14; Mark 15:1b-5; Luke 23:1-7; John 18:28-38**) is held before Pilate, the governor of Judea. The accusation against Jesus is treason. However, he was found innocent. So Jesus was sent to Herod Antipas for a fifth trial (**Luke 23:8-12**), where there was no formal accusation leveled against Jesus. But he was severely mistreated and mocked.

The final trial was held before Pilate (**Matt 27:15-26; Mark 15:6-15; Luke 23:18-23; John 18:39-19:16**). Again, the accusation was treason which was not proven. Wishing to absolve himself of guilt, Pilate left the decision to the mob, allowing them to choose between Jesus and Barabbas. Pilate washed his hand and allowed Jesus to be crucified.

## HOW TO SAY IT

Barabbas.        buh-RAB-uhs..

Caiaphas.        KAH-ee-af-as.

Levitical.        lih-VI-tih-kuhl.

## DAILY HOME BIBLE READINGS

### MONDAY
Lead by Truth and Light
(Psalm 43)

### TUESDAY
Walking in God's Truth
(Psalm 86:8–13)

### WEDNESDAY
Arrest of Jesus
(John 18:1–11)

### THURSDAY
Denial of Jesus
(John 18:12–18)

### FRIDAY
Questioning of Jesus
(John 18:19–24)

### SATURDAY
What Is Truth?
(John 8:31–38)

### SUNDAY
"Are You the King?"
(John 18:28–37)

## PREPARE FOR NEXT SUNDAY

Read **John 20:1–10, 19–20** and study "The Living Word."

**Sources:**

Bauer, Walter. A Greek-English Lexicon of the New Testament and Other Early Christian Literature (BACD). Chicago, IL: University of Chicago Press, 1979.

Bonnet, Louis. Evangile Selon Jean. Bible Annotée NT2. St-Légier, Suisse, 1983.

Bruce, F. F. The Gospel of John. Grand Rapids, MI: W. B. Eerdmans Publishing Company, 1983.

The Holy Bible. Contemporary English Version (CEV). New York, NY: American Bible Society, 1995.

New Testament Greek Lexicon. Bible Study Tools.com. http://www.biblestudytools.com/hebrew/dictionary. (accessed May 13, 2010).

Old Testament Hebrew Lexicon. Bible Study Tools.com. h t t p : / / w w w . biblestudytools.com/hebrew/dictionary. (accessed May 13, 2010).

Passage Lookup. Bible Gateway.com. http://www.biblegateway.com/passage (accessed May 26, 2010).

Pfeiffer, Charles F., Howard F. Vos, and John Rea, eds. Wycliffe Bible Dictionary.          Peabody, MA: Hendrickson Publishers, 1998. 1043.

"Pilate." Merriam-Webster Dictionary Online. http://www.merriam-webster.com/dictionary/pilate (accessed September 30, 2010).

Rochedieu, Charles. Les Trésors du Nouveau Testament. Saint-Légier, Suisse: Editions Emmaüs, 1972.

Strong's Concordance with Hebrew and Greek Lexicon. Eliyah.com. http://www.eliyah.com/lexicon.html (accessed September 30, 2010).

Thompson, Frank Charles. Thompson Chain-Reference Bible. Indianapolis, IN: B. B. Kirkbride Bible Co., 1982.

## COMMENTS / NOTES:

# THE LIVING WORD

**BIBLE BASIS:** John 20:1–10, 19–20

**BIBLE TRUTH:** The disciples responded to Jesus' death and resurrection.

**MEMORY VERSE:** And when he had so said, he shewed unto them his hands and his side. Then were the disciples glad, when they saw the Lord (John 20:20, KJV).

**LESSON AIM:** By the end of this lesson, we will: DESCRIBE the disciples' response to Jesus' death and resurrection; APPRECIATE the beginning of a new life in Christ; and INVITE someone to Sunday School or Bible study to learn more about Christ.

**BACKGROUND SCRIPTURES:** John 20:1–23—Read and incorporate gained from the Background Scriptures into your lesson.

## TEACHER PREPARATION

**MATERIALS NEEDED:** Bibles (several different versions), Quarterly Commentary/Teacher Manual, Adult Quarterly, teaching resources such as charts, worksheets/handouts, paper, pens, and pencils.

**OTHER MATERIALS NEEDED / TEACHER'S NOTES:**

_____

_____

## LESSON OVERVIEW

**LIFE NEED FOR TODAY'S LESSON**
To allow our fear to give way to hope in Christ Jesus.

**BIBLE LEARNING**
Inviting others to know about Christ is sharing the Gospel of Jesus Christ.

**BIBLE APPLICATION**
Inviting others to know about Christ is sharing the Gospel of Jesus Christ.

**STUDENTS' RESPONSES**
Students will plan how to share the Good News of Jesus with others.

## LESSON SCRIPTURE

### JOHN 20:1-10, 19-20, KJV

1 The first day of the week cometh Mary Magdalene early, when it was yet dark, unto the sepulchre, and seeth the stone

### JOHN 20:1-10, 19-20, AMP

1 Now on the first day of the week Mary Magdalene came to the tomb early, while it was still dark, and saw the stone [already]

**taken** away from the sepulchre.

2 Then she runneth, and cometh to Simon Peter, and to the other disciple, whom Jesus loved, and saith unto them, They have taken away the Lord out of the sepulchre, and we know not where they have laid him.

3 Peter therefore went forth, and that other disciple, and came to the sepulchre.

4 So they ran both together: and the other disciple did outrun Peter, and came first to the sepulchre.

5 And he stooping down, and looking in, saw the linen clothes lying; yet went he not in.

6 Then cometh Simon Peter following him, and went into the sepulchre, and seeth the linen clothes lie,

7 And the napkin, that was about his head, not lying with the linen clothes, but wrapped together in a place by itself.

8 Then went in also that other disciple, which came first to the sepulchre, and he saw, and believed.

9 For as yet they knew not the scripture, that he must rise again from the dead.

10 Then the disciples went away again unto their own home.

20:19 Then the same day at evening, being the first day of the week, when the doors were shut where the disciples were assembled for fear of the Jews, came Jesus and stood in the midst, and saith unto them, Peace be unto you.

20 And when he had so said, he shewed unto them his hands and his side. Then were the disciples glad, when they saw the Lord.

removed from the [groove across the entrance of the] tomb.

2 So she ran and went to Simon Peter and to the [a]other disciple (John), whom Jesus loved (esteemed), and said to them, "They have taken away the Lord out of the tomb, and [b]we do not know where they have laid Him!"

3 So Peter and the other disciple left, and they were going to the tomb.

4 And the two were running together, but the other disciple outran Peter and arrived at the tomb first.

5 Stooping down and looking in, he saw the linen [c]wrappings [neatly] lying there; but he did not go in.

6 Then Simon Peter came up, following him, and went into the tomb and saw the linen wrappings [neatly] lying there;

7 and the [burial] [d]face-cloth which had been on Jesus' head, not lying with the [other] linen wrappings, but [e]rolled up in a place by itself.

8 So the other disciple, who had reached the tomb first, went in too; and he saw [the wrappings and the face-cloth] and [f]believed [without any doubt that Jesus had risen from the dead].

9 For as yet they did not understand the Scripture, that He must rise from the dead.

10 Then the disciples went back again to their own homes.

20:19 So when it was evening on that same day, the first day of the week, though the disciples were [meeting] behind barred doors for fear of the Jews, Jesus came and stood among them, and said, "[a]Peace to you."

**20** After He said this, He showed them His hands and His side. When the disciples saw the Lord, they were filled with great joy.

## BIBLICAL DEFINITIONS

A. **Sepulchre (John 20:1–4, 6, 8)** *mnemeion (Gk.)*—A grave or tomb. Jesus was buried in a sepulchre, which was a room carved out of a rocky hill.

B. **Resurrection** *anastasis (Gk.)*—The act of having life restored after death.

## LIGHT ON THE WORD

For three years, Jesus walked the earth teaching His disciples and demonstrating before the Jewish religious authorities that He was their long-awaited Messiah. Finally, in an ultimate show of rejection and contempt, the religious authorities conspired with the Roman government and the Jewish populace to kill the Lord. The Roman form of capital punishment was chosen, and Jesus was hung on a cross until He died. After all were certain of Jesus' death, Joseph of Arimathea and Nicodemus were permitted to take His body down from the cross and lay it in Joseph's unused tomb. On the first day of the week, Mary Magdalene was returning to the tomb to tend to the body of the Lord when she discovered that the stone covering the tomb's opening had been rolled away and the body was no longer there.

## TEACHING THE BIBLE LESSON

## LIFE NEED FOR TODAY'S LESSON

AIM: That your students will appreciate the beginning of a new life in Christ.

## INTRODUCTION

### Two of Jesus' Followers

**Mary Magdalene.** She was first introduced to us by Luke, the physician **(Luke 8:2–3)**, as one of the women from whom Jesus cast demons. Mary had been delivered from seven demons and apparently spent her days joining the other women who devoted themselves to ministering to Jesus.

**Simon Peter.** He served as the head of the band of disciples. The other disciples recognized Peter's authority after the Lord entrusted him with the keys of the kingdom. It is not surprising, therefore, that Mary and John would defer to his leadership upon seeing the empty tomb.

## BIBLE LEARNING

AIM: That your students will appreciate that Jesus is no longer dead.

## I. MARY MAGDALENE AT THE TOMB (John 20:1-3)

Faithful to Jesus even after His death, John presents Mary Magdalene's rising early and going to Jesus' tomb to anoint His body with precious ointments and spices, as was the custom of the day. Both Mark **(15:47)** and Luke **(23:55)** record that Mary and the other women had watched Jesus' burial and the sealing of the tomb. While we are not surprised that Mary could locate the tomb in the darkness of the early morning hours, it is not clear how Mary expected to remove the huge stone placed at the entrance of the tomb. Perhaps she expected the Roman soldiers, who were guarding the tomb, to roll the stone for her.

### Early in the Morning (verses 20:1-3)

**1 The first day of the week cometh Mary Magdalene early, when it was yet dark, unto the sepulchre, and seeth the stone taken away from the sepulchre. 2 Then she runneth, and cometh to Simon Peter, and to the other disciple, whom Jesus loved, and saith unto them, They have taken away the Lord out of the sepulchre, and we know not where they have laid him. 3 Peter therefore went forth, and that other disciple, and came to the sepulchre.**

On the first day of the week, Mary Magdalene arrived at the tomb only to discover that its stone covering had been rolled away and the body of Jesus was gone. The tomb belonged to Joseph of Arimathea's family (**Matthew 27:59**). She promptly returned to the city where she informed John and Peter of her discovery.

### Run, Mary, Run (verses 1-3)

At this point in John's narrative, Mary Magdalene runs to tell Peter and the other disciples that Jesus' body is missing. John does not tell us that Mary has yet to enter the interior of the tomb. In John's account, Mary does not enter the tomb until after she notifies the men (**John 20:11–12**). John is the only writer who was actually an eyewitness to this event. It is quite possible that he prioritized the notification of Peter and himself and simply chose to leave out details that occurred before his arrival at the tomb. The fact that Mary announces that the body is missing implies she has indeed entered the sepulchre.

## SEARCH THE SCRIPTURES

### QUESTION 1

Mary ran to tell the disciples about the empty tomb. Which disciples did she see first?

Simon Peter and the disciple Jesus loved (John).

## LIGHT ON THE WORD

### The No-Named Disciple

Interesting, too, is the fact that John does not name the other disciple, the one "whom Jesus loved" (**John 20:2**). There is no doubt that it can only be the writer of the Gospel, John, the brother of James. John never identifies himself in his own Gospel, choosing instead to refer to himself only as the son of Zebedee or, as he does in this account, the one Jesus loved.

## II. PETER AND JOHN AT THE TOMB (John 20:4–10)

The two disciples began running toward the site where they knew that Jesus had been buried. Because he was younger, John outran Peter and arrived at the tomb first, but out of respect for Peter's position as the leader of the disciples, he did not enter. Rather, John waited until Peter arrived and then followed him into the grave.

### The Linen Cloth Left Behind
#### (verses 4-10)

**4 So they ran both together: and the other disciple did outrun Peter, and came first to the sepulchre. 5 And he stooping down, and looking in, saw the linen clothes lying; yet went he not in. 6 Then cometh Simon Peter following him, and went into the sepulchre, and seeth the linen clothes lie, 7 And the napkin, that was about his head, not lying with the linen clothes, but wrapped together in a place by itself. 8 Then went in also that other disciple, which came first to the sepulchre, and he saw, and believed. 9 For as yet they knew not the scripture, that he must rise again from the dead. 10 Then the disciples went away again unto their own home.**

Peter didn't hesitate before entering the Lord's tomb, the same eagerness and impulsiveness that characterized his life before the Lord's death remained. Once inside, Peter could observe that the burial cloth (napkin), which had been used to cover the Lord's face, was neatly folded together in a place separate from the other grave clothes. John, after following Peter into the cave, was also able to observe the burial cloth. Scripture does not record Peter's response to what he observed, however, John saw, and because of what he saw he believed.

## QUESTION 2

The disciples left the empty tomb and went where?

**Home. Answers will vary.**

## LIGHT ON THE WORD

### A Faith Booster

The physical evidence of the empty grave clothes bolstered John's faith, and he was able to believe what he did not understand. In time, Peter would believe as well. Perhaps his exposure to the empty tomb and John's faith helped him.

## III. JESUS APPEARS TO HIS DISCIPLES (John 20:19–20)

The other disciple is almost certainly the apostle John, also identified in Scripture as the disciple whom Jesus loved (**John 13:23; 21:20**). While hanging from the Cross, Jesus would instruct John to care for His mother (**19:25**). Later, John was confined to the Isle of Patmos where he received the vision that became our book of Revelation. He is also the author of the Gospel of John.

### Resurrection Day (verses 19-20)

**19 Then the same day at evening, being the first day of the week, when the doors were shut where the disciples were assembled for fear of the Jews, came Jesus and stood in the midst, and saith unto them, Peace be unto you. 20 And when he had so said, he shewed unto them his hands and his side. Then were the disciples glad, when they saw the Lord.**

It was now the evening of Resurrection Day. In spite of the appearance of the Risen Lord to Mary and the evidence of the folded cloth, the disciples were very much afraid. If the authorities would kill the Lord, what would they do to His followers? So they gathered together and locked the doors, probably in the same room where they had eaten the Last Supper with the Lord. We can imagine them trying to sort out the strange things that had happened that day.

Then suddenly Jesus appeared without the doors opening and was suddenly visible among them. The appearance may have occurred among 10 of the disciples, Judas had committed suicide, and Thomas was not there. (Although others who followed Jesus were considered His disciples, the original 12 apostles had a unique role.) Jesus' first words to them were, "Peace be unto you" (**John 20:19**). Maybe the men were expecting some sort of reprimand. After all, they had all run away when Jesus was captured in the Garden of Gethsemane. Instead, Jesus offered a lovely greeting, with no recriminations.

## SEARCH THE SCRIPTURES

### QUESTION 3

Jesus' first words to the disciples were what?

**"Peace be unto you." Answers will vary.**

## LIGHT ON THE WORD

### Jesus' Wounded Hands and Side

We know from Luke 24:37 that the disciples thought they were seeing a ghost, but Jesus proved to them that He was their Lord in the flesh. Although a resurrected kind of flesh, Jesus showed them His hands and His side to prove that He was indeed the same Jesus who had died on the Cross for them. At this, they believed and were overjoyed.

## BIBLE APPLICATION

**AIM: That your students will begin to understand that believers in Christ should not fear death.**

### Peace in Christ

When we lose a loved one to death, our response to that realm as Christians should not be full of fear. If we are sure that they have trusted in Christ, our fear gives way to a hope that they have gone to a place of light, rest, and peace in the presence of our Lord. How does our relationship with God change the way we view death? Which would you prefer to have: the popularity and wealth of this world or the assurance that when you die, you will go to live with Jesus?

## STUDENTS' RESPONSES

**AIM: That your students will know the victory of Christ over death.**

Jesus, by living a life pleasing to God, broke the bonds of death over those who believe in Him. God confirmed this by raising Jesus from the dead. Write a poem or song celebrating the victory of Christ over death.

## PRAYER

Lord, we thank You and praise You for giving us Jesus, His death, and His resurrection. He gave His life so that we can have life eternal. Thank You! In Jesus' name we pray. Amen.

## DIG A LITTLE DEEPER

### The Resurrection Appearances of Jesus in the New Testament

How do we know that Jesus rose from the dead? What is the evidence of his resurrection? The following facts support the historicity of the empty tomb:

In addition, the Bible records multiple resurrection appearances:

To Mary Magdalene (**John 20:11, 18**)

To the women (**Matt 28:1-10**)

To Peter (**Luke 24:34; 1 Cor 15:5**)

To the disciples on the road to Emmaus (**Luke 24:13-35**)

To the ten disciples (**Luke 24:36-40; John 20:19-23; 1 Cor 15:5**)

To the eleven disciples in Galilee (**John 21:1-23**)

To 500 disciples at one time (**1 Cor 15:5**)

To James (**1 Cor 15:7**)

To the disciples at the Ascension (**Luke 24:50-52; Acts 1:3-8**)

Besides those already mentioned, the witnesses in Acts attest to the bodily resurrection of Jesus (2:32; 3:15; 5:32; 10:39-41).

## HOW TO SAY IT

Recriminations.     Re-KRIM-i-NA-shuns.

Sepulchre.          SEP-ul-ker.

Populace.           POP-u-lus.

## DAILY HOME BIBLE READINGS

### MONDAY
To Save Sinners Like Me
(1 Timothy 1:12–17)

### TUESDAY
Judgment of Jesus
(John 19:4–16)

### WEDNESDAY
"We Have a Law"
(Leviticus 24:10–16)

### THURSDAY
Crucifixion of Jesus
(John 19:17–25)

### FRIDAY
"Father, into Your Hands"
(Psalm 31:1–5)

### SATURDAY
Burial of Jesus
(John 19:38–42)

### SUNDAY
Resurrection of Jesus
(John 20:1–10, 19–20)

## PREPARE FOR NEXT SUNDAY

Read **John 2:13-22**, and study "Cleansing the Temple."

**Sources:**

Better Days Are Coming http://www.betterdaysarecoming.com. Accessed November 30, 2009

Hayford, Jack W., gen. ed. Spirit Filled Life Bible. New King James Version. Nashville, TN: Thomas Nelson, 1991.

Jakes, T. D., gen. ed. New King James Version, Holy Bible, Woman Thou Art Loosed Edition. Nashville, TN: Thomas Nelson, 1998.

Life Application Study Bible, New Living Translation. Wheaton, IL: Tyndale House, 1996. pp. 1679, 2014, 2281.

Lockyer Sr., Herbert, gen. ed. Nelson's New Illustrated Bible Dictionary. Nashville, TN: Thomas Nelson, 1995. p. 1331.

Smith, William. Smith's Bible Dictionary. Peabody, MA: Hendrickson, 2000.

**COMMENTS / NOTES:**

# CLEANSING THE TEMPLE

**BIBLE BASIS:** John 2:13-22

**BIBLE TRUTH:** Jesus wants us restore honor in the church as the central place of worship in the lives of God's people. .

**MEMORY VERSE:** And said unto them that sold doves, Take these things hence; make not my Father's house an house of merchandise (John 2:16, KJV).

**LESSON AIM:** By the end of this lesson, we will: DESCRIBE how Jesus' cleansing the Temple represents restoration in our lives; DESIRE a fresh revelation of God in the church; and CREATE a list of ways that we see God's power in our daily lives.

**BACKGROUND SCRIPTURES: JOHN 2:13-22**—Read and incorporate insights gained from the Background Scriptures into your lesson.

## TEACHER PREPARATION

**MATERIALS NEEDED:** Bibles (several different versions), Quarterly Commentary/Teacher Manual, Adult Quarterly, teaching resources such as charts, worksheets/handouts, paper, pens, and pencils.

**OTHER MATERIALS NEEDED / TEACHER'S NOTES:**

_____

_____

## LESSON OVERVIEW

**LIFE NEED FOR TODAY'S LESSON**
To observe the church as God's central place of worship.

**BIBLE LEARNING**
Through Jesus' actions, recognize how God requires us individually and collectively (as the church) to reverence His presence.

**BIBLE APPLICATION**

To begin to understand through Jesus' actions of cleansing the Temple, the restoring work of God

**STUDENTS' RESPONSES**
Students will plan how to keep the church and themselves pleasing to God by keeping those things committed to Him sacred.

## LESSON SCRIPTURE

### JOHN 2:13-22, KJV

13 And the Jews' passover was at hand, and Jesus went up to Jerusalem,

### JOHN 2:13-22, AMP

13 Now the Passover of the Jews was approaching, so Jesus went up to Jerusalem.

14 And found in the temple those that sold oxen and sheep and doves, and the changers of money sitting:

15 And when he had made a scourge of small cords, he drove them all out of the temple, and the sheep, and the oxen; and poured out the changers' money, and overthrew the tables;

16 And said unto them that sold doves, Take these things hence; make not my Father's house an house of merchandise.

17 And his disciples remembered that it was written, The zeal of thine house hath eaten me up.

18 Then answered the Jews and said unto him, What sign shewest thou unto us, seeing that thou doest these things?

19 Jesus answered and said unto them, Destroy this temple, and in three days I will raise it up.

20 Then said the Jews, Forty and six years was this temple in building, and wilt thou rear it up in three days?

21 But he spake of the temple of his body.

22 When therefore he was risen from the dead, his disciples remembered that he had said this unto them; and they believed the scripture, and the word which Jesus had said.

14 And in the temple [enclosure] He found the [a]people who were selling oxen and sheep and doves, and the money changers sitting at their tables

15 He made a whip of cords, and drove them all out of the temple, with the sheep and the oxen; and He scattered the coins of the money changers and overturned their tables;

16 then to those who sold the doves He said, "Take these things away! Stop making My Father's house a place of commerce!"

17 His disciples remembered that it is written [in the Scriptures], "ZEAL (love, concern) FOR YOUR HOUSE [and its honor] WILL CONSUME ME."

18 Then the Jews retorted, "What sign (attesting miracle) can You show us as [proof of] your authority for doing these things?"

19 Jesus answered them, "Destroy this temple, and in three days I will raise it up."

20 Then the Jews replied, "It took forty-six years to build this temple, and You will raise it up in three days?"

21 But He was speaking of the temple which was His body.

22 So when He had risen from the dead, His disciples remembered what He had said. And they believed and trusted in and relied on the Scripture and the words that Jesus had spoken.

## BIBLICAL DEFINITIONS

A. **Passover (John 2:13)** *pascha* **(Gk.)**— "A celebration in memory of the day on which the Israelites' fathers, who were preparing to leave Egypt, were told by God to sprinkle their doorposts with lamb's blood, so that the destroying angel, seeing the blood, could pass over their dwellings" (Strong, 1996).

B. **Scourge (v. 15)** *phragellion* (Gk.)—A whip.

## LIGHT ON THE WORD

The apostle John, the son of Zebedee and brother of James, is the author of the Gospel of John. He and his brother were called "Sons of Thunder." John wrote to prove that Jesus Christ is not just a man, but is indeed the eternal Son of the Living God, and all who believe in Him will have everlasting life (reign with Him forever and ever in His kingdom). In other words, Jesus is fully God and fully man. In addition, because Jesus offers the gift of eternal life to all who believe in Him, He is also the Light of the world. He is the Word and the long-awaited Messiah. John not only reveals Jesus to us in both power and magnificence, he also shows us Jesus' power over everything created, as well as His love for all humanity.

## TEACHING THE BIBLE LESSON

## LIFE NEED FOR TODAY'S LESSON

**AIM: That your students will pray that God's House will always be respected as a house of worship and prayer.**

## INTRODUCTION

### The Temple

Located in Jerusalem, the Temple was the religious and political seat of Palestine, on a hill overlooking the city. During their festivals, Jewish families from all over the world traveled there for the grand celebrations. "(King) Solomon had the first Temple built on this same site almost 1,000 years earlier (959 B.C.), but his Temple had been destroyed by the Babylonians, who took many of the Jews into captivity (**2 Kings 2:5**). The Temple was rebuilt in 515 B.C. and Herod the Great enlarged and remodeled it" (The Life Application Study Bible, 1622). According to Strong, the temple embraces "the entire aggregate of buildings, balconies, porticos, courts (that is that of the men of Israel, that of the women, and that of the priests), belonging to the temple. The latter designates the sacred edifice properly so called, consisting of two parts, the 'sanctuary' or 'Holy Place' (which no one except the priests was allowed to enter), and the 'Holy of Holies' or 'the most holy place' (which was entered only on the great day of atonement by the high priest alone). Also there were the courts where Jesus or the apostles taught or encountered adversaries, and the like, 'in the temple'; also the courts of the temple, of the Gentiles, out of which Jesus drove the buyers and sellers and the money changers, court of the women" (1996).

## BIBLE LEARNING

**AIM: That your students will understand the importance of keeping the church as a sacred house of worship.**

## I. JESUS SAW THEM CHEATING IN THE TEMPLE (John 2:13-14)

The "Passover" was "the festival instituted by God for Israel at the time of the Exodus in order to commemorate the night when Yahweh spared all the firstborn of the Israelites but struck dead all those of the Egyptians (**Exodus 12:1–30, 43–49**)" (Wycliffe, 1283). It was a time when thousands came from all over the world to participate in the celebration of what God had done to save His people by delivering them from slavery. The Passover, "the paschal feast" or "the feast of the Passover", extends from the 14th to the 20th day of the month Nisan" (Strong, 1996). Nisan is the first month of the Jewish sacred calendar (**Nehemiah 2:1; Esther 3:7**), called "Abib" in the Pentateuch (The Books of the Law—Genesis, Exodus, Leviticus, Numbers, and Deuteronomy). Nisan "corresponds to our March-April" (Wycliffe, 1210).

### Selling in the Temple Distracts Worship (verses 13-14)

**13 And the Jews' passover was at hand, and Jesus went up to Jerusalem. 14 And found in the temple those that sold oxen and sheep and doves, and the changers of money sitting:**

In the outer courts of the Temple, the Court of the Gentiles and the animal merchants and moneychangers were allowed to set up booths to do business. Since there were thousands of out-of-town visitors who came to celebrate the Passover, business was booming. The religious leaders gave these merchants and moneychangers permission to carry out their trades so that the leaders could make money for the Temple's upkeep. The Temple's tax had to be paid in the local currency, many of the foreigners who came to the Passover celebration had to have their money converted. The moneychangers, however, cheated or exploited the people by charging exorbitant exchange rates. Therefore, their business interfered with worship, and they were cheating the people at the place of worship. Adding to these infractions was the fact that after the cattle, sheep, oxen, and doves that foreigners brought for the sacrifices were rejected for imperfections, the animal merchants sold new ones at inflated prices.

## SEARCH THE SCRIPTURES

### QUESTION 1
What were merchants and moneychangers doing in the Temple and why was it a problem?

They were selling and changing money to Jews coming for Passover; they were exploiting the people and distracting the people from the worship.

## LIGHT ON THE WORD

### Jesus Was Angry
Jesus was angry at the exploitation and greedy practices of these merchants and moneychangers. As we will see, when Jesus saw

their blatant disrespect for the Temple and for those worshiping there He did something about it.

## II. GOD'S HOUSE IS A HOUSE OF WORSHIP (John 2:15-17)

Here we see the righteous anger of Jesus. His ire was so aroused by what He saw in His Father's House that "he made a scourge of small cords" (**John 2:15**), which in today's terms would be a whip, to drive them out of the Temple.

### Jesus Cleanses the Temple of Distractions (verses 15-17)
**15 And when he had made a scourge of small cords, he drove them all out of the temple, and the sheep, and the oxen; and poured out the changers' money, and overthrew the tables.**

Not only did He drive out the merchants and moneychangers, but He also drove out the sheep and oxen and then overturned the tables.

**16 And said unto them that sold doves, Take these things hence; make not my Father's house an house of merchandise.**

Jesus told the people selling the doves to get their merchandise out of the Temple and admonished them not to turn His "Father's house into a marketplace!" Jesus knew that turning the area into a marketplace was misusing God's Temple; they had insulted Almighty God--His Father.

**17 And his disciples remembered that it was written, THE Zeal of thine house hath eaten me up.**

When the disciples saw how Jesus responded to such disrespect, they remembered the prophecy from the Scriptures: "Zeal for your house will consume me (Jesus)" (**verse 17, NIV**). In other words, Jesus saw the wrong being done and would not stand still and let it continue. He set out to correct the matter, pursuing and defending. He was consumed with correcting the situation, therefore He took action and did not wait for someone else to right the wrong.

## QUESTION 2

What did Jesus do to restore order in the Temple?

**Jesus drove out the merchants and all their merchandise, overthrew the money changers' tables and told them to not make His "Father's house an house of merchandise". Answers will vary.**

## LIGHT ON THE WORD

### The Jewish Leaders Did Not Approve

The Jewish leaders' beliefs were in fundamental conflict with Jesus, and they demanded to know by what authority He carried out these acts. They insisted that Jesus show them a miraculous sign to prove that His authority was from God. However, Jesus was telling them that His body is God's temple and would be crucified and resurrected in three days. Jesus' words would, of course, mean more to the disciples after Jesus' resurrection. These words would prove that indeed He is the Messiah,the Son of the Living God!

## III. JESUS REVEALS ANOTHER MEANING OF THE TEMPLE (John 2:18-22)

The religious leaders were expecting Jesus to show them a sign to prove His authority to rid the Temple of the merchants and moneychangers as well as their merchandise. The word "sign" means "of miracles and wonders by which God authenticates the men sent by him, or by which men prove that the cause they are pleading is God's" (Strong, 1996).

### Jewish Leaders Question Jesus' Authority (verses 18-22)

**18 Then answered the Jews and said unto him, What sign shewest thou unto us, seeing that thou doest these things?**

In other words, these religious leaders were in charge of the Temple and they would not just accept Jesus' word that He was who He said He was. They wanted to see a miracle to prove that He was sent by God. They wanted Him to demonstrate that He received His authority from God.

**19. Jesus answered and said unto them, Destroy this temple, and in three days I will raise it up.**

Here Jesus speaks of His body as a temple, and the leaders thought He was still talking about the Temple where He had disrupted business and where He had driven out the merchants and moneychangers. The Temple with all of its parts was sacred and was to be kept holy as unto the Lord. Jesus in applying this word to Himself shifts attention to something else that was more sacred, His body that would be sacrificed for the sins of humanity. He predicts His crucifixion on that cruel Cross at Calvary. Three days He would be in the grave, but He would rise again on the third day. Death could not and would not keep Him in the grave!

**20 Then said the Jews, Forty and six years was this temple in building, and wilt thou rear it up in three days? But He spake of the temple of His body.**

Again, the religious leaders were not on the same page as Jesus. They thought He was speaking of the Temple that Zerubbabel had built over 500 years earlier and Herod the Great had begun enlarging and enhancing. Herod's efforts with the Temple were still under way, even though the remodeling project had started 46 years prior. Knowing how long it took to build the Temple, they were startled. The religious leaders thought that Jesus was telling them this earthly temple could be torn down and rebuilt in three days but in actuality Jesus was speaking of His body as a temple.

**22 When therefore He was risen from the dead, his disciples remembered that He had said this unto them; and they believed the scripture, and the word which Jesus had said.**

Again, Jesus was speaking of His own body as "the temple" in verse 21. Yet, even the disciples who still did not fully appreciate who Jesus was, remembered after He was risen from the dead that He had told them about rising again. The word "remembered" means "to be recalled or to return to one's mind, to remind one's self of" (Strong, 1996). Jesus was true to His Word, He did rise again, just as He said He would.

## SEARCH THE SCRIPTURES

### QUESTION 3

What did Jesus mean when He said "Destroy the Temple, in three days I will raise it up?

**Jesus was referencing His body and His own death, burial, and resurrection.**

## LIGHT ON THE WORD

### Jesus Cleans the Temple

Today's lesson dealt with Jesus cleansing the Temple of everything that was not of God and everything that hindered true worship of the Living God. The church is a sacred place where congregants assemble to praise, lift up the name of Jesus, and hear from His inerrant Word.

## BIBLE APPLICATION

**AIM: That your students will appreciate God's Temple.**

Sometimes congregants do not respect the sanctuary and forget that they are entering into the presence of Holy God. Some may even throw paper on the floor and leave their bulletins on the seats after the service. You take the lead in respecting God's House!

## STUDENTS' RESPONSES

**AIM: That your students will be excellent examples of true worshipers in God's House.**

Pray that His Word will always go forth with authority and power, and those who do not know Him as Lord and Savior will find Him. As well, pray that your life will be a demonstration of God's power as you are yielded to Him.

## PRAYER

Father in heaven, I pray that my local church would be a place where Your Spirit is pleased to dwell. I pray that every sanctuary is a place of honor where Your holiness is revered. I pray to examine myself daily and quickly repent of anything that does not please You. Because Your Son gave His life for me, I present my body as a living sacrifice, holy and acceptable unto You, which is my reasonable service. In Jesus' name, Amen.

## DIG A LITTLE DEEPER

### Jesus' use of metaphors in John's Gospel

John makes frequent use of metaphorical language in his Gospel. For example, Jesus' seven "I am" sayings (I am the bread of life [6:35, 48, 51]; I am the light of the world [8:12; 9:5]; I am the door of the sheep [10:7, 9]; I am the good shepherd [10:11, 14]; I am the resurrection and the life [11:25]; I am the way, the truth, and the life [14:6]; I am the true vine [15:1]) are not intended to be taken literally. Rather, they give Jesus the opportunity to talk about himself and his mission using symbolic language. As a matter of fact, the very words "I am" to identify himself as the "I am" of the Old Testament, i.e., the LORD God (cf. Exod 3:14).

Another example of Jesus' use of symbolic language is in talking about his death. This feature of Jesus' language is highlighted in a comparison of Mark and John.

In Mark's Gospel, Jesus predicts his suffering and death (i.e., his passion) three times.

And he began to teach them that the Son of Man must suffer many things and be rejected by the elders and the chief priests and the scribes and be killed and after three days rise again (Mark 8:31-32).

He was teaching his disciples, saying to them, "The Son of Man is going to be delivered into the hands of men, and they will kill him. And when he is killed, after three days he will rise" (Mark 9:31).

And taking the twelve again, he began to tell them what was to happen to him, saying, "See, we are going up to Jerusalem, and the Sion of Man will be delivered over to the chief priests and the scribes, and they will condemn him to death and deliver him over to the Gentiles. And they will mock him and spit on him, and flog him and kill him. And after three days he will rise" (Mark 10:32b-34).

In John's Gospel, Jesus speaks of his passion as being "lifted up" three times.

And as Moses lifted up the serpent in the wilderness, so must the Son of Man be lifted up, that whoever believes in him may have eternal life (John 3:14).

So Jesus said to them, "When you have lifted up the Son of Man, then you will know that I am he … (John 8:28a).

And I, when I am lifted up from the earth, will draw all people to myself (John 12:32).

It's the last reference where John is explicit in clarifying that Jesus is referring specifically to his death on the cross (v. 33). Accordingly, although it may be a popular hymn,

## HOW TO SAY IT

| | |
|---|---|
| Herod. | HER-uhd. |
| Nisan. | NI-san. |

### DAILY HOME BIBLE READINGS

**MONDAY**
Building the Temple
(1 Chronicles 28:1–10)

**TUESDAY**
The Lord Has Chosen Zion
(Psalm 132:1–14)

**WEDNESDAY**
Keeping the Passover
(2 Chronicles 30:1–9)

**THURSDAY**
The House of the Lord
(Psalm 122)

**FRIDAY**
My Father's House
(Luke 2:41–51)

**SATURDAY**
Zeal for God's House
(Psalm 69:6–15)

**SUNDAY**
Cleansing the Temple
(John 2:13–22)

## PREPARE FOR NEXT SUNDAY

Read **John 4:7–15, 23–26, 28–30** and study "Woman of Samaria."

**Sources:**

E-Bible Teacher.com. http://www.ebibleteacher.com/images.html (accessed October 15, 2010).

Life Application Study Bible, New Living Translation. Wheaton, IL: Tyndale House Publishers, 1996. 1622–23.

Merriam-Webster Online Dictionary. http://www.merriam-webster.com (accessed October 14, 2010).

New Testament Greek Lexicon. Bible Study Tools.com. http://www.biblestudytools.com/lexicons/hebrew (accessed January 8, 2011).

Passage Lookup. Bible Gateway.com. http://www.biblegateway.com/passage (accessed January 7, 2011).

Pfeiffer, Charles F., Howard F. Vos, and John Rea, eds. Wycliffe Bible Dictionary. Peabody, MA: Hendrickson, 1998. 1210, 1672–78.

Strong, James. The Exhaustive Concordance of the Bible. electronic ed. Woodside Bible Fellowship: Ontario, 1996 (accessed October 13, 2010).

## COMMENTS / NOTES:

# WOMAN OF SAMARIA

**BIBLE BASIS:** John 4:7–15, 23–26, 28–30

**BIBLE TRUTH:** God's love and gift of salvation is for all people.

**MEMORY VERSE:** But whosoever drinketh of the water that I shall give him shall never thirst; but the water that I shall give him shall be in him a well of water springing up into everlasting life (John 4:14, KJV).

**LESSON AIM:** By the end of this lesson, we will: DISCUSS who and what is acceptable based on societal norms; BE EMPOWERED to know that we can change because of Jesus; and SHARE how our perception of others influences our actions toward them.

**BACKGROUND SCRIPTURES:** JOHN 4:1–42— Read and incorporate the insights gained from the Background Scriptures into your study of the lesson.

## TEACHER PREPARATION

**MATERIALS NEEDED:** Bibles (several different versions), Quarterly Commentary/Teacher Manual, Adult Quarterly, teaching resources such as charts, worksheets/handouts, paper, pens, and pencils.

**OTHER MATERIALS NEEDED / TEACHER'S NOTES:**

_____

_____

## LESSON OVERVIEW

**LIFE NEED FOR TODAY'S LESSON**
Remember that through Christ we are all accepted and loved.

**BIBLE LEARNING**
Jesus broke down societal barriers to give a life-changing experience.

**BIBLE APPLICATION**
To appreciate how to walk in the love of Christ and share His love with others.

**STUDENTS' RESPONSES**
Students will work on developing their own love walk by reaching out to people different from themselves.

## LESSON SCRIPTURE

### JOHN 4:7-15, 23-26, 28-30, KJV

**7** There cometh a woman of Samaria to draw water: Jesus saith unto her, Give me to drink.

### JOHN 4:7-15, 23-26, 28-30, AMP

**7** Then a woman from Samaria came to draw water. Jesus said to her, "Give Me a drink"—

8 (For his disciples were gone away unto the city to buy meat.)

9 Then saith the woman of Samaria unto him, How is it that thou, being a Jew, askest drink of me, which am a woman of Samaria? for the Jews have no dealings with the Samaritans.

10 Jesus answered and said unto her, If thou knewest the gift of God, and who it is that saith to thee, Give me to drink; thou wouldest have asked of him, and he would have given thee living water.

11 The woman saith unto him, Sir, thou hast nothing to draw with, and the well is deep: from whence then hast thou that living water?

12 Art thou greater than our father Jacob, which gave us the well, and drank thereof himself, and his children, and his cattle?

13 Jesus answered and said unto her, Whosoever drinketh of this water shall thirst again:

14 But whosoever drinketh of the water that I shall give him shall never thirst; but the water that I shall give him shall be in him a well of water springing up into everlasting life.

15 The woman saith unto him, Sir, give me this water, that I thirst not, neither come hither to draw.

23 But the hour cometh, and now is, when the true worshippers shall worship the Father in spirit and in truth: for the Father seeketh such to worship him.

24 God is a Spirit: and they that worship him must worship him in spirit and in truth.

25 The woman saith unto him, I know that Messias cometh, which is called Christ: when he is come, he will tell us all things.

8 For His disciples had gone off into the city to buy food—

9 The Samaritan woman asked Him, "How is it that You, being a Jew, ask me, a [a]Samaritan woman, for a drink?" (For Jews have nothing to do with Samaritans.)

10 Jesus answered her, "If you knew [about] God's gift [of eternal life], and who it is who says, 'Give Me a drink,' you would have asked Him [instead], and He would have given you living water (eternal life)."

11 She said to Him, "Sir, [b]You have nothing to draw with [no bucket and rope] and the well is deep. Where then do You get that living water?

12 Are You greater than our father [c]Jacob, who gave us the well, and who used to drink from it himself, and his sons and his cattle also?"

13 Jesus answered her, "Everyone who drinks this water will be thirsty again.

14 But whoever drinks the water that I give him will never be thirsty again. But the water that I give him will become in him a spring of water [satisfying his thirst for God] welling up [continually flowing, bubbling within him] to eternal life."

15 The woman said to Him, "Sir, give me this water, so that I will not get thirsty nor [have to continually] come all the way here to draw."

23 But a time is coming and is already here when the true worshipers will worship the Father in spirit [from the heart, the inner self] and in truth; for the Father seeks such people to be His worshipers.

24 God is spirit [the Source of life, yet invisible to mankind], and those who worship Him must worship in spirit and truth."

**26** Jesus saith unto her, I that speak unto thee am he.

**28** The woman then left her waterpot, and went her way into the city, and saith to the men,

**29** Come, see a man, which told me all things that ever I did: is not this the Christ?

**30** Then they went out of the city, and came unto him.

**25** The woman said to Him, "I know that Messiah is coming (He who is called Christ—the Anointed); when that One comes, He will tell us everything [we need to know]."

**26** Jesus said to her, "I who speak to you, am He (the Messiah)."

**28** Then the woman left her water jar, and went into the city and began telling the people,

**29** "Come, see a man who told me all the things that I have done! Can this be the Christ (the Messiah, the Anointed)?"

**30** So the people left the city and were coming to Him.

## BIBLICAL DEFINITIONS

A. **Living water (John 4:10–11)** *zao* (Gr.)—Living water has vital power in itself and exerts the same upon the soul; represents the Holy Spirit in this text.

B. **Messias (v. 25)** *Messias* (Gr.)—The Greek form of Messiah, meaning, "anointed"; a name of Christ.

## LIGHT ON THE WORD

Jesus had been traveling and preaching for many days. Like most travelers during this time, He was poor and journeyed on foot. He then became fatigued, which reveals that He was truly human. Because sin, toil, and strife are part of human existence, Christ became weary because He submitted Himself to our human condition. The roads through Samaria were accessible, but the country was full of hills and mountains, which required great energy and strength to climb. On this trip, Jesus was headed to Galilee. He decided to leave Judea and return to Galilee because the Pharisees had heard that Jesus was baptizing more disciples than John, even though they were actually His disciples (**John 4:1–3**).

## TEACHING THE BIBLE LESSON

## LIFE NEED FOR TODAY'S LESSON

AIM: Students will see how Jesus accepts all people regardless of societal standards.

## INTRODUCTION

### Samaria

This country is located north of the Dead Sea and west of the Jordan River. The land is inhospitable for use and difficult for travel, full of mountains, deep cracks in the earth, and valleys. During Bible times, mountain passes connected Samaria with other countries, which made them accessible. The well where Jesus met the "woman of Samaria" was located in a town called Sychar, which was near a plot of ground that Jacob had given to his son, Joseph (**John 4:5–7**). Therefore, the well is often referred to as "Jacob's Well."

During this time, Samaritans and Jews hated one another. Because of this strained relationship, it was not common or safe to see a Jew traveling through Samaria. In this passage, Christ is traveling from Judea to Galilee, and He has taken the road leading directly through Samaria. Being a Jew, Jesus was vulnerable to mistreatment and even violence from the Samaritan people, making this story even more significant because Jesus befriended a Samaritan woman and showed her love and kindness. Typically, a man of Jesus' heritage would have been on high alert while traveling through Samaria, but Jesus extinguished the fires of hatred with the healing waters of love.

## BIBLE LEARNING

AIM: **Students will understand that Jesus orchestrates life-changing encounters.**

## I. LIVING WATER (John 4:7-15)

At the beginning of this story, we find Jesus in a rather unique circumstance: He's alone. He was becoming a celebrity primarily by performing miracles. People followed Him wherever He went, and His disciples constantly surrounded Him. On this rare occasion, the disciples had gone into town to buy food, and Jesus was left alone.

Being tired from His journey, Jesus sat by a well. A Samaritan woman approached to fill her water jar. Jesus asked her for a drink of water. Surprised and confused, the Samaritan woman questioned Jesus. She didn't understand why He would speak to her, let alone even acknowledge her existence. She knew the cultural rules of her time. There were three reasons why she was shocked by Jesus' actions: (1) Jewish men did not initiate conversation with unknown women; (2)

Jewish teachers did not host public discussions with women; and (3) Jews and Samaritans hated each other and did not converse.

Regardless of societal standards, Jesus continued to engage in conversation with the woman, revealing her sinfulness and need for a Savior (**John 4:16–18**). Throughout the discussion, it is obvious that the woman was knowledgeable. She asked Jesus questions based on her knowledge of culture, history, and religious beliefs. She knew the history of the land, the cultural drama between the Jews and Samaritans, and the prophecy of a coming Messiah. She was eager, or "thirsty," to learn more and hung on Jesus' every word (**verse 15**).

### Jesus Meets the Samaritan Woman (verses 7-15)

**7 There cometh a woman of Samaria to draw water: Jesus saith unto her, Give me to drink. 8 (For his disciples were gone away unto the city to buy meat.)**

While the disciples were in the town of Sychar to buy some food, a Samaritan woman came to draw water from the well. Jesus did something astonishing. He started a conversation with a woman He had never met before (**see verse 9**). In verse 8, the particle "for" shows why Jesus asked a service of the woman that no one else could have done for Him, because the disciples had gone away into the city. Jesus' request was simple and sincere. He was tired and thirsty (verse 6). He used a personal need as a point of contact with the woman (**cp. Luke 5:1–3**).

**9 Then saith the woman of Samaria unto him, How is it that thou, being a Jew, askest drink of me, which am a woman of Samaria? for the Jews have no dealings with the Samaritans.**

Essentially, the woman said to Jesus, "How is it that you, 'being' a Jew would ask for a drink from me, a Samaritan woman?" Jesus' request to the woman of Samaria presents two difficulties for her: She was a woman and a Samaritan. The custom in many areas during the time of Jesus and as reinforced by the rabbinic laws was that a man was not allowed to talk to a woman in public places. Secondly, over the course of the Jews' history, they did not associate with Samaritans. The reasons dated from the annexation of the Northern Kingdom of Israel by the Assyrians in 722–721 B.C. (**2 Kings 17:24–41; Ezra 4:1–5; cp. Luke 9:52; Acts 1:8; 8:5–25**). The Samaritans were the progeny of Israelites who intermarried with them after the deportation to Assyria and pagans brought from the East by the king of Assyria.

Surprised and curious, the woman could not understand how He dared to ask her for water. The Samaritan woman asked why Jesus would want to "have dealings with," "make use of," or "associate with her on friendly terms." The relationship between the two nations was not friendly.

**10  Jesus answered and said unto her, If thou knewest the gift of God, and who it is that saith to thee, Give me to drink; thou wouldest have asked of him, and he would have given thee living water.**

Having caught her full attention and stimulated her curiosity, Jesus replied metaphorically to make her think more deeply. She needed to ponder the answer to these questions: Who is Jesus? What is the gift of God? What does "living water" mean? Jesus was progressively revealing Himself to the woman as He did with Nicodemus (**see John 3**). Basically, Jesus said to her, "Jesus answered her, If you had only known and had recognized God's gift and Who this is that is saying to you, Give Me a drink, you would have asked Him [instead] and He would have given you living water (**John 4:10 AmpV**)."

The word "gift" used in this context always applied to a divine gift in Acts and the Epistles (**Acts 2:38; 8:20; 10:45**). Here it refers to the Holy Spirit (**see John 7:38–39**). The "spring water" or "living water" is used metaphorically to refer to the Holy Spirit (**see John 7:38–39**); in Jeremiah, spring water is opposed to stagnant cistern water; (**see Jeremiah 2:13; cp. 17:13**).

**11 The woman saith unto him, Sir, thou hast nothing to draw with, and the well is deep: from whence then hast thou that living water? 12 Art thou greater than our father Jacob, which gave us the well, and drank thereof himself, and his children, and his cattle?**

The Samaritan woman interpreted the metaphor literally. She knew about the living water in the well near her. This well belonged to her and her people. Thus, it was absurd to her that Jesus, without a bucket, would offer to give her water from a deep well. Such an exploit would outrank what Jacob did in digging the well. It is interesting to notice that in John 4:12 she called Jacob "our father" or "ancestor" since Jews considered him the founder of their nation. The Samaritans also considered Jacob their ancestor. The implied answer to the woman's question is "no" or "never." What she meant was that Jesus could not do what He was saying. She could not conceive that Jesus was greater than Jacob.

**13 Jesus answered and said unto her, Whosoever drinketh of this water shall thirst again: 14 But whosoever drinketh of the water that I shall give him shall never thirst; but the water that I shall give him shall be in him a well of water springing up into everlasting life.**

Jesus contrasted water that quenched thirst temporarily with water that quenched thirst permanently. The latter is superior because it leads to eternal life. Jesus was trying to get to the woman's fundamental longing, which was spiritual thirst, so He was speaking of the Holy Spirit (**see John 7:38–39**). He was telling her that at the Holy Spirit's coming; holy places such as the well of Jacob would lose their meaning. Religious and ethnic identities based on holy sites would give way to a new identity whose source would be in the Holy Spirit (**see John 4:21, 23; cp. Acts 7:47–48**).

**15 The woman saith unto him, Sir, give me this water, that I thirst not, neither come hither to draw.**

The woman misunderstood Jesus' words. She was still hearing "water" in merely physical terms. She was thinking of some magical source of water that would keep her from the need of laborious drawing from a well. She asked Jesus to give her the water He was speaking of so that she would not keep coming to this place to "draw" or "pump out water." In using the verb "come," in this context she meant that she didn't want to keep coming day by day, referring to a repeated action in the present.

## SEARCH THE SCRIPTURES

### QUESTION 1

What was the significance of Jesus asking the Samaritan woman for a drink of water?

**Because He was a Jew and she was a Samaritan, the two nations did not have a good relationship. Answers will vary.**

## LIGHT ON THE WORD

### Worshipers Welcome

At this point, Jesus continued to tell the woman that the time has come where true worshipers will worship the Father in truth and spirit. Interestingly, she knew what He was telling her. She told Him that she had heard the Messiah was coming. Up until this point in the conversation, the woman did not seem quite in sync with Jesus. He had been talking about living water, and she had been talking about H2O (the water we drink). He was breaking barriers, while she

was abiding by them.

## II. THE MESSIAH REVEALED (John 4:23-26)

During this entire time of His discourse, Jesus had been talking about Himself to the Samaritan woman. She was oblivious to the fact that Jesus was revealing His identity to her. "Then Jesus declared, 'I, who speak to you—am he'" (**John 4:26, NIV**). What a shock it must have been when the Samaritan woman realized to whom she was speaking!

### In Spirit and in Truth (verses 23-26)
**23 But the hour cometh, and now is, when the true worshippers shall worship the Father in spirit and in truth: for the Father seeketh such to worship him.**

The true question about worship is not "where" but "how." The time of "true" or "genuine" worship is now at hand because the Messiah is now at hand. "The true worshippers" genuinely understand that Jesus is the truth of God (**John 3:21; 14:6; Acts 4:12**). The Father wants people of this kind as His worshipers. They are to worship in spirit and in truth. To worship in spirit is to worship in a new way revealed by God to humanity in Jesus. To worship in truth is to worship God through Jesus. True worship is offered through Jesus by the means of the Holy Spirit. True worship is in contrast with religious formalism such as that of the Pharisees. The Father is seeking true worshipers because its authentic nature requires that worship be spiritual.

**24 God is a Spirit: and they that worship him must worship him in spirit and in truth.**

By this affirmation of the essence of God ("God is a Spirit"), Jesus justified what He had said about genuine worship in John 4:23. Worship must be in harmony with the nature of the one being worshiped. We cannot relate to God satisfactorily in physical terms since He is Spirit. He is invisible and intangible. For God to be known, He must reveal Himself to us. He did so in the Scriptures. His fuller revelation is now at hand in Jesus (**see John 1:18**). True and satisfactory worship is worship offered in and through Jesus.

**25 The woman saith unto him, I know that Messias cometh, which is called Christ: when he is come, he will tell us all things.**

The Samaritans had a messianic anticipation based on the Pentateuch (**Deuteronomy 18:15–18**). They were waiting for the Messiah they called Taheb (meaning the "converter" or "restorer"), a second Moses who would reveal the truth, restore true belief, and renew true worship. They did not expect the Messiah to be the King born of David. The Samaritan woman was beginning to understand part of what Jesus was telling her. She was waiting with nostalgia for the coming of the Messiah who "will tell us all things" (**John 4:25**). The verb "tell" means "to report" (**such as in Acts 14:27; 15:4; II Corinthians 7:7**), but it is generally rendered as "announce," "proclaim," or "teach." All these meanings can be understood in the Messiah's ministry.

**26 Jesus saith unto her, I that speak unto thee am he.**

Jesus revealed to the concerned woman that she was speaking with the Messiah in person. "I am . . . he" (**cp. John 6:20; 8:24, 58; Exodus 3:14–15**). Jesus had never before expressed His messianic title so clearly. The situation here was different from when He was among Jews. Many Jews had false messianic hope. They were expecting a political figure to deliver them from their enemies, the Romans (**see John 6:14–15; 18:36**). It was dangerous for Jesus to declare openly that He was the Messiah (**cp. Matthew**

16:20; Mark 8:30; Luke 9:21).

## SEARCH THE SCRIPTURES

### QUESTION 2

What did Jesus reveal to the Samaritan about His identity?

**Jesus revealed that He was the Messiah spoken of in the Old Testament Scriptures. Answers will vary.**

## LIGHT ON THE WORD

### Come See a Man

The Samaritan woman heard the good news. Could this be the promised Messiah here in her town? She had to tell somebody so she ran off to tell others to come see a man who told her about herself (**John 4:28**). Because of her excitement, people left what they were doing and headed to see Jesus. How authentic the woman's amazement and faith must have been! She, a woman of questionable reputation, convinced an entire town of Samaritans to stop their work, leave their businesses, and put their livelihoods on hold to see a Jewish man who might be the Messiah. Her faith and joy were contagious, and she broke down more cultural barriers. Christ had changed her life in a significant way.

## III. JESUS GIVES SOMETHING TO TALK ABOUT (John 4:28-30)

Amazed by what she heard, the Samaritan left her water jar and went to tell others about Jesus. Perhaps her excitement simply made her forget. It is plausible that she did not want to lug the heavy vessel with her because she wanted to hurry and bring others to see the Christ before He left. Once she reached the town, the Samaritan woman told people what Jesus had told her. She suggested that He might very well be the Christ. Just like the Samaritan woman, others had heard the prophecy of a coming Messiah, and now they had the chance to see

Him. The Samaritan woman's words about Jesus being the Christ sparked the interest of others.

### Jesus Reaches Other Samaritans
### (verses 28-30)

**28 The woman then left her waterpot, and went her way into the city, and saith to the men, 29 Come, see a man, which told me all things that ever I did: is not this the Christ?**

Leaving her water jar, the woman hurried back to town to share her discovery with her people. She said, "Come", and she pointed out two things about Jesus: (1) He told her "all (the) things" she "ever did" everything, **(see John 4:10–19; cp. 1:48). (2)** He might be the Messiah. Her first impression of Jesus was that He was a prophet **(John 4:19).** As their conversation continued, she wondered if He was indeed the long-awaited Messiah.

**30 Then they went out of the city, and came unto him.**

Just as Jesus caught her attention by awakening her curiosity, she was able to get people to listen to her. They were impressed by her words and decided to see for themselves. Despite the woman's likely unpopular lifestyle, the people hastened to leave town to go to see if Jesus was the Christ. One can easily picture the Samaritans coming out of the town like a stream and going toward Jesus.

## SEARCH THE SCRIPTURES

### QUESTION 3

What happened when the Samaritan woman reached town to tell others what she experienced?

**Those who heard her came out to meet Jesus for themselves. Answers will vary.**

## LIGHT ON THE WORD

### Overcoming Cultural Barriers

Life is full of unfair discrimination, but God does not discriminate. In today's lesson, we learned how Jesus accepts all people, regardless of societal standards, and welcomes them into the kingdom of heaven.

## BIBLE APPLICATION

**AIM: Students will understand their responsibility to share the love of Christ.**

African Americans know how societal norms can promote discrimination and unbiblical principles. People have been inflicting these kinds of boundaries since the beginning of time, and it all comes down to a selfish struggle for power. Skin color, religious beliefs, health, age, gender, and financial worth are just a few of the futile reasons people have turned on each other. In the United States, African Americans have the unique opportunity to show forgiveness and share Christ's love with others, in spite of this country's history of slavery and abuse. People of faith must overcome cultural barriers in order to grow as Christians and share the message of salvation.

## STUDENTS' RESPONSES

**AIM: Students will be a witness of Christ to others.**

Jesus revealed to the Samaritan woman (and to us) that His love extends beyond societal boundaries to all people. He loves everyone, regardless of gender, nationality, and social class. Therefore, as Christians, we must follow Christ's example and reach out to everyone, including societal outcasts, in order to share Christ's love with others. Challenge yourself to extend a loving hand and share the message of Jesus Christ to someone who has a difficult time because of societal or cultural factors.

## PRAYER

Father in heaven, I am to be a carrier of Your light everywhere I go. I pray for those I encounter through the course of my day to receive Your love through me. Help me Lord to love like You, and to see people beyond their exterior and reach their spirit. I pray to bring the best out of everyone I meet and that they see the best of You in me. In Jesus' name I pray, Amen.

## DIG A LITTLE DEEPER

### The mutual hatred of Jews and Samaritans for one another

What was the problem? Why didn't the Jews and the Samaritans get along (v. 9)? The narrative reaches back to the Assyrian Captivity recorded in 2 Kings 17:22-23. The narrative continues 2 Kings 17:24-41. The king of Assyria brought people from Assyria and moved them into the cities of Samaria. They intermarried with the Jews who remained in Samaria. Accordingly, Samaritans were considered to be a mixed-race: Jewish-Gentile. Moreover, they combined the worship of the Lord with the worship of their idol gods.

In the first century, Jews who lived in Galilee who traveled to Jerusalem to celebrate the various feast days were often met with hostility from those living in Samaria (Luke 9:51-56) – even murder (Josephus, Jewish War 2.232-46 and Antiquities of the Jews 20.118-36).

Despite their sordid history, Jesus demonstrated his love for them and others who were social outcasts, like the poor, widows, orphans, shepherds. Jesus carried on a conversation with a Samaritan woman that leads to the conversion of many in that region (John 4:1-45). Shockingly, he told a parable about a good Samaritan (Luke 10:25-37). And Evangelist Peter traveled to the city of Samaria, preached the gospel, healed the sick, and cast out demons (Acts 8:4-8).

For further study, see Joachim Jeremias, Jerusalem in the Time of Jesus: An Investigation into Economic and Social Conditions during the New Testament Period (Philadelphia: Fortress, 1969) 352-58.

## HOW TO SAY IT

Judea.      Joo-DEE-uh.

Samaria.      Suh-MER-ee-uh

### DAILY HOME BIBLE READINGS

**MONDAY**
Planted by Streams of Water
(Psalm 1)

**TUESDAY**
Longing for God
(Psalm 42)

**WEDNESDAY**
The Water of Life
(Revelation 22:10–17)

**THURSDAY**
The Samaritans' Heresy
(2 Kings 17:26–34)

**FRIDAY**
Worshiping What You Do Not Know
(John 4:16–22)

**SATURDAY**
Fields Ripe for Harvest
(John 4:35–42)

**SUNDAY**
"Come and See"
(John 4:7–15, 23–26, 28–30)

## PREPARE FOR NEXT SUNDAY

Read **John 9:1–17** and next week's lesson, "Healing the Blind Man."

**Sources:**
Bauer, Walter. A Greek-English Lexicon of the New Testament and Other Early Christian
Literature (BACD). Chicago, IL: University of Chicago Press, 1979.

Bonnet, Louis. Evangile Selon Jean. Bible Annotée NT2. St-Légier, Suisse, 1983.

Bruce, F. F. The Gospel of John. Grand Rapids, MI: W. B. Eerdmans Publishing Company, 1983.

"Dictionary and Word Search for 'Living Water' in the KJV." Blue Letter Bible.org., 1996–2010. http://www.blueletterbible.org/search/translationResults.cfm?Criteria=living+water&t=KJV (accessed July 30, 2010).
"Dictionary and Word Search for "Messias" (Strong's 3323)." Blue Letter Bible. org., 1996–2010. http://www.blueletterbible.org/lang/lexicon/lexicon.cfm?Strongs=G3323&t=KJV (accessed July 30, 2010).

Henry, Matthew. Matthew Henry's Concise Commentary on the Whole Bible. Nashville,
TN: Thomas Nelson, 1997. 986–87.

The Holy Bible. Contemporary English Version (CEV). New York: American Bible
Society, 1995.

New Testament Greek Lexicon. Bible Study Tools.com. http://www.biblestudytools.com/lexicons/greek (accessed January 9, 2011).

Packer, J. I., Merrill C. Tenney, and William White Jr. Nelson's Illustrated Encyclopedia of Bible Facts. Nashville, TN: Thomas Nelson, 1995. 191–93.

Passage Lookup. Bible Gateway.com. http://www.biblegateway.com/passage (accessed January 9, 2011).

Rochedieu, Charles. Les Trésors du Nouveau Testament. Saint-Légier, Suisse: Editions
Emmaüs, 1972.

Yancey, Philip, and Tim Stafford. The Student Bible: New International Version. Grand Rapids, MI: Zondervan, 1986. 931–932.

## COMMENTS / NOTES:

# HEALING THE BLIND MAN

**BIBLE BASIS:** John 9:1–17

**BIBLE TRUTH:** Jesus ministered to people by meeting their need.

**MEMORY VERSE:** "Therefore said some of the Pharisees, This man is not of God, because he keepeth not the sabbath day. Others said, How can a man that is a sinner do such miracles? And there was a division among them". (John 9:16, KJV)

**LESSON AIM:** By the end of this lesson, we will: KNOW that traditions should not be used to ignore human suffering or needs; REFLECT on a situation where we felt discriminated against or ostracized; and PARTICIPATE in activities that help people in need.

**BACKGROUND SCRIPTURES:** Read John 9 and incorporate the insights gained from the Background Scriptures into your study of the lesson.

## TEACHER PREPARATION

**MATERIALS NEEDED:** Bibles (several different versions), Quarterly Commentary/Teacher Manual, Adult Quarterly, teaching resources such as charts, worksheets/handouts, paper, pens, and pencils.

**OTHER MATERIALS NEEDED / TEACHER'S NOTES:**

_____

_____

## LIFE NEED FOR TODAY'S LESSON
Remember that Jesus cared for those who are considered the least.

## BIBLE LEARNING
Jesus put the blind man's need to see before the Jewish rules about Sabbath observance.

## BIBLE APPLICATION
To understand that Jesus expects us to participate in meeting the needs of others.

## STUDENTS' RESPONSES
Students will discern opportunities to be a blessing to someone in need.

## LESSON SCRIPTURE

### JOHN 9:1-17, KJV

1 And as Jesus passed by, he saw a man which was blind from his birth.

### JOHN 9:1-17, AMP

1 While He was passing by, He noticed a man [who had been] blind from birth.

**2** And his disciples asked him, saying, Master, who did sin, this man, or his parents, that he was born blind?

**3** Jesus answered, Neither hath this man sinned, nor his parents: but that the works of God should be made manifest in him.

**4** I must work the works of him that sent me, while it is day: the night cometh, when no man can work.

**5** As long as I am in the world, I am the light of the world.

**6** When he had thus spoken, he spat on the ground, and made clay of the spittle, and he anointed the eyes of the blind man with the clay,

**7** And said unto him, Go, wash in the pool of Siloam, (which is by interpretation, Sent.) He went his way therefore, and washed, and came seeing.

**8** The neighbours therefore, and they which before had seen him that he was blind, said, Is not this he that sat and begged?

**9** Some said, This is he: others said, He is like him: but he said, I am he.

**10** Therefore said they unto him, How were thine eyes opened?

**11** He answered and said, A man that is called Jesus made clay, and anointed mine eyes, and said unto me, Go to the pool of Siloam, and wash: and I went and washed, and I received sight.

**12** Then said they unto him, Where is he? He said, I know not.

**13** They brought to the Pharisees him that aforetime was blind.

**2** His disciples asked Him, "Rabbi (Teacher), who sinned, this man or his parents, that he would be born blind?"

**3** Jesus answered, "Neither this man nor his parents sinned, but it was so that the works of God might be displayed and illustrated in him.

**4** We must work the works of Him who sent Me while it is day; night is coming when no one can work.

**5** As long as I am in the world, I am the Light of the world [giving guidance through My word and works]."

**6** When He had said this, He spat on the ground and made mud with His saliva, and He spread the mud [like an ointment] on the man's eyes.

**7** And He said to him, "Go, wash in the pool of Siloam" (which is translated, Sent). So he went away and washed, and came back seeing.

**8** So the neighbors, and those who used to know him as a beggar, said, "Is not this the man who used to sit and beg?"

**9** Some said, "It is he." Still others said, "No, but he looks like him." But he kept saying, "I am the man."

**10** So they said to him, "How were your eyes opened?"

**11** He replied, "The Man called Jesus made mud and smeared it on my eyes and told me, 'Go to Siloam and wash.' So I went and washed, and I received my sight!"

**12** They asked him, "Where is He?" He said, "I do not know."

**13** Then they brought the man who was formerly blind to the Pharisees.

**14** Now it was on a Sabbath day that Jesus made the mud and opened the man's eyes.

**14** And it was the sabbath day when Jesus made the clay, and opened his eyes.

**15** Then again the Pharisees also asked him how he had received his sight. He said unto them, He put clay upon mine eyes, and I washed, and do see.

**16** Therefore said some of the Pharisees, This man is not of God, because he keepeth not the sabbath day. Others said, How can a man that is a sinner do such miracles? And there was a division among them.

**17** They say unto the blind man again, What sayest thou of him, that he hath opened thine eyes? He said, He is a prophet.

**15** So the Pharisees asked him again how he received his sight. And he said to them, "He smeared mud on my eyes, and I washed, and now I see."

**16** Then some of the Pharisees said, "This Man [Jesus] is not from God, because He does not keep the Sabbath." But others said, "How can a man who is a sinner (a non-observant Jew) do such signs and miracles?" So there was a difference of opinion among them.

**17** Accordingly they said to the blind man again, "What do you say about Him, since He opened your eyes?" And he said, "[It must be that] He is a prophet!"

## BIBLICAL DEFINITIONS

A. **Sin (John 9:2)** *hamartano* (Gk.)—To wander from the law of God; violate God's law.

B. **Should be made** *manifest* (v. 3) *phaneroo* (Gk.)—Made visible or known what has been hidden or unknown.

## LIGHT ON THE WORD

In the first-century world, blindness was a severe hardship. Usually, it meant that blind people had to support themselves by begging. Some scholars report that mud made from spittle was a common treatment for eye problems in Jewish medicine of the time (Vincent, 182). Modern medical science suggests that, for that remedy to work, it would take a miracle.

## TEACHING THE BIBLE LESSON

## LIFE NEED FOR TODAY'S LESSON

AIM: Students will examine how they approach people in need, and follow Jesus'

example.

## INTRODUCTION

### Pharisees

The Pharisees were a group of orthodox Jews who prided themselves on strict faithfulness to their rigid interpretations of the Law of Moses. Jesus' emphasis on the proper interpretation and spirit of the law and the hypocrisy of self-righteousness led to many clashes with them.

### Siloam

The pool of Siloam was a spring-fed pool located in the southeastern corner of Jerusalem. The Gospel writer points out that the Hebrew word Siloam means "sent," probably referring originally to the outflow of water from the spring, but in this context serving as a symbol connected to Christ's messianic ministry as well. Jesus was the Messiah sent by God, and He sent the blind man to be healed.

## BIBLE LEARNING

AIM: Students will understand the importance

of reserving judgment about people who are different.

## I. WHOSE FAULT WAS IT? (John 9:1-7)

As long as people have talked about theology, they have debated the problem of evil. Why does a loving God allow people to suffer? Why do bad things happen to good people? These are deeply troubling concerns, but sometimes doctrinal debates about them cause us to miss the point.

That seems to be what happened with Jesus' disciples. John begins the story: "And as Jesus passed by, he saw a man which was blind from his birth. And his disciples asked him, saying, Master, who did sin, this man, or his parents, that he was born blind?" (**John 9:1–2**).

When the disciples saw the man who had been born blind, their minds jumped to an old theological argument. Many people (going all the way back to Job's friends) believe that suffering is a punishment for sin or lack of faith. Among the many problems with this belief, it doesn't explain how a person could suffer from blindness since the moment he was born. Some might argue that the man's parents had sinned. The disciples were curious about Jesus' opinion.

### Jesus Is the Light of the World (verses 1-7)

**1 And as Jesus passed by, he saw a man which was blind from his birth.**

Jesus saw a blind man as He was walking along in the city of Jerusalem or probably outside the Temple (**see John 8:59; cp. Acts 3:2**). The man had been blind from birth. His case was desperate (**[cp.] John 5:5–6**). Jesus is all-powerful (**cp. Luke 1:37**). He is able to help even in a hopeless situation.

**2 And his disciples asked him, saying, Master, who did sin, this man, or his parents, that he was born blind?**

For the disciples, and for the Jews of the time of Jesus, personal suffering of this nature was supposedly due to personal sin. Here, since the suffering began at birth, the problem was in identifying who was responsible: either this man sinned in the womb, or his parents had committed a sin before the man's birth (**cp. Ezekiel 18:4; Exodus 20:5**).

While the Bible allows a general relationship between suffering and sin due to the Fall, it refuses to permit the principle to be individualized in every case (**cp. Genesis 3; Romans 5; Job**). A person's suffering is not always due to a particular sin he or she committed.

**3 Jesus answered, Neither hath this man sinned, nor his parents: but that the works of God should be made manifest in him.**

Jesus told the disciples that this man's blindness was not due to his sin or the sin of his parents. It occurred so that the work of God might be displayed in his life (**cp. Exodus 4:11; 2 Corinthians 12:9**). This is not to suggest that God made this man blind (or allowed it) in order to use him to reveal His glory (**see James 1:12–18**). As in all seemingly hopeless cases, the man's blindness allows the works of God to be revealed. The man's story is a sign revealing the glory of Jesus sent by God. One of the marks of the coming of the messianic age is the receiving of sight by the blind (**Isaiah 29:18; 35:5**).

**4 I must work the works of him that sent me, while it is day: the night cometh, when no man can work. 5 As long as I am in the world, I am the light of the world.**

Jesus pointed out to the disciples an urgency to be reckoned with (**cp. John 4:34; Matthew 24:36–51**). Jesus used a short parable about day and night to talk primarily about His ministry and later the ministry of the disciples.

He compared His ministry to light shining in darkness (see **John 1:9; 3:19; 8:12**). His life is compared to one day of labor, and it will finish with the night of His death (**John 5:17; Luke 13:32**). Thus, He must take advantage of the hours of the day in order to finish the job before the coming of the night (see **John 11:9–10**). He was talking about His imminent death. This is an explicit connection to Jesus' earlier claim (**John 8:12**). As the Light of the world, Jesus offers salvation to all human beings. After His death, His disciples will be called to be His witnesses (**John 4:34–38; 11:7, 15; Acts 1:8**).

**6 When he had thus spoken, he spat on the ground, and made clay of the spittle, and he anointed the eyes of the blind man with the clay,**

Jesus proceeded to heal the blind man using a mudpack made from saliva. No reason is given for using a mudpack instead of just saying a word as in previous healings (see **John 4:50, 53**). It may be that the man needed to be involved in the healing process by an act of obedience to Jesus. Jesus probably used the mudpack, not as medicine, to stimulate the man's faith (**cp. 2 Kings 5:13**).

**7 And said unto him, Go, wash in the pool of Siloam, (which is by interpretation, Sent.) He went his way therefore, and washed, and came seeing.**

Jesus sent the man to the pool called "Siloam", meaning "explained," "interpreted," or "sent" (**cp. 2 Kings 20:20; 2 Chronicles 32:30**). Water flowed from the spring at Gihon into a pool in the city of Jerusalem. Jesus sent the man, and He Himself was sent by the Father. In John 9:7, having obeyed the command to go and wash in Siloam, the man "came (back) seeing," meaning "he came away seeing or able to see." Healing was the reward of his obedience (**cp. 1 Samuel 15:22–23**). It is not that the water of Siloam had a curative virtue; it is his faith leading him to

where he had been sent (**cp. Luke 17:14, 19**).

## SEARCH THE SCRIPTURES
### QUESTION 1

What answer did Jesus give to the disciples' question about the cause of the beggar's blindness?

**Jesus told the disciples that this man's blindness was not due to his sin or the sin of his parents. It occurred so that the work of God might be displayed in his life. Answers will vary.**

## LIGHT ON THE WORD
### A New Creation

Not surprising, the sight of a blind beggar created a stir in the neighborhood. Some of the neighbors tentatively recognized him; others thought he was a different person who happened to look the same.

The man used to sit and beg, but after Jesus healed him, he could walk and run on his own and would be able to earn his own living. By giving the man the ability to see, Jesus transformed his entire life.

This miraculous healing is one of many fulfillments of prophecies foretelling that the Messiah would give sight to the blind. God declares through Isaiah, "I will keep you and will make you to be a covenant for the people and a light for the Gentiles, to open eyes that are blind, to free captives from prison and to release from the dungeon those who sit in darkness" (**Isaiah 42:6–7, NIV; compare Isaiah 35:5; Matthew 11:2–6**). Miracles, like this one, point directly to Jesus' identity as God's promised Servant.

## II. THE BLIND MAN RECEIVES HIS SIGHT (John 9:8-12)

Blind eyes being opened is also used throughout

Scripture as a metaphor for spiritual insight or visions that people could only have received from God (**Numbers 22:31; 2 Kings 6:17; Luke 24:31**).

The healed man is eager to claim his identity as the former blind beggar: "I am the man" (John 9:9, NIV). When his neighbors pressed him for details of this extraordinary event, he replied with a simple, matter-of-fact retelling of his story, centered on Jesus. Later, he summarized his experience in a brilliant, pithy statement: "One thing I do know. I was blind but now I see!" (**John 9:25, NIV**).

### Jesus Heals the Blind Man
### (verses 8-12)

**8 The neighbours therefore, and they which before had seen him that he was blind, said, Is not this he that sat and begged? 9 Some said, This is he: others said, He is like him: but he said, I am he. 10 Therefore said they unto him, How were thine eyes opened?**

As a result of the miracle the man's neighbors started discussing his identity. They were used to seeing him when he was a beggar (**cp. Acts 3:2**), but they were seeing a different person. They were not sure he was the same person who used to be a blind beggar. They explored different opinions. The man assured them that he was the same person. He used the same self-identifying expression used by Jesus: "I am he" (**cp. John 6:20; 8:24, 28, 58**). He was asked to tell them what happened to him.

**11 He answered and said, A man that is called Jesus made clay, and anointed mine eyes, and said unto me, Go to the pool of Siloam, and wash: and I went and washed, and I received sight.**

The how of a miracle is always difficult to explain, but the man stuck to the facts. He explained very simply how the miracle happened and who did it. The man who healed him was called Jesus.

**12 Then said they unto him, Where is he? He said, I know not.**

They asked the man where Jesus was. In F. F. Bruce's view, "The question 'Where is he?' suggests that those who questioned the man would have liked to question Jesus too, to see if the two accounts tallied" (Bruce, 211). Since the man could not see when Jesus made mud and smeared his eyes with it, when he went back home after his healing, he could not really know where Jesus was.

## SEARCH THE SCRIPTURES
### QUESTION 2

How did the beggar explain what happened to him to his neighbors?

**He explained very simply how Jesus anointed his eyes with clay and told him to go wash in the pool of Siloam, and he received his sight. Answers will vary.**

## LIGHT ON THE WORD
### The Poison of Legalism

Not all the witnesses of this remarkable event were enthusiastic. The neighbors brought the healed man before the Pharisees, religious authorities who (perhaps they expected) would be interested to see a real-life miracle. Instead, the Pharisees grilled the man with questions, observing that Jesus healed him on the Sabbath (John 9:13–14).

According to the Pharisees' interpretation of Moses' Law, activities such as making clay or washing your eyes were considered work that was unlawful on the day of rest (Vincent, 184). Some of them reasoned, "This man is not from God, for he does not keep the Sabbath" (**John 9:16, NIV**).

This is a clear case of legalism. The law—or worse, someone's interpretation of it—is set as a measure for judging a person's standing with God. While the law itself is not a bad thing, God never intended it to be the foundation of our relationship with Him. The law points out our sinfulness, but it has no power to keep us from sinning or make us live better. For those things, we need faith in Christ alone. "The law was our schoolmaster to bring us unto Christ, that we might be justified by faith" (**Galatians 3:24**).

## III. JESUS PLACES NEEDS BEFORE RULES AND REGULATIONS (John 9:13-17)

Some of the Pharisees pointed out the flaw in the legalistic logic: "How can a man that is a sinner do such miracles?" (**John 9:16**). This led to a disagreement and a quarrel. In the end, all the Pharisees missed the point. They were judging people based on their own inflexible understanding of the law, rather than allowing for any compassion toward their neighbors or understanding of the fact that God doesn't always work the way we expect.

Though he lacked specifics, the healed man knew what he thought about Jesus: "He is a prophet" (**verse 17**).

Jesus rebuked the Pharisees, saying that insistence on one's self-righteousness is the real form of blindness. Jesus' miraculous healing, His acceptance of the blind man, and His refusal to work within the system of legalism show that the Pharisees' approach missed the point. The point is to allow God to transform us supernaturally into something new. It is similar to what Paul said, "Neither circumcision nor uncircumcision means anything; what counts is a new creation" (**Galatians 6:15, NIV**).

### Jewish Leaders Challenge Miraculous Healing (verses 13-17)
**13 They brought to the Pharisees him that aforetime was blind.**

They took the man to the Pharisees "aforetime", meaning at some time or "once." They "brought" "to lead to a court of justice" or "to a magistrate" (in this context) him to the Pharisees, probably because the miracle was so out of the ordinary and religious issues related to the Sabbath were involved (**see verse 14**). The Pharisees as religious authorities would know how to handle the situation.

**14 And it was the sabbath day when Jesus made the clay, and opened his eyes.**

The day on which the healing occurred was the Sabbath day. At this point, the reader is told that the healing of the man, who was born blind, had happened on the Sabbath. "One of the categories of work specifically forbidden on the sabbath in the traditional interpretation of the law was kneading, and the making of mud or clay with such simple ingredients as earth and saliva was construed as a form of kneading" (Bruce, 212). For the Pharisees, the healing of this man violated the laws of the Sabbath. The making of clay constituted work and caused the worker to be a Sabbath-breaker.

**15 Then again the Pharisees also asked him how he had received his sight. He said unto them, He put clay upon mine eyes, and I washed, and do see.**

The Pharisees asked the man "again" or in context "anew," to explain how he was healed. They repeated the same question as the neighbors' in verse 10: "How can you see?" It was important for them to find out a basis for an accusation of the breaking of the law (see verse 16). The man explained the healing very simply and briefly using three verbs: "put," in context meaning "to lay on" or "put upon"; "wash," meaning in context "to wash oneself," "to bathe," and "see." Basically, the man told them, "He put clay upon my eyes, I washed myself, and now I see."

**16 Therefore said some of the Pharisees, This man is not of God, because he keepeth not the sabbath day. Others said, How can a man that is a sinner do such miracles? And there was a division among them.**

The man's account of what happened was so persuasive that some of the Pharisees were clearly impressed (**cp. John 3:2**). They said, "How can a man that is a sinner do such miracles?" Others, however, accused Jesus of breaking the Sabbath instituted by God and of being a false prophet trying to lead the people away from God (**cp. Deuteronomy 13:3–5**). So, they were divided (**see John 7:43; 10:19**).

**17 They say unto the blind man again, What sayest thou of him, that he hath opened thine eyes? He said, He is a prophet.**

They asked for the man's opinion of Jesus. His opinion did not count much among the hostile Pharisees. They probably just wanted to get some words out of the man that would allow them to make an accusation against Jesus and even the man. The man said that Jesus was a prophet maybe "in the succession of Elijah and Elisha … [or] perhaps he simply used 'prophet' as a synonym for 'man of God'" (Bruce, 214). It may also have been that it was the highest category the man could think of at this point (**see John 4:19; 6:14**).

## SEARCH THE SCRIPTURES

### QUESTION 3
What law was Jesus accused of breaking by healing the beggar?

**Jesus was accused of breaking the Sabbath by placing mud on the man's eyes. Answers will vary.**

## LIGHT ON THE WORD

### Legalism or True Faith?
Legalistic religion can make people judgmental, but true faith in Jesus results in a supernaturally transformed life.

## BIBLE APPLICATION

**AIM: Students will make every effort not to prejudge people.**

In this story, the Pharisees show several characteristics of what modern researchers call "spiritual abuse," such as legalism, judgmentalism, authoritarianism, rejection, and placing doctrine above people. If you're not familiar with the topic of spiritual abuse, study a list of its characteristics. Have you seen spiritually abusive or legalistic behaviors in religious groups in your experience? How can you avoid these in your own church or ministry? What facts about Jesus might you point to if you needed to encourage someone who had suffered this kind of abuse in His name?

## STUDENTS' RESPONSES

**AIM: Students will examine themselves and show compassion toward others.**

Examine your own approach to people in need. Is it theoretical like the disciples, judgmental like the Pharisees, or compassionate like Jesus? If there are any people or groups of people you've been avoiding unintentionally or on purpose, take the initiative to offer them some tangible help or encouragement in Jesus' name.

## PRAYER

Father in heaven, I ask You to forgive me for any time this week I made judgments about people, even if I didn't say it but I thought about it. Help me to accept people for who they are and see the best in them. I pray for those who are in need and when You show me their need, I pray to promptly obey You in meeting their need, even if it is inconvenient. If it is money, I pray not to judge how they use it but leave that between You and them. In the name of Jesus. Amen.

## DIG A LITTLE DEEPER

### The authorship of John's Gospel and the identity of the beloved disciple

John's Gospel claims to be based on the testimony of one who is identified as the disciples whom Jesus loved. He is never named but appears frequently on the pages of this Gospel leaning on Jesus' chest at the Last Supper (13:23) and acting as an intermediary between Peter and Jesus (13:24-25). He follows Jesus into Pilate's court during his trial (18:15-16) and was at the foot of the cross during Jesus' crucifixion (19:26-27). On that resurrection morning, he outruns Peter to the tomb (20:4), looks in, and believes (20:8). In the epilogue of the Gospel, this disciple identifies Jesus to Peter (21:7) and questions Peter's fate (21:20-23).

Who is this disciple? Early church tradition identifies him as John, one of the sons of Zebedee, who, with James, Jesus called Boanerges (i.e., Sons of Thunder [Mark 3:17]). Irenaeus (ca. 180), a disciple of Polycarp (d. 156 in Smyrna), said:

John himself, the disciple of the Lord, who also had leaned back on Jesus' chest, he too, published the Gospel while he was staying at Ephesus in Asia (Against Heresies 3.1.1.).

I can remember the events of that time …so that I am able to describe the very place where the blessed Polycarp sat … and the accounts he gave of his conversation with John, and with others who had seen the Lord (Eusebius as quoted by Irenaeus, Church History 5.20.5-6).

Therefore, we may conclude that John is the author of the Gospel that bears his name.

[Because of the overlap (John 9:16), readers should see the Digging Deeper discussions on religious groups in first-century Israel (Lesson 4), the seven signs of John's Gospel (Lesson 3), and metaphors in John's Gospel (Lesson 7)].

## HOW TO SAY IT

| | |
|---|---|
| Pharisees. | FAIR-uh-see. |
| Sabbath. | SAB-ay-oth'. |

## DAILY HOME BIBLE READINGS

### MONDAY
Hope for the Future
(Isaiah 29:17–21)

### TUESDAY
Separating Light from Darkness
(Genesis 1:14–19)

### WEDNESDAY
Light for the Journey
(Exodus 13:17–22)

### THURSDAY
The Blind Questioning Blindness
(John 9:18–23)

### FRIDAY
Teaching the Unteachable
(John 9:24–34)

### SATURDAY
Seeing but Not Seeing
(John 9:35–41)

### SUNDAY
The Light of the World
(John 9:1–17)

## PREPARE FOR NEXT SUNDAY

Read **John 6:22–35** and next week's lesson, "The Bread of Life."

**Sources:**
Bauer, Walter. A Greek-English Lexicon of the New Testament and Other Early Christian Literature (BACD). Chicago, IL: University of Chicago Press, 1979.

Bonnet, Louis. Evangile Selon Jean. Bible Annotée NT2. Saint-Légier, Suisse, 1983.

Bruce, F. F. The Gospel of John. Grand Rapids, MI: W. B. Eerdmans Publishing Company, 1983. 211–12, 214.

The Holy Bible. Contemporary English Version (CEV). New York, NY: American Bible Society, 1995.

Merriam-Webster Online Dictionary. http://www.merriam-webster.com (accessed October 4, 2010).

New Testament Greek Lexicon. Bible Study Tools.com. http://www.biblestudytools.com/lexicons/greek (accessed January 9, 2011).

Passage Lookup. Bible Gateway.com. http://www.biblegateway.com/passage (accessed January 9, 2011).

Provender: A Clearinghouse of Sources on Spiritual Abuse and Cult-like Practices in Churches and Groups. http://pureprovender.blogspot.com (accessed July 26, 2010).

Rochedieu, Charles. Les Trésors du Nouveau Testament. Saint-Légier, Suisse: Editions Emmaüs, 1972.

Vincent, Marvin R. Word Studies in the New Testament. Vol. 2. Grand Rapids, MI: W. B. Eerdmans Publishing Company, 1957. 182, 184.

## COMMENTS / NOTES:

# THE BREAD OF LIFE

**BIBLE BASIS:** John 6:22–35

**BIBLE TRUTH:** God in Christ is our source for everything..

**MEMORY VERSE:** And Jesus said unto them, I am the bread of life: he that cometh to me shall never hunger; and he that believeth on me shall never thirst (John 6:35, KJV).

**LESSON AIM:** By the end of this lesson, we will: EXPLAIN why Jesus is the Bread of Life; TRUST that Jesus is our Bread of Life; and LIST the ways that we can share the Bread of Life with others.

**BACKGROUND SCRIPTURES:** John 6—Read and incorporate the insights gained from the Background Scriptures into your study of the lesson.

## TEACHER PREPARATION

**MATERIALS NEEDED:** Bibles (several different versions), Quarterly Commentary/Teacher Manual, Adult Quarterly, teaching resources such as charts, worksheets/handouts, paper, pens, and pencils.

**OTHER MATERIALS NEEDED / TEACHER'S NOTES:**

_____

_____

## LESSON OVERVIEW

**LIFE NEED FOR TODAY'S LESSON**
Remember that Jesus is the Bread of Life.

**BIBLE LEARNING**
Trust Jesus as the Bread of Life and Provider of our every need.

**BIBLE APPLICATION**
To understand how to trust Jesus for every need in our life.

**STUDENTS' RESPONSES**
Students will repent for trying to meet their own needs and reflect on areas where they can trust God more.

## LESSON SCRIPTURE

### JOHN 6:22-35, KJV

22 The day following, when the people which stood on the other side of the sea saw that there was none other boat there, save that

### JOHN 6:22-35, AMP

22 The next day the crowd that stood on the other side of the sea realized that there had been only one small boat there, and that Jesus

one whereinto his disciples were entered, and that Jesus went not with his disciples into the boat, but that his disciples were gone away alone;

23 (Howbeit there came other boats from Tiberias nigh unto the place where they did eat bread, after that the Lord had given thanks:)

24 When the people therefore saw that Jesus was not there, neither his disciples, they also took shipping, and came to Capernaum, seeking for Jesus.

25 And when they had found him on the other side of the sea, they said unto him, Rabbi, when camest thou hither?

26 Jesus answered them and said, Verily, verily, I say unto you, Ye seek me, not because ye saw the miracles, but because ye did eat of the loaves, and were filled.

27 Labour not for the meat which perisheth, but for that meat which endureth unto everlasting life, which the Son of man shall give unto you: for him hath God the Father sealed.

28 Then said they unto him, What shall we do, that we might work the works of God?

29 Jesus answered and said unto them, This is the work of God, that ye believe on him whom he hath sent.

30 They said therefore unto him, What sign shewest thou then, that we may see, and believe thee? What dost thou work?

31 Our fathers did eat manna in the desert; as it is written, HE GAVE THEM BREAD FROM HEAVEN TO EAT.

32 Then Jesus said unto them, Verily, verily, I say unto you, Moses gave you not that bread

had not boarded the boat with His disciples, but that His disciples had gone away alone.

23 [Now some] other small boats from Tiberias had come in near the place where they ate the bread after the Lord had given thanks.

24 So when the crowd saw that neither Jesus nor His disciples were there, they boarded the small boats themselves and came to Capernaum looking for Jesus.

25 And when they found Him on the other side of the sea, they asked Him, "Rabbi, when did You get here?"

26 Jesus answered, "I assure you and most solemnly say to you, you have been searching for Me, not because you saw the signs (attesting miracles), but because you ate the loaves and were filled.

27 Do not work for food that perishes, but for food that endures [and leads] to eternal life, which the Son of Man will give you; for God the Father has authorized Him and put His seal on Him."

28 Then they asked Him, "What are we to do, so that we may habitually be doing the works of God?"

29 Jesus answered, "This is the work of God: that you believe [adhere to, trust in, rely on, and have faith] in the One whom He has sent."

30 So they said to Him, "What sign (attesting miracle) will You do that we may see it and believe You? What [supernatural] work will You do [as proof]?

31 Our fathers ate the manna in the wilderness; as it is written [in Scripture], 'HE GAVE THEM BREAD OUT OF HEAVEN TO EAT.'"

32 Then Jesus said to them, "I assure you and most solemnly say to you, it is not Moses who has given you the bread out of heaven, but it

from heaven; but my Father giveth you the true bread from heaven.

**33** For the bread of God is he which cometh down from heaven, and giveth life unto the world.

**34** Then said they unto him, Lord, evermore give us this bread.

**35** And Jesus said unto them, I am the bread of life: he that cometh to me shall never hunger; and he that believeth on me shall never thirst.

is My Father who gives you the true [b]bread out of heaven.

**33** For the Bread of God is He who comes down out of heaven, and gives life to the world."

**34** Then they said to Him, "Lord, always give us this bread."

**35** Jesus replied to them, "I am the Bread of Life. The one who comes to Me will never be hungry, and the one who believes in Me [as Savior] will never be thirsty [for that one will be sustained spiritually]."

## BIBLICAL DEFINITIONS

**A. Labour (John 6:27)** *ergazomai* (Gr.)—To work, to do, to commit.

**B. Believe (vv. 29, 30)** *pisteuo* (Gr.)—To accept as true, to place confidence in, to rely on.

## LIGHT ON THE WORD

In today's lesson, the day before coming to Capernaum, Jesus and His disciples had been on the other side of the Sea of Galilee. At this time in Jesus' earthly ministry, He was often surrounded by huge crowds, who were intrigued by the miracles He performed. The particular crowd in John 6 presented the occasion for another miracle--the feeding of the 5,000 with five loaves and two fish (**John 6:1–13**). The enthusiastic crowd wanted to make Jesus king in that moment. The king they had in mind was one who would free them from Roman domination, restoring their national glory. They did not understand, even as Jesus compassionately satisfied their physical hunger, His deeper purpose was to show that He is the

Messiah. He had come to make the way for eternal salvation. Consequently, Jesus slipped from the crowd and went to the hills to pray. In the night, the disciples boarded their boat and attempted to cross the sea, but they were embattled by a storm. Jesus came walking on the water to aid them, and when He entered the boat, the storm ceased (**Matthew 14:22–35**). The crowd that had dispersed earlier did not witness this miracle.

## TEACHING THE BIBLE LESSON

### LIFE NEED FOR TODAY'S LESSON

**AIM: Students will learn how they can come to Jesus to meet their basic life needs.**

### INTRODUCTION

#### Capernaum

Located on the northwestern shore of the Sea of Galilee, Capernaum, a city in the Galilean province, was a central location for Jesus' earthly ministry. Jesus lived in Nazareth until He came to Galilee and was baptized by John the Baptist (**Mark 1:9**). After John the Baptist was imprisoned, Jesus returned to Galilee and resided in Capernaum (**Matthew 4:12–16**). Here, on the shore of the Sea of Galilee, the Lord called His first disciples--Peter, Andrew, James, and John (**Matthew 4:18–22**). Peter's home in Capernaum became the residence for Jesus and the apostles when they were not traveling (**Mark 1:29; Luke 4:38**). The Lord often preached in the synagogue in Capernaum (**Mark 1:21; John 6:52–59**) and performed many miracles in the city. These miracles included the healing of the centurion's servant (**Matthew 8:5–13**), the healing of the man with palsy (**Mark 2:1–12**), and the casting out of a demon in a man in the synagogue (**Luke 4:31–36**). After having performed so many miracles in Capernaum and the people still had not repented, Jesus said, "And you, Capernaum, will you be lifted to the skies? No, you will go down to the depths of Hades. If the miracles that were performed in you had been performed in Sodom, it would have remained to this day. But I tell you that it will be more bearable for Sodom on the day of judgment than for you." (**Matthew 11:23–24, NIV**).

### Bread

Bread was considered a staple in the ancient world. It was either baked in a loaf or round cake form. Barley bread usually was baked in the round form and was broken into pieces when eaten. It was barley bread that was used in the miraculous feeding of the 5,000 (**John 6:9**), indicating the crowd consisted of mostly poor people. In the Roman Empire, those with money could afford to make bread from wheat, but barley bread was relegated to the poor. The Romans had such a disdain for barley bread that soldiers regarded having to eat it as a punishment.

## BIBLE LEARNING

**AIM: Students will know what Jesus means when He says He is the Bread of Life.**

## I. SEARCHING FOR JESUS (John 6:22-25)

Some of the crowd of the previous day had lingered in the night near the shore of the Sea of Galilee, fully expecting the next morning to see Jesus and witness more miracles. The crowd was very excited to have been fed the day before, so much so, that they wanted to make Jesus their king (**John 6:14**). The people expected Jesus to deliver them from Roman rule, just as they believed Moses had delivered their ancestors. You can imagine that as they desperately searched for Jesus, excitement was again welling up in their hearts, only to be dashed by the realization that He was not there. They were, of course, disheartened by the prospect of not seeing Jesus, but also, on a very practical note, they would not get a meal, to which Jesus alludes later in the text. The people saw the disciples board the only boat the night before, and they remembered that Jesus had not left with them, but had gone to the mountains. By the time the people realized Jesus must have somehow left that side of the sea, boats from Tiberias had docked. Jesus stepped into a boat, crossed over and came to his own town, Capernaum (**Matthew 9:1, NIV**). Because Jesus could often be found teaching in the synagogue, the people knew where to find Him (**see John 6:59**). At the lakeshore, they addressed Him as Rabbi--a title of respect for Jewish teachers--and asked when He had arrived there. Though their inquiry seemed simple, their question also led to others: By what means had He arrived there since no one saw Him get on the boat with His disciples? Had they missed a miracle?

### Followers Look for a Miracle (verses 22-23)

**22 The day following, when the people which stood on the other side of the sea saw that there was none other boat there, save that one whereinto his disciples were entered, and that Jesus went not with his disciples into the boat, but**

**that his disciples were gone away alone; 23 (Howbeit there came other boats from Tiberias nigh unto the place where they did eat bread, after that the Lord had given thanks:)**

"The day following" in **verse 22** refers to the miracle of the feeding of the 5,000 the day prior, which happened on the Tiberias side of the Sea of Galilee. Jesus had crossed over from Capernaum with the disciples in one boat. The crowd apparently did not miss this detail because when the disciples left in the same boat, they knew Jesus had not gone with them. In Matthew 14:22 and Mark 6:45, it was Jesus who directed or "constrained" the disciples to return to the other side.

In the first century, boats were not nearly as prolific as they are today, and every arrival and departure was a memorable event. Now, via John's inserted parenthetical clarification, the crowd witnessed "other boats" returning to Tiberias, but Jesus was not on any of them either.

**24 When the people therefore saw that Jesus was not there, neither his disciples, they also took shipping, and came to Capernaum, seeking for Jesus. 25 And when they had found him on the other side of the sea, they said unto him, Rabbi, when camest thou hither?**

Not to be deterred, the crowd got into boats (not everyone; perhaps many) and went looking for Jesus. To their great surprise, because they had been carefully watching the coming and going of boats, Jesus was already on the Capernaum side. Even though they had just witnessed a major feeding miracle, they did not assume Jesus had crossed miraculously. In their thinking, He would have had to walk most of the night to get there by foot or found a boat they did not know about. What they did not even conceive of was that He had walked across the water to meet the disciples in the middle of the lake and then rode the rest of the way with them. This was another miracle–– important to the context and symbolic of Jesus' ability to be present in any situation.

The collective account in the Gospels tells the whole story (**Matthew 14:22–26; Mark 6:45–51; John 6:16–21**). The disciples had been rowing across at dusk when the water typically was its choppiest. They seemed to have encountered a strong headwind and made little progress. They were only halfway, about 3.5 miles, when Jesus suddenly appeared. They knew the shore was nowhere near, so they assumed He had to be a ghost. The writer has crossed the Sea of Galilee in a boat, which took at least 30 minutes under the power of a diesel engine. Merrill Tenney captures the moment: "Jesus calmed their fears by speaking to them. When they recognized his voice, they were willing to take him into the boat" (Tenney, 73). Jesus had just proven His power over matter by feeding the 5,000, and now He proved His power over nature. He was eminently qualified for the teaching He was about to deliver. The version of the incident in Matthew captures the story of Peter walking on water (**Matthew 14:28–31**).

## SEARCH THE SCRIPTURES

### QUESTION 1
What did Jesus do for the people following Him the day before?

**Jesus had miraculously fed 5,000 people the day before. Answers will vary.**

## LIGHT ON THE WORD

### Jesus Uncovers True Motives
Jesus, being a searcher of hearts (**2 Chronicles 28:9; Jeremiah 17:10; Romans 8:27**), knows every motivation. For this reason, He did not answer the questions the people asked about His whereabouts, but instead addressed their true

motive: "Jesus answered, 'I tell you the truth, you are looking for me, not because you saw the miraculous signs I performed but because you ate the loaves and had your fill'" (**John 6:26, NIV**).

## II. THE PERISHABLE FOOD
## (John 6:26-31)

Because many in the crowd were severely poor, the meal Jesus provided may have been the first in a long while in which they ate until full. In addition to the quantity of food, perhaps the quality was better than that to which they were accustomed. Barley bread was usually harsh on the stomach, but because Jesus had a hand in this meal, the quality was better. For this reason, the people diligently sought Jesus with the hope of having another good meal. However, Jesus told them not to be consumed with laboring for perishable food, or the things of this world, but rather focus on eternal life, the gift the Father had ordained Him to give. It is not that their physical needs were unimportant, but they needed to "seek first the kingdom of God and His righteousness" and trust that "all these things shall be added to you" (**Matthew 6:33, NKJV**). The people then wanted to know how they could do God's work and what tasks they must perform. Their question reflects their understanding that to please God was to do acts of the Law, but the Law could not save (**Romans 8:3**). Jesus told them the only work God wanted was for them to "believe in the one he has sent" (**John 6:29, NIV**).

### Jesus Teaches on Eternal Rewards
### (verses 26-31)

**26 Jesus answered them and said, Verily, verily, I say unto you, Ye seek me, not because ye saw the miracles, but because ye did eat of the loaves, and were filled. 27 Labour not for the meat which perisheth, but for that meat which endureth unto everlasting life, which the Son of man shall give unto you: for him hath God the Father sealed.**

When the crowd caught up with Jesus back on the Capernaum side, He began to teach them again, as was His custom and as He had done the entire day before. Jesus' message was similar to a previous word He had given to the Samaritan woman (**John 4:7–15**). Physical water only temporarily satisfies, but spiritual water gives eternal life. Likewise, physical food only temporarily satisfies (and also spoils), but spiritual food gives eternal life.

In verse 27, "labour" used in this context is the same as in business, working for a goal or reward. In the next verse, the crowd zeroes in on the meaning. What the Father "sealed," means the Father gave divine approval to (**see also John 3:33**). This event also is indicated but by a different word ("pleased") at Jesus' baptism (**Matthew 3:17; see also John 1:32-34**). In Christ we can rest assured that God gives His seal of approval and safekeeping of the saints (**2 Corinthians 1:22; Ephesians 1:13; 4:30**).

**28 Then said they unto him, What shall we do, that we might work the works of God? 29 Jesus answered and said unto them, This is the work of God, that ye believe on him whom he hath sent.**

"Labour" in verse 27 and "work" here come from the same word, but the phrase "works of God" in verse 28 uses the noun for "work." Thus, it is a straightforward question, which Jesus answers just as directly. One can believe in biblical facts, concepts, and ethics about Jesus but still not have faith in Him. For many, the "work of God" is the hardest work of all because it requires belief—suspending disbelief, stifling mistrust, and ignoring fear. It is a courageous prayer of confidence, from a humble heart—not as easy as it sounds or everyone would believe. Verse 29 contains the Gospel message in a sentence. Jesus also may have referenced Malachi 3:1.

**30 They said therefore unto him, What sign shewest thou then, that we may see, and believe thee? What dost thou work? 31 Our fathers did eat manna in the desert; as it is written, HE GAVE THEM BREAD FROM HEAVEN TO EAT.**

This is quite an amazing question by the same crowd that just the day before had witnessed the miraculous feeding of more than 5,000 people. Yet the very next day they were asking for a sign, ironically pointing to the miraculous feeding of the Israelites in the desert as an example of what they wanted to see. It is as though they were saying, "Feeding this crowd was nothing compared to the crowd Moses fed, and food for one day is nothing compared to food for 40 years." What the crowd seemed to have forgotten was that in spite of the daily miracle in the desert, the Israelites quickly abandoned their faith. Their memory had been no better than that of the crowd Jesus faced. David Ball notes, "The crowd's misunderstanding of Jesus' sign becomes the basis for his explanation of the true understanding of the miracle" (Ball, 1996).

In John 6:31, "manna" refers specifically to the manna given to the Israelites in the desert, which also was kept in the Ark of the Covenant (see also "bread of God" and "food of God" in Leviticus 21:6, 8, 17). "Bread from heaven" as a phrase clearly has original language alliteration. Psalm 78:23–25 refers to the wilderness manna, calling it the corn of heaven and food of angels, raining down from the open doors of heaven. This manna from heaven in the wilderness prefigured the Bread of Life from heaven, which was Jesus.

### SEARCH THE SCRIPTURES

### QUESTION 2
According to Jesus what did the people have to do to "do the works of God"?

**To believe in Him, the One sent from God.**

Answers will vary.

## LIGHT ON THE WORD
### Jesus Is the Bread of Life
Jesus is the Bread of Life who would make eternal life possible by fulfilling His messianic purpose. Anyone who would believe in Him would never hunger and thirst again. Manna sustained physically, but Jesus sustains spiritually, making the way for eternal redemption.

## III. BETTER THAN MANNA (John 6:32-35)

Jesus explained Himself yet again. The people were mistaken in believing Moses had given their ancestors manna. In fact, God had provided it for them. Manna was a precursor to the true Bread God was now giving them. It was of greater value than any food their ancestors received, because it more than sustains the body; this Bread provides eternal life, not just for the Jews but also for the whole world. However, the people were still focused on physical things. When they asked Jesus to give them this bread every day, they were talking about actual food. They had not perceived that Jesus spoke of the One who God had sent to redeem them.

### Jesus Reveals True Bread from Heaven (verses 32-35)
**32 Then Jesus said unto them, Verily, verily, I say unto you, Moses gave you not that bread from heaven; but my Father giveth you the true bread from heaven. 33 For the bread of God is he which cometh down from heaven, and giveth life unto the world.**

In John 6:32, "true" means genuine or original; also veracious or sincere. Jesus reminded the people that Moses' bread was merely ordinary bread that had been provided miraculously; besides, it had not come from Moses but from God, who used Moses as His agent. The Israelites hadn't even been able to save it until the next day. And the next day they were hungry again. Jesus' bread was not like that (see also Deuteronomy 8:3). Both the bread from heaven and Jesus' true bread from heaven were gifts from God (see John 3:16), provided for all, and the permanent answer to their true hunger. Physical bread is needed to sustain physical life, but only spiritual bread can sustain spiritual life. As David Thomas wrote, "Men want bread, not theories of bread."

**34 Then said they unto him, Lord, evermore give us this bread.**

The response by the crowd was uncannily similar to the response of the Samaritan woman (**John 4:15**). Once the Samaritan woman heard about Jesus' living water, she wanted some. Likewise, once the crowd heard about Jesus' spiritual bread, they wanted some.

**35 And Jesus said unto them, I am the bread of life: he that cometh to me shall never hunger; and he that believeth on me shall never thirst.**

The book of John uniquely contains six of these "I AM" statements by Jesus. Merrill Tenney writes, "Each represents a particular relationship of Jesus to the spiritual needs of men" (Tenney, 76). In order, the bread of life is spiritual food (**John 6:35, 48, 51**); the light of the world is for sight in spiritual darkness (**John 8:12**); the door of the sheep is for safety in a dangerous world (**John10:7–11**); the resurrection is for power over death and eternal life (**John 11:25**); the way, truth, and life is for clarity and guidance in spiritual confusion (**John 14:6**); and the true vine is for spiritual nourishment (**John 15:1**). The bottom line in each instance of Jesus' messages is that He is the answer for their human needs. According to Tenney, "He desired that men should receive him not simply for what he might *give* them, but for what he might *be* to

them" (Tenney, 76, emphasis added). Belief is a core theme of the sixth chapter (**see also verses John 6:36, 40, 64, 69**).

The conditions for receiving the Bread of Life are simple—no payment or work is needed; only the "work" of trust and belief. In the Gospel of John, Jesus stated six times that He was the bread from heaven and four times that He was the bread of life. He also repeatedly explained that eating regular bread still resulted in death, but eating spiritual bread resulted in eternal life.

## SEARCH THE SCRIPTURES
### QUESTION 3
What was the people's response to Jesus' offer of true bread from heaven?

**Just as the Samaritan woman they wanted what Jesus was offering. Answers will vary.**

## LIGHT ON THE WORD
### Jesus Makes Our Lives Complete
There are certain things we need in order to function well in society: food, clothes, shelter, and an income. In and of themselves, these things are not bad. However, letting our pursuit of them consume our lives is the problem. Christians need these things too, but we must live with the understanding that Jesus, not material things, makes our lives complete. Make Him your focus always.

## BIBLE APPLICATION
**AIM: Students will trust in the Lord at all times**

In recent years, many people have lost much of their material wealth and their lives have spiraled out of control, as a result. It is a good time to witness to them, but make sure your life reflects your belief that Jesus is the Bread of Life.

## STUDENTS' RESPONSES

**AIM: Students will continue to seek the Lord for their needs.**

### Be in Constant Prayer

This week, be in constant prayer as you examine your life to ensure you are trusting in the Lord. Then also pray about to whom you can witness and the best way to witness to them.

## PRAYER

Father in heaven, thank You for supplying my every need; I am so grateful to You! You are my source, my portion and my provider. I look to You for everything I need, and Your Word promises that if I seek first Your Kingdom and Your righteousness that all other things will be added unto me. Help me to be content in whatever state I am in, and to always give thanks for this is Your will, concerning me. I pray that my life will be a testimony of Your goodness and draw others unto You. In Jesus' name I pray. Amen.

## DIG A LITTLE DEEPER

### The Manna and the Messiah

One story that every Jew knew was the Exodus from Egypt and the miraculous provisions of God for his people in the wilderness for forty years. Special attention was always given to his providing manna (from the Hebrew word meaning "What is it?").

When the people grumbled against Moses (and God) because of the lack of food, God promised to send bread to them.

In the evening, quail came up and covered the camp, and in the morning, dew lay around the camp. And when the dew had gone up, there was on the face of the wilderness a fine, flake-like thing, fine as frost on the ground. When the people of Israel saw it, they said to one another, "What is it?" For they did not know what it was.

And Moses said to them, "It is the bread that the Lord has give you to eat" (Exod 16:13-15; cf. Num 11:4-9; 21:5; Deut 8:3, 16; Josh 5:12; Neh 9:15, 20; Ps 78: 23-25; 105:40; cf. 1 Cor 10:3).

Part of Jewish hope included the expectation of the renewal of manna from heaven. For example, one ancient writer describes it like this:

And it shall come to pass when all is accomplished … that the Messiah shall then begin to be revealed. And it shall come to pass at that selfsame time that the treasury of manna shall again descend from on high, and they will eat of it in those years, because these are they who have come to the consummation of time (2 Baruch 29:3, 8).

Later rabbis also use similar terms when describing their expectation of the Messiah:

As the former redeemer (i.e., Moses) caused manna to fall, so the latter redeemer will cause manna to descend (Ecclesiastes Rabbah 1:9).

When Jesus says, "I am the bread of life" (John 6:35) or "I am the living bread" (John 6:51), he is affirming that he is the fulfillment of those promises made to the people of God. Just as belief in Jesus leads to eternal life, so receiving (metaphorically eating) him grants life (John 10:51).

See also Lesson 7 Digging Deeper: Jesus' use of metaphors in John's Gospel.

## HOW TO SAY IT

| | |
|---|---|
| Capernaum. | kuh-PUHR-nee-uhm. |
| Galilee. | GAL-uh-lee. |
| Manna. | MAN-uh. |
| Sodom. | SOD-uhm. |
| Tiberias.t | ti-BIHR-ee-uhs. |

## DAILY HOME BIBLE READINGS

### MONDAY
Feeding the Hungry
(John 6:1–15)

### TUESDAY
Walking on Water
(John 6:16–21)

### WEDNESDAY
Giving Eternal Life
(John 6:36–40)

### THURSDAY
Offering Living Bread
(John 6:41–51)

### FRIDAY
The Life-Giving Spirit
(John 6:60–65)

### SATURDAY
To Whom Can We Go?
(John 6:66–71)

### SUNDAY
The True Bread of Heaven
(John 6:22–35)

## PREPARE FOR NEXT SUNDAY

Read **John 10:7–18** and next week's lesson, "The Good Shepherd."

**Sources:**

Alcock, Joan P. Food in the Ancient World: Food through History. Westport, CT: Greenwood Press, 2006. 33.

Ball, David M. 'I Am' in John's Gospel: Literary Function, Background & Theological Implications. Sheffield, England: Sheffield Academic Press, 1996. 237.

Barrett, C. K. The Gospel according to St. John: An Introduction with Commentary and Notes on the Greek Text. 2nd ed. Philadelphia, PA: Westminster Press, 1978. 282.

Bruce, F. F. The Gospel of John: Introduction, Exposition and Notes. Grand Rapids, MI: William B. Eerdmans Publishing Company, 1983. 149–53.

Henry, Matthew. Complete Commentary on the Whole Bible. Bible Study Tools.com. http://www.biblestudytools.com/commentaries/matthew-henry-complete/john6.html (accessed January 10, 2011).

Lindars, Barnabas. Behind the Fourth Gospel. London, England: SPCK, 1971. 137.

Merriam-Webster Online Dictionary. http://www.merriam-webster.com/dictionary (accessed October 6, 2010).

Old and New Testament Concordances, Lexicons, Dictionaries, Commentaries, Images, and Bible Versions. Blue Letter Bible.org. http://www.blueletterbible.org/ (accessed July 10, 2010).

Strong's Concordance with Hebrew and Greek Lexicon. Eliyah.com. http://www.eliyah.com/lexicon.html (accessed October 4, 2010).

Tenney, Merrill C. John, Acts. The Expositor's Bible Commentary, vol. 9. Edited by Frank E. Gaebelein. Grand Rapids, MI: Zondervan, 1981. 70–78.

## COMMENTS / NOTES:

_____

_____

_____

_____

_____

_____

_____

_____

_____

_____

_____

_____

_____

_____

_____

_____

_____

_____

_____

_____

_____

_____

_____

_____

_____

# THE GOOD SHEPHERD

**BIBLE BASIS:** John 10:7–18

**BIBLE TRUTH:** God anoints and equips good leaders for His people. .

**MEMORY VERSE:** And when he putteth forth his own sheep, he goeth before them, and the sheep follow him: for they know his voice (John 10:4, KJV).

**LESSON AIM:** By the end of this lesson, we will: DISCUSS why good leadership is important; TRUST and REJOICE that Jesus is the Good Shepherd; and DESCRIBE the characteristics of a good shepherd that we follow in others.

**BACKGROUND SCRIPTURES:** John 10:1–18— Read and incorporate the insights gained from the Background Scriptures into your study of the lesson.

## TEACHER PREPARATION

**MATERIALS NEEDED:** Bibles (several different versions), Quarterly Commentary/Teacher Manual, Adult Quarterly, teaching resources such as charts, worksheets/handouts, paper, pens, and pencils.

**OTHER MATERIALS NEEDED / TEACHER'S NOTES:**

_____

_____

## LESSON OVERVIEW

**LIFE NEED FOR TODAY'S LESSON**
To apply Jesus' example of good leadership.

**BIBLE LEARNING**
To trust and rejoice that Jesus is the Good Shepherd.

**BIBLE APPLICATION**
To begin to understand and recognize good leadership in every area of their lives.

**STUDENTS' RESPONSES**
Students will discern characteristics of good leadership and work to develop them in their own lives.

## LESSON SCRIPTURE

### JOHN 10:7-18, KJV

**7** Then said Jesus unto them again, Verily, verily, I say unto you, I am the door of the sheep.

### JOHN 10:7-18, AMP

**7** So Jesus said again, "I assure you and most solemnly say to you, I am [a]the Door for the sheep [leading to life].

8 All that ever came before me are thieves and robbers: but the sheep did not hear them.

9 I am the door: by me if any man enter in, he shall be saved, and shall go in and out, and find pasture.

10 The thief cometh not, but for to steal, and to kill, and to destroy: I am come that they might have life, and that they might have it more abundantly.

11 I am the good shepherd: the good shepherd giveth his life for the sheep.

12 But he that is an hireling, and not the shepherd, whose own the sheep are not, seeth the wolf coming, and leaveth the sheep, and fleeth: and the wolf catcheth them, and scattereth the sheep.

13 The hireling fleeth, because he is a hireling, and careth not for the sheep.

14 I am the good shepherd, and know my sheep, and am known of mine.

15 As the Father knoweth me, even so know I the Father: and I lay down my life for the sheep.

16 And other sheep I have, which are not of this fold: them also I must bring, and they shall hear my voice; and there shall be one fold, and one shepherd.

17 Therefore doth my Father love me, because I lay down my life, that I might take it again.

18 No man taketh it from me, but I lay it down of myself. I have power to lay it down, and I have power to take it again. This commandment have I received of my Father.

8 All who came before Me [as false messiahs and self-appointed leaders] are thieves and robbers, but the [true] sheep did not hear them.

9 I am the Door; anyone who enters through Me will be saved [and will live forever], and will go in and out [freely], and find pasture (spiritual security).

10 The thief comes only in order to steal and kill and destroy. I came that they may have and enjoy life, and have it in abundance [to the full, till it overflows].

11 I am the Good Shepherd. The Good Shepherd lays down His [own] life for the sheep.

12 But the hired man [who merely serves for wages], who is neither the shepherd nor the owner of the sheep, when he sees the wolf coming, deserts the flock and runs away; and the wolf snatches the sheep and scatters them.

13 The man runs because he is a hired hand [who serves only for wages] and is not concerned about the [safety of the] sheep.

14 I am the Good Shepherd, and I know [without any doubt those who are] My own and My own know Me [and have a deep, personal relationship with Me]—

15 even as the Father knows Me and I know the Father—and I lay down My [very own] life [sacrificing it] for the benefit of the sheep.

16 I have other sheep [beside these] that are not of this fold. I must bring those also, and they will listen to My voice and pay attention to My call, and they will become one flock with one

Shepherd.

**17** For this reason the Father loves Me, because I lay down My [own] life so that I may take it back.

**18** No one takes it away from Me, but I lay it down voluntarily. I am authorized and have power to lay it down and to give it up, and I am authorized and have power to take it back. This command I have received from My Father."

## BIBLICAL DEFINITIONS

A. **Door (John 10:7)** *thura* (Gk.)—A portal, gate, or entrance.

B. **Shepherd (v. 11)** *poimen* (Gk.)—A shepherd or pastor; used in this instance to illustrate Jesus' ownership and committment to those who follow Him.

## LIGHT ON THE WORD

Jesus described Himself as both the "good shepherd" and the "door" **(John 10:7, 9, 14)**. As a good shepherd, He owned His sheep and was not a hired hand. As owner, the shepherd was on intimate terms with his sheep; that is, he knew their names and personalities. He invested great amounts of time in the sheep. Unlike the hired hand, the owner will give his life, if necessary, to save his sheep from wolves or other predators.

Jesus also described Himself as the "door" through which one must come to become one of His sheep. There was normally only one entrance into the sheep pen, which reduced the likelihood of unwanted persons entering and harming the sheep.

The door is the main entrance. Jesus explained that anyone who tried to get in any other way besides going through the gate (door) would be a thief—that person would be up to no good. In this passage, Jesus compares Himself to a shepherd who enters the gate; Jesus went on to say that only the shepherd enters through the gate. Only the shepherd has the right to enter the sheepfold and call his own sheep out to follow him.

When the shepherd arrived, he would call his own sheep by name. Because sheep recognize the voice of their shepherd, they follow him out to pasture. Just as a sheep would respond to the voice of the shepherd calling its name, when the Good Shepherd Jesus came, all believers recognized His voice and followed Him.

## TEACHING THE BIBLE LESSON

## LIFE NEED FOR TODAY'S LESSON

**AIM: Students will know Jesus as the Good Shepherd and allow Him to lead their lives.**

## INTRODUCTION

### The Shepherd

Jesus pointed out that the most important trait of the good shepherd is that he lays down his life for the sheep. A shepherd's life could at times be dangerous. Wild animals were common in the countryside of Judea, and oftentimes the shepherd had to risk life and limb to save his sheep.

### The Sheepfold

In biblical times, a communal sheepfold held everyone's sheep at night. A strong door protected the sheepfold, and only the guardian of the door had a key.

## BIBLE LEARNING

**AIM: Students will learn the voice of Jesus and follow.**

## I. YOU MUST COME IN AT THE DOOR (John 10:7-14)

These verses consist of a series of four "I am" statements. These statements reveal who Jesus is in relationship to those that follow Him. There are four characteristics that set this good shepherd apart from the thief or robber: (1) He approaches directly—He enters at the gate; (2) He has God's authority—the gatekeeper allows Him to enter; (3) He is trustworthy and meets real needs—the sheep recognize His voice and follow Him; and (4) He has sacrificial love—He is willing to lay down His life for the sheep.

At the same time, there is also a vast difference between the good shepherd, the thief, and the hired hand. The thief comes to steal, kill, and destroy the sheep. The hired hand protects the sheep, but does the job only for money and quickly flees when danger comes. In contrast, the "good" shepherd is committed to the sheep. Jesus is not merely doing a job; He is committed to loving us and even laying down His life for us.

### Jesus Is the Dedicated and Devoted Shepherd (verses 7-14)

**7 Then said Jesus unto them again, Verily, verily, I say unto you, I am the door of the sheep.**

In the first six verses of this chapter, Jesus has spoken to the Pharisees' situation figuratively. He realized His audience would certainly understand the inferences to be drawn from the illustration of the shepherd/sheep relationship; unfortunately, they missed the spiritual lesson Jesus was trying to teach. So Jesus shifts metaphors and declares, "I am the door of the sheep." Again, Jesus' hearers would be familiar with the figure of a shepherd as a "door" of the sheep. Since shepherds habitually lie down across the entrance of the sheepfold with their bodies forming a barrier to thieves and wild beasts, they speak of themselves as the door to let the flock in or out and to protect the flock from intruders. Through the door, the flock goes in and out to graze and to rest. If attacked or frightened, the sheep can retreat into the security of the fold.

Several times in the Gospel of John, Jesus describes Himself using the phrase "I am" (**cf. John 6:35; 8:12, 58; 9:5**). Christ's usage of "I am" in this manner leaves no question about His claim to deity. In fact, to a perceptive Jew who understood the term "I am" as used in Exodus 3:14, Jesus was making Himself equal to God (**cf. John 10:33**).

**8 All that ever came before me are thieves and robbers: but the sheep did not hear them.**

This verse is not a reference to Old Testament prophets, but to all messianic pretenders and religious charlatans, like many of the Pharisees and chief priests of the time. Here, Jesus describes them as "thieves" who divest the unwary of their precious possessions, and "robbers" who plunder brazenly by violence. They were the type that did not care about the spiritual good of the people, but only about themselves. As a result, the sheep (i.e., those who are faithful) would not heed their voice.

**9 I am the door: by me if any man enter in, he shall be saved, and shall go in and out, and find pasture.**

Christ claims to be the door, not just a door.

Jesus is explicitly identifying Himself here as the means to salvation (cf. **Psalm 118:19–21**). As the Shepherd, Jesus provides safety and sustenance for His flock. He is the only way of salvation. Through Him, believers find "pasture" or provision for all of their daily needs.

## 10 The thief cometh not, but for to steal, and to kill, and to destroy: I am come that they might have life, and that they might have it more abundantly.

The thief's motive is diametrically opposed to that of the shepherd. His interest is selfish. He steals the sheep in order to kill them and feed himself, thus destroying part of the flock. In this description, we see a veiled glimpse into the character of the Pharisees and religious authorities who opposed Jesus. In contrast, Christ is the Life-Giver and Life-Sustainer. His interest is the welfare of the sheep. He enables the sheep to have full and secure lives. Conversely, the thief takes life, but Christ gives life abundantly.

## 11 I am the good shepherd: the good shepherd giveth his life for the sheep.

The adjective "good" carries the meaning of being a true or a model shepherd. Here, Jesus is referring to the model of a shepherd found in Ezekiel 34:11–16. According to Ezekiel, the good shepherd gathers, feeds, and protects the sheep. A strong bond exists between sheep and shepherd. It was not unusual for Palestinian shepherds to risk their lives for their flocks. Wild beasts, lions, jackals, wolves, and bears were on the prowl. In his experience as a shepherd, David's fights with a lion and a bear over the life of his flock convinced him that God was also able to give Goliath into his hands (**2 Samuel 17:34–37**). When Jesus says in John 10:11, "I am the good shepherd" (i.e., the true Shepherd), He is expressing the manner in which He carries out His mission of salvation.

## 12 But he that is an hireling, and not the shepherd, whose own the sheep are not, seeth the wolf coming, and leaveth the sheep, and fleeth: and the wolf catcheth them, and scattereth the sheep.

A "hireling" or hired servant, denotes someone who both has no real interest in his duty and is unfaithful in the discharge of it. As a wage earner, a hireling's interest is in the money he makes and in self-preservation. He has no real commitment to the sheep. Therefore, if a wolf shows up, he runs to save his own life, leaving the sheep to fend for themselves. The result is devastating for the sheep. His carelessness exposes the flock to fatal danger. As is the case today, Israel (the Old Testament church) had many false religious leaders, selfish kings, and imitation messiahs; as a result, the flock of God suffered constantly from their abuse.

## 13 The hireling fleeth, because he is a hireling, and careth not for the sheep. 14 I am the good shepherd, and know my sheep, and am known of mine.

The "hireling" is just that—a hired hand. The image of the hired hand is reflective of Israel's selfish kings and false prophets found in the Old Testament (**Ezekiel 34:5–6; Jeremiah 23:1–3; Zechariah 11:15, 17**). Both here and in the Old Testament passages, the hired hand's main concern is for himself. The sheep are only a means to an end.

By contrast, the "good" (meaning "noble" or "true") shepherd cares for the sheep—so much so that he is willing to lay down his life for them. It is important to note that there is a bond of intimacy between the shepherd and his sheep, as indicated by the phrase in John 10:14, "I . . . know." The use of the word "know" implies Christ's ownership and watchful oversight of the sheep. The reciprocal point that the sheep know their shepherd identifies the sheep's response to Christ's love and intimate care. Moreover, the use of "know" indicates that this knowledge is of high value to the shepherd.

## SEARCH THE SCRIPTURES

### QUESTION 1

According to Jesus what does a good shepherd do for His sheep?

**A good shepherd lays down His life for the sheep, knows His sheep, and they know His voice. Answers will vary.**

## LIGHT ON THE WORD

### Jesus Knows His Sheep

Jesus' followers know Him to be their Messiah—they love and trust Him. Such knowledge and trust between Jesus and His followers is compared to the relationship between Jesus and the Father. Thus, Jesus is the Good Shepherd, not only because of His relationship with the sheep, but also because of His relationship with God the Father.

## II. JESUS GATHERS THE SHEEP (John 10:15-16)

Jesus tells the Pharisees that He has other sheep. By using this metaphor, Jesus is letting the Pharisees know that He came to save Gentiles as well as Jews. This is an insight into Jesus' worldwide mission: to die for sinful people all over the world. The new Gentile believers and the Jewish believers would form one flock and have one Shepherd.

### Jesus Reclaims All to the Father (verses 15-16)

**15 As the Father knoweth me, even so know I the Father: and I lay down my life for the sheep.**

The deep mutual knowledge between Christ (the Shepherd) and His sheep is likened to the relationship between the Father and the Son.

God the Father and Jesus, His Son, "know" one another (**verse 15, NIV**); they have a uniquely intimate relationship. The connection between the sheep and the shepherd who knows his sheep and lays down his life for them shows unity of purpose between the Father and the Son. Jesus is more than the Good Shepherd; He is the fulfillment of God's promises to God's people. Christ voluntarily laid down His life for us. His death was not an unfortunate accident, but part of the planned purpose of God.

**16 And other sheep I have, which are not of this fold: them also I must bring, and they shall hear my voice; and there shall be one fold, and one shepherd.**

Jesus was addressing His immediate audience—those already in the fold, the Israelites who believed. But the phrase "other sheep" is a direct reference to the Jews and Gentiles who had not yet come to believe. Therefore, they were still outside of Jesus' protection. The fold, then, is a metaphor for God's covenant people--the church--and none other than the Shepherd Jesus will gather His sheep together into one fold. As they hear His voice, His people from among Jews and Gentiles will come and be formed into one body of Christ as one flock with one Shepherd. There is one people of God, comprised of believers inside and outside of ethnic Israel.

## SEARCH THE SCRIPTURES

### QUESTION 2

Who is Jesus referring to when He says there are "other sheep" that He has in His fold?

**Jesus is referring to the Gentiles. Answers will vary.**

## LIGHT ON THE WORD

### A Willing Sacrifice

Jesus abandons the sheep metaphor and speaks

directly about His relationship with God. Jesus laid down His life of His own accord, and of His own accord He would also take it up again in resurrection. Jesus was living out God's commission (**John 3:16**). When Jesus said He laid down His life voluntarily and that He had the power to take it up again, He was claiming His authority to control His own death and resurrection.

## III. JESUS IS THE GOOD SHEPHERD (John 10:17-18)

Jesus, the Good Shepherd, has the best interests of His sheep in mind at all times. He is on constant guard to keep His sheep upright and in the fold. He is prepared to meet every need and even to give His life to rescue the sheep from danger. As the Good Shepherd, He protects us from danger and provides for our sustenance. Like the Pharisees of Jesus' day, we need to be reminded that it was Jesus' choice to give up His life; it was not taken from Him. It is because of His sacrifice that we can have eternal life. The Son's authority to lay down His life and take it up again did not originate with Himself; it came from the Father.

### Jesus Lays Down His Life for the Sheep (verses 17-18)

**17 Therefore doth my Father love me, because I lay down my life, that I might take it again.**

Jesus reaffirms the love the Father has for Him and picks up again on the theme of His death and resurrection. He will voluntarily lay down His life for the salvation of the world. The Father's "love" is linked with the Son's willingness to lay down His life for the world. The mutual love of the Father and Son come together in one divine purpose of salvation for humankind. The Father in love arranged for the salvation of His people, and the Son in love freely gave His all to accomplish salvation for His people. Naturally, the Father's everlasting love always endures for the Son. However, His death is the supreme manifestation of His sacrificial obedience to the will of God the Father.

**18 No man taketh it from me, but I lay it down of myself. I have power to lay it down, and I have power to take it again. This commandment have I received of my Father.**

In choosing to die for the sins of the world, Jesus once again proved His sovereign authority over His own destiny. If Christ had not chosen to die, no one would have had the power to kill Him. The work of redemption is done by the Father through the Son. Jesus laid down His life in order to take it up again. In Jesus' death, the penalty for sin is paid in full, and the Resurrection is the vindication of the Son as the atonement for sin. In death, the Son becomes the sacrifice for our sins and reconciles us to God. In resurrection, the Son is glorified and the victory of God's kingdom is announced.

## SEARCH THE SCRIPTURES

### QUESTION 3

By whose command does Jesus give His life?

Jesus gives His life on the command of His Father. Answers will vary.

## LIGHT ON THE WORD

### Jesus Supplies All Our Needs

Today's lesson revealed Christ as the Good Shepherd who invests great amounts of time to redeem and protect His sheep as well as to provide sustenance for all our needs.

## BIBLE APPLICATION

AIM: Students will understand how to listen for the voice of the Good Shepherd.

### Jesus Cares

We live in a society where people make daily decisions to live by pleasure principles rather than God's principles. Such pleasure principles lead to acts of adultery, stealing, debauchery, deceitfulness, and so on. Jesus died to rescue us from these pitfalls. God commands us to live for Him and in Him.

As the Good Shepherd, Jesus cares for us and protects us from evil. Yet many of us are living outside of the door of His will. What changes are you willing to make in order to know the voice of the Good Shepherd?

## STUDENTS' RESPONSES

**AIM: Students will make a commitment to always follow Christ.**

### Following the Good Shepherd's Voice

People seek protection from those things that pose a threat to their well-being. Think about your own life. Into what category do you fall? Have you followed the voice of the Good Shepherd, Jesus Christ, our Lord and Savior, for protection? If you have, thank God for opening your ears, your heart, and your eyes so that you recognize the voice of the Good Shepherd. Or are you a hired hand, a thief, or a robber? If you are a leader, do you only care about yourself? If so, ask God to strengthen you so that you might know the voice of the Shepherd and follow Him when He calls.

## PRAYER

Father in heaven, I thank You for the privilege of relationship with You through Your Son Jesus Christ. And thank You for being able to recognize Your voice. My desire is to follow You closely. I pray to rightly discern and obey Your promptings in my spirit by Your Holy Spirit. Help me to be a good leader in my sphere of influence and to draw people to You. In Jesus' name, I pray. Amen.

## DIG A LITTLE DEEPER

### The Exclusivity of Jesus

Jesus is the only way of salvation. It may seem like an obvious conclusion for believers. However, we live in a society where it is often asserted that there are multiple ways of salvation. In other words, it is not uncommon to hear proclamations that Jesus is one among many paths to God that include Muhammad, the Buddha, Confucius, et al.

However, Jesus emphatically states the opposite. It is especially evident in his consistent use of the definite article "the" in his "I Am" statements. The definite article denotes exclusivity or only-ness. Jesus claims to be the only true and living way to God. For example, Jesus says to his disciple Thomas:

I am the way, and the truth, and the life. No one comes to the Father except through me (John 14:6).

During his extended metaphor, Jesus identifies himself as "the door of the sheep" (John 10:7). He says:

I am the door. If anyone enters by me, he will be saved … (John 10:9).

Therefore, it is belief in Jesus (i.e., committed trust in him) and Jesus alone that saves and yields eternal life. If one does not believe in him, it results in damnation:

Whoever believes in [Jesus] is not condemned, but whoever does not believe is condemned already, because he has not believed in the name of the only Son of God (John 3:18).

Whoever has the Son has life; whoever does not have the Son of God does not have life (1 John 5:12).

Lest one think that this theme is peculiar to John's writings, one need only to consider the teachings of the early church as reflected in the preaching of the apostles.

There is salvation in no one else, for there is no other name under heaven given among men by which we must be saved (Acts 4:12).

Salvation is found in Jesus alone.

See also Lesson 7 Digging Deeper: Jesus' use of metaphors in John's Gospel.

See also Lesson 13 Digging Deeper: Belief in the Gospel of John.

## HOW TO SAY IT

Debauchery. De-BAW-cher-e.

Ezekiel. E-ZEE-ke-el.

Palestinian. Pal-e-STIN-e-en.

### DAILY HOME BIBLE READINGS

**MONDAY**
Sheep without a Shepherd
(2 Chronicles 18:12–22)

**TUESDAY**
A New Shepherd for Israel
(Numbers 27:12–20)

**WEDNESDAY**
The Shepherd David
(Psalm 78:67–72)

**THURSDAY**
Lord, Be Our Shepherd
(Psalm 28)

**FRIDAY**
Shepherd of Israel, Restore Us
(Psalm 80:1–7)

**SATURDAY**
The Sheep Follow
(John 10:1–6)

**SUNDAY**
I Am the Good Shepherd
(John 10:7–18)

## PREPARE FOR NEXT SUNDAY

Read **John 11:17–27** and next week's lesson, "The Resurrection and the Life."

**Sources:**

New Testament Greek Lexicon. Bible Study Tools.com. http://www.biblestudytools.com/lexicons/greek (accessed January 10, 2011).

Passage Lookup. Bible Gateway.com. http://www.biblegateway.com/passage (accessed January 10, 2011).

# THE RESURRECTION AND THE LIFE

**BIBLE BASIS:** John 11:17–27

**BIBLE TRUTH:** Jesus is the resurrection and the life..

**MEMORY VERSE:** Jesus said unto her, I am the resurrection, and the life: he that believeth in me, though he were dead, yet shall he live (John 11:25, KJV).

**LESSON AIM:** By the end of this lesson, we will: DISCUSS what the Resurrection and the Life in Christ means for us; RECALL a time when we experienced joy in a situation that looked hopeless; and SHARE with others the Good News that Jesus is the Resurrection and the Life.

**BACKGROUND SCRIPTURES:** John 11:1 – 27—Read and incorporate the insights gained from the Background Scriptures into your study of the lesson.

## TEACHER PREPARATION

**MATERIALS NEEDED:** Bibles (several different versions), Quarterly Commentary/Teacher Manual, Adult Quarterly, teaching resources such as charts, worksheets/handouts, paper, pens, and pencils.

**OTHER MATERIALS NEEDED / TEACHER'S NOTES:**

_____

_____

## LESSON OVERVIEW

### LIFE NEED FOR TODAY'S LESSON
To recall that nothing in life is hopeless as long as Jesus is on the throne.

### BIBLE LEARNING
To know Jesus' promise of new life to those who believe in Him.

### BIBLE APPLICATION
To appreciate how to live a righteous life by having the joy of the Lord during times of trial.

### STUDENTS' RESPONSES
Students will choose to live a righteous life and have joy in the Lord.

## LESSON SCRIPTURE

### JOHN 11:17-27, KJV

**17** Then when Jesus came, he found that he had lain in the grave four days already.

### JOHN 11:17-27, AMP

**17** So when Jesus arrived, He found that Lazarus had already been in the tomb [a]four days.

18 Now Bethany was nigh unto Jerusalem, about fifteen furlongs off:

18 Bethany was near Jerusalem, about two miles away;

19 And many of the Jews came to Martha and Mary, to comfort them concerning their brother.

19 and many of the Jews had come to see Martha and Mary, to comfort them concerning [the loss of] their brother.

20 Then Martha, as soon as she heard that Jesus was coming, went and met him: but Mary sat still in the house.

20 So when Martha heard that Jesus was coming, she went to meet Him, while Mary remained sitting in the house.

21 Then said Martha unto Jesus, Lord, if thou hadst been here, my brother had not died.

21 Then Martha said to Jesus, "Lord, if You had been here, my brother would not have died.

22 But I know, that even now, whatsoever thou wilt ask of God, God will give it thee.

22 Even now I know that whatever You ask of God, God will give to You."

23 Jesus saith unto her, Thy brother shall rise again.

23 Jesus told her, "Your brother will rise [from the dead]."

24 Martha saith unto him, I know that he shall rise again in the resurrection at the last day.

24 Martha replied, "I know that he will rise [from the dead] in the resurrection on the last day."

25 Jesus said unto her, I am the resurrection, and the life: he that believeth in me, though he were dead, yet shall he live:

25 Jesus said to her, "I am the Resurrection and the Life. Whoever believes in (adheres to, trusts in, relies on) Me [as Savior] will live even if he dies;

26 And whosoever liveth and believeth in me shall never die. Believest thou this?

26 and everyone who lives and believes in Me [as Savior] will never die. Do you believe this?"

27 She saith unto him, Yea, Lord: I believe that thou art the Christ, the Son of God, which should come into the world.

27 She said to Him, "Yes, Lord; I have believed and continue to believe that You are the Christ (the Messiah, the Anointed), the Son of God, He who was [destined and promised] to come into the world [and it is for You that the world has waited]."

## BIBLICAL DEFINITIONS

A. **Resurrection (John 11:25)** *anastasis* (Gk.)—A rising from the dead.

B. **Life (v. 25)** *zoe* (Gk.)—Denotes life in the fullest sense; life as God has it.

C. **Believeth (v. 25)** *pisteuo* (Gk.)—To put confidence in; to trust or be persuaded.

## LIGHT ON THE WORD

Only in the book of John do we find the recounting of Jesus raising Lazarus from the dead. This is a family that Jesus loved, and He was loved by them. When He needed a rest, He knew He could find it with these three adults, so when they had a need, they immediately sent for Jesus.

At the start of John 11, Martha and Mary notify Jesus that their brother Lazarus is very sick (**John 11:3**). But instead of rushing to Bethany, Jesus stays where He is for two more days. In biblical times, it was common to bury the dead either on the same day or very close to the time of death. It was also believed that a person's soul hovered around the body for three days after physical death. But by the time Jesus finally arrives in Bethany, Lazarus has been dead four days.

Obviously, Jesus was not in a rush to get to Bethany. He informs His disciples that Lazarus is in fact dead and that He is glad that He was not there to keep Lazarus from dying, so that they may believe (**John 11:15**). This statement shapes the theological heart of today's lesson.

Jesus wants us to put our complete confidence in Him because He is in control of all the affairs of life. When things look bad and we cannot see any way out, Jesus wants us to run to Him, like Martha, and place all of our trust in Him alone.

## TEACHING **THE BIBLE LESSON**

## LIFE NEED FOR TODAY'S LESSON

**AIM: Students will know that Jesus promised that those who believe in Him will—even though they die—have a new relationship with God.**

## INTRODUCTION
### Martha

It is thought by some scholars that Martha was the elder sister of Mary and Lazarus. This is because she is referred to as the owner of the house (**Luke 10:38**). In an earlier meeting with Jesus, it was Martha who became distraught when her sister Mary sat at Jesus' feet instead of helping her serve (**Luke 10:39–42**).

### Bethany

This is a village on the eastern slope of the Mount of Olives, two miles east of Jerusalem. It appears that Jesus preferred to lodge there instead of in Jerusalem. Today, it is known as el-Azariyeh (i.e., "place of Lazarus").

## BIBLE LEARNING

**AIM: Students will understand that God will sometimes use trying circumstances for His glory.**

## I. JESUS IS IN CONTROL (John 11:17-20)

When Jesus arrives in Bethany, Lazarus had already been dead four days. The professional mourners had arrived, and the situation looked hopeless to the human eye. Everything around Martha and Mary was telling them that it was time to give up hope—that there was nothing more to be done. Mary and Martha must have begun to wonder whether Jesus had forgotten about them or, worse yet, had decided not to do anything about their brother's condition. But why does He linger and not rush to the scene? Could it be that He waited to demonstrate His power until all hope in human effort was exhausted?

Ultimately, Jesus is in complete control of the situation. His delay is for the benefit of His disciples and Lazarus' sisters, Martha and Mary, so they may come to trust in the Lord with all their hearts, instead of leaning on their own understanding (**compare [cf.] Proverbs 3:5**).

### Jesus Delays His Arrival
### (verses 17-20)

**17 Then when Jesus came, he found that he had lain in the grave four days already. 18 Now Bethany was nigh unto Jerusalem, about fifteen furlongs off: 19 And many of the Jews came to Martha and Mary, to comfort them concerning their brother.**

Lazarus had been dead and buried for four days. Bethany (now called el-Azariyeh, or "place of Lazarus") is approximately two miles east of Jerusalem. This fact is significant because it shows how close Jesus was to Jerusalem. The nearness of Bethany to Jerusalem accounts for the large presence of Jews at the scene of this miracle. Jewish custom provided for a 30-day period of mourning. To console the bereaved during this period of mourning was considered a pious act among the Jews. Here, John draws attention to two things. First, Jesus' proximity to Jerusalem would have allowed Him to get to Lazarus' house within the first three days of his death. Second, because Bethany was so close to Jerusalem, there were many Jews present to witness the great miracle that was about to take place.

**20 Then Martha, as soon as she heard that Jesus was coming, went and met him: but Mary sat still in the house.**

Upon hearing of Jesus' arrival, Martha hastened to meet Him, while Mary sat in the house. The different responses of Martha and Mary may indicate their personality types: Martha was the outgoing activist and Mary was the contemplative type. It can also be said that because Martha was the older of the two sisters, it was her duty to go out to meet Jesus, while Mary stayed home to continue the mourning rituals with the other mourners.

## SEARCH THE SCRIPTURES

## QUESTION 1

How long was Lazarus dead before Jesus arrived in Bethany?

**Lazarus was in the grave for four days prior to Jesus' arrival. Answers will vary.**

## LIGHT ON THE WORD
### Jesus Is the Answer

Martha expects Jesus to do something. She says "Lord, if You had been here, my brother would not have died" **(John 11:21, NKJV)**. Mary also challenged Jesus. "Then when Mary was come where Jesus was, and saw him, she fell down at his feet, saying unto him, Lord, if thou hadst been here, my brother had not died" **(John 11:32, KJV)**. Some scholars suggest that Martha's remarks to Jesus were ones of reproach instead of words of grief. Some consider Martha a woman of practical duty, eager to put everybody in their rightful place. After all, it was Martha who questioned Jesus regarding her sister Mary's lack of service when Jesus visited their home **(see Luke 10:38–41)**. But here in John 11:22, we realize that Martha's faith in Jesus' ability to heal her brother is undiminished. She tells Jesus, "I know" that God will do whatever we ask, which implies that intuitively Martha's assessment of Jesus is that of a righteous man to whom God listens and for whom nothing is impossible.

## II. JESUS IS ALWAYS ON TIME (John 11:21-24)

In response to Martha's statement, Jesus tells her, "Thy brother shall rise again" **(verse 23)**. Judging from Martha's response to Jesus, it appears that she is disappointed. Martha answered, "I know he will rise again in the resurrection at the last day." **(verse 24, NIV)**. Martha's response to the Master implies that she does not yet grasp the full implication of what Jesus was saying. She understood that in the "last day" all would rise, but Martha yearned for a more immediate solution—she wanted her brother back!

Initially, the way Martha addressed Jesus is similar to how we often address Him when things do not go the way we think they should. Oftentimes we ask, "Lord, where were You? If You would have showed up when I called You, this might not have happened." The Lord may not show up when we think He ought to, but we can be sure that He is always right on time.

### Jesus Declares Life (verses 21-24)

**21 Then said Martha unto Jesus, Lord, if thou hadst been here, my brother had not died. 22 But I know, that even now, whatsoever thou wilt ask of God, God will give it thee.**

Martha's words were a confession of her faith in the Lord; they were not intended as a reproach of Jesus, but were the response of a person in great grief. It is probable that the sisters expressed the same ideas to one another as they awaited the coming of Jesus.

Martha believed that through Christ nothing was impossible with God. She firmly believed that Jesus would have saved Lazarus from death had He been present. But even now that Lazarus was dead, she believed that Jesus could still bring him back to life. In verse 22, the use of the phrase "thou wilt ask" means "desire, call for, or crave" implies that she hoped that Jesus would and that He should pray for an immediate resurrection in spite of Lazarus' decomposing body.

**23 Jesus saith unto her, Thy brother shall rise again. 24 Martha saith unto him, I know that he shall rise again in the resurrection at the last day.**

The phrase "shall rise" means to "stand up." This statement has a double meaning. It relates to the recall of Lazarus from death to life that was about to take place, as well as to his final resurrection at the close of time. Martha seems

to understand Jesus' words to mean that her brother will rise again during the last days. If she understood Jesus' words only in this sense, the assumption is that she had no thought of Lazarus' immediate resurrection (**verse 22**).

## SEARCH THE SCRIPTURES

### QUESTION 2

What did Jesus declare to Martha about her brother?

**Jesus declared that Lazarus would rise again. Answers will vary.**

## LIGHT ON THE WORD

### Jesus Holds the Power

When Jesus heard Martha's reply, He responded to her by stating emphatically, "I am the resurrection and the life" (**verse 25, NIV**). In essence, Jesus was telling Martha, "You keep looking forward to some event in the future, but what you are looking for is standing right in front of you." Jesus challenged Martha to place her trust in Him as the One who holds the power of life and death in His hands.

Placing faith in Jesus has implications for the present and is not relegated to some "pie in the sky, we'll do better in the sweet by and by" mind-set. Jesus wants to effect change in our lives right now. As Christians, we must reach the point where our trust in Christ transcends our understanding of the world around us. When things look impossible from a human perspective, we cannot let this diminish our faith in the One who "sustains all things by his powerful word" (**Hebrews 1:3, NIV**). Jesus cares about the troubles of our lives, and more important than that, He has the power and desire to do something about it.

## III. JESUS IS THE RESURRECTION AND THE LIFE (John 11:25-27)

The word Jesus used for "life" speaks of life in the fullest sense. Jesus has the power to give life because He is Life itself. The power that Jesus has extends beyond merely the physical; He also holds the power to give life to the spiritually dead. Ephesians 2:1 (**NKJV**) says that we "were dead in trespasses and sins," and God "made us alive" or raised us from our spiritual death (**Ephesians 2:5**). On another occasion, addressing a mob of angry Jews, Jesus said, "For just as the Father raises the dead and gives them life, even so the Son gives life to whom he is pleased to give it" (**John 5:21**, **NIV**). The Lord wants us to know that all power in heaven and on earth is in Jesus' hand (**Matthew 28:18**), and for this reason we should place all of our trust in Him.

### Martha Believes Jesus for New Life (verses 25-27)

**25 Jesus said unto her, I am the resurrection, and the life: he that believeth in me, though he were dead, yet shall he live: 26 And whosoever liveth and believeth in me shall never die. Believest thou this?**

Like most Jews, Martha believed in the final resurrection of the dead and the coming rule of God. Therefore, when Jesus stated, "I am the resurrection, and the life," He was saying that the promise of resurrection and life is not only some future event, but also was immediately available. To Martha, this would have been a startlingly new revelation. Christ embodies that kingdom with all of its blessings for humankind for which Martha and her people hoped. The power to initiate eternal life and resurrection through which humankind may gain entry into life resides in Jesus. This revelation was both an assurance of resurrection to the eschatological kingdom of God and of life in the present through Him who is Life.

It was crucial that Martha grasp the full importance of what Christ was about to do for Lazarus. In Christ, death will never triumph over the believer. Moreover, Jesus was saying that the person, who believes in Him, though they die, will live; and the person who lives and believes in Him will never die.

In verse 26, Jesus asks Martha a question that is the basis for determining her faith and the faith of all believers. Jesus asked, "Believest thou this?" Jesus was asking Martha if she had the faith to believe what He said. Did she believe that He (Jesus) is the Resurrection, and that He has the power of life over death? That is, does she believe in His sovereignty? Unless a person believes in Jesus and His Word, the eternal life He offers cannot be found.

**27 She saith unto him, Yea, Lord: I believe that thou art the Christ, the Son of God, which should come into the world.**

Here, Martha's reply is a full-fledged confession of her faith in Jesus. In her confession, Martha states, "I believe" which means "accept as true, be persuaded of, credit, or place confidence in." This is a belief that includes commitment. Martha was agreeing with Jesus' exposition about eternal life for those who believe in Him. Martha's magnificent confession contains some principal elements of the Person of Christ: He is the Christ (God's anointed One) and the Son of God.

## SEARCH THE SCRIPTURES

### QUESTION 3

What was Martha's response to Jesus' promise to resurrect her brother?

**Martha believed Jesus. Answers will vary.**

## LIGHT ON THE WORD

### Jesus Is the Giver of Life

Jesus is the Resurrection and the Life. In the book of John, we are reminded that He is the giver of physical as well as spiritual life.

## BIBLE APPLICATION

**AIM: Students will understand in times of trouble to place their hope in Christ.**

### Divine Intervention

When a wife gave birth to her son, she had complications that threatened her life. Her uterus ruptured, and she was losing a tremendous amount of blood. The doctors were doing everything they could, but the situation was looking worse by the minute. Her husband had a choice to make: either put his hope solely in the impersonal practices of medical science or primarily trust in the personal Lord and Savior, Jesus Christ. He expected the physicians to do their best, but he relied on the Lord for the healing. When faced with tough circumstances, let us look to Jesus, the One who is able not only to raise us from the dead, but also to powerfully intervene in the dead circumstances of our lives.

## STUDENTS' RESPONSES

**AIM: Students will share the benefits of placing their trust in the Lord.**

### Hopeless Situations

We have all been in situations that looked hopeless. Undoubtedly, we have been tempted to give up hope and count our losses. Think about some of the times that you have given up hope and the Lord came in and "resurrected" the situation. Think about the effect this had on you and what effect it should have on your faith. Challenge yourself to extend a loving hand and share the message of Jesus Christ to someone who has a difficult time because of societal or cultural factors.

## PRAYER

Father in heaven, You are mighty to save and to redeem. Thank You that in the toughest of times we can confidently place our hope in You. I pray to always be reminded of the truth of Your love and care for me and my loved ones. Your Word tells us to call to mind, to tell of Your wondrous works. Give me opportunities to share with others who are going through so that they, too, may be encouraged to place their trust in You. In Jesus' name, I pray. Amen.

## DIG A LITTLE DEEPER

### Jewish burial practices

Upon death (described as "he lay with his fathers" [e.g., 1 Kgs 14:31; 2 Chron 12:16] or "he was gathered to his people" [e.g., Gen 25:8; Deut 32:50]), the faithful Jew is buried before sunset. For example, after Jairus' daughter dies, mourners gathered immediately to weep and wail loudly (Mark 5:38). On the other hand, sinners were cursed with a lack of burial (e.g., Deut 28:25-26; 1 Kgs 14:10-11; Jer 16:4).

During the time of Jesus, Jews customarily followed the following procedure for the burial of the dead:

• Close the eyes of the deceased.

Wash the body.

• Men would wash men, but either men or women could wash women. The body would also be anointed with perfumes and ointments. Remember that because of his hasty burial, this practice was postponed until after the Sabbath. This explains why the women were going to his tomb to complete this task (Mark 16:1-2).

• Wrap the body in cloths. When Lazarus comes out of the tomb, Jesus gives the command that the onlookers unbind his hands and feet that had been bound with linen strips (John 11:44).

• Burial would take place at the family tomb – usually, a cave and a stone rolled in front (see, e.g., John 11:38).

• This would be followed by seven days

of mourning at the home of the deceased. The only time that the family would leave the house would be to mourn at the tom (see John 11:31).

• After one year, the children of the deceased were expected to conduct a secondary burial (According to Jewish texts: Once the flesh of the deceased had decomposed, they would gather his bones and bury them in their proper place in his ancestral burial plot (Sanhedrin 47). This practice involves gathering the bones from the shelf of the tomb and placing them into an ossuary, i.e., a stone box, often with the name of the deceased inscribed on it. Jesus assumes this ongoing practice when he tells a prospective follower: "Leave the dead to bury their dead" (Matt 8:21-22; Luke 9:59-60).

See also Lesson 7 Digging Deeper: Jesus' use of metaphors in John's Gospel.

## HOW TO SAY IT

Didymus. DID-e-mus.

Furlongs. FUR-longs.

## PREPARE FOR NEXT SUNDAY

Read **John 14:1-14** and next week's lesson, "The Way, the Truth, and the Life."

**Sources:**
Adeyemo, Tokunboh, ed. Africa Bible Commentary. Grand Rapids, MI: Zondervan,
2006.
Barclay, William. The Gospel of John. Vol. 2. Philadelphia, PA: The Westminster Press,
1956.
"Bethany." Smith's Bible Dictionary. Bible Study Tools.com. http://www.biblestudytools.com/dictionaries/smiths-bible-dictionary/bethany.html (accessed January 8, 2011).
Carson, D. A. The Gospel According to John. Grand Rapids, MI: William B. Eerdmans
Publishing Company, 1991.
New Testament Greek Lexicon. Bible Study Tools.com. http://www.biblestudytools.com/lexicons/greek (accessed January 10, 2011).
Passage Lookup. Bible Gateway.com. http://www.biblegateway.com/passage (accessed January 10, 2011).
Strong's Exhaustive Concordance of the Bible. McLean, VA: MacDonald Publishing
Company. n.d.

## DAILY HOME BIBLE READINGS

**MONDAY**
The Power of Christ's Resurrection
(Philippians 3:7–11)

**TUESDAY**
The Son Gives Life
(John 5:19–24)

**WEDNESDAY**
Life or Condemnation
(John 5:25–29)

**THURSDAY**
"I Give Eternal Life"
(John 10:22–28)

**FRIDAY**
For God's Glory
(John 11:1–10)

**SATURDAY**
So That You May Believe
(John 11:11–16)

**SUNDAY**
The Resurrection and the Life
(John 11:17–27)

## COMMENTS / NOTES:

_____

_____

_____

_____

_____

_____

_____

_____

_____

_____

_____

_____

# THE WAY, THE TRUTH, AND THE LIFE

**BIBLE BASIS:** John 14:1-14

**BIBLE TRUTH:** The only way to the Father is through Jesus Christ..

**MEMORY VERSE:** Jesus saith unto him, I am the way, the truth, and the life: no man cometh unto the Father, but by me (John 14:6, KJV).

**LESSON AIM:** By the end of this lesson, we will: KNOW why Jesus is the Word in our lives; REFLECT on how Jesus gives us direction; and

DECIDE to affirmly trust Jesus as "the way, the truth, and the life" for the world.

**BACKGROUND SCRIPTURES:** John 14:1 – 14—Read and incorporate the insights gained from the Background Scriptures into your study of the lesson.

## TEACHER PREPARATION

**MATERIALS NEEDED:** Bibles (several different versions), Quarterly Commentary/Teacher Manual, Adult Quarterly, teaching resources such as charts, worksheets/handouts, paper, pens, and pencils.

**OTHER MATERIALS NEEDED / TEACHER'S NOTES:**

_____

_____

## LESSON OVERVIEW

### LIFE NEED FOR TODAY'S LESSON
Remember that Jesus has the answers for everyday life.

### BIBLE LEARNING
To know that Jesus is the living Word of God.

### BIBLE APPLICATION
To understand why it is important to seek Jesus for everyday decisions.

### STUDENTS' RESPONSES
Believers will plan to do the work of God by receiving instructions from Him through prayer and His Word.

## LESSON SCRIPTURE

### JOHN 14:1-14, KJV

**1** Let not your heart be troubled: ye believe in God, believe also in me.

### JOHN 14:1-14, AMP

**1** "Do not let your heart be troubled (afraid, cowardly). Believe [confidently] in God and

2 In my Father's house are many mansions: if it were not so, I would have told you. I go to prepare a place for you.

3 And if I go and prepare a place for you, I will come again, and receive you unto myself; that where I am, there ye may be also.

4 And whither I go ye know, and the way ye know.

5 Thomas saith unto him, Lord, we know not whither thou goest; and how can we know the way?

6 Jesus saith unto him, I am the way, the truth, and the life: no man cometh unto the Father, but by me.

7 If ye had known me, ye should have known my Father also: and from henceforth ye know him, and have seen him.

8 Philip saith unto him, Lord, show us the Father, and it sufficeth us.

9 Jesus saith unto him, Have I been so long time with you, and yet hast thou not known me, Philip? he that hath seen me hath seen the Father; and how sayest thou then, Show us the Father?

10 Believest thou not that I am in the Father, and the Father in me? the words that I speak unto you I speak not of myself: but the Father that dwelleth in me, he doeth the works.

11 Believe me that I am in the Father, and the Father in me: or else believe me for the very works' sake.

12 Verily, verily, I say unto you, He that believeth on me, the works that I do shall he do also; and greater works than these shall he do; because I go unto my Father.

trust in Him, [have faith, hold on to it, rely on it, keep going and] believe also in Me.

2 In My Father's house are many dwelling places. If it were not so, I would have told you, because I am going there to prepare a place for you.

3 And if I go and prepare a place for you, I will come back again and I will take you to Myself, so that where I am you may be also.

4 And [to the place] where I am going, you know the way."

5 Thomas said to Him, "Lord, we do not know where You are going; so how can we know the way?"

6 Jesus said to him, "[a]I am the [only] Way [to God] and the [real] Truth and the [real] Life; no one comes to the Father but through Me.

7 If you had [really] known Me, you would also have known My Father. From now on you know Him, and have seen Him."

8 Philip said to Him, "Lord, show us the Father and then we will be satisfied."

9 Jesus said to him, "Have I been with you for so long a time, and you do not know Me yet, Philip, nor recognize clearly who I am? Anyone who has seen Me has seen the Father. How can you say, 'Show us the Father?'

10 Do you not believe that I am in the Father, and the Father is in Me? The words I say to you I do not say on My own initiative or authority, but the Father, abiding continually in Me, does His works [His attesting miracles and acts of power].

11 Believe Me that I am in the Father and the Father is in Me; otherwise believe [Me] because of the [very] works themselves [which you have witnessed].

**13** And whatsoever ye shall ask in my name, that will I do, that the Father may be glorified in the Son.

**14** If ye shall ask any thing in my name, I will do it.

**12** I assure you and most solemnly say to you, anyone who believes in Me [as Savior] will also do the things that I do; and he will do even greater things than these [in extent and outreach], because I am going to the Father.

**13** And I will do whatever you ask in My name as My representative], this I will do, so that the Father may be glorified and celebrated in the Son.

**14** If you ask Me anything in My name [as My representative], I will do it.

## BIBLICAL DEFINITIONS

A. **Troubled (John 14:1)** *tarasso* (Gk.)—Agitated, anxious, or causing commotion.

B. **Mansions (v. 2)** *mone* (Gk.)—Abodes or dwellings.

C. **Works (v. 12)** *ergon* (Gk.)—Denotes a deed or act.

## LIGHT ON THE WORD

During His ministry, Jesus repeatedly prepared the disciples for His suffering and death. In John 13, Jesus tells the disciples that one of them would betray Him **(verse 21)**. At the same time, He also informs the disciples that He will soon be leaving them and that they could not follow Him (verse 33). Undoubtedly, these things disturbed the disciples. When Peter asks Jesus where He was going, Jesus responds, "Where I am going, you cannot follow now, but you will follow later" **(John 13:36, NIV)**. It is not difficult to see why the disciples would have been troubled. They were coming to grips with the fact that the One they had given up everything to follow was now telling them that He was about to leave them to go to a place where they could not follow. It must have seemed as though they were losing the very reason for which they had existed for the past three years.

## TEACHING THE BIBLE LESSON

## LIFE NEED FOR TODAY'S LESSON

**AIM: Students will seek comfort in the promises of God through Jesus Christ.**

## INTRODUCTION

### Philip

He was one of the 12 disciples whom Jesus called directly. Philip, along with Peter and Andrew, was from Bethsaida of Galilee (John 1:44).

### Thomas

Also called Didymus, or "the twin," Thomas was one of Jesus' 12 disciples. He is the one who said that he would not believe that Jesus was resurrected from the dead unless he could touch the nail prints in Jesus' hands and the wound from the spear in His side.

## BIBLE LEARNING

**AIM: Students will place their confidence and trust in Jesus.**

# I. IN MY FATHER'S HOUSE
## (John 14:1-4)

In John 13, Jesus told His disciples of His approaching suffering and departure. Now, He aims to calm the turmoil raging in their hearts. Jesus encourages them by telling them, "Do not let your hearts be troubled" (**John 14:1, NIV**). Jesus' news apparently throws the disciples' minds into disarray and sends them into a spiritual tailspin, but Jesus provides the key that will lead them out of their mental anguish. He points to Himself as the basis for sustaining peace in the midst of the storm of difficult circumstances by telling them if "you believe in God, believe also in Me" (**verse 1, NKJV**). Even though He will no longer be present with the disciples physically, He assures them that where He is going, He is preparing a place for them. This provides great comfort, not only for the apostles, but also for us. Even though Jesus no longer walks the earth in bodily form, we have His promise that He is with us "even to the very end of the age" (**Matthew 28:20, NIV**), and that He still has the power to calm the storms that rage in our lives. In our times of anxiety and uncertainty, we are directed to place our faith not in our own ingenuity, wit, or financial savvy, but in Jesus Christ, the Sovereign Lord, who is in control of all the circumstances of our lives.

### Jesus, the Way to Comfort
### (verses 1-4)
**1 Let not your heart be troubled: ye believe in God, believe also in me.**

In his letter to the Romans, the apostle Paul says, "Whatsoever is not of faith is sin" (**Romans 14:23**). Many have included worry in this list to counter those who treat worry as if it falls somehow harmlessly between sin and virtue. Jesus emphasizes this truth by pointing to faith as the relief or antidote for worry or anxiety. Here, Jesus tells the disciples not to let their hearts become troubled. The word "troubled" means "agitated, disquieted, or stirred up."

In the context of this passage, Jesus ushers in faith as a comfort to relieve the anxious disciples, much like a welcome medicine for a nagging illness or parental reassurance about a child's nightmare. In this scenario, the disciples' concern was well founded, since they had just learned that one would betray Jesus, that one would deny Him, and that they couldn't go with Him wherever it was He was going (**John 13**). Jesus' own heart was "troubled" when He announced that one would betray Him (**John 13:21**). It is remarkable that Jesus ministered to them with compassion in spite of the fact that His much more serious anguish was now only hours away.

Peter must have been the most visibly shocked to learn he would deny Jesus, since Jesus immediately responded to his concern with His declaration that Peter would be disloyal (**John 13:38**). Jesus immediately follows this with His words of comfort. When our hearts are troubled, when things look their worst, our best response is faith or belief in our Lord; nothing less will open the door to His peace and comfort (**Psalm 42:5**). Nothing is more important than guarding our hearts (**Proverbs 4:23; 1 Corinthians 16:13–14; 2 Peter 3:17**), but at the same time, we as believers have good reason to take courage, unlike those without the hope that is ours.

**2 In my Father's house are many mansions: if it were not so, I would have told you. I go to prepare a place for you.**

The hope of a home in heaven was given as a source of comfort, not only for the disciples, but also for countless believers through the ages, confronting all the multiple anxieties they as individuals and the church as a whole would face. Jesus' intent was to minister comfort in the face of potentially overwhelming distress; His response (**begun in verse 1**) was thorough and multifaceted. Added to faith in God and Himself was the reminder of the disciples' (and our) final reward. Here, Jesus reassures them that He would not deceive them by promising them something that was so grand but wasn't the truth. Along with having our name written in the book of life (**Isaiah 62:2; Revelation 2:17; 3:12; 21:27**), everything becomes new in Christ (**2 Corinthians 5:17**), including our coming new home in God's kingdom.

### 3 And if I go and prepare a place for you, I will come again, and receive you unto myself; that where I am, there ye may be also.

This isn't an impersonal second coming to which Jesus refers; He won't be sending a butler, an angel, or anyone else to escort us to our heavenly home. He will come Himself and receive us personally (**1 Thessalonians 4:17**). In John 14:3, the phrase "I will come" is a common, single word that refers to individuals arriving or returning, appearing or making an appearance. The emphasis is on "again," just as being born is common but being born "again" is noteworthy (**John 3:3**).

As many have said, "Heaven is where Jesus is, and it wouldn't be heaven without Him." According to Acts 7:31, 49 (**KJV**), the voice of the Lord came unto Moses saying, "Heaven is my throne, and earth is my footstool . . . ." Then according to Revelation 11:19, "And the temple of God was opened in heaven." Indeed, heaven would be sufficient if we just got to be with Him. Wherever He is should be where we want to be; wherever He is not should be the place to avoid at all costs. Nonetheless, it is to His Father's house that we will be going, the home of the King of kings and Lord of lords, the Creator of the universe—being ushered by Christ at His Second Coming to God's eternal home will be glorious beyond words (**Luke 22:30; Revelation 21**).

### 4 And whither I go ye know, and the way ye know.

Jesus is trying to tell or remind His disciples that they already know in their hearts where He is going and how to get there. Surely this would be one of the things of which the coming Comforter would continue to remind them after Jesus' departure, and about which He would continue to teach them (**cf. John 14:26**).

## SEARCH THE SCRIPTURES
### QUESTION 1
Why did Jesus say to His disciples "Let not your heart be troubled"?

He was preparing the disciples for His return to the Father. Answers will vary.

## LIGHT ON THE WORD
### There's Only One Way
We live in a religiously pluralistic society. The overarching theme preached from some pulpits is tolerance. To some, it is considered nothing short of arrogance to claim that a religion has the exclusive right to the truth. The mainstream view—that all religions worship the same God—is best expressed in a statement made by nineteenth-century Indian saint Sri Ramakrishna: "God has made different religions to suit different aspirations, times, and countries. All doctrines are only so many paths, but a path is by no means God Himself. Indeed, one can reach God if one follows any of the paths with wholehearted devotion" (Smith, 1991).

However, what Ramakrishna expresses is in direct opposition to what Jesus Himself says: "I am the way, the truth, and the life: no man cometh unto the Father but by me" (John 14:6). Jesus declares that there are not many ways to God; there is only one way. Therefore, no matter how sincere one is in following a particular path, if it is not the one true path, it will ultimately lead to a dead end.

Jesus, unlike Ramakrishna, does not point His followers to a path but to a person, namely, Himself: "I am the way." Jesus is not claiming to have uncovered some hidden truth. He is not telling His disciples, "I have experienced enlightenment and now I am able to point you in the direction you must travel." He is claiming something much stronger than that. Jesus declares, "Anyone who has seen me has seen the Father" (**John 14:9, NIV**).

## II. THE FATHER AND I ARE ONE (John 14:5-11)

Jesus reveals the character and personality of God to us, just as John writes earlier in chapter 1, "No one has seen God at any time. The only begotten Son, who is in the bosom of the Father, He has declared Him" (**John 1:18, NKJV**). We are to place faith in Christ as the way to the Father because it is only through Him that we can know the Father.

### Jesus, the Way to the Father (verses 5-11)

**5 Thomas saith unto him, Lord, we know not whither thou goest; and how can we know the way?**

With childlike innocence, Thomas asks about what Jesus just told them that they already knew. Perhaps Thomas's response is an illustration of our own level of spiritual awareness, in reality knowing more than we think we do and being less in the dark than we believe we are at times. The disciples had received a full load of bad news, and perhaps, had they had more time to digest Jesus' discourse, they might have been less reactive. In any case, Jesus doesn't entrust the matter to their faulty memories and previous knowledge, but continues to explain in order to be certain they do in fact know what they need to know.

**6 Jesus saith unto him, I am the way, the truth, and the life: no man cometh unto the Father, but by me.**

By His blood, Jesus opened up for us the "new and living way" into the Holy of Holies (**Hebrews 10:20**). Even the Old Testament speaks of there being only one way: "Ask for the old paths, where is the good way, and walk therein, and ye shall find rest for your souls" (**Jeremiah 6:16**). The word "way" refers to a traveler's way or a way of thinking, feeling, and deciding; it is used over 100 times in the New Testament and normally has the aforementioned common interpretation—until Jesus says He is the way.

John clearly establishes that the Word is God (**John 1:1**), the Word became flesh (**John 1:14**), and the Word is truth (**John 17:17**). "Thy word is true from the beginning" (**Psalm 119:160**). Jesus completes the circle by stating that He is the truth and is one with God (**John 10:30**); other writers are more explicit regarding His deity (**Colossians 1:16; 2:9; Philippians 2:6; 1 John 5:20**). It is truth that sets us free (**John 8:32**) and that leads us to salvation (**Ephesians 1:13**). Even His critics know that, as truth, Jesus would never deceive anyone (**Luke 20:21**). However, people are able to deceive themselves (**1 John 1:8**). As the embodiment of truth, Jesus stands in perfect contrast to the devil, in whom there is no truth (**John 8:44**). The word "truth" is used in a variety of contexts, including references to personal excellence and to truth pertaining to God. Again, it is a common word that is used in these ways over 100 times in the New Testament—until Jesus says He is the truth. Only because of Christ, we are "dead indeed unto sin, but alive unto God" (**Romans 6:11**); likewise, He is the only cure for sin (**Romans 6:23**).

**7 If ye had known me, ye should have known my Father also: and from henceforth ye know him, and have seen him.**

Jesus' words are a not-so-subtle rebuke of the disciples' for their lack of awareness of just who had been with them for so long. Regardless of the disciples' shortsightedness, Jesus patiently continues to explain that in seeing and knowing Him, they have already seen and known the Father. Almost before they can realize they have been rebuked for their lack of awareness, Jesus immediately extends comfort in His reassurance that, at least from this point forward, they no longer need to be unaware of the Father. As Jesus stated (**John 10:30**), He and the Father are one. Jesus is God and reveals God to us. The disciples' common awakening experience, which came soon enough and was similar in essence for all of them (and us), is captured by the apostle Paul's pen: "God . . .hath shined in our hearts, to give the light of the knowledge of the glory of God in the face of Jesus Christ" (**2 Corinthians 4:6; cf. 4:4; Colossians 1:15**). God does this by sending the Holy Spirit after Jesus ascended to heaven.

**8 Philip saith unto him, Lord, show us the Father, and it sufficeth us. 9 Jesus saith unto him, Have I been so long time with you, and yet hast thou not known me, Philip? he that hath seen me hath seen the Father; and how sayest thou then, Show us the Father? 10 Believest thou not that I am in the Father, and the Father in me? the words that I speak unto you I speak not of myself: but the Father that dwelleth in me, he doeth the works.**

Philip wanted a sign. One cannot help but empathize with Philip, since he sounds like so many today who, no matter how much they know or are told, insist on saying, "If I could just see God once, that would settle it for me. If just once I could witness a real miracle, then I'd become a believer. Why can't God just show His face for one split second?" Just like Philip, modern skeptics ignore what is before them. In Philip's case, it was the living Jesus, God in the flesh, worker of miracles, standing before him

and talking to him. Yet he didn't understand what he was hearing. In this light, Jesus' response (**verse 9**) is both understandable and appropriate.

On closer examination, it seems evident that more of Jesus' exasperation is showing. Jesus is asking Philip, "How could you not know after all this time? Haven't you been paying attention at all? Do you really not get it? If you've seen Me, you've seen the Father. How can you look right at Me and ask to see the Father?"

Jesus' response continues (**verse 10**): "Philip, do you really not comprehend that I am in the Father, and the Father is in Me? The Father lives in Me; it is He who does the works I do." Jesus stresses His unity with the Father once again. When we read these passages consecutively, we see the patient Teacher gently guiding His future apostles, who soon will faithfully carry out His Great Commission to the four corners of the world—that is, once they get it straight who He is.

**11 Believe me that I am in the Father, and the Father in me: or else believe me for the very works' sake.**

Although Jesus' conversation is in response to questions from Thomas and Philip, all the disciples are present and Jesus is addressing all of them in His typical teaching fashion. In this passage, Jesus continues in the same "read-my-lips" tone: "Philip—all of you—it is imperative that you listen very closely and hear Me well. Again, I repeat, I am in the Father and the Father is in Me." It is no wonder that the early church continued to struggle with the essence of Jesus' words. One can hardly imagine how He could have communicated His deity any more clearly than He did.

## SEARCH THE SCRIPTURES

### QUESTION 2

How did Jesus answer Thomas when he asked Him to show them the way?

Jesus answered: "I am the way, the truth, and the life: no man cometh unto the Father, but by me. Jesus is the only way to the Father. Answers will vary.

## LIGHT ON THE WORD

### Greater Works

In verses 12 through 14, Christ notifies His disciples that placing their faith in Him will cause them to lead lives that exhibit the power of God. He says, "He who believes in Me, the works that I do he will do also; and greater works than these he will do, because I go to My Father" (**verse 12, NKJV**). It is important to note that Jesus says that the works testified of His relationship with the Father: "Believe Me that I am in the Father and the Father in Me, or else believe Me for the sake of the works themselves" (**verse 11, NKJV**). These were not gratuitous or pointless displays of power, but a demonstration of His authenticity as the Son of God. Furthermore, Jesus lets us know that it is the Father who is at work through Him: "The words that I speak to you I do not speak on My own authority; but the Father who dwells in Me does the works" (**verse 10, NKJV**). This reveals the unity of Jesus and the Father.

## III. JESUS GIVES THE PROMISE OF POWER (John 14:12-14)

Placing all our trust in Jesus produces two results. First, faith in Christ yields fruitful lives that both demonstrate our relationship with Him and glorify the Father. "This is to my Father's glory, that you bear much fruit, showing yourselves to be my disciples" (**John 15:8, NIV**). When we ask for things in Jesus' name, we are to ask for things that are consistent with His character and purpose. Putting all our trust in Christ guarantees that we will experience power-filled lives because He aims to glorify His Father's name.

Second, placing faith in Christ gives us the power we need to live out the Christian life. The only way we can live powerful lives that reflect Christ's presence is by being indwelt with the Holy Spirit. It is the Holy Spirit who gives us power to live the Christian life, and He is only accessible through faith in Christ.

### Jesus, the Way to Powerful Living (verses 12-14)

**12 Verily, verily, I say unto you, He that believeth on me, the works that I do shall he do also; and greater works than these shall he do; because I go unto my Father.**

At this point, Jesus moves on to a different subject, one of many He would address on that auspicious night. One has to wonder if the disciples grasped the fact that the "greater works" to which Jesus referred in verse 12 would not be possible if He had stayed with them, but were only going to be possible because He was leaving them. Jesus' words were not only about the fantastic advances in ministry that they were going to accomplish when the Holy Spirit came, He also offered them another facet of His multilayered message of comfort and courage regarding His impending death and subsequent departure. His message was entirely about comfort, assurances, and taking heart for the great things that awaited them. These 11 men—the original pillars of the faith and the architects of the New Testament church—needed at that moment to hear some words of encouragement, reassurance, and hope from their departing Master.

**13 And whatsoever ye shall ask in my name, that will I do, that the Father may be glorified in the Son.**

Jesus would deny these particular men nothing. He left in their charge the greatest task ever given to any human, and He knew what they would need in order to accomplish the work He had given them. Many people have heard some preacher at some time try to interpret this as some kind of mysterious combination or formula by implying or claiming that all you have to do is say all the right words and include all the potential caveats and specific disclaimers, and God is almost obliged to accommodate you. Unfortunately, many in the church have a gross misconception of what it means to abide in Christ, which impairs their understanding of how things work in God's kingdom.

When we abide in Christ, His power flows through us to accomplish His purposes in the world. The Holy Spirit is the agent, sent by the resurrected Christ, and we are the vehicles through which He flows. It is not our confession or religious invocation that garners the forces of heaven to do our bidding. It is only when our hearts are surrendered, when we are living in and for God, when our will is attuned to His, and when our prayers are for His purposes, in His name, and for His glory that He will answer, even beyond all we ask or think (**Ephesians 3:20**).

**14 If ye shall ask any thing in my name, I will do it.**

It is here that we find some of the most poignant parting words known to humankind. Jesus, the Savior, is preparing for His death, burial, and resurrection. He is equipping His disciples with the most important things they will need to know as they carry out His work without His physical presence. The reiteration of John 14:13 must be heard in the context of the whole passage. This kind of repetitive reassurance is the type one gives a loved one who needs comfort. We tend to say things more than once when we want someone to believe us, especially if there is an impending separation.

## QUESTION 3

How would Jesus' disciples do greater works?

**Jesus declared that the disciples would do greater works because He's going to the Father and the disciples would receive the power of the Holy Ghost to do the work.**

## LIGHT ON THE WORD
### A Faithful Declaration

In our society, many believe science is the only way by which we can access the truth about the world around us. Many of our scientists believe that faith is a superstitious concept embraced by those who are weak. In what ways does Jesus' declaration, "I am the way, the truth, and the life" challenge that notion? What are some ways that we can share with our family, neighbors, and coworkers the importance of this declaration?

## BIBLE APPLICATION

**AIM: That your students will affirm for themselves that Christ is the only way to be saved.**

Jesus said that He is the only way. Was He merely on an ego trip? If so, why did He go to the Cross? And if He was just another martyr, why did God raise Him from the dead? Look at the words of Jesus and contemplate what they mean for our lives today.

## STUDENTS' RESPONSES

**AIM: Students will share their testimony and declare Christ as the way.**

This week, share with someone that Jesus is the only way to a relationship with God and that He wants to reconcile him or her to God. Also, pray that God will give you the faith to trust Him and allow Him to guide you throughout your everyday life.

## PRAYER

Father in heaven, You sent your Son Jesus to show us the way to You. I pray that You will help each of us to know You more and more every day. I repent for times that I tried to run my own life; I give my ambitions, my hopes, and my dreams to You. I commit my way unto You so that Your plan can be my plan. I ask for the courage to share with others the way, the truth, and the life I have found in You. In Jesus' name I pray. Amen.

## DIG A LITTLE DEEPER

### Belief in the Gospel of John

The key verse that unlocks the Gospel of John is found in chapter 20:

Now Jesus did many other signs in the presence of his disciples that are not written in this book. But these are written that you might believe that Jesus is the Christ, the Son of God, and that believing you might have life in his name (vv. 30-31).

John states that the ultimate goal of what has been recorded is belief. Upon expressing this belief, one begins to experience eternal life.

This verb believe (Greek: *pisteuo*), and its noun form (Greek: *pistis*) occurs more than 100 times in John's Gospel. It has the idea of personal trust. It goes beyond mere intellectual assent and demands that one commit themselves to another. This theme is introduced by the Baptizer at the beginning of the Gospel.

[Jesus] came to his own, and his own people did not receive him. But to all who did receive him, who believed in his name, he gave the right to become children of God (1:12).

Belief in Jesus comes about as one witnesses or hears about the signs/miracles of Jesus.

For example, during his conversation with Martha, note Jesus' concentrated uses of the word just before he raises Lazarus from the dead.

Jesus said to her, "I am the resurrection and the life. Whoever believes in me, though he die, yet shall he live, and everyone who lives and believes in me shall never die. Do you believe this? She said to him, "Yes, Lord; I believe that you are the Christ, the Son of God, who is coming into the world (11:25-27).

Although, after the miracle resuscitation, John states that many of the Jews "believed in him" (v. 45; cf. v. 48), signs do not compel faith.

Though [Jesus] had done so many signs before them, they still did not believe in him (12:37).

In other words, simply seeing or witnessing miracles does not strong-arm one into believing in Jesus. Again, there must be that willingness to trust Jesus in order for one to obtain eternal life.

Finally, belief in Jesus comes about as one hears Jesus testify as to who he is and his mission. Once again, note the concentrated use of the verb believe during his conversation with the Pharisee Nicodemus – seven times in the short space of 3:9-21.

See also Lesson 3 Digging Deeper: The seven signs of John's Gospel.

See also Lesson 7 Digging Deeper: Jesus' use of metaphors in John's Gospel.

## HOW TO SAY IT

Sri Ramakrishna. SRE Ra-ma-KRISH-na.

## DAILY HOME BIBLE READINGS

### MONDAY
Making Known the Way of God
(Exodus 18:13–23)

### TUESDAY
Turning Aside from the Way
(Exodus 32:7–14)

### WEDNESDAY
Seeking Truth Within
(Psalm 51:1–7)

### THURSDAY
Speaking Truth from the Heart
(Psalm 15)

### FRIDAY
Telling the Whole Message
(Acts 5:17–21)

### SATURDAY
Choosing the Hard Road
(Matthew 7:13–20)

### SUNDAY
"How Can We Know the Way?"
(John 14:1–14

## COMMENTS / NOTES:

## PREPARE FOR NEXT SUNDAY

Read **Exodus 23:1-9** and study "Rules For Just Living."

**Sources:**

Henry, Matthew. Commentary on the Whole Bible. Christian Classics Ethereal Library.org. http://www.ccel.org/h/henry/mhc5John.xv.html (accessed October 1, 2010).

New Testament Greek Lexicon. Bible Study Tools.com. http://www.biblestudytools.com/lexicons/greek (accessed January 10, 2011).

Passage Lookup. Bible Gateway.com. http://www.biblegateway.com/passage (accessed January 10, 2011).

Smith, Huston. The World's Religions. San Francisco, CA: Harper, 1991. 56.

Tenney, Merrill C. The Expositor's Bible Commentary. Edited by Frank E. Gaebelein.
Grand Rapids, MI: Zondervan Publishing House, 1981.

# QUARTERLY COMMENTARY

## TEACHER'S TIPS

### " CHECKING FOR UNDERSTANDING"
Patrick Guy

### " THE RELEVANT SUNDAY SCHOOL – 2021 & BEYOND: HOW TO "KEEP THE BURNING"
Ja'Qyrie Wheeler

### QUARTERLY QUIZ

# CHECKING FOR UNDERSTANDING

## By Patrick Guy

*"This is at the heart of all good education, where the teacher asks students to think and engages them in encouraging dialogues, constantly checking for understanding and growth."*

– William Glasser, M.D.

Through the years, many churches and denominations have been birthed out of misunderstandings of key scripture. Fallacies or misconceptions are often preached and taught in churches, and the best way to break the cycle of false doctrine is to bring clarity and truth, which leads to understanding. King Solomon wrote, "and with all thy getting get understanding" (Proverbs 4:7). As a Sunday School teacher, it is essential to remember that you are an educator, and educators always check for understanding. The overarching question for any educator is, "how do I know they know?" Checking for understanding is an integral part of teaching, primarily when we are tasked with teaching the most significant content given to the Church – His Word!

Many churches utilize Sunday School lessons that publishers have already prepared. However, every teacher should review the lessons, ensure doctrinal alignment, and adjust them specifically to meet the class's needs. Sunday School teachers should include opportunities for collaborations within that lesson and ensure the student's voice is manifest. "Student voice" means that students should be encouraged to reflect out loud and contribute to the discussion. Through the interaction from student to student and student to teacher, the teacher takes on the role of facilitator. Through the facilitation of classroom dialogue, the teacher can check for understanding. Here are a few tips for checking for understanding while facilitating the lesson:

**Ask Open-Ended Questions:** If you want to help your Sunday school students understand ideas in class, be intentional in your line of questioning. Ask questions that require more than a yes or no. Ask questions that require students to think about their answer before responding to your question; such questions require students to lean on their prior knowledge or seek new knowledge when the questions challenge them to revisit a concept. Remember, asking open-ended questions is not about right or wrong answers. You want to hear what the students are thinking and their perceptions about the concepts.

**Give Students Time to Reflect:** Allot 4-5 minutes to reflect on text or topic. Ask students to reflect on the lesson, write down what they have learned, and if time permits further, ask them to briefly share how they would apply what they have learned in a real-world scenario. The Word is already reverent, but activities like this help make it relevant. Reflection time is important because the study of scripture is not just knowledge but ultimately application – living it. "But be ye doers of the word" (James 1:22).

**Complete a Misconception Check:** Often, in studying the scriptures, there are delusions and misunderstandings. There are multiple steps to correctly dissecting and understanding scripture; application is the final step. Three of the frequent shortfalls in interpreting application are (1) inattention to context, (2) not considering the complete historical and literary contexts, and or (3) using literary and historical contexts correctly but applying the principles to modern-day circumstances for which they were not meant to be applied. Such shortfalls create misreading and error, so the Sunday School teacher needs to check for misconceptions. Present students with frequent or probable fallacies about a text or topic you are covering that day. Ask them whether they agree or disagree and explain their position. As they explain, the teacher should listen for what to correct and what to affirm. Always remember, your students cannot apply what they do not understand.

Patrick Guy is a native of Fort Worth, Texas. He has been awarded degrees from the University of Memphis and Texas Christian University; Currently, he is a 2021 doctoral candidate. For the past twenty-two years, Guy has served as an elementary and middle school educator and a k-12 school administrator. During this time, he has established himself as a transformational leader committed to the "learning for all, whatever it takes" resolve. Guy serves in ministry at the Grace Cathedral COGIC in Dallas, Texas, under the pastoral leadership of Superintendent Nathaniel Green. He is a member of the Texas Northeast 3rd Ecclesiastical Jurisdiction led by Bishop Nelson J. Gatlin, Prelate, and Mother Patricia Roach, Supervisor of the department of Women.

# THE RELEVANT SUNDAY SCHOOL 2021 & BEYOND: HOW TO "KEEP THE BURNING."

By Ja'Qyrie Wheeler

In Acts 1:1-4, Jesus promises us the Holy Spirit to help us. His Spirit comes to help us live right and allows others to see his light in us. God's Spirit also helps the church and Sunday School to be relevant. So, the question is: What does relevant mean, and how can the church and Sunday School BE relevant??

Relevant means what is happening currently. It is how we do things NOW. Our church and our Sunday School cannot stay the same. We must change. Change happens to meet the needs of what is happening in this moment or season for all ages.

2020 was a tough year. From the pandemic to racial injustice, it was a lot for me to handle. I had never even heard the Word pandemic before. Suddenly, COVID changed my entire life. Instantly I was separated from family, friends, and activities I loved to do. All these changes left me feeling sad, nervous, confused, and scared. As I watched the news, people were dying all over the world from a sickness called COVID that had no cure. I began to pray more, especially for my grandparents. I was taught in church that prayer changes things. When things are out of our control, the best thing you can do is pray. First Thessalonians 5:16-18 says to rejoice always and pray without ceasing, give thanks in all things.

Due to COVID, the church too had to adapt to change to stay relevant. We were not able to meet in person or be together. Our school year was virtual. It was a big adjustment. But it was what we had to do to be relevant at that time.

I thank God for protecting my family during COVID. Although my mom got laid off, COVID gave us more time together to bond and create new memories. I learned to adapt to this new way of living. God continued to provide all our needs. And God helped our ministry be flexible, adapt, and learn new ways of reaching people for God.

**Why should the church and Sunday School be relevant?**

If we don't stay relevant, we won't have an opportunity to grow? Acts 2:46-47 talks about the church growing daily. The church cared about people and met their needs. When we adapt to care about people, God helps us to grow. At my church, we started virtual service on Zoom. I was still able to do Sunday School. We started playing Kahoot to help check and reinforce our Bible learning. I REALLY loved Kahoot. We even had great prizes. I won a pizza. This kept me excited and interested in church and Sunday School.

How do we know how to be relevant in the church and in Sunday School?

We don't always have the answers. But if we pray to God, he tells us what to do. The Bible tells us, if my people would pray and ask for God's help, he will show us the way (from 2 Chronicles 7:14, paraphrased).

**How can we be relevant in 2021 and beyond?**

I believe the church and Sunday School can be relevant in 2 ways:

- We can be relevant by using technology to reach the community outside of the church.

- Involving young people in the operational work of the ministry helps us to be relevant. I actually run the Zoom at my church, and I love it. I also had a chance to march for justice and attended rallies with my church members. We met some really nice people in the community.

- Finally, I think we can add in more fun activities for our youth. I missed coming together with the Sunshine Band. We have fun and learn about God at the same time.

In conclusion, if we seek God, pray daily, follow His directions, reach outside our church, we can keep the burning in 2021 and beyond. The world changes, but God's Word stays relevant.

Ja'Qyrie Wheeler is the ten years old daughter of Erie Wheeler. She is in the fifth grade, and her hobbies include science, art. and singing. Ja'Qyrie is not only a gifted singer, but God has also given her a brilliant mind that has put her years above her grade level. She is a member of Bible Way Victory Community Church in Everett, WA, under the leadership of her grandfather, Elder A. C. Darby, Jr. She is a member of Washington State Jurisdiction, under the leadership of Bishop Designee, Alvin C. Moore, Sr. and Supervisor, Mother Curlie Davis.

# DIG DEEPER WRITERS
## SUMMER QUARTER

## Elder Joseph W. Gill

Elder Joseph W. Gill was ordained under Bishop James R. Wright of the New York Western First Ecclesiastical Jurisdiction in 2012. He is a member of Four Square Gospel Church Of God In Christ, where he serves under the leadership of his pastor, Administrative Assistant W. Steven Williams. In the local church, Elder Gill has served as a deacon; as a teacher of Sunday School, Prayer & Bible Band, and New Believer's classes; and as a trustee.

Elder Gill earned a Bachelor's degree in Religion from Vassar College, and is a lifelong student of the Bible. He is a staff member, and part-time instructor, at the Bethel Bible Institute, in Syracuse, New York. Elder Gill is mission-minded, and has lived abroad. He and his wife, Missionary Krystal Gill, taught English in Tsuruoka, Japan for two years.

B. A. in Religion, from Vassar College, Poughkeepsie, NY
Four Square Gospel C.O.G.I.C., Syracuse, NY (Pastor Steve Williams)
New York Western First Ecclesiastical Jurisdiction (Bishop James Wright, Mother Althea Chaplin)

# QUARTERLY QUIZ

These questions may be used in two ways: as a pretest at the beginning of the quarter; as a review at the end of the quarter; or as a review after each lesson. Questions are based on the Scripture text of each lesson (King James Version).

## LESSON 1

1. According to Exodus 23:1, to raise a false report is to be an _____ witness.

_____

_____

2. What should one do if he/she sees "thine enemy's ox or his ass going astray" (Exodus 23:4)?

_____

_____

## LESSON 2

1. "Ye shall not _____, neither deal _____, neither _____ one to another" (Leviticus 19:11).

_____

_____

2. Ye shall do no _____ in judgment: thou shalt not respect the person of the _____, nor _____ the person of the _____: but in _____ shalt thou judge thy neighbour" (Leviticus 19:15).

_____

_____

## LESSON 3

1. "And ye shall _____ the _____ year, and proclaim _____ throughout _____ the land unto _____ the inhabitants thereof" (Leviticus 25:10).

_____

_____

2. Who was the LORD to Israel (Leviticus 25:55)?

_____

_____

## LESSON 4

1. What five things does the Lord require of the Israelites (Deuteronomy 10:12-13)?

_____

_____

2. Which body organ were the people to circumcise, metaphorically (Deuteronomy 10:16)?

_____

_____

## LESSON 5

1. What did the pouring of water by the Israelites mean (I Samuel 7:6)?

_____

_____

2. "And Samuel took a _____ lamb, and _____ it for a _____ offering wholly unto the _____" (I Samuel 7:9).

_____

_____

# QUARTERLY QUIZ

## LESSON 6

1. What are some of the phrases that King David uses to describe himself (II Samuel 23:1–4)?

_____

_____

1. Who came to King Solomon for justice (I Kings 3:16)?

_____

_____

## LESSON 7

1. Who came to King Solomon for justice (I Kings 3:16)?

_____

_____

2. What problem did they bring to Solomon (I Kings 3:17–22)?

_____

## LESSON 8

1. Who called for the famine (II Kings 8:1)?

_____

_____

2. Who was Gehazi (II Kings 8:4)?

_____

_____

## LESSON 9

1. "And said to the judges, Take heed what ye _____: for ye _____ not for _____, but for the _____, who is _____ _____ in the judgment" (II Chronicles 19:6).

_____

_____

2. "And he charged them, saying, Thus shall ye _____ in the _____ of the _____, _____, and with a _____ _____" (II Chronicles 19:9).

_____

_____

## LESSON 10

1. "Put not your trust in _____, nor in the _____ of _____, in whom there is _____ help" (Psalm 146:3).

_____

_____

2. "The LORD openeth the _____ of the _____: the _____ raiseth them that are _____ _____: the _____ loveth the _____" (Psalm 146:8).

_____

_____

# QUARTERLY QUIZ

## LESSON 11

1. Who was going to be upon the shoulder of the child that is born (Isaiah 9:6)?

_____

_____

2. List five names that the child will be called (Isaiah 9:6).

_____

_____

## LESSON 12

1. What had the pastors done that displeased God (Jeremiah 23:1)?

_____

_____

2. What was going to be their punishment (Jeremiah 23:2)?

_____

_____

## LESSON 13

1. What will be the responsibility of the Good Shepherd that God will send (Ezekiel 34:23)?

_____

_____

2. Who will be the Israelites' God (Ezekiel 34:24)?

_____

_____

*Answers to Quarterly Quiz Can be found on  page 480

# RULES FOR JUST LIVING

**BIBLE BASIS:** Exodus 23:1-9

**BIBLE TRUTH:** We should seek justice for all.

**MEMORY VERSE:** "Thou shalt not follow a multitude to do evil; neither shalt thou speak in a cause to decline after many to wrest judgment" (Exodus 23:2, KJV).

**LESSON AIM:** By the end of the lesson, we will: KNOW that God is not pleased with injustice; FEEL the joy that comes from observing justice; and SEEK justice for all.

**BACKGROUND SCRIPTURES:** Exodus 22:1-23:9- Read and incorporate the insights gained from the Background Scriptures into your study of the lesson.

## TEACHER PREPARATION

**MATERIALS NEEDED:** Bibles (several different versions), Quarterly Commentary/Teacher Manual, Adult Quarterly, teaching resources such as charts, worksheets/handouts, paper, pens, and pencils.

**OTHER MATERIALS NEEDED / TEACHER'S NOTES:**

_____

_____

## LESSON OVERVIEW

**LIFE NEED FOR TODAY'S LESSON**
To seek justice for all.

**BIBLE LEARNING**
To learn that God is a just God.

**BIBLE APPLICATION**
To know that there is joy in bringing about justice for all.

**STUDENTS' RESPONSES**
Students will seek justice for all.

## LESSON SCRIPTURE

### EXODUS 23:1-9 KJV

**1** Thou shalt not raise a false report: put not thine hand with the wicked to be an unrighteous witness.

### EXODUS 23:1-9 AMP

**1** "You shall not give a false report; you shall not join hands with the wicked to be

2 Thou shalt not follow a multitude to do evil; neither shalt thou speak in a cause to decline after many to wrest judgment:

3 Neither shalt thou countenance a poor man in his cause.

4 If thou meet thine enemy's ox or his ass going astray, thou shalt surely bring it back to him again.

5 If thou see the ass of him that hateth thee lying under his burden, and wouldest forbear to help him, thou shalt surely help with him.

6 Thou shalt not wrest the judgment of thy poor in his cause.

7 Keep thee far from a false matter; and the innocent and righteous slay thou not: for I will not justify the wicked.

8 And thou shalt take no gift: for the gift blindeth the wise, and perverteth the words of the righteous.

9 Also thou shalt not oppress a stranger: for ye know the heart of a stranger, seeing ye were strangers in the land of Egypt.

a malicious witness [promoting wrong and violence].

2 You shall not follow a crowd to do [something] evil, nor shall you testify at a trial or in a dispute so as to side with a crowd in order to pervert justice;

3 nor shall you favor or be partial to a poor man in his dispute [simply because he is poor].

4 "If you meet your enemy's ox or his donkey wandering off, you must bring it back to him.

5 If you see the donkey of one who hates you lying helpless under its load, you shall not leave the man to deal with it [alone]; you must help him release the animal [from its burden].

6 "You shall not pervert (bend) the justice due to your poor in his dispute.

7 Keep far away from a false charge or action, and do not condemn to death the innocent or the righteous, for I will not justify and acquit the guilty.

8 "You shall not accept a bribe, for a bribe blinds the clear-sighted and subverts the testimony and the cause of the righteous.

9 "You shall not oppress a stranger, for you know the soul [the feelings, thoughts, and concerns] of a stranger, for you were strangers in Egypt.

## BIBLICAL DEFINITIONS

A. **Gift (Exodus 23:8)** *shachad* (Heb.)— This word means the same in Hebrew and English, but the context is a present being used as a bribe.

B. **Oppress (Exodus 23:9)** *lachats* (Heb.)—To take advantage of, restrict, or pervert justice regarding someone's human rights.

## LIGHT ON THE WORD
### A Covenant People.

For the first time, the people of Israel under Moses' leadership were ready to pledge themselves in covenant with the God who had delivered them from slavery to the Egyptians. In Walter Brueggemann's words, "The proclamation of commands and the oath of allegiance are the defining elements of the covenant that bind Israel to YHWH (God) in obedience" (61). Along with the new laws that God gave to Moses came instructions for the construction of a holy place where God's presence would confirm his faithfulness to the new covenant.

The Sinai Tradition. The place of the giving of the law to Moses at Mt. Sinai in effect becomes an extended "Sinai Tradition" that extends through Leviticus and into Numbers. Overall, this is the core tradition of God working in covenant with man that makes Israel and eventually Judaism unique among all nations. The "law collection" or "law codes" created while God's people lingered at Mt. Sinai were normative for all that followed.

## TEACHING THE BIBLE LESSON

## LIFE NEED FOR TODAY'S LESSON

AIM: That your students will learn that when they act with justice and mercy whether toward a friend or foe they reflect the heart and character of God.

## INTRODUCTION
### Time for a Covenant

This was a foundational, formative time for God's people. During their "sojourn tradition," they had just been miraculously delivered from the horrible oppression in Egypt. Now they were ready to commit to a covenantal relationship with God. The giving of the Decalogue (the Ten Commandments) and the Covenant Code that followed define the formation of God's nation of Israel. In the words of John Rogerson and Philip Davies regarding the Covenant Code, "It sets out what it means to live as the people of Yhwh. . . Israel is also marked out as a people with a special relationship with Yhwh" (242).

## BIBLE LEARNING

AIM: That your students will learn that they should do justice.

## I. FIVE IMPERATIVES THAT BELIEVERS SHOULD KNOW (Exodus 23:1-3)

The lesson Scriptures focus on the arena of law called "social justice" legislation. The first set of judicial imperatives is addressed to witnesses in a legal proceeding. These are given as examples of the types of things that constitute injustice, which are to be avoided under penalty of judgment. The list was not meant to be exhaustive, and there are many other similar situations that would involve the same principles of not only avoiding injustice but also doing justice.

### Social Justice Legislation
### (verses 1-3)

**1 Thou shalt not raise a false report: put not thine hand with the wicked to be an unrighteous witness. 2 Thou shalt not follow a multitude to do evil; neither shalt thou speak in a cause to decline after many to wrest judgment: 3 Neither shalt thou countenance a poor man in his cause.**

(A): "Thou shalt not raise a false report" (verse 1). This refers to someone being an untruthful witness. Today, before witnesses may testify during a trial, they must swear to "tell the truth, the whole truth, and nothing but the truth." This reinforces the law of perjury, and if violated and proven that one has lied under oath, it carries a serious penalty. In non-legal settings, the justice principle of speaking truthfully about others extends to gossip and slander.

(B): "Put not thine hand with the wicked to be an unrighteous witness" (**verse 1**). This means do not cooperate with wicked people and give false testimony about someone who is guilty. This is the inverse of the previous. Just as one must not testify falsely if someone is innocent, by the same justice principle, one must not testify falsely if someone is guilty.

(C): "Thou shalt not follow a multitude to do evil" (**verse 2**). This means do not go along with the crowd if justice is being perverted. God holds each person to a personal standard of holiness and justice, and it is no excuse to say that one was just going along to get along. The child of God must be willing to refuse to follow the majority when he or she sees injustice being committed.

(D): "Neither shalt thou speak in a cause to decline after many to wrest judgment" (**verse 2**). This means do not fail to speak up when you see injustice, even if your voice is outnumbered or unpopular. This is the inverse of the third injunction. Not only must the just person not follow the crowd to participate in injustice, but also he or she must be willing to speak out against it.

(E): "Neither shalt thou countenance a poor man in his cause" (**verse 3**). This means do not automatically show partiality for a poor person, just because he or she is poor; the same goes for a rich person. The poor are not always innocent, nor are the rich always guilty. Such axiomatic statements were true in Old Testament times, and they are still true today. People tend to believe in stereotypes regarding a certain type or class of people for whom they have reason to disagree. The just child of God must be blind to both poverty and wealth when called on to make such a judgment.

## SEARCH THE SCRIPTURES
### QUESTION 1
What does it mean to "raise a false report" ?

**It means to be an unrighteous (false) witness.**

## LIGHT ON THE WORD
### Two Cases for Your Study
The following two examples are outside of a legal environment and uniquely refer to how one treats one's enemies.

## II. GIVE ME EXAMPLES!
## (Exodus 23:4-5)

Verses **4** and **5** are two case laws showing examples of impartiality, which uniquely address justice for one's enemies. It was a common misunderstanding—and still is—to think that the Old Testament taught people to hate their enemies. On the contrary, benevolence and mercy were frequent themes (see **2 Kings 6:18–23; Proverbs 25:21–22; Jeremiah 29:7**). Even the famous "eye for an eye" assertion (**Exodus 21:24**) was a matter of straight justice and not revenge or hatred. In reality, vengeance often far exceeds the original incident. What Jesus clarified and overruled in **Matthew 5:38–39** was a misinterpreted oral tradition and not a matter of actual law. **Exodus 23:4–5** are examples of the practical application of justice, a dominant and explicit theological theme of the Old Testament.

### How to Treat One's Enemy (verses 4-5)
**4 If thou meet thine enemy's ox or his ass going astray, thou shalt surely bring it back to him again. 5 If thou see the ass of him that hateth thee lying under his burden, and wouldest forbear to help him, thou shalt surely help with him.**

(A): "If thou meet thine enemy's ox or his ass going astray, thou shalt surely bring it back to him again" (**verse 4**). The meaning is clear that the just person is to help a man whose donkey has strayed, even if that person is an enemy. Through the ages, this has been the testimony that often has won converts because they saw God's people being kind and just, even to their enemies.

(B): "If thou see the ass of him that hateth thee lying under his burden, and wouldest forbear to help him, thou shalt surely help with him" **(verse 5).** Similar to the above point, the just person is to help a person whose donkey has fallen with a load, even if that person is an enemy. The parable of the "Good Samaritan" is a perfect New Testament parallel to this Old Testament injunction. If, for example, a person is lying trapped under a fallen animal, the just person is compelled to help—the principle is timeless, whether it is someone trapped under a car, a tree, or in a burning building. The just person must act justly in all situations, whether the person needing help is a friend or foe.

## QUESTION 2

Why did God instruct His people to be kind and just, even to their enemies?

**Being kind and just, even to one's enemies, can win converts. Answers will vary.**

## LIGHT ON THE WORD

### Judges Must Also Exercise Justice

The final five judicial imperatives of this portion of Scripture are addressed specifically to judges. After all, who other than a judge is more often in a position to determine the fate of others and to exercise either justice or injustice?

## III. INSTRUCTIONS TO JUDGES (Exodus 23:6-9)

The injunction now returns to courtroom procedural laws, this time addressing corrupt judges who put vulnerable people at a great disadvantage. There are two types of poor in this section: "poor" in **Exodus 23:3** in Hebrew is a basic term, while "poor" in **verse 6** in Hebrew refers to an extremely needy person, in danger of oppression and abuse; someone who is destitute or indigent.

### Just Judges (verses 6-9)

**6  Thou shalt not wrest the judgment of thy poor in his cause. 7 Keep thee far from a false matter; and the innocent and righteous slay thou not: for I will not justify the wicked. 8 And thou shalt take no gift: for the gift blindeth the wise, and perverteth the words of the righteous. 9 Also, thou shalt not oppress a stranger: for ye know the heart of a stranger, seeing ye were strangers in the land of Egypt.**

(A): "Thou shalt not wrest the judgment of thy poor in his cause" **(verse 6).** Just as one should not deny justice to a rich person, just because he or she is rich, so the just person must not deny justice to a poor person, just because he or she is poor.

(B): "Keep thee far from a false matter" **(verse 7).** The just person must at all costs avoid evil and injustice. One must consciously and deliberately steer clear of such things. Conversely, the clear implication is to maintain God's standard of justice at all times.

(C): "And the innocent and righteous slay thou not, for I will not justify the wicked" **(verse 7).** This passage could not be clearer. A judge must never falsely charge anyone and must never put an innocent person to death. Particularly when it comes to matters of life and death, God specifically will not excuse the one with innocent blood on his or her hands. This is the only injunction in the passage that comes with an attached warning that such wickedness will not go unpunished. God will judge the unjust judge.

(D): "And thou shalt take no gift: for the gift

blindeth the wise, and perverteth the words of the righteous" **(verse 8).** Sadly, bribing judges and other officials is a sin that has been committed countless times through the centuries. The frequency of the sin, however, does not relieve the sinners of the responsibility. If that were the case, then God would be guilty of going along with the crowd! No one who is in a position of authority should take a bribe, especially a judge who is often solely responsible for the fate of others. Bribes blind judges to justice, when instead judges are to be blind to partiality.

(E): "Also thou shalt not oppress a stranger: for ye know the heart of a stranger, seeing ye were strangers in the land of Egypt" **(verse 9).** As with the previous verse, this injunction comes with an explanation. Just as the Israelites once were oppressed strangers in Egypt, so they are not to oppress strangers (e.g., foreigners and travelers). Referring specifically to judges, again few others are so often responsible for the fate of so many others, and in this case, the person on trial must not be judged by their nationality or ethnicity.

## SEARCH THE SCRIPTURES

### QUESTION 3
What will happen to the unjust judge?

**God will judge him—"I will not justify the wicked."**

## LIGHT ON THE WORD

### A Cry for Justice
One hears a lot about social justice in the news, and it is only natural for victims of injustice to cry out for justice in every aspect of society. Studying the Scriptures on social justice presents a clear picture of what it means for God's people to embody justice in society—how they are to both avoid injustice and exercise justice. This clear picture must be preserved in a world where so many believe that only political solutions or new laws will fulfill God's requirements for justice. While governments are capable of doing things that individuals cannot, according to God's Word, individuals are always responsible for their actions and decisions. Even governments are made up of individuals, and each will give an account of every decision, whether it was just or unjust. Ultimately, no one will be excused for inflicting or enabling injustice.

## BIBLE APPLICATION
**AIM: That your students will know that they are responsible for their actions.**

### God Still Calls His People to Holiness—Justice
Even though today's believers live in the New Covenant, God's holy character and standards have not changed. He still does not tolerate injustice among His people. He still calls His people to be holy and to come out from among those in the world who commit such evil, as stated in **1 Peter 2:9,** "But ye are a chosen generation, a royal priesthood, an holy nation, a peculiar people; that ye should shew forth the praises of him who hath called you out of darkness into his marvellous light." The challenge for believers today is to correct injustices when they are found and to act justly, even when there is a compelling reason or temptation to do otherwise.

## STUDENTS' RESPONSES
**AIM: That your students will embrace justice.**

The focus of this week's lesson is on the horizontal aspect of the Covenant Code, addressing one's behavior toward others. A just and righteous God expects His children to do justice and righteousness.

## PRAYER

Dear Father, help us to practice justice toward others. Help us to treat them as we wish to be treated. In Jesus' Name we pray. Amen.

## DIG A LITTLE DEEPER

After the Ten Commandments were delivered to the children of Israel directly by God **(Exodus 20),** there followed several dozen additional laws that built upon the commandment principles. In **chapters 21–24** we find a large collection of what is called "case law." In these instances, the broader principles that embody the commandments are applied to specific cases that would predictably arise. For example, in order to apply the dictum "Thou shalt not steal" **(Exodus 20:15)** to the case of an actual thief, the Israelites were told what punishments to mete out **(Exodus 22:1).**

Sometimes Jewish case law seemed to address practical concerns not even alluded to in the decalogue. There was case law dealing with the treatment of slaves, the care for the poor, lending practices and the conduct of commercial business, to describe only a few examples. Although the aforementioned cases do not enlarge upon particular commandments, they do derive from the overall spirit of justice underlying the Ten Commandments.

Christian blogger Peter Krol has an excellent article on his Knowable Word website: "6 Principles for Understanding the Case Law of Exodus." Krol provides some tools to help us properly read the case laws, particularly in the light of New Testament revelation. You can search for that article at https://www. knowableword.com, where you can also learn more about this bible study ministry.

Ref.:

Krol, Peter. "6 Principles for Understanding the Case Law of Exodus." Knowable Word (blog). June 23, 2017, https://www. knowableword.com/2017/06/23/6-principles-for-understanding-the-case-laws-of-exodus/.

## HOW TO SAY IT

| | |
|---|---|
| Decalogue. | DEK-uh-log. |
| Deuteronomy. | Doo'tuh-RON-uh-mee. |
| Sinai. | SI-nī also -nē-ī. |

### DAILY HOME BIBLE READINGS

**MONDAY**
Punishment for False Witnesses
(Deuteronomy 19:15–20)

**TUESDAY**
God Holds Court
(Psalm 82)

**WEDNESDAY**
The Day of Punishment
(Isaiah 10:1–4)

**THURSDAY**
Rescued from the Wicked and Unjust
(Psalm 71:1–6)

**FRIDAY**
A God of Justice
(Isaiah 30:18–22)

**SATURDAY**
God's Ways Are Just
(Deuteronomy 31:30–32:7)

**SUNDAY**
Justice for All
(Exodus 23:1–9)

## PREPARE FOR NEXT SUNDAY

Read **Leviticus 19:9–18, 33–37,** and next week's lesson "Living as God's Just People."

**Sources:**

Bruckner, James K. Exodus. Old Testament Series. New International Biblical Commentary. Peabody, MA: Hendrickson Publishers, 2008. 216–17.

Brueggemann, Walter. An Introduction to the Old Testament: The Canon and Christian
Imagination. Louisville, KY: Westminster John Knox Press, 2003. 60–66.

Hebrew and Greek Lexicons. Bible Study Tools.com. http://www.biblestudytools.com/lexicons (accessed November 5, 2010).

Kaiser, Walter C. Genesis, Exodus, Leviticus, Numbers. The Expositor's Bible Commentary, vol. 2. Edited by Frank E. Gaebelein. Grand Rapids, MI: Zondervan, 1990. 442–43.

Mackay, John L. Exodus: A Mentor Commentary. Ross-Shire, Great Britain: Christian
Focus Publications, 2001. 398–401.

Merriam-Webster Online Dictionary. Merriam-Webster, Inc. http://www.merriam-webster.com (accessed November 5, 2010).

Old and New Testament Concordances, Lexicons, Dictionaries, Commentaries, Images, and Bible Versions. Blue Letter Bible.org. http://www.blueletterbible.org/ (accessed July 10, 2010).

Passage Lookup. Bible Gateway.com. http://www.biblegateway.com/passage (accessed January 17, 2011).

Rogerson, John, and Philip Davies. The Old Testament World. Englewood Cliffs, NJ:
Prentice Hall, 1989. 238–42.

## COMMENTS / NOTES:

# LIVING AS GOD'S JUST PEOPLE

**BIBLE BASIS:** Leviticus 19:9-18, 33-37

**BIBLE TRUTH:** We should love our neighbor as we do ourselves..

**MEMORY VERSE:** But the stranger that dwelleth with you shall be unto you as one born among you, and thou shalt love him as thyself; for ye were strangers in the land of Egypt: I am the LORD your God (Leviticus 19:34, KJV).

**LESSON AIM:** By the end of the lesson, we will: KNOW what it means to love one's neighbor as one's self; REFLECT on ways to act with compassion; and PRAY to live a life of justice and compassion.

**BACKGROUND SCRIPTURES:** Leviticus 19:9-18, 33-37- Read and incorporate the insights gained from the Background Scriptures into your study of the lesson.

## TEACHER PREPARATION

**MATERIALS NEEDED:** Bibles (several different versions), Quarterly Commentary/Teacher Manual, Adult Quarterly, teaching resources such as charts, worksheets/handouts, paper, pens, and pencils.

**OTHER MATERIALS NEEDED / TEACHER'S NOTES:**

_____

_____

## LESSON OVERVIEW

**LIFE NEED FOR TODAY'S LESSON**
To apply the principles of treating others fairly, justly, and respectfully.

**BIBLE LEARNING**
To know what it means to love one's neighbor as one's self.

**BIBLE APPLICATION**
To reflect on ways to act with compassion.

**STUDENTS' RESPONSES**
Students will act with love and compassion toward others.

## LESSON SCRIPTURE

### LEVITICUS 19:9-18, 33-37 KJV

**9** And when ye reap the harvest of your land, thou shalt not wholly reap the corners of thy

### LEVITICUS 19:9-18, 33-37 AMP

**9** 'Now when you reap the harvest of your land, you shall not reap to the very corners of field, neither shalt thou gather the gleanings of thy harvest.

10 And thou shalt not glean thy vineyard, neither shalt thou gather every grape of thy vineyard; thou shalt leave them for the poor and stranger: I am the LORD your God.

11 Ye shall not steal, neither deal falsely, neither lie one to another.

12 And ye shall not swear by my name falsely, neither shalt thou profane the name of thy God: I am the LORD.

13 Thou shalt not defraud thy neighbour, neither rob him: the wages of him that is hired shall not abide with thee all night until the morning.

14 Thou shalt not curse the deaf, nor put a stumblingblock before the blind, but shalt fear thy God: I am the LORD.

15 Ye shall do no unrighteousness in judgment: thou shalt not respect the person of the poor, nor honour the person of the mighty: but in righteousness shalt thou judge thy neighbour.

16 Thou shalt not go up and down as a talebearer among thy people: neither shalt thou stand against the blood of thy neighbour: I am the LORD.

17 Thou shalt not hate thy brother in thine heart: thou shalt in any wise rebuke thy neighbour, and not suffer sin upon him.

18 Thou shalt not avenge, nor bear any grudge against the children of thy people, but thou shalt love thy neighbour as thyself: I am the LORD.

19:33 And if a stranger sojourn with thee in your land, ye shall not vex him.

34 But the stranger that dwelleth with you shall be unto you as one born among you,

your field, nor shall you gather the gleanings (grain left after reaping) of your harvest.

10 And you shall not glean your vineyard, nor shall you gather its fallen grapes; you shall leave them for the poor and for the stranger. I am the Lord your God.

11 'You shall not steal, nor deal deceptively, nor lie to one another.

12 You shall not swear [an oath] falsely by My name, so as to profane the name of your God; I am the Lord.

13 'You shall not oppress or exploit your neighbor, nor rob him. You shall not withhold the wages of a hired man overnight until morning.

14 You shall not curse a deaf man nor put a stumbling block before the blind, but you shall fear your God [with profound reverence]; I am the Lord.

15 'You shall not do injustice in judgment; you shall not be partial to the poor nor show a preference for the great, but judge your neighbor fairly.

16 You shall not go around as a gossip among your people, and you are not to act against the life of your neighbor [with slander or false testimony]; I am the Lord.

17 'You shall not hate your brother in your heart; you may most certainly rebuke your neighbor, but shall not incur sin because of him.

18 You shall not take revenge nor bear any grudge against the sons of your people, but you shall love your neighbor (acquaintance, associate, companion) as yourself; I am the Lord.

33 'When a stranger resides with you in your land, you shall not oppress or mistreat him.

and thou shalt love him as thyself; for ye were strangers in the land of Egypt: I am the LORD your God.

**35** Ye shall do no unrighteousness in judgment, in meteyard, in weight, or in measure.

**36** Just balances, just weights, a just ephah, and a just hin, shall ye have: I am the LORD your God, which brought you out of the land of Egypt.

**37** Therefore shall ye observe all my statutes, and all my judgments, and do them: I am the LORD.

**34** But the stranger who resides with you shall be to you like someone native-born among you; and you shall love him as yourself, for you were strangers in the land of Egypt; I am the Lord your God.

**35** 'You shall do no wrong in judgment, in measurement of weight or quantity.

**36** You shall have just and accurate balances, just weights, a just ephah, and a just hin. I am the Lord your God, who brought you out of the land of Egypt.

**37** You shall observe and keep all My statutes and all My ordinances and do them. I am the Lord.'"

## BIBLICAL DEFINITIONS

A. **Stranger (Leviticus 19:10)** *ger* (Heb.)—A sojourner; a newcomer, or a foreigner.

B. **Unrighteousness (Lev. 19:15)** *`evel* (Heb.)—Injustice, iniquity, and wickedness.

## LIGHT ON THE WORD

A Holy People. God's people have always had a special relationship with Him, one that is based on God's nature and character. When Israel agreed to be God's people and to obey His covenant—following His miraculous deliverance of them from the Egyptians—they bound themselves to ethical and religious responsibilities. These were delivered to them in the form of legal codes (i.e., the Covenant Code and the Holiness Code), which included both positive and negative injunctions. The vertical relationship of God's people was outlined in the Decalogue (the Ten Commandments) and

was fairly simple and straightforward—they were to have no other gods, they were not to use the Lord's name in vain, and they were to honor the Sabbath. The horizontal relationship was more complicated and came in the form of numerous specific injunctions, all provided as guiding examples and principles for how they were to govern themselves both at home and in the world.

## TEACHING THE BIBLE LESSON

## LIFE NEED FOR TODAY'S LESSON

**AIM: That your students will pray to live a life of justice and compassion.**

## INTRODUCTION

### The Holiness Code

The Holiness Code of **Leviticus 18:1–24:9** was given to the Israelites as a set of ethical and religious responsibilities, which includes both positive and negative injunctions. John Rogerson and Philip Davies write, "The basis of the regulations in **19:11–18** about fair dealing with one's neighbours [sic] is not so much social solidarity as mutual religious responsibility" (145). A large part of Leviticus deals with priestly matters, while **chapters 18** and **20** address sexual relations. **Chapter 19,** the focus of today's lesson, deals primarily with Israel's horizontal relationships with others, particularly addressing justice and fairness as examples of holiness.

## BIBLE LEARNING

**AIM: That your students will apply God's Word to their daily living.**

## I. HOW SHOULD WE TREAT OTHERS?(Leviticus 19:9-16)

Jesus summarized the horizontal part of a proper relationship with God as "love thy neighbour as thyself" (**see Matthew 22:38–39; Luke 10:27**). Inherent in every aspect of God's holy nature and His laws regarding holiness is His heart of love. Every injunction contained in the entire Sinai Tradition reflects God's heart of love. Treating others right, or loving one's neighbor, is the ultimate expression of social justice. Contained within this overriding principle are the following details:

### Love Your Neighbor
### (Leviticus 19:9-16)

**9 And when ye reap the harvest of your land, thou shalt not wholly reap the corners of thy field, neither shalt thou gather the gleanings of thy harvest. 10 And thou shalt not glean thy vineyard, neither shalt thou gather every grape of thy vineyard; thou shalt leave them for the poor and stranger: I am the LORD your God. 11 Ye shall not steal, neither deal falsely, neither lie one to another. 12 And ye shall not swear by my name falsely, neither shalt thou profane the name of thy God: I am the LORD. 13 Thou shalt not defraud thy neighbour, neither rob him: the wages of him that is hired shall not abide with thee all night until the morning. 14 Thou shalt not curse the deaf, nor put a stumblingblock before the blind, but shalt fear thy God: I am the LORD. 15 Ye shall do no unrighteousness in judgment: thou shalt not respect the person of the poor, nor honour the person of the mighty: but in righteousness shalt thou judge thy neighbour. 16 Thou shalt not go up and down as a talebearer among thy people: neither shalt thou stand against the blood of thy neighbour: I am the LORD.**

Proper handling of the land (**verses 9–10**). Inherent in treating others right is the matter of strangers (e.g., travelers), but also includes the ubiquitous poor and those who perhaps once were better off but have fallen on hard times. By generously leaving the corners of one's fields or vines for those less fortunate, the Israelite demonstrated a godly attitude toward others. Today, one's surplus can be shared with others in any number of ways.

Honesty with everyone (**verses 11–13**). It might seem obvious at first, but the injunctions against committing perjury, stealing, and lying (which parallel the third, eighth, and ninth commandments respectively) are sometimes harder to obey when the boundaries are less clear. When the cases are obvious, the choices between right and wrong are clear. But often deception, deceit, and fraud can take very subtle and more easily justified forms. The godly person avoids all such acts, however minor, that dishonor God and harms others.

Not taking advantage of others (**verses 14–16**). Much like the previous injunctions, these specify taking advantage of the disadvantaged. In particular, singling out weak or easy "marks," such as the handicapped or someone in a desperate situation, is injustice defined. The opposite type of person is also included—God's holy people also are not to act dishonorably toward the privileged. An easy example would be filing unjust lawsuits against "deep pockets." In all cases, embodying social justice excludes all forms of gossip, backstabbing, and slander, as these are harmful to others and dishonoring to God.

## SEARCH THE SCRIPTURES

### QUESTION 1
What did God command that the Israelites do with the corners of their field?

"Thou shalt not wholly reap the corners of thy field."

## LIGHT ON THE WORD

### What's in Your Heart?
In **Matthew 5:43,** Jesus quoted **Leviticus 19:17–18** (part of the Mosaic Law), understanding clearly that hate in one's heart is what leads to murder. Thus, hate has always been condemned in both testaments of Scripture, with or without the act of murder. The specific expressions of revenge and bearing a grudge in **verse 18** are a sharper focus of the general injunction against hatred. Other parts of the Old Testament zoom in even further on the subject of revenge, specifying repeatedly that God alone has the right, and God alone is able to exact perfect justice, regardless of the severity of the act or actions that inspired the hate and revenge (**see Jeremiah 15:15; Nahum 1:2; Psalm 94:1**). It is common knowledge that resentment and anger fester and invariably result in unholy expressions and deeds. It is also commonly known that such attitudes often harm the bearers more than their targets.

## II. WHERE DOES SOCIAL JUSTICE START? (Leviticus 19:17-18)

Juxtaposed against, and antithetical to, all forms of injustice, hatred, and evil, love stands as the quintessential solution and antidote. The do's and don'ts of loving one's neighbor could have been listed by the thousands, but this list in Leviticus, expanded from the Decalogue in Exodus, should have served as sufficient extension to make the clear point that love for God translates into love for neighbors, and that love does not inflict injustice, hatred, vengeance, and so on. Jesus quoted from the now-famous citation of the second greatest commandment, captured by all three Synoptic Gospel writers (**Matthew 5:43; 19:19; 22:39; Mark 12:31; Luke 10:27**), Paul (**Romans 13:9; Galatians 5:14**), and James (**James 2:8**). Again, the only rationale needed is that God is God.

The Scriptures are very clear on whom "others" are and to whom we should "do unto (others) as we would have them do unto us" (**from Matthew 7:12; Luke 6:31, NIV**). Just in this lesson, the "others" are the poor (**Leviticus 19:10, 15**); the stranger (**verses 10, 33, 34**); the neighbor (**verses 13, 15, 16, 17, 18**); the deaf and blind (**verse 14**); the brother (**verse 17**); people (**verse 16**); and children of the people (**verse 18**). Clearly, the list includes more than one's physical neighbors or same-status peers. Rather, it specifically includes the disadvantaged, the weak, and the vulnerable.

### How to Treat Others (verses 17-18)
**17 Thou shalt not hate thy brother in thine heart: thou shalt in any wise rebuke thy neighbour, and not suffer sin upon him. 18 Thou shalt not avenge, nor bear any grudge against the children of thy people, but thou shalt love thy neighbour as thyself: I am the LORD.**

Don't hate and don't seek revenge. Jesus was very clear when He commanded in **Matthew 5:43–44** to love even one's enemies, which would more than encompass these verses speaking primarily about "neighbors." Jesus knew that murder started with hate and frequently originated with a grudge that morphed into vengeance.

An injunction against this evil root would preclude much trouble, grief, and heartache, not to mention it would spare lives. God is fully capable of exercising vengeance, as eloquently captured in the prayer of **Psalm 94:1,** "O Lord God, to whom vengeance belongeth; O God, to whom vengeance belongeth, shew thyself." In **verse 3, Psalm 94** asks the timeless question, "How long shall the wicked triumph?" The answer is that however long it is, their judgment belongs to God and God alone.

Love your neighbor as yourself. The second greatest commandment is reiterated in both testaments and reinforced by Jesus and others. This is presented as one of several positive injunctions, but it happens to capture the heart of the entire Holiness Code—in fact, all the law codes. Nothing better defines the child of God or social justice than loving one's neighbor as one's self.

## QUESTION 2

"Thou shalt not _____ thy brother in thine _____".

**Hate, heart. Answers will vary.**

## LIGHT ON THE WORD

### Who Is the Stranger and My Neighbor?

As stated, the Hebrew word for "stranger" can include a sojourner. It is easy to see the proper way to treat strangers in a brief sentence: "Love them as you love yourself." In a literal sense, the Israelites had been "stranger sojourners" in Egypt not long before, so the reference in **verse 34** to their former place of slavery was appropriate and the connection vivid. God loved the Israelites when they were sojourners in the foreign land of Egypt, and He also loved them when they rebelled against Him and practiced evil. Likewise, He loves us while we have been strangers and sinners to Him.

## III. HOW TO TREAT THE STRANGER AND MY NEIGHBOR (Leviticus 19:33-37)

Strangers also may be newcomers or foreigners (aliens), and God's children are to treat them as they would be treated—again invoking the second greatest commandment. This clarifies beyond question the New Testament rhetorical question, "Who is my neighbour?" (**Luke 10:29**).

### Our Role in Social Justice
### (Leviticus 19:33-34)

**33 And if a stranger sojourn with thee in your land, ye shall not vex him. 34 But the stranger that dwelleth with you shall be unto you as one born among you, and thou shalt love him as thyself; for ye were strangers in the land of Egypt: I am the LORD your God.**

Strangers are sojourners (travelers). The answer is abundantly clear—our neighbor is everyone! None are excluded from the injunction, as clarified by the various specific examples. Whether they are visitors just passing through, settlers from another culture, or foreign outsiders, all are to be treated like blood relatives and loved as one's self. Clearly, the lawyer asking the question of Jesus should have been familiar with the Holiness Code and should not have been surprised when Jesus told him by a parable that one's neighbor includes even the despised Samaritans.

Israel once was a stranger in Egypt. Considering that the great Exodus from Egypt had not happened very long before the time of these injunctions, the reminder should have been a very familiar example. Nothing drives a point home better than a personal example, especially a recent one. For Christians, the parallel is with their personal deliverance from the bondage of sin, which more often than not is remembered with great fondness, no matter how many years transpire. Occasionally, however, some need to be reminded that they once had been delivered from oppression and bondage, and they should not even consider mistreating others or inflicting them with any kind of injustice.

## SEARCH THE SCRIPTURES
### QUESTION 3
Israel was a stranger in what land?

**Egypt.**

## LIGHT ON THE WORD
### Being Just in Business and Law
Few Old Testament theological concepts emerge quite as strongly as the twin themes of justice and righteousness **(see Proverbs 21:3; Isaiah 16:5; Amos 5:24).** We are to embody or model our love and obedience to God through our love for and service to others, without exception.

Jesus further underscored the Levitical amplifications of the Decalogue by removing all listed specifics and replacing them with even more impossible-to-achieve holiness—namely that to simply think about acting unjustly would make one guilty of the whole law **(Matthew 5:22).** In contrast to unjust weights used in unrighteousness, those in **Leviticus 19:36** who use "just weights" both exercise justice and are evidence of righteousness. We must obey God's commands!

## IV. JUSTICE IN BUSINESS AND LAW (Leviticus 19:35-37)
Just scales, righteous dealings, and fairness toward all. Occasionally, some Old Testament laws translate perfectly into modern society without the need for any kind of cultural filter. The injunction about unjust scales is preceded by a general command of not doing any unrighteousness in "judgment" or in weighing any matter, but specifically when scales

determine values and deception is difficult to detect. This could find countless modern applications, such as gas stations not setting their pumps accurately; taxi drivers "running up the meter"; expense accounts or invoices being "padded"; accountants doing "creative" bookkeeping.

### Justice and Righteousness in Business and Law (verses 35-37)
**35 Ye shall do no unrighteousness in judgment, in meteyard, in weight, or in measure. 36 Just balances, just weights, a just ephah, and a just hin, shall ye have: I am the LORD your God, which brought you out of the land of Egypt. 37 Therefore shall ye observe all my statutes, and all my judgments, and do them: I am the LORD.**

Obeying God's just ordinances is evidence for righteousness. Even where there is an unbridgeable cultural distance between the laws of the "Sinai Tradition" and today, God's people are still called to a standard of holiness measured against God's holiness. Nothing demonstrates personal righteousness more than being faithful to living in a way that honors God. Nothing more explicitly defines such a life as one who is committed to loving others through practical expressions of social justice.

## SEARCH THE SCRIPTURES
### QUESTION 4
"Ye shall do no _____ in _____, in meteyard, in _____, or in _____."

**Unrighteousness, judgment, weight, measure. Answers will vary.**

## LIGHT ON THE WORD
### Walking in God's Word
Often, the lofty matters of holiness and justice

become elusive principles when confronted with complex, emotional, and controversial events and circumstances—such as the nation's concern for border security and how that should be translated into laws and actions. As much as one wants to obey God's Word and love one's neighbor, how are those realities impacted when a neighbor is breaking the law? Should everyone crossing the border illegally be granted unlimited freedom to enter the U.S., even if some of them are criminals from the Mexican drug cartel, murderers, kidnappers, and drug and weapons dealers? How should the thinking of law-abiding Christians be balanced to reflect the concerns for the innocent poor seeking a better life as well as the safety of fellow American citizens? These are not easy questions or simple issues. God's people must be careful to weigh (judge) the issues and allow themselves to be driven by principles of biblical justice and not let God's definitions be confused by the vested interests of politics.

## BIBLE APPLICATION

**AIM: That your students will begin to understand that God expects us to live just lives.**

### Holiness, Justice, and Righteousness

Locate some of the examples given in the Holiness Code of specific examples of injustice. Try to find modern examples that would parallel the same principles. Now think about some of your personal experiences with injustice or unrighteousness. How did these experiences make you feel? Now contrast these memories and feelings with a memorable time when you witnessed holiness, justice, or righteousness. Finish by thinking about how you have treated others justly and unjustly.

## STUDENTS' RESPONSES

**AIM: That your students will know that they are called to "holy" living.**

### A Call to Holy Living

God's people are to be in the world but not of it. Theirs is a higher calling to the kingdom of God and to holy living as defined by Scripture—which translates to a timeless command to treating others as we would be treated, to love others as we would be loved, and a determination to be just and fair in all one's human relationships. Surely, there are enough challenges in this one paragraph to last a lifetime.

## PRAYER

Dear Lord, thank You for Your justice. Help me to meet Your call to holy living. In Jesus' Name I pray. Amen.

## DIG A LITTLE DEEPER

The call for righteous business practices must be honored by the Church's business leaders and owners. In the marketplace, there is a particular disdain for compromised and belied Christian testimonies. Not only are saints in business expected to be trustworthy and reliable, but also to demonstrate excellence in product and customer service. Mediocrity may be tolerated by non-believers, but Christians are held to the highest standards.

This is why we're thankful to groups like the Business and Professional Women's Federation (B&PWF), a unit of the C.O.G.I.C. Department of Women. According to the mission statement of the B&PWF, its participants strive to share "God-given resources and expertise" with other businesswomen. A major goal is to promote networking and mentorship for young women who aspire to professional careers. To that end, the auxiliary often sponsors meetings and mixers, seminars and workshops, fundraisers and scholarships, on the local, district, and jurisdictional levels. Of course, the national chapter hosts important events at the Women's Convention and the Holy Convocation.

Make contact with the B&PWF on the local, jurisdictional or national level to see what they may be able to offer you.

Ref.:

Church of God in Christ, Inc. Official Handbook for the Department of Women. 3rd ed. (2002), p. 42.

## HOW TO SAY IT

Decalogue.          DEK-uh-log.

Ephah.              EE-fuh.

Leviticus.          Lih-VI-tih-kuhs

Zechariah.          Zek'uh-RI-ah

## PREPARE FOR NEXT SUNDAY

Read **Leviticus 25:8–12, 25, 35–36, 39–40, 47–48, 55,** and next week's lesson " Celebrate Jubilee."

**Sources:**
Balentine, Samuel E. Leviticus. Interpretation: A Bible Commentary for Teaching and
Preaching. 2nd ed. Louisville, KY: John Knox Press, 2002. 160–67.

Bellender, W. H., Jr. Leviticus, Numbers. Old Testament Series. New International
Biblical Commentary. Peabody, MA: Hendrickson Publishers, 2001. 116–21.

Bible Pronunciation Chart. Better Days Are Coming.com. http://www.betterdaysarecoming/bible/pronunciation.html (accessed January 29, 2011).

Brueggemann, Walter. An Introduction to the Old Testament: The Canon and Christian
Imagination. Louisville, KY: Westminster John Knox Press, 2003. 67–74.

Harris, R. Laird. Genesis, Exodus, Leviticus, Numbers. The Expositor's Bible Commentary, vol. 2. Edited by Frank E. Gaebelein. Grand Rapids, MI: Zondervan, 1990. 604–09.

Hebrew and Greek Lexicons. Bible Study Tools.com. http://www.biblestudytools.com/lexicons (accessed November 8, 2010).

Merriam-Webster Online Dictionary. Merriam-Webster, Inc. http://www.merriam-webster.com (accessed November 8, 2010).

Old and New Testament Concordances, Lexicons, Dictionaries, Commentaries, Images, and Bible Versions. Blue Letter Bible.org. http://www.blueletterbible.org/ (accessed July 10, 2010).

## DAILY HOME BIBLE READINGS

**MONDAY**
God's Indignation over Injustice
(Ezekiel 22:23–31)

**TUESDAY**
No Safety for Sinners
(Jeremiah 7:8–15)

**WEDNESDAY**
Deliver Me from Evildoers
(Psalm 140:1–8)

**THURSDAY**
Occasions for Stumbling
(Matthew 18:1–9)

**FRIDAY**
If You Truly Amend Your Ways
(Jeremiah 7:1–7)

**SATURDAY**
"Who Is My Neighbor?"
(Luke 10:25–37)

**SUNDAY**
"I Am the LORD"
(Leviticus 19:9–18, 33–37)

Passage Lookup. Bible Gateway.com. http://www.biblegateway.com/passage (accessed January 17, 2011).

Robinson, Haddon W. "A Prejudiced Usher." Our Daily Bread. March 6, 1994. http://www.odb.org/1994/03/06/a-prejudiced-usher/ (accessed January 29, 2011).

Rogerson, John, and Philip Davies. The Old Testament World. Englewood Cliffs, NJ: Prentice Hall, 1989. 242–45.

# CELEBRATE JUBILEE

**BIBLE BASIS:** Leviticus 25:8–12, 25, 35–36, 39–40, 47–48, 55

**BIBLE TRUTH:** Jubilee was an opportunity to begin anew.

**MEMORY VERSE:** And ye shall hallow the fiftieth year, and proclaim liberty throughout all the land unto all the inhabitants thereof: it shall be a jubile unto you; and ye shall return every man unto his possession, and ye shall return every man unto his family (Leviticus 25:10,KJV).

**LESSON AIM:** By the end of the lesson, we will: EXPLAIN why jubilee was an opportunity to begin anew; REFLECT on a time when we needed to begin again; and SUMMARIZE the principles of jubilee.

**BACKGROUND SCRIPTURES:** Leviticus 25:8-55-Read and incorporate insights gained from the Background Scriptures into your study of the lesson.

## TEACHER PREPARATION

**MATERIALS NEEDED:** Bibles (several different versions), Quarterly Commentary/Teacher Manual, Adult Quarterly, teaching resources such as charts, worksheets/handouts, paper, pens, and pencils.

**OTHER MATERIALS NEEDED / TEACHER'S NOTES:**

_____

_____

## LESSON OVERVIEW

**LIFE NEED FOR TODAY'S LESSON**
To be reminded of how God gave us many second chances to do things right.

**BIBLE LEARNING**
To understand God's principles of Jubilee.

**BIBLE APPLICATION**
To praise God for giving us times of Jubilee.

**STUDENTS' RESPONSES**
That your students will be thankful for a merciful God giving them times of Jubilee.

## LESSON SCRIPTURE

### LEVITICUS 25:8–12, 25, 35–36, 39–40, 47–48, 55 KJV

**8** And thou shalt number seven sabbaths of years unto thee, seven times seven years; and

### LEVITICUS 25:8–12, 25, 35–36, 39–40, 47–48, 55 AMP

**8** 'You are also to count off seven Sabbaths of years for yourself, seven times seven years, so the space of the seven sabbaths of years shall be unto thee forty and nine years.

**9** Then shalt thou cause the trumpet of the jubile to sound on the tenth day of the seventh month, in the day of atonement shall ye make the trumpet sound throughout all your land.

**10** And ye shall hallow the fiftieth year, and proclaim liberty throughout all the land unto all the inhabitants thereof: it shall be a jubile unto you; and ye shall return every man unto his possession, and ye shall return every man unto his family.

**11** A jubile shall that fiftieth year be unto you: ye shall not sow, neither reap that which groweth of itself in it, nor gather the grapes in it of thy vine undressed.

**12** For it is the jubile; it shall be holy unto you: ye shall eat the increase thereof out of the field.

**25:25** If thy brother be waxen poor, and hath sold away some of his possession, and if any of his kin come to redeem it, then shall he redeem that which his brother sold.

**25:35** And if thy brother be waxen poor, and fallen in decay with thee; then thou shalt relieve him: yea, though he be a stranger, or a sojourner; that he may live with thee.

**36** Take thou no usury of him, or increase: but fear thy God; that thy brother may live with thee.

**25:39** And if thy brother that dwelleth by thee be waxen poor, and be sold unto thee; thou shalt not compel him to serve as a bondservant:

**40** But as an hired servant, and as a sojourner, he shall be with thee, and shall serve thee unto the year of jubile:

that you have the time of the seven Sabbaths of years, namely, forty-nine years.

**9** Then you shall sound the ram's horn everywhere on the tenth day of the seventh month (almost October); on the Day of Atonement you shall sound the trumpet throughout your land.

**10** And you shall consecrate the fiftieth year and proclaim freedom [for the slaves] throughout the land to all its inhabitants. It shall be a Jubilee (year of remission) for you, and each of you shall return to his own [ancestral] property [that was sold to another because of poverty], and each of you shall return to his family [from whom he was separated by bondage].

**11** That fiftieth year shall be a Jubilee for you; you shall not sow [seed], nor reap what reseeds itself, nor gather the grapes of the uncultivated vines.

**12** For it is the Jubilee; it shall be holy to you; you shall eat its crops out of the field.

**25** 'If a fellow countryman of yours becomes so poor he has to sell some of his property, then his nearest relative is to come and buy back (redeem) what his relative has sold.

**35** 'Now if your fellow countryman becomes poor and his hand falters with you [that is, he has trouble repaying you for something], then you are to help and sustain him, [with courtesy and consideration] like [you would] a stranger or a temporary resident [without property], so that he may live among you.

**36** Do not charge him usurious interest, but fear your God [with profound reverence], so your countryman may [continue to] live among you.

**39** 'And if your fellow countryman becomes so poor [in his dealings] with you that he sells

**25:47.** And if a sojourner or stranger wax rich by thee, and thy brother that dwelleth by him wax poor, and sell himself unto the stranger or sojourner by thee, or to the stock of the stranger's family:

**48.** After that he is sold he may be redeemed again; one of his brethren may redeem him:

**25:55.** For unto me the children of Israel are servants; they are my servants whom I brought forth out of the land of Egypt: I am the LORD your God.

himself to you [as payment for a debt], you shall not let him do the work of a slave [who is ineligible for redemption],

**40** but he is to be with you as a hired man, as if he were a temporary resident; he shall serve with you until the Year of Jubilee,

**47** 'Now if the financial means of a stranger or temporary resident among you become sufficient, and your fellow countryman becomes poor in comparison to him and sells himself to the stranger who is living among you or to the descendants of the stranger's family,

**48** then after he is sold he shall have the right of redemption. One of his relatives may redeem him:

**55** For the children of Israel are My servants; My servants, whom I brought out of the land of Egypt. I am the Lord your God.

## BIBLICAL DEFINITIONS

A. **Jubile (Leviticus 25:10, 11, 12, 40)** *teruw`ah, yowbel* (Heb.)—Also spelled "jubilee"; a season of celebration; a year of emancipation and restoration.

B. **Hallow (v. 10)** *qadash* (Heb.)—To consecrate or sanctify.

## LIGHT ON THE WORD

Moses. Moses had been instructed to teach the Children of Israel about the Feasts and what was required in each (**Leviticus 23**). He then speaks to them on the proper care of the Tabernacle lamps and the bread for the Tabernacle (**Leviticus 24**). The Children of Israel were also warned about blaspheming God and how any person committing this act would be handled.

So leading into **chapter 25,** the people were receiving instructions from their leader, Moses. In **Leviticus 25–27,** Moses gives the Israelites practical guidelines for holiness.

Levites. The tribe of Levi was separated by God from the other tribes and placed in charge of the dismantling, carrying, and erecting of the tabernacle (**Numbers 1:47–54**). The Levites were dedicated to the ministry of priesthood, especially in regards to caring for the tabernacle.

## TEACHING THE BIBLE LESSON

## LIFE NEED FOR TODAY'S LESSON

**AIM: That your students will learn how to care for others.**

## INTRODUCTION

### What Has God Done for You Lately?

There is a vintage song of the church entitled, "He Broke the Chains." This very heart-stirring song extols what God has done for humanity when He gave His life on that cruel Cross at Calvary. One verse says, "My life was lost in sin and shame, The way I could not see, But Jesus came, oh, bless His name, And set my spirit free." The chorus proclaims, "I can't forget the day He spoke to my troubled soul, Words of peace that made my burdens roll, He broke the chains that bound and set all my joybells ringing, Praise to His matchless name."

"He Broke the Chains" should remind us that we were in captivity, as well. We needed a Savior to set us free, and we needed to believe in the Lord Jesus Christ so that we could be saved. It should also remind us that sometimes even after we are saved, we can find ourselves in captivity to bills, credit cards, jobs, families, busy schedules, etc. Still, we need that same God to help set us free.

## BIBLE LEARNING

AIM: That your students will celebrate their times as well as others' times of Jubilee—Restoration.

## I. LET JUBILEE BEGIN!
### (Leviticus 25:8-12)

Too often, the Mosaic Law is viewed with 21st century eyes and is not sufficiently appreciated for the pivotal and normative role it played in the lives of our faith's ancestors. As Samuel Balentine writes about the Holiness Code of **Leviticus (18:1–24:9)**, "[It is] an integral part of the instructions that under gird God's covenantal relationship with Israel" (193). In addition to the many prohibitions of the Law in general and in the Holiness Code, God included many positive injunctions and did not neglect celebrations such as the Sabbath year (just prior

to this lesson, explained in **25:2–7**). In this climactic portion of Leviticus, the Jubilee year is in focus, which is the ultimate Sabbath year. God's ongoing desire for liberty and justice for all continues in the laws regarding the Jubilee **(see also Exodus 23:10–11 and Deuteronomy 15:1–6)**.

The concept of crop rotation was unknown in pre-Deuteronomic times, but God knew all about soil depletion and it was embedded in the Law, including miraculous provision during the land Sabbaths. Even while oblivious to modern farming techniques, if Israel obeyed God and trusted Him, He would provide for them. The lesson revolves around obedience regarding giving the land a Sabbath rest and culminating in the ultimate Sabbath rest, the Jubilee, which in turn expands into lessons on justice for God's people.

### God Restores His People
### (Leviticus 25:8-12)

**8 And thou shalt number seven sabbaths of years unto thee, seven times seven years; and the space of the seven sabbaths of years shall be unto thee forty and nine years. 9 Then shalt thou cause the trumpet of the jubile to sound on the tenth day of the seventh month, in the day of atonement shall ye make the trumpet sound throughout all your land. 10 And ye shall hallow the fiftieth year, and proclaim liberty throughout all the land unto all the inhabitants thereof: it shall be a jubile unto you; and ye shall return every man unto his possession, and ye shall return every man unto his family. 11 A jubile shall that fiftieth year be unto you: ye shall not sow, neither reap that which groweth of itself in it, nor gather the grapes in it of thy vine undressed. 12 For it is the jubile; it shall be holy unto you: ye shall eat the increase thereof out of the field.**

In the prelude to this lesson, God expanded the Sabbath rest for people to include a Sabbath rest for the land (**Leviticus 25:1–7**). People rested every seventh day, and the land now would rest every seven years. In such a year, none would starve as the land would still produce naturally (**verses 6–7**) and all were welcome to enjoy its bounty. As the lesson opens, the Sabbath year itself now is extended to seven cycles, each lasting seven years, after which, in the 50th year, a type of super Sabbath would ensue, appropriately named the Year of Jubilee. The Sabbath was held in very high regard as the sign of the Mosaic Covenant (**Exodus 31:12–17; Ezekiel 20:12**). A seventh Sabbath would invoke an even higher respect, and a Jubilee year would be a high point in the life of an Israelite.

**Leviticus 25:9** specifies the day and month for the blowing of the shofar "trumpet," proclaiming the commencement of the ultimate Sabbath. There are two uses for the word "jubile" in Hebrew. The first in **Leviticus 25** is in the phrase "trumpet of the jubile" and it means "a shout or blast of warning or joy." The announcement appropriately came on the Day of Atonement, which was a somber occasion for national repentance that continues to the present. It appears that God's plans and schedule put people—especially sellers and creditors—in the right frame of mind for generosity. There is an indication in **2 Chronicles 36:21** that the Jubilees and Sabbaths occasionally were not observed. (**See also Isaiah 61:1; Jeremiah 34:8, 15, 17; Ezekiel 46:17** for releasing of those enslaved for debt.)

"Hallow" in Hebrew means to consecrate or sanctify. To "hallow the fiftieth year" is to make the entire year holy, to set it apart, as God's people are to be holy and set apart (**Leviticus 20:26**). In this use, "liberty throughout all the land" refers to the mass relief regarding land mortgages, which many would have undertaken (as many still do) to survive hard economic times. The "jubile" in **25:10** means "to lead, bring, or carry." Put together, the jubilee trumpet is sounded to carry forth the joyful news. In the Year of Jubilee, so appropriately named, there would be much expected celebration as properties were either reclaimed or repurchased, and those who had been forced to move now could come back home.

It must be noted that such national sharing and communal wealth redistribution was a far cry from communism, which is government-forced redistribution. By the same token, New Testament communal sharing also was not communism (**Acts 4:32**). A social unit as small as a family can have unity when all are in agreement; likewise, Israel enjoyed God's blessing when everyone for the most part obeyed and engaged properly with the Levitical Jubilee. As time passed, the more self-seeking people everywhere became, including Israelites, the less the passages were observed.

"Holy unto you" in **verse 12** is another reminder that this is part of God's Holiness Code and Law, which contains good news along with its prohibitions. No one could harvest, yet everyone could eat, including slaves, the poor, and animals. Not only that, God would see to it that the year prior to the Jubilee yielded an abundant enough crop to sustain them through the Jubilee year and until the harvest of the following year—a total of three years. At the same time, it was not entirely a vacation, as the law was to be read to the people, perhaps resembling a kind of national year of study (**see Deuteronomy 31:10–13**).

## SEACH THE SCRIPTURES

### QUESTION 1

On what year did Jubilee occur, and what were farmers supposed to do when Jubilee happened?

**"A jubile shall that fiftieth year be unto you: ye shall not sow, neither reap that which groweth of itself in it, nor gather the grapes in it of thy**

vine undressed."

## LIGHT ON THE WORD
### Why Redeem?
In **Leviticus 25:25,** "redeem" is a familiar concept of Old Testament times in the person of the "kinsman-redeemer" **(see Ruth 4:4, 6).** In ancient Israel, the well-being of the community was more important than that of the individual. This theme resonates throughout the Holiness Code.

## II. HELP A BROTHER OR SISTER OUT (Leviticus 25:25, 35-36, 39-40)

Moses informs the people that if a person has become poor and has sold his or her possessions, a family member may come and redeem what was sold. We must always know that God has a way to restore us. Even when we have given up our best and given our all, God can restore us.

### May I Help You
### (verses 25, 35-36, 39-40)?
**25 If thy brother be waxen poor, and hath sold away some of his possession, and if any of his kin come to redeem it, then shall he redeem that which his brother sold.**

**25:35 And if thy brother be waxen poor, and fallen in decay with thee; then thou shalt relieve him: yea, though he be a stranger, or a sojourner; that he may live with thee. 36 Take thou no usury of him, or increase: but fear thy God; that thy brother may live with thee.**

**25:39 And if thy brother that dwelleth by thee be waxen poor, and be sold unto thee; thou shalt not compel him to serve as a bondservant: 40 But as an hired servant, and as a sojourner, he shall be with thee, and shall serve thee unto the year of jubile:**

Three specific cases are presented in **Leviticus 25:25, 35–36, and 39–40.** In each case, there is a person who has fallen on hard times. In today's volatile economic climate, many have lost their homes to foreclosure. What if America had a Jubilee year, where all would have the right (or their descendants) to repurchase, refinance, or "redeem" their home at a fair and just price?

"Usury," found in **verse 36,** in Hebrew means the added charge of interest, which is forbidden in the Jubilee year. Even in the majority of normal years, general protections for the poor were in place, of which any excessive interest was prohibited **(see Deuteronomy 23:20; Ezekiel 18:8; 22:12).** In ancient times (as today), interest on loans was collected in advance, and if the loan was not paid off on time, more interest was added. Since many borrowers could never repay the accruing total, they often became indentured servants.

In this second case (which includes **Leviticus 25:37–38**), rather than a home having been sold, someone had been forced to surrender the property's title to a creditor but remained as a tenant or renter, working off his debt by tending his own crops. Unlike greedy modern financial institutions that evict families without showing an ounce of compassion, the people of God, who had been set free from slavery, did not, in turn, exploit their fellow Israelites, and the Holiness Code ensured that this would not happen. In **verse 36,** a kind of no-interest loan is granted—out of fear of God—so that the unity of God's people might not be broken. Imagine this in the modern world!

In another variation of the same case, the owner who is unable to maintain his payments or work off his debt often would become a "bondservant" to the creditor. In Hebrew, it means slave but not in the anachronistic (old-fashioned) sense. The creditor would "own" him, much like the term continues in use even today. For the Israelites, however, anything more than financially driven indentured servitude was not to be permitted. Bellinger writes, "The notion of one Israelite owning another and putting the slave to hard service is anathema" (153). While, technically, servitude to repay a debt is a form of slavery, what was prohibited was the element of harshness. Rather, whatever the person was able to earn was to be applied to his debt, and he was not to be mistreated. Also, his "contract" could not be unending—as many today experience hopeless indebtedness, where they will never be free of the debt regardless of how long or hard they work.

At the onset of the Year of Jubilee, this debtor is relieved of the outstanding balance. When God's Word includes "all the inhabitants," it means it literally. "Times of economic difficulties and the intent to mitigate such circumstances and break the spiral into poverty motivate these rules," writes Bellinger (154). This inherent justice for all stands in stark contrast to today's world where credit card companies and other lenders refuse to retract exorbitant rates and other fees, even in a severe recession.

## QUESTION 2
Why did God want the Israelites to help the poor?

**He wanted them to practice loving their neighbor as themselves—They were to treat the poor just as they wanted to be treated in similar circumstances. Answers will vary.**

## LIGHT ON THE WORD
### A Debt Relationship with a Gentile
The third case is similar to the others but involves a debt relationship with a Gentile. Amazingly, the same basic proscription applies even to non-Israelites, that the Israelite be released in the Year of Jubilee.

## III. REDEEM (Leviticus 25:47-48)

The biblical scholar, Balentine, offers this insight: "Israelites must not be treated harshly; they are servants to God alone and owe ultimate allegiance to no other power" (197). **Verse 49** has an interesting statement that a slave might amass the funds to redeem himself, which speaks to the much different status of slaves in ancient times compared to the modern association with the word. In a sense, it was not a lot different from modern contracts, which "bind" one to another for the term of the contract.

### Buy Back One's Relative
### (verses 47-48)
**47 And if a sojourner or stranger wax rich by thee, and thy brother that dwelleth by him wax poor, and sell himself unto the stranger or sojourner by thee, or to the stock of the stranger's family: 48 After that he is sold he may be redeemed again; one of his brethren may redeem him:**

When they sold themselves to someone who was rich, slaves could be bought back or redeemed by family members or persons who were willing to pay the price. God will and has made provision for us to be spiritually redeemed. Jesus paid the price for our salvation and redeemed us from a path of unrighteousness.

## SEARCH THE SCRIPTURES
### QUESTION 3
Who was to redeem an Israelite who was sold to a sojourner or stranger?

**"One of his brethren may redeem him."**

## LIGHT ON THE WORD
### God, Our Deliverer?
God brought the Israelites out of Egypt, and He expected them to serve Him only—He was to be their only God. We must also remember

our deliverance and whom we are to honor with our lives. God is the One we owe our all to for everything that He has done for us, and He is to be our one true God.

## IV. GOD IS OUR DELIVERER
### (Leviticus 25:55)

**Verse 47** supports **verse 55**—God delivered Israel, Israel belongs to God, and Israel's allegiance belongs to none other (**see also verse 53**). The rationale was clean and simple: because God is the Lord and it was His will. Any non-Israelite who wished to contest the Hebrew Scriptures surely would be quickly reminded of how things had gone for Israel's enemies through the years. Since the God of the Old Testament is the same God of the New Testament, one would expect similar principles to be found in both testaments. Consider the close parallel here with **Colossians 4:1**: "Masters, give unto your servants that which is just and equal; knowing that ye also have a Master in heaven."

### God Calls His People to Holiness
### (Leviticus 25:55)
**55 For unto me the children of Israel are servants; they are my servants whom I brought forth out of the land of Egypt: I am the LORD your God.**

God calls His people to holiness, which involves horizontal relationships with others. God instituted the Year of Jubilee at a time when liberty and justice for all was embedded in the law of the land. Among its inherent provisions for the land were those involving crop rotation, not allowing anyone to ever be indebted for a lifetime. There was also a forbidding of the kind of enslavement as they had experienced in Egypt; and, further, no one would be permitted to mistreat others, even enemies, or God would judge them because of His perfect compassion (for the oppressed) and justice (for oppressors).

## QUESTION 4
Why did God institute Jubilee?

**He called His people to holy living—He is the LORD their and our God. Answers will vary.**

## LIGHT ON THE WORD

### God Is the True Owner of All Properties!
It is interesting to note that even if the people fully obeyed the Jubilee, it would not work without God's blessing of the fallow ground the year prior. While it is a false gospel to "give to get," there is truth in the reality that the obedient will be aligned for more blessings than the disobedient. The Old Testament is replete with examples of both.

Not only were mortgages renegotiated to return the land to the original owners or to assist with interest free loans to help reunite owners with property, but the Year of Jubilee also was a yearlong vacation from work, during which both planting and harvesting ceased. Ultimately, the message from God is a reminder that even landowners and property owners, in reality, are only stewards or custodians, dwelling on God's land and God's property—all of creation belongs to Him (see **verse 23**, "the land is mine").

## BIBLE APPLICATION

**AIM: That your students will begin to understand that God is their Deliverer, too.**

### When Believers Are in Captivity....
Captivity sometimes comes in the lives of Christians. We must know that God is still on our side and in due season He will deliver us. Our mission is to continue to believe God, trust God, and know that everything will work out for our good.

## STUDENTS' RESPONSES

**AIM: That your students will practice generosity toward others.**

### The Prosperity of the Whole Earth Is in God's Hands

The principles of not taking advantage of one another, of looking out for the poor, and of acting generously out of fear and reverence for God are still wise attitudes and practices. We are still aliens who only own what we own temporarily; this is still God's creation, and He still controls the crops, the weather, and indeed the prosperity of the whole earth.

## PRAYER

Dear LORD, thank You for all that You have provided for us on this earth. Help us to always remember that we are just stewards and should always be willing to share with those who are less fortunate. In Jesus' Name we pray. Amen.

## DIG A LITTLE DEEPER

Here in the United States we are facing a business and household debt crisis that has only been exacerbated by the recent Coronavirus shut-downs. Now, with sky-high unemployment, many Americans cannot even pay on the interest, much less service their debt. As the public falls further and further behind, the country seems to be teetering on the edge of a depression.

As early as March 2020 Michael Hudson, a professor of economics at the University of Missouri–Kansas City, advocated for a debt jubilee in the op-ed pages of The Washington Post. Prof. Hudson reminded readers that after the subprime mortgage crisis of 2007–2008, the American government bailed out the banks, but allowed middle- and working-class Americans to sink in debt. The situation was exacerbated by radical home devaluation and a "jobless" recovery. Much of the debt incurred persists to this day. But this new crisis affords an opportunity for the government to be more proactive, and avoid another decade of stagnation. Hudson explained that only bad debts would have to be cancelled outright; the heavy lifting could be done by subsidizing interest accruals, late fees and penalties for most people.

In the face of the world-wide economic disaster, debts are being incurred that objectively will never be repaid. The numbers are astronomical, and if all the debtors defaulted, it would be catastrophic for their creditors as well. We may need to implement the biblical principle of jubilee to avoid the collapse of the American economy. Moreover, we need to discuss this issue with our friends, neighbors and church families.

Ref.:

Hudson, Michael. "A Debt Jubilee Is the Only Way to Avoid a Depression." The Washington Post, March 21, 2020.

## HOW TO SAY IT

Levite. LE-vīt.

## DAILY HOME BIBLE READINGS

### MONDAY
Turning Back from Repentance
(Jeremiah 34:8–17)

### TUESDAY
If You Return to Me
(Nehemiah 1:5–11)

### WEDNESDAY
Walking at Liberty
(Psalm 119:41–48)

### THURSDAY
The Spirit and Freedom
(2 Corinthians 3:12–18)

### FRIDAY
When Liberty Becomes a Stumbling Block
(1 Corinthians 8)

### SATURDAY
The Perfect Law of Liberty
(James 1:19–27)

### SUNDAY
Proclaiming Liberty throughout the Land
(Leviticus 25:8–12, 25, 35–36, 39–40, 47–48, 55)

## PREPARE FOR NEXT SUNDAY

Read **Deuteronomy 10:12-22; 16:18-20,** and next week's lesson "The Heart of the Law."

**Sources:**
Balentine, Samuel E. Leviticus. Interpretation: A Bible Commentary for Teaching and
Preaching. Louisville, KY: John Knox Press, 2002. 193–97.

Bellenger, W. H., Jr. Leviticus, Numbers. Old Testament Series. New International
Biblical Commentary. Peabody, MA: Hendrickson Publishers, 2001. 140–54.

Brown, David, A. R. Fausset, and Robert Jamieson. A Commentary, Critical and Explanatory on Old and New Testaments. Logos Bible Software.

Evans, Tony. Tony Evans' Book of Illustrations. Chicago, IL: Moody Publishers, 2009. 113–14.

Hebrew and Greek Lexicons. Bible Study Tools.com. http://www.biblestudytools.com/lexicons (accessed November 8, 2010).

Harris, R. Laird. Genesis, Exodus, Leviticus, Numbers. The Expositor's Bible Commentary, vol. 2. Edited by Frank E. Gaebelein. Grand Rapids, MI: Zondervan, 1990. 632–40.

MacArthur, John. The MacArthur Study Bible: NASB. Nashville, TN: Thomas Nelson, 2006. 150–53.

Merriam-Webster Online Dictionary. Merriam-Webster, Inc. http://www.merriam-webster.com (accessed November 8, 2010).

Douglas, James D., et al., eds. The New Bible Dictionary. London, U.K.: InterVarsity Press, 1962. 794–99, 1120–21.

Old and New Testament Concordances, Lexicons, Dictionaries, Commentaries, Images, and Bible Versions. Blue Letter Bible.org. http://www.blueletterbible.org/ (accessed July 10, 2010).

Passage Lookup. Bible Gateway.com. http://www.biblegateway.com/passage (accessed January 28, 2011).

## COMMENTS / NOTES:

_____

_____

_____

_____

_____

_____

_____

_____

_____

_____

_____

_____

_____

_____

_____

_____

_____

_____

_____

_____

_____

_____

_____

_____

# THE HEART OF THE LAW

**BIBLE BASIS:** Deuteronomy 10:12-22; 16:18-20

**BIBLE TRUTH:** God's love is unconditional, and He is always just.

**MEMORY VERSE:** And now, Israel, what doth the LORD thy God require of thee, but to fear the LORD thy God, to walk in all his ways, and to love him, and to serve the LORD thy God with all thy heart and with all thy soul, To keep the commandments of the LORD, and his statutes, which I command thee this day for thy good? (Deuteronomy 10:12-13, KJV).

**LESSON AIM:** By the end of the lesson, we will: EXPLAIN what our response should be to God's unconditional love; REFLECT on God's love and justice; and EVALUATE how loving and just we are toward others.

**BACKGROUND SCRIPTURES:** Deuteronomy 10:1-22; 16:18-20- Read and incoporate the insights gained from the Background Scriptures into your study of the lesson.

## TEACHER PREPARATION

**MATERIALS NEEDED:** Bibles (several different versions), Quarterly Commentary/Teacher Manual, Adult Quarterly, teaching resources such as charts, worksheets/handouts, paper, pens, and pencils.

## OTHER MATERIALS NEEDED / TEACHER'S NOTES:

_____

_____

## LESSON OVERVIEW

### LIFE NEED FOR TODAY'S LESSON
To apply biblical principles in loving God and others.

### BIBLE LEARNING
As recipients of God's love, we are expected to be fair.

### BIBLE APPLICATION
To live a righteous life that reflects God's love and justice.

### STUDENTS' RESPONSES
Students will evaluate how loving and just they are toward others and develop a plan to align with God's principles.

## LESSON SCRIPTURE

**DEUTERONOMY 10:12-22; 16:18-20 KJV**

**10:12** And now, Israel, what doth the LORD thy God require of thee, but to fear the LORD thy God, to walk in all his ways, and to love him,

**DEUTERONOMY 10:12-22; 16:18-20 AMP**

**12** "And now, Israel, what does the Lord your God require from you, but to fear [and worship]

and to serve the LORD thy God with all thy heart and with all thy soul,

13 To keep the commandments of the LORD, and his statutes, which I command thee this day for thy good?

14 Behold, the heaven and the heaven of heavens is the LORD's thy God, the earth also, with all that therein is.

15 Only the LORD had a delight in thy fathers to love them, and he chose their seed after them, even you above all people, as it is this day.

16 Circumcise therefore the foreskin of your heart, and be no more stiffnecked.

17 For the LORD your God is God of gods, and Lord of lords, a great God, a mighty, and a terrible, which regardeth not persons, nor taketh reward:

18 He doth execute the judgment of the fatherless and widow, and loveth the stranger, in giving him food and raiment.

19 Love ye therefore the stranger: for ye were strangers in the land of Egypt.

20 Thou shalt fear the LORD thy God; him shalt thou serve, and to him shalt thou cleave, and swear by his name.

21 He is thy praise, and he is thy God, that hath done for thee these great and terrible things, which thine eyes have seen.

22 Thy fathers went down into Egypt with threescore and ten persons; and now the LORD thy God hath made thee as the stars of heaven for multitude.

16:18 Judges and officers shalt thou make thee in all thy gates, which the LORD thy God giveth thee, throughout thy tribes: and they shall judge the people with just judgment.

the Lord your God [with awe-filled reverence and profound respect], to walk [that is, to live each and every day] in all His ways and to love Him, and to serve the Lord your God with all your heart and with all your soul [your choices, your thoughts, your whole being],

13 and to keep the commandments of the Lord and His statutes which I am commanding you today for your good?

14 Behold, the heavens and the highest of heavens belong to the Lord your God, the earth and all that is in it.

15 Yet the Lord had a delight in loving your fathers and set His affection on them, and He chose their descendants after them, you above all peoples, as it is this day.

16 So circumcise [that is, remove sin from] your heart, and be stiff-necked (stubborn, obstinate) no longer.

17 For the Lord your God is the God of gods and the Lord of lords, the great, the mighty, the awesome God who does not show partiality nor take a bribe.

18 He executes justice for the orphan and the widow, and [e]shows His love for the stranger (resident alien, foreigner) by giving him food and clothing.

19 Therefore, show your love for the stranger, for you were strangers in the land of Egypt.

20 You shall fear [and worship] the Lord your God [with awe-filled reverence and profound respect]; you shall serve Him and cling to Him [hold tightly to Him, be united with Him], and you shall swear [oaths] by His name.

21 He is your praise and glory; He is your God, who has done for you these great and awesome things which you have seen with your own eyes.

**19.** Thou shalt not wrest judgment; thou shalt not respect persons, neither take a gift: for a gift doth blind the eyes of the wise, and pervert the words of the righteous.

**20.** That which is altogether just shalt thou follow, that thou mayest live, and inherit the land which the LORD thy God giveth thee.

22 Your fathers went down to Egypt, seventy persons [in all], and now the Lord your God has made you as numerous as the stars of heaven.

18 "You shall appoint judges and officers in all your cities (gates) which the Lord your God is giving you, according to your tribes, and they shall judge the people with righteous judgment.

19 You shall not distort justice; you shall not be partial, and you shall not take a bribe, for a bribe blinds the eyes of the wise and perverts the words of the righteous.

20 You shall pursue justice, and only justice [that which is uncompromisingly righteous], so that you may live and take possession of the land which the Lord your God is giving you.

## BIBLICAL DEFINITIONS

### A. Fear (Deuteronomy 10:12, 20)

*yare'* (Heb.)—Dreading punishment or destruction; feeling overwhelming awe, wonder and amazement.

### B. Heart (v. 12) *lebab* (Heb.)—The seat of thought and will.

## LIGHT ON THE WORD

"The book of Deuteronomy concentrates on the events that took place in the final weeks of Moses' life. The major event of that period was the verbal communication of divine revelation from Moses to the people of Israel" (MacArthur Study Bible, 243). These speeches were then written and given to the priests and elders to pass on to future generations of Israel. It is estimated that they were written somewhere in the 11th month of the 40th year after the Exodus from Egypt. Some other scholars place the time frame from January-February, 1405 B.C. "Having shown the impossibility of self-dependence (**chapter 8**) and the impossibility of spiritual pride in light of her rebellious history (**9:1—10:11**), Moses called Israel to exercise her only option for survival: total commitment to the LORD" (Walvoord, 281).

## TEACHING THE BIBLE LESSON

## LIFE NEED FOR TODAY'S LESSON

**AIM: That your students, through His chosen people, will understand what God expects of them.**

## INTRODUCTION

### God

Known as YHWH (YAHWEH), Lord of Hosts, Almighty, Spirit of the Lord, Holy One, God Most High, Master, Sovereign Lord.

## Israelites

An Israelite can be: (a) a descendant of the patriarch Jacob; (b) a member of the holy and inclusive community of those who follow the God of Israel, keeping the laws divinely revealed to the prophet Moses, without any ethnic identification; (c) a member of the holy and exclusive community of Israel defined by ethnic and religious purity.

## Central Rift Valley

Israel was encamped in the Central Rift Valley to the East of the Jordan River. Referred to as "the plains of Moab", the valley is an area north of the Arnon River across the Jordan River from Jericho.

## BIBLE LEARNING

AIM: That your students will understand how the Israelites were called to walk in God's love and justice.

## I. FEAR THE LORD BY WALKING IN HIS WAYS (Deuteronomy 10:12-22)

Moses lets the Children of Israel know that God requires some things of them. There must be a fear of God because of who He is—His greatness. When the Israelites are instructed to fear God, Moses is not telling them to be afraid. He simply wants them to hold God in awe and submit to Him. We, too, must surrender and submit to God, who should be the Head of our lives. Moses also instructs the people to love God. We know that God is love, and He loved us first. But because of all that God has done for us, we need to love Him in return. And if we truly love Him, we will willingly serve and obey Him. Our love for God will move us to serve Him with our whole heart and soul. And while serving Him, we will have a true desire to walk in all His ways. In addition, when our love for God is pure, it will be our desire to please Him in all that we do. One thing that always pleases

God is our obedience. When we are obedient, we demonstrate our sincere love for God.

### Let Your Love Show (verses 12-22)

**12 And now, Israel, what doth the LORD thy God require of thee, but to fear the LORD thy God, to walk in all his ways, and to love him, and to serve the LORD thy God with all thy heart and with all thy soul. 13 To keep the commandments of the LORD, and his statutes, which I command this day for thy good?**

In essence, Moses' question was, "If you're going to be one of God's people, what does that involve? What does God expect of you?" Then in **verses 12-13,** he listed five responses that honored God's grace to them. The first is to "fear" Him. Fear could mean "dreading punishment or destruction," but just as often, it meant "feeling overwhelming awe, wonder, and amazement." The second meaning fits better here for those who choose to include themselves as one of God's people. Second, Moses said God asked His people "to walk in all his ways" **(verse 12)**. "To walk" indicates the Israelites' actions. The word "ways" could refer literally to "a path or a road," but also figuratively to "habits or behavior." Moses said God wanted His people to model themselves after Him and His behavior toward them in all their relationships **(Ephesians 5:1, NIV)**. These first two instructions parallel Jesus' declaration that the two greatest commandments are to love God with complete devotion and to love your neighbor as yourself **(Deuteronomy 6:5; Leviticus 19:18; Matthew 22:37-39)**.

In **Deuteronomy 10:12,** the third instruction for the Israelites was "to love the LORD thy God" by trusting Him, being thankful for their deliverance from slavery, and His forgiveness of their stubborn rebellion **(9:5-8, 26-27)**.

Moses' fourth instruction in **Deuteronomy 10:12** tells how to express that loving trust and gratitude: "serve the LORD thy God with all thy heart and with all thy soul." It's easy to miss what Moses meant here. In English, we connect the "heart" with feelings. But the Israelites viewed the heart as "the seat of thought and will." The "soul" referred here to a person's seat of human passion and energy. Moses urged the Israelites to show their love for God by faithfully obeying God's will with all their energy and determination.

In **Deuteronomy 10:13,** Moses summed up God's instructions in practical terms: "keep the commandments of the LORD, and his statutes." Commandments gave basic general principles; "statutes" referred to specific ways of applying those laws in various situations. Moses saved the most important truth for last. God said the intent behind all His instructions was "for thy good." God wanted to pattern life among His chosen people on His caring and generous attitude toward them, to create a just world where each of them cared about each other like He cared about them.

**14 Behold, the heavens and the heaven of heavens is the LORD's thy God, the earth also, with all therein is. 15 Only the LORD had a delight in thy fathers to love them, and he chose their seed after them, even you above all people, as it is this day.**

Approximately 3,000 years ago, God inspired Moses to imagine a reality beyond what anyone could see or imagine—a heaven beyond the heavens. Moses declared what seldom crosses the minds of most of the world's population even today—that God is the Creator and Owner of all anyone can see and what we can still only imagine.

**Deuteronomy 10:15,** in the KJV, begin with the word "only." At least four modern translations start the verse with "yet" (e.g., NLT, NIV, CEV, and NASB). Both words are weaker than the one Moses used which indicated a complete contrast

with what was just stated. He "had a 'delight' in thy fathers to 'love' them." The word used in this context was often translated as "love," but meant more than strong affection. Rather, it involved being actively committed to what you love. From all God created, He was especially tied to the Israelites, not just to one generation of ex-slaves wandering in the wilderness. God wanted the Israelites to understand that He chose them from everything He made as His chosen people.

## 16. Circumcise therefore the foreskin of your heart, and be no more stiffnecked.

In Israel's early days, circumcision was performed on not only baby boys, but also on young men approaching puberty and marriage as they became part of God's covenant people (**Genesis 17:9-25; 34:14-15; Exodus 4:25-26**). Here circumcision symbolized the intentional commitment to God, the knowing choice of an adult, not an act performed on a helpless newborn infant. To circumcise the heart symbolized a covenantal agreement and was intended to be a permanent, life-altering change, a spiritual transformation in how an Israelite, especially a man, thought of a relationship with God.

Moses used the word "stiffnecked" repeatedly to describe an obstinate unwillingness by Israel toward giving God the love, faith, and obedience His grace toward them deserved (**Exodus 32:9; 33:5; Deuteronomy 9:6,13**).

**10:17 For the LORD your God is God of gods and Lord of lords, a great God, a mighty, a terrible, which rewardeth not persons, nor taketh reward. 18 He doth execute the judgment of the fatherless and widow, and loveth the stranger, in giving him food and raiment.**

Moses declared that many kings exerted lordly power over peoples and nations, but the

Israelites' God was "Lord Supreme" of all other lords. Here Moses explained the reasons for that claim. Their LORD was the only true God, not a minor god, and thus "great" in the extent of His influence (see Deuteronomy 11:7). "Mighty" was used in Deuteronomy 10:17 to describe a warrior in battle whose breadth of power could overcome whatever opposition he faced (Psalm 65:5-8a). The word "terrible" (or "awesome," NKJV) in Deuteronomy 10:17 had the basic meaning of "fearful," but here Moses referred to a trusting awe of their God because of His past powerful acts (Exodus 34:10).

Too often their treatment of other Israelites was influenced by the status of people seeking justice or by the possibility of material inducements. Without a father or a husband, children and women were especially vulnerable to abuse and injustice, but when God acts, He does so without any partiality for one person over another. That fairness applied even to the "stranger" a word in verse 18 which is often translated as "foreigner" (NIV). However, it didn't necessarily mean the person wasn't an Israelite. It could refer to an Israelite from another tribe, anyone who was an outsider, someone with no property rights, living temporarily or permanently in their midst. Not only could the outsider expect fair treatment from their God, Moses told them that God "'loveth' the stranger," using the same term he used toward the Israelites in verse 15.

### 19 Love ye therefore the stranger: for ye were strangers in the land of Egypt.

To share in God's holiness required sharing His merciful attitude toward people (Deuteronomy 5:15). Jesus made this the heart of the Gospel: "By this shall all men know that ye are my disciples, if ye have love one to another" (John 13:35). Again using the same word that referred to His love for them, He instructs them to have love for the outsider. He reminds them that for hundreds of years they had been homeless, penniless outsiders in Egypt. They knew the injustice and abuse such people went through (Exodus 2:19-24). The NIV of Deuteronomy 10:19 pinpoints their duty as God's chosen people to embody love for the powerless outsider: "And you are to love those who are foreigners, for you yourselves were foreigners in Egypt."

### 20. Thou shalt fear the LORD thy God: him shalt thou serve, and to him shalt thou cleave, and swear by his name.

To uphold God's awe-inspiring greatness confirmed belief in His fearful power. Faithful pursuit of His expressed will and purposes nailed down the reality of that belief. Taking a sworn oath in the LORD's name declared acceptance of God as their highest authority. Talk about God's grandeur meant little unless it was backed up "in truth or righteousness" (Isaiah 48:1, NIV). In Deuteronomy 10:20, Moses urged them to "cleave" or hold tightly to that belief. Later in Deuteronomy 30:20 (NIV), he charged them to "hold fast to him. For the LORD is your life."

### 10:21 He is thy praise, and he is thy God, that hath done for thee these great and terrible things, which thine eyes have seen. 22 Thy fathers went down into Egypt with threescore and ten persons; and now the LORD thy God hath made thee as the stars of heaven for multitude.

The word "praise" in Deuteronomy 10:21 meant a hymn of praise; the word "hallelujah" is derived from Hebrew. Scholars debate whether the praise mentioned here was for God or Israel. Both were true. God's acts of delivering them from slavery and sustaining them despite hunger, thirst, and enemies brought them wary respect. Yet despite their fearful stubbornness, their lifesaving deliverance came about only because of God's grace through visible acts of power (Exodus 19:4).

Moses reminded them that God had sustained them through years of abusive treatment and multiplied their numbers and strength for a new future. God had braced the Israelites through centuries of slavery and mistreatment for a greater future. By doing so, He demonstrated His great love and power.

## SEARCH THE SCRIPTURES

### QUESTION 1

Why was the treatment of the fatherless, widows, and strangers important to God?

**God wanted the Israelites to remember that they too were once strangers in a foreign land and how they were treated. Since He dispenses justice without partiality He expected them to do the same.**

## LIGHT ON THE WORD

### God's Choice

Moses instructs the people on how to select the judges and officials in the land. He lets them know that God has a say in this selection as well. There are judges that the Lord gives that will provide righteous judgment. We must make sure that we seek God's advice on persons that we put in leadership positions.

## II. GOD'S SPIRIT IN LEADERSHIP (Deuteronomy 16:18-20)

Those who are called to serve must serve through the leading of God's Spirit. God does not want His leaders being bought and bribed by persons who want things to always go their way. There must be justice in the world, and this comes through those who judge with the Spirit of God leading them. Those who are just in their judging will be blessed by God.

### God's Administrators (16:18-20)
**18 Judges and officers shalt thou make thee in all thy gates, which the LORD thy God giveth thee, throughout thy tribes: and they shall judge the people with just judgment.**

This brief passage lays out the guidelines God gave in His covenant with Israel at Mt. Sinai for building a just society (**Exodus 23:1-9**). "Judges and officers" referred to those who decided how to settle disputes and those who enforced judges' decisions. Several modern translations of **Deuteronomy 16:18,** such as NIV, and NKJV say "appoint" judges and officers, which specified intentionally setting persons in a particular place. In other words, both judges and their assistants were to be chosen with care for fairness and honesty.

Moses inserted a reminder that their land was a gift from God. By their covenant with God, they obligated themselves to abide by its laws and apply them to all persons and circumstances (**Exodus 19:8; 23:1-9; 24:3**). The mention in **Deuteronomy 16:18** of "all thy gates" and "throughout thy tribes" shows that God intended to ensure justice both locally and nationally.

**19 Thou shalt not wrest judgment; thou shalt not respect persons, neither take a gift: for a gift doth blind the eyes of the wise, and pervert the words of the righteous.**

The word "wrest" means "to bend or twist something away from its intended use." In other words, God said: "Don't twist My law around to say whatever you want it to say." **Proverbs 17:23** says only a wicked person does that (see, for example, **1 Samuel 8:3**).

To "not respect persons" (**Deuteronomy 16:19**) literally meant "do not . . . show partiality" (NIV). When a judge learned that a dispute involved one of his friends or someone rich or influential from his community, Moses said he should not allow that recognition to influence how he interpreted the law or how it was enforced.

Another warning to judges was not to accept a "gift". Most modern translations such as NIV use the word "bribe" because accepting gifts can often create a sense of obligation on the part of the recipient. Gifts could cause a judge to say what wasn't true or look away from what he or she was smart enough to see wasn't right. Moses' concern was that the influence of personal relationships, social standing, or material reward should never be allowed to undermine justice for all, rich or poor, insiders or outsiders.

**20 That which is altogether just thou shalt follow, that thou mayest live, and inherit the land which the LORD thy God giveth thee.**

Only "justice (that) is a joy to the righteous" could ensure the stability of the community God wanted His chosen people to show the rest of the world (**Proverbs 21:15, NIV**). Only certainty of fairness for all could ensure life at its fullest, not for one generation but for those who inherit what the Israelites left behind. During World War II, Dr. Ralph Sockman wrote, "The task of our generation is to keep faith with the greatness of those who have gone before us so that we shall not betray those who come after us" **(8)**. That was God's will for the Israelites as they approached the opportunity to create a just and godly society.

### QUESTION 2
What did God require of those chosen to be judges or officials?

**God required that judges and officials judge with just judgment, show no partiality, and not pervert the law for personal use. Answers will vary.**

### LIGHT ON THE WORD
### The Greatest Love of All

Our lesson today reiterated that love is sweet, kind, understanding, and love conquers all. God's love for us is so great that He gave His only begotten Son, Jesus, to die for our sins. There is no greater love. If we love God, we will follow His command and serve Him with our hearts and souls. God commands that we love one another, including all of those who have come to live in our community as well.

## BIBLE APPLICATION

**AIM: That your students will understand God's mandate for us to show mercy to others.**

In America, we have many who were not born on American soil but have begun to call America home. We must not mistreat others just because they are foreign to this land. It is our duty to treat everyone with love and kindness, as God has treated us. Sometimes in order to love others, we must strip our hearts of all the baggage that we are carrying: strip our hearts of prejudice; strip our hearts of the stereotypes that hinder us from helping others who do not look like us or speak like us. We must remove all of those unloving things, and allow our hearts to be open to the Lord and all that He is doing around us.

## STUDENTS' RESPONSES

**AIM: That your students will glorify God by walking in love.**

### Showing Love Everywhere You Go
Begin to show love everywhere that you go. Recipients of your love shouldn't always have to be family members or friends. God calls for us to love one another, as He has loved us. That means we must love all of our neighbors, near and far. Love is what makes the world a better place. Let people see the love of God in you each day.

### PRAYER

Father in heaven, I pray to live my life as You require of me according to **Micah 6:8,** "to act justly, and to love mercy, and to walk humbly with my God." I pray to stay close to You and revere Your presence in my life by walking in Your ways. Forgive me for times this week I did not exemplify Your love and mercy to others, and I ask for strength. In Jesus' Name, I pray. Amen.

## DIG A LITTLE DEEPER

Our lesson text posed a challenging question at the outset: "And now, Israel, what does the LORD your God require of you?" Writer and Bible teacher Samuel Whitefield posed the same question in his new work What Does God Want? Aligning Your Life with God's Desire (OneKing, Inc., 2020). It is the first part of a series on discipleship, and it explains through scripture that our Heavenly Father's greatest interest is in His Son and His Son's people. Whitefield therefore argues that If we share God's zeal, we will give our lives to make disciples. In the language of **Deuteronomy 10,** our love for God is reflected by our love for others. If we fully align our lives to God's purposes, Whitefield explains, we will live lives worthy of emulation, and we will inspire others to imitate us as we imitate Christ. It is a quick read and easy to digest. Find What Does God Want? at your local bookstore or library.

Ref:

Whitefield, Samuel. What Does God Want? Aligning Your Life with God's Desire. Grandview, MO: OneKing Publishing, 2020.

## HOW TO SAY IT

| | |
|---|---|
| Amorite. | AM-uh-rit. |
| Ashtoreth. | ASH-tuh-reth. |
| Balak. | BAY-lak. |
| Bashan. | BAY-shuhn. |
| Chemosh. | KEE-mosh. |
| Moab. | 'mō-ab. |
| Molech. | MOH-lok. |

### DAILY HOME BIBLE READINGS

**MONDAY**
God of Gods, Lord of Lords
(Psalm 136:1-9)

**TUESDAY**
Spiritual Matters of the Heart
(Romans 2:25-29)

**WEDNESDAY**
God's Faithfulness and Justice
(Romans 3:1-9)

**THURSDAY**
Hold Fast to the Traditions
(2 Thessalonians 2:13-17)

**FRIDAY**
What the Lord Requires
(Micah 6:1-8)

**SATURDAY**
Just and True Are Your Ways
(Revelation 15:1-4)

**SUNDAY**
Loving God and Justice
(Deuteronomy 10:12-22; 16:18-20)

## PREPARE FOR NEXT SUNDAY

Read **1 Samuel 7:3–11, 15–17** and next week's lesson "Samuel Administers Justice."

**Sources:**

Bible Pronunciation Chart. Better Days Are Coming.com. http://www.betterdaysarecoming/bible/pronunciation.html (accessed January 29, 2011).

Brown, Francis, et al. The New Brown-Driver-Briggs-Gesenius Hebrew and English Lexicon. Peabody, MA: Hendrickson Publishers, 1985.

Evans, Tony. Tony Evans' Book of Illustrations. Chicago, IL: Moody Publishers, 2009.
199.

Hebrew and Greek Lexicons. Bible Study Tools.com. http://www.biblestudytools.com/lexicons (accessed November 8, 2010).

Mayes, A. D. H. New Century Bible: Deuteronomy. London, England: Morgan, Marshall
& Scott Publications, 1979. 207-212, 264-265.

Sockman, Ralph W. Date with Destiny: A Preamble to Christian Culture. New York, NY: Abingdon-Cokesbury Press, 1944. 8.

Takadi, Midori. "Jasper, John J. (1812-1901)." Black Past.org. http://www.blackpast.org/?q=aah/jasper-john-j-1812-1901 (accessed January 29, 2011).

Von Rad, Gerhard. The Old Testament Library: Deuteronomy, A Commentary. Philadelphia, PA: Westminster Press, 1966. 83-84, 114-115.

Walvoord, John F., and Roy B. Zuck. The Bible Knowledge Commentary: An Exposition of the Scriptures, Old Testament. Wheaton, IL: Victor Books, 1985. 281. Logos Bible Software – Dallas Theological Seminary.

## COMMENTS / NOTES:

# SAMUEL ADMINISTERS JUSTICE

**BIBLE BASIS:** 1 Samuel 7:3–11, 15–17

**BIBLE TRUTH:** God hears the prayers of the righteous.

**MEMORY VERSE:** And Samuel took a sucking lamb, and offered it for a burnt offering wholly unto the LORD: and Samuel cried unto the LORD for Israel: and the LORD heard him (1 Samuel 7:9,KJV).

**LESSON AIM:** By the end of the lesson, we will: KNOW the power of prayer and the purpose of praying for justice; SENSE God's call for justice in our community; and PRAY for justice in our community (the country).

**BACKGROUND SCRIPTURES:** 1 Samuel 7:3-17-Read and incorporate the insights gained from the Background Scriptures into your study of the lesson.

## TEACHER PREPARATION

**MATERIALS NEEDED:** Bibles (several different versions), Quarterly Commentary/Teacher Manual, Adult Quarterly, teaching resources such as charts, worksheets/handouts, paper, pens, and pencils.

**OTHER MATERIALS NEEDED / TEACHER'S NOTES:**

_____

_____

## LESSON OVERVIEW

### LIFE NEED FOR TODAY'S LESSON
To apply the power of prayer for God's justice in our communities.

### BIBLE LEARNING
To learn how Samuel used the power of prayer to bring God's justice to his nation.

### BIBLE APPLICATION
To begin to understand how prayer is a tool God gives us to bring His will on earth as it is in heaven.

### STUDENTS' RESPONSES
Students will discern opportunities to strategically pray for God's justice in. their community (and the country).

## LESSON SCRIPTURE

### 1 SAMUEL 7:3-11, 15-17 KJV

**3** And Samuel spake unto all the house of Israel, saying, If ye do return unto the LORD with all your hearts, then put away the strange

### 1 SAMUEL 7:3-11, 15-17 AMP

**3** Then Samuel said to all the house of Israel, "If you are returning to the Lord with all your heart, remove the foreign gods and the gods and Ashtaroth from among you, and prepare your hearts unto the LORD, and serve him only: and he will deliver you out of the hand of the Philistines.

4 Then the children of Israel did put away Baalim and Ashtaroth, and served the LORD only.

5 And Samuel said, Gather all Israel to Mizpeh, and I will pray for you unto the LORD.

6 And they gathered together to Mizpeh, and drew water, and poured it out before the LORD, and fasted on that day, and said there, We have sinned against the LORD. And Samuel judged the children of Israel in Mizpeh.

7 And when the Philistines heard that the children of Israel were gathered together to Mizpeh, the lords of the Philistines went up against Israel. And when the children of Israel heard it, they were afraid of the Philistines.

8 And the children of Israel said to Samuel, Cease not to cry unto the LORD our God for us, that he will save us out of the hand of the Philistines.

9 And Samuel took a sucking lamb, and offered it for a burnt offering wholly unto the LORD: and Samuel cried unto the LORD for Israel; and the LORD heard him.

10 And as Samuel was offering up the burnt offering, the Philistines drew near to battle against Israel: but the LORD thundered with a great thunder on that day upon the Philistines, and discomfited them; and they were smitten before Israel.

11 And the men of Israel went out of Mizpeh, and pursued the Philistines, and smote them, until they came under Beth-car.

7:15 And Samuel judged Israel all the days of his life.

Ashtaroth (pagan goddesses) from among you and direct your hearts to the Lord and serve Him only; and He will rescue you from the hand of the Philistines."

4 So the Israelites removed the Baals and the Ashtaroth and served the Lord alone.

5 Samuel said, "Gather all Israel together at Mizpah and I will pray to the Lord for you."

6 So they gathered at Mizpah, and drew water and poured it out before the Lord, and fasted on that day and said there, "We have sinned against the Lord." And Samuel judged the Israelites at Mizpah.

7 Now when the Philistines heard that the Israelites had gathered at Mizpah, the lords (governors) of the Philistines went up against Israel. And when the Israelites heard it, they were afraid of the Philistines.

8 And the sons of Israel said to Samuel, "Do not cease to cry out to the Lord our God for us, so that He may save us from the hand of the Philistines."

9 So Samuel took a nursing lamb and offered it as a whole burnt offering to the Lord; and Samuel cried out to the Lord for Israel and the Lord answered him.

10 As Samuel was offering up the burnt offering, the Philistines approached for the battle against Israel. Then the Lord thundered with a great voice that day against the Philistines and threw them into confusion, and they were defeated and fled before Israel.

11 And the men of Israel came out of Mizpah and pursued the Philistines, and struck them down as far as [the territory] below Beth-car.

7:15 Now Samuel judged Israel all the days of his life.

**16.** And he went from year to year in circuit to Beth-el, and Gilgal, and Mizpeh, and judged Israel in all those places.

**16** He used to go annually on a circuit to Bethel, Gilgal, and Mizpah, and he judged Israel in all these places.

**17.** And his return was to Ramah; for there was his house; and there he judged Israel; and there he built an altar unto the LORD.

**17** Then he would return to Ramah, because his home was there; and there he judged Israel, and there he built an altar to the Lord.

## BIBLICAL DEFINITIONS

A. **Pray (1 Samuel 7:5)** *palal* (Heb.)—To plead, to intervene, to interpose, to arbitrate, or even judge.

B. **Sinned (v. 6)** *chata'* (Heb.)—Missed the mark; erred.

## LIGHT ON THE WORD

Samuel was a judge, prophet, and priest who was obedient to God. He was familiar with the power of God. Samuel knew that the Israelites were worshiping false gods; they were not committed to the true and living God.

The Israelites had suffered defeat by the Philistines when they had tried to use the power of the Ark of the Covenant to gain victory in battle. The Lord had given the Children of Israel strict instructions concerning the Ark. Instead of keeping the Ark in the most holy place, they were disobedient by moving it to the battlefield. Earlier, God had killed the men of Beth-shemesh because they had gazed upon the Ark. The Israelites had experienced 20 years of sorrow because they had not repented of their sins. Samuel urged the Israelites to repent and called them to meet him at Mizpah so that he could pray on their behalf. The Israelites believed that God had left them, but they did not do anything about it. Samuel urged them to make a change—to repent.

## TEACHING THE BIBLE LESSON

### LIFE NEED FOR TODAY'S LESSON

**AIM: That your students will see through Israel why they must repent from sin and walk in obedience to God's Word.**

## INTRODUCTION

### Samuel

Samuel was the son of Elkanah and Hannah. He served as a prophet, judge, and priest. He was born in answer to the prayers of his barren mother, Hannah. Hannah gave Samuel to Eli, the high priest at Shiloh, for dedicated service to God. When Samuel was dedicated to God, he listened to God. Samuel was the last judge in Israel, and he encouraged the Israelites to commit themselves to God and serve Him only.

### Mizpah

The name means "watchtower" or "lookout." Samuel called the Israelites to come to Mizpah to pray and fast in sorrow for their sins. Mizpah was the capital of Judah after the fall of Jerusalem. Later, Saul would be chosen at Mizpah as Israel's first king. Saul had the blessings but not the approval of God and Samuel.

### Ashtaroth

The name of the Canaanite goddess of fertility, sexuality, and war, she was the companion of Baal. Ashtaroth worship usually involved prostitution. The ground was believed to be fertile when she was worshiped in sexual rituals.

## BIBLE LEARNING

**AIM: That your students will understand the importance of turning away from anything that does not please God.**

## I. A NATION IN SIN (1 Samuel 7:3-7)

Eleazar, whose name means "God is power" or "God is help," had been selected to take care of the Ark of the Covenant. The Ark was taken to a city named Kirjath-jearim, which was near the battlefield because the Israelites wanted to be victorious in battle. Unfortunately, their faith was focused on the Ark of the Covenant, not on God. Therefore, they believed it would bring them victory if it was nearby when they fought the Philistines. In essence, the Ark had become an idol for them. God, Himself should have been the focus of their faith, not the Ark. Because God will not tolerate such misplaced faith, they were defeated. Because of this defeat, the Israelites realized that God was no longer blessing them. They needed to repent and return to God. Samuel, who was judge, called the assembly at Mizpah. He directed the Israelites to pray and ask God for forgiveness.

### Samuel Leads Israel to Repent (verses 3-7)

**3. And Samuel spake unto all the house of Israel, saying, If ye do return unto the LORD with all your hearts, then put away the strange gods and Ashtaroth from among you, and prepare your hearts unto the LORD, and serve him only: and he will deliver you out of the hand of the Philistines.**

The Ark of the Covenant was returned to Israel and brought to Kirjath-jearim, "and all the house of Israel lamented after the LORD" **(verse 2).** Afterward, Samuel, functioning as judge, prophet, and priest (and king) over God's chosen people, sets forth the condition for deliverance, whereby covenantal fellowship may be restored with the true and living God. That covenantal fellowship had been broken because of their sin. The phrase in **verse 3** "with all your hearts" in Hebrew is meaning "seat of emotions and passions; the seat of courage" (Strong, 1994).

As judge, Samuel wants the Israelites to give their hearts back to the one true God. He guides the house of Israel through the prescription of consecrating themselves before God. As God's chosen people, they must walk in obedience to the stipulations in order to receive His promise of mercy and favor **(Exodus 19:5).** First, then, they must repent and turn from worshiping their detestable idols. The word "Ashtaroth" is the plural in Hebrew for Ashtoreth, the goddess of fertility and sexual union; consequently, there were sexual rites surrounding her worship at her many shrines in the land of Canaan.

**4. Then the children of Israel did put away Baalim and Ashtaroth, and served the LORD only.**

God fashions, through tests and discipline, the hearts and minds of His people as they turn toward Him. After a period of estrangement because of their rebellion and apostasy, during which the promise of blessing and protection is deferred, the Israelites return to their God as prodigals—not just agreeing to abide by the dictates of God's Law, but wholeheartedly committing themselves to have no other god and to serve Him only. They readily comply with Samuel's call to repentance. "Baalim" is the plural form for the son of Dagon, the god of the sky who brought forth thunder and rain to fertilize the earth. Of the many strange gods, Baal and Ashtoreth were perhaps the most popular and therefore the most prevalent.

**5. And Samuel said, Gather all Israel to Mizpeh, and I will pray for you unto the LORD.**

Samuel directs the people to gather at Mizpeh ("Mizpah" in other translations) that he might intercede for them before God. Mizpeh, several miles north of Jerusalem, is a familiar setting. It was the place of national assembly where the people of Israel conferred to bring the Benjamites to justice for the atrocity committed against the concubine of a Levite (**see Judges 20:1**). Mizpeh would also be the place for the national convention of all the tribes of Israel at which Saul would be elected king, and it would become the capital of Judah after the fall of Jerusalem (**1 Samuel 10:17; 2 Kings 25:21–24**).

**6. And they gathered together to Mizpeh, and drew water, and poured it out before the LORD, and fasted on that day, and said there, We have sinned against the LORD. And Samuel judged the children of Israel in Mizpeh.**

That the people would pour water on the ground is an acknowledgment that they deserved to be cursed for violating the terms of the covenant—they had sinned. In Hebrew, the word "sin" means "miss the mark; to bring into guilt or condemnation or punishment" (Strong, 1994).

But underlying this act is the appeal for mercy and the knowledge that God honors a contrite heart that knows its bankruptcy. He is a merciful God who says that "the soul that sinneth, it shall die" (**Ezekiel 18:4**). But He also provides a legal refuge—with Samuel as His leader and judge of Israel at Mizpeh—whereby He remains true to His word; some transgressors find refuge by the means of grace He provides. Thus, the people fasted and confessed their sin. The word "fasted" means "abstain(ed) from food" (Strong, 1994). The Israelites felt compelled to also abstain from food in acknowledgment of their sin and repentance.

**7. And when the Philistines heard that the children of Israel were gathered together to Mizpeh, the lords of the Philistines went up against Israel. And when the children of Israel heard it, they were afraid of the Philistines.**

Perhaps the Philistines sensed an opportunity, now that all the Israelites have gathered at Mizpeh, to decimate the Israelites once and for all; or perhaps they felt threatened and mobilized their army. Certainly, the reality of the attack of the enemy becomes more evident when God's people turn away from and against the evil influence of the world. God's way is never without opposition and challenge. In any case, the people are afraid. (Fear is the potential enemy within because it tempts us with getting momentary expediency of relief without waiting on God.)

## SEARCH THE SCRIPTURES
### QUESTION 1
What did Samuel call the people to do in order to receive deliverance from the Philistines?

**Samuel called the people to return to the Lord in their hearts, put away strange gods, and prepare their hearts to serve the Lord only.**

## LIGHT ON THE WORD
### Victorious Through Prayer
The Philistines knew that the Israelites were not gathered at Mizpah for a religious observance; they suspected that the Israelites were united in an uprising. The Philistines planned to attack the Israelites, who wanted Samuel to continue to pray for them. The Israelites wanted Samuel to pray for their victory. At Aphek, they had depended on the Ark for victory. Now the Israelites depended on the power of God for victory.

## II. GOD EXECUTED JUSTICE (1 Samuel 7:8-11, 15-17)

The Philistines had endured a final defeat at

the hands of God. There were no other battles between the Israelites and the Philistines when Samuel was judge. Because of the Israelites' obedience, then, God executed justice through Samuel.

Like the Philistines, we may need to remember the personal victories that God has given us. When we are experiencing difficult moments, the memories will help us to endure. When we remember the victories that God has given us, we can endure the present suffering with confidence. We have faith that God has already given us the victory if we endure.

### Samuel Leads Israel to Victory
### (verses 8-11, 15-17)

**8. And the children of Israel said to Samuel, Cease not to cry unto the LORD our God for us, that he will save us out of the hand of the Philistines.**

The people look to and beseech Samuel, God's provision and chosen instrument, as mediator on their behalf. Samuel, in this sense, is a type of Christ, and the deliverance sought from the Philistines foreshadows the greater deliverance and salvation affected in the Person of Christ.

**9. And Samuel took a sucking lamb, and offered it for a burnt offering wholly unto the LORD: and Samuel cried unto the LORD for Israel; and the LORD heard him.**

Acting as priest, Samuel sacrifices a lamb. The stage is set. The Lord's face and the promise of His mercies are no longer eclipsed by the iniquity of His people. When Samuel cries out, God accepts and answers his prayer.

**10. And as Samuel was offering up the burnt offering, the Philistines drew near to battle against Israel: but the LORD thundered with a great thunder on that day upon the Philistines, and discomfited them; and they were smitten before Israel.**

The Philistines are poised for attack, but the Lord's hand against the Philistines is sure, swift, and unmistakable—they were smitten before Israel. The Israelites—as they had done so many times before, from the day of their liberation from the hand of Pharaoh—see the miracle of what the Lord has done.

**11. And the men of Israel went out of Mizpeh, and pursued the Philistines, and smote them, until they came under Beth-car.**

"Who is this King of glory? the LORD strong and mighty, the LORD mighty in battle" (**Psalm 24:8**). So it is when the battle is the Lord's, and all that is left for the Israelites to do is to pursue the scattered Philistines and slay them.

**1 Samuel 7:15-17.** Samuel judged Israel all the days of his life. And he went from year to year in circuit to Beth-el, and Gilgal, and Mizpeh, and judged Israel in all those places. And his return was to Ramah; for there was his house; and there he judged Israel; and there he built an altar unto the LORD.

God won the battle for the Israelites and He used Samuel until Samuel's death to continue to judge the Israelites. In Hebrew, the word "judged" means ruled, governed; decided about a controversy; exercised judgment. Therefore, Samuel administered justice when he helped the people to repent and turn their hearts back to the true and living God.

### QUESTION 2
What did God do in response to Samuel's prayer and sacrifice and what was the result?

**God heard the prayer and received Samuel's sacrifice and gave them victory over the Philistines. Answers will vary.**

## LIGHT ON THE WORD

### Follow God, No Excuses

The Israelites desired to remove any obstacles or sins that had led to their defeat and subjection by the Philistines. They needed to reaffirm their covenantal loyalty to God to receive His blessings. Samuel prayed to God on the Israelites' behalf, and God saved them—He brought justice.  As with Samuel, our commitment to God should be continual. If we are distracted and place anything before God, we should seek Him and repent. When we follow God, there will be distractions; but we must focus on Him. We can easily make excuses, but we must follow God. When we seek God daily with a sincere heart, we can endure and keep our focus on Him.

## BIBLE APPLICATION

**AIM: That your students will recognize God's love and respond by living a life that pleases Him.**

As humans, we live in a world of sin. As believers, we serve a loving God, who hears our prayers and knows our need for help. When we are disobedient, we cannot stay in our current state. We must make a change. We must repent—turn from our sin, and return to God. If you know someone who has stopped seeking God's guidance, pray for that person. Encourage him or her to return to God.

## STUDENTS' RESPONSES

**AIM: That your students will seek God at all times and encourage others through prayer.**

Seek God at all times. The standards of the world are different from God's standards. Remember that God has complete control; therefore, we can be victorious in all situations. Success defined by the world's standards cannot compare with success as a child of God. While we live in the world, we can be strengthened to endure difficult situations by associating with others who will encourage and pray for us.

Seek out a Christian group that has community involvement, or support a community group that encourages those who are alone or homeless. We receive strength when we pray for others and encourage them with our actions and lifestyles. Seek to help those in need; by so doing, you are serving God. When you join a group that prays and seeks to help those in need, you will stay encouraged to do God's will.

## PRAYER

Father in heaven, I pray to be steadfast, immovable, always abounding in the work of the Lord. I pray to be more fervent and strategic in prayers for myself and others, and quick to repent of my sins or anything that does not please You. I seek to have a heart that is tender to You, and that I walk in obedience to Your commands. I also pray for my community and our country, to put away our idols and turn our faces back to You. In Jesus' Name, Amen

## DIG A LITTLE DEEPER

Racial justice became a catch phrase even in evangelical churches in 2020, and many believers awoke to the evidence of police violence against communities of color. The Church wanted to pray about the issue but found it difficult to articulate the godly position. For this purpose the American Bible Society released a prayer guide, directing readers to a comprehensive list of scriptures that reveal God's heart regarding racial justice. If we base our intercessory prayer on these expressions of God's concern for righteousness, we will find our words seasoned with wisdom and relevance. You will find the list of scriptures at the American Bible Society's blogsite (https://news.americanbible.org); download it and meditate over it. Then pray for justice with newfound power and urgency.

Ref.:

Podbury, Nena. "20 Scriptures that Teach Us How to Pray for Justice." American Bible Society News (blog). September 29, 2020. https://news.americanbible.org/blog/entry/prayer-blog/20-scriptures-that-teach-us-how-to-pray-for-justice.

## HOW TO SAY IT

| | |
|---|---|
| Ashtaroth. | ASH-tuh-reth. |
| Mizpah. | MIZ-puh. |
| Philistine. | fuh-LIS-teen. |
| Shiloh. | SHī-lō. |

### DAILY HOME BIBLE READINGS

**MONDAY**
Repent and Turn
(Ezekiel 18:25–32)

**TUESDAY**
An Earnest Petition
(1 Samuel 1:12–20)

**WEDNESDAY**
A Gift to the Lord
(1 Samuel 2:11–21)

**THURSDAY**
A Voice in the Night
(1 Samuel 3:1–14)

**FRIDAY**
A Trustworthy Prophet
(1 Samuel 3:15–4:1a)

**SATURDAY**
A Revered Prophet
(Psalm 99)

**SUNDAY**
A Faithful Judge
(1 Samuel 7:3–11, 15–17)

## PREPARE FOR NEXT SUNDAY

Read **2 Samuel 23:1–7; 1 Chronicles 18:14** and next week's lesson "David Embodies God's Justice."

**Sources:**

Bible Pronunciation Chart. Better Days Are Coming.com. http://www.betterdaysarecoming/bible/pronunciation.html (accessed January 29, 2011),

Hebrew and Greek Lexicons. Bible Study Tools.com. http://www.biblestudytools.com/lexicons (accessed June 18, 2010).

Life Application Study Bible: New Living Translation. Wheaton, IL: Tyndale House Publishers, 1996. 402–18.

Merriam-Webster Online Dictionary. Merriam-Webster, Inc. http://www.merriam-webster.com (accessed October 20, 2010).

Passage Lookup. Bible Gateway.com. http://www.biblegateway.com/passage (accessed January 17, 2011).

Strong, James. New Exhaustive Strong's Numbers and Concordance with Expanded
Greek-Hebrew Dictionary. Seattle, WA: Biblesoft, and International Bible Translators, 1994.

## COMMENTS / NOTES:

_____
_____
_____
_____
_____
_____
_____
_____
_____
_____
_____
_____
_____
_____
_____
_____
_____
_____
_____
_____
_____
_____
_____

# DAVID EMBODIES GOD'S JUSTICE

**BIBLE BASIS:** 2 Samuel 23:1–7; 1 Chronicles 18:14

**BIBLE TRUTH:** God is faithful to His covenant, even when we are not..

**MEMORY VERSE:** So David reigned over all Israel, and executed judgment and justice among all his people (1 Chronicles 18:14, KJV).

**LESSON AIM:** By the end of the lesson, we will: UNDERSTAND the importance of promoting justice and equity in our relationships; BE ASSURED that God has a covenant with us; and BE A VOICE for God and justice in our church and community.

**BACKGROUND SCRIPTURES:** 2 Samuel 22:1, 23:7; 1 Cronicles 9:8-Read and incorporate the insights gained from the Background Scriptures into your study of the lesson.

## TEACHER PREPARATION

**MATERIALS NEEDED:** Bibles (several different versions), Quarterly Commentary/Teacher Manual, Adult Quarterly, teaching resources such as charts, worksheets/handouts, paper, pens, and pencils.

**OTHER MATERIALS NEEDED / TEACHER'S NOTES:**

_____

_____

## LESSON OVERVIEW

### LIFE NEED FOR TODAY'S LESSON
Remember that God has a covenant with us through Jesus Christ.

### BIBLE LEARNING
Learn how David expressed God's love of justice and equity.

### BIBLE APPLICATION
To begin to understand why it is important to promote God's justice and equity in our relationships.

### STUDENTS' RESPONSES
Students will plan how to be a voice for God and justice in their community.

## LESSON SCRIPTURE

| 2 SAMUEL 23:1–7; 1 CHRONICLES 18:14 KJV | 2 SAMUEL 23:1–7; 1 CHRONICLES 18:14 AMP |
| --- | --- |
| 2 Samuel 23:1. Now these be the last words of David. David the son of Jesse said, and the | 23 Now these are the last words of David. David the son of Jesse declares,The man who |

man who was raised up on high, the anointed of the God of Jacob, and the sweet psalmist of Israel, said,

2 The Spirit of the LORD spake by me, and his word was in my tongue.

3 The God of Israel said, the Rock of Israel spake to me, He that ruleth over men must be just, ruling in the fear of God.

4 And he shall be as the light of the morning, when the sun riseth, even a morning without clouds; as the tender grass springing out of the earth by clear shining after rain.

5 Although my house be not so with God; yet he hath made with me an everlasting covenant, ordered in all things, and sure: for this is all my salvation, and all my desire, although he make it not to grow.

6 But the sons of Belial shall be all of them as thorns thrust away, because they cannot be taken with hands:

7 But the man that shall touch them must be fenced with iron and the staff of a spear; and they shall be utterly burnt with fire in the same place.

1 Chron. 18:14 So David reigned over all Israel, and executed judgment and justice among all his people.

was raised on high declares,The anointed of the God of Jacob, And the sweet psalmist of Israel,

2 "The Spirit of the Lord spoke by me, And His word was on my tongue.

3 "The God of Israel, The Rock of Israel spoke to me, 'He who rules over men righteously, Who rules in the fear of God,

4 Is like the morning light when the sun rises, A morning without clouds, When the fresh grass springs out of the earth Through sunshine after rain.'

5 "Truly is not my house so [blessed] with God? For He has made an everlasting covenant with me, Ordered in all things, and secured. For will He not cause to grow and prosper All my salvation and my every wish? Will He not make it grow and prosper?

6 "But the wicked and worthless are all to be thrown away like thorns, Because they cannot be taken with the hand;

7 "But the man who touches them Must be armed with iron and the shaft of a spear, And they are utterly burned and consumed by fire in their place." I Chronicles

18:14 So David reigned over all Israel and administered justice and righteousness for all his people.

## BIBLICAL DEFINITIONS

A. **Anointed (2 Samuel 23:1)** *mashiyach* (Heb.)—A consecrated person, such as a king or priest; can refer to the Messiah.

B. **Just (v. 3)** *tsaddiyq* (Heb.)—Lawful, righteous.

## LIGHT ON THE WORD

God called David a man who followed Him with all his heart (**1 Kings 14:8**). David did some terrible things, but his heart was tender toward

God so that when he sinned, he repented deeply. Before his sin with Bathsheba and his murder of her husband, Uriah, David had a desire to build a beautiful temple for the Lord. God denied his desire because as a warrior David had blood on his hands. But God had a far greater blessing for David. God promised to send Jesus, the eternal King, through the ancestry of David. For a complete account of this story and all the many blessings promised to David, see **2 Samuel 7.**

## TEACHING THE BIBLE LESSON

## LIFE NEED FOR TODAY'S LESSON

**AIM: That your students will learn through King David how to seek the heart of God.**

## INTRODUCTION

### David, the Psalmist

We first meet a teenage David when Samuel anointed him as the future king. The next time we meet him is as a musician. Music seems to have always been a big part of David's life. We can imagine him as he spent long days minding the sheep as he sang and composed songs. He probably took his portable harp with him to the pasturelands. Sometime after his anointing, he sang and played his harp to calm the troubled heart of King Saul. Evidently, the news of his musical talent had reached all the way to the king's palace. As the narrative of David's life is recorded in **1 and 2 Samuel and 1 Chronicles,** we see little of the thoughts in David's mind. But many of the psalms are inscribed to tell us where they fit in David's life and so we enter his thoughts and heart. In today's Scripture passage, he calls himself "the sweet psalmist of Israel" (**2 Samuel 23:1**). Psalms are the prayer and praise songs of the Bible. We .have little idea about the tunes and types of music for the psalms, but the God-inspired words are preserved for us, so we are free to interpret the musical style as fits our culture, history, and personal taste.

### The United Kingdom

Only three kings ruled over the united kingdom of Israel and Judah—King Saul, King David, and King Solomon. Just a little over a thousand years before the birth of Christ (1050 B.C.), Saul was anointed to be king over all of Israel. God had already planned for the Israelites to have a king, but not by setting aside the Lord God as their true King. Tall and impressive Saul was just who people might choose for a king, but soon after his reign began, it became obvious that Saul was going to do things his way, not God's way. Twenty-five years later, David was anointed king, but another 15 years passed before he actually took possession of the kingdom. David reigned as king in Hebron for seven years and overall Israel for 33 years…a total of 40 years (**1 Kings 2:11**), until his son, Solomon, became the king. Solomon reigned for 40 years. He started well, but by marrying 700 wives and having 300 concubines, he was clearly disobedient to the Lord and his heart was turned away from following God. Under Solomon's son, Rehoboam, the kingdom was divided into Israel and Judah and that was the end of the united kingdom.

## BIBLE LEARNING

**AIM: That your students will seek to leave a lasting legacy by living a life that honors God.**

## I. DAVID HONORS GOD

## (2 Samuel 23:1-7)

As our lives here on earth come to an end, every person wants to sum up his or her life at its best. King David was no different. These first seven verses in **2 Samuel 23** are written in the Hebrew form of poetry. This was used often in the Old Testament to make it easier to remember. Until Gutenberg invented the printing press and produced the first printed Bible in 1440, every Bible before that time was hand-copied. Priests and elders in the temple were among the few with access to a Bible (**2 Chronicles 34:14; 2 Kings 22:8–12**). As a result, most people only learned God's Word by hearing it read in worship and classes and then memorizing what they heard (**Exodus 24:7; Deuteronomy 31:11; Nehemiah 8:1–5, 13**). This emphasizes how important the writer of II Samuel thought it was for all Israelites, both priests, and laypeople, to remember David's final words.

### David's Last Words in Tribute to God (23:1-2)

**1 Now these be the last words of David. David the son of Jesse said, and the man who was raised up on high, the anointed of the God of Jacob, and the sweet psalmist of Israel, said, 2 The Spirit of the LORD spake by me, and his word was in my tongue.**

Many nations revere their founders and first great leaders. David was both. He was an unlikely soldier, much less a military leader. He was the youngest of eight sons of Jesse, a shepherd from the village of Bethlehem. His three oldest brothers were already in Israel's army. Four other older brothers were still at home. His father Jesse made use of David to care for his sheep and to carry supplies to replenish the needs of his older brothers in the army (**1 Samuel 17:13–22**).

Yet, God told the prophet, Samuel, that He had chosen young David for a special purpose. In **2 Samuel 23:1** we read that God ordered young David to be "anointed" with oil, marking him as God's choice to become the next king of Israel. Decades later, David had been "raised up" from a simple shepherd and errand boy to his nation's exalted leader. God endowed David with bravery, aptitude as a warrior, and great leadership skills. Being called "the sweet psalmist of Israel" indicates that he was also blessed with musical and poetic talents, as **1 Samuel 16:23 and 2 Samuel 22:1–51** show.

In spite of his moral failings, the memory of what God brought about through David's life at his best symbolized the fulfillment of God's promise through David's ancestors Abraham, Isaac, and Jacob.

**2 Samuel 23:1** begins with "the last words of David." "Words" here referred to human words or statements. **Verse 2** refers to "spake" primarily found in the Old Testament, meaning a message or utterance by God, often with "the LORD" or some other reference to God attached (**1 Samuel 2:30; Amos 6:8**). Many modern versions translate "spake" or, "said," as "oracle" (NIV). This indicates that what David said was not just his opinion of himself, but God's evaluation of his reign as king. Thus, David said, "The Spirit of the LORD spake by me" (**2 Samuel 23:2**).

## SEARCH THE SCRIPTURES

### QUESTION 1

How did David seek to honor God toward the end of his life?

**He spoke directly by the Spirit of God.**

## LIGHT ON THE WORD

### Ruled in Righteousness

Politicians who exercise their offices with integrity and justice sometimes seem to be rare. But David ruled in righteousness because of his relationship with God. The fear of God may be defined as a profound sense of the holiness of God. This fear leads us to worship God and obey Him. Leaders of any sort, who are keenly aware of God's omniscience (all-knowing), His omnipotence (all-powerful), and His omnipresence (everywhere present), would be very careful to do what is right. Such leaders know that God knows everything we think, say, and do. And having such great knowledge of God causes us to desire to please Him and obey Him. We pray that our leaders will rule injustice because they have a true sense of who God is.

## II. GOD'S REIGN THROUGH DAVID (2 Samuel 23:3-4)

No matter how powerful, wealthy, or talented a person becomes, and David certainly was all three, none of us ever escapes the reality that "sin is crouching at the door, it desires to have you" (**Genesis 4:7, NIV; see also 1 Peter 5:8–9a; 1 Corinthians 10:12**). These verses also show that despite the seriousness of our sins, God can speak and work through our lives to bring enrichment to individuals and society as a whole and bring honor to Himself. But, for that to happen, a person must be willing to return to God in repentance as David did (**Psalm 51**).

Leaders who rule with justice are beautiful to see––as beautiful as the sun coming up on a cloudless day, or like the sun coming out after a rainy day. Not only is the sun lovely to look at, but it causes green plants to sprout forth from the earth. Therefore, we are happy to see compassionate and just rulers, but we are also happy with the results of their leadership.

### David's Ruling Justice (2 Samuel 23:3-4)

**3. The God of Israel said, the Rock of Israel spake to me, He that ruleth over men must be just, ruling in the fear of God.**

Once again David emphasized that he was declaring not his own point of view but God's. By calling God "the Rock" he pictured God as a great cliff of protection in the storms of life, a place of security on which to mount a defense against an enemy or an unmovable foundation when crushing problems threatened to wash him away (**2 Samuel 22:1–2; Psalm 61:2–3**). He remains so for today's believers.

In the middle of **2 Samuel 23:3,** David stated God's inventory of the importance of his reign as king. God concludes that as head of state, the most important quality of David's reign was that Israel's governance under him was just. Despite David's moral failings, his reign was characterized by judgments on national issues that were "just" (**See 2 Samuel 8:15; Jeremiah 23:5.**)

What enabled a ruler to do that then, as well as officials in authority today, is a fearful concern for honoring and acting in keeping with God's unchanging nature and values. Righteousness did not require that justice be harsh. Zechariah prophesied of God's revelation of Himself in the coming of His Messiah: "Look, your king is coming to you. He is righteous and victorious, yet he is humble (KJV, "lowly"), riding on a donkey" (**Zechariah 9:9**). Likewise, **Psalm 89:14** declared, "Justice and judgment are the habitation of thy throne: mercy and truth shall go before thy face."

**4. And he shall be as the light of the morning, when the sun riseth, even a morning without clouds; as the tender grass springing out of the earth by clear shining after rain.**

Bible translators have struggled with getting the meaning out of this verse. The King James Version gets the meaning across as well as most modern translations. David starts by picturing a bright sunrise on a cloudless day. The sky is clear. But then he talks about rain on the grass—from a sunny cloudless sky? For some, the imagery might seem perplexing.

The lesson from this verse is that when a ruler is committed to doing what's right, the assurance of justice makes life better. That's true whether everything's perfect as on a bright, clear morning, or in difficult times such as on a rainy day. Right after it rains, leaves of grass are rising up from the ground and "shining" with glittering raindrops on them. David's point was that commitment to God's righteous will and faithfulness in executing justice in human relations had positive effects in easy or difficult times (**Leviticus 19:14–15; Isaiah 55:10–11; Jeremiah 21:10–16; 22:16**).

## QUESTION 2
According to David how must leaders rule?

**Rulers must be just and do so in the fear of the Lord. Answers will vary.**

## LIGHT ON THE WORD

### David, the Ideal King
Is David the ideal king, like the sunlight coming up, the new growth after the rain? No, David was not perfect and Scripture makes sure that we see him in all his weaknesses. But because David loved God and repented when he did wrong, God loved David and made a special covenant with him. This covenant was made before David sinned with Bathsheba and Uriah. And because the covenant was with God, God was keeping His word. Even though Solomon did not follow God to the end and most of the rulers after him did not follow God, God kept His promise to send His Son through the lineage of David. David was well aware of the awesomeness of God's promises to him.

But those who refuse to live in covenant with God are just the opposite of the beautiful sunny day. Instead of lush grass, their lives are patches of thorns. You can't use your hands to pull them up. You must use some sort of tool to pull them up, and then you burn them so they cannot reseed themselves.

## III. DAVID'S LEGACY OF GOD'S JUSTICE (2 Samuel 23:5-7; 1 Chronicles 18:14)

King David's rule is summarized as just and right. Other nations may be richer and stronger, but the nation of Israel is to be special because it is governed according to God's justice.

### God's Enduring Covenant to David
### (verses 5-7; 1 Chronicles 18:14)
**5. Although my house be not so with God; yet he hath made with me an everlasting covenant, ordered in all things, and sure; for this is all my salvation, and all my desire, although he did not make it to grow.**

This is another verse with many layers of meaning. The key to understanding its truths is keeping in mind that God was speaking through David and David responded to what God inspired him to say. First, David admitted that his royal family, "my house," had not all bought into his commitment to doing God's righteous will. Several examples could be cited, but two involving David's children illustrate why David said this. David's son, Ammon, raped David's daughter, Tamar, Ammon's half-sister (**2 Samuel 13:14**). In revenge, David's son Absalom, Tamar's brother, had Ammon murdered (**2 Samuel 13:22, 28–29**).

In spite of his own and his family's failure to follow God's purposes fully, **2 Samuel 23:5** points out that David was convinced of the enduring certainty of God's "covenant" with him and his descendants. David cited that the basis for his confidence about his family's future was God's purposes and pleasure. God had a plan "ordered…and sure." The "salvation" of God's purposes through David's descendants lay in God's power to rescue them from whatever difficulty they encountered and ensure their welfare, generation after generation. That was God's desire, which gave David pleasure to fulfill. That, however, did not mean that God caused to prosper those things in David's life or in his family that were contrary to His nature.

**6 But the sons of Belial shall be all of them as thorns thrust away, because they cannot be taken with hands: 7 But the man that shall touch them must be fenced with iron and the staff of a spear; and they shall be utterly burnt with fire in the same place.**

2 **Samuel 23:6** begins with the phrase "the

sons of Belial"; this is the one time in the Old Testament that Belial is mentioned as an individual. The translator of the KJV likely added the phrase here because all the other 14 times that Belial is mentioned, the biblical writers speak of the sons, daughters, or children of Belial. The word meant a worthless, witless person who causes needless destruction or evil events. The Israelites did not have as clear an image of the evil spiritual being who opposed God's involvement with humanity as the New Testament writers did. Belial was a personal name used in the Old Testament similar to Satan. Satan, which means "adversary," was often used as a descriptive title, "the Satan," rather than as a personal name.

God's purpose in **verses 6** and **7** was to illustrate that the lives of David's descendants would only have lasting meaning if they maintained a just society and followed David's example of trying to implement God's righteous values in their lives. He compared an unjust ruler to thorny vines. He said briar vines should be chopped down with a stout, durable tool, taking care not to be pierced by their thorns. Once cut off, they should be moved out of the way using a spear's wooden shaft. A pile of chopped-down, thorny briars was worthless. Their only value after that was to serve as fuel for a fire (**John 15:6**). Likewise, unjust rulers or officials remained a constant danger to society. These verses were David's poetic way of saying they should be dealt with carefully and pushed aside where they could cause no harm.

**1 Chronicles 18:14.** So David reigned over all Israel, and executed judgment and justice among all his people.

The two books of Chronicles were written after the Israelites returned from exile and captivity in Babylon. They show that even hundreds of years after David lived and the monarchy David founded had collapsed, the justice experienced during David's reign was still held up as a model that society should aspire to.

## SEARCH THE SCRIPTURES
### QUESTION 3
What was the final legacy of David's life as King of Israel?

"**David reigned over Israel, and executed judgment and justice among his people.**" **Answers will vary.**

## LIGHT ON THE WORD
### God Knows and Sees
During the recent economic meltdown, many bankers and other people in high-placed financial positions were caught doing things that were illegal or at least seemed to be very unethical. The things they did destroyed the pensions of elderly people, took away the homes of families, and otherwise caused economic ruin for their wealthy peers. Not only did they not seem to care about the poor and middle class, but they seemed to have no concept that God knows and sees everything they are doing and have done. Why do you think they are so indifferent to the situations of others, especially those who have much less than they do? How can they have forgotten about God?

## BIBLE APPLICATION

**AIM: That your students will understand their responsibility to seek God's counsel and to act justly.**

### King David
Today's lesson shared King David's final words and what he thought was the most important legacy he had to leave behind. Before and after being anointed king, David for the most part sought to honor God and consulted with Him before making decisions. He was humble before God and strived to rule with His people justly.

## STUDENTS' RESPONSES

**AIM: That your students will examine themselves to make sure they are showing compassion to others.**

### Examine Yourself!

It's easy to criticize the rich and famous, but if we examine ourselves, we will discover some of those same tendencies within us. How can we demonstrate justice and compassion toward our coworkers or neighbors this week?

## PRAYER

Father in heaven, I want to leave a lasting legacy as one who lived life for Your glory. I pray for Your wisdom and to know Your will so that I can make good decisions. I also pray for leaders in every realm and every level to know You so that they can execute justice, make good decisions, and lead with compassion. In the Name of Jesus, I pray. Amen.

## DIG A LITTLE DEEPER

We may not be monarchs or rulers of nations, but we still can make direct application of the principles in this lesson regarding our personal commitment to justice. Most of us have some sphere of influence and power, however small it may be. We are parents or guardians of children; we're bosses or supervisors on the job; we're auxiliary leaders in our local churches. We have some area of authority in which we operate; we have agency—the capacity to exert power—over other people's lives. Therefore, we have to answer an important question: Are we behaving justly in our own areas of authority?

Our protagonist David had a few tools to assess his own righteousness. David famously prayed, "Search me, O God, and know my heart: try me, and know my thoughts" (**Psalm 139:23**). He invited God to point out anything in his deeds or character that was an offense. The Lord

sometimes honored this request by sending other people to confront David, as happened when the prophet Nathan challenged him about his sin against Uriah (**2 Samuel 12:7**). When confronted, the king was contrite and confessed.

Like David, we must engage in self-reflection, and be courageous enough to face our failings and foibles. We will have to receive whomever the Lord sends to chastise us. We'll have to sincerely repent and seek restoration. In order to be considered just persons, we will have to perform the humbling work of self-discovery and improvement.

## HOW TO SAY IT

Ammon. AM-uhn.

Belial. BEE-lee-uhl.

Tamar. TAY-mahr.

## DAILY HOME BIBLE READINGS

### MONDAY
Inquiring of the Lord
(2 Samuel 2:1–7)

### TUESDAY
Rejoicing in God's Deliverance
(2 Samuel 22:8–20))

### WEDNESDAY
Depending on God's Guidance
(2 Samuel 22:26–31)

### THURSDAY
Living in God's Strength
(2 Samuel 22:32–37)

### FRIDAY
Praising God's Steadfast Love
(2 Samuel 22:47–51)

### SATURDAY
Reigning in Righteousness
(Isaiah 32:1–8)

### SUNDAY
Ruling in the Fear of God
(2 Samuel 23:1–7; 1 Chronicles 18:14)

## PREPARE FOR NEXT SUNDAY

Read **1 Kings 3:16–28; 2 Chronicles 9:8** and next week's lesson "Solomon Judges with Wisdom and Justice."

**Sources:**

Bible Pronunciation Chart. Better Days Are Coming.com. http://www. betterdaysarecoming/bible/pronunciation.html (accessed January 29, 2011).

Brown, Francis, et al. The New Brown-Driver-Briggs-Gesenius Hebrew and English Lexicon. Peabody, MA: Hendrickson Publishers, 1985.

Hertzberg, Hans Wilhelm. The Old Testament Library: I & II Samuel, A Commentary.
4th ed. Philadelphia, PA: Westminster Press, 1976. 398–402.

Mauchline, John. New Century Bible: 1 and 2 Samuel. London, England: Morgan, Marshall & Scott Publications, 1971. 312–15.

Merriam-Webster Online Dictionary. Merriam-Webster, Inc. http://www. merriam-webster.com (accessed January 29, 2011).

Passage Lookup. Bible Gateway.com. http://www.biblegateway.com/ passage (accessed January 17, 2011).

Peterson, Eugene H. First and Second Samuel. Louisville, KY: Westminster John Knox
Press, 1999.

Robinson, Gnana. Let Us Be Like the Nations: A Commentary on the Books of 1 and 2
Samuel. Grand Rapids, MI: William B. Eerdmans Publishing Co., 1993.

Wilcock, Michael. The Message of Chronicles: One Church, One Faith, One Lord.
Downers Grove, IL: InterVarsity Press, 1987. 13–18, 78.

Williamson, Hugh G. M. New Century Bible Commentary: 1 and 2 Chronicles. Grand
Rapids, MI: William B. Eerdmans Publishing Co., 1982. 15–17.

## COMMENTS / NOTES:

_____
_____
_____
_____
_____
_____
_____
_____
_____
_____
_____
_____
_____
_____
_____
_____
_____
_____
_____
_____
_____
_____
_____
_____
_____

# SOLOMON JUDGES WITH WISDOM AND JUSTICE

**BIBLE BASIS:** 1Kings 3:16–28; 2 Chronicles 9:8

**BIBLE TRUTH:** Using godly wisdom is the only way to make good decisions..

**MEMORY VERSE:** And all Israel heard of the judgment which the king had judged; and they feared the king: for they saw that the wisdom of God was in him, to do judgment (1 Kings 3:28, KJV).

**LESSON AIM:** By the end of the lesson, we will: UNDERSTAND the importance of seeking divine wisdom; REFLECT on a time when acting with compassion and justice brought about a fair result; and CHOOSE to act with wisdom and justice.

**BACKGROUND SCRIPTURES:** 1 Kings 3, 2 Chronicles 9:8-Read and incorporate the insights gained from the Background Scriptures into your study of the lesson.

## TEACHER PREPARATION

**MATERIALS NEEDED:** Bibles (several different versions), Quarterly Commentary/Teacher Manual, Adult Quarterly, teaching resources such as charts, worksheets/handouts, paper, pens, and pencils.

**OTHER MATERIALS NEEDED / TEACHER'S NOTES:**

_____

_____

## LESSON OVERVIEW

**LIFE NEED FOR TODAY'S LESSON**
To apply God's wisdom in our daily living.

**BIBLE LEARNING**
Solomon was the wisest man who ever lived because he sought the Lord to make just decisions.

**BIBLE APPLICATION**
To understand how to make wise decisions, even in unjust situations.

**STUDENTS' RESPONSES**
Students will seek to discern how to act with wisdom and justice.

## LESSON SCRIPTURE

**1 KINGS 3:16–28; 2 CHRONICLES 9:8 KJV**

1 Kings 3:16. Then came there two women, that were harlots, unto the king,

**1 KINGS 3:16–28; 2 CHRONICLES 9:8 AMP**

16 Then two women who were prostitutes came to the king and stood

and stood before him.

17 And the one woman said, O my lord, I and this woman dwell in one house; and I was delivered of a child with her in the house.

18 And it came to pass the third day after that I was delivered, that this woman was delivered also: and we were together; there was no stranger with us in the house, save we two in the house.

19 And this woman's child died in the night; because she overlaid it.

20 And she rose at midnight, and took my son from beside me, while thine handmaid slept, and laid it in her bosom, and laid her dead child in my bosom.

21 And when I rose in the morning to give my child suck, behold, it was dead: but when I had considered it in the morning, behold, it was not my son, which I did bear.

22 And the other woman said, Nay; but the living is my son, and the dead is thy son. And this said, No; but the dead is thy son, and the living is my son. Thus they spake before the king.

23 Then said the king, The one saith, This is my son that liveth, and thy son is the dead: and the other saith, Nay; but thy son is the dead, and my son is the living.

24 And the king said, Bring me a sword. And they brought a sword before the king.

25 And the king said, Divide the living child in two, and give half to the one, and half to the other.

26 Then spake the woman whose the living child was unto the king, for her bowels yearned upon her son, and she said, O my lord, give her the living child, and in no wise

before him.

17 And the one woman said, "O my lord, this woman and I live in the same house; and I gave birth to a child while she was in the house.

18 And on the third day after I gave birth, this woman also gave birth. And we were [alone] together; no one else was with us in the house, just we two.

19 Now this woman's son died during the night, because she lay on him [and smothered him].

20 So she got up in the middle of the night and took my son from [his place] beside me while your maidservant was asleep, and laid him on her bosom, and laid her dead son on my bosom.

21 When I got up in the morning to nurse my son, behold, he was dead. But when I examined him carefully in the morning, behold, it was not my son, the one whom I had borne."

22 Then the other woman said, "No! For my son is the one who is living, and your son is the dead one." But the first woman said, "No! For your son is the dead one, and my son is the living one." [This is how] they were speaking before the king.

23 Then the king said, "This woman says, 'This is my son, the one who is alive, and your son is the dead one'; and the other woman says, 'No! For your son is the dead one, and my son is the one who is alive.'"

24 Then the king said, "Bring me a sword." So they brought a sword before the king.

25 Then the king said, "Cut the living child in two, and give half to the one [woman] and half to the other."

slay it. But the other said, Let it be neither mine nor thine, but divide it.

**27** Then the king answered and said, Give her the living child, and in no wise slay it: she is the mother thereof.

**28** And all Israel heard of the judgment which the king had judged; and they feared the king: for they saw that the wisdom of God was in him, to do judgment.

**2 Chron 9:8** Blessed be the LORD thy God, which delighted in thee to set thee on his throne, to be king for the LORD thy God: because thy God loved Israel, to establish them forever, therefore made he thee king over them, to do judgment and justice.

**26** Then the woman whose child was the living one spoke to the king, for she was deeply moved over her son, "O my lord, give her the living child, and by no means kill him." But the other said, "He shall be neither mine nor yours; cut him!"

**27** Then the king said, "Give the first woman [who is pleading for his life] the living child, and by no means kill him. She is his mother."

**28** When all [the people of] Israel heard about the judgment which the king had made, they [were in awe and reverently] feared the king, for they saw that the wisdom of God was within him to administer justice.

**2 Chron 9:8** Blessed be the LORD your God, who delighted in you, setting you on His throne as king for the LORD your God; because your God loved Israel, establishing them forever, therefore He made you king over them, to do justice and righteousness."

## BIBLICAL DEFINITIONS

A. **Wisdom (1 Kings 3:28)** *chokmah* (Heb.)—Ability to discern inner qualities and relationships.

B. **Judgment (v. 28; 2 Chronicles 9:8)** *mishpat* (Heb.)—A formal utterance of an authoritative opinion.

## LIGHT ON THE WORD

At 20 years of age, King Solomon felt very young and unprepared to assume the throne of his father, the great King David. (We only need to look at Solomon's son, Rehoboam, as he ascended to the throne, to see how some youths can make very unwise decisions.) Solomon had already married Pharaoh's daughter—not a wise decision—and here he was worshiping at a high place, another forbidden thing. But God was able to see that in his heart, Solomon was worshiping the true God. Therefore, when young Solomon lay down to sleep that night, God appeared to him in a dream. God made the wonderful offer to Solomon that He would give him whatever he wanted God to give him.

Solomon could have asked for riches and fame, for long life, and for the death of his enemies. Instead, he asked God to give him wisdom to rule Israel. This answer showed that already Solomon was wise enough to know that he needed the Lord's help to govern the nation. God was delighted with Solomon's answer. He promised to make him wiser than any other king of that time. God also gave him riches and fame.

He promised to give Solomon long life, too, if he would obey God all his life. Unfortunately, he was distracted from obeying the Lord by his many wives and their foreign gods, and his story ends in a lamentable fashion.

Today's Scripture passage shows how God answered Solomon's request and gave him great wisdom in governing the people.

## TEACHING THE BIBLE LESSON

## LIFE NEED FOR TODAY'S LESSON

AIM: That your students will see how God gives wisdom.

## INTRODUCTION

### Prostitution

Prostitution is defined as selling sexual favors. Even in the Bible, people seemed to have a double standard regarding the female prostitute and the male who patronizes her. In **Genesis 38** we read that Judah paid for sex from a woman he thought was a prostitute, but who was actually his widowed daughter-in-law. He acted as though he were scandalized when she became pregnant but had a change of attitude when it came out that he was the father of the baby. However, the Bible always condemns any sex outside of marriage.

Prostitutes in every culture are looked down upon, and it is very surprising seeing Solomon, the king of Israel, judging a case with two such women. This incident highlights the wisdom of Solomon, but it also shows that every human being deserves justice and fair treatment.

### Wisdom

Wisdom is more than mere book knowledge; it involves knowing the right thing to do and doing it. Social scientists today have observed that the heads of major corporations are rarely younger than 50 years old. There are certain mental processes that seem to come only with maturity.

This was something that young King Solomon was lacking, but God granted him wisdom at the beginning of his reign **(1 Kings 3:3–15)**. True wisdom comes from God. We read in **James 1:5** that if we lack wisdom, we should ask God and He will give it to us. At many points in life, we are challenged to make decisions, and if we are wise, we will ask God for His help.

## BIBLE LEARNING

AIM: That your students will understand that God gives us wisdom in tough situations when asked.

## I. A PROBLEM BEFORE THE KING (1 Kings 3:16-23)

Two mothers, who are prostitutes, are before King Solomon arguing their cases. Both claim to be the mother of the living baby. We are surprised that a case of two prostitutes would come up before the king of the land. But perhaps they went before a lower court first, and no solution could be found. So they are appearing before the "Supreme Court," so to speak.

### Two Prostitutes, Two Babies, One Dilemma (verses 16-23)

**16. Then came there two women, that were harlots, unto the king, and stood before him.**

In the time of Israel's first kings, "to rule" meant "to judge, to make life-changing decisions, to be society's final authority." Few matters could be more important than the custody of a child. Direct access to a nation's king was a widespread practice then. So, two women brought their dispute over a baby boy's rightful custody for King Solomon to settle. His responsibility was to referee and decide the baby's true mother.

Although prostitution was never viewed as an attractive occupation, and by definition requires behavior contrary to God's standards, it was accepted then as lawful, permissible work. For example, there is no hint of censure when Hebrew spies went to scout out Canaan and "went…into an harlot's house…and lodged there" (Joshua 2:1). Nor is there any condemnation of the widowed Judah, when he hired a woman he thought was a prostitute, only to learn later that it was his daughter-in-law in disguise (Genesis 38:13–17, 24–26).

A pregnant prostitute has a dilemma. Pregnancy and child care prevent her from working. She probably also knows that bringing a child into her world gives a child a poor environment in which to grow up. The two women in the narrative probably lived in a brothel. Brothels have always been common in cities, and they may provide some protection and company for the women in a very lonely business. A baby will also provide some solace to a prostitute. Prostitution was viewed as a tawdry trade even in Solomon's time, yet the two harlots were accepted by Israel's king and their dispute received his full attention. The lesson for our time from this incident is that regardless of a person's social standing, he or she deserves the full benefits of the government's system of justice.

**17 And the one woman said, O my lord, I and this woman dwell in one house; and I was delivered of a child with her in the house. 18 And it came to pass the third day after I was delivered, that this woman was delivered also: and we were together; there was no stranger with us in the house, save we two in the house.**

The first woman makes clear Solomon's task: whom to believe. Only two people were present. Being prostitutes, the women were young and unmarried. No husbands or children were present to confirm or contradict either woman's claim. Both women gave birth to a child; both babies were boys.

**19 And this woman's child died in the night; because she overlaid it. 20 And she rose at midnight, and took my son from beside me, while thy handmaid slept, and laid it in her bosom, and laid her dead child in my bosom.**

Although 1 Kings 3:19 says "midnight," that only meant sometime in the midst of the night's passage. The dead baby seemed to have been crushed and smothered when the sleeping mother unknowingly rolled onto ("overlaid") him. In a time centuries before delivery rooms, hospital nurseries, or watchful nurses, the young mothers may have heard that such tragic happenings had occurred before. A congenital birth defect or Sudden Infant Death Syndrome (SIDS) may have been the true cause of death, but these were not the categories in use then. Neither woman could know the cause of death for sure. Both were probably exhausted by the labor of what was likely a first birth and were deep asleep. The first speaker admitted she was.

**21. And when I arose in the morning to give my child suck, behold, it was dead: but when I had considered it in the morning, behold, it was not my son, which I did bear.**

The woman who first gave birth admitted that she slept soundly all night, waking only when "morning" arrived. We can only imagine the mother's horror as she lifted her baby toward her breast and realized the baby was dead. She then mentioned "morning" again, which suggests the brightness of daylight. As she carefully "considered" or looked closely at the child, she concluded he was not the child she had given birth to three days before. At least she did not want to believe her son was dead or perhaps chose not to believe it. Whatever her exact reaction was, her response to the baby's death is understandable. The most natural human response to grief is to refuse to accept it as real. Whether the woman honestly believed the baby wasn't hers or refused to believe it, we see the need for a fair judicial system where honest people can exercise clearheaded, fair-minded judgment in difficult, sometimes confusing, situations.

**22 And the other woman said, Nay; but the living is my son, and the dead is thy son. And this said, No; but the dead is thy son, and the living is my son. Thus they spake before the king. 23 Then said the king, the one saith, This is my son that liveth, and thy son is the dead: and the other saith, Nay: but thy son is the dead, and my son is the living.**

Finally, the second mother interjected, but only to argue the opposite of the first woman's assertions. Then the first woman responded, reasserting her initial claims. Rather than making their cases to Solomon, the women argued back and forth with each other.

As King Solomon watched and listened, he tried to decide how to uncover the truth. Who to believe was his problem. As the women's emotions heightened, they forgot their royal audience and challenged each other directly: "the dead is thy son....No; the dead is thy son, and the living is my son."

Solomon didn't know which mother to believe.

## SEARCH THE SCRIPTURES
### QUESTION 1
What was the problem brought before King Solomon?

**Two women (prostitutes) were arguing because both had given birth, one child died and both were claiming the living child.**

## LIGHT ON THE WORD
### Wisdom to Decide
This story appears right after God has agreed to make Solomon the wisest king of his day, and it demonstrates how wise Solomon was. Solomon called for a sword and threatened to cut the baby in half and give half of a dead baby to each mother. Was Solomon taking a risk? No, God gave him insight into a mother's heart.

## II. GOD PROVIDES KING SOLOMON WITH WISDOM (1 Kings 3:24-28; 2 Chronicles 9:8)

For the protection of the human race, God puts love in a mother's heart for her baby. "Good" mothers would do anything to protect their children. God gave King Solomon the wisdom to understand this. There are many kinds of wisdom and one type is the ability to understand human emotions, which Solomon displayed in this situation. God gave wisdom to Solomon so that he would rule with justice and righteousness.

### King Solomon Provokes Resolution (verses 24-28; 2 Chronicles 9:8)
**24. And the king said, Bring me a sword. And they brought a sword before the king.**

Finally, Solomon concluded there was a way to unravel the contradictory claims over who was the baby's mother. The solution was one that would work only in an absolute monarchy and would never be considered in our modern judicial system. He gave the decisive and ominous command, "Bring me a sword." The literal Hebrew response to the king's command was "they brought a sword 'before' [to the face of] the king." Solomon never took the sword in hand; one was simply fetched and placed before him.

**25 And the king said, Divide the living child in two, and give half to the one and half to the other.**

He then gave a horrifying order. One of his

attendants was told to "divide" the child into two parts. The word was more often used to mean cut, chop, or destroy. In **2 Kings 6:3-6,** the same word is used for chopping down trees with an ax to build a house for the prophet Elisha. "Divide" carries a much less horrific image than "cut" or "chop."

Although in English it isn't clear, Solomon's order was plural. Two, or maybe three, attendants were to cut the child in two. One attendant would hold the baby by one leg, another was to grip the opposite leg, and a third would use the sword to slice the baby boy down the middle into two pieces.

In **1 Kings 3:25** the second part of his command was again in the plural: "give" a bloody half of the baby to each mother. Our text from KJV includes a grave but accurate contrast from the original Hebrew. Solomon instructs his attendants, "give half to the one," and then he commands, "and half to the other," rather than just telling them "Divide the living child in two, and give half to one, and half to the other!" (NKJV). Solomon's instructions forced each woman to visualize herself receiving the bloody fulfillment of his orders.

**26 Then spake the woman whose the living child was unto the king, for her bowels yearned upon her son, and she said, O my lord, give her the living child, and in no wise slay it. But the other said, Let it be neither mine nor thine, but divide it. 27 Then the king answered and said, Give her the living child, and in no wise slay it: she is the mother thereof.**

The response that Solomon hoped for immediately developed in **verse 26.** The baby's true mother felt the pit of her stomach roil at the thought of the baby's slaughter. The ancient Israelites thought of a woman's "bowels" literally her womb, as the seat of her emotions. Feelings of compassion for her helpless newborn son

caused intense warmth to churn in the depth of his mother's being. She could not bear the image of her baby boy chopped in two and begged the king to let the other woman have the baby.

That outcry and the response of the other woman convinced Solomon of the identity of the baby's real mother. If the first woman had objected to the baby's slaughter, Solomon might have wondered if that might simply be a natural, motherly distress about such an event. But the second woman's bitter agreement confirmed the king's judgment. The second woman's encouragement of Solomon's order revealed her harsh acceptance of having lost a son. Her only remaining possibility was that another woman should suffer what was denied her.

**28. And all Israel heard of the judgment which the king had judged; and they feared the king: for they saw that the wisdom of God was in him, to do judgment.**

There were apparently many examples that could be recalled of Solomon's wisdom. The book of Proverbs contains several collections of his wise observations (**Proverbs 1:1; 10:1a; 25:1**). This incident perhaps best summed up both his wisdom and sense of justice. It was retold often until Solomon's wisdom and justice were revered throughout the nation. If two women at the bottom of social status by reason of their gender and their occupation could gain an audience before the king, receive his full attention and the benefit of his best reasoning and a just decision, no one in society should expect any less. Christians are right to pray for God's guidance for those in authority (**1 Timothy 2:1–3a**).

When **1 Kings 3:28** asserts "the wisdom of God was in him," the term "in him" means within the depths of Solomon's being. His ability to administer wise justice was not simply a matter of will or talent. It was God's gift to him. That gift was endowed on Solomon for a purpose:

"to do judgment". That meant not simply giving a legal ruling, but a just one (**2 Chronicles 9:8,** "judgment and justice"). Mere knowledge of facts according to testimony could not ensure a just ruling for the baby's true mother. Only a commitment to justice at their nation's highest level and a desire among leaders to know and follow God's leading made that a reality.

**2 Chronicles 9:8.** Blessed be the LORD thy God, which delighted in thee to set thee on his throne, to be king for the LORD thy God: because thy God loved Israel, to establish them for ever, therefore made he thee king over them, to do judgment and justice.

From over a thousand miles away, the queen of Sheba had heard about Solomon's incredible insight into personal, relational, and governmental affairs. So she brought a great store of wealth to persuade him to share its benefits with her (**1 Kings 10:1–8; 2 Chronicles 9:1–7**). Her conclusions are distilled in **2 Chronicles 9:8.**

When the Israelites were released after decades in Babylonian exile and returned to Judah, they rewrote their history as God's chosen people. Special attention was given to emphasizing God's central place and purposes for them as His people. This verse quotes the queen of Sheba almost exactly as found in **1 Kings 10:9.** The differences, however, are hugely important.

She first concluded that God deserved praise as the source of Solomon's success as king. In **2 Chronicles 9:8,** the chronicler adds one letter to the Hebrew word for "throne" and changes the emphasis from Solomon's rule over Israel to God's rule over them as His people (Williamson, 234; see also **1 Chronicles 17:14**). Then, to make clear what so many of Israel's kings after David's and Solomon's reigns had missed, he adds, "to be king for the LORD thy God" (**2 Chronicles 9:8**). God's purpose went far beyond simply making Solomon the sovereign ruler of God's people. God's purpose in installing him was so that Solomon might implement God's just, merciful, and righteous purposes. Ultimately, Solomon's task was to make decisions that fully implemented the purposes of a merciful and just Creator.

## QUESTION 2
How does King Solomon resolve the matter, and how does the real mother respond?

**King Solomon proposes cutting the child in two and splitting him between the two women. The real mother willingly gives the child to the other woman to save the child's life. Answers will vary.**

## LIGHT ON THE WORD
### Wisdom for Life
What circumstances have you found yourself in that called for wisdom that seemed to be beyond your own abilities? What did you do about the situation? Today's lesson taught us how God's leading is critical to executing wisdom and justice.

## BIBLE APPLICATION
**AIM: That your students will understand that good leaders need the wisdom of God to bring justice.**

### Wise Leaders
There are many kinds of leaders in society today. There are arrogant leaders, corrupt leaders, and many other types of persons in charge who are not showing justice and righteousness in their leadership. We always can use more leaders who are full of wisdom. Read **Romans 13:1–7** to see what we can do to encourage our leaders to operate as God wants them to.

## STUDENTS' RESPONSES

**AIM: That your students will seek the wisdom of God and bring Him glory.**

### The Wisdom That Comes from God

What kind of wisdom do you need in your life? Look up **James 1:5.** This verse tells us that if we lack wisdom, we should ask God to give it to us and He will do so. Start at the same place as young Solomon—recognizing that you need God's wisdom.

## PRAYER

Father in heaven, apart from You I can do nothing. I pray to have an undivided heart that I may know Your ways so that Your good Spirit can lead me. Help me to seek Your counsel in every area of my life. I pray to yield to Your will, and as a result, people will talk about Your greatness through me. In Jesus' Name, Amen.

## DIG A LITTLE DEEPER

"The Front Porch" is a multimedia platform where black preachers and scholars have discussions among themselves about the church and the art of ministry. The website boasts a blog that is one of the most informative in the black church world. A post in 2019 by Isaac Adams, the Assistant Pastor of Capitol Hill Baptist Church, came to mind while reflecting on this week's lesson. In "Wisdom to Live Justly," Adams explored the idea that justice is an outgrowth of biblical wisdom. He traced the theme of justice throughout Solomon's Proverbs, and identified in the scriptures "seven requirements in seeking justice as God's people." It is a relatively short piece, and well worth the time for anyone contemplating Solomon's reputation for wisdom and justice.

Ref.:

Adams, Isaac. "Wisdom to Live Justly." The Front Porch (blog). 2019. https://thefrontporch.org/2019/02/wisdom-to-live-justly/.

## HOW TO SAY IT

| | |
|---|---|
| Chronicles. | KRON-ih-kuhlz. |
| Babylonian. | bab'uh-LOH-nee-uhn. |
| Sheba. | SHE-bah. |

### DAILY HOME BIBLE READINGS

**MONDAY**
A Prayer for Wisdom
(Ephesians 1:15–23)

**TUESDAY**
The Lord Loves Justice
(Psalm 37:27–34)

**WEDNESDAY**
Jedidiah—Beloved of the Lord
(2 Samuel 12:20–25)

**THURSDAY**
Solomon Anointed Israel's King
(1 Kings 1:28–37)

**FRIDAY**
Grace for a Competitor
(1 Kings 1:41–53)

**SATURDAY**
Solomon's Unsurpassed Wisdom
(1 Kings 4:29–34)

**SUNDAY**
Solomon Puts Wisdom into Practice
(1 Kings 3:16–28; 2 Chronicles 9:8)

## PREPARE FOR NEXT SUNDAY

Read **2 Kings 8:1-6** and next week's lesson "A King Acts on a Widow's Behalf."

**Sources:**
Adeyemo, Tokunboh, et al., eds. Africa Bible Commentary. Grand Rapids, MI: Zondervan, 2006.

Bible Pronunciation Chart. Better Days Are Coming.com. http://www.betterdaysarecoming/bible/pronunciation.html (accessed January 29, 2011).

Brown, Francis, et al. The New Brown-Driver-Briggs-Gesenius Hebrew and English Lexicon. Peabody, MA: Hendrickson Publishers, 1985.

Gray, John. Old Testament Library: I & II Kings, A Commentary. 2nd ed., revised.
Philadelphia, PA: The Westminster Press, 1970. 127–29.

Morris, Wilda W. "Prostitution." Holman Illustrated Bible Dictionary. Chad Brand, et al., eds. Nashville, TN: Holman Bible Publishers, 2003. 1336–37.

Passage Lookup. Bible Gateway.com. http://www.biblegateway.com/ passage (accessed January 17, 2011).

The Revised English Bible (REB). New York, NY: Oxford University Press, 1989. 288.

Williamson, Hugh G. M. 1 and 2 Chronicles: New Century Bible Commentary. Grand Rapids, MI: Wm. B. Eerdmans Publishing Co., 1982. 233–34.

## COMMENTS / NOTES:

# A KING ACTS ON A WIDOW'S BEHALF

**BIBLE BASIS:** 2 Kings 8:1–6

**BIBLE TRUTH:** The Shunammite woman appealed to the king for the return of her house and property, and the Lord intervened to help her..

**MEMORY VERSE:** And when the king asked the woman, she told him. So the king appointed unto her a certain officer, saying, Restore all that was hers, and all the fruits of the field since the day that she left the land, even until now (2 Kings 8:6, KJV).

**LESSON AIM:** By the end of the lesson, we will: IDENTIFY scriptural support that justice can restore people and communities; FEEL blessed and appreciate the wonderful things we have seen accomplished by God's power; and PRAISE God for guiding us to pursue justice when we have been deprived of it.

**BACKGROUND SCRIPTURES:** 2 Kings 4:1-37; 8:1-6-Read and incorporate the insights gained from the Background Scriptures into your study of the lesson.

## TEACHER PREPARATION

**MATERIALS NEEDED:** Bibles (several different versions), Quarterly Commentary/Teacher Manual, Adult Quarterly, teaching resources such as charts, worksheets/handouts, paper, pens, and pencils.

**OTHER MATERIALS NEEDED / TEACHER'S NOTES:**

_____

_____

## LESSON OVERVIEW

### LIFE NEED FOR TODAY'S LESSON
That students will be encouraged in seeking justice.

### BIBLE LEARNING
To understand that God will help us as we seek justice for ourselves and others.

### BIBLE APPLICATION
To learn how God intervened on the behalf of a widow who had been treated unjustly.

### STUDENTS' RESPONSES
Students will praise God for guiding us to pursue justice when we have been deprived of it.

## LESSON SCRIPTURE

### 2 KINGS 8:1-6 KJV

**1** Then spake Elisha unto the woman, whose son he had restored to life, saying, Arise, and go thou and thine household, and sojourn

### 2 KINGS 8:1-6 AMP

**8** Now Elisha had said to the [Shunammite] woman whose son he had restored to life, "Prepare and go, you and your household, and wheresoever thou canst sojourn; for the LORD hath called for a famine; and it shall also come upon the land seven years.

**2** And the woman arose, and did after the saying of the man of God: and she went with her household, and sojourned in the land of the Philistines seven years.

**3** And it came to pass at the seven years' end, that the woman returned out of the land of the Philistines: and she went forth to cry unto the king for her house and for her land.

**4** And the king talked with Gehazi the servant of the man of God, saying, Tell me, I pray thee, all the great things that Elisha hath done.

**5** And it came to pass, as he was telling the king how he had restored a dead body to life, that, behold, the woman, whose son he had restored to life, cried to the king for her house and for her land. And Gehazi said, My lord, O king, this is the woman, and this is her son, whom Elisha restored to life.

**6** And when the king asked the woman, she told him. So the king appointed unto her a certain officer, saying, Restore all that was hers, and all the fruits of the field since the day that she left the land, even until now.

stay temporarily wherever you can; for the LORD has called for a famine, and moreover, it will come on the land [and continue] for seven years."

**2** So the woman set out and did everything in accordance with the word of the man of God. She and her household went and stayed temporarily as foreigners in the land of the Philistines for seven years.

**3** At the end of the seven years the woman returned from the land of the Philistines; and she went to appeal to the king [of Israel] for her house and for her land.

**4** Now the king was talking with Gehazi, the servant of the man of God, saying, "Tell me all the great things that Elisha has done."

**5** And [just] as Gehazi was telling the king how Elisha had restored the dead to life, behold, the woman whose son he had restored to life appealed to the king for her house and for her land. And Gehazi said, "My lord, O king, this is the woman and this is her son, whom Elisha restored to life."

**6** When the king asked the woman, she told him [everything]. So the king appointed for her a certain high official, saying, "Restore everything that was hers, including all the produce of the field since the day that she left the land until now."

## BIBLICAL DEFINITIONS

**A. Servant (2 Kings 8:4)** `ebed (Heb.)—A minister, ambassador, and a worshiper of God.

**B. Officer (v. 6)** *cariyc* (Heb.)—A man in the royal court who is a "eunuch"; a castrated male.

## LIGHT ON THE WORD

The author of 2 Kings focuses on the history of the divided kingdoms of Israel and Judah. One of the main prophetic characters in the early part of the book was Elisha, the servant of Elijah, and he was endowed with a "double portion" of His spirit (see 2 Kings 2:8–9). Some suggest that Elisha's ministry continued where Elijah's left off, but with a greater anointing and effect, especially during the apostasy that was prevalent in Israel. Elisha's ministry seems to have centered on Gilgal and Shunem. The Gilgal mentioned in the earlier part of 2 Kings indicates that this was in the hill country of Ephraim, north of Bethel. Shunem was a town in the territory of Issachar near Jezreel on the slopes of Mount Moriah, overlooking the eastern end of the Jezreel Valley.

It was here that Elisha had a divine contact with the Shunammite woman, a woman of great wealth and social prominence. The prophet, and his servant Gehazi, stayed in her home and, through the power of God, caused the woman to conceive a child, though her husband was old.

## TEACHING THE BIBLE LESSON

## LIFE NEED FOR TODAY'S LESSON

**AIM: That your students will feel blessed and appreciate the wonderful things we have seen accomplished by God's power.**

## INTRODUCTION

### Famine

A famine is an extreme shortage of food that God oftentimes used on the Israelites in response to their continued disobedience. One of the common forms of famine was a drought, which is the excessive dryness of the land. Famines and droughts are recorded throughout the Bible during the time of Abraham (Genesis 12:10), Isaac (Genesis 26:1), Joseph (Genesis 41:27), the Judges (Ruth 1:1), and the Israelites in the days of David (2 Samuel 21:1), Elijah (1 Kings 18:2), Elisha (2 Kings 4:38), Haggai (Haggai 1:11), and Nehemiah (Nehemiah 5:3). Some famines were predicted by prophets, as seen in 2 Kings 8:1 when Elisha tells the Shunammite woman to take her household and leave the land because the Lord has called for a famine that will last seven years. Famines appeared also as a natural cause. Joel 1:2-4 states, "Hear this, you elders, And give ear, all you inhabitants of the land! Has anything like this happened in your days, or even in the days of your fathers? Tell your children about it, Let your children tell their children, and their children another generation. What the chewing locust left, the swarming locust has eaten; What the swarming locust left, the crawling locust has eaten; And what the crawling locust left, the consuming locust has eaten" (NKJV).

Wind, hail, and mildew were other ways that famine appeared. Warfare, as experienced by the Israelites, was another example of famines. "Now it came to pass in the ninth year of his reign, in the tenth month, on the tenth day of the month, that Nebuchadnezzar king of Babylon and all his army came against Jerusalem and encamped against it; and they built a siege wall against it all around. So the city was besieged until the eleventh year of King Zedekiah. By the ninth day of the fourth month the famine had become so severe in the city that there was no food for the people of the land" (2 Kings 25:1–3, NKJV). Either because of disobedience to God or natural causes or war, families frequently migrated from one place to another seeking food and water because of the frequent famines on the land.

## BIBLE LEARNING

**AIM: That your students will learn that sometimes we have to appeal for what is ours by right.**

## I. THE GIFT OF SPIRITUAL

## LEADERS (2 Kings 8:1-4)

The beginning of restoration is obedience to the will of God and obedience to the leaders God sends for us. The people of God have a history just as we do today of obeying God, disobeying God, following false teachings, worshiping false gods, only to eventually return to God. Because of God's continuous faithfulness for us, God provides leaders to help us to obey God's will in our lives. "And He Himself gave some to be apostles, some prophets, some evangelists, and some pastors and teachers, for the equipping of the saints for the work of ministry, for the edifying of the body of Christ, till we all come to the unity of the faith" (**Ephesians 4:11–13a, NKJV**).

### The Process of Seeking Restoration
### (2 Kings 8:1–4)

**1 Then spake Elisha unto the woman, whose son he had restored to life, saying, Arise, and go thou and thine household, and sojourn wheresoever thou canst sojourn; for the LORD hath called for a famine; and it shall also come upon the land seven years. 2 And the woman arose, and did after the saying of the man of God: and she went with her household, and sojourned in the land of the Philistines seven years. 3 And it came to pass at the seven years' end, that the woman returned out of the land of the Philistines: and she went forth to cry unto the king for her house and for her land. 4 And the king talked with Gehazi the servant of the man of God, saying, Tell me, I pray thee, all the great things that Elisha hath done.**

The Shunammite woman accepted Elisha as a holy man because of the relationship she had built with him. With our verbal confession of faith in Jesus Christ and belief in our heart of His resurrection, we begin to participate in a life of faith, which is our faith walk. Our faith walk is based on a life of obedience to God's purpose for our lives. Our faith walk matures as we actively begin a prayer life and daily renewal of our minds from reading the Word of God. As our faith in God and His Son, Jesus Christ, grows, we can learn to accept and desire restoration.

After the famine, which lasted seven years, the Shunammite woman returned to her land to discover that her property has been taken. There is no recording of how her property was taken. Despite no record of Elisha's presence or of Elisha directing the woman to go to the king to petition for her property, the woman goes to the king to appeal to him to have her property restored to her.

The king said to Gehazi, the servant of Elisha, "'Tell me, please, all the great things Elisha has done'" (**2 Kings 8:4, NKJV**). As Gehazi told the king how Elisha restored the woman's son from the dead to life, the woman appeared to ask the king for her property.

## SEARCH THE SCRIPTURES

### QUESTION 1
Why did the woman go to the king?

**She came to plead for the return of house and land.**

## LIGHT ON THE WORD

### Gehazi Speaks to the King

Gehazi says, "'My lord, O king, this is the woman, and this is her son whom Elisha restored to life'" (**2 Kings 8:5, NKJV**). After the king asks the woman if she is indeed that woman whose son was restored back to life by Elisha, the king appoints a certain man and says, "'Restore all that was hers, and all the proceeds of the field from the day that she left the land until now'" (**2 Kings 8:6, NKJV**).

## II. A PROVIDENTIAL ARRIVAL BEFORE THE KING (2 Kings 8:5-6)

As Gehazi told about Elisha's exploits, providentially the woman arrived to appeal to the king about her "property." Gehazi turned and proclaimed, "My lord, O king, this is the woman and this is her son whom Elisha restored to life" (**2 Kings 8:5, KJV**).

God has a way of making all things work together for His good. Only God would have orchestrated Gehazi's appearance at the same time that the Shunammite came in the presence of the king. Not only was Gehazi able to give the king an account of Elisha's work, but also a specific demonstration of the prophet's ministry in the person of the Shunammite woman and her son.

As Gehazi shared how Elisha raised the young boy from the dead, the same woman, who cried out for Elisha to help her (**see 2 Kings 4:30–37**), now had the attention of the king who wanted to hear her story and had the power to restore her farm and other property.

Although the text does not say, we can assume that the king was "floored" at the providential nature of all that took place. In a similar manner, we are often stunned when God works in our lives in ways that seem impossible. But we must always remember that what is impossible with people, is possible with God (**see Luke 1:37**).

### The Fulfillment of Restoration (2 Kings 8:5–6)

**5 And it came to pass, as he was telling the king how he had restored a dead body to life, that, behold, the woman, whose son he had restored to life, cried to the king for her house and for her land. And Gehazi said, My lord, O king, this is the woman, and this is her son, whom Elisha restored to life. 6 And when the king asked the woman, she told him. So the king appointed unto her a certain officer, saying, Restore all that was hers, and all the fruits of the field since the day that she left the land, even until now.**

Certainly, the woman had a personal testimony to share with the king. Not only was she intimately involved in the ministry of Elisha, but she also received specific instructions from the prophet to leave her home and property and spend seven years in the land of the Philistines to escape the famine. God's hand was upon this woman in a powerful manner, because of her obedience and trust in the ministry of Elisha, the man of God.

The king commanded an officer to act on his behalf; everything the woman had lost—her home, farm, and personal possessions—was to be restored in the same quantity that it was taken from her during the seven-year famine. And so the woman received the blessing of the Lord in the form of her property, because of her faithfulness to the man of God, and the intervention of the king.

### QUESTION 2
How did the king know of the woman?

**Gehazi shared the story of the Shunammite woman and her son and then identified her when she came before the king.**

## LIGHT ON THE WORD
### The Woman Returned Home

After the famine, which lasted seven years, the Shunammite woman returned to her land to discover that her property had been taken. There is no recording of how her property was taken. Despite no record of Elisha's presence or of Elisha directing the woman to go to the king to petition for her property, the woman went to the king to appeal to him to have her property restored to her. Sometimes we must take the initiative to appeal for justice for ourselves.

## BIBLE APPLICATION

**AIM: That your students will work for justice in their own lives and the lives of others.**

### God Works on Our Behalf

The Shunammite woman's testimony is ours, as well. We, too, have a King acting on our behalf as we share our stories and declare His truth with those we encounter in our life journeys. Let us not be afraid to make Him known and the miracles He manifests in our lives every day **(see Revelation 12:11).** God is able to work on our behalf for justice denied.

## STUDENTS' RESPONSES

**AIM: That your students will seek the Lord's help in the times when they are fighting for justice.**

### Heroes Working for Justice

Review with your students some of the heroes and heroines of African American history who relied on God's help when working for justice. Discuss situations of injustice that they have encountered this week and spend time in prayer asking the Lord if these are situations in which they should intervene and if so, what they can do.

## PRAYER

Dear Father, thank You that You are so concerned that we receive justice. Help us to also seek justice on behalf of others. In Jesus' Name, Amen.

## DIG A LITTLE DEEPER

When the Apostle Paul had returned to Jerusalem after his final missionary journey, he nearly incited a riot by simply visiting the temple **(Acts 21:27, ff.).** False accusations were spread about the congregation, and an angry mob drew him out of the sanctuary. Seeing the tumult, a company of Roman soldiers inserted themselves into the midst to prevent Paul's lynching. They arrested Paul, meaning to carry him back to their encampment and scourge him there. But Paul identified himself as a Roman citizen to the captain of the guard to escape any rough treatment. "Is it lawful for you to scourge a man that is a Roman, and uncondemned?" he asked rhetorically **(Acts 22:25).** His self-advocacy admonished the soldiers to treat him with fairness and respect.

We can emulate the great apostle, and assert our own rights and privileges as citizens. As a principle, pursuing our rights of citizenship is the flip side of fulfilling our civic duties. For example, a believer in America should embrace all the freedoms and protections afforded by the U.S. Constitution. There will also be state and local laws that exist for our benefit. We should learn our rights and not be afraid to exert them. Contact your State Attorney General's office, and you can access free information about your rights of citizenship.

## HOW TO SAY IT

| | |
|---|---|
| Elisha. | Ih-LI-shuh. |
| Gehazi. | Ge-HA-zi. |
| Philistine. | FIL-uh-steen. |
| Shunammite. | SHOO-na-mite. |

## DAILY HOME BIBLE READINGS

### MONDAY
A Son Restored
(Luke 15:11–24)

### TUESDAY
The Protector of Widows
(Psalm 68:1–6)

### WEDNESDAY
Greed and Generosity
(Luke 20:45–21:4)

### THURSDAY
A Promised Son
(2 Kings 4:8–17)

### FRIDAY
Seeking Help from the Prophet
(2 Kings 4:18–27)

### SATURDAY
A Child Restored
(2 Kings 4:28–37)

### SUNDAY
Justice for a Widow
(2 Kings 8:1–6)

## PREPARE FOR NEXT SUNDAY

Read **2 Chronicles 19:4–11,** and next week's lesson "Jehoshaphat Makes Judicial Reforms."

**Sources:**
Berlin, Adele, and Marc Brettler. The Jewish Study Bible. New York, NY: Oxford University Press, 1999. 740.

Bible Pronunciation Chart. Better Days Are Coming.com. http://www.betterdaysarecoming/bible/pronunciation.html (accessed January 29, 2011).

Bruce, F. F., gen. ed. Zondervan Bible Commentary. Grand Rapids, MI: Zondervan
Publishing Company, 2008. 373.

Hayford, Jack W., Litt.D., et al., eds. The New Spirit-Filled Life Bible, NKJV. Nashville, TN: Thomas Nelson Publishers, 2002. 357.

Hebrew and Greek Lexicons. Bible Study Tools.com. http://www.biblestudytools.com/lexicons (accessed November 9, 2010).

MacArthur, John. The MacArthur Study Bible: NASB. Nashville, TN: Thomas Nelson
Publishing Company, 2006. 511–13, 519.

Meeks, Wayne, et al. The Harper Collins Study Bible, NRSV. New York, NY: HarperCollins Publishers, 1993. 565–71.

Myers, Allen C., ed. The Eerdmans Bible Dictionary. Grand Rapids, MI: William B. Eerdmans Publishing Company, 1996.

Old and New Testament Concordances, Lexicons, Dictionaries, Commentaries, Images, and Bible Versions. Blue Letter Bible.org. http://www.blueletterbible.org/ (accessed January 29, 2011).

The Old Testament of the Jewish Bible. Alexander Jones, gen. ed. Garden City, NY: Doubleday, 1966. 463.

Zodhiates, Spiros. The Hebrew-Greek Key Word Study Bible, King James Version.
Chattanooga, TN: AMG Publishers, 1991. 1666.

## COMMENTS / NOTES:

_____
_____
_____
_____
_____
_____
_____
_____
_____
_____
_____
_____
_____
_____
_____
_____
_____
_____
_____
_____
_____
_____
_____
_____
_____
_____

# JEHOSHAPHAT MAKES JUDICIAL REFORMS

**BIBLE BASIS:** 2 Chronicles 19:4–11

**BIBLE TRUTH:** King Jehoshaphat instituted a system of reform that followed the biblical commands for civil law and was organized to promote justice without corruption.

**MEMORY VERSE:** And said to the judges, Take heed what ye do: for ye judge not for man, but for the LORD, who is with you in the judgment (2 Chronicles 19:6, KJV).

**LESSON AIM:** By the end of the lesson, we will: UNDERSTAND that God is the ultimate authority to whom we are accountable; REFLECT on a time when choosing the "fair" or "just" option worked out for good; and JUDGE fairly when given the responsibility.

**BACKGROUND SCRIPTURES:** 2 Chronicles 18:28, 19:11-Read and incorporate the insights gained from the Background Scriptures into your study of the lesson.

## TEACHER PREPARATION

**MATERIALS NEEDED:** Bibles (several different versions), Quarterly Commentary/Teacher Manual, Adult Quarterly, teaching resources such as charts, worksheets/handouts, paper, pens, and pencils.

**OTHER MATERIALS NEEDED / TEACHER'S NOTES:**

_____

_____

## LESSON OVERVIEW

### LIFE NEED FOR TODAY'S LESSON
That students will see the need for a justice system that is organized and built upon integrity.

### BIBLE LEARNING
To understand that God can help rulers institute governmental systems that are just.

### BIBLE APPLICATION
To learn how biblical law contributes to just systems of government.

### STUDENTS' RESPONSES
Students will actively pursue justice inour court systems.

## LESSON SCRIPTURE

### 2 CHRONICLES 19:4-11 KJV

4 And Jehoshaphat dwelt at Jerusalem: and he went out again through the people from

### 2 CHRONICLES 19:4-11 AMP

4 So Jehoshaphat lived in Jerusalem, and he went out again among the people from Beersheba to the hill country of Ephraim and

Beer-sheba to mount Ephraim, and brought them back unto the LORD God of their fathers.

5 And he set judges in the land throughout all the fenced cities of Judah, city by city,

6 And said to the judges, Take heed what ye do: for ye judge not for man, but for the LORD, who is with you in the judgment.

7 Wherefore now let the fear of the Lord be upon you; take heed and do it: for there is no iniquity with the LORD our God, nor respect of persons, nor taking of gifts.

8 Moreover in Jerusalem did Jehoshaphat set of the Levites, and of the priests, and of the chief of the fathers of Israel, for the judgment of the LORD, and for controversies, when they returned to Jerusalem.

9 And he charged them, saying, Thus shall ye do in the fear of the LORD, faithfully, and with a perfect heart.

10 And what cause soever shall come to you of your brethren that dwell in their cities, between blood and blood, between law and commandment, statutes and judgments, ye shall even warn them that they trespass not against the LORD, and so wrath come upon you, and upon your brethren: this do, and ye shall not trespass.

11 And, behold, Amariah the chief priest is over you in all matters of the LORD; and Zebadiah the son of Ishmael, the ruler of the house of Judah, for all the king's matters: also the Levites shall be officers before you. Deal courageously, and the LORD shall be with the good.

brought them back to the Lord, the God of their fathers.

5 He appointed judges in the land in all the fortified cities of Judah, city by city,

6 and he said to the judges, "Be careful what you do, for you do not judge for man, but for the Lord who is with you in the matter of judgment.

7 So now let the fear (reverent awe) of the Lord be on you [to keep you from making unjust decisions]; be careful in what you do, for there is no injustice with the Lord our God, or partiality, or acceptance of a bribe."

8 In Jerusalem also Jehoshaphat appointed some of the Levites, priests, and heads of the fathers' households of Israel to render judgment of the Lord and to judge disputes among the inhabitants of Jerusalem.

9 Then the king commanded them, "Do this in the fear of the Lord, faithfully and wholeheartedly.

10 Whenever any dispute comes to you from your brothers (relatives) who live in their cities, between blood and blood, between law and commandment, or between statutes and judgments, you are to warn [and instruct] them so that they may not be guilty before the Lord; otherwise [God's] wrath will come on you and your brothers. Do this and you will not be guilty.

11 Behold, Amariah the chief priest will be over you in all matters of the Lord, and Zebadiah the son of Ishmael, the governor of the house of Judah, in all the king's matters; and the Levites will serve you as officers. Deal courageously, and may the Lord be with the upright."

## BIBLICAL DEFINITIONS

A. **Judges (2 Chronicles 19:5)** *mishpat* (Heb.)—Men chosen to exercise authority over God's chosen people to lead them back to the one true God.

B. **Judgment (v. 6)** *mishpat* (Heb.)—A verdict that is pronounced judicially; a formal decree or ordinance.

## LIGHT ON THE WORD

Jehoshaphat was the son of Asa and his successor as king of Judah **(1 Kings 15:24),** and he "turned not aside from . . . doing that which was right in the eyes of the LORD **(1 Kings 22:43).** He occupied the throne for 25 years. Jehoshaphat's concern was that the people of Judah would receive and obey the Word of the Lord. To help them accomplish this, he sent Levites and priests into the cities of Judah to teach the people the law of the Lord **(2 Chronicles 17:7–9).**

## TEACHING THE BIBLE LESSON

## LIFE NEED FOR TODAY'S LESSON

**AIM: That your students will learn that they can contribute to a good system of government by basing their own lives on the Word of God.**

## INTRODUCTION

### Establishing a Judicial System

Jehoshaphat created a system of reform by establishing judges for the people of Judah. "Also in the third year of his reign he sent his leaders, . . . to teach in the cities of Judah. So they taught in Judah, and had the Book of the Law of the LORD with them; they went throughout all the cities of Judah and taught the people" **(2 Chronicles 17:7, 9, NKJV).** Jehoshaphat reminded the judges: "Take heed to what you are doing, for you do not judge for man but for the LORD, who is with you in the judgment" **(19:6, NKJV).**

## BIBLE LEARNING

**AIM: That your students will learn that a good judicial system is based upon certain biblical principles.**

## I. The Need for a Judicial System Based upon the Old Testament Law (2 Chronicles 19:4-7)

The people of Judah had forsaken the Law of the Lord. They engaged in the worship of foreign gods, built altars for those gods, and built wooden images of those gods. Many of us, because we are under His grace and mercy, have also disobeyed God. Like the people of Judah, each of us with our disobedience has experienced God's wrath and ultimately God's forgiveness. Jehoshaphat made the mistake of making an alliance with the ungodly King Ahab. "And Jehu the son of Hanani the seer went out to meet him, and said to King Jehoshaphat, 'Should you help the wicked and love those who hate the LORD? Therefore the wrath of the LORD is upon you. Nevertheless good things are found in you, in that you have removed the wooden images from the land, and have prepared your heart to seek God.' So Jehoshaphat dwelt at Jerusalem; and he went out again among the people from Beersheba to the mountains of Ephraim, and brought them back to the LORD God of their fathers" **(2 Chronicles 19:2-4).** So it was at this time that King Jehoshaphat began to build a judicial system based on the Old Testament law.

### God's People Return to Justice
### (verses 4–7)

**4-7. And Jehoshaphat dwelt at Jerusalem: and he went out again through the people from Beer-sheba to mount Ephraim, and brought them back unto the LORD God of their fathers. 5 And he set judges in the land throughout all the fenced cities of Judah, city by city, 6 And said to the judges, Take heed what ye**

**do: for ye judge not for man, but for the LORD, who is with you in the judgment. 7 Wherefore now let the fear of the Lord be upon you; take heed and do it: for there is no iniquity with the LORD our God, nor respect of persons, nor taking of gifts.**

The judicial system of reform was established in levels to prevent abuse of power. Jehoshaphat taught the Levites and priests to "act in the fear of the LORD, faithfully and with a loyal heart" **(verse 9, NKJV)**. He reminded the Levites and the priests that some of the decisions would be made by others. "And take notice: Amariah the chief priest is over you in all matters of the LORD; and Zebadiah the son of Ishmael, the ruler of the house of Judah, for all the king's matters; also the Levites will be officials before you" **(verse 11, NKJV)**.

With the creation of a layered system of reforms, Jehoshaphat was able to bring the people of Judah back to the authority of God. We also see this divine concern for justice expressed in the New Testament: "Let every soul be subject to the governing authorities. For there is no authority except God, and the authorities that exist are appointed by God. Therefore whoever resists the authority resists the ordinance of God, and those who resist will bring judgment on themselves" **(Romans 13:1–2, NKJV)**.

## SEARCH THE SCRIPTURES

### QUESTION 1
Why did Jehoshaphat send judges to the people of Judah?

**King Jehoshaphat wanted the people to come back to the Lord.**

## LIGHT ON THE WORD

### A Delegation of Responsibility
The reform that King Jehoshaphat instituted involved a delegation of responsibility from the king to his officials and a possible regaining by the priests of some of the authority they had lost in the highly centralized days of David and Solomon.

## II. THE SUPREME COURT (2 Chronicles 19:8-11)

Jehoshaphat set up a central court in Jerusalem to deal with major cases, including homicide and appeals. Notice that Jehoshaphat wanted these cases to be heard by the Levites and chiefs of Israel, and only in Jerusalem. These cases were to be brought before those who could interpret the religious laws and the civil laws. This would imply that the cases had civil and religious overtones. The king's primary objectives were that all judgment must be done in the fear of the Lord and with a heart that is focused on justice and truth.

### The Equipping of the Judges (verses 8–11)
**8-11. Moreover in Jerusalem did Jehoshaphat set of the Levites, and of the priests, and of the chief of the fathers of Israel, for the judgment of the LORD, and for controversies, when they returned to Jerusalem. 9 And he charged them, saying, Thus shall ye do in the fear of the LORD, faithfully, and with a perfect heart. 10 And what cause soever shall come to you of your brethren that dwell in their cities, between blood and blood, between law and commandment, statutes and judgments, ye shall even warn them that they trespass not against the LORD, and so wrath come upon you, and upon your brethren: this do, and ye shall not trespass. 11 And, behold, Amariah the chief priest is over you in all matters of the LORD; and Zebadiah the son of Ishmael, the ruler of the house of Judah, for all the king's matters: also the Levites shall be officers before you. Deal**

**courageously, and the LORD shall be with the good.**

God places people in our lives to equip us for service to Him. "So they taught in Judah, and had the Book of the Law of the LORD with them; they went throughout all the cities of Judah and taught the people" (**2 Chronicles 17:9, NKJV**). When we are prepared to go out and serve, God tells us what our assignment is. "'Take heed to what you are doing, for you do not judge for man but for the LORD, who is with you in the judgment'" (**2 Chronicles 19:6, NKJV**). God instructs us on our assignment and cautions us to not abuse the authority He has placed within us. "And he commanded them, saying, 'Thus you shall act in the fear of the LORD, faithfully and with a loyal heart'" (**verse 9, NKJV**). God reminds each of us that we are accountable for what God has instructed us to do. "And take notice: Amariah the chief priest is over you in all matters of the LORD; and Zebadiah the son of Ishmael, the ruler of the house of Judah, for all the king's matters; also the Levites will be officials before you. Behave courageously, and the LORD will be with the good" (**verse 11, NKJV**).

## QUESTION 2
What warning did Jehoshaphat give to the judges?

**They are judging for the Lord, who is with them in the judgment. Answers will vary.**

## LIGHT ON THE WORD

### Judging Fairly
Many people within the African American community are being judged unfairly, simply because of choices related to their lifestyles. Perhaps those of us within our community who are doing the judging should go back to emphasizing that God and education are the keys to a positive lifestyle. Perhaps those of us who are judging should become positive role models by mentoring, going back to the community, and sharing the stories of our successes. For instance, we should tell the story of the importance of obtaining and maintaining a strong work ethic. In addition, we should make a commitment to avoid condemnation without truly understanding the person's situation. "So Jehoshaphat dwelt at Jerusalem, and he went out again among the people from Beersheba to the mountains of Ephraim, and brought them back to the LORD God of their fathers" (**2 Chronicles 19:4, NKJV**). Maybe God can use us in restoring many of our people.

## BIBLE APPLICATION
**AIM: That your students will see the need for a good system of justice.**

### Needed: Reformation of Our Judicial System
In America, we need reformation in our judicial system that is focused on justice and truth. All too many African Americans know what it is like to be accused of a crime they have not committed. Our penal system is littered with innocent people who do not have the resources or influence to overturn wrong decisions. But one day, all of this will change as God will establish true righteousness and justice in the land.

## STUDENTS' RESPONSES
**AIM: That your students will seek to be agents of change with God's help and direction**

### Reformation
Note the king's final word to the judges as the reformation is put in place: "Deal courageously, and the LORD shall be with the good" (**2 Chronicles 19:11c**). Reformation is never easy, whether in a church, family, business, or community. It takes someone like Jehoshaphat to challenge the status quo and recognize

that despite the naysayers that fight against reformation, God is with us to bring about the needed change for His honor and praise. Are you a Jehoshaphat?

## PRAYER

Dear Father, thank You for being so concerned that we receive justice. Help us to also seek justice on behalf of others. In Jesus' Name, Amen.

## DIG A LITTLE DEEPER

Chuck Colson (1931–2012) had the distinction of being the first associate of President Richard Nixon to be incarcerated for crimes related to the Watergate scandal. Colson had had a midlife conversion to evangelical Christianity the year before he served his prison sentence. The one-time political fixer radically changed his life, and ultimately started an influential and successful prison ministry. In the 45 years since its founding, Prison Fellowship has grown to become the largest nonprofit organization for convicts and their families.

Prison Fellowship is now a major advocate for federal and state criminal justice reform. For example, the organization heavily promoted the rollback of onerous Clinton-era drug laws, as was accomplished by the First Step Act, signed into law in December 2018. But, of course, lobbying of lawmakers is only part of their story. Prison Fellowship is a hands-on ministry, with staff and volunteers running programs and special events for prisoners throughout the country. Their affiliated ministry, Angel Tree, provides Christmas gifts and summer camps for the children of imprisoned parents. They are unapologetically Christian, sharing the gospel within the largest incarcerated population in the world. If you have a like-minded concern for criminal justice reform, please contact them at prisonfellowship.org to find out how to donate time or treasure.

## HOW TO SAY IT

Amariah.  am'uh-RI-uh.

Beer-sheba.  bee'uhr-SHEE-buh.

Jehoshaphat.  juh-HOSH-uh-fat(').

### DAILY HOME BIBLE READINGS

**MONDAY**
The Lord Is Our Judge
(Isaiah 33:13–22)

**TUESDAY**
May Righteousness Flourish
(Psalm 72:1–7)

**WEDNESDAY**
Steadfast in Keeping God's Statutes
(Psalm 119:1–8)

**THURSDAY**
Fear the Lord, Depart from Evil
(Job 28:20–28)

**FRIDAY**
The Battles Is God's
(2 Chronicles 20:5–15)

**SATURDAY**
Walking in God's Commandments
(2 Chronicles 17:1–6)

**SUNDAY**
Judging on the Lord's Behalf
(2 Chronicles 19:4–11)

## PREPARE FOR NEXT SUNDAY

Read **Psalm 146:1-10,** and next week's lesson "Praise for God's Justice."

**Sources:**
Berlin, Adele, and Marc Brettler. The Jewish Study Bible. New York, NY: Oxford University Press, 2004. 144, 404–5, 1790–94.

Bible Pronunciation Chart. Better Days Are Coming.com. http://www.
betterdaysarecoming/bible/pronunciation.html (accessed January 29,
2011).

Brand, Chad, and Charles Draper, eds. Holman Illustrated Bible Dictionary.
Nashville, TN: Holman Bible Publishers, 2003. 500, 877–78.

Bruce, F. F., gen. ed. Zondervan Bible Commentary. Grand Rapids, MI:
Zondervan
Publishing Company, 2008. 426.

Hebrew and Greek Lexicons. Bible Study Tools.com. http://www.
biblestudytools.com/lexicons (accessed November 11, 2010).

MacArthur, John. The MacArthur Study Bible: NASB. Nashville, TN: Thomas
Nelson
Publishing Company, 2006. 605.

Meeks, Wayne, et al., eds. The HarperCollins Study Bible, NRSV. New York, NY:
HarperCollins Publishers, 1993. 667–71.

Myers, Allen C., ed. The Eerdmans Bible Dictionary. Grand Rapids, MI: William
B. Eerdmans Publishing Company, 1996.

The Old Testament of the Jewish Bible. Alexander Jones, gen. ed. Garden City,
NY: Doubleday, 1966. 547.

Passage Lookup. Bible Gateway.com. http://www.biblegateway.com/
passage (accessed January 24, 2011).

Zodhiates, Spiros. The Hebrew-Greek Key Word Study Bible, King James
Version.
Chattanooga, TN: AMG Publishers, 1991. 1632, 1674.

## COMMENTS / NOTES:

# PRAISE FOR GOD'S JUSTICE

**BIBLE BASIS:** Psalm 146:1–10

**BIBLE TRUTH:** This psalm praises God for His care for those whom society overlooks and despises..

**MEMORY VERSE:** Happy is he that hath the God of Jacob for his help, whose hope is in the LORD his God: Which executeth judgment for the oppressed: which giveth food to the hungry. The LORD looseth the prisoners (Psalm 146:5, 7, KJV).

**LESSON AIM:** By the end of the lesson, we will: EXPLAIN how prayer and faith can bring about justice; REFLECT upon God's role as Promise Keeper; and AFFIRM that God has promised to help people who are oppressed.

**BACKGROUND SCRIPTURES:** Psalm 146:1-10, Exodus 21-23 Isaiah 58-Read and incorporate the insights gained from the Background Scriptures into your study of the lesson.

## TEACHER PREPARATION

**MATERIALS NEEDED:** Bibles (several different versions), Quarterly Commentary/Teacher Manual, Adult Quarterly, teaching resources such as charts, worksheets/handouts, paper, pens, and pencils.

**OTHER MATERIALS NEEDED / TEACHER'S NOTES:**

_____

_____

## LESSON OVERVIEW

### LIFE NEED FOR TODAY'S LESSON
That students will seek God's help when they face unfair situations.

### BIBLE LEARNING
To understand that God cares for all those who are treated unfairly.

### BIBLE APPLICATION
To learn that we can count on God for help when all people fail us.

### STUDENTS' RESPONSES
Students will praise God because He is worthy.

## LESSON SCRIPTURE

### PSALM 146:1-10 KJV

1 Praise ye the LORD. Praise the LORD, O my soul.

### PSALM 146:1-10 AMP

1 Praise the LORD! (Hallelujah!) Praise the LORD, O my soul!

448

2 While I live will I praise the LORD: I will sing praises unto my God while I have any being.

3 Put not your trust in princes, nor in the son of man, in whom there is no help.

4 His breath goeth forth, he returneth to his earth; in that very day his thoughts perish.

5 Happy is he that hath the God of Jacob for his help, whose hope is in the LORD his God:

6 Which made heaven, and earth, the sea, and all that therein is: which keepeth

 truth for ever:

7 Which executeth judgment for the oppressed: which giveth food to the hungry. The LORD looseth the prisoners:

8 The LORD openeth the eyes of the blind: the LORD raiseth them that are bowed down: the LORD loveth the righteous:

9 The LORD preserveth the strangers; he relieveth the fatherless and widow: but the way of the wicked he turneth upside down.

10 The LORD shall reign for ever, even thy God, O Zion, unto all generations. Praise ye the LORD.

2 While I live I will praise the LORD; I will sing praises to my God as long as I live.

3 Do not trust in princes, In mortal man, in whom there is no salvation (help).

4 When his spirit leaves him, he returns to the earth; In that very day his thoughts and plans perish.

5 How blessed and graciously favored is he whose help is the God of Jacob (Israel), Whose hope is in the LORD his God,

6 Who made heaven and earth, The sea, and all that is in them, Who keeps truth and is faithful forever,

7 Who executes justice for the oppressed, Who gives food to the hungry. The LORD sets free the prisoners.

8 The LORD opens the eyes of the blind; The LORD lifts up those who are bowed down; The LORD loves the [a]righteous [the upright in heart].

9 The LORD protects the strangers; He supports the fatherless and the widow; But He makes crooked the way of the wicked.

10 The LORD shall reign forever, Your God, O Zion, to all generations. Praise the LORD! (Hallelujah!)

## BIBLICAL DEFINITIONS

A. **Executes (Psalm 146:7)** `asah (Heb.)—Undertakes a deliberate action with a specific or distinct purpose.

B. **Oppressed (v. 7)** `ashaq (Heb.)—Someone who has been cheated or otherwise exploited.

## LIGHT ON THE WORD

Some psalms reflect thanksgiving, praise,

confession of sin, pursuit of wisdom, or devotion; other psalms concentrate on prayer or petitions. Of the five groupings of psalms, the last group, **Psalms 107–150** are unique in that they each begin and end with the exuberant exclamation of both joy and gratitude "Praise ye the LORD," which is often translated as "Hallelujah."

## TEACHING THE BIBLE LESSON

## LIFE NEED FOR TODAY'S LESSON

AIM: **That your students will learn that God cares for the poor and all those that society rejects, ignores and oppresses.**

## INTRODUCTION

### God Turns Society Upside Down

The concepts of oppression and justice are both universal and ancient. Access to abundance and fair judgment is often reserved for the powerful. This means that equity and justice are frequently denied to the oppressed. In the ancient world, human-made social order dictated the "haves" and the "have nots." The widows, orphans, and immigrants occupied the lowest stratum of society; hence, justice was not within their reach. In today's lesson, the psalmist recognizes that God reverses this perverse pecking order, and the psalmist praises God for His righteous judgment and affirms his trust in the Lord. The psalmist expresses his confidence that because He is righteous in nature, our God will bless those whom people had found insignificant. God will listen to and fairly judge the petitions of those that humankind has ignored. In the presence of an all-knowing, ever-present, all-powerful Creator, the poor and needy will be exalted, while the wealthy and powerful will be rendered frail and useless. This blessed assurance gives us reason to place our trust in God and in God alone.

## BIBLE LEARNING

AIM: **That your students will learn that praise is a good way to begin.**

## I. PRAISE THE LORD (Psalm 146:1-2)

This psalm begins with an undeniable declaration of praise. Praise is reserved generally for someone that we recognize as great. In today's world, we sometimes praise our friends or family for kind or notable actions or deeds. We even praise politicians or celebrities for their works or performances. This type of praise is subjective. These people do something that benefits us, and we express our gratitude by praising them. Unfortunately, we are equally quick to censure and even condemn these same people if they do something that evokes our disapproval.

### A Promise of Praise (verses 1–2)
**1 Praise ye the LORD. Praise the LORD, O my soul. 2 While I live will I praise the LORD: I will sing praises unto my God while I have any being.**

The subject of the psalmist's adoration is neither fleeting nor capricious. The earnestness of the psalmist is apparent to us in the very personalization of the praise. With his entire being (his "soul," **verse 1**), the psalmist will praise the Lord. This praise is leveled at God who has covenanted to love and protect His people. The psalmist's praise echoes the Israelites' covenant to obey, honor, and love God with all of their being. Unconditional praise should be our response as Christians to our understanding that Jesus, the Christ, is our Savior, and it is only through Him that we are reconciled to the one, true, and righteous God. As mature Christians, we should begin and maintain a pattern of praise in our lives, which will continue through all eternity like the psalmist.

## SEARCH THE SCRIPTURES

### QUESTION 1

How long does the psalmist promise to praise God?

**The psalmist promises to praise God for as long as he lives.**

## LIGHT ON THE WORD

### A Warning

The psalmist now turns his attention from praise to issue an important warning. We are instructed not to place our trust in human leadership. When we "trust" (**verse 3**), we have confidence and assurance that someone will do what he or she promises to do. In the ancient world of the psalmist, the "princes" were the kings and rulers. While many in authority today do as they promise, many others do not. In recent years, failure to exercise proper authority led to a global financial crisis and an unprecedented oil spill that resulted in catastrophic ecological and economic damage. We must always remember that those in authority only hold temporary positions. Because they are human, they will eventually "perish" or die (**verse 4**).

## II. OUR ONLY TRUST IS IN GOD (Psalm 146:3-4)

While highly positioned men and women may hold authority in government or be in positions that assist in our employment, education, finances, and so on, not one of them can offer us help after we die! Because only God can assure us of eternal salvation, the psalmist insists that our trust is only safe in Him who can assure us that our souls will not die. For the Christian, our very salvation lies in this acknowledgment that our only security is God; we are objects of His incredible love and grace.

### The Perils of Misplaced Trust (verses 3–4)

**3 Put not your trust in princes, nor in the son of man, in whom there is no help. 4 His breath goeth forth, he returneth to his earth; in that very day his thoughts perish.**

The psalmist warns his audience of the absurdity of trusting in human beings as life's foundation and source of justice, whether they are princes or common persons. The end of life on earth is the same for the prince or the pauper—the bodies of each decay and turn into dust.

### QUESTION 2

What happens to the princes at the end of their lives?

**Their bodies will decay. Answers will vary.**

## LIGHT ON THE WORD

### God Is Worthy of Praise

The psalmist's reference to "the God of Jacob" means the God of the people of Israel (**Psalm 146:5**). The psalmist identifies God as the Creator of everything (heaven, earth, and the seas) and everyone. Clearly, God is worthy of praise not only because He is the Creator, but because He makes provision for the most beloved of His creations: human beings. The psalmist goes on to list some of the ways God cares for the "oppressed" or those who most need His care and protection. God feeds the hungry, sets prisoners free, makes the blind to see, and lifts up the fallen (**verse 7**).

## III. GOD'S JUDGMENT OF THE ABUSERS (Psalm 146:5-9)

It is important to note that God's provisional care goes beyond the poor and downtrodden. These are people who have been abused, usually by someone in power who took advantage of them. The psalmist tells us that God will bring judgment upon the people who are responsible for these abuses. Those who think they are getting away with oppressing others will encounter God, who protects and vindicates the righteous.

### Declaration of God's Righteousness (verses 5–9)

**5 Happy is he that hath the God of Jacob for his help, whose hope is in the LORD his God: 6 Which made heaven, and earth, the sea, and all that therein is: which keepeth truth for ever: 7 Which executeth judgment for the oppressed: which giveth food to the hungry. The LORD looseth the prisoners: 8 The LORD openeth the eyes of the blind: the LORD raiseth them that are bowed down: the LORD loveth the righteous: 9 The LORD preserveth the strangers; he relieveth the fatherless and widow: but the way of the wicked he turneth upside down.**

The psalmist's reference to "the God of Jacob" probably means the God of the people of Israel (**Psalm 146:5**). The psalmist identifies God as the Creator of everything (heaven, earth, and the seas) and everyone. Clearly, God is worthy of praise not only because He is the Creator, but because He makes provision for the most beloved of His creations: human beings. The psalmist goes on to list some of the ways God cares for the "oppressed" or those who most need His care and protection. God feeds the hungry, sets prisoners free, makes the blind to see, and lifts up the fallen (**verse 7**).

It is important to note that God's provisional care goes beyond the poor and downtrodden. These are people who have been abused, usually by someone in power who took advantage of them. The psalmist tells us that God will bring judgment upon the people who are responsible for these abuses. Those who think they are getting away with oppressing others will encounter God, who protects and vindicates the righteous.

We should also note that our righteous God acknowledges His creation as righteous, too. "The righteous" refers to those who are faithful to God's covenant (**verse 8**); after Christ's advent, we obtain righteousness through faith in Christ. The reference to "strangers" in **verse 9** refers to people who were from other countries living among the Jews. God's provisional care is extended to these immigrants and refugees, too.

## SEARCH THE SCRIPTURES

### QUESTION 3
Who will defend the oppressed?

**God will defend the oppressed.**

## LIGHT ON THE WORD

### God's Present and Future Reign

As the psalmist concludes his thoughts, he circles back to where he began: an outburst of praise and a proclamation that our God, our righteous Judge, will reign over us forever. This sentiment is echoed in **Exodus 15:18**, "The LORD shall reign for ever and ever." Similarly, the eternity of God's reign is confirmed when we read, "And the seventh angel sounded; and there were great voices in heaven, saying, The kingdoms of this world are become the kingdoms of our Lord, and of his Christ; and he shall reign for ever and ever" (**Revelation 11:15**). This is a promise to all generations who hear and respond to the message of salvation revealed in Jesus.

## IV. REASON TO PRAISE THE LORD (Psalm 146:10)

Just considering God's immeasurable love for us can cause joy for the love of our Lord to well up and erupt in praise. He is not only the Creator of the universe, but He also faithfully keeps truth for all time. Our praise, like that of the psalmist, lies in the fact that we can have absolute security in knowing, "God is not a man, that he should lie; neither the son of man, that he should repent: hath he said, and shall he not do it? or hath he spoken, and shall he not make it good?" (**Numbers 23:19**).

### Confidence in the Eternity of the Righteous Judge (Psalm 146:10)
**10. The LORD shall reign for ever, even thy God, O Zion, unto all generations. Praise ye the LORD.**

Like David in **Psalm 10:16** and **145:13**, and at the end of Moses' song (**Exodus 15:18**), in **Psalm 146:10** the psalmist sings of the majesty of a mighty God who will reign to the end of days. In **Revelation 11:15**, the apostle John affirms, "The kingdoms of this world are become the kingdoms of our Lord, and of his Christ; and he shall reign for ever and ever." Though wickedness abounds today, we who are Christians have the assurance of an everlasting God who shall reign in Zion throughout all of life. Hallelujah!

## QUESTION 4
When does God reign?

**He reigns forever. Answers will vary.**

## LIGHT ON THE WORD
### Lasting Justice
People appreciate receiving lasting justice. Where can we look to find unshakable justice? God is the source of steadfast justice.

## BIBLE APPLICATION

**AIM: That your students will understand the justice of God.**

### Dealing with Unfair Situations
The notion of justice is sometimes a tricky one. When we face unfair situations, we often try to use common sense or logic to rectify things. Sometimes we take on the operation of judgment ourselves—"to get even." The very term "getting even" implies making someone else carry the appropriate weight so that there is an even distribution. Compare and contrast our understanding of justice with the justice described in **Psalm 146**.

## STUDENTS' RESPONSES
**AIM: That your students will seek to share the hope that is in God.**

### Share the Good News
One need only listen to friends, family members, and coworkers to hear the discouragement of those around us. Many of the people we see every day are without hope and trust in anything and anyone. Make it a point to reach out to someone this week. Share your testimony with them, and more importantly, share the Word of God with them. Encourage them to put their confidence in God.

## PRAYER

Dear Father, we praise You! We thank You that You care for us when we are down. In fact, You care for all people. Help us to demonstrate Your love to others this week. In Jesus' Name, Amen.

## DIG A LITTLE DEEPER

We serve a God Who identifies with downtrodden and persecuted people. As Jesus Christ taught at the end of his Olivet Discourse (**Matthew 25:31–46**), the Son of Man would consider feeding the hungry, hosting the stranger, clothing the naked, and visiting the sick and the prisoners to be ministering to him personally: "Inasmuch as ye have done it unto one of the least of these my brethren, ye have done it unto me" (**v. 40**). Scripture instructs us that God is "a father to the fatherless, a defender of widows" (**Ps. 68:5, NLT**) and that a person "that hath pity upon the poor lendeth unto the LORD" (**Prov. 19:17**). Our heavenly Father has frequently shown us His heart for the vulnerable.

If we are the children of God, we should share His interests and reflect His values. If we do not have a zeal and a burden for the oppressed, it is time to pray that God gives them to us.

## HOW TO SAY IT

Hallelujah.          ha'lul-LOO-yuh.

---

### DAILY HOME BIBLE READINGS

#### MONDAY
Where Is the God of Justice?
(Malachi 2:10–17)

#### TUESDAY
God's Ways Are Justice
(Daniel 4:34–37)

#### WEDNESDAY
The Fast That God Chooses
(Isaiah 58:1–9b)

#### THURSDAY
God's Continued Guidance
(Isaiah 58:9c–14)

#### FRIDAY
God Will Grant Justice
(Luke 18:1–8)

#### SATURDAY
Love God and Establish Justice
(Amos 5:8–15)

#### SUNDAY
Happy Are Those Who Execute Justice
(Psalm 146)

---

## PREPARE FOR NEXT SUNDAY

Read **Isaiah 9:2-7,** and next week's lesson "God Promised a Righteous Lord."

**Sources:**
Berlin, Adele, and Marc Brettler. The Jewish Study Bible. New York, NY: Oxford University Press, 2004. 17–18, 1280–81, 1398, 1442–43.

Bible Pronunciation Chart. Better Days Are Coming.com. http://www.betterdaysarecoming/bible/pronunciation.html (accessed January 29, 2011).

Blank, Wayne, ed. Daily Bible Study. http://www.keyway.ca (accessed June 17, 2010).

Exploring the Word of God. Psalms: Thematic Collections. http://www.wcg.org/lit/bible/poetry/psalms5.htm (accessed June 1, 2010).

"Hallel." Answers.com. http://www.answers.com/topic/hallel (accessed January 29, 2011).

Merriam-Webster Online Dictionary. Merriam-Webster, Inc. http://www.merriam-webster.com (accessed January 29, 2011).

The Old Testament of the Jewish Bible. Alexander Jones, gen. ed. Garden City, NY: Doubleday, 1966.

Stern, David H. Complete Jewish Bible: An English Verson of the Tanakh and B'rit adashah. Clarksville, MD: Jewish New Testament Publications, 1998.

Wigram, George V. The Englishman's Hebrew and Chaldee Concordance of the Old Testament. Nashville, TN: Broadman Press, 1980.

## COMMENTS / NOTES:

_____

_____

_____

_____

_____

_____

_____

_____

_____

_____

_____

_____

_____

_____

_____

_____

_____

_____

_____

_____

_____

_____

_____

_____

_____

# GOD PROMISED A RIGHTEOUS LORD

**BIBLE BASIS:** Isaiah 9:2-7

**BIBLE TRUTH:** Our hope is found in the coming Messiah who established a just and right kingdom..

**MEMORY VERSE:** For unto us a child is born, unto us a Son is given: and the government shall be upon his shoulder: and his name shall be called Wonderful, Counsellor, The mighty God, The everlasting Father, The Prince of Peace (Isaiah 9:6, KJV).

**LESSON AIM:** By the end of the lesson, we will: KNOW the relationship between Isaiah's prophecy and its fulfillment in Jesus Christ; REFLECT on God's promise of justice to those who are without hope; and IDENTIFY signs of hope in conflict-ridden areas such as inner cities and our government.

**BACKGROUND SCRIPTURES:** Isaiah 9:1-7- Read and incorporate the insights gained from the Background Scriptures into your study of the lesson.

## TEACHER PREPARATION

**MATERIALS NEEDED:** Bibles (several different versions), Quarterly Commentary/Teacher Manual, Adult Quarterly, teaching resources such as charts, worksheets/handouts, paper, pens, and pencils.

**OTHER MATERIALS NEEDED / TEACHER'S NOTES:**

_____

_____

## LESSON OVERVIEW

**LIFE NEED FOR TODAY'S LESSON**
That students will learn that God sent Jesus to bring us peace.

**BIBLE LEARNING**
To understand that God sent the Savior for everyone.

**BIBLE APPLICATION**
To learn that Jesus is both God and man.

**STUDENTS' RESPONSES**
Students will trust in Jesus our wonderful Savior as their LORD and Savior.

## LESSON SCRIPTURE

### ISAIAH 9:2-7 KJV

2 The people that walked in darkness have seen a great light: they that dwell in the land of the shadow of death, upon

### ISAIAH 9:2-7 AMP

2 The people who walk in [spiritual] darkness Will see a great Light; Those who live in the dark land, The Light will shine

them hath the light shined.

**3.** Thou hast multiplied the nation, and not increased the joy: they joy before thee according to the joy in harvest, and as men rejoice when they divide the spoil.

**4.** For thou hast broken the yoke of his burden, and the staff of his shoulder, the rod of his oppressor, as in the day of Midian.

**5.** For every battle of the warrior is with confused noise, and garments rolled in blood; but this shall be with burning and fuel of fire.

**6.** For unto us a child is born, unto us a Son is given: and the government shall be upon his shoulder: and his name shall be called Wonderful, Counsellor, The mighty God, The everlasting Father, The Prince of Peace.

**7.** Of the increase of his government and peace there shall be no end, upon the throne of David, and upon his kingdom, to order it, and to stablish it with judgment and with justice from henceforth even for ever. The zeal of the LORD of hosts will perform this.

on them.

3 You [O God] will increase the nation, You will multiply their joy; They will rejoice before You Like the joy and jubilation of the harvest, As men rejoice when they divide the spoil [of victory].

4 For You will break the yoke of Israel's burden and the staff (goad) on their shoulders, The rod of their oppressor, as at the battle of Midian.

5 For every boot of the marching warrior in the battle tumult, And [every soldier's] garment rolled in blood, will be used for burning, fuel for the fire.

6 For to us a Child shall be born, to us a Son shall be given; And the government shall be upon His shoulder, And His name shall be called Wonderful Counselor, Mighty God, Everlasting Father, Prince of Peace.

7 There shall be no end to the increase of His government and of peace, [He shall rule] on the throne of David and over his kingdom, To establish it and to uphold it with justice and righteousness From that time forward and forevermore. The zeal of the LORD of hosts will accomplish this.

## BIBLICAL DEFINITIONS

A. **Shadow of Death (Isaiah 9:2)** *tsal-maveth* (Heb.)—Distress or extreme danger.

B. **Yoke (v. 4)** *'ol* (Heb.)—Denotes a condition of servitude or slavery.

## LIGHT ON THE WORD

Isaiah was one of the most influential Old Testament prophets. He lived and ministered in the southern kingdom of Judah for 58 years. Isaiah lived through one of his nation's most turbulent periods during which he witnessed Judah's defeat by the Babylonian Empire and actually saw his fellow citizens taken into captivity. He prophesied during the reign of five kings: Uzziah, Jotham, Ahaz, Hezekiah, and Manasseh. His free access to the palace in Jerusalem and his familiarity with court life imply that Isaiah belonged to Judah's wealthy class and may have been related to the ruling family. However, this did not keep Isaiah from verbally attacking the aristocracy in defense of the common people. Scripture refers to his wife as a "prophetess" and identifies him as the father of at least two sons: Shear-jashub and Maher-shalal-hash-baz (**Isaiah 7:1–3; 8:1–3**).

## TEACHING THE BIBLE LESSON

## LIFE NEED FOR TODAY'S LESSON

**AIM:** That your students will learn that God sent Jesus into a dark and turbulent world.

## INTRODUCTION

### Living with War Due to Sinfulness

Much of Isaiah's writings strongly criticize the people of Judah for their sinfulness and unwillingness to be faithful to the one true God. During the reign of King Ahaz, the kings of Israel and Damascus waged war against Judah. Instead of looking to God for support, King Ahaz foolishly allied himself with the Assyrian king, Tiglath-pileser. Judah soon found itself a vassal state under the Assyrians. In 721 B.C., Israel was invaded and the capital city of Samaria was destroyed. The tribute demanded by the Assyrians from Judah was so great that Ahaz's successor and son, King Hezekiah, formed an alliance with the nations of Egypt, Moab, and Edom, and plotted with them to revolt against the Assyrians. The revolt was squashed in 711 B.C. Isaiah warned that their continued refusal to be faithful to God would result in disaster for the entire nation. King Hezekiah didn't listen, and in 705 B.C., he participated in another attempted revolt, this time enlisting the aid of the Babylonians. King Hezekiah refused to heed the prophet, and Judah was almost destroyed

before the people turned back to God and begged Him to come to their aide. Throughout his ministry, Isaiah repeatedly called on the nation to rely on God, rather than military strength or political alliances. The northern kingdom had refused to listen to their prophets, Amos and Hosea. Instead, Israel had resorted to military might to assert their nationhood, and as a result, had been soundly defeated and no longer existed as a nation. By the grace of God, Judah was for a time spared.

## BIBLE LEARNING

**AIM:** That your students will learn that we need a Savior.

## I. Living under Bleak Spiritual Conditions (Isaiah 9:2-5)

During the time Isaiah lived, Assyria was a major military force that was defeating many countries. It is understandable that the future appeared foreboding and hopeless to the people of Judah. In the previous chapter, the prophet Isaiah describes the bleak spiritual conditions when he writes, "And when they shall say unto you, Seek unto them that have familiar spirits, and unto wizards that peep, and that mutter: should not a people seek unto their God? for the living to the dead? To the law and to the testimony: if they speak not according to this word, it is because there is no light in them. And they shall pass through it, hardly bestead and hungry: and it shall come to pass, that when they shall be hungry, they shall fret themselves, and curse their king and their God, and look upward. And they shall look unto the earth; and behold trouble and darkness, dimness of anguish; and they shall be driven to darkness" (**Isaiah 8:19-22**). It is reasonable to assume that this text occurs after Assyria invaded Syria and Israel around 734–32 B.C. Judah was in a state of spiritual darkness and political distress as it helplessly watched the scorched earth policy of the invading Assyrians in the northern portion of Palestine.

### End of the Darkness (9:2–5)

**2 The people that walked in darkness have seen a great light: they that dwell in the land of the shadow of death, upon them hath the light shined. 3 Thou hast multiplied the nation, and not increased the joy: they joy before thee according to the joy in harvest, and as men rejoice when they divide the spoil. 4 For thou hast broken the yoke of his burden, and the staff of his shoulder, the rod of his oppressor, as in the day of Midian. 5 For every battle of the warrior is with confused noise, and garments rolled in blood; but this shall be with burning and fuel of fire.**

Into a scene of national tumult and despair, the prophet Isaiah introduces a wonderful prophecy of hope. Isaiah makes it clear that he is addressing Judah. They are the people who had walked in "darkness" and dwelled "in the land of the shadow of death" (Isaiah 9:2). It is ironic that the people, who dwell in the Promised Land, have been plunged into spiritual darkness. This kind of darkness is a frightening but apt description of sin. The lost person foolishly believes that he "understands" or is in the light, when he actually operates in perpetual darkness. It is this spiritual darkness that contributes to the encompassing sense of hopelessness and helplessness.

Conversely, God's presence is equated with light. "God is light, and in Him is no darkness at all" (1 John 1:5b, NKJV). The great light that will appear is Jesus, Christ Jesus, the Messiah. Seven hundred years later, Jesus would begin His ministry and bring light into this very land that is now plunged into darkness. It is Jesus who will stand in the Temple and declare, "I am the light of the world; he who follows Me shall not walk in darkness, but shall have the light of life" (John 8:12, NKJV). Isaiah insists that because a Messiah is coming, there will be joy instead of gloom (verse 3). The hope of the people is to be placed in the Lord, not in reliance on military strength or political savvy. Their "joy" would come from the Messiah, not human allies. Only then would they be able to rejoice. Present-day saints should be reminded that we are not bound by our present conditions and circumstances; we can rejoice in our hope in the only One who can remove the gloom from our lives. From his dark and dank Roman prison cell, the apostle Paul rejoiced in his chains: "Rejoice in the Lord always. I will say it again: Rejoice!" (Philippians 4:4, NIV).

## SEARCH THE SCRIPTURES

### QUESTION 1

What has happened to the people that walked in darkness?

**They have seen a great light.**

## LIGHT ON THE WORD

### The Promised Child

The promise of a child named Immanuel in Isaiah 7:14 (see also 8:8,) is fulfilled by the promised birth in 9:6 of the Son, who was both God and King. It is beyond question that both prophecies foretell Jesus. "Immanuel" means "God with us." God did not come as a great authoritarian figure, but rather as a child. As the son of David, He would reign from David's throne, but as the Son of God, He would be "God with us." One can imagine the prophet Isaiah questioning whether or not he was hearing correctly when God inspired him to pen these words. This royal descendant of David and heir to his throne would not rise as other kings nor would anything be the same as with other kings.

## II. GOD'S GIFT TO US (Isaiah 9:6-7)

How wonderful it is for Christians to note that the birth of this child, introduced by Isaiah, is a gift to us from God Himself. A child, but not just any child--He will be the Son of God. Here, Isaiah's prophecy recognizes that the Messiah will be a legitimate heir to the Davidic throne, a point of paramount importance to the people living in the time of this writing. Even though the Messiah would be "born" as human beings are, Isaiah stresses that He will be "given" (**Isaiah 9:6**). The King of whom Isaiah speaks will be both human and divine, possessing the power of the Creator (God) and the frailties and characteristics of the creation (humankind). However, He was without sin. When we read "the government will rest on his shoulders" (**9:6, NLT**), we see Isaiah's poetic description of the Messiah as a capable and sovereign Ruler, not to be confused with a mere human king.

## Gift of Forthcoming Peace
### (verses 6–7)

**6 For unto us a child is born, unto us a Son is given: and the government shall be upon his shoulder: and his name shall be called Wonderful, Counsellor, The mighty God, The everlasting Father, The Prince of Peace. 7 Of the increase of his government and peace there shall be no end, upon the throne of David, and upon his kingdom, to order it, and to establish it with judgment and with justice from henceforth even for ever. The zeal of the LORD of hosts will perform this.**

Isaiah identifies the Messiah as "Wonderful, Counsellor" (**verse 6**). Here, we are assured that the Messiah will rule with infinite wisdom that exceeds human limitations. He will be efficient and effective in the planning and implementation of His divine plans. It is in this role that Jesus invites us, "Come to me, all who are weary and burdened, and I will give you rest. Take my yoke upon you and learn from me, for I am gentle and humble in heart, and you will find rest for your souls. For my yoke is easy and my burden is light" (**Matthew 11:28–30, NIV**).

In **Isaiah 9:6,** the prophet's description of the Messiah as "mighty God" recognizes the full omnipotence (having all-power) and absolute deity of the Savior. The qualities of eternal tenderness and protection are evoked with the title "The everlasting Father." Jesus offers us the same compassion and provision that the loving and caring Father shows toward His children who love, fear, and obey Him.

Finally, Isaiah declares that the Messiah is the "Prince of Peace" (**verse 6**). Not only will He bring peace, but He will rule with peace. Christians have the blessed assurance that at the very moment we place our trust in Jesus, He gives us His perfect peace. This does not mean that all of our problems will go away. Rather, it means that we can have confidence that we will never face our problems alone—He will always be with us, guiding and providing protection through our darkest hours. His promise to us is the same promise He gave to the disciples following His resurrection, "My peace I give unto you" (**John 14:27a**). The psalmist warns his audience of the absurdity of trusting in human beings as life's foundation and source of justice, whether they are princes or common persons. The end of life on earth is the same for the prince or the pauper—the bodies of each decay and turn into dust.

As an elaboration of the divine names of the Child, the implications also are nothing short of supernatural. A king might enlarge a kingdom (e.g., David, **2 Samuel 8**), but only a divine king can enlarge His kingdom infinitely—this kingdom will be so much greater than the kingdoms of Israel or David. Not only that, everything will be built on righteousness (see again **Isaiah 11:1–9**). In **Isaiah 9:7,** government refers to a rule or dominion. Nothing will corrupt this princely administration. The last sentence of **verse 7** changes the prior prophetic perfect tense to simple future tense: It will happen—God Himself will make sure it happens (see parallel language in **Isaiah 37:32**).

## QUESTION 2

What title identifies Jesus as God?

**Jesus is the mighty God. Answers will vary.**

## LIGHT ON THE WORD

### Turn to Jesus

The growing number of global military conflicts and an economic meltdown that has left millions jobless and homeless only add to a growing sense of helplessness throughout the world. The alarming crime rates have also left many frightened and insecure. Few if any leave their doors unlocked, and many are afraid to travel. Every day we see examples of people with money, power, and position afforded one form of treatment within the judicial system and the poor and disadvantaged are treated radically different. There are some rich people who steal millions and get away with little more than a slap on the wrist, and often the poor are sentenced to prison for stealing hundreds. What a joy to know that in this fast-paced, restless, and insecure world we live in, we can still turn to Jesus for hope, comfort, and perfect peace.

## BIBLE APPLICATION

**AIM: That your students will see those around them who need a Savior.**

### Helping Those Who Are Living with Turmoil

The prophet Isaiah lived in a time of political turmoil and spiritual confusion. The people of Judah were understandably anxious as the powerful Assyrian army gathered at the gates of Jerusalem. Their world was very similar to ours in some ways. Many people are stressed out and feel powerless, hopeless, and helpless. Similar to Isaiah, reach out to someone this week and let them know that God is still in control. Speak words of comfort to them and let them know that God knows and He cares.

## STUDENTS' RESPONSES

**AIM: That your students will seek to share the hope that is in God.**

### The Light of Immanuel

Just as the Pharisees in Jesus' day struggled with Isaiah's words, unable to make the leap from the human son of David to the divine Son of God named Immanuel, "God with us," so modern Pharisees are equally confounded and reject what they cannot comprehend. Even Mary questioned at first, "How shall this be?" **(Luke 1:34),** but soon enough she came to full awareness of the miracle of Jesus' conception and birth. The question for today goes beyond the miraculous facts and asks, "Does the light of Immanuel shine in our hearts—does the Prince of Peace rule our hearts?" Until He both shines and rules, we will not personally know this God who is with us, nor will we know the everlasting light, joy, justice, and peace He came to bring.

## PRAYER

Dear Father, we praise You! We thank You for being our Light in a dark and sinful world. Thank You for sending us Jesus, Your One and Only Son. In Jesus' Name, Amen.

## DIG A LITTLE DEEPER

If you have heard the Pause to Pray broadcast on your local Christian radio station, you are already familiar with the Presidential Prayer Team. This national ministry is a full-time nonpartisan endeavor that encourages people to pray for the president and leadership of the United States of America. The Presidential Prayer Team uses prayer lists and other tools disseminated through many media: 1-minute radio spots and messages via phone, email, print, and the web.

The Presidential Prayer Team is certainly operating with the conviction that the government is borne on the shoulders of the Lord. As they explain on their website, "we believe that Almighty God rules over the affairs of men and moves in response to the prayers of His people." Because there is efficacy in prayer, and believers are exhorted to pray for governmental leaders, the ministry wants to "aggressively grow the active number of praying members of the Prayer Team." They are looking for volunteers committed to fervent and consistent intercession on behalf of our legislative, executive, and judiciary officers. The lists they provide give us the names and occupations of people in government, for whom we can then pray individually and specifically. Check out their website or engage with the ministry at www.presidentialprayerteam.org.

Ref.:

https://www.presidentialprayerteam.org/about-us/

## HOW TO SAY IT

| | |
|---|---|
| Gideon. | GID-ee-uhn. |
| Hezekiah. | hez'uh-KI-uh |
| Jotham. | Otham, YOtham. |
| Midian. | MID-ee-uhn. |
| Tiglath-pileser. | til'gath-pil-NEE-zuhr. |
| Zebulun. | ZEB-yuh-luhn. |

## DAILY HOME BIBLE READINGS

**MONDAY**
A Heart Hardened to God's Righteousness
(Exodus 9:27–35)

**TUESDAY**
Before God in Our Guilt
(Ezra 9:10–15)

**WEDNESDAY**
Take Your Stand
(1 Samuel 12:6–16)

**THURSDAY**
If We Confess Our Sins
(1 John 1:5–9)

**FRIDAY**
The Righteous Judge
(2 Timothy 4:1–8)

**SATURDAY**
The Light of the World
(John 8:12–19)

**SUNDAY**
The Promise of a Righteous King
(Isaiah 9:2–7)

## PREPARE FOR NEXT SUNDAY

Read **Jeremiah 23:1-6; 33:14-18** and next week's lesson "God Promised a Righteous Branch."

**Sources:**

Bible Pronunciation Chart. Better Days Are Coming.com. http://www.betterdaysarecoming/bible/pronunciation.html (accessed January 29, 2011).

Blenkinsopp, Joseph. Isaiah 1–39: A New Translation with Introduction and Commentary. The Anchor Bible, vol. 19. New York, NY: Doubleday, 2000. 245–51.

Grogan, Geoffrey W. Isaiah–Ezekiel. The Expositor's Bible Commentary, vol. 6. Edited by Frank E. Gaebelein. Grand Rapids, MI: Zondervan, 1986. 73–75.

"Isaiah." Biblical Resources. www.biblicalresources.info/pages/isaiah/ biography.html (accessed June 24, 2010).

Merriam-Webster Online Dictionary. Merriam-Webster, Inc. http://www. merriam-webster.com (accessed January 29, 2011).

Old and New Testament Concordances, Lexicons, Dictionaries, Commentaries, Images, and Bible Versions. Blue Letter Bible.org. http:// www.blueletterbible.org/ (accessed November 17, 2010).

Passage Lookup. Bible Gateway.com. http://www.biblegateway.com/ passage (accessed January 24, 2011).

Seitz, Christopher R. Isaiah 1–39. Interpretation: A Bible Commentary for Teaching and
Preaching. Louisville, KY: John Knox Press, 1993. 84–87.

## COMMENTS / NOTES:

# GOD PROMISED A RIGHTEOUS BRANCH

**BIBLE BASIS:** Jeremiah 23:1–6; 33:14–18

**BIBLE TRUTH:** Jeremiah prophesied that Jesus would come as the Righteous Branch..

**MEMORY VERSE:** Behold, the days come, saith the LORD, that I will raise unto David a righteous Branch, and a King shall reign and prosper, and shall execute judgment and justice in the earth (Jeremiah 23:5, KJV).

**LESSON AIM:** By the end of the lesson, we will: UNDERSTAND the relationship between the "Righteous Branch" in Jeremiah and the coming of Jesus; REFLECT on examples of good leaders; and LIST ways we can become better leaders.

**BACKGROUND SCRIPTURES:** Jeremiah 23:1-6, 33:14-18-Read and incorporate the insights gained from the Background Scriptures into your study of the lesson.

## TEACHER PREPARATION

**MATERIALS NEEDED:** Bibles (several different versions), Quarterly Commentary/Teacher Manual, Adult Quarterly, teaching resources such as charts, worksheets/handouts, paper, pens, and pencils.

**OTHER MATERIALS NEEDED / TEACHER'S NOTES:**

_____

_____

## LESSON OVERVIEW

### LIFE NEED FOR TODAY'S LESSON
That students will learn that God cares about how Christian leaders care for the sheep.

### BIBLE APPLICATION
To learn that Christian leaders will be held accountable for how they care for the sheep.

### BIBLE LEARNING
To understand that Jesus is in the process of bringing judgment and justice to Earth.

### STUDENTS' RESPONSES
Students will take seriously any Christian leadership positions they hold.

## LESSON SCRIPTURE

### JEREMIAH 23:1–6; 33:14–18 KJV

**23:1** Woe be unto the pastors that destroy and scatter the sheep of my pasture! saith the LORD.

### JEREMIAH 23:1–6; 33:14–18 KJV

1 "Woe to the shepherds (civil leaders, rulers) who are destroying and scattering the sheep of My pasture!" says the LORD. 2 Therefore

2 Therefore thus saith the LORD God of Israel against the pastors that feed my people; Ye have scattered my flock, and driven them away, and have not visited them: behold, I will visit upon you the evil of your doings, saith the LORD.

3 And I will gather the remnant of my flock out of all countries whither I have driven them, and will bring them again to their folds; and they shall be fruitful and increase.

4 And I will set up shepherds over them which shall feed them: and they shall fear no more, nor be dismayed, neither shall they be lacking, saith the LORD.

5 Behold, the days come, saith the LORD, that I will raise unto David a righteous Branch, and a King shall reign and prosper, and shall execute judgment and justice in the earth.

6 In his days Judah shall be saved, and Israel shall dwell safely: and this is his name whereby he shall be called, THE LORD OUR RIGHTEOUSNESS.

33:14 Behold, the days come, saith the LORD, that I will perform that good thing which I have promised unto the house of Israel and to the house of Judah.

15 In those days, and at that time, will I cause the Branch of righteousness to grow up unto David; and he shall execute judgment and righteousness in the land.

16 In those days shall Judah be saved, and Jerusalem shall dwell safely: and this is the name wherewith she shall be called, The LORD our righteousness.

17 For thus saith the LORD; David shall never want a man to sit upon the throne of the house of Israel;

18 Neither shall the priests the Levites want a man before me to offer burnt offerings, and

thus says the LORD, the God of Israel, in regard to the shepherds who care for and feed My people: "You have scattered My flock and driven them away, and have not attended to them; hear this, I am about to visit and attend to you for the evil of your deeds," says the LORD.

3 "Then I will gather the remnant of My flock out of all the countries to which I have driven them and bring them back to their folds and pastures; and they will be fruitful and multiply.

4 I will set up shepherds over them who will feed them. And they will not be afraid any longer, nor be terrified, nor will any be missing," says the LORD.

5 "Behold (listen closely), the days are coming," says the LORD, "When I will raise up for David a righteous Branch; And He will reign as King and act wisely And will do [those things that accomplish] justice and righteousness in the land.

6 "In His days Judah will be saved, And Israel will dwell safely; Now this is His name by which He will be called; 'The LORD Our Righteousness.'

14 'Behold, the days are coming,' says the LORD, 'when I will fulfill the good word and promise which I have made regarding the house of Israel and the house of Judah.

15 In those days and at that time I will cause a righteous Branch of David to spring forth; and He (the Messiah) shall execute justice and righteousness on the earth.

16 In those days Judah will be saved and [the people of] Jerusalem will live in safety; and this is the name by which she will be called: the LORD Our Righteousness (Justice).'

to kindle meat offerings, and to do sacrifice continually.

17 For thus says the LORD, 'David shall never lack a man (descendant) to sit on the throne of the house of Israel;

18 and the Levitical priests shall never lack a man (descendant) to offer burnt offerings before Me and to burn grain offerings and to prepare sacrifices all day long.'"

## BIBLICAL DEFINITIONS

A. **Fruitful (Jeremiah 23:3)** *para'* (Heb.)—Abundant, successful, showing an ability to bear fruit.

B. **Righteous (v. 5)** *tsaddiyq* (Heb.)— Just, lawful, righteous.

## LIGHT ON THE WORD

The Old Testament tells many stories of how kings ruled over the Israelites in the northern kingdom and the southern nation of Judah, but most of them did not obey God. All of the northern kings were evil and a number of Judah's kings worshiped idols, married heathens, sacrificed children, and committed other sins that disobeyed God's Law and the keeping of His way. Judah's bad kings promoted their own self-serving interests with little regard for the people they served. God put the practice of kingship in place so they could watch over the Children of Israel, His people. Instead, they were corrupt, unjust, and led the people away from God—into sin and wrongdoing.

Zedekiah, the last king to reign over Judah, disobeyed God as so many who came before him. He acted pridefully and sinned greatly, which caused a heathen nation to conquer Judah and force them into exile after slavery. Zedekiah would not submit to God's way and led the nation into utter collapse and ruin, which marked the end of Judah reigning as a free and self-governing country (Nelson's Illustrated Bible Dictionary, 1986). As a result, Judah no longer held its former fame and honor.

## TEACHING THE BIBLE LESSON

## LIFE NEED FOR TODAY'S LESSON

**AIM: That your students will learn that Jesus is the Righteous Shepherd.**

## INTRODUCTION

### The Sinfulness of King Zedekiah

The plight of Judah looked hopeless when other nations pummeled everything linked to their beliefs, way of life, and society. The prospect of rebuilding or restoring themselves looked impossible. Before Zedekiah, a handful of kings did right in the sight of God. When these kings reigned, they led the people and the nation back to God. At other times, when the ungodly kings ruled, God raised prophets to foretell blessings if the king and nation repented, or judgment if they did not.

During the reign of Zedekiah, God called Jeremiah as a prophet to speak against the rampant sin occurring in the nation of Judah and declare His judgment. Zedekiah's name means the "righteousness of Yahweh." However, instead of Zedekiah ruling Judah in righteousness as his name suggests, under Zedekiah's rule, the nation adopted many strange ways that did not align with God's direction for them. They rebelled against the Law of God.

So Jeremiah's woe stresses the atrocities of their time. He cries out, "Woe be unto the pastors that destroy and scatter the sheep of my pasture! saith the LORD" (**Jeremiah 23:1**). The language used highlights Jeremiah and God's sorrow and distress at the cruelty, idolatry, evil, and selfishness of the leaders. However, as we will see later in his prophecy, all was not lost and a promise of a better future and idyllic king would come.

## BIBLE LEARNING

**AIM: That your students will learn that God can step into their lives and change them.**

## I. GOD WILL STEP IN TO TAKE CARE OF THE MESS (Jeremiah 23:1-4)

God promised to step in and take control over the scattered nation in spite of the lack of care and attention and despite the harm, they suffered. God takes ownership and calls them "my people" and "my flock." Repetition of the word "my" emphasizes the importance of Judah to God and the seriousness of their state. Regardless of how far the people were scattered, how far they had strayed, or how damaged they were, Jeremiah prophesizes hope. No longer did they need to suffer at the hands of ungodly leaders. God says, "I myself" (**verse 3, NIV**)— He is concerned and will move on their behalf. God, who is holy, faithful, and righteous in contrast to Zedekiah and other Old Testament kings who acted unrighteously will provide and lead His people back to a location of fruitfulness and increase.

### Promise of Restoration (23:1–4)

**1 Woe be unto the pastors that destroy and scatter the sheep of my pasture! saith the LORD. 2 Therefore thus saith the LORD God of Israel against the pastors that feed my people; Ye have scattered my flock, and driven them away, and have not visited them: behold, I will visit upon you the evil of your doings, saith the LORD. 3 And I will gather the remnant of my flock out of all countries whither I have driven them, and will bring them again to their folds; and they shall be fruitful and increase. 4 And I will set up shepherds over them which shall feed them: and they shall fear no more, nor be dismayed, neither shall they be lacking, saith the LORD.**

Under the unrighteous kings, the nation no longer lived within their inheritance or the right location—their exile deprived them of their true heritage. With the promise of restoration and a change of leadership back to God's rule, He would bring them to their pasture ("their folds")—a place of covering, accountability, purpose, destiny, and fellowship. As with the nation of Judah, Christians can lose their way when they do not allow God to lead them. Allowing God's leadership to govern our actions will facilitate productivity, increase, and fruitfulness. Fruitfulness, a product of engaging in a right relationship with God and abiding in the right place spiritually, cannot be produced apart from God.

A further distinction between Old Testament leadership was that it scattered the nation, but the promised coming leadership gathers and unites. Zedekiah abused his charge, but God will attend to and care for His flock and will even raise up other leaders to tend them. As a result, God's people would no longer be confined to kings and leaders who did not promote the way of God. The leaders God promised to put in place would tend them (i.e., provide for them) and not lead them astray. He says, "And I will give you pastors according to mine heart, which shall feed you with knowledge and understanding" (**Jeremiah 3:15**).

## SEARCH THE SCRIPTURES

### QUESTION 1

What does God say He will raise up over the nation of Judah?

**God will raise up shepherds which shall feed them.**

## LIGHT ON THE WORD

### The Promised Shepherd

At first glance, God's promise of a shepherd could potentially look like nothing would change from Zedekiah. If God raised more shepherds, they possibly would also be subject to human failures, which could fall into the same lack of control as those who came before them, like Zedekiah—after all, his name means "the righteousness of Yahweh." However, a shift occurs from the promise of more individual shepherds to the promise of a "righteous Branch" whose very nature cannot tolerate sin. Unlike Zedekiah, His name, "the Lord our Righteousness," defines the very core of His existence. The character of the "righteous Branch" would exude everything related to righteousness, truth, and purity. Jeremiah's prophecy about the righteous Branch refers to the coming of Jesus Christ, the only Leader and Shepherd who cannot and will not fail. Jesus would spring forth from the line of King David to fulfill the promise to David that the throne will not lack any man sitting on the throne to rule over the Children of Israel.

## I. THE NEED FOR A RIGHTEOUS SHEPHERD (Jeremiah 23:5-6; 33:14-18)

Psalm 145:17 says, "The LORD is righteous in all his ways, and holy in all his works." Therefore, the people of God and His leaders, who rule or lead on His behalf, should exhibit righteousness or "conformity to an ethical or moral standard" as presented in God's Word (Harris, 752).

Jeremiah's lament further reflects this ideal about the offense of Judah's kings: "Shalt thou reign, because thou closest thyself in cedar? did not thy father eat and drink, and do judgment and justice, and then it was well with him? He judged the cause of the poor and needy; then it was well with him: was not this to know me? saith the LORD" (**Jeremiah 22:15–16**).

### The Righteous Branch
### (23:5–6; 33:14–18)

**23:5 Behold, the days come, saith the LORD, that I will raise unto David a righteous Branch, and a King shall reign and prosper, and shall execute judgment and justice in the earth. 6 In his days Judah shall be saved, and Israel shall dwell safely: and this is his name whereby he shall be called, THE LORD OUR RIGHTEOUSNESS.**

**33:14 Behold, the days come, saith the LORD, that I will perform that good thing which I have promised unto the house of Israel and to the house of Judah. 15 In those days, and at that time, will I cause the Branch of righteousness to grow up unto David; and he shall execute judgment and righteousness in the land. 16 In those days shall Judah be saved, and Jerusalem shall dwell safely: and this is the name wherewith she shall be called, The LORD our righteousness. 17 For thus saith the LORD; David shall never want a man to sit upon the throne of the house of Israel; 18 Neither shall the priests the Levites want a man before me to offer burnt offerings, and to kindle meat offerings, and to do sacrifice continually.**

As the righteous Branch, Jesus embodies the true character of a king and leader. Jesus would show justice and righteousness, instead of corruption and sin. Jesus would save His people from trouble, delivering them from their enemies, while providing safety and security.

Christ's coming would fulfill God's promise to David and His promise of restoration to His people from exile back into their rightful place in their inheritance.

The verses in **chapter 33** are an almost exact parallel to the previous section. Jeremiah expands and modifies the messianic oracle just discussed, with some notable parallel constructs, such as the phrases "The days come" or "the time is coming" **(23:5)**. **Verse 15** has the same name for the branch; **verse 16** contains the same play on Zedekiah's name **(23:6)**. Clearly, the passage has a messianic interpretation (the promise that Jesus would come to be our Savior).

## QUESTION 2

Why will Jesus be called the Lord our Righteousness**?**

**He will execute judgment and justice in the land. Answers will vary.**

## LIGHT ON THE WORD

### Good Versus Bad Shepherds

While bad shepherds scatter, good shepherds gather. While bad shepherds don't do their job, don't feed the sheep, and don't protect them, good shepherds will do their job well, and the fears and terrors of the sheep will subside; all their needs will be met and they will be content. Jesus is the Good Shepherd who feeds us, protects us, and fills all our needs.

## BIBLE APPLICATION

**AIM: That your students will pray for their leaders and hold them accountable.**

### Christian Leaders in the Media

We hear, through Christian media, about the alarming trend in the church regarding the large number of leaders' moral and ethical failures occurring across the nation. It would seem that the principle of righteousness is taboo and accountability is no longer required. The level of righteousness required for leaders still stands today as indicated in **Romans 6:12–14.**

## STUDENTS' RESPONSES

**AIM: That your students will examine themselves to see if they are living up to God's standards in their relationships with others.**

### The Lord Our Righteousness

As leaders and believers, our uprightness should be defined in God's terms, not ours. When we accept Christ, we accept the "the Lord our righteousness." Jesus is our righteousness. Just as God promised restoration through the coming of Christ to the nation of Judah, we possess an even greater hope for experiencing fruitfulness and success because He lives within us; He is with and in us. God accredits the virtue of Jesus' character to us when we believe in Him. We have the power this week and every week to obey and commit to God's will and way for our lives.

Over the next week, review the quality of your relationships with others and how you interact. Decide if you are demonstrating God's conduct. Did your actions demonstrate fairness or justice? Did they reflect truthfulness or uprightness? Make a commitment this week to mirror the character and righteousness of Jesus Christ.

## PRAYER

Dear Father, we praise You! Help us to reflect You in our leadership. In Jesus' Name, Amen.

## DIG A LITTLE DEEPER

Moral failure in the clergy challenges the modern church as much as the faithless shepherds plagued ancient Israel. The Christian world—the Black Church included—has endured so many scandals in the last quarter-century that we lose count of them. If you've ever asked why there seem to be so many failed leaders in the church, there is an essential resource that you should explore. Overcoming the Dark Side of Leadership, by Gary L. McIntosh and Samuel D. Rima, examines the five basic characteristics of personal dysfunction that, to some extent, affect every person. Although these characteristics may be hidden from view—like the dark side of the moon—they, in fact, often motivate a person to become a leader. The dysfunction may initially be a driver of success, but it will ultimately cripple and perhaps even ruin a minister if never recognized and mitigated. McIntosh and Rima give us biblical and current examples of personality disorders, which help illustrate the phenomena vividly. Yet, the most valuable aspect of the book is the set of tools it provides for self-assessment and the advice the authors give us for dealing with our dark sides. If you are in leadership or aspire to be, you need this invaluable resource.

Ref.:

McIntosh, Gary L., and Rima, Samuel D. Overcoming the Dark Side of Leadership: How to Become an Effective Leader by Confronting Potential Failures, rev. ed. Grand Rapids, MI: Baker Books, 2007.

## HOW TO SAY IT

| | |
|---|---|
| Jehoahaz. | juh-HOH-uh-haz. |
| Jehoiachin. | juh-HOI-uh-kin. |
| Judah. | JOO-duh. |
| Levite. | LE-vīt. |
| Nebuchadnezzar. | neb'uh-kuhd-NEZ-uhr. |
| Zedekiah. | zed'uh-KI-uh. |

## DAILY HOME BIBLE READINGS

**MONDAY**
Pursue Righteousness
(1 Timothy 6:11–16)

**TUESDAY**
God's Children Now
(1 John 2:28–3:3)

**WEDNESDAY**
The Righteous Will Flourish
(Proverbs 11:27–31)

**THURSDAY**
All Shall Be Righteous
(Isaiah 60:17–22)

**FRIDAY**
The Lord Loves Righteousness and Justice
(Psalm 33:1–5)

**SATURDAY**
The Gracious and Righteous Lord
(Psalm 116:5–19)

**SUNDAY**
The Lord Is Our Righteousness
(Jeremiah 23:1–6; 33:14–18)

## PREPARE FOR NEXT SUNDAY

Read **Ezekiel 34:23–31,** and next week's lesson "God Promised to Be with Us."

**Sources:**
Bible Pronunciation Chart. Better Days Are Coming.com. http://www.betterdaysarecoming.com/bible/pronunciation.html#z (accessed December 3, 2010).

Clements, R. E. Jeremiah. Interpretation: A Bible Commentary for Teaching and
Preaching. Atlanta, GA: John Knox Press, 1988. 137–40, 199–201.

Feinberg, Charles L. Isaiah–Ezekiel. The Expositor's Bible Commentary, vol. 6. Edited by Frank E. Gaebelein. Grand Rapids, MI: Zondervan, 1986. 517–20, 590–92.

Fretheim, Terence E. Jeremiah. Smyth & Helwys Bible Commentary. Macon, GA:
Smyth & Helwys, 2002. 324–330, 477–81.

Lundbom, Jack R. Jeremiah 21–36: A New Translation with Introduction and Commentary. The Anchor Bible, vol. 21B. New York, NY: Doubleday, 2004. 164–76, 537–42.

Merriam-Webster Online Dictionary. Merriam-Webster, Inc. http://www. merriam-webster.com (accessed January 29, 2011).

Old and New Testament Concordances, Lexicons, Dictionaries, Commentaries, Images, and Bible Versions. Blue Letter Bible.org. http:// www.blueletterbible.org/ (accessed November 18, 2010).

"Saddiq." Theological Wordbook of the Old Testament. R. Laird Harris, gen. ed.
Chicago, IL: Moody Press, 1980. 752–55 (accessed through PC Study Bible, September 1, 2010).

"Zedekiah." Merriam-Webster Online Dictionary. http://www.merriam-webster.com/dictionary/zedekiah (accessed December 3, 2010).

"Zedekiah." Nelson's Illustrated Bible Dictionary. Herbert Lockyer, Sr., gen. ed.
Nashville, TN: Thomas Nelson Publishers, 1986. 1326–27 (accessed through PC Study Bible, September 1, 2010).

## COMMENTS / NOTES:

# GOD PROMISED TO BE WITH US

**BIBLE BASIS:** Ezekiel 34:23–31

**BIBLE TRUTH:** Ezekiel prophesied that when God sent the Son of David, there would be no more oppression, enslavement, or hunger.

**MEMORY VERSE:** And I will set up one shepherd over them, and he shall feed them, even my servant David; he shall feed them, and he shall be their shepherd (Ezekiel 34:23, KJV).

**LESSON AIM:** By the end of the lesson we will: KNOW and understand the new covenant between God and God's people; FEEL the tranquility of a lasting relationship with Christ; and PERFORM acts of justice so that others can find peace and wholeness.

**BACKGROUND SCRIPTURES:** Ezekiel34-Read and incorporate the insights gained from the Background Scriptures into your study of the lesson.

## TEACHER PREPARATION

**MATERIALS NEEDED:** Bibles (several different versions), Quarterly Commentary/Teacher Manual, Adult Quarterly, teaching resources such as charts, worksheets/handouts, paper, pens, and pencils.

**OTHER MATERIALS NEEDED / TEACHER'S NOTES:**

_____

_____

## LESSON OVERVIEW

**LIFE NEED FOR TODAY'S LESSON**
That students will learn that Jesus cares about everything that affects them in their lives.

**BIBLE APPLICATION**
To learn that Jesus cares about needs for food, protection, security, and even blessings.

**BIBLE LEARNING**
To understand that when Jesus comes again, He will make everything right.

**STUDENTS' RESPONSES**
Students will be involved in supplying the needs of others as Jesus supplies their., needs.

## LESSON SCRIPTURE

### EZEKIEL 34:23–31 KJV

23 And I will set up one shepherd over them, and he shall feed them, even my servant David; he shall feed them, and he

### EZEKIEL 34:23–31 AMP

23 "Then I will appoint over them one shepherd and he will feed them, [a ruler like]

**shall** be their shepherd.

24 And I the LORD will be their God, and my servant David a prince among them; I the LORD have spoken it.

25 And I will make with them a covenant of peace, and will cause the evil beasts to cease out of the land: and they shall dwell safely in the wilderness, and sleep in the woods.

26 And I will make them and the places round about my hill a blessing; and I will cause the shower to come down in his season; there shall be showers of blessing.

27 And the tree of the field shall yield her fruit, and the earth shall yield her increase, and they shall be safe in their land, and shall know that I am the LORD, when I have broken the bands of their yoke, and delivered them out of the hand of those that served themselves of them.

28 And they shall no more be a prey to the heathen, neither shall the beast of the land devour them; but they shall dwell safely, and none shall make them afraid.

29 And I will raise up for them a plant of renown, and they shall be no more consumed with hunger in the land, neither bear the shame of the heathen any more.

30 Thus shall they know that I the LORD their God am with them, and that they, even the house of Israel, are my people, saith the Lord GOD.

31 And ye my flock, the flock of my pasture, are men, and I am your God, saith the Lord GOD.

My servant David; he will feed them and be their shepherd.

24 And I the LORD will be their God, and My servant David will be a prince among them; I the LORD have spoken.

25 "I will make a covenant of peace with them and will eliminate the predatory animals from the land so that they may live securely in the wilderness and sleep [safely] in the woods.

26 I will make them and the places around My hill (Jerusalem, Zion) a blessing. And I will make showers come down in their season; there will be [abundant] showers of blessing (divine favor).

27 Also the tree of the field will yield its fruit and the earth will yield its produce; and My people will be secure on their land. Then they will know [with confidence] that I am the LORD, when I have broken the bars of their yoke and have rescued them from the hand of those who made them slaves.

28 They will no longer be prey to the nations, and the predators of the earth will not devour them; but they will live safely, and no one will make them afraid [in the day of the Messiah's reign].

29 I will prepare for them a place renowned for planting [crops], and they will not again be victims of famine in the land, and they will not endure the insults of the nations any longer.

30 Then they will know [with assurance] that I the LORD their God, am with them and that they, the house of Israel, are My people," says the Lord GOD.

31 "As for you, My flock, the flock of My pasture, you are men, and I am your God," says the Lord GOD.

## BIBLICAL DEFINITIONS

A. **Shepherd (Ezekiel 34:23)** *ra`ah* (Heb.)—Pastor, ruler, teacher.

B. **Prince (v. 24)** *nasiy', nasa'* (Heb.)— Captain, leader.

## LIGHT ON THE WORD

Shepherding was a key occupation of the Children of Israel, and it was also used as a term to compare the reign of the Old Testament kings to their reign over God's people—the Israelites. God's Law charged the kings with the care of the people. However, throughout the Old Testament, we see many examples of kings disobeying God and adopting the practices of non-believing nations. They did not keep their charge and often abused their authority. Because of their "bad shepherding," the Israelites did whatever they wanted with little guidance or direction. They behaved like sheep without a shepherd to guide them.

As a result, other nations conquered Israel and forced them into exile away from the land God gave to them as an inheritance. These heathen nations took over and ripped their land away from them while forcing the Israelites into slavery and bondage. The Israelites lived in constant fear as they faced war, conflict, and defeat. The Israelites' defeat and ruin annulled any opportunity to recover on their own.

## TEACHING THE BIBLE LESSON

## LIFE NEED FOR TODAY'S LESSON

AIM: **That your students will learn that God cares about people's basic needs.**

## INTRODUCTION

### The Downfall of Israel

A lack of good leadership points to the primary reason for Israel's downfall. Many of the Old Testament kings did not lead well, because they did not obey God's edicts or commands. They did not shepherd properly. Scriptures use the shepherding allegory throughout based on its familiarity among the people of its times to clarify or describe a truth. The Hebrew root for "shepherding" means "to pasture" and denotes the key term for feeding domestic animals. Figuratively, the shepherd signifies a leader, and sheep symbolized the people under his rule.

Historically, not only were shepherds responsible for the physical survival and welfare of their own sheep or their master's flocks, but they also had to provide shelter, medication, and provision for lameness and weariness of the sheep. Because the shepherd watched over, cared for, and met the sheep's needs to keep them safe, the sheep were helpless without the shepherd's guidance and protection. Thus, if the shepherds could not perform these basic tasks, the sheep could not survive. Thus, the shepherd must maintain a clear understanding of his role to watch and tend the sheep. The kings of Israel and Judah failed to live up to this standard.

## BIBLE LEARNING

AIM: **That your students will learn that God planned to replace Israel's shepherds.**

## I. GOD IS THE GOOD SHEPHERD (Ezekiel 34:23-24)

In contrast to the kings of Judah and Israel, who did not shepherd or pasture the people properly, God declares that He will restore order and everything taken from these nations. Order would come through God as He reestablished His rule over His people. Ezekiel uses the shepherd imagery to describe His leadership and the restoration of His kingdom. Of course, God is the supreme Good Shepherd (**Psalm 23**). Whereas many Old Testament kings failed and sinned greatly due to their self-serving interests and inevitably scattered the people, God as their

Shepherd is infallible. He rules perfectly without constraints of human frailty or human error.

### The Good Shepherd
#### (Ezekiel 34:23–24)

**23 And I will set up one shepherd over them, and he shall feed them, even my servant David; he shall feed them, and he shall be their shepherd. 24 And I the LORD will be their God, and my servant David a prince among them; I the LORD have spoken it.**

The New Testament also uses shepherd imagery as described in **John 10:11–15,** "I am the good shepherd: the good shepherd giveth his life for the sheep. But he that is an hireling, and not the shepherd, whose own the sheep are not, seeth the wolf coming, and leaveth the sheep, and fleeth: and the wolf catcheth them, and scattereth the sheep. The hireling fleeth, because he is an hireling, and careth not for the sheep. I am the good shepherd, and know my sheep, and am known of mine. As the Father knoweth me, even so know I the Father: and I lay down my life for the sheep."

The attributes described in the Old Testament interconnect with the New Testament description of Jesus as the Good Shepherd. Jesus is caring and selfless to the point of laying down His life for the sheep. Jesus is the Son of David, that Ezekiel was prophesying about. He becomes your sheep the minute you receive Him as Your Lord and Savior.

## SEARCH THE SCRIPTURES

### QUESTION 1
Who is the one shepherd that God is going to place over His people?

One ruler like David will be the King. That King is Jesus.

## LIGHT ON THE WORD

### Our Shepherd Provides for All Our Needs

Now that we know about the character of the Shepherd, what does He do on behalf of the sheep? He protects, He blesses, He frees, and He feeds. The kings of Israel and Judah were bad shepherds; they were self-serving and neglected the needs of the people. The result of the shepherds' neglect is that the sheep were scattered and unprotected. In this Scripture, we see that God will one day restore order and justice. When He restores, there will be no more oppression, enslavement, or hunger. The Good Shepherd imagery is also reflected in the New Testament (**Matthew 9:36; 18:12-14; Mark 14:27; Luke 15:1-7; John 10:1-30; 21:15-17**).

## II. OUR SHEPHERD PROTECTS US (Ezekiel 34:25-31)

No one likes to live in fearful or traumatic conditions. Fear can become a normal part of life depending on where one lives, negative experiences, or enemies we confront. When God committed to a covenant of peace, He reversed His people's status as the bane of society. The covenant established His role to protect the Israelites, prevent their enemies from pillaging and defeating them, and allow them to feel safe. Security, a basic human need, frees us from living in anxiety and fear.

### God Supplies All of Our Needs
#### (verses 25–31)

**25 And I will make with them a covenant of peace, and will cause the evil beasts to cease out of the land: and they shall dwell safely in the wilderness, and sleep in the woods. 26 And I will make them and the places round about my hill a blessing; and I will cause the shower to come down in his season; there shall be showers of blessing. 27 And the tree of the field shall yield her fruit, and the earth shall yield her increase, and they shall be safe in**

**their land, and shall know that I am the LORD, when I have broken the bands of their yoke, and delivered them out of the hand of those that served themselves of them. 28 And they shall no more be a prey to the heathen, neither shall the beast of the land devour them; but they shall dwell safely, and none shall make them afraid. 29 And I will raise up for them a plant of renown, and they shall be no more consumed with hunger in the land, neither bear the shame of the heathen any more. 30 Thus shall they know that I the LORD their God am with them, and that they, even the house of Israel, are my people, saith the Lord GOD. 31 And ye my flock, the flock of my pasture, are men, and I am your God, saith the Lord GOD.**

Our Good Shepherd provides showers of blessings for us. A "blessing" is the "pronouncement of the favor of God upon an assembled congregation." A blessing is also "based upon the widespread biblical precedent" **(see Genesis 27:27–29; Numbers 6:22–27; Tyndale Bible Dictionary, 226–227).** When God shepherds, He not only meets the basic needs of the sheep or His people, but He also blesses them or puts them in a position of favor. As His people, when we allow God to shepherd, lead, guide, and direct us, we can enjoy a state of spiritual favor. We can rest securely in Him for He cares for us and desires for us to live abundantly, successfully, and productively.

Our Good Shepherd gives us real freedom. Under the Shepherd's care, He will break the yoke of bondage from the Israelites' captors. No longer would they be enslaved, restricted, or subject to another nation's rule. Under the Good Shepherd, they would possess freedom—from slavery, fear, and worry, free to live. And our heavenly Shepherd promises spiritual freedom for us—freedom from sin, freedom to follow Him and obey Him.

Our Good Shepherd feeds us. All creatures must eat in order to survive, but if they do not maintain the means to find food, this can prove difficult. Forced into exile, the Israelites fended for themselves for the basic necessity of food. God promised that they would no longer hunger or question where their food would come from as He would allow their barren land to produce again. Food provides the basic foundation for strength and sustenance in order to function effectively. We can see not only the literal aspect but the spiritual implication, as well. If Christians do not properly feed on the Word of God, we will weaken spiritually.

**QUESTION 2**
How did God promise to bless His sheep?

**There will be showers of blessings—many blessings! Answers will vary.**

## LIGHT ON THE WORD
### A Lasting Relationship with God
What can meet our deepest need? People are searching for tranquility and wholeness. Where can these things be found? A lasting relationship with God and an assurance that God is with us meet our deepest need.

## BIBLE APPLICATION

**AIM: That your students will pray for Black America.**

### People Are Drifting Away
The past few decades reflect a slow shift in Black America away from Christian principles to a reliance on self, which is also evident across all cultural groups. Historically, Blacks held strong spiritual relationships as we needed to depend on God for basic needs. But as the country has increased in wealth, our tendency to rely on our jobs and our education for food, shelter, and safety for our families has increased. How can the Black church help us to maintain our

dependence on God and a rich relationship with Him when, for most of us, so many of our basic daily needs, such as food and shelter, are already met?

## STUDENTS' RESPONSES

**AIM: That your students will examine themselves to see if they are living up to God's standards in their relationships with others.**

### We Are God's People

"For He is our God, And we are the people of His pasture, And the sheep of His hand" (**Psalm 95:7, NKJV**). As the sheep of God's pasture, we must completely depend upon God for our well-being, endurance, and our lives. Take time this week to acknowledge Him in everything you do. Do not allow the busyness of life to overwhelm you where you do not seek direction from Him and obtain your strength to accomplish all that He purposes for you.

## PRAYER

Dear Father, we thank You that Jesus, our Good Shepherd, has come. We thank You that He is holding out His hands for all people to believe in Him and follow Him. In Jesus' Name, Amen.

## DIG A LITTLE DEEPER

We can yet play a role in reviving the awareness of the Lord's provision and care for His people. Each of us has an influence on family members, neighbors, co-workers, and colleagues. It is essential to share our testimonies broadly. There are lives that have been assigned to us, folks to whom we are uniquely qualified to witness. The Holy Ghost can use us to initiate revival and resurgence in the church. We need only seek the boldness to proclaim what we already know of the Good Shepherd.

## HOW TO SAY IT

| | |
|---|---|
| Babylonian. | bab'uh-LOH-nee-uhn. |
| Ezekiel. | i-ZEE-kee-uhl. |
| Judah. | JOO-duh. |
| Yahweh. | yä-WA, -vä. |

---

### DAILY HOME BIBLE READINGS

**MONDAY**
The Lord Is My Shepherd
(Psalm 23)

**TUESDAY**
I Will Be with You
(Genesis 28:10–17)

**WEDNESDAY**
God Will Be with You
(Genesis 48:17–21)

**THURSDAY**
I AM Has Sent Me
(Exodus 3:9–15)

**FRIDAY**
I Am with You
(Haggai 1:7–14

**SATURDAY**
I Am with You Always
(Matthew 28:16–20)

**SUNDAY**
"I Am Your God"
(Ezekiel 34:23-31)

## PREPARE FOR NEXT SUNDAY

Read **Hebrews 10:19-31,** and next week's lesson "Faith Calls for Perseverance."

**Sources:**

"Bless, Blessing." Tyndale Bible Dictionary. Walter A. Elwell and Philip W. Comfort, eds. Wheaton, IL: Tyndale House Publishers, 2001. 226–27.

"Blessing." Nelson's Illustrated Bible Dictionary. Herbert Lockyer, Sr., gen. ed. Nashville, TN:
Thomas Nelson Publishers, 1986 (accessed through PC Study Bible, September 1, 2010).

Briscoe, Stuart. All Things Weird and Wonderful: Ezekiel and His Mysterious Book of Whirling
Wheels and Dry Bones Can Help You Be a Better Communicator to a Spiritually Dead Generation. Wheaton, IL: Victor Books, 1977. 125.

Merriam-Webster Online Dictionary. Merriam-Webster, Inc. http://www.merriam-webster.com (accessed January 29, 2011).

"Ra'ah." Theological Wordbook of the Old Testament, vol. 2. R. Laird Harris, gen. ed. Chicago, IL: Moody Press, 1980. 852-853 (accessed through PC Study Bible, September 1, 2010).

Taylor, John B. Ezekiel: An Introduction & Commentary. Downers Grove, IL: InterVarsity Press, 1969. 223–24.

## COMMENTS / NOTES:

# ANSWERS TO THE QUARTERLY QUIZZES

**SEPTEMBER • OCTOBER • NOVEMBER 2021**

**LESSON 1**    1. Those who seek God's will in all they do; 2. He corrects those He loves.

**LESSON 2**    1. Holding on to instruction gives life; 2. The issues of life flow from the heart.

**LESSON 3**    1. He destroys it; 2. the prayers of the righteous are of particular interest to God.

**LESSON 4**    1. "It is the glory of God to conceal a thing"; 2. His throne will be established in righteousness.

**LESSON 5**    1. You will have rest rather than anxiety over your child's actions and the quality of life you lead. In addition, your soul will be delighted with the child throughout his or her life; 2: The hasty and rash person is more helpless than a fool!

**LESSON 6**    1. The king besieged the city and built great bulwarks; 2. A sinner.

**LESSON 7**    1. vanity; 2. Creator, youth, days, draw nigh.

**LESSON 8**    1. Mountains of Lebanon, including Amana, Shenir, and Hermon; 2. garden.

**LESSON 9**    1. merciful, mercy; 2. peacemakers.

**LESSON 10**   1. Allow the saints to explore different ways to make peace—answers will vary; 2. answers will vary.

**LESSON 11**   1. Answers will vary; 2. perfect.

**LESSON 12**   "And when thou prayest, thou shalt not be as the hypocrites are: for they love to pray standing in the synagogue and in the corners of the streets, that they may be seen of men" (Matthew 6:5); 2. God will not forgive us.

**LESSON 13**   1. first, kingdom, God, righteousness; 2. thought, morrow, morrow, thought, Sufficient, evil.

**DECEMBER 2021 • JANUARY • FEBRUARY 2022**

**LESSON 1**    1. Jesus wanted to make a contrast between Himself and His disciples from the religious leaders, the Pharisees, and Sadducees.  2. Anxiety causes stress, which can cause stroke, heart failure, and in some cases, death. Instead of adding to life, worry shortens life. Answers will vary.

**LESSON 2**    1. Only God rules nature. Answers will vary. 2. Jesus is fully God and fully man. He was tired.

**LESSON 3**    1. Answers will vary. 2. She knew the Word so she knew what to do. Answers will vary.

**LESSON 4**    1. Answers will vary. 2. It is remarkable that Peter walked on water at all. His faith was evident in his first step out of the boat. Answers will vary.

**LESSON 5**   1. Lepers were outcasts isolated from society.  2. Although isolated from society, the lepers heard the good news that Jesus is a healer.

**LESSON 6**   1. Paul's purpose is to a) impart a spiritual gift and b) for mutual strengthening. 2. Paul is eager and excited to preach.

**LESSON 7**   1. Because Abraham trusts God's promise, God trusts Abraham with righteousness/justice. 2. They do not have to "work" to be saved. Gentiles need only have faith in Jesus Christ. Males do not have to be circumcised.

**LESSON 8**   1. Justification is a sentence of acquittal—God acquits us of guilt on the condition of His grace. God sees me, "Just-as-if-I'd never sinned." 2. Reconciliation means that we are no longer God's enemies. We are at peace with God. Atonement means to be "at one" with God.

**LESSON 9**   1. Without the Law—the Ten Commandments—we would not know what sin is. 2. Righteousness is right standing with God, which results in right living and treating one another right.

**LESSON 10**   1. Examples from the past teach and encourage us to have faith in God. Answers will vary. 2. Faith respects God and has reverence for who He is. Faith obeys God even without understanding why. Answers will vary.

**LESSON 11**   1. The early church was persecuted, and some may have considered returning to Judaism.  2. The writer urges believers to remain faithful to Christ, even when life becomes difficult. Answers will vary.

**LESSON 12**   1. According to 1 John 2–3, how do we recognize the spirit of the antichrist in false teachers? 2. The Holy Spirit lives in us to keep us connected to Jesus. Answers will vary.

**LESSON 13**   1. Suffering is temporary. Sharing in God's glory is eternal. Answers will vary. 2. Moving from a temporary tent to a permanent building puts the present in perspective and magnifies the hope of the future. Answers will vary.

## MARCH • APRIL • MAY 2022

**LESSON 1**   1. I (wisdom); 2. blessed

**LESSON 2**   1. Light; 2. world, was made by him

**LESSON 3**   1. Cana; 2. Yes. The servants and Jesus' mother knew that Jesus had provided the wine

**LESSON 4**   1. Son, man; 2. save

**LESSON 5**   1. Passover; 2. True

**LESSON 6**   1. Mary Magdalene; 2. linen clothes and the napkin (that was wrapped around

His head)

| | |
|---|---|
| **LESSON 7** | 1. merchandise; 2. temple, three days |
| **LESSON 8** | 1. Jesus was offering her salvation—eternal life; 2. She became an evangelist telling others about Jesus. |
| **LESSON 9** | 1. night; 2. Siloam |
| **LESSON 10** | 1. Labour; 2. The Bread of Life is God and He offers eternal life. |
| **LESSON 11** | 1. I am the door; 2. thief, steal, kill, destroy |
| **LESSON 12** | 1. Martha said, "if thou hadst been here, my brother had not died;" 2. She said, "I know that he shall rise again in the resurrection at the last day." |
| **LESSON 13** | 1. Jesus told them to believe in Him; 2. He said that if we know Him, we know the Father. |

## JUNE • JULY • AUGUST 2022

| | |
|---|---|
| **LESSON 1** | 1. unrighteous; 2. "thou shalt surely bring it back to him again." |
| **LESSON 2** | 1. steal, falsely, lie; 2. unrighteousness, poor, honour, mighty, righteousness |
| **LESSON 3** | 1. hallow, fiftieth, liberty, all, all; 2. He was their God. |
| **LESSON 4** | 1. fear the LORD, walk in all His ways, love God, serve the LORD with all their heart and with all their soul, and keep the commandments of the LORD and His statutes; 2. foreskin of their heart |
| **LESSON 5** | 1. It was a show of repentance; 2. sucking, offered, burnt, LORD |
| **LESSON 6** | 1. the son of Jesse, the man who was raised up on high, the anointed of the God of Jacob, and the sweet psalmist of Israel; 2. the God of Israel, the Rock of Israel |
| **LESSON 7** | 1. two women who were harlots (prostitutes); 2. They both had a baby and one died. Both were claiming the live baby. |
| **LESSON 8** | 1. The LORD called for a famine; 2. Gehazi was a servant of the man of God. |
| **LESSON 9** | 1. do, judge, man, LORD, with you; 2. do, fear, LORD, faithfully, perfect heart |
| **LESSON 10** | 1. princes, son, man, no; 2. eyes, blind, LORD, bowed down, LORD, righteous |
| **LESSON 11** | 1. the government; 2. Wonderful, Counsellor, The mighty God, The everlasting Father, The Prince of Peace |
| **LESSON 12** | 1. They had destroyed and scattered God's sheep (His people); 2. He will visit on them the evil of their doings. |
| **LESSON 13** | 1. The Good Shepherd will feed them and will be their shepherd; 2. The LORD will be their God. |

# 2021 - 2022
# UNIFORM LESSONS SERIES OUTLINE

**YEAR 6: Fall 2021-2022**
**IDENTIFICATION: Worship**
**PERIOD: Fall Quarter, September-November 2021 (13 Sundays)**
**TITLE: Celebrating God**

This quarter focuses upon acts of worship and praise that celebrate who God is and what God has done for God's people. The lessons offer several examples of biblical people who celebrate God, psalms that call God's people to praise and celebration, and visions of praise for God's ultimate work in establishing an eternal realm of justice and righteousness.

Unit I, "God's People Offer Praise," has four lessons that give examples of persons who celebrate God. Both Moses and the prophet Miriam sing songs of praise for God's mighty acts. David dances before the ark as he brings it into Jerusalem. Bartimaeus glorifies God in Mark. In Acts, after their experience of Pentecost and Peter's sermon, early believers enter into a life of praise for God's redemption through Jesus Christ.

Unit II, "Called to Praise God," has five lessons that explore psalms calling God's people to celebrate what God has done. The psalms speak of making joyful noise to praise God, of praising God for justice and righteousness, of giving thanks for deliverance, of the joy of worship, and of music as a way to celebrate and praise God.

Unit III, "Visions of Praise," has four lessons that share John's visions of celebration for God's ultimate victory in establishing a realm of peace and justice. In Revelation, people from every nation praise God and all heaven rejoices. In the passage from Acts, believers praise God that the good news now includes everyone as Gentiles receive the gift of the Holy Spirit.

Children Unit I: God's People Offer Praise
Youth/Adult Unit I: God's People Offer Praise

| 1. September 5 | Moses and Miriam Praise God | Exodus 14:1–15:1-21 |
| | | Print: Exodus 15:11-21 |
| | Moses and Miriam Praise God | Exodus 14:1–15:1-21 |
| | | Print: Exodus 15:11-21 |

People compose poems and songs for different celebrations. How can songs and poems express thankfulness and rejoicing in victory? After their deliverance from Egyptian slavery, Moses and Miriam composed songs and led the people in praising God.

| 2. September 12 | David Dances before the Ark | 2 Samuel 6 |
| | | Print: 2 Samuel 6:1-5, 14-19 |
| | David Dances before the Ark | 2 Samuel 6 |
| | | Print: 2 Samuel 6:1-5, 14-19 |

Celebrations can be diverse in form and include various actions. How do we celebrate great events in our lives? King David expressed his joy and celebration of God by leading God's people in music and dance.

3. September 19      Glorifying God      Mark 10:46-52; Luke 18:35-43
Print: Mark 10:46-52

Glorifying God      Mark 10:46-52; Luke 18:35-43
Print: Mark 10:46-52

People respond to life challenges and victories differently. How can we respond in ways that are encouraging for ourselves and others? Bartimaeus's boldness and faith in Jesus gave him the courage to ask for and receive his sight from Jesus.

4. September 26      Believers Praise God      Acts 2:32-33, 37-4
Print: Same

Believers Praise God      Acts 2:32-33, 37-47
Print: Same

Celebrations bring about unity and a new way of seeing and being in the world. How can our celebrations unify a divided community and world? The first Christian community heard the gospel, was inspired by the Holy Spirit to see the world differently, and united to live, worship, and evangelize together.

Children Unit II: Called to Praise God
Youth Adult Unit II: Called to Praise God

5. October 3      Make a Joyful Noise      Psalm 100
Print: Same

Make a Joyful Noise      Psalm 100
Print: Same

Life provides us with many opportunities to praise and find delight in people and things. How do we decide what has more value and is more worthy of our praise? Psalm 100 highlights that God is the object of the earth's praise and joy.

6. October 10      Praise God for Being Just      Psalm 9; Ecclesiastes 3:16-22
Print: Psalm 9:1-12

Praise God for Justice and Righteousness      Psalm 9; Ecclesiastes 3:16
Print: Psalm 9:1-12

People choose to praise and have joy in particular things that may not be the best for them. Why do we choose those things that may harm us or others? Psalm 9 proclaims that God will bring justice and this is cause for our joyful praise.

| 7. October 17 | Give Thanks for Deliverance | Psalm 107 |
| | | Print: Psalm107:1-9, 17-22 |
| | Give Thanks for Deliverance | Psalm 107 |
| | | Print: Psalm 107:1-9, 39-43 |

People seek deliverance when they are in trouble. How should we respond when we are delivered? Psalm 107 encourages us to be thankful to God for God's deliverance.

| 8. October 24 | The Joy of Worship | Psalm 84 |
| | | Print: Same |
| | The Joy of Worship | Psalm 84 |
| | | Print: Same |

There are times when the pressures of life are a heavy burden to carry. Where can people go to find the pressures of life lifted and then enjoy a period of celebration? The psalmist recounts a uniquely joyful experience when worshiping in the temple.

| 9. October 31 | Praise God with Music | Psalms 149; 150 |
| | | Print: Psalm 150 |
| | Praise God with Music | Psalms 147; 148; 149; 150 |
| | | Print: Psalms 149:1-5; 150:1-6 |

People choose different ways to express their emotions. What are some of the ways that expressions of victory and joy can be shared? Psalms 149 and 150 share great praise for who God is and the joy of praising God with all of who we are.

Children Unit III: Visions of Praise
Youth Adult Unit III: Visions of Praise

| 10. November 7 | Let Everyone Praise God | Revelation 7:9-17 |
| | | Print: Revelation 7:9-14 |
| | All People Praise God | Revelation 7:9-17 |
| | | Print: Same |

Celebrations that unite people from all over the world are significant and magnificent. How can we celebrate in spite of persecution and a hostile world? The writer of Revelation proclaims that God will preserve believers from every nation, tribe, people group, and language who remain faithful to him despite hardship.

| 11. November 14 | Praise for God's Eternal Reign | Revelation 11 |
| | | Print: Revelation 11:15-19 |
| | Praise for God's Eternal Reign | Revelation 11 |
| | | Print: Revelation 11:15-19 |

Celebrations are ways of culminating a unique event, and creating new ways of being in community. How do people celebrate in a hostile world? Revelation helps us to understand that all of the world is moving toward the just, eternal reign of God.

| 12. November 21 | Rejoicing in Heaven | Revelation 19 |
| | | Print: Revelation 19:1-8 |
| | Rejoicing in Heaven | Revelation 19 |
| | | Print: Revelation 19:1-8 |

People want to have victory over the wicked people in their lives and in the world. How will they find victory over the wicked? God has the final judgment of the world, and God is worthy of all praise.

| 13. November 28 | Good News for All | Acts 10:34-47 |
| | | Print: Same |
| | Good News for All | Acts 10:34-47 |
| | | Print: Same |

Barriers often keep people from becoming part of particular groups. How are barriers removed? God reveals to Peter that the Gospel of Jesus Christ is for all, and the power of the Holy Spirit is God's gift to everyone who accepts Christ.

**YEAR 6: Winter 2021-2022**
**IDENTIFICATION: Justice**
**PERIOD: Winter Quarter 2021-2022, December 2021-February 2022 (13 Sundays)**
**TITLE: Justice, Law, History**

GENERAL INTRODUCTION:
The study this quarter focuses on justice as presented in a variety of Old Testament Scriptures. Justice originates in the nature of God and is given to God's people as a gift under the Law. The history of God's covenant people shows that kings who exercised God's justice according to God's law were considered good kings. Over time, adverse circumstances caused God's people to raise questions about God's justice.

Unit I, "God Requires Justice," has four lessons that explore how leaders of God's people must rely on God's Law as they administer justice. Deuteronomy demands that God's people be just and equitable. In 2 Samuel, King David demonstrates justice by showing kindness to Mephibosheth. Isaiah describes a reign of justice and righteousness. The Christmas lesson shows foreign "kings" respecting God's justice more than Israel's own king.

Unit II, "God: the Source of Justice," has five lessons that focus on God's justice in the lives of God's people and in the gift of the Law. Stories in Genesis reveal God's justice in the face of human injustice. Included are stories of Cain's murder of his brother Abel as well as Hagar and Ishmael being cast out of Abraham's household. Exodus demands justice for all people including one's enemies. In Deuteronomy, judges, officials, and priests work together to administer justice for God's people In particular, Deuteronomy demands justice for marginalized people.

Unit III, "Justice and Adversity," has four lessons that deal with situations in which justice seems absent. In Second Samuel, Nathan condemns David for his acts of injustice toward Uriah the Hittite, Bathsheba's husband. In Ezra, after years of exile in Babylon, Ezra returns to Jerusalem and determines to restore respect for God's Law. Session 3 tells the story of Job's faithfulness to God after several tragic events in his life. The Scriptures in Job question the presence of God's justice when Job has suffered greatly.

Children Unit I: God Requires Justice
Youth/Adult Unit I: God Requires Justice

| | | |
|---|---|---|
| 1. December 5 | Remember God's Just Laws | Deuteronomy 5; 10; 27; 28:1-2<br>Print: Deuteronomy 5:1-3;<br>10:12-13; 27:1-10 |
| Justice and Obedience to the Law | | Deuteronomy 5; 10; 27; 28:1-2<br>Print: Deuteronomy 5:1-3;<br>10:12-13; 27:1-10 |

People often struggle to do what they know is right. How can people find the strength and motivation to do what is right? Deuteronomy 10 teaches that obedience to God's Law is for our own well-being.

2. December 12        David Is a Just King        2 Samuel 9

| 2. December 12 | David Is a Just King | 2 Samuel 9 |
| | | Print: 2 Samuel 9:1-12 |
| | David Administers Justice and Kindness | 2 Samuel 9 |
| | | Print: 2 Samuel 9:1-12 |

People rely on the kindness and support of others. How can people show radical kindness to one another? King David acted justly, remembered his promise to Jonathan, and was kind to Jonathan's son.

| 3. December 19 | Hail the Righteous King! | Isaiah 9:1-7 |
| | | Print: Isaiah 9:2-7 |
| | Justice and Righteousness Reign | Isaiah 9:1-7 |
| | | Print: Isaiah 9:2-7 |

People suffer injustices and ill treatment. Will there be a time when people can count on being treated fairly? God's kingdom will be one of justice and righteousness.

| 4. December 26 | A Just King is Born | Matthew 2 |
| | | Print: Matthew 2:1–12 |
| | A Just King is Born | Matthew 2 |
| | | Print: Matthew 2:1–12 |

People look for someone to bring justice in spite of injustice. To whom can people turn to address issues of injustice? The Wise Men searched and found the King of Justice, Jesus, and worshiped Him.

Children Unit II: God Is Just
Youth Adult Unit II: God: The Source of Justice

| 5. January 2 | A Just and Merciful God | Genesis 4 |
| | | Print: Genesis 4:1-16 |
| | Justice, Vengeance, and Mercy | Genesis 4 |
| | | Print: Genesis 4:1-16 |

Some people become angry when their best efforts don't result in the anticipated outcome. How do people deal with their anger and disappointment? God punished Cain because he allowed his anger to turn to rage and then to murder.

| 6. January 9 | A Just God Remembers Everyone | Genesis 21:8-21 |
| | | Print: Genesis 21:8-20 |
| | Hagar and Ishmael Not Forgotten | Genesis 21:8-21 |
| | | Print: Genesis 21:8-20 |

People sometimes face situations that feel hopeless. How can people find assurance when their circumstances change? Genesis shows that even though Hagar and Ishmael's circumstances changed, God was still with them.

7. January 16          A Just God Says, "Remember Others"          Exodus 23
Print: Exodus 23:1-12

The Laws of Justice and Mercy          Exodus 23
Print: Exodus 23:1-12

It can be tempting to treat friends with more leniency and enemies with more harshness than they deserve. How can people treat others justly? Exodus demands justice for all people including one's enemies.

8. January 23          God's Just Judges and Priests    Deuteronomy 16:18-20; 17:8-13; 19:15-21
Print: Deuteronomy 16:18-20; 17:8-13

Justice, Judges, and Priests    Deuteronomy 16:18-20; 17:8-13; 19:15-21
Print: Deuteronomy 16:18-20; 17:8-13

People sometimes distort justice. What actions can we take to prevent manipulations of justice? In Deuteronomy, judges, officials, and priests work together to administer justice for God's people.

Children Unit III: Justice during the Storm
Youth Adult Unit III: Justice and Adversity

9. January 30          Justice and the Outsiders          Deuteronomy 24:10-21
Print: Same

Justice and the Marginalized          Deuteronomy 24:10-21
Print: Same

Some people are poor and marginalized. How can their dignity and worth be respected? Deuteronomy demands justice for all who are poor or marginalized.

10. February 6          Nathan Condemns David          2 Samuel 12
Print: 2 Samuel 12:1-9, 13-15

Nathan Condemns David          2 Samuel 12
Print: 2 Samuel 12:1-9, 13-15

People often see acts of injustice being committed. How are we called to respond when we witness unjust acts? Nathan sought God's guidance and received wisdom for how to address David's sin.

11. February 13          Ezra Seeks God's Law          Ezra 7:1-26
Print: Ezra 7:1-10, 23-26

Law and Order          Ezra 7:1-26
Print: Ezra 7:1-10, 23-26

People sometimes face situations in which they fear others will oppose their efforts. What motivates people to behave benevolently toward others? God's hand was on Ezra, and he was able to return to Jerusalem in an effort to restore respect for God's Law.

12. February 20         Facing Life's Storms                              Job 1:1–2:10

Print: Job 1:8-15, 18-19; 2:3-7

Bildad Misunderstands God's Justice            Job 8
Print: Job 8:1-10, 20-22

People tend to rationalize why bad things happen. How do people respond when they are faced with tragedy—natural disasters, birth defects, atrocious crimes, etc.? Job remained faithful to God after several tragic events in his life, even while his friends questioned God's justice and Job's innocence.

13. February 27         Serving a Just God                                Job 42
Print: Job 42:1-6, 10-17

Serving a Just God                                       Job 42
Print: Job 42:1-6, 10-17

Even the most downcast people can still have hope. How does our hope keep us focused on what is important? Job had a frank, heart-to-heart conversation with God, and God blessed Job's faithfulness.

**YEAR 6: Spring 2022**
**IDENTIFICATION: God**
**PERIOD: Spring Quarter, March-May 2022 (13 Sundays)**
**TITLE: God Frees and Redeems**

GENERAL INTRODUCTION:
This quarter uses the lens of liberation, Christian freedom, to examine and experience the nature of God who acts to deliver and free people in different situations. This liberation is experienced in the story of the Passover and in the good news of Easter. Liberation is experienced in God's new covenant community.

Unit I, "Liberating Passover," consists of four lessons that explore the memory of the liberating event of the Exodus. The memory of the Exodus, relived in the Passover liturgy, cultivated a desire for restoration and liberation for the Hebrew people as told in the books of Ezra and Deuteronomy.

Unit II, "Liberating Gospels," offers four lessons that explore the liberating freedom found in events beginning with Jesus' triumphal entry into Jerusalem and continuing through his death and resurrection. These lessons are drawn from the Gospel of Matthew. The text from John describes the liberating freedom found by following Jesus.

Unit III, "Liberating Letters," contains five lessons based on the letters to the Romans and Galatians that explore Paul's understanding of the radical nature of Christian freedom. The final lesson in the unit focuses on the fruit of the Spirit emanating from Christian freedom.

Children Unit I: Liberating Passover
Youth/Adult Unit I: Liberating Passover

| | | |
|---|---|---|
| 1. March 6 | Free to Go Home | Ezra 1; 2:64-70 |
| | | Print: Ezra 1:1-8, 11; 2:64-70 |
| | Babylonian Captivity Ends | Ezra 1; 2:64-70 |
| | | Print: Ezra 1:1-8, 11; 2:64-70 |

Sometimes people are given a challenging job, which requires a change or risk. Where can we find resources to meet these challenges? Israel's release from Babylonian captivity reveals that we can have faith that God will provide persons and resources to fulfill God's purposes.

| | | |
|---|---|---|
| 2. March 13 | Free to Talk to God | Ezra 6:1-12 |
| | | Print: Same |
| | Freedom to Worship | Ezra 5; 6:1-12; 10:1-5 |
| | | Print: Ezra 6:1-12 |

Sometimes people focus on their own adverse situations rather than seeking guidance. Why do we act and speak according to our situations rather than seeking liberation from them? Ezra shows us that when we recognize and confess our failings God is ready to listen and support us, even in unexpected ways.

| 3. March 20 | Free to Celebrate Passover | Ezra 6:13-22; Leviticus 23:4-8 |
| | | Print: Ezra 6:13-22 |
| | Celebrate Passover Liberation | Ezra 6:13-22; Leviticus 23:4-8 |
| | | Print: Ezra 6:13-22 |

Celebrations provide opportunities for persons to rejoice after a difficult task. How can we celebrate and show thanksgiving to the person who made the victory possible? After the temple was completed, the Israelites celebrated God by sharing the Passover together.

| 4. March 27 | Let's Remember God's Blessings | Deuteronomy 8 |
| | | Print: Deuteronomy 8:1-11 |
| | Lest We Forget | Deuteronomy 8 |
| | | Print: Deuteronomy 8:1-11 |

Humility can be thought of as a weakness in today's society. Why do people forget the road they traveled in life and who helped them in their accomplishments? Deuteronomy extols humility as liberating and explains its purpose.

Children Unit II: Liberating Gospels
Youth Adult Unit II: Liberating Gospels

| 5. April 3 | The Passover with the Disciples | Matthew 26:17-30 |
| | | Print: Same |
| | The Passover with the Disciples | Matthew 26:17-30 |
| | | Print: Same |

People need reminders of times of liberation in history. How do people deal with the burdens of daily life? In celebrating the Passover with his disciples, Jesus reminded them of the freedom he gave from fear and want.

| 6. April 10 | King Jesus Enters Jerusalem | Matthew 21:1-11 |
| (Palm Sunday) | | Print: Same |
| | Triumphal Entry into Jerusalem | Matthew 21:1-11 |
| | | Print: Same |

People long for leaders who can liberate them from tyranny and be worthy of their praise. What does humility teach us about leadership? Matthew describes Jesus' humility and the crowd blessing him.

| 7. April 17 | He's Alive! | Matthew 27; 28:1-10 |
| (Easter) | | Print: Matthew 28:1-10 |
| | The Paschal Lamb Lives! | Matthew 27; 28:1-10 |
| | | Print: Matthew 28:1-10 |

The world is full of sadness and despair. How can we find hope in the midst of our anguish? In Matthew, Jesus allays our fears and gives courage to face the future.

8. April 24          Jesus Makes Me Free                              John 8:31-38
                                                                      Print: Same
                     Freedom in Christ Jesus                          John 8:31-38
                                                                      Print: Same

Many people are bound by bad habits and vices. How can one experience deliverance? Jesus is the truth that sets us free and enables us to be his disciples.

Children Unit III: Liberating Letters
Youth Adult Unit III: Liberating Letters

9. May 1             Freed to Do Right                              Romans 6:1-14
                                                                      Print: Same
                     Freedom from Sin                               Romans 6:1-14
                                                                      Print: Same

In life, we are constantly struggling to do what is morally right. How can we overcome temptations? Through Jesus' death and resurrection, we become dead to sin and instruments of righteousness.

10. May 8            The Spirit Sets Me Free                       Romans 8:18-30
                                                                      Print: Same
                     Freedom for the Future                        Romans 8:18-30
                                                                      Print: Same

Living in the world we sometimes suffer because of evildoers. Where can one find inspiration and hope for the future? God promises to bring good out of our suffering and give us a blessed future.

11. May 15           Free to Be Faithful                             Galatians 3
                                                              Print: Galatians 3:18-29
                     Freedom and the Law                             Galatians 3
                                                              Print: Galatians 3:18-29

Laws are provided to govern and ensure a functioning society. If there were no laws, what would guide human behavior? Paul taught that God's Law served a purpose, but when Christ came grace made it possible for all people to become children of God and heirs of God's promises.

12. May 22           Free to Love Others                          Galatians 5:1-15
                                                                      Print: Same
                     The Nature of Christian Freedom             Galatians 5:1-15
                                                                      Print: Same

Sometimes people feel bound by laws and desires that keep them in chains. Where can we find freedom to experience life in transforming ways? According to Galatians, God calls us to a freedom that is guided by love for others.

| 13. May 29 | Free to Live on Spiritual Fruit | Galatians 5:16-26 |
| | | Print: Same |
| | The Spiritual Fruit of Freedom | Galatians 5:16-26 |
| | | Print: Same |

In the world many opposing forces influence our lives. When we feel conflicted, what can we do? Paul reminds us that choosing to be guided by the Spirit will result in good fruit.

**YEAR 6: Summer 2022**
**IDENTIFICATION: Creation**
**PERIOD: Summer Quarter 2022, June-August (13 Sundays)**
**TITLE: Partners in a New Creation**

GENERAL INTRODUCTION:
Members of Christ's body have the grand opportunity to be co-laborers with the ever-abiding Spirit of God in reconciling, re-creating, and rightly restoring all things in the eternal reign of God. This summer quarter considers ways in which believers are partners with God in creation.

Unit I, "God Delivers and Restores," has four lessons. Using three chapters of Isaiah, this study explores God's predictions of the future destruction of Babylon and deliverance for Israel. These events were evidence of God's power at work to grant mercy and redemption to the penitent and to restore God's people to a state of peace and prosperity.

Unit II, "The Word: The Agent of Creation," has five lessons taken from John's Gospel. The lessons stress how the Creating Word, at work in and with humanity, became flesh, healed the sick, saved the lost, resurrected the dead and granted—through the Holy Spirit—peace.

Unit III, "The Great Hope of the Saints," is a four-lesson study drawn from Revelation. The study helps learners envision the new home and city God has prepared for the redeemed. In this new heavenly environment, the saints will enjoy the new water of eternal life.

Children Unit I: God Delivers and Restores
Youth Adult Unit I: God Delivers and Restores

| | | |
|---|---|---|
| 1. June 5 | God Sees Everything | Isaiah 47 |
| | | Print: Isaiah 47:10-15 |
| | God Foretells Destruction | Isaiah 47 |
| | | Print: Isaiah 47:10-15 |

Humans trust in their own abilities and the systems they develop to control their lives and the lives of others. How does this confidence shape us? Isaiah affirms that God, the Creator of all, humbles the proud and the powerful.

| | | |
|---|---|---|
| 2. June 12 | God Will Make Things Better | Isaiah 49:1-17 |
| | | Print: Isaiah 49:1-11 |
| | God Foretells of Redemption | Isaiah 49:1-17 |
| | | Print: Isaiah 49:1-11 |

Individuals and nations aspire to accomplish great things even in the midst of great challenges. How can we make a difference? Creator God covenants with us to redeem us—even when we don't realize it—for a higher purpose and important mission.

3. June 19      God Gives a Better Life      Isaiah 49:18-26

| 3. June 19 | God Gives a Better Life | Isaiah 49:18-26 |
|---|---|---|
| | | Print: Isaiah 49:18-23 |
| | God's Restored People Shall Prosper | Isaiah 49:18-26 |
| | | Print: Isaiah 49:18-23 |

When freedom from oppression is realized, it is hard to believe. From where do freedom and blessings come? Creator God will restore relationships between God's people, nations, the land, and the next generation in ways that confirm God's Lordship.

| 4. June 26 | God Wants to Free Us | Isaiah 51 |
|---|---|---|
| | | Print: Isaiah 51:1-8 |
| | God Offers Deliverance | Isaiah 51 |
| | | Print: Isaiah 51:1-8 |

People of integrity find it difficult to ignore criticism. Where do they find affirmation in the face of adversity? God delivers the righteous from the judgment of others when they are faithful to God's teachings.

Children Unit II: The Word: An Agent of Creation
Youth Adult Unit II: The Word: The Agent of Creation

| 5. July 3 | Jesus Becomes Flesh | John 1:1-14 |
|---|---|---|
| | | Print: Same |
| | The Creating Word Becomes Flesh | John 1:1-14 |
| | | Print: John 1:1-14 |

People are often curious about how things began. How do we understand the origins of life? John begins by explaining that Jesus, the Word, was God's creating and redeeming agent in the world.

| 6. July 10 | Jesus Heals | John 4:46-54 |
|---|---|---|
| | | Print: Same |
| | The Word Heals | John 4:46-54 |
| | | Print: Same |

When we or our loved ones are sick, we seek restoration and healing. When all efforts fail, what can we do? Jesus invites our active, faith-filled participation with his power to create new life through healing—even at a distance.

| 7. July 17 | The Word Raises the Dead | John 11:17-44 |
|---|---|---|
| | | Print: John 11:17-27, 38-44 |
| | The Word Resurrects the Dead | John 11:17-44 |
| | | Print: John 11:17-27, 38-44 |

When people experience tragic situations, they long for comfort. Where can we find hope and strength for the future? Our faith in Jesus releases the power of God to bring resurrection and new life.

| 8. July 24 | The Word Saves | John 12:27-50 |
| | | Print: John 12:44-50 |
| | The Word Saves | John 12:27-50 |
| | | Print: John 12:44-50 |

Most people acknowledge a sense of a higher, spiritual power that exceeds our human capabilities. How do we understand the mysteries of the universe, the world, and our lives? Jesus' mission is to save the world so that the world can live in an eternal relationship with his Father, the Creator God.

| 9. July 31 | The Word Gives Peace | John 14:15-31 |
| | | Print: John 14:15-29 |
| | The Word Gives Peace | John 14:15-31 |
| | | Print: John 14:15-29 |

People seek trustworthy guidance for their lives. How can we find guidance? Our love for Jesus, shown through our obedience to his words and the Holy Spirit's teachings, creates an incredible peace.

Children Unit III: The Great Hope of the Saints
Youth Adult Unit III: The Great Hope of the Saints

| 10. August 7 | A New Home | Revelation 21:1-8 |
| | | Print: Revelation 21:1-7 |
| | A New Home | Revelation 21:1-8 |
| | | Print: Same |

People long for a place and time when life's stresses and death will not exist. Where can we find such a peaceful existence? The vision in Revelation 21 foretells that God will create a new heaven and earth where life's challenges will be banished forever.

| 11. August 14 | A New City | Revelation 21:9-27 |
| | | Print: Revelation 21:9-21 |
| | A New City | Revelation 21:9-27 |
| | | Print: Revelation 21:9-21 |

It is difficult for people to imagine living in a place that is totally different from the one in which they presently live. What will the new place be like? Revelation 21 uses figurative language to describe the brilliant new city God will create.

| 12. August 21 | The River of Life | Revelation 22:1-7 |
| | | Print: Same |
| | The River of Life | Revelation 22:1-7 |
| | | Print: Same |

Rivers give life and nourishment to the things that exist around them. How do rivers nourish our lives? In God's new creation, God's power will be in the river, nourishing and healing people and nations in the New Jerusalem.

13. August 28        Come and Enjoy        Revelation 22:8-21
Print: Revelation 22:10-21

Come and Enjoy        Revelation 22:8-21
Print: Revelation 22:10-21

Everything has a beginning and an end. What is the source and ultimate purpose of human life? Revelation affirms that God, who is the Alpha and Omega, creates and controls all things.

# GLOSSARY

## A

**Anointed**—A consecrated person, such as a king or priest; can refer to the Messiah.

## B

**Begotten**—The one who is born; brought forth.
**Believe**—To accept as true, to place confidence in, to rely on.
**Believeth**—To put confidence in; to trust or be persuaded.
**Blessing**—Prosperity, benediction, benefit, favor, peace, invocation of good.
**Bowels**—Womb, intestines, the abdomen.

## C

**Covenant**—A promise, contract, or a will.
**Curse**—The act of denouncing.

## D

**Defilement**—Unclean. No Hebrew, especially a priest could partake of the Passover Feast and be unclean. To be in a Gentile's presence or building rendered that person unclean.
**Door**—A portal, gate, or entrance.

## E

**Earing**—Plowing; plowing time.
**Ephraim**--Joseph's younger son, born of Joseph and Asenath before the seven years of famine in Egypt; he was the ancestor of an Israelite tribe, and his name came to designate the Northern Kingdom of Israel.
**Executes**—Undertakes a deliberate action with a specific or distinct purpose.

## F

**Faith**—A strong conviction that Jesus is the Messiah and the One through whom we can by faith obtain eternal salvation.

**Fear**—Dreading punishment or destruction; feeling overwhelming awe, wonder and amazement.
**Firkins**—A measure of capacity for liquids (each firkin equals about 10 gallons).
**Fruitful**—Abundant, successful, showing an ability to bear fruit.

## G

**Gift**—This word means the same in Hebrew and English, but the context is a present being used as a bribe.

## H

**Hallow**—To consecrate or sanctify.
**Heart**—The seat of thought and will.
**Hebrew Servant**—Proper name for a servant, slave, or attendant.
**Hypostatize (Hy-POST–a-tize)**—To think of a concept, abstraction, etc., as having a real, objective existence.

## I

**Jubile**—Also spelled "jubilee"; a season of celebration; a year of emancipation and restoration.
**Judges**—Men chosen to exercise authority over God's chosen people to lead them back to the one true God.
**Judgment**—A formal utterance of an authoritative opinion.
**Just**—Lawful, righteous.

## K

**Know**—To ascertain by seeing, be assuredly aware, with certainty.

## L

**Labour**—To work, to do, to commit.
**Life**—Denotes life in the fullest sense; life as God has it.

**Living water**—It has vital power in itself and exerts the same upon the soul; represents the Holy Spirit.

**Longsuffering**—The patience and selfrestraint of people who could quickly and easily avenge themselves against wrongdoers.

## M

**Magnify**—Glorify.

**Manasseh**—Grandson of Jacob; the firstborn son of Joseph and his Egyptian wife, Asenath; the name means "causing to forget"

**Mansions**—Abodes or dwellings.

**Messias**—The Greek form of Messiah, meaning "anointed"; a name of Christ.

**Metaphor**—A figure of speech in which a word or phrase is likened to
  something, but is not to be taken literally.

Mock—To laugh and make fun of.

**Mocked**—Turned up one's nose at someone as a gesture of ridicule, scorn, or contempt.

## N

**Nature**—The way of feeling and acting which has become "normal."

**Nourish**—Feed, attend to, contain, sustain, endure.

## O

**Officer**—A man in the royal court who is a "eunuch"; a castrated male.

**Oppress**—To take advantage of, restrict, or pervert justice regarding someone's human rights.

**Oppressed**—Someone who has been cheated or otherwise exploited.

## P

**Passover**—A Jewish celebration commemorating their exodus from bondage in Egypt

**Pray**—To plead, to intervene, to interpose, to arbitrate, or even judge.

**Prince**—Captain, leader.

**Purifying**—The process of ritual cleansing, either legal or ceremonial, to purge from the pollution of sin and guilt.

## R

**Redeem**—To buy something from someone to establish ownership.

**Resurrection**—The act of having life restored after death.

**Righteous**—Just, lawful.

**Requite**—Return again, turn back, turn away, restore, bring, render, answer, recompense, recover, deliver, put, withdraw.

**Righteousness**—Rightness, rectitude, virtue, prosperity, piety.

## S

**Salvation**—Deliverance, victory, or help.

**Scourge**—A whip.

**Seed**—Offspring, issue, progeny, posterity, family, race.

**Sent**—Charged or commanded by another with a verbal communication.

**Sepulchre**—A grave or tomb. Jesus was buried in a sepulchre, which was a room carved out of a rocky hill.

**Servant**—A minister, ambassador, and a worshiper of God.

**Shadow of Death**—Distress or extreme danger.

**Shepherd**—A pastor; used to illustrate Jesus' ownership and commitment to those who follow Him.

**Should be made manifest**—Made visible or known what has been hidden or unknown.

**Sin**—To wander from the law of God; violate God's law, miss the mark.

**Sinned**—Missed the mark; erred.

**Son of Man**—The phrase appears in the Old Testament primarily to specify a member of humanity (cf. Psalm 8:4).

**Soul**—The seat of feelings, emotion, desire, and affection.

**Stranger**—A sojourner; a newcomer, or a foreigner.

## T

**Tempt**—To test, prove, try, put to the proof, to qualify.

**Transgressor**—A person who violates a command or law; someone who goes beyond a boundary or limit.

**Triumphed**—Rose up or was exalted in victory.

**Troubled**—Agitated, anxious, or causing commotion.

# U

**Unrighteousness**—Injustice, iniquity, and wickedness.

# W

**Wisdom**—Ability to discern inner qualities and relationships.

**Witness**—Someone who has seen or heard or knows the Gospel and testifies to it

**Word**—The Word denotes the expression of thought, not the mere name of an object. In John 1:1 and 1:14, Jesus is called "the Word." He became flesh and dwelled among us as fully human and fully divine.

**Works**—Denotes a deed or act

# Y

**Yoke**—Denotes a condition of servitude or slavery

# OUR AFFIRMATION OF FAITH

is a reminder of the basic beliefs of the Church Of God In Christ. It witnesses to the reality that God has been active in creation, history, and our lives. Being Trinitarian, our affirmation focuses on the work of the Father, Son, and Holy Spirit, while proclaiming the Gospel holistically. God tells us through Scripture that salvation is available to all through Jesus Christ.

Our Affirmation of Faith is woven throughout the testifying, singing, praying, preaching, and teaching of the Church. Hence, one can hear the cardinal beliefs through these events.

The Affirmation makes no pretense of being exhaustive, or being a complete statement of all our beliefs. It presents a set of key beliefs that are grounded in Scripture.

The Affirmation echoes the classic testimony: "Giving honor to God in the highest and to the Lord Jesus Christ, I thank God that I'm saved, sanctified, and filled with the Holy Ghost." Our theology begins with God; the doctrine of God shapes all other doctrines for the Church Of God In Christ.

### The Church Of God In Christ — Affirmation of Faith

**We Believe** the Bible to be the inspired and only infallible written Word of God,

**We Believe** that there is One God, eternally existent in three Persons; God the Father, God the Son, and God the Holy Spirit.

**We Believe** in the Blessed Hope, which is the rapture of the Church of God, which is in Christ at His return.

**We Believe** that the only means of being cleansed from sin, is through repentance and faith in the precious Blood of Jesus Christ.

**We Believe** that regeneration by the Holy Ghost is absolutely essential for personal salvation.

**We Believe** that the redemptive work of Christ on the Cross provides healing for the human body in answer to believing prayer.

**We Believe** that the Baptism in the Holy Ghost, according to Acts 2:4, is given to believers who ask for it.

**We Believe** in the sanctifying power of the Holy Spirit, by whose indwelling, the Christian is enabled to live a Holy and separated life in this present world.

Amen.

# THE SYMBOL OF THE CHURCH OF GOD IN CHRIST

The Symbol of the Church Of God In Christ is an outgrowth of the Presiding Bishop's Coat of Arms, which has become quite familiar to the Church. The design of the Official Seal of the Church was created in 1973 and adopted in the General Assembly in 1981 (July Session).

The obvious GARNERED WHEAT in the center of the seal represents all of the people of the Church Of God In Christ, Inc. The ROPE of wheat that holds the shaft together represents the Founding Father of the Church, Bishop Charles Harrison Mason, who, at the call of the Lord, banded us together as a Brotherhood of Churches in the First Pentecostal General Assembly of the Church, in 1907.

The date in the seal has a two-fold purpose: first, to tell us that Bishop Mason received the baptism of the Holy Ghost in March 1907 and, second, to tell us that it was because of this outpouring that Bishop Mason was compelled to call us together in February of 1907 to organize the Church Of God In Christ.

The RAIN in the background represents the Latter Rain, or the End-time Revivals, which brought about the emergence of our Church along with other Pentecostal Holiness Bodies in the same era. The rain also serves as a challenge to the Church to keep Christ in the center of our worship and service, so that He may continue to use the Church Of God In Christ as one of the vehicles of Pentecostal Revival before the return of the Lord.

This information was reprinted from the book So You Want to KNOW YOUR CHURCH by Alferd Z. Hall, Jr.

# The Doctrines of the Church Of God In Christ

## THE BIBLE

We believe that the Bible is the Word of God and contains one harmonious and sufficiently complete system of doctrine. We believe in the full inspiration of the Word of God. We hold the Word of God to be the only authority in all matters and assert that no doctrine can be true or essential if it does not find a place in this Word.

## THE FATHER

We believe in God, the Father Almighty, the Author and Creator of all things. The Old Testament reveals God in diverse manners, by manifesting His nature, character, and dominions. The Gospels in the New Testament give us knowledge of God the "Father" or "My Father," showing the relationship of God to Jesus as Father, or representing Him as the Father in the Godhead, and Jesus himself that Son (St. John 15:8, 14:20). Jesus also gives God the distinction of "Fatherhood" to all believers when He explains God in the light of "Your Father in Heaven" (St. Matthew 6:8).

## THE SON

We believe that Jesus Christ is the Son of God, the second person in the Godhead of the Trinity or Triune Godhead. We believe that Jesus was and is eternal in His person and nature as the Son of God who was with God in the beginning of creation (St. John 1:1). We believe that Jesus Christ was born of a virgin called Mary according to the Scripture (St. Matthew 1:18), thus giving rise to our fundamental belief in the Virgin Birth and to all of the miraculous events surrounding the phenomenon (St. Matthew 1:18–25). We believe that Jesus Christ became the "suffering servant" to man; this suffering servant came seeking to redeem man from sin and to reconcile him to God, his Father (Romans 5:10). We believe that Jesus Christ is standing now as mediator between God and man (I Timothy 2:5).

## THE HOLY GHOST

We believe the Holy Ghost or Holy Spirit is the third person of the Trinity; proceeds from the Father and the Son; is of the same substance, equal to power and glory; and is together with the Father and the Son, to be believed in, obeyed, and worshiped. The Holy Ghost is a gift bestowed upon the believer for the purpose of equipping and empowering the believer, making him or her a more effective witness for service in the world. He teaches and guides one into all truth (John 16:13; Acts 1:8, 8:39).

## THE BAPTISM OF THE HOLY GHOST

We believe that the Baptism of the Holy Ghost is an experience subsequent to conversion and sanctification and that tongue-speaking is the consequence of the baptism in the Holy Ghost with the manifestations of the fruit of the spirit (Galatians 5:22–23; Acts 10:46, 19:1–6). We believe that we are not baptized with the Holy Ghost in order to be saved (Acts 19:1–6; John 3:5). When one receives a baptismal Holy Ghost experience, we believe one will speak with a tongue unknown to oneself according to the sovereign will of Christ. To be filled with the Spirit means to be Spirit controlled as expressed by Paul in Ephesians 5:18,19. Since the charismatic demonstrations were necessary to help the early church to be successful in implementing the command of Christ, we, therefore, believe that a Holy Ghost experience is mandatory for all believers today.

## MAN

We believe that humankind was created holy by God, composed of body, soul, and spirit. We believe that humankind, by nature, is sinful and unholy. Being born in sin, a person needs to be born again, sanctified and cleansed from all sins by the blood of Jesus. We believe that one is saved by confessing and forsaking one's sins, and believing on the Lord Jesus Christ, and that having become a child of God, by being born again and adopted into the family of God, one may, and should, claim the inheritance of the sons of God, namely the baptism of the Holy Ghost.

## SIN

Sin, the Bible teaches, began in the angelic world (Ezekiel 28:11–19; Isaiah 14:12–20) and is transmitted into the blood of the human race through disobedience and deception motivated by unbelief (I Timothy 2:14). Adam's sin, committed by eating of the forbidden fruit from the tree of knowledge of good and evil, carried with it permanent pollution or depraved human nature to all his descendants. This is called "original sin." Sin can now be defined as a volitional transgression against God and a lack of conformity to the will of God. We, therefore, conclude that humankind by nature is sinful and has fallen from a glorious and righteous state from which we were created, and has become unrighteous and unholy. We therefore, must be restored to the state of holiness from which we have fallen by being born again (St. John 3:7).

## SALVATION

Salvation deals with the application of the work of redemption to the sinner with restoration to divine favor and communion with God. This redemptive operation of the Holy Ghost upon sinners is brought about by repentance toward God and faith toward our Lord Jesus Christ which brings conversion, faith, justification, regeneration, sanctification, and the baptism of the Holy Ghost. Repentance is the work of God, which results in a change of mind in respect to a person's relationship to God (St. Matthew 3:1–2, 4:17; Acts 20:21). Faith is a certain conviction wrought in the heart by the Holy Spirit, as to the truth of the Gospel and a heart trust in the promises of God in Christ (Romans 1:17, 3:28; St. Matthew 9:22; Acts 26:18). Conversion is that act of God whereby He causes the regenerated sinner, in one's conscious life, to turn to Him in repentance and faith (II Kings 5:15; II Chronicles 33:12,13; St. Luke 19:8,9; Acts 8:30). Regeneration is the act of God by which the principle of the new life is implanted in humankind, the governing disposition of soul is made holy, and the first holy exercise of this new disposition is secured. Sanctification is that gracious and continuous operation of the Holy Ghost, by which He delivers the justified sinner from the pollution of sin, renews a person's whole nature in the image of God, and enables one to perform good works (Romans 6:4, 5:6; Colossians 2:12, 3:1).

## ANGELS

The Bible uses the term "angel" (a heavenly body) clearly and primarily to denote messengers or ambassadors of God with such Scripture references as Revelations 4:5, which indicates their duty in heaven to praise God (Psalm 103:20), to do God's will (St. Matthew 18:10), and to behold His face. But since heaven must come down to earth, they also have a mission to earth. The Bible indicates that they accompanied God in the Creation, and also that they will accompany Christ in His return in Glory.

## DEMONS

Demons denote unclean or evil spirits; they are sometimes called devils or demonic beings. They are evil spirits, belonging to the unseen or spiritual realm, embodied in human beings. The Old Testament refers to the prince of demons, sometimes called Satan (adversary) or Devil, as having power and wisdom, taking the habitation of other forms such as the serpent (Genesis 3:1). The New Testament speaks of the Devil as Tempter (St. Matthew 4:3), and it goes on to tell the works of Satan, the Devil, and demons as combating righteousness and good in any form, proving to be an adversary to the saints. Their chief power is exercised to destroy the mission of Jesus Christ. It can well be said that the Christian Church believes in demons, Satan, and devils. We believe in their power and purpose. We believe they can be subdued and conquered as in the commandment to the believer by Jesus. "In my name they shall cast out Satan and the work of the Devil and to resist him and then he will flee (WITHDRAW) from you" (St. Mark 16:17).

## THE CHURCH

The Church forms a spiritual unity of which Christ is the divine head. It is animated by one Spirit, the Spirit of Christ. It professes one faith, shares one hope, and serves one King. It is the citadel of the truth and God's agency for communicating to believers all spiritual blessings. The Church then is the object of our faith rather than of knowledge. The name of our Church, "CHURCH OF GOD IN CHRIST," is supported by I Thessalonians 2:14 and other passages in the Pauline Epistles. The word "CHURCH" or "EKKLESIA" was first applied to the Christian society by Jesus Christ in St. Matthew 16:18, the occasion being that of His benediction of Peter at Caesarea Philippi..

## THE SECOND COMING OF CHRIST

We believe in the second coming of Christ; that He shall come from heaven to earth, personally, bodily, visibly (Acts 1:11; Titus 2:11–13; St. Matthew 16:27, 24:30, 25:30; Luke 21:27; John 1:14, 17; Titus 2:11); and that the Church, the bride, will be caught up to meet Him in the air (I Thessalonians 4:16–17). We admonish all who have this hope to purify themselves as He is pure.

## DIVINE HEALING

The Church Of God In Christ believes in and practices Divine Healing. It is a commandment of Jesus to the Apostles (St. Mark 16:18). Jesus affirms His teachings on healing by explaining to His disciples, who were to be Apostles, that healing the afflicted is by faith (St. Luke 9:40–41). Therefore, we believe that healing by faith in God has scriptural support and ordained authority. St. James's writings in his epistle encourage Elders to pray for the sick, lay hands upon them and to anoint them with oil, and state that prayers with faith shall heal the sick and the Lord shall raise them up. Healing is still practiced widely and frequently in the Church Of God In Christ, and testimonies of healing in our Church testify to this fact.

## MIRACLES

The Church Of God In Christ believes that miracles occur to convince people that the Bible is God's Word. A miracle can be defined as an extraordinary visible act of divine power wrought by the efficient agency of the will of God, which has as its final cause the vindication of the righteousness of God's Word. We believe that the works of God, which were performed during the beginnings of Christianity, do and will occur even today where God is preached, faith in Christ is exercised, the Holy Ghost is active, and the Gospel is promulgated in the truth (Acts 5:15, 6:8, 9:40; Luke 4:36, 7:14, 15, 5:5, 6; St. Mark 14:15).

## THE ORDINANCES OF THE CHURCH

It is generally admitted that for an ordinance to be valid, it must have been instituted by Christ. When we speak of ordinances of the church, we are speaking of those instituted by Christ, in which by sensible signs the grace of God in Christ and the benefits of the covenant of grace are represented, sealed, and applied to believers, and these in turn give expression to their faith and allegiance to God. The Church Of God In Christ recognizes three ordinances as having been instituted by Christ himself and, therefore, are binding upon the church practice..

## THE LORD'S SUPPER (HOLY COMMUNION)

The Lord's Supper symbolizes the Lord's death and suffering for the benefit and in the place of His people. It also symbolizes the believer's participation in the crucified Christ. It represents not only the death of Christ as the object of faith, which unites the believers to Christ, but also the effect of this act as the giving of life, strength, and joy to the soul. The communicant by faith enters into a special spiritual union of one's soul with the glorified Christ.

## FOOT WASHING

Foot washing is practiced and recognized as an ordinance in our Church because Christ, by His example, showed that humility characterized greatness in the kingdom of God, and that service rendered to others gave evidence that humility, motivated by love, exists. These services are held subsequent to the Lord's Supper; however, its regularity is left to the discretion of the pastor in charge.

## WATER BAPTISM

We believe that Water Baptism is necessary as instructed by Christ in St. John 3:5, "UNLESS MAN BE BORN AGAIN OF WATER AND OF THE SPIRIT..."

However, we do not believe that water baptism alone is a means of salvation, but is an outward demonstration that one has already had a conversion experience and has accepted Christ as his personal Savior. As Pentecostals, we practice immersion in preference to sprinkling because immersion corresponds more closely to the death, burial, and resurrection of our Lord (Colossians 2:12). It also symbolizes regeneration and purification more than any other mode. Therefore, we practice immersion as our mode of baptism. We believe that we should use the Baptismal Formula given to us by Christ for all "...IN THE NAME OF THE FATHER, AND OF THE SON, AND OF THE HOLY GHOST..." (Matthew 28:19).

# Suggested Order of Service

1. Call to order.

2. Singing.

3. Prayer.

4. Responsive reading:

**Supt.:** Behold, how good and how pleasant it is for brethren to dwell together in unity!
*Psalm 133:1*

**School:** And let the peace of God rule in your hearts, to the which also ye are called in one body; and be ye thankful.
*Colossians 3:15*

**Supt.:** Blessed are they that dwell in thy house: they will be still praising thee.
*Psalm 84:4*

**School:** Praise ye the LORD. I will praise the LORD with my whole heart, in the assembly of the upright, and in the congregation.
*Psalm 111:1*

**Supt.:** And the LORD said unto him, I have heard thy prayer and thy supplication, that thou hast made before me: I have hallowed this house, which thou hast built, to put my name there for ever; and mine eyes and mine heart shall be there perpetually.
*1 Kings 9:3*

**School:** Ye shall keep my sabbaths, and reverence my sanctuary: I am the LORD.
*Leviticus 19:30*

**Supt.:** And I say also unto thee, That thou art Peter, and upon this rock I will build my church; and the gates of hell shall not prevail against it.
*Matthew 16:18*

**School:** My soul longeth, yea, even fainteth for the courts of the LORD: my heart and my flesh crieth out for the living God.
*Psalm 84:2*

**Supt.:** And other sheep I have, which are not of this fold: them also I must bring, and they shall hear my voice; and there shall be one fold, and one shepherd.
*John 10:16*

**School:** But if I tarry long, that thou mayest know how thou oughtest to behave thyself in the house of God, which is the church of the living God, the pillar and ground of the truth.
*1 Timothy 3:15*

**All:** Lift up your hands in the sanctuary, and bless the LORD.
*Psalm 134:2*

5. Singing.

6. Reading lesson by school and superintendent.

7. Classes assemble for lesson study.

8. Sunday School offering.

9. Five-minute warning bell.

10. Closing bell.

11. Brief lesson review by pastor or superintendent.

12. Secretary's report.

13. Announcements.

14. Dismissal.

# NOTES

# NOTES